P9-DVJ-200

Praise for H. W. Brands's

REAGAN

"Reagan's legacy continues to fuel the ideas and frame the choices facing his would-be successors, and this astute biography is further evidence that the fortieth president continues to cast a long shadow over a still largely conservative political order."
—*The Washington Post*

"Brands is the rare academic historian who can write like a best-selling novelist. Through meticulous research, he recreates decades-old dialogue and puts the reader inside the Oval Office, the Cabinet Room and the house in Reykjavík, Iceland—allegedly haunted—where Reagan and Soviet leader Mikhail Gorbachev debated the fate of the world and laid the groundwork for the end of the Cold War."
—*USA Today*

"Brands's work draws richly from Reagan's presidential diaries and other recently released sources that earlier biographers couldn't tap."
—*The Philadelphia Inquirer*

"Brands's book stands out in the canon of works on Reagan. . . . With an expert's talent for synthesizing earlier works, access to previously unavailable sources and new interviews, Brands creates a riveting narrative. His prose flows as smoothly as his subject's speeches, and his insights provide a fresh look at a transformative president that celebrates his accomplishments but never ignores his blunders. A brilliant example of the biographer's craft, *Reagan* deftly and boldly provides a balanced portrait of a man whose personality remains elusive but whose legacy continues to resonate."
—*Richmond Times-Dispatch*

"Readers will be greatly attracted to Brands's skills as a narrative historian. [He] delivers high drama in treating Reagan's handling of diplomatic affairs, tensions with the press corps and squabbles with Congress. Few American historians and biographers can compete with Brands as a powerful historical storyteller. Make no mistake, this is a first-rate presidential biography. . . . The definitive biography of Reagan." —*The Oregonian*

"Brands is an immensely talented writer. . . . [*Reagan*] is a pleasurable read." —*The Daily Beast*

"A keenly researched book, filled with fascinating stories."
—*Tampa Bay Times*

"A superb biographer writing at the top of his game has found the perfect subject for his narrative skills and profound understanding of the American presidency. Over the years H. W. Brands has produced an extraordinary body of historical and biographical works. This is his masterpiece." —Doris Kearns Goodwin, Pulitzer Prize–winning author of *The Bully Pulpit*

"Ronald Reagan understood what was best about America, and expected the best for it—which is why he led it so successfully. In *Reagan*, H. W. Brands expresses, with deep, deft strokes, what will become the accepted view of a great man."
—Richard Brookhiser, author of
Founders' Son: A Life of Abraham Lincoln

H. W. Brands

REAGAN

H. W. Brands holds the Jack S. Blanton Sr. Chair in History at the University of Texas at Austin. A *New York Times* bestselling author, he was a finalist for the Pulitzer Prize for Biography or Autobiography for *The First American* and *Traitor to His Class*.

www.hwbrands.com

Also by H. W. Brands

The Reckless Decade:
America in the 1890s

T.R.:
The Last Romantic

The First American:
The Life and Times of Benjamin Franklin

The Age of Gold:
The California Gold Rush and the New American Dream

Lone Star Nation:
The Epic Story of the Battle for Texas Independence

Andrew Jackson:
His Life and Times

Traitor to His Class:
The Privileged Life and Radical Presidency of Franklin Delano Roosevelt

American Colossus:
The Triumph of American Capitalism, 1865–1900

The Murder of Jim Fisk for the Love of Josie Mansfield:
A Tragedy of the Gilded Age

The Man Who Saved the Union:
Ulysses Grant in War and Peace

The Heartbreak of Aaron Burr

REAGAN

The Life

H. W. Brands

ANCHOR BOOKS
A Division of Penguin Random House LLC
New York

FIRST ANCHOR BOOKS EDITION, MAY 2016

Copyright © 2015 by H. W. Brands

All rights reserved. Published in the United States by Anchor Books,
a division of Penguin Random House LLC, New York, and distributed in
Canada by Random House of Canada, a division of Penguin Random House
Canada Limited, Toronto. Originally published in hardcover in the United
States by Doubleday, a division of Penguin Random House LLC,
New York, in 2015.

Anchor Books and colophon are registered trademarks of
Penguin Random House LLC.

Photograph of the ABC story on the Reagan family © Bettmann/CORBIS.
All other photographs courtesy of the Ronald Reagan Library.

The Library of Congress has cataloged the Doubleday edition as follows:
Brands, H. W.
Reagan: the life / H. W. Brands.
pages cm
1. Reagan, Ronald.   2. Presidents—United States—Biography.
3. United States—Politics and government—1981–1989.   I. Title.
E877.B73 2015   973.927092—dc23   [B]   2014038054

Anchor Books Trade Paperback ISBN: 978-0-307-95114-4
eBook ISBN: 978-0-385-53640-0

Author photograph © Marsha Miller
Book design by Michael Collica

www.anchorbooks.com

Printed in the United States of America
10 9 8 7 6 5 4 3 2 1

CONTENTS

REAGAN

PROLOGUE

TONIGHT
Don't miss
"A Time for Choosing"
with
Ronald Reagan
9:30 to 10:00
WNBC-TV
Channel 4
Sponsored by T.V. for
Goldwater Committee

DESPERATE TIMES CALLED for desperate measures. Barry Goldwater's campaign was nearly broke, and the candidate was floundering. His opponent, Lyndon Johnson, the craftiest politician in the country, had wrapped himself in the mantle of the martyred John Kennedy to launch a revolution in civil rights and had portrayed himself as the coolheaded commander in chief to parry a communist insurgency in Southeast Asia. In the process Johnson had made Goldwater look like a closet racist and a trigger-happy warmonger. Goldwater hadn't helped his cause by calling himself an extremist, albeit in the defense of liberty, and by suggesting that nuclear weapons be used in Vietnam. The more he spoke, the deeper his hole grew and the more remote his chances of victory. In his desperation, a week before the election he turned to a proxy speaker, a political unknown from California, Ronald Reagan.

Reagan faced desperation of a different kind, less public but more protracted. A washed-up actor last seen hawking the wares and bromides of corporate America, Reagan was at a turning point in his life. As a child he had discovered the allure of an audience, the soothing effect of applause on one's anxieties. He stepped from the stage of church skits and school plays to broadcast radio, which multiplied his audience into the hundreds of thousands, and then to movies, which put his face and voice before millions. But in Hollywood he hit the limits of his talent. He never captured the movie-house marquees, never cracked the A-list of leading men. By his mid-thirties he couldn't get good roles. He moonlighted in the politics of the film industry, representing actors in negotiations with the studios. But that gig ran out, and he was hard up for work. He took a job with General Electric that got him back on-screen, but the much-reduced screen of television, in the much-reduced role of series host. His contract required him to schlep the country for GE, speaking to company employees and to local business boosters about the blessings of big industry and its essential role in the American dream. His own dreams meanwhile faded, and when the GE job ended, they all but disappeared. The invitation to speak for Barry Goldwater came as a godsend, but one fraught with risk. It put him before an audience again and gave him a chance to be heard, but he knew if he flubbed this opportunity, he might never get another.

The Goldwater campaign didn't expect much. It bought a single-column notice on page 79 of the October 27 issue of the *New York Times*; comparable ads ran equally deep in papers around the country. In 1964 political campaigns were still figuring out how to employ television. They hesitated to use spot advertising, from fear that they would be seen as packaging their candidates like cereal or cigarettes. In this case the Goldwater campaign created a faux political event. It hired a hall in Los Angeles and enlisted a few hundred supporters who received Goldwater placards and signs. It placed Reagan on a podium draped in bunting the television audience took for red, white, and blue, though the broadcast was in black and white. He spoke as though at a campaign rally of the sort that had characterized American politics for more than a century.

But this staged event lacked the spontaneity of a genuine rally, and the speech started awkwardly. The audience awaited its cue, the name Goldwater, but Reagan spoke for many minutes before mentioning the candidate, and the audience sat mute. Reagan nervously talked too fast. His standard speech for the GE circuit was longer than this evening's television time allowed, yet rather than edit it down, he tried to pack it all in. The silence of his listeners caused him to talk through his laugh lines, making the awkwardness worse. During his years with GE he had abandoned the pro-government liberalism of his young adulthood in favor of a pro-business conservatism; in doing so, he accumulated note-card decks of statistics documenting government waste and excess. On this occasion he rattled the statistics off in numbing order. Then, without warning, he swerved from domestic politics to foreign policy, leaving his audience confused as to what the American federal debt had to do with the Castro revolution in Cuba. His gestures didn't suit his words, and his principal gesture, a wagging of the right index finger, looked decidedly schoolmarmish.

Yet something happened midway into the half-hour speech. A belated mention of Goldwater got the crowd to respond, and their encouragement calmed Reagan down. He gave his jokes their moments to sink in. "Anytime you and I question the schemes of the do-gooders, we're denounced as being against their humanitarian goals," he said. "They say we're always 'against' things—we're never 'for' anything. Well, the trouble with our liberal friends is not that they're ignorant; it's just that they know so much that isn't so."

The audience perked up the more. American conservatives were a combative tribe who didn't speak of liberals as their "friends," but here Reagan did. His tone was serious, but it wasn't angry, the way Goldwater's often was. Reagan criticized Democratic leaders, but he didn't criticize Democrats. He condemned the direction the American government was going, but he professed confidence in the American people.

At the outset he had said that the Goldwater campaign had not provided him with a script; the words he spoke were his own. He didn't say they were words he had tested on hundreds of audiences. But the polish showed. "This idea that government is beholden to the people, that it has no other source of power except the sovereign people, is still the newest and the most unique idea in all the long history of man's relation to man," he said. "This is the issue of this election: Whether we believe in our capacity for self-government or whether we abandon the American revolution and confess that a little intellectual elite in a far-distant capital can plan our lives for us better than we can plan them ourselves."

He made his points with images and examples. "We have so many people who can't see a fat man standing beside a thin one without coming to the conclusion the fat man got that way by taking advantage of the thin one," he said in a swipe at government redistribution schemes. Government welfare programs were a racket. "A judge called me here in

Los Angeles. He told me of a young woman who'd come before him for a divorce. She had six children, was pregnant with her seventh. Under his questioning, she revealed her husband was a laborer earning $250 a month. She wanted a divorce to get an $80 raise. She's eligible for $330 a month in the Aid to Dependent Children Program. She got the idea from two women in her neighborhood who'd already done that very thing." A job-training program was typically profligate. "We're going to spend each year just on room and board for each young person we help $4,700 a year. We can send them to Harvard for $2,700!" He cracked a smile. "Of course, don't get me wrong. I'm not suggesting Harvard is the answer to juvenile delinquency."

The audience laughed and applauded. Some remembered to wave their Goldwater signs, but most were focused on the man in front of them. "No government ever voluntarily reduces itself in size," Reagan said. "So government programs, once launched, never disappear. Actually, a government bureau is the nearest thing to eternal life we'll ever see on this earth." The audience laughed again and clapped more loudly.

His pace hit a rhythm that swept them along. Government regulation was the creeping edge of socialism. "It doesn't require expropriation or confiscation of private property or business to impose socialism on a people. What does it mean whether you hold the title to your business or property if the government holds the power of life and death over that business or property? And such machinery already exists. The government can find some charge to bring against any concern it chooses to prosecute. Every businessman has his own tale of harassment. Somewhere a perversion has taken place. Our natural, unalienable rights are now considered to be a dispensation of government, and freedom has never been so fragile, so close to slipping from our grasp as it is at this moment."

The danger to freedom was double-edged, from communism abroad and from socialism at home. Both threats drew from the same liberal source. "Those who would trade our freedom for the soup kitchen of the welfare state have told us they have a utopian solution of peace without victory. They call their policy 'accommodation.' And they say if we'll only avoid any direct confrontation with the enemy, he'll forget his evil ways and learn to love us. All who oppose them are indicted as warmongers. They say we offer simple answers to complex problems. Well, perhaps there is a simple answer—not an easy answer—but simple: if you and I have the courage to tell our elected officials that we want our national policy based on what we know in our hearts is morally right."

Reagan had the audience in his hand. He let them cheer, then gave them more of the same. "We cannot buy our security, our freedom from the threat of the bomb by committing an immorality so great as saying to a billion human beings now enslaved behind the Iron Curtain, 'Give up your dreams of freedom because to save our own skins, we're willing to make a deal with your slave masters.' Alexander Hamilton said, 'A nation which can prefer disgrace to danger is prepared for a master, and deserves one.' Now let's set the record straight. There's no argument over the choice between peace and war, but there's only one guaranteed way you can have peace, and you can have it in the next second: surrender."

He borrowed from Patrick Henry: "You and I know and do not believe that life is so dear and peace so sweet as to be purchased at the price of chains and slavery." He delved further into history: "If nothing in life is worth dying for, when did this begin—just in the face of this enemy? Or should Moses have told the children of Israel to live in slavery under the pharaohs? Should Christ have refused the cross? Should the patriots at Concord Bridge have thrown down their guns and refused to fire the shot heard 'round the world? The martyrs of history were not fools, and our honored dead who gave their lives to stop the advance of the Nazis didn't die in vain."

He drew toward the close. "Where, then, is the road to peace? Well, it's a simple answer after all. You and I have the courage to say to our enemies: There is a price we will not pay. There is a point beyond which they must not advance." He quoted Winston Churchill: "The destiny of man is not measured by material computations. When great forces are on the move in the world, we learn we're spirits, not animals." Churchill again: "There's something going on in time and space, and beyond time and space, which, whether we like it or not, spells duty." He pivoted, surprisingly for a Republican, to Franklin Roosevelt. "You and I have a rendezvous with destiny," Reagan said. He finished with a nod to Lincoln: "We'll preserve for our children this, the last best hope of man on earth, or we'll sentence them to take the last step into a thousand years of darkness."

THE SPEECH CAME too late to rescue Goldwater, who lost in a landslide to Johnson. But it earned Reagan a future. His listeners in the hall leaped to their feet and stamped their approval as he finished; the reaction of the national television audience was almost as positive. Editorials and letters praised the energy and conviction this newcomer brought to the defense of American freedom at home and abroad. Many Republicans concluded that their party had nominated the wrong man. Reagan had never run for political office, but his name at once surfaced in discussions about the governorship of California. Conservatives in other states formed Reagan-for-president committees.

Reagan professed surprise at the sudden reversal in his fortunes. Perhaps he *was* surprised. But he wasn't unprepared. He had been honing his broadcast skills since his days in radio, and all those talks for GE had served like a long off-Broadway run before a main-stage premiere. Seven years as head of the Screen Actors Guild had exposed him to a species of politics as conniving as politics could be. The decade when he thought he would never again reach a big audience had sharpened his hunger for the satisfaction only applause could bring.

Those who afterward read the transcript of his speech realized it could not have been better composed to draw attention to Reagan, rather than Goldwater. The most quotable lines had nothing of Goldwater in them, beyond the fact that Goldwater shared Reagan's conservative values. Reagan positioned himself as a spokesman for conservatism who happened to be campaigning for Goldwater. The Goldwater defeat, far from damaging Reagan, made him more appealing as the one around whom conservatives might rally.

Reagan couldn't know that his speech had launched one of the most remarkable careers in American politics. He couldn't know that he would be twice elected governor of the most populous state in the Union and twice elected president of the United States. He couldn't know that he would leave a deeper impression on the country and the world than any but a handful of other presidents. All he could know in the autumn of 1964 was that at a time of life when career doors begin to close, at a time in his own life when the obvious doors had already closed, he had suddenly kicked a new door wide open.

He got ready to step through. "I have never aspired to public office, nor looked upon a political career with any particular favor," he told reporters soberly. He said he still viewed government skeptically. But a patriotic American had to listen to his fellow citizens. "I'm honored and flattered that so many people would think of me in connection with public office." Their opinions deserved careful consideration. "I will review my thinking, and whatever decision I make will be based on what I think will provide the most good."

PART ONE

PRAIRIE IDYLL

1911–1934

1

R EAGAN REMEMBERED THREE things from childhood: that his father was a drunk, that his mother was a saint, and that his ability to make an audience laugh afforded an antidote to life's insecurities and embarrassments.

"When I was eleven, I came home from the YMCA one cold, blustery, winter's night," Reagan recalled decades later. "My mother was gone on one of her sewing jobs, and I expected the house to be empty." Nelle Reagan worked to supplement her husband's earnings. "As I walked up the stairs, I nearly stumbled over a lump near the front door; it was Jack lying in the snow, his arms outstretched, flat on his back." Reagan and his older brother, Neil, called his mother and father by their first names. "I leaned over to see what was wrong and smelled whiskey. He had found his way home from a speakeasy and had just passed out right there. For a moment or two, I looked down at him and thought about continuing on into the house and going to bed, as if he weren't there. But I couldn't do it. When I tried to wake him he just snored—loud enough, I suspected, for the whole neighborhood to hear him. So I grabbed a piece of his overcoat, pulled it, and dragged him into the house."

The boy watched his father during several years and drew inferences. "Jack wasn't one of those alcoholics who went on a bender after he'd had a run of bad luck or who drowned his sorrows in drink," Reagan said. "No, it was prosperity that Jack couldn't stand. When everything was going perfectly, that's when he let go, especially if during a holiday or family get-together that gave him a reason to do it. At Christmas, there was always a threat hanging over our family. We knew holidays were the most likely time for Jack to jump off the wagon. So I was always torn between looking forward to Christmas and being afraid of its arrival."

Jack Reagan's drinking made him an unreliable breadwinner, and the family bounced around Illinois during his younger son's first decade. Ronald Wilson Reagan was born in Tampico on February 6, 1911. The family moved to Chicago when he was two, then to Galesburg, to Monmouth, and back to Tampico. The places passed like scenes outside a car window. Reagan remembered a noisy fire engine from Chicago that made him want to be a fireman. America entered World War I in April 1917, when the family was in Galesburg; the soldiers on the troop trains passing through seemed to a six-year-old to embody adventure and heroism. The war ended in November 1918, with the family in Monmouth, where the celebrations almost overwhelmed the lad. "The parades, the torches, the bands, the shoutings and drunks, and the burning of Kaiser Bill in effigy created in me an uneasy feeling of a world outside my own," he remembered.

The family landed in Dixon when Reagan was nine. The town of ten thousand became his home until he left for college. Jack Reagan pulled himself together a bit, or perhaps Nelle simply put a stop to the serial moves. But as his sons grew into teenagers, they encountered challenges of a different sort. Dixon had few Catholics and disliked most of those. The boys didn't practice their father's faith, but the malignant papism the town bullies saw in Jack Reagan was imputed to them, and they were forced to defend themselves, sometimes with fists. More insidious and less amenable to riposte was the scorn they endured on account of Jack's boozing.

NELLE REAGAN EXPLAINED her husband's weakness in terms intended to elicit the boys' sympathy and understanding. "Nelle tried so hard to make it clear he had a *sickness* that he couldn't help, and she constantly reminded us of how good he was to us when he wasn't drinking," Reagan recalled. Nelle was Scots-English by ancestry, to Jack's Irish, and she displayed the proverbial thriftiness of the Scot. Not that she had much choice, given her husband's uncertain earnings. She mended and re-mended Neil's clothes for passing down to Ronnie. She sent Neil to the butcher to cadge liver for a mythical family cat. She filled the stew pot with oatmeal and passed it off as a delicacy. "I remember the first time she brought a plate of oatmeal meat to the table," Reagan recounted. "There was a thick, round patty buried in gravy that I'd never seen before. I bit into it. It was moist and meaty, the most wonderful thing I'd ever eaten."

Nelle schooled her boys in religion, by precept and especially by example. She spent every Sunday at the Disciples of Christ Church and took the boys with her, to Sunday school at first and then to the regular services. She never thought ill of anyone, so far as her sons could tell. "While my father was a cynic and tended to suspect the worst of people, my mother was the opposite," Reagan remembered. "She always expected to find the best in people and often did, even among the prisoners at our local jail to whom she frequently brought hot meals." She preached and practiced the Golden Rule. "My mother always taught us: 'Treat thy neighbor as you would want your neighbor to treat you.'" She put others ahead of herself, and her sons foremost. "While my father was filled with dreams of making something of himself, she had a drive to help my brother and me make something of ourselves."

In one respect Jack Reagan seemed entirely admirable to his sons. Their youth witnessed the revival of the Ku Klux Klan, which added Catholics, Jews, and immigrants to African Americans as targets of its venom. Jack forbade the boys to see *The Birth of a Nation*, the D. W. Griffith film that made heroes out of the white-robed vigilantes. In vain did Neil and Ronnie point out that all the other kids were seeing the picture and that, anyway, the Klan in the movie was of a different time and place. "The Klan's the Klan, and a sheet's a sheet, and any man who wears one over his head is a bum," Reagan recalled Jack saying.

Reagan told another story that Jack had told him. On the road for work, Jack checked into a hotel where the proprietor assured him, "You'll like it here, Mr. Reagan. We don't permit a Jew in the place." Jack grabbed his suitcase and turned to leave. "I'm a Catholic," he declared. "If it's come to the point where you won't take Jews, then some day you won't take *me* either." Jack Reagan spent that cold night in his car.

NEIL REAGAN WAS socially adept and a good athlete, with little trouble finding a niche after each of the family's moves. Ronnie, two and a half years younger, wasn't so lucky. The frequent relocations left him disconcerted. "I was forever the new kid in school," he remembered with retrospective anxiety. "During one period of four years, I attended four different schools." Neil's grace at sports eluded him. "I was small and spent a lot of time at the bottom of pile-ons in sandlot football games. In baseball, I was forever striking out or suffering the indignity of missing an easy fly ball. I was so lousy at baseball that when our group was choosing up sides for a game, I was always the last kid chosen. I remember one time when I was in the eighth grade. I was playing second base and a ball was hit straight toward me but I didn't realize it. Everybody was looking at me, expecting me to catch it. I just stood there. The ball landed behind me and everybody said, 'Oh, no!'" Decades later the memory still stung. "You don't forget things like that."

Some of his trouble was myopia, which glasses partially remedied, albeit at the cost of his being taunted as "Four-Eyes." He preferred the nickname Dutch, originally for the way Nelle cut his hair. But the damage to his psyche had been done. "I had a lot of trouble convincing myself I was good enough to play with the other kids, a deficiency of confidence that's not a small matter when you're growing up in a youthful world dominated by sports and games. I was always the first to think: *I can't make the team. I'm not as good as Jack or Jim or Bill.*"

In one respect, though, he was as good as the others. Nelle Reagan contributed to the cultural life of Dixon by organizing amateur performances at her church, where participants delivered passages from books, plays, poems, or speeches they had committed to memory. Nelle performed and loved the experience. She encouraged her sons to join her. Neil accepted readily; Dutch required convincing. But she persisted and eventually won him over. "Summoning my courage," he recalled, "I walked up to the stage that night, cleared my throat, and made my theatrical debut. I don't remember what I said, but I'll never forget the response: *People laughed and applauded.* That was a new experience for me and I liked it. I liked that approval. For a kid suffering childhood pangs of insecurity, the applause was music."

THE MUSIC FED his fondness for stories. Reagan was an early reader, with a sticky memory. The tales of the Rover Boys, of Tarzan and Frank Merriwell, provided escape from his father's drinking and smoothed the rough edges of life for the new kid struggling to fit in. Someday, he dreamed, his world would be like that of the popular, athletic Merriwell. Stories also provided a rare chance to bond with his father, who taught him how to spin a yarn. "He had a wry, mordant humor," Reagan remembered of Jack. "He was the best raconteur I ever heard, especially when it came to the smoking-car sort of stories." Nelle took exception to her husband's bawdy tales, but on this point her son sided with his father. "Jack always made clear to us that there was a time and place for this sort of anecdote; he drew a sharp line between lusty vulgar humor and filth. To this day I agree with his credo and join Jack and Mark Twain in asserting that one of the basic forms of American humor is the down-to-earth wit of the ordinary person, and the questionable language is justified if the point is based on real humor."

An inspiring teacher encouraged young Reagan's storytelling. B. J. Frazer informed the students in his ninth-grade English class that good writing should be entertaining as well as informative. "That prodded me to be imaginative with my essays," Reagan recalled. "Before long he was asking me to read some of my essays to the class, and when I started getting a few laughs, I began writing them with the intention of entertaining the class. I got more laughs and realized I enjoyed it as much as I had those readings at church."

His stories displayed various motifs. "'Twas the night of Hallowe'en, but nothing was still," he wrote in one. "The good people went to sleep that memorial"—presumably "memorable"—"Saturday night with the sounds of laughter, running feet, and muffled shouts ringing in their ears. Then they were peaceful, and only then, at twelve o'clock, a gasping, panting roar awakened the town." The town's pranksters have been at work in the dark beyond the rail station. "The freight due from the north was vainly fighting to get over a hundred foot stretch of greased track." Eventually, the engineer coaxes his engine and cars beyond the slippery spot. "But the next morning a greater shock came. The city was transformed, but less beautiful. The telephone poles were artistically draped with porch furniture, signs, and various parts of buggys and wagons. The streets looked like rummage sales, while schools and stores found their doorways piled with representatives of the last nights"—here the sentence ends, short a word or two and an apostrophe. The story concludes with a flourish: "But alas! Except for an occasional chair on a telephone pole, the scene was soon shattered by the respective owners of the collected articles."

In eleventh grade he crafted a longer tale. "Mark had, with an air of mystery and promise, insisted that I dine with him," it began. Mark and the narrator are students at Yale—the alma mater of Frank Merriwell—and they are visiting New York City for the day. "Here we were, in one of those little cafes tucked in a cranny just off Broadway, a place without the elegance of famous places, and without the soiled squalor of the Bowery, a place that defied any attempt to classify it." They overhear two men seated nearby discussing a nefarious plot. "One was a tall dark man with glittering black eyes and a lean hard jaw. His companion, who seemed to do most of the talking, was a swarthy, dark haired man, short and stout with a pointed Van Dyke beard and a pointed waxed mustache. Suddenly we heard the talkative man hiss, 'Fool! bombs are too bungling. Gas is smooth and silent.' My heart suddenly cross-blocked my liver and my adams apple drop-kicked a tonsil." The conspirators depart the restaurant but leave behind a piece of paper, which Mark snatches up. The paper has a diagram of the U.S. Treasury building in Washington. "The word gas seared through my brain like a hurtling meteorite. For outlined in red ink on the map was the complete ventilation system of the Treasury building." Mark and the narrator stare at each other. "We were speechless. It did not seem possible that two mere undergraduates of Yale should stand alone between this gang of maniacs and the horrible tragedy outlined on that soiled paper." But they have to try. They race to the local police station and convey their intelligence to the sergeant, who piles them into his squad car to chase down the plotters. They catch them, only to have the desperate pair laugh in their faces. They are not criminals at all, but fugitives from a mental asylum, as Mark discovers from a newspaper conveniently at hand. "He held before our startled eyes a screaming headline, 'Lunatics Escape. Reward.' Beneath these startling words were photographs of our new found friends. So the honor of 'old Eli' was upheld."

B. J. Frazer headed Dixon High's drama program when he wasn't teaching English, and he encouraged Reagan to try out. Reagan did so gladly, seeking more of that welcome music. By this time he had outgrown a bit of his shyness, not least by discovering a sport, football, that required neither keen eyesight nor particular coordination in those who played the line. Yet the sensitivities of earlier days remained, and performing onstage continued to ease them. "For a teenager still carrying around some old feelings of insecurity, the reaction of my classmates was more music to my ears," he said. The experience grew more habit-forming with each curtain call. "By the time I was a senior, I was so addicted to student theatrical productions that you couldn't keep me out of them."

In later years he would reflect on the phenomenon. "There's something about the entertainment world that attracts people who may have had youthful feelings of shyness or insecurity," he observed. "After I went to Hollywood, some of the most successful people I met—a lot of actors and great comedians like Jack Benny, for example—would just sit quietly, even shyly, at a party while some of the funniest people were writers who took center stage and became the real show-offs. It made me wonder if some entertainers hadn't gravitated to their calling because they'd been a little insecure and the job gave them a chance to be someone they're not, at least for a while."

AMERICANS LIKED STORIES as much as Reagan did, and for similar reasons. America's national youth had been difficult. Where the inhabitants of other countries drew their common identities from shared histories and long attachment to particular pieces of ground, Americans—overwhelmingly immigrants and their offspring—shared little except a rejection of the lands whence they came. New kids all, they sought a common story, a cultural glue that gave their disparate experiences a collective meaning.

They found their most satisfying story in what they came to call American exceptionalism. John Winthrop, governor of the Massachusetts Bay Colony, declared the Puritan settlement a "city upon a hill": a model to people everywhere. Thomas Jefferson and the signers of the Declaration of Independence placed their dispute with Britain squarely in "the course of human events," not simply events of North America or the British Empire. The exponents of Manifest Destiny in the 1840s spoke of America's divinely ordained mission to spread the blessings of liberty and democracy from sea to sea. Abraham Lincoln at Gettysburg declared the Civil War a struggle to determine whether government of, by, and for the people would perish not merely from America but from the earth. Advocates of overseas expansion during the 1890s updated the Manifest Destiny argument, alternately asserting a Christian duty to baptize heathens and citing Darwin to explain American superiority as the result of the competitive struggle among peoples and cultures.

By the early twentieth century the concept of American exceptionalism was rooted firmly in the national psyche. Woodrow Wilson led America into World War I contending that only the example and guidance of the United States, the most selfless of nations and the most developed democracy, could enable Western civilization to survive the horrendous destruction it was inflicting on itself. Western civilization did survive, but barely, and American exceptionalism turned inward as it became clear that the world wasn't ready for America's regenerative leadership. Young Reagan adopted the widely held belief that Wilson had made a terrible misjudgment in leading America to war. Recalling the fate of the troops he'd cheered off to battle, he reflected, "I think the realization that some of those boys to whom I'd waved on the troop train later died on European soil made me an isolationist for a long time."

The reaction against the Wilsonian project included a rejection of the liberalism that had carried Wilson into office. The 1920s were the most conservative decade in memory. A ban on alcohol was written into the Constitution; state legislatures outlawed the teaching of evolution; a "red scare" swept the land in the wake of the foreign revolutions the world war spawned; xenophobia inspired a drastic curtailment of immigration and contributed to the revival of the Ku Klux Klan. After nearly two decades during which the powers of government had consistently grown, Americans turned away from government toward the private sector. "The chief business of America is business," Calvin Coolidge said, and most of his compatriots agreed.

It helped Coolidge's case that American business thrived during the 1920s. The automobile industry became a mainstay of the industrial sector after General Motors introduced annual model changes that caused motorists to view their vehicles as assertions of identity rather than mere instruments of locomotion. Electrical appliances entered millions of households, transforming daily life and creating the perception of needs where none had existed before. Real estate and housing boomed, especially in Florida and other sunny climes. The stock market soared, quadrupling in value and creating millionaires too many to count.

Yet the wealth wasn't spread evenly. The cities flourished, but the farm sector languished. Commodity prices never regained their wartime levels, though farmers continued to hope they would. And when the farmers planted according to their hopes, overproduction and low prices became chronic.

YOUNG REAGAN DIDN'T analyze the nation's economy, but he felt the effects of the farm squeeze. While his father's line of work was selling shoes, not corn or hogs, when the farmers who lived near Dixon and might have been Jack Reagan's customers couldn't sell their corn and hogs, they didn't buy his shoes. Neil and Dutch never went hungry, but they knew the family was living month to month. They worked when they could, Dutch most regularly as a lifeguard in Dixon's riverside Lowell Park. He liked the job, not least because it conferred a certain stature. He wore a shirt with "Life Guard" emblazoned on the chest and exercised authority over his waterfront domain. He afterward boasted of saving seventy-seven people in several summers on the job, although more than a few of these denied needing rescue. "'I would have been fine if you'd let me alone,' was their theme," Reagan remarked later. "'You made a fool out of me trying to make a hero out of yourself.'" But whatever the rescue count, which he meticulously notched in a tree branch by the river, he carried an important responsibility on his broadening shoulders. And his paycheck helped cover the family bills.

Yet lifeguarding wasn't a career, or even a year-round job. As high school graduation approached, he had to consider alternatives. College in the 1920s was the preserve of the few; neither of his parents had attended college, nor had Neil made a start. But a girl in his class had her sights on college, and he had his sights on her. Margaret Cleaver was the daughter of the minister of the church Reagan attended with Nelle. She was pert and pretty and less enamored of him than he was of her. "She was (strange as it sounds) grown up enough to know we weren't any of us grown up enough to call this anything but friendship," he recalled. "Me? I was in love." Margaret's older sisters had gone to Eureka College, a Disciples of Christ school between Peoria and Bloomington, a hundred miles south of Dixon. Margaret intended to follow their lead.

Reagan would likely have gone to college even without Margaret's positive example. His mother continued to insist that her sons make something of themselves, something more than their father. Neil resisted the urging, identifying more and more openly with Jack. He had Jack's dark charm and discovered a liking for alcohol. He announced that he was forsaking his mother's church, the Disciples, for his father's Catholicism—prompting Nelle to explain tearfully that he had been baptized a Catholic as an infant. And he defied Nelle's wish that he go to college, opting instead for wage labor at the local cement plant.

Reagan, by contrast, identified with his mother. Some of this was her doing: she kept him out of the Catholic baptismal font and cultivated those interests of his that matched hers. Dutch repaid her by being the good boy, the polite one who made people laugh, who worshipped with the Disciples, who took up with the minister's daughter. He was the one Nelle would be proud of. He saw his mother trapped in Dixon, in a dismal marriage to a man who lacked competence and ambition. For her vicarious sake as well as his own future, he determined that he had to get out of Dixon. College was his escape.

Nelle approved of Eureka College on religious grounds; Reagan was more taken by its football team. A Dixon football hero had gone to greater fame at Eureka; Reagan imagined himself doing likewise. "I had never seen Eureka College but it was my choice," he explained later. Margaret Cleaver's decision for Eureka sealed the deal.

Money was a problem, but Reagan talked his way into a partial scholarship and a job that would cover the cost of his meals; the rest of his expenses would come from a savings account he had built with his pay from lifeguarding.

REAGAN'S DREAMS OF football glory at Eureka weren't unreasonable, for the college was tiny, with a mere 250 students, many of them girls. Surely he could stand out among such a small group. But he lacked talent. "Dutch? I put him at end on the fifth string," his coach, Ralph McKinzie, recalled decades later. There was no lower string than fifth, and the team turned no one away. "The first year I never let him on the field to play a game. Guess he hated me for it. But I had a team to consider. He was nearsighted, you know. Couldn't see worth a damn. Ended up at the bottom of the heap every time and missed the play because he couldn't see the man or the ball moving on him." McKinzie acknowledged Reagan's resolve. "Gotta say he was a regular at practice. And took his knocks." But he just wasn't cut out for the gridiron. "Don't know why he persisted at football. He had this dream I guess of becoming a big football star. He liked being close to the field even when he wasn't playing a game. Used to take an old broom from the locker room and pretend it was a microphone and 'announce' the game play by play afterwards." Reagan learned the formations and plays, but to no avail. "Just couldn't execute what he knew," McKinzie said.

He fared better on the stage. He appeared in several campus dramatic productions, taking the lead in some. The drama coach entered her troupe in a one-act competition at Northwestern University, near Chicago. The Eureka team came in third of twelve, and Reagan was recognized individually. "The head of Northwestern's Drama Department sent for me and asked if I'd ever considered the stage as a career," Reagan recalled afterward.

Margaret's father and mother took Reagan and Margaret to see a touring production of the play *Journey's End*, set in wartime France. Reagan later remembered the leading character's effect on him. "War-weary, young but bitterly old Captain Stanhope carried me into a new world.

For two and a half hours I was in that dugout on the Western front—but in some strange way, I was also on stage. More than anything in life I wanted to speak his lines to the young replacement officer who misunderstands and sees callousness in his effort to hide grief. That deep silence, the slow coming to his feet, then the almost whispered, 'My God, so that's it! You think I don't care! You bloody little swine, you think I don't care—the only one who knew—who really understood.'"

Yet Reagan's most memorable performance at Eureka came not onstage, and certainly not on the football field, but in student politics. The college was chronically strapped for money, and in his freshman year its president proposed to balance the books by eliminating various courses and laying off the faculty who taught them. The trustees supported the president. The faculty resisted the reductions, but it was the student response that had the larger effect. Seniors and juniors discovered that courses they required for graduation were suddenly unavailable; they complained that the college was reneging on its commitment to them. The students formed a committee to weigh their options; Reagan served as a representative of the freshman class.

Members of the committee suggested a strike, a student boycott of classes. The idea caught on, but the committee leaders judged that it would carry the greatest weight if put forward by a freshman, a member of the class with the least immediate self-interest in the matter. Someone knew Reagan and suggested him. He accepted the assignment.

"I'd been told that I should sell the idea so there'd be no doubt of the outcome," he remembered. He took the advice and prepared an elaborate brief on behalf of the students and against the president and trustees. "I reviewed the history of our patient negotiations with due emphasis on the devious manner in which the trustees had sought to take advantage of us." Reagan was thrilled by the response. "I discovered that night that an audience has a feel to it and, in the parlance of the theater, that audience and I were together. When I came to actually presenting the motion there was no need for parliamentary procedure: they came to their feet with a roar—even the faculty members present voted by acclamation. It was heady wine." Thirty years later he could still taste the victory. "Hell, with two more lines I could have had them riding through 'every Middlesex village and farm'—without horses yet," he said, riffing on Longfellow's rendering of Paul Revere's ride.

The strike prompted the trustees to reconsider and the president to resign. It made Reagan a presence on campus. He never became a football hero, though he eventually earned more playing time. He was a first-rate swimmer, from his years as a lifeguard, and he represented the college in meets. But swimming was a minor sport and didn't have the cachet of football. He was active in student government, working his way to election as student body president.

He joined the Tau Kappa Epsilon fraternity, where he enjoyed a fraternal comeuppance. Manual labor had lost its charm for Neil, and he decided to give college a try. He came to Eureka and pledged Reagan's fraternity, a year behind his younger brother, who was expected to haze him along with the rest of the pledges. Reagan later claimed to have faked the whacks, delivered to the buttocks with a wooden paddle drilled with holes to raise blisters. Neil remembered things differently. "I became the younger brother," he said. And he was treated like a younger brother, only more harshly. "Anytime I heard the shout 'Assume the position, Reagan' and grabbed my ankles, I knew the whack I got from him was going to be worse than the others because he felt he had to; otherwise they'd accuse him of showing partisanship."

Reagan loved everything about Eureka except its reason for being: academics. He was a thoroughly indifferent student, unmotivated and insufficiently brilliant to make top grades without effort. He studied economics, the closest thing Eureka offered to a curriculum in business, in hopes it might prove practical after graduation. But he was an optimist at heart, and neither the theory nor the practice of the dismal science engaged him. History was too backward-looking for a young man with an eye on the future. French might be good for the French, but what did an American need with it? Reagan's attitude toward his studies was purely instrumental: he worked no harder than his extracurriculars required. "My principal academic ambition at Eureka was to maintain the C average I needed to remain eligible," he confessed afterward.

English was the rare subject that sometimes inspired him, when he could exercise his storytelling skills. One of his short stories involved what the protagonist called "the A.E.F. suicide club," for the doomed soldiers of World War I. A doughboy named Edwards reflects on the experience of a younger soldier, Bering. "Edwards was not old himself, but his thirty years had robbed him of some of Bering's optimism, his idealism and youth. A lump came to his throat as he listened to the boy talk of sacrifice and glory and heroism and he cursed mentally at a world so ordered that once every generation it must be bathed in the blood of youth like this one." A half century later Reagan would offer public paeans to the sacrifice of men like Bering, but in 1931 he could see little but folly in their efforts. Bering, in Reagan's story, survives the war yet sustains permanent physical and emotional injuries. He never regains his grounding in life. Reagan's story ended with Edwards, years later, reading a short piece in the newspaper: "A tramp, David Bering, met his death today beneath the wheels of a Santa Fe freight. Bering, an ex–service man, had been gassed in the war and was bumming his way to the Speedway veterans hospital for treatment. He attempted to board the moving train and lost his footing. He was thrown under the wheels when he fell. Notices have been broadcasted but no relatives or friends have claimed the body. He will be buried in the potters field."

2

AFTER WE MOVED to Dixon, I fell in love with the movies," Reagan recalled. "I couldn't count the number of hours I spent in the darkness of our only moviehouse with William S. Hart and Tom Mix galloping over the prairie or having my eyes turned misty by the cinematic perils that befell Mary Pickford and Pearl White." His mother's sister came for a visit, and the whole family went to the theater to watch the weekly silent film. "I don't remember its name, but it featured the adventures of a freckle-faced young boy and I enjoyed it a lot. Afterward, I overheard my aunt talking to my mother about this young star and saying she thought I had the potential to become a child actor. 'If he was mine,' she said, 'I'd take him to Hollywood if I had to walk all the way.'"

Nelle Reagan wasn't about to walk to Hollywood; she had her hands full holding the family together in Dixon. But her sister's attitude was widely shared in the years after World War I. Hollywood's grip on the American imagination was new but more seductive for its novelty. Photographers and inventors had tried to get pictures to move in the late nineteenth century; Thomas Edison's Kinetoscope accomplished the feat, for one viewer at a time, in 1894. By the turn of the century peep shows had become picture shows, and the 1903 *Great Train Robbery*, a twelve-minute drama set in the West but shot in New Jersey, promised a heady future for the new medium.

That future unfolded in California. Early movie cameras required daylight to make their recordings, and Southern California's glorious weather allowed more days of outdoor shooting than almost anywhere else in the country. By 1910, Hollywood, a community west of downtown Los Angeles that had begun life as the brainchild of real estate developers, was attracting some of the budding industry's best talent. D. W. Griffith shot *The Birth of a Nation* there; the tendentious depiction of the Civil War and Reconstruction that appalled Jack Reagan and other advocates of racial equality riveted large audiences who paid the exorbitant price of $2 to see the three-hour film. By 1920 several motion-picture studios, Hollywood's answer to Henry Ford's assembly line, were together churning out hundreds of movies per year.

In the process they were making stars. The actors in the earliest films hadn't been credited, but audiences nonetheless came to have favorites. Some studios resisted promoting these favorites, fearing they would demand higher wages. Yet the shrewder executives recognized the potential for establishing brand names, and they signed the crowd-pleasers to long-term contracts. The star system was born.

It was the star system that drew the attention of Nelle Reagan's sister and the millions of Americans who dreamed that they or their children would go to Hollywood and acquire fame and wealth. Both attributes were on gaudy display in the movie capital in the 1920s. Mary Pickford, the object of Dutch Reagan's filmic affections, earned half a million dollars a year before becoming a movie mogul herself as a founding partner— with Griffith, Charlie Chaplin, and Douglas Fairbanks—of the United Artists studio. Pickford and Fairbanks were romantic partners as well as business associates; their romance was a sensation, partly because it began while each was married to someone else but mostly because it seemed a match made in Hollywood heaven. Their lavish wedding provided reams of copy for the rapidly growing movie press; their Beverly Hills estate, Pickfair, was soon the most popular stop on the homes-of-the-stars tours that became a staple of Southern California tourism.

THE MAGIC OF Hollywood grew more essential to the American psyche when the 1920s crashed to a close with a stock market collapse in the final months of the decade. The bubble in share prices had grown unsustainable, and when it burst, it knocked the wind out of Wall Street. The woes of the financial industry became the agony of America when the country was rudely awakened to the fact that bankers had been playing the market with depositors' money. Their losses triggered defaults by their banks, leaving depositors without cash or recourse. The federal government might have salvaged the situation by flooding the financial markets with money; in fact the dominant figure on the Federal Reserve Board,

Benjamin Strong, had advocated readying just such a response as the stock bubble grew. But Strong died untimely and his successors lacked the nerve to open the spigots, and the money supply shrank by a strangling one-third. Prices plunged, merchants canceled orders, and manufacturers laid off workers in a vicious circle that continued until a quarter of the work-force lacked jobs.

Reagan had the good luck to be in college during the first two years of the depression but the bad luck to graduate, in June 1932, when conditions were worse than ever. He recalled the Christmas Eve of his senior year; he and Neil were at home when Jack received a special-delivery letter. Jack read the letter and muttered, "Well, it's a hell of a Christmas present." He had lost his job. Reagan sent Nelle money during his last semester to help with the grocery bill, and he resolved anew not to wind up like Jack.

He returned to lifeguarding for his postgraduation summer, but this bought him barely two months. Come autumn, he'd have to compete with the many other unemployed for a permanent job. He knew what he wanted to do; he just couldn't figure out *how* to do it. His love for movies had only grown, as had his appetite for the applause that kept his anxieties at bay. He had followed the careers of Tom Mix and Mary Pickford, and he imagined himself on the screen beside them. "By my senior year at Eureka, my secret dream to be an actor was firmly planted," he remembered. But he kept it secret lest his friends and acquaintances consider him egotistically odd. "To say I wanted to be a movie star would have been as eccentric as saying I wanted to go to the moon," he explained. "If I *had* told anyone I was setting out to be a movie star, they'd have carted me off to an institution."

To disguise his dream, he charted a path he considered more conventional. Radio was a newer medium than movies, with the first regular broadcasts postdating the war. But it caught on quickly, and soon radio sets—typically large consoles, often in handsome wood cabinets—had become a standard feature in middle-class households. Sports broadcasts were an early staple of programming; for many Americans the age of radio began when the Radio Corporation of America, or RCA, aired the 1921 heavyweight boxing championship fight between Jack Dempsey and Georges Carpentier. Soon the voices of sports announcers were almost as familiar as the faces of Hollywood movie stars.

Reagan spent his teens listening to radio stations broadcasting from Chicago; their signals covered Dixon and much of the rest of northern Illinois. He supposed that sports radio could be a step on his road to the movies; at least it was in the field of public entertainment. And its announcers enjoyed the fame he sought. So he decided that after his last season as a lifeguard ended, he would try to find a job in radio. He bade farewell to Margaret Cleaver, who herself was departing to take a teaching job in a distant Illinois town, and headed to Chicago.

He arrived with high hopes. Chicago had lots of stations and, presumably, room for at least one more announcer. Yet several fruitless visits to stations produced nothing. A kindly woman in one of the offices told him why. "This is the big time," she said. "No one in the city wants to take a chance on inexperience." He should go out to smaller cities and towns and interview with stations there. "They can't afford to compete with us for experienced talent, so they are often willing to give a newcomer a chance."

Reagan returned to Dixon and talked his father into lending him the family car, a worn Oldsmobile, for a small-town tour. Davenport, Iowa, was just across the Mississippi River from Illinois, seventy-five miles west of Dixon. A series of futile visits to radio stations there made him think the Chicago woman had simply wanted to get rid of him. Eventually, he found himself at station WOC. The program director told him he had arrived too late; the station had had an opening but had filled it just the day before. Reagan's frustration overcame his usual politeness. He stalked out of the office saying, in a voice loud enough for all to hear, "How the hell can you get to be a sports announcer if you can't even get a job at a radio station?"

Something about Reagan appealed to the program director, who followed him out into the hall. Peter MacArthur was a blunt-spoken Scotsman with arthritic knees; his two canes clacked on the wooden floor while his brogue demanded, "Hold on, you big bastard!" Reagan stopped. "What was that you said about *sports* announcing?" MacArthur inquired. Reagan replied that he wanted to be a sports announcer someday. "Do you know anything about football?" MacArthur asked. Reagan said he had played in high school and college. MacArthur offered him an audition. He took Reagan to an empty sound studio and put him in front of a microphone. "I'll be in another room listening. Describe an imaginary football game to me and make me *see* it."

Reagan hadn't been expecting this, but he wasn't going to miss the first opportunity his job search had yielded. He recalled a game Eureka had won in the last seconds. He knew the action and the players' names, and he launched in. "Here we are in the fourth quarter with Western State University leading Eureka College six to nothing." He added color:

"Long blue shadows are settling over the field and a chill wind is blowing in through the end of the stadium." Eureka didn't have a stadium, only bleachers, but Reagan guessed MacArthur wouldn't know the difference. He proceeded to the decisive final play. In real life Reagan had missed his assigned block in the secondary, but the ballcarrier got through anyway to score the tying touchdown. In Reagan's retelling, he obliterated the linebacker, creating the crucial opening for the game-tying score. The extra point sealed the victory. Reagan described the delirious fans, recapped the outcome, and closed: "We return you now to our main studio."

MacArthur clattered in from the control booth. "Ye did great, ye big SOB," he said. "Be here Saturday, you're broadcasting the Iowa-Minnesota Homecoming game. You'll get $5 and bus fare."

The game day came. Reagan discovered that he wouldn't be alone in the press box; a veteran announcer would share the duties. Reagan called the first quarter, the other man the second, Reagan the third. He expected to hand off the microphone again for the fourth quarter, but MacArthur phoned Reagan's partner and told him to let the new fellow finish. Reagan concluded that he had passed his live test.

MacArthur offered him $10 a game for Iowa's three remaining home games. Reagan was thrilled to accept and delighted to be a high-profile sports announcer. The Big Ten was the best football conference in the country, and to call its games was a remarkable feat for someone so new to the business.

Unfortunately, his job terminated with the season's end. Basketball and other winter sports had nothing like football's following, and the station had no work for him. MacArthur said he'd keep him in mind for the following season, but he couldn't make any promises.

REAGAN COULD NOT have lost his job at a bleaker time. The depression had prompted thousands of jobless, often homeless veterans of the war to march to Washington to petition for early payment of the pension they had been promised, lest they expire before they reached the statutory age. Herbert Hoover, the self-made millionaire whose precrash election had seemed confirmation of the business-oriented policies of that Republican era, grew alarmed at their presence. He envisioned a Bolshevik revolution toppling America's capitalist democracy, and he ordered the army to drive the petitioners away. The operation, headed by Chief of Staff Douglas MacArthur, who shared Hoover's red fears, proved a tragic fiasco as the soldiers scattered the pitiful vets, burned their makeshift shelters and many of their meager belongings, and, in the process, killed the baby daughter of one of the protesters. The country recoiled at Hoover's over-reaction; Franklin D. Roosevelt, the Democratic nominee for president, turned to his friend Felix Frankfurter and declared, "Well, Felix, this will elect me."

It, and the deepening depression, did just that. Reagan was one of the twenty-three million Americans who in November 1932 voted for Roosevelt, and with them and more than a few of the sixteen million who voted for Hoover, he looked to the new president to stanch the econo-my's bleeding. But Roosevelt wouldn't be inaugurated until four months after the election, as inaugurations occurred in March in those days, and it wasn't clear the country could survive until then. The banking system staggered under the weight of stock losses and bad loans; its distress caused depositors to fear for the security of their deposits. Few deposits were insured, and the depositors raced to withdraw their funds before the banks collapsed. These "runs" precipitated the very result the depositors feared; dozens, then scores, then hundreds and thousands of banks closed their doors. The entire financial structure of the United States teetered at the edge of an abyss.

As if the moment weren't fraught enough, Roosevelt was nearly assassinated just weeks before he was to take his inaugural oath. The deranged gunman missed Roosevelt but killed a member of his traveling party, the mayor of Chicago. The incident intimated that Hoover had been right in declaring democracy in danger, if perhaps wrong about the direction from which the danger came.

Reagan didn't record his reaction to Roosevelt's instantly famous inaugural address, with its reassurance that America had nothing to fear but fear itself. Nor did he comment directly on the initial measures Roosevelt adopted to stem the bank panic. But after Congress, convened in special session at Roosevelt's summons, rubber-stamped an emergency banking bill sent from the White House to the Capitol, Reagan listened with rapt attention as Roosevelt explained the measure to the American people. A radio man himself, Reagan heard the master radio performer of his political generation deliver the first of what came to be called Fireside Chats. Reagan listened and learned. "His strong, gentle, confident voice resonated across the nation with an eloquence that brought comfort and resilience to a nation caught up in a storm and reassured us that we could lick any problem," Reagan recalled. "I will never forget him for that."

Roosevelt's bold action and calming words saved the banks, and the president turned to the other challenges facing the country. He sent fifteen major bills to Congress during the hundred days of the special session, and the legislature approved every one. The aim of the New Deal, as Roosevelt's program was called, was relief for suffering individuals, recovery for the economy, and reform to prevent a recurrence of the depression. The sum was an enormous expansion of government authority over the private sector and of government responsibility for the welfare of the American people.

Conservative Republicans were appalled. The virtues of individual initiative and personal responsibility that had formed the bedrock of the republic were in danger, they said. American self-reliance had long held Leviathan, the insatiable beast of big government, at bay. But in the frenzy of the moment the Democrats had unchained the beast, whose appetite would grow with the eating.

Some Democrats were sobered, too. Southern conservatives, Democrats by virtue of bad memories of the Civil War and Reconstruction, chafed at the takeover of the party of Jefferson and Jackson—skeptics of big government both—by its northeastern liberal wing. For the moment they heeded the demands of party solidarity, but they remained unconvinced of the New Deal's virtues.

Yet Reagan was in awe. The poor kid from the struggling family was thrilled that a patrician like Roosevelt had taken the part of ordinary people. "I soon idolized FDR," Reagan remembered. "He'd entered the White House facing a national emergency as grim as any the country has ever faced and, acting quickly, he had implemented a plan of action to deal with the crisis."

THE REAGAN HOUSEHOLD benefited directly from the New Deal. Democrats in Dixon weren't numerous, and Jack Reagan was one of the most visible. He was still unemployed and for this reason was delighted to accept a job helping administer federal relief. Reagan visited Jack's office when he was in town. "I was shocked to see the fathers of many of my schoolmates waiting in line for handouts—men I had known most of my life, who had had jobs I'd thought were as permanent as the city itself," he remarked later.

Reagan's own unemployment was of shorter duration than that of many of Jack's clients. In early 1933, Pete MacArthur at WOC telephoned to say that one of his regular announcers had quit; did Reagan want the job? Reagan said he did, and he left for Davenport the next day.

He discovered that regular programs posed a different challenge than football games. At the games, Reagan chiefly had to report. He elaborated and embellished, to be sure, but the story unfolded in front of him. In the regular programs, by contrast, he had to create stories. He played recorded music and read advertisements, but he had to craft a narrative that held the disparate parts of the show together. He had to convey his personality and develop a rapport with listeners.

It didn't come easily. By his own admission he was stiff and uncomfortable. He nearly got fired, but the man he was supposed to train as his replacement had second thoughts about entering the entertainment world; he thought his current job, teaching, provided greater security. Reagan got a second chance. He asked for and received coaching to improve his on-air performance, and he gradually learned to feel more comfortable in front of the microphone.

Meanwhile, though, the parent company of WOC decided to consolidate operations and fold WOC into a more powerful station, WHO, in Des Moines. Reagan and the other Davenport staffers were told they could keep their jobs if they were willing to move to Des Moines.

Most were, including Reagan. The depression still blighted the land, notwithstanding Roosevelt's efforts at relief and recovery, but the radio industry surged forward. The Davenport station had broadcast at 1,000 watts, limiting its range to the environs of Davenport; the Des Moines station broadcast at 50,000 watts, sending its signal across much of the Midwest—and at night, when the signals bounced off the ionosphere, across the country. One result of the switch to more powerful transmitters was the industry consolidation Reagan experienced; another was the deeper penetration of radio into American homes and American lives. Radio stations broadcast music, with bands and orchestras performing live in radio studios. They broadcast drama, from highbrow plays by distinguished playwrights to the popular detective series *The Shadow* and the comedy *Amos 'n' Andy*.

And they broadcast ever more sports. The bigger stations reached larger audiences and commanded higher fees for advertisements; these fees supported bigger staffs that could cover events previously ignored. Reagan's new employer sent him to football games, baseball games, automobile races, track meets, and swimming championships.

Yet the budget wasn't boundless, and he sometimes announced games from a distance. His station would arrange for telegraphic summaries to be wired to the station from the ballpark where the Chicago Cubs or White Sox were playing. A telegraph operator at the station would pass the summaries to Reagan, who would convert them into a narrative. The numbers "6-4-3" meant a double play from the shortstop to the second baseman to the first baseman. Reagan would relate how the batter Jones hit a sharp grounder or a high hopper to Smith at shortstop, who would field it cleanly or perhaps bobble it a moment before tossing it to Murphy at second, who would leap over the sliding runner from first, Young, while firing it to the first baseman, Greenberg, who would stretch to catch it just in time to nip Jones barreling down the first-base line.

The system left ample scope for Reagan's imagination, especially when technical malfunctions occurred. "One summer's day—and this is a story that I've probably repeated more times in my life than any other—my imagination was tested to its maximum," he remembered. "The Cubs and St. Louis Cardinals were locked in a scoreless ninth-inning tie with Dizzy Dean on the mound and the Cubs' Billy Jurges at bat. I described Dean winding up and releasing his pitch. Then Curly, our telegraph operator, shook his head and passed me a slip of paper, and I looked for a description of the pitch. Instead his note read, 'The wire's gone dead.' Well, since I had the ball on the way to the plate I had to get it there. Although I could have told our listeners that the wire had gone dead, it would have sent them rushing toward their dials and a competitor. So I decided to let Jurges foul off the pitch, figuring Western Union would soon fix the problem. To fill in some time, I described a couple of kids in the stands fighting over the foul ball. When Curly gestured that the wire was still dead, I had Jurges foul off another ball; I slowed Dean down, had him pick up the resin bag and take a sign, shake it off, get another sign, and let him pitch; I said he'd fouled off another one, but this time he'd just missed a home run by only a few inches." Eventually, the wire came alive again, but not before Reagan's Jurges had fouled off a record number of pitches. Then he popped out.

How many of Reagan's listeners were actually fooled by his performances is impossible to say. His wasn't the only radio station that made do with the telegraphic hookups, which were common across the country during the 1930s and for years after. Nor was Reagan the only announcer to fill dead time with faux fouls and spurious pitches. Other announcers added sound effects: toy bats hitting marbles to re-create the crack of bat against ball, recorded cheers for crowd noise, canned organ music for the seventh-inning stretch, even sheets of metal to provide rumbles of thunder for rain delays. What captured and held listeners wasn't so much the game at the actual ballpark as the story the announcer crafted around it. Reagan's audience didn't care that he couldn't see the game as long as he spun a good yarn that let *them* see it, in their minds' eyes. He did, and they kept tuned in.

PART TWO

THE GOLDEN WEST

1935–1962

3

YET REAGAN WANTED more. He always wanted more. Even as it honed his skill at spinning stories, radio whetted Reagan's appetite for the larger audiences of movies. He worked at the Des Moines station for four years, but as time passed, he plotted his escape to the silver screen. He talked his bosses into sending him to Southern California in 1935 to cover spring training of the Chicago Cubs; to offset the cost, he agreed to count the trip as his annual vacation. He hoped to visit Hollywood while in the area and discover what he could about the magical place where movies were made. Maybe the magic would touch him.

He told no one about this ulterior part of his plan. And during his first trip to California, little came of it. Catalina Island, where the Cubs held their training camp, was farther from Hollywood than he had thought, and the journey by ferry and streetcar wasn't convenient. Nor did anything of substance emerge on his second trip, in the spring of 1936. But on his third visit, in April 1937, he got help from the weather. A storm system sat over Southern California, canceling baseball and giving the reporters covering the team time off. Reagan took the opportunity to go to Los Angeles and visit the Biltmore Hotel. He had the name of a woman who had worked at WHO before he arrived and who had left the station to have a try at Hollywood. She hadn't caught on in movies yet, beyond bit parts, but she had landed a gig singing with a band that played the Biltmore. Reagan took in one of the shows and sent her a message inviting her to meet him afterward.

Her name was Joy Hodges and she was happy to see a fellow midwesterner. He brought greetings from mutual friends; they swapped reminiscences of Iowa. Eventually, he screwed up his courage and admitted he had a secret wish to break into movies.

He was wearing the glasses he regularly wore to correct his nearsightedness. She told him to take them off. Movie actors didn't wear glasses, at least not on-screen. She looked him over and decided he might do. She said she had an agent who was looking for clients. Reagan said he'd love to meet the man.

The next morning she called Reagan and said she had set up an appointment. Reagan arrived for the ten o'clock meeting without his glasses; he felt his way through the receptionist's office to his meeting with Bill Meiklejohn. He described his experience acting onstage and broadcasting on radio, exaggerating where he thought he could get away with it. Meiklejohn doubtless discounted the description but liked the new fellow's appearance sufficiently to call Warner Brothers. "Max," he told Max Arnow, a casting director at the studio, "I have another Robert Taylor sitting in my office."

Arnow heard such statements from agents every day. "God made only one Robert Taylor," he replied, loud enough for Reagan to hear. But the studios were always looking for new talent and fresh faces, and he told Meiklejohn to bring Reagan over.

They took Meiklejohn's car, and Reagan soon found himself sitting in front of Arnow. After they were introduced, Arnow asked, "Is that your real voice?" Reagan thought the question strange but replied that it was. Arnow didn't elaborate, but Reagan learned afterward that he sounded like an actor who had worked for Warner Brothers and recently died.

Arnow sized Reagan up while Meiklejohn preached his virtues. Arnow agreed to give Reagan a screen test. He handed him a few pages from the script of *The Philadelphia Story* and told him to memorize them and wait for a call.

Reagan couldn't believe his swift good fortune. He took the script to Catalina, where he found he couldn't concentrate on his baseball reporting. He returned to the mainland by ferry several days later and reported to the studio. The screen test lasted but a few minutes. Reagan exchanged lines with a young actress brought in for the purpose and then was dismissed.

The next day Arnow called Meiklejohn and said the test had gone well enough that he wanted to show it to Jack Warner, the head of the studio. But Warner was busy and might not be able to look at it for a couple of weeks. Reagan should sit tight.

Reagan was hopeful but not unrealistic. Amid the continuing depression, he couldn't afford to jeopardize his radio job on the chance Warner might like him. He said the Cubs were breaking camp and heading to Chicago; he had to be on the eastbound train with them.

Reagan only later reflected that his apparent nonchalance about an acting career might have served him well. "I didn't realize that Hollywood was a place where everyone knocked down the doors trying to get in, and they weren't used to someone telling them that he had another job and couldn't wait around. It must have intrigued them a little." At the time he thought he might have ruined his one chance of fame. "I said to myself, 'What a damn fool.'"

And so when, two days after arriving back in Des Moines, he received a telegram from Meiklejohn, he was stunned. "Warner offers contract seven years," it said. "One year option. Starting $200 a week. What shall I do?"

Reagan replied at once: "Sign before they change their minds."

JACK WARNER DIDN'T change his mind easily. He didn't do much of anything easily, because nothing in life had come easily to him. A son of Polish Jews who had fled pogroms in the Russian Empire, Warner grew up hearing stories of Cossacks raiding the shtetlach and burning houses and raping women and girls. He spent his boyhood in Youngstown, Ohio, where Mafia mobsters and labor thugs broke heads and slit throats for profit and influence. He gravitated to vaudeville to escape the gang life of the steel town, performing onstage until his elder brother Sam persuaded him to move to the production side of the business, where the money was. He and Sam got into movies just after the turn of the twentieth century, showing early films in makeshift theaters around Ohio and Pennsylvania. In time they turned to film production. But this threw them athwart Thomas Edison's movie trust, which controlled most production on the East Coast, and they decided to relocate west. Jack planted the family flag on Sunset Boulevard in Hollywood as the Roaring Twenties were beginning, and the Warner Brothers studio—Sam and Jack were joined by Harry and Albert—rode the rising tide of consumer spending and technological improvement in the years that followed.

The studio's first star was a dog, a German shepherd named Rin Tin Tin who drew huge audiences into the theaters to watch his canine heroics. Jack Warner dubbed Rin Tin Tin the "mortgage lifter" for his ability to erase debts the studio and its affiliates incurred. Warner liked the canine better than he liked most human actors. "He didn't ask for a raise or a new press agent or an air-conditioned dressing room or more close-ups," he said. In fact Rin Tin Tin got a raise, to $1,000 per week; he also acquired doubles to relieve him of the most onerous and dangerous stunts.

But he didn't survive the shift from silent films to movies with sound tracks, not at Warner at any rate. Sam Warner persuaded his brothers to purchase a technology that allowed the attachment of sound recordings to film. The initial appeal was that sound would permit theaters to dispense with the orchestras that played accompaniment to otherwise silent films. When Sam suggested that the technology could also record actors' voices, Harry snorted, "Who the hell wants to hear actors talk? The music—that's the big plus about this." The studio produced *The Jazz Singer* in 1927; the film contained orchestral music, singing, and only a few lines of spoken dialogue. But it was the talking that captivated audiences and shortly rendered silent films obsolete. Rin Tin Tin received his walking papers. "The making of any animal pictures, such as we have in the past with Rin Tin Tin," the studio informed its erstwhile star, through his master and agent, "is not in keeping with the policy that has been adopted by us for talking pictures, very obviously of course because dogs don't talk."

Rin Tin Tin caught on with a different studio, which was more than could be said for some other silent-film stars, who lacked voices for the talkies and couldn't even bark. Jack Warner and the rest of the industry learned that voices counted a great deal in the new films, a fact that worked in Ronald Reagan's favor when his radio-trained voice recorded well in his screen test. Meanwhile, the Warner brothers elbowed their way forward, until their firm became one of the five major Hollywood studios.

And the one that took the grittiest view of life. The leading brand in Hollywood belonged to Metro-Goldwyn-Mayer, the movie conglomerate headed by Louis B. Mayer, who consorted with the Southern California establishment and upheld the conservative business virtues personified by Herbert Hoover, California's gift to America, as it seemed in those predepression days. Mayer dined at the Hoover White House and benefited from the tax cuts implemented by the Republican administrations of the 1920s.

Jack Warner was, in many ways, the self-conscious opposite of Mayer. Warner applauded Franklin Roosevelt and the New Deal, and his studio shot movies that showed the seamier side of American life. Gangster films became a Warner Brothers staple; James Cagney was Jack Warner's personal discovery. Keepers of the American conscience chided Warner Brothers for touring the gutter; Harry Warner defended their films by saying, "The motion picture presents right and wrong, as the Bible does. By showing both right and wrong, we teach the right."

REAGAN HELPED. HE headed for Hollywood in May 1937 in a used Nash convertible packed with nearly all his earthly possessions. His journey recapitulated the trek Americans had been making since the days of the California gold rush; the West had long been the land of opportunity, the glittering destination of the American dream. Hollywood was simply its latest incarnation. Reagan stopped at the Biltmore to thank Joy Hodges for her part in opening opportunity's door, and he presented himself, a week early, at the Warner Brothers studio.

His reception took him aback. "Where in hell did you get that coat?" Max Arnow demanded. Reagan had had the white sport jacket specially tailored; he admired it very much. "You can't wear that outfit," Arnow snorted. "The shoulders are too big—they make your head look too small." Arnow called in an aide. "Take him over to wardrobe and see what the tailor can do with this outfit. He looks like a Filipino." The tailor sliced and reconfigured Reagan's jacket, narrowing the shoulders and fitting it closer to his chest. He ordered special shirts with custom collars to make Reagan's neck, judged too short, look longer.

From wardrobe Reagan was sent to makeup, where his self-esteem suffered further blows. "That Arnow guy must think I'm Houdini," the makeup director groused. "Some of the mugs he signs up!" In fact there was little to do, or perhaps just little that could be done. A new haircut erased the vestiges of Reagan's college-boy look. His face had good color; he could keep that.

His voice was fine, though he would need coaching for particular dialects or accents. But his name would have to be changed. No one outside Holland would pay to see an actor called Dutch. Reagan hesitantly suggested his given first name. Arnow and the Warner Brothers publicity team rolled the moniker around their tongues: "Ronald Reagan . . . Ronald Reagan." It sounded okay. It would fit a marquee. They would give it a try.

NEITHER THEY NOR he had any idea how much hinged on this snap decision. Reagan's highest hope was to make his career in movies; he had no inkling he would carry his Hollywood name into another field, one that insisted on real names.

Instead, he concentrated on getting his first role. Studios tested their new talent in B movies, the low-budget features that filled out the double bills that made moviegoers feel they were getting their money's worth. The Bs were shot quickly and forgotten even faster. Reagan seemed a natural for one that was beginning production when he arrived; called *Love Is on the Air*, it had a part for a radio announcer of roughly Reagan's description.

Reagan confessed to unaccustomed stage fright as the hour of his first take approached. For years he had dreamed of this opportunity; he had no fallback if he botched it. Another member of the cast, a veteran character actor, noticed his nerves. "Kid, don't worry," he said. "Just take it easy and everything will be all right." The makeup crew applied some final touch-ups. The lights came on. The director said, "Camera . . . Action!"

Reagan remembered the moment decades later. "Suddenly, my jitters were gone," he said. "The old character actor had been right. As soon as I heard the director's words, I forgot all about the camera and the lights and the crew and concentrated on delivering my lines."

It was his second stroke of luck, or fate, in just a few days. The ability to act for a camera, as opposed to an audience, is a talent not given to every thespian. Nor is it a talent vouchsafed to every politician. From the beginning, Reagan loved the camera, and the camera loved him. The affair would last a lifetime.

The early notices were favorable. Besides filling out theater bills, the B films served as the studios' equivalent of baseball's minor leagues; scouts and reviewers paid less attention to the movies themselves than to the new talent they introduced. The reviewers liked Reagan, and about the time he discovered that his seven-year contract actually guaranteed him only six months of work, Warner Brothers extended the option another six months and gave him a raise.

ALREADY HE EYED his next step. Dreams of the A-list danced in his head. He made a triumphal return to Dixon, which proclaimed him its favorite son. He brought his parents west to California and set them up in the first house they had ever owned. He suggested roles for himself and even movies to his bosses at Warner.

One suggestion resulted in a picture about Knute Rockne, a Norwegian immigrant who became the football coach at Notre Dame. Rockne was respected but not revered until his 1931 death in an airplane crash, which made him an irresistible subject for mythmakers in multiple genres. Reagan talked up a Rockne movie around the Warner lot and subsequently took offense when Warner bought the rights to Rockne's life without crediting or paying him. Perhaps he was correct to conclude he had been poached, but the idea was obvious enough to occur to any number of people in Hollywood.

He took further offense when he learned that Warner was testing other actors for the role he envisioned for himself: George Gipp, a halfback who, like Rockne but before him, died young and touched similar heartstrings. Reagan demanded an opportunity to test for the role. The producer rebuffed him, saying he didn't look like a football player. Reagan dug out a yearbook photograph of himself in a Eureka College uniform and returned with it to the producer's office. The next day he got his test, and he won the role.

He loved playing a football hero, someone far better at the game than he had ever been. And though the Gipp part was modest in scope, it gave Reagan a line that would be associated with him for decades. Gipp has been diagnosed with an incurable illness; on his deathbed he tells Rockne, "Some day when the team's up against it and the breaks are beating the boys, ask them to go in there with all they've got and win just one for the Gipper."

REAGAN WAS PROUD of his Gipp role, though not as proud as his father was. Sons eventually outstrip their fathers, but in Reagan's case the eclipse came swiftly and dramatically. The family's move to California showed how well Reagan was doing; it simultaneously confirmed what a failure Jack was. On his own or at his mother's suggestion, Reagan softened the blow of his generosity to the older man. He asked Jack if he would mind taking charge of the fan mail that was beginning to arrive for him at the Warner studio. "Look," he remembered explaining, "you don't have to do this if you don't want to, but you could really help me. I've got a heck of a problem with this fan mail, mailing out autographed pictures and so forth.

What would you say if I got you a secretary's pass and a regular salary at the studio and you came in every day to pick up the mail, look it over, order the pictures, and so forth."

His father liked the idea. "Jack jumped at it," Reagan said. "It was a real job, it gave him self-respect, and he did a great job at it." Whether Jack understood that his son was paying his salary, Reagan didn't say. He did say that Jack handled the work better than he himself could have. "One day he showed me a letter from a young woman who had written that she was dying and wanted a photo of me before she did. I thought it was a story invented by someone who believed that's what it took to get an autographed picture. Jack urged me to sign the picture anyhow and I did. About ten days later I got a letter from a nurse who told me that the woman, who was named Mary, had died with my picture in her hands and that it had made her very happy to have it." Reagan added, "Jack never said, 'I told you so.'"

Jack lived only a few years in California. He died in 1941 at the age of fifty-seven. Reagan was pleased to relate his father's last days as a tale of redemption, with himself in a supporting role. "When he died so young, I blamed it at first on his problem with alcohol," Reagan wrote decades afterward. "Now I think his heart may have finally failed because of smoking. I'd always thought of Jack as a three-pack, one-match-a-day man: In the morning he'd use one match to light his first cigarette of the day, and from then on, he'd light the next one from the old one." Reagan claimed partial credit for saving Jack from booze, if not tobacco. "The home he loved in California and his job at the studio may have helped him finally lick the curse that had hounded him so long. I was in the East on an errand for the motion picture industry when my mother called and told me that he had died," he said. "During the call, she told of finding Jack one night standing in the house, looking out the window, and he began talking about his drinking and wondering how their lives might have been different if he hadn't been a drinker. Then he told my mother that he had decided he was never going to take another drink, and she said, 'Jack, how many times have I heard you say that?' 'Yes,' Jack said, 'but you've never seen me do this before,' and he disappeared and came back with a big jug of wine he'd hidden from my mother. Then he dumped the wine into the sink and smashed the jug."

His mother went on to say that Jack had started going to church, and that he was proud of his son's success. Jack had closely followed the filming of the Knute Rockne movie, and when it was ready for its premiere at

Notre Dame, the emotional alma mater of every Irishman in America, he wanted to attend. But he didn't want to ask his son. Nelle quietly passed the word along, and Reagan made the arrangements. "I invited him to join us on the Warner Brothers train that took us to South Bend for the ceremonies and premiere," Reagan recalled. "Before he died, Nelle told me, Jack told her what the trip had meant to him: 'I was there,' he said, 'when our son became a star.'"

HE BECAME A husband about the same time. The end of college had ended Reagan's romance with Margaret Cleaver, in the manner often effected by such life transitions. Physically separated by their need to find jobs, they drifted apart emotionally. Margaret went off to France, where she met a young man in the American consular service whom she eventually married. Reagan went to Iowa and then Hollywood, where he met young women as suddenly detached from their roots as he was.

The studios understandably emphasized the romantic appeal of their actors, and the movie press sold papers relating which actor was dating which actress, where they dined, and what clubs they haunted. Reagan received his share of coverage, much of it courtesy of Louella Parsons, the doyenne of the gossip columnists, who happened to be from Dixon, Illinois. She took a liking to Reagan, with whom she had a minor role in one of his first films, *Hollywood Hotel*.

Parsons considered matchmaking part of the mythmaking of Hollywood, and when Reagan and a young actress named Jane Wyman appeared together in the 1938 B comedy *Brother Rat*, about three cadets at the Virginia Military Institute, Parsons publicized a budding romance. Wyman's childhood and youth had been even more challenging than Reagan's. She had been born Sarah Jane Mayfield in St. Joseph, Missouri, in 1917. Her father left the family when she was five, and her overwhelmed, or distracted, mother farmed her out to some neighbors. Her foster mother lost her husband when Jane was eleven, and the two relocated to Los Angeles, where Jane found independence of a sort in marriage, at sixteen, to a salesman named Wyman. The marriage didn't last, but the name did, and as Jane Wyman she made her way to Hollywood, where she signed a contract with Warner Brothers a year before Reagan arrived. She married again, but this marriage failed even more quickly than the first, and by the time she and Reagan encountered each other on the set of *Brother Rat*, she was again in the mood for romance.

Or perhaps for security. Wyman guarded her innermost feelings, but a few years later she told an interviewer that until she met Reagan, she had never been able to entrust her feelings to anyone. She had hardly known her father and had scant experience of a stable home. Reagan, tall and strong, six years her elder, offered emotional assurance that warmed her from within. "He was such a sunny person . . . genuinely and spontaneously *nice*," she said. He seemed a rock of stability. She couldn't overstate what his love did for her. "Marrying Ronnie worked a miracle for me."

As for what Reagan saw in Wyman, it doubtless started with her physical attractiveness. She was young and vulnerable looking, in a way that men, including her two husbands and then Reagan, found irresistible. Her mercurial personality added to the appeal; at one moment she could coo, at the next hiss and spit. Had Wyman not expressed interest in Reagan, he might have paid her little mind. He had formed no serious attachments since parting with Margaret Cleaver. In his own way he was as cautious and distrustful of love as Jane. No more in his background than in hers did childhood afford a model for happy marriage. His parents, unlike hers, had stayed together, but he certainly did not intend to become a husband like his father had been to his mother.

Nor did he possess, or was he possessed by, an ungovernable libido. A Hollywood veteran of that era, a woman, later distinguished Reagan from the lions of the boudoir. "When Clark Gable or Errol"—Flynn—"or Ty Power came into the room, you could just feel the heat waves shimmering," she told an interviewer. But not Reagan? the interviewer asked. "Oh no, *never* Ronnie." Why not? the interviewer asked. Wasn't he as handsome as the others? "Yes," she responded. "But female desire is attuned to male desire. Clark, Errol, obviously were crazy about women. Ronnie just wasn't. I don't think he ever looked at Ann Sheridan"—with whom Reagan starred in *Kings Row*—"and she was *luscious*."

In any event, Wyman seems to have initiated the romance, and Reagan offered little resistance. She might have been more eager to secure a commitment than he: Hollywood gossip and bits of circumstantial evidence suggest that she staged a suicide attempt to dramatize that she couldn't live without him. On the other hand, her hospital stay might have been caused by a nasty stomach bug. Yet the story went around that he held her hand at her bedside and said that of course he would marry her.

The wedding took place in a chapel in Forest Lawn Memorial Park in Glendale, north of Los Angeles, in January 1940. The bride had just turned twenty-three; the groom was almost twenty-nine.

4

WHILE REAGAN'S CAREER and personal life were blossoming, Franklin Roosevelt's fortunes appeared to be fading. The New Deal had stalled in the spring of 1935 when the Supreme Court toppled a central pillar of government planning of the economy, the National Recovery Administration. Roosevelt riposted with the Social Security Act, which expanded the welfare state into individual lives as nothing in American history before it had. The federal government assumed responsibility for the well-being of the elderly, for those unable to work, and for their dependents. Social Security meant what the name implied: individuals would be secured from the great vicissitudes of life in an industrial society. Roosevelt originally intended to wrap medical insurance into the package, but he decided not to press his luck and left health care to future generations.

Social Security proved wildly popular at the polls, not least because the greatest cost was pushed to those future generations. Roosevelt ran for reelection in 1936, and though one out of every seven American workers remained unemployed, he trounced Republican Alf Landon by the largest electoral margin in history until then. Roosevelt interpreted the result as an endorsement of the New Deal and a repudiation of the Supreme Court, and in early 1937 he prepared a measure to bend the court to the people's will. Roosevelt's plan would add justices to the court, nominally to ease the workload of the most elderly justices but transparently to add liberal voices and votes to its decision-making process.

Roosevelt's political instincts rarely failed him, but this time they led him badly astray. His "court-packing plan," as it was quickly called, revived conservatives who had been dispirited by the 1936 election results, and it added to the ranks of Roosevelt critics many moderates who cherished the constitutional separation of powers. A president less intoxicated by his victory at the polls would have heeded the warnings, but Roosevelt stubbornly demanded that the Democratic leaders in Congress drive his court measure forward. They tried and failed, and Roosevelt suffered a stinging political defeat.

The setback proved all the more painful when the economy shortly plunged. After four years of recovery, during which the unemployment rate had declined from 25 percent to 15, the economy unexpectedly lurched into reverse gear. Unemployment leaped while production collapsed; most of the gains of Roosevelt's first term were undone. Economists then and later argued the causes of the recession, variously blaming premature tightening of fiscal policy by the administration and Congress, clumsy monetary policy by the Federal Reserve, and sabotage by capitalists willing to cut off their noses to spite Roosevelt's face.

Whatever the causes of the recession, the consequence was to weaken Roosevelt further. Conservative southern Democrats now challenged him openly, and Republicans scored big victories in the 1938 midterm elections. The once powerful president found himself sorely beset and staggering into what appeared certain to be his final two years in office.

AMONG THE EARLY movies Reagan appeared in were several cops-and-robbers films. Hollywood wrestled with the issue of crime, notwithstanding Harry Warner's appeal to the authority of the Bible. Movies were perceived as more powerful emotionally than the other mass media of the day—the press and radio—and the industry itself and certain outside agencies took pains to ensure that films not contribute to the delinquency of youth or other impressionable people. The Motion Picture Producers and Distributors of America, headed by Will Hays, established a production code designed to protect the morals of America—and, not coincidentally, preserve the industry from profit-threatening negative publicity. The Roman Catholic Church created the Legion of Decency, which likewise policed movie morals, with less concern for the industry's bottom line and more for the influence of the church.

Few themes were taboo per se. Crime and violence could be treated, likewise sex. But they had to be placed in the context of broadly accepted community values. Crime passed muster so long as the criminals met their comeuppance in the final reel. Physical violence had to stop short of the gross or shocking, but fisticuffs were fine as representing a manly out-let for righteous anger and an occasional necessity for the defense of the vulnerable. Marriage was the appropriate setting for sex; if extramarital sex took place, it ought to produce unhappy results.

Reagan negotiated the code easily. The sexy parts went to other actors, and in films involving crime, he battled for good, often with his clenched hands. "When do I fight?" he asked the director of *Code of the Secret Service* upon arrival on the set, according to Warner Brothers publicity. The studio account went on to explain that within the hour the actor had "five skinned knuckles, a bruised knee, and a lump the size of an egg on his head." Reagan played Brass Bancroft, a Secret Service agent who foils counterfeiters and other miscreants with some cleverness but much brute force. The industry paper *Film Daily* called *Code of the Secret Service* a "rip-roaring thriller of bare-fisted walloping action," while Warner Brothers boasted that a companion film, *Secret Service of the Air*, featured "a cafe brawl that is an all-time high for the rough and tumble."

The Brass Bancroft movies—Reagan starred in four—hewed to the mandate that crime not pay. This was a critical matter during the 1930s, when abundant evidence indicated that crime *did* pay. Prohibition had prompted criminals to organize, the better to assuage the thirst of urban tipplers who had never supported the alcohol ban and saw nothing wrong with taking a drink. Prohibition ended during Franklin Roosevelt's first year in office, but the crime cartels carried on. Roosevelt's attorney general, Homer Cummings, declared a war on crime and mobilized the newly named Federal Bureau of Investigation, headed by J. Edgar Hoover, against it. The actions of the G-men weren't universally applauded; in the depths of the depression popular sentiment sometimes gravitated toward flamboyant criminals like the dapper John Dillinger and the photogenic Bonnie Parker and Clyde Barrow.

Yet the appeal of the outlaws simply intensified the pressure imposed on Hollywood by government and respectable opinion not to glamorize the gangsters. Government's leverage was the threat of antitrust action against the studios, which oligopolized their market and stifled competi-tion. Respectable opinion could orchestrate boycotts of theaters and films, as when the Catholic cardinal of Philadelphia, offended by a provocative Warner Brothers billboard, forbade his flock to attend movies. The prel-ate's action got Hollywood's attention. An industry executive recalled a meeting of top executives: "There was Harry Warner, standing up at the head of the table, shedding tears the size of horse turds, and pleading for someone to get him off the hook. And well he should, for you could fire a cannon down the center aisle of any theater in Philadelphia, without danger of hitting anyone!"

The campaign against crime segued into a fight against other challenges to the status quo. In a decade when capitalism appeared to have run aground, more than a few Americans sought alternatives. Communism appealed to many who noted that the Soviet Union, the homeland of communism, wasn't suffering from the depression that had paralyzed the capitalist world. The fact that international communists were among the few standing up to fascism added to the allure of the Marxist-Leninist doctrine. Hollywood actors and writers might or might not have been drawn to communism in greater proportion than Americans at large, but they were more visible, and as a result their actions were more closely monitored. When Errol Flynn, Warner Brothers' most valuable property, traveled to Spain to see how the communists there were doing against the fascists in Spain's civil war, the Hearst newspaper syndicate condemned him as a communist fellow traveler. Jack Warner fretted that Flynn's career was over. "If any more stuff comes out in the American papers like this, the public certainly won't want him," Warner said. He informed Flynn how dire his situation was, and Flynn stepped back.

The lesson wasn't lost on other actors. Reagan's Illinois upbringing and education hadn't exposed him to much in the way of radicalism; his knowledge of communism wouldn't have filled a short scene in a skimpy screenplay. Yet his early experience in Hollywood made him realize that whatever it promised for the rest of the proletariat, communism would be nothing but trouble for a studio contract player. He would stick with the forces of law and order, on screen and off.

No CODES GOVERNED Hollywood's treatment of foreign affairs, but the studios nonetheless touched the subject at their peril. The isolationism that had gripped the country in the wake of World War I remained strong, causing American elected officials to keep their distance from the troubles of Europe and Asia. Franklin Roosevelt had been an ardent advocate of the League of Nations and other forms of American foreign engagement until the election of 1920, in which he took the second spot on the Democratic ticket. But after he and James Cox, the presidential nominee, went down to a disastrous defeat, in no small part on account of the League's unpopularity, Roosevelt kept his internationalist views to himself. He spent his first term as president dodging foreign affairs, pointedly refusing to accept responsibility for any multilateral approach to ending the depression.

But isolation had serious drawbacks. Japan had exited the world war and the postwar peace conference miffed at not having been accorded the respect received by the other members of the victorious alliance; the Japanese government spent the next two decades devising means for compelling respect. It severed Manchuria from China in 1931 and applied increasing pressure against the rest of the country. In 1937 it launched an open war against China, seizing the capital city of Nanking in especially brutal fashion.

The affairs of Europe were even more alarming. Italian democracy succumbed to the blows of Benito Mussolini and his fascist thugs; in 1935 the thuggery spread to Africa when Italian forces invaded Abyssinia, as Ethiopia was then called. Spain's civil war produced horrific bloodshed and an evil premonition that if fascism triumphed there, as it seemed likely to do, it might conquer much of Europe.

The greatest danger developed in Germany. Adolf Hitler took office as chancellor just weeks before Franklin Roosevelt became America's president. Hitler's hatred of Jews was no secret, but only gradually did the world discover how fully that hatred informed the policy of Germany. The National Socialist, or Nazi, Party and its allies in the German parliament imposed increasing debilities on the Jews living in what Hitler called the Third Reich (the empires of Charlemagne and then the Wilhelms having been the first two). Hitler denounced the postwar settlement and rebuilt the German military; he demanded territorial adjustments to restore Germany's prewar borders.

The reaction in America to all this took two forms. On one side were internationalists who believed Hitler and the other fascists represented an existential threat that the remaining democracies, including America, could ignore only at grave peril. On the other side were isolationists who declared the danger overblown and likely to produce the same sucker's sentiments that had drawn the United States into the world war in 1917. Franklin Roosevelt agreed with the internationalists yet couldn't afford to provoke the isolationists. In October 1937 he tested the waters of internationalism with a speech in which he called for a "quarantine" of foreign aggressors. The timid response by his fellow internationalists, however, and the denunciations by the isolationists, coming amid the grief he was getting over his court-packing plan and the recession, deterred him from doing more.

Hollywood had no responsibility for American foreign policy, but it reflected the same divisions that paralyzed Roosevelt. The Warners, Louis Mayer, and most other leaders of the industry in the 1930s were Jews, and they naturally looked on Hitler's ascendance with apprehension. But precisely because they were Jews, they often felt marginally positioned in American society. To pay special notice to the Jews of Europe would underline their difference from other Americans, a difference many had taken pains to diminish.

So they waffled. Louis Mayer asked news baron William Randolph Hearst to inquire of Hitler about Germany's aims and plans, and he accepted Hitler's assurances, relayed through Hearst, that Berlin had no aggressive designs. Irving Thalberg, who worked with Mayer at MGM, was less hopeful but not more willing to challenge the Nazi regime. "A lot of Jews will lose their lives," Thalberg said upon returning from a visit to Germany in 1934. Yet as a people, he predicted, the Jews would survive. "Hitler and Hitlerism will pass; the Jews will still be there."

The Warners took a stronger stand, in part because Hitlerism hit them sooner than it did some of their colleagues. During an early out-break of anti-Jewish violence in Germany, Nazi goons murdered the Warner Brothers representative there. The company responded by closing its German distribution office. As individuals, Jack and Harry Warner embraced the cause of European Jews, supporting Jewish refugees from Germany and speaking out against Hitler.

Yet even the Warners hesitated to use their most compelling platform, the pictures their studio made. Harry Warner blasted Hitler in speeches but was cautious in approving film ideas. "Are we making it because we're Jews or because it can make a good movie?" he asked of one potentially controversial project. In this they aligned with Adolph Zukor, the head of Paramount, who carefully distinguished politics from entertainment. "I don't think Hollywood should deal with anything but entertainment," Zukor said. "The newsreels take care of current events. To make films of political significance is a mistake." Audiences could find their politics elsewhere. "When they go to a theatre they want to forget."

REAGAN'S ROLE AS George Gipp was the one that would be remembered the longest, but the part he was proudest of was Drake McHugh in *Kings Row*. The film, based on a best-selling novel of the same name, almost didn't get made. The novel was steamy, involving incest and nymphomania in addition to more-pedestrian extramarital sex and physical violence. Industry and outside censors at first tried to block its conversion to film, then settled for its bowdlerization. Yet the dramatic centerpiece of the story remained for Reagan's character, when the disapproving surgeon father of his romantic interest takes the opportunity of a rail-yard accident to gratuitously amputate his legs. "I started preparing for this scene days before it was filmed," Reagan recalled. He imagined what it would be like to wake up from the anesthesia and discover that his legs were gone. Even so, he wasn't ready for the shock he received when he mounted the special bed the propmen had constructed for him, with holes for his legs to disappear through. He looked down and for a moment imagined he had suffered the fate of his character. "I just stayed there looking at where my body ended. The horror didn't ease up." He told the director to forgo a rehearsal take. "Just shoot it," he said. The cameras rolled; Reagan opened his eyes, reached down to where his legs had been, and screamed, "Where is the rest of me?!"

Of all his film roles this was the one Reagan thought might have won him an Academy Award nomination. But Warner Brothers put its weight behind James Cagney, who starred that same year in *Yankee Doodle Dandy*, and Reagan was left out. Warner nonetheless gave him a raise and a new contract and expressed unbounded confidence in his future.

5

REAGAN WOULD LATER derive great benefit from lucky timing, from being in the right place at the right time. But in the early 1940s his timing could hardly have been worse. While *Kings Row* was in production, Japan attacked Pearl Harbor, exploding the premise on which American isolationism had traditionally been based. The oceans no longer afforded protection; the world's problems—the ambitions of aggressors, the struggles for empire and influence—were America's problems, whether Americans liked it or not. Until that fateful day—December 7, 1941—the parting counsel George Washington had given his countrymen about avoiding foreign entanglements had provided a plausible basis for American policy; in the flames of Pearl Harbor, the Father of His Country's hoary counsel became stunningly obsolete.

Franklin Roosevelt had anticipated the moment, though not the locale. For many months tension had been rising between the United States and Japan. Tokyo was determined to gain predominance in East Asia and the western Pacific; Roosevelt was equally determined to keep this from happening. He warned the Japanese diplomatically; when his warnings failed, he ordered a halt to shipments of American oil and steel to Japan. The Japanese interpreted Roosevelt's embargo as a declaration of economic war, which it was. Both he and they understood that the embargo threatened to bring Japan's war machine, engaged heavily in China, to a shuddering halt. The Japanese high command prepared a strike to the south and east, toward the resource-rich East Indies. Roosevelt, who had learned military strategy during seven years' service as assistant navy secretary during World War I, fully expected such a strike. What he did not expect—what no one in the American chain of command expected—was that the Japanese would inaugurate their southwestern offensive with a blow to their far east, against the American fleet at Pearl Harbor. Consequently, the surprise was total and the damage to American battleships, the heart of the fleet, overwhelming. The deaths of more than two thousand Americans added to the pain the nation felt and to the culpability that might have been charged against Roosevelt.

But Roosevelt deflected the blame downward and outward. He launched an investigation of the navy commanders responsible for Hawaii and the Pacific, and he went before Congress to register the nation's outrage at Japan's murderous violation of the rules of civilized behavior. The day of the attack would "live in infamy," he said. He asked for a declaration of war, which Congress delivered at once. When Germany, Japan's Axis ally, declared war on the United States three days later, Americans rallied around their president as they have always done at the start of wars. The only critics leveling serious charges against Roosevelt were the most die-hard of the isolationists, who charged him not with knowing too little about the Japanese plans but with knowing too *much*. Realizing that events had cut the ground from beneath them, they alleged that Roosevelt had engineered the Pearl Harbor attack in order to stampede the American people into war.

Roosevelt didn't dignify the charge with denial. He recognized that he had won the argument over America's international role as definitively as arguments are ever won in political life. He knew that what had been impossible just weeks before was now not merely possible but necessary. For two decades he had believed that the United States must play the leading role in world affairs, but for most of that time he had been compelled by America's popular aversion to foreign involvement to keep this belief to himself. Finally he could speak his mind, confident that the American people would follow where their commander in chief led. The few isolationists left could only gnash their teeth in vain.

PEARL HARBOR PROVED the starting point for Reagan's long march across the political spectrum. It was a complicated journey, for it required moving along two axes. In the 1930s, Reagan was a liberal isolationist: Rooseveltian in domestic affairs but anti-Rooseveltian on foreign policy. In the next two decades he would undergo a double transformation, becoming a conservative internationalist: anti-Rooseveltian domestically but Rooseveltian in foreign policy.

The march began in foreign policy. Reagan's work had kept him too busy to develop strong views about America's role in the world; he leaned toward the anti-German opinions of the Warners and others in the film industry's Jewish community, but he hadn't considered matters closely enough to develop convictions of his own. His patriotism was sporadic and opportunistic. While working in radio in Iowa, he had encountered a member of the U.S. Army reserve who informed him that the local cavalry regiment was recruiting. The cavalry was a dying branch of the army; though horses had played a larger role in World War I than was generally appreciated, no one expected they would have much to offer in the next war. Yet the army clung to the past in many things, and it clung to its horses. And it was looking for new horsemen. Reagan had become enamored of horses watching movies as a boy, and the chance to ride at the army's expense made the recruitment pitch appealing. Equestrian skills certainly wouldn't hurt his film career; to be the next Tom Mix, he'd have to learn to ride. So he enlisted. "I didn't have a burning desire to be an army officer," he conceded afterward. "I still thought we'd fought the war to end all wars. But it was a deal too good to turn down."

The rising tension with Japan changed the terms of the bargain. As Roosevelt applied economic pressure against Tokyo, the army called up reserve officers like Reagan. He received a letter telling him to put his affairs in order and prepare to report on short notice. He was in the middle of filming *Kings Row* with Warner Brothers, and the studio set its lawyers to securing a deferment lest the project, with its $1 million budget and large crew of workers, be jeopardized. Such deferment requests were neither unusual nor particularly unpopular at a moment when most Americans still hoped and many expected to avoid a war. The Warner lawyers succeeded, and in October 1941 Reagan was informed he would not be called before January 1, 1942. But the army told him to be ready to report at "any time after that date."

The studio sought an additional extension. It had other movies in the works, and Reagan's impressive performance in *Kings Row* made the Warner executives think they had a valuable property in him. They strove to keep him working.

Pearl Harbor spoiled their plans. The onset of war accelerated the army's timetable for mobilization, and it altered the public's perception of military service. Special treatment for celebrities no longer sat well with those the film industry relied on to fill the theaters. Reagan's screen persona as a defender of the public weal would have been badly damaged had he dodged service. And so, after a final reflexive effort to delay the inevitable, Warner dropped its lobbying on his behalf, and in April 1942 off to the army he went.

BUT HE DIDN'T go very far. Warner's surrender on Reagan was part of a larger reorientation of the film industry. Hollywood had survived the depression better than most industries; the dream machine allowed Americans to put their troubles out of their minds for a few hours at modest cost. Whether Hollywood would survive the onset of war was unclear at first. The manufacturing industries and everything connected to armaments and war provisions took precedence in government planning, and these were subject to dictates from Washington. Auto production was halted as Detroit's assembly lines were converted to making airplanes and tanks; the sale of consumer goods was strictly controlled lest their frivolous use by noncombatants weaken the war effort. The escapist entertainment that formed a staple of the Hollywood studios was about as frivolous as anything could be; in the weeks and months after Pearl Harbor, movie executives faced the distinct possibility that the government would order them to suspend production until the war ended.

But no such order was given. Its withholding reflected the resourcefulness of Jack Warner and other movie executives; it also owed to the vision of Hap Arnold and certain fellow officers in the U.S. Army. Warner's commitment to the war effort was unimpeachable; having warned about the Nazis for years, he was determined to see Hitler crushed as quickly as possible. But Warner was no less devoted to the welfare of Warner Brothers, and he calculated that by making the movie industry a wing of the War Department, he could ensure that the studio not suffer in the anti-Axis struggle. Warner went to Washington with a proposal that the army publicize the brave work its officers and men were doing on behalf of the nation's security. He met General Henry Arnold, called Hap, who headed the U.S. Army Air Forces and believed his fliers were the future of warfare. Arnold enlisted Warner—literally, as a lieutenant colonel—to create a motion-picture unit.

The two men served each other's purposes. Warner made Arnold and the air force look good, giving Arnold an edge in the competition for resources that became a central aspect of the politics of the war effort. Arnold and the army ensured that the movie industry was classified as essential to the nation's struggle against fascism.

An early collaboration, *Winning Your Wings*, starring Jimmy Stewart, depicted army pilots as heroes and dramatically stimulated recruitment. In fact the prospective pilots enlisted faster than Arnold's air force could handle them. "Jack, we've got enough pilots to fly every plane in the world since you released *Winning Your Wings*," Arnold told Warner.

"Good," Warner replied.

"Not good," Arnold rejoined. "We need rear gunners on the planes, too, and we're not getting them. Can you put something together in a hurry? Give it some romantic appeal."

"I couldn't see anything very romantic about the duties and hazards of a rear gunner's job," Warner observed later. "But we turned out a quickie at General Arnold's request." *The Rear Gunner* had the desired effect, and within weeks the rear-gunner enlistees exceeded Arnold's capacity, too.

REAGAN REPORTED TO Fort Mason, which had guarded the entrance to San Francisco Bay since the Civil War. It still guarded the bay, but after an initial panic that the Pearl Harbor attack presaged a Japanese assault on the American mainland, Fort Mason served chiefly as a point of embarkation for American army units headed to the western Pacific.

Reagan assisted with the embarkation. Any thought that he would join the departures dissipated when army doctors discovered his near-sightedness. "If we sent you overseas you'd shoot a general," one of the doctors told him. "And you'd miss him," the doctor's colleague added.

Reagan remained at Fort Mason just long enough for the army to find a higher use for his gifts and experience. Jack Warner's film outfit, the First Motion Picture Unit, had set up shop in Culver City, ten miles from Hollywood. The unit gathered top movie talent, including such stars as Jimmy Stewart, Clark Gable, and William Holden. Reagan seemed a natural, having played a pilot in prewar films and possessing a voice well suited to the narration many of the films featured.

He was ordered to Culver City and subsequently took part in the production of dozens of films. He played a lieutenant in *The Rear Gunner* who recognizes the aptitude and grit in the young man who becomes the movie's hero and thereby a model for other young men who might want to enlist. He narrated *Beyond the Line of Duty*, about an actual airman who won the Distinguished Service Cross on a mission over the western Pacific. He helped fan the enthusiasm for war with *Westward Is Bataan* and *Target Tokyo*, which respectively celebrated early American victories in the Pacific and the onset of the strategic bombing of Japan's home islands. *The Fight for the Sky* portrayed the exploits of American airmen over Europe. *This Is the Army*, a musical produced with the assistance of the army but not by the film unit, included Reagan as a World War I veteran's son who, in a metaphor for America collectively, receives the task of completing the unfinished work of his father.

His wartime movies made Reagan more familiar to audiences than ever. Millions saw him in uniform on-screen and came to recognize his voice as the voice of those protecting America against aggression. They learned to associate him with American power and American patriotism. Reagan discovered that the role of defender of the nation suited him, and he happily added it to his repertoire.

WORLD WAR II changed Americans' thinking about much more than their country's place in the world. It radically reshaped their attitudes toward one another. Advocates of women's political rights had won a signal victory when Reagan was too young to notice, with the 1920 ratification of the Nineteenth Amendment. But though women could subsequently vote, most remained economically dependent on the men in their lives. During the Great Depression many employers unashamedly laid women off first, assuming that their female employees were not the principal breadwinners in their families. The entry of the United States into the war dramatically increased job opportunities for women, who replaced the millions of men pulled from the civilian workforce into the military. As women assumed jobs previously reserved for men, they brought home paychecks previously claimed by men. For some the experience of economic independence was unsettling; for many it was empowering.

African Americans were similarly drawn into the industrial workforce. Blacks had begun moving from the rural South to the urban North and Midwest during World War I, but amid the Great Depression the migration slowed and in some places reversed. World War II again opened employment opportunities, and blacks once more moved to the industrial cities. For centuries America's race question had been a southern issue; now it became a national one. And it grew entwined with the war effort. A. Philip Randolph, the head of the Brotherhood of Sleeping Car Porters, a largely black union, organized a march on Washington to spotlight segregation by federal war contractors. Franklin Roosevelt did his best to stop Randolph's march, believing it would distract from the war effort. A deal was struck: no march and no discrimination in war industries. The bargain bought Roosevelt the war focus he desired; it taught African Americans that in organization lay strength.

Yet the war's largest result in domestic life was its validation of the New Deal belief that big government could solve America's big problems. This belief had faded during the late 1930s, as the depression dragged on and the New Deal ran out of steam. Republicans and Democrats alike looked beyond Roosevelt to the 1940 election, and both parties assumed that whoever replaced him would be less willing or able to expand government than he had been.

The war changed everything. Its bow wave, in advance of American entry, refloated the American economy by justifying heavy federal spending on military readiness. After Pearl Harbor the federal spending on defense, and on myriad activities related to defense, increased even more rapidly, lifting the country to levels of production, employment, and income it had never before experienced. The approach of the war meanwhile allowed Roosevelt to run for a third term and win. The attack on Pearl Harbor caused Americans to look to their president for leadership and to support the government he headed.

The onset and prosecution of the war retrospectively rehabilitated and prospectively entrenched the New Deal. Absent the war, Roosevelt would have left office under the cloud of the continuing depression; with the war, he got credit for the recovery it brought. And the New Deal, despite having nothing to do with the war and little to do with the recovery, shared the credit, such being the correlational logic of democratic politics. The war, moreover, provided time for such New Deal programs as Social Security to become woven into the fabric of the national consciousness. Not until 1940 did Social Security issue its first monthly retirement checks; until then, and for some years after, Social Security was a net drain on the finances of most participants. A hostile successor to Roosevelt—and had the depression continued, his successor almost certainly would have been hostile—would likely have limited and might even have undone the system. Instead, Roosevelt remained in office and Social Security prospered.

Most tellingly, the war showed big government at its best. The patriotic reaction the war elicited in Americans caused them to cooperate with government and with each other in the common war effort. This cooperation made government more effective than it ever had been before or would be after. Government commanded the economy, telling workers they couldn't have higher wages and manufacturers they couldn't charge higher prices, and the workers and the manufacturers went along. Government provided medical care, and doctors didn't complain. Government built housing, and the real estate and construction industries didn't protest. Government increased taxes drastically, and taxpayers paid up.

What rendered it all acceptable was that government won the war, in astonishingly short order. Had the war dragged on or ended badly, the trust reposed in government might have been withdrawn. But the greatest conflict in human history was brought to a victorious conclusion for the United States only three and a half years after American entry. America's unprecedentedly large government defeated fascism; America's big government placed the United States at the pinnacle of world power. In the process, big government restored the nation's economic vitality and self-confidence. By 1945 most Americans found big government thoroughly acceptable, even necessary, and they had ample reason for feeling the way they did.

6

R EAGAN WAS AMONG those who took comfort in the arms of big government. "At the end of World War II, I was a New Dealer to the core," he remembered later. "I thought government could solve all our postwar problems just as it had ended the Depression and won the war. I didn't trust big business. I thought government, not private companies, should own our public utilities; if there wasn't enough housing to shelter the American people, I thought government should build it; if we needed better medical care, the answer was socialized medicine." Neil Reagan had left the family fold to become a Republican, and Reagan berated him for the apostasy. "We spent hours arguing—sometimes with pretty strong language—over the future of the country," he said. "He complained about the growth of government, claimed Washington was trying to take over everything in the American economy from railroads to the corner store, and said we couldn't trust our wartime ally, Russia, any longer. I claimed he was just spouting Republican propaganda."

Reagan didn't at first intend to carry the arguing beyond his family. Three and a half years in the army had made him long for life as a civilian again, as well as for the civilian pay that came with it. His responsibilities were growing: he and Jane had had their first child, Maureen, in January 1941. For a second child they chose to adopt; Michael entered the Reagan home shortly after his birth in March 1945. The money Jane made from acting meant that the family didn't have to live on the $300 per month the army paid Reagan while he was in the service, but they both were delighted for him to return to his Warner Brothers salary, which was many times higher.

Warner wanted him to earn that money, and it looked for suitable projects. They weren't easy to find. Tastes had changed; the audience had changed. For Reagan to flop in his first postwar feature might have been fatal to his career and to the investment the studio had made in him. Warner moved slowly, and Reagan took what amounted to a paid vacation. "I was well fixed," he explained afterward. "My $3,500-a-week contract was running." He was healthy and still young: thirty-four when the war ended. "I didn't have a practical thought in my head. I hoped it would be a long time before I got one." He visited Lake Arrowhead, in the San Bernardino Mountains east of Los Angeles, and spent days speeding around in a motorboat. He returned to Hollywood and devoted two months to building a pair of model ships. He had never done anything like this in his life before and would never do it again. "But then it seemed exactly the right thing to do," he said later.

Warner still had nothing for him, so he looked for other ways to fill his time. His celebrity and wealth made him appealing to people and groups with causes to promote. He was invited to join the Hollywood Independent Citizens Committee of the Arts, Sciences, and Professions, or HICCASP, which had begun life as a New Deal support group and persisted as a gathering ground for liberal-minded activists in the film industry. Reagan was flattered by the invitation and became an earnest member.

The group took vocal positions on numerous issues. It opposed atomic weapons, emphasizing not the role of the atomic bomb in precipitating Japan's surrender but the danger of atomic weapons to civilization. In HICCASP, as in the day jobs of its members, there was a division of labor. Writers wrote and actors spoke. This was fine with Reagan, who appreciated his innocence on the issues that engaged the group and was willing to read lines written by others. Norman Corwin was a writer for radio, film, and print and had devoted himself to numerous social and political causes; in the autumn of 1945 he grew most exercised about the impending doom that hung over humanity in the shape of a mushroom cloud. He wrote a poem titled "Set Your Clock at U-235," which he and others in HICCASP persuaded Reagan to read to a large gathering of the likeminded. "The secrets of the earth have been peeled, one by one, until the core is bare," Reagan declaimed. "The latest recipe is private, in a guarded book, but the stink of death is public on the wind from Nagasaki." Reagan continued, "Unless we work at it together, at a single earth . . . there will be others out of the just-born and the not-yet-contracted-for who will die for our invisible daily mistakes . . . Oneness is our destination, has long been, is far the best of places to arrive at."

The poem wasn't especially controversial. Singer and actor Paul Robeson had read the same lines to a well-heeled gathering at New York's Waldorf Astoria hotel; appearing on the same program was General George C. Marshall, the architect of the American victory in the war. But Reagan's bosses at Warner decided that public one worldism might upset conservative audiences. Arguing that his reading was a dramatic performance in violation of his exclusive contract, the studio ordered him to cease and desist. Reagan chose not to challenge the order and stepped off that particular stage.

But he mounted others, slightly chastened and somewhat more skeptical of the company he was keeping. Dozens of committees and leagues had formed among the sixteen million veterans of the war; some were straightforwardly self-interested and lobbied Congress for such measures as extensions to the GI Bill, which already provided mortgage assistance, college grants, and unemployment pay to veterans. Reagan, among the top earners in the country, didn't require government help and consequently chose his affiliation on other grounds. The American Veterans Committee had a slogan that appealed to him: "Citizens First, Veterans Second." So he joined. "I expected great things of the AVC," he recalled.

He threw himself into its work. He helped arrange venues for fundraisers, and he gave speeches to Rotary Clubs and other civic organizations. His famous name and familiar face ensured large crowds, and most of the audiences responded favorably when he lauded America's victory over fascism and spoke of the need to be vigilant against any sort of neofascism. One listener, however, approached him after an address to the men's club of the Hollywood Beverly Christian Church, where Reagan regularly worshipped. This man, the congregation's pastor, remarked that he liked everything Reagan had said but thought he should say more. "I think your speech would be even better if you mentioned that if communism looked like a threat, you'd be just as opposed to it as you are to fascism."

Reagan confessed that he had never thought of this. But it seemed so obvious that he said of course he would. A short while later he gave a speech to another local group, a citizens' organization that supported various political and social causes. He repeated his praise of the late war effort and his defiance of fascism should it again appear. The audience loved him, until the closing paragraph. "I've talked about the continuing threat of fascism in the postwar world," he said, "but there's another 'ism,' communism, and if I ever find evidence that communism represents a threat to all that we believe in and stand for, I'll speak out just as harshly against communism as I have fascism."

A heavy silence fell upon the room.

A few days later he heard from a woman who had been there. "I have been disturbed for quite some time, suspecting there is something sinister happening in that organization that I don't like," she wrote. "I'm sure you noticed the reaction to your last paragraph when you mentioned communism. I hope you recognize what that means. I think the group is becoming a front for communists. I just wanted you to know that that settled it for me. I resigned from the organization the next day."

Looking back, Reagan considered this period a turning point in his political education. "Thanks to my minister and that lady," he said, "I began to wake up to the real world."

ANOTHER LESSON OCCURRED a few months later. In the summer of 1946, Reagan was asked to join the executive council of HICCASP. He was pleased by the recognition and eager to participate. But his first council meeting proved disillusioning. Held at the home of a prominent council member, it brought out some sixty people, including James Roosevelt, the eldest son of Franklin Roosevelt. Like Reagan, James Roosevelt thought it proper to strike what he considered a balance between the threats to America from the right and from the left. Roosevelt told the group that HICCASP was being assailed by outsiders as a communist front; it would behoove the executive council to go on record as opposing communism as well as fascism.

"It sounded good to me," Reagan remarked later, "sort of like that last paragraph I had inserted in my speech." But it didn't sound good to many of the people at the meeting. "I was amazed at the reaction. A well-known musician sprang to his feet. He offered to recite the U.S.S.R. constitution from memory, yelling that it was a lot more democratic than that of the United States. A prominent movie writer leaped upward. He said that if there was ever a war between the United States and Russia, he would volunteer for Russia."

Reagan took Roosevelt's side, thereby attracting the leftists' ire. "I found myself waist-high in epithets such as 'Fascist' and 'capitalist scum' and 'enemy of the proletariat' and 'witch-hunter' and 'Red-baiter' before I could say boo," he recalled. One man, screenwriter John Howard Lawson, grew especially incensed. "He persisted in waving a long finger under my nose and telling me off."

The meeting dissolved in disorder. As Reagan left, he was approached by Dore Schary, an executive with MGM. "Come up to Olivia de Havilland's apartment," Schary said quietly.

Reagan did so. "I found a solid group of about a dozen gathering in glee," he recounted. His puzzlement at their high spirits showed, and the group explained that the blowup at the HICCASP meeting hadn't been accidental. De Havilland said she had grown suspicious of HICCASP when she had been given a speech written by author and screenwriter Dalton Trumbo to deliver to a gathering in Seattle. She had decided it was too communist tinged. She had suggested to James Roosevelt that they put the HICCASP council on the spot; Roosevelt's proposal did just that, with the results Reagan had witnessed.

Reagan laughed as he heard the story. De Havilland thought unmasking the communists more serious than amusing, and she asked Reagan what he found so funny. "Nothing," he replied, "except that I thought you were one."

"I thought *you* were one," she rejoined.

7

MEANWHILE, HE STILL got no good movie roles. He blamed his unlucky timing. If not for the war, which pulled him from the screen at the moment of his dramatic breakthrough in *Kings Row*, he might have become the next Jimmy Stewart or Henry Fonda. The war had set him on a side track. Now, in the wake of conflict, Warner Brothers gave the best parts to actors the younger postwar audiences found more appealing.

His complaint had merit; great success on the screen, like great success in any number of endeavors, requires the complicity of fate. The stars must align in the heavens for stars to shine in Hollywood. Yet there was more to the faltering of Reagan's career. If he was being brutally honest, he had to acknowledge his own narrow acting range and limited sex appeal. During his life many acquaintances would comment on Reagan's unwillingness to share his deepest feelings. He could know people for years but never let them close. His reserve might have been partly innate, but it doubtless reflected the need for the son of an alcoholic father to shield himself from the disappointments that come from seeing the one who should be your emotional pillar lying drunk in the snow.

Reagan could play light roles, the ones that let him skate on the fragile surface of human existence. But the dark parts, those that required digging deep and conveying essential inner conflict, were too risky. He liked to think his Drake McHugh role showed what he could do. And in that role he did indeed display terror at a profound personal loss. Yet this was just a moment in a career, a moment he wasn't able to reproduce. He blamed the war. But other actors' careers survived the war. The simple fact was that Reagan wasn't temperamentally suited to serious acting. The same defenses that kept acquaintances at a distance personally kept audiences at a distance dramatically.

As for the limited sex appeal, it might have had similar roots. Love is the riskiest of all endeavors. Or it might have been something different. But in any event, Reagan didn't exude the sexual desire and desirability that made contemporaries like Errol Flynn irresistible to female audiences and instructive to their male escorts.

HOLLYWOOD'S LOSS WOULD be America's gain. But not yet. For now, Reagan simply knew, or rather felt, that he had to find a new stage. Most of the youthful insecurity was gone. And why not? He was rich, famous, and married to a beautiful woman. What more could a man of thirty-five want? But he still looked outward to quiet the inner voices, to prove he wasn't like his father. He still craved the applause of an audience. If Warner wouldn't give him one, he would find his own.

He had joined the Screen Actors Guild in 1937, at the start of his Hollywood career. In 1941 he attended a meeting of the SAG board, in the place of a temporarily indisposed member. His connection to the board continued, indirectly, during the war years, through Jane Wyman, who became a board member in 1942. He returned to the board in early 1946, as a replacement for a departing member, and he won sufficient notice among the other members that he was chosen third vice president that autumn.

He discovered he liked the politics of the film industry. He came to relish the give-and-take of SAG affairs. And he gradually realized he possessed a gift for writing his own lines, lines that reflected the opinions he was developing about the film industry and the broader world.

Reagan's return to the SAG board coincided with a labor battle that split Hollywood and inflicted scars on the movie industry that would last for decades. The American labor movement had long been riven by disagreements over workers' relationship to the capitalist system. Unions that represented skilled workers typically accepted the permanence of capitalism and simply sought better pay and conditions for their members within the existing system. Unions that represented unskilled workers, by contrast, often adopted the more radical position of challenging the existence or structure of capitalism and calling for workers' governance or outright socialism. The American Federation of Labor, or AFL, was the prime exponent of the former, more conservative view; the Congress of Industrial Organizations (CIO) was its radical counterpart. Since the mid-1930s the two organizations had been locked in a bitter, sometimes violent dispute for control of organized labor in particular industries and for primacy in the labor movement as a whole.

The struggle of labor ideologies spilled into Hollywood. The Screen Actors Guild represented actors, the elite of the Hollywood workforce. A new organization, the Conference of Studio Unions (CSU), attempted to gain a foothold in the movie industry by organizing the behind-the-camera workforce. In doing so, it took on an existing union, the International Alliance of Theatrical Stage Employees (IATSE). The CSU called a series of strikes designed to win attention for the union and demonstrate the muscle it could deliver on its members' behalf. The strikes attracted attention, but it wasn't all positive, for the IATSE matched the CSU muscle with muscle of its own. IATSE members challenged the CSU picket lines, leading to riots in which dozens were injured by rocks, knives, clubs, and fists.

Reagan and the SAG board initially tried to avoid choosing sides between the CSU and the IATSE. Those comparatively few guild members with strong labor affinities were reluctant to cross any picket line, almost regardless of its origin. A somewhat larger group, uniformly liberal in political views, accepted the claims of the CSU and its leader, Herbert Sorrell, that the new union represented a democratic alternative to the corrupt, autocratic IATSE. But the largest contingent of actors saw little to choose between the rival backstage unions and were willing to be guided by their own self-interest, which was, chiefly, to keep working. Like Reagan, many of them had been in the military during the war and were eager to be back to their old jobs and their old pay scale.

The fact that the IATSE disputed the authority of the CSU made crossing the picket lines easier than it might have been. Union practice mandated solidarity when workers were clearly arrayed against owners, but when workers were pitted against workers, in jurisdictional disputes such as the present case, other unions could exercise their discretion. The Screen Actors did just that, and they chose to cross the CSU picket lines.

Yet crossing entailed risks. While Warner Brothers let the IATSE line crossers fend for themselves, it took greater care of the actors, in whom it had more invested. The studio would call the actors each morning and name an obscure off-studio site where they should meet. The sites changed daily to foil CSU spies. Buses would roll up to the site, and the actors would board; the buses, with guards, would then drive to Warner and enter the lots. Reagan, who had finally found a part in a project called *Night unto Night*, recalled being advised to lie down on the floor as his bus crossed the picket line, lest he attract rocks or more lethal projectiles. "I couldn't do that," he explained. "So instead they made me sit by myself. They figured that if I was going to get it, nobody else would be hurt." On one occasion he got to the rendezvous point just as his bus was going up in flames.

Reagan at times found himself targeted more specifically. His anti-communist position in HICCASP hadn't gone unnoticed by the leaders of the CSU, who considered him a knee-jerk defender of the status quo and therefore a threat to their union. His decision to cross the picket line appeared to confirm the judgment. Reagan rejected the legitimacy of the union's action. "The CSU strike was a phony," he asserted afterward. "It wasn't meant to improve the wages and working conditions of its members, but to grab something from another union that was rightfully theirs." He said much the same thing at the time, in a meeting in early October 1946. The session had been called by some SAG members who were dissatis-fied with the direction provided by the board, and it was held at the home of actress Ida Lupino. Reagan learned of the meeting from fellow actor and SAG member William Holden, who suggested they attend. Sterling Hayden, a leftist among the actors, explained the strike in terms favor-able to the CSU and, in Reagan's judgment, inaccurate. Reagan wanted to rebut each point, but Holden held him back until Hayden finished. "Now!" Holden said.

Reagan stood up and began speaking. "I confronted one of the most hostile audiences I ever hope to address," he remembered. He had been studying the strike at the behest of the SAG board and was preparing a report for a meeting of the full membership. He had concluded that the dispute was jurisdictional and told the group so at Lupino's. "I launched into a dress rehearsal of the same report I was to give to the mass SAG meeting two nights later. It was giving the opposition ammunition but it was also a chance to spike their guns."

The next morning Reagan went back to work on *Night unto Night*. The filming that day took place on a beach. Amid the session he was summoned to a telephone. The caller refused to identify himself. "There's a group being formed to deal with you," he said, according to Reagan's recollection. "They're going to fix you so you won't ever act again."

Reagan didn't treat the threat seriously until other actors and the executives at Warner told him he should. The studio called the police, who licensed him to carry a gun and placed a security detail at his house. He was informed what the man on the phone might have had in mind: throwing acid into his face. "Thereafter I mounted the holstered gun religiously every morning and took it off the last thing at night," he recalled.

BUT THIS WAS no way to live. While the strike lasted, Reagan and other opponents of the CSU would be in danger. So would their livelihoods. The violence at Warner Brothers cast the entire film industry in a bad light, and the dream machine, like many of its individual stars, had long depended on *good* lighting to work the magic that kept the money rolling in.

There was a related issue for the studios. Critics of the movie industry complained that the studios monopolized business by operating their own theaters and giving those theaters exclusive rights to show their films. Potential competitors were effectively barred from entry. Congress and the courts had allowed the current system to develop and persist, but they might not always be so supportive. Whatever brought the industry into the public eye in a negative way—a protracted strike, for example— threatened to raise the monopoly question anew and perhaps prompt a change in government policy. The studios, and the actors, preferred the security and profitability of the status quo.

A convention of the AFL was about to begin in Chicago; because the CSU, the IATSE, and SAG were all associated with the AFL, it made sense for the SAG leadership to appeal to the federation to arbitrate the Hollywood dispute. The AFL had dipped its toe into the fray already; a panel of three AFL vice presidents, sardonically but universally called the Three Wise Men, had laid down guidelines for a division of labor between the CSU and the IATSE. The guidelines bought a truce, but it didn't hold for long. A subsequent clarification by the Wise Men had only muddied the waters. Yet the precedent, that the AFL would employ its prestige and influence to try to resolve the Hollywood strike, encouraged the SAG board sufficiently that it dispatched a delegation to Chicago.

Reagan was one of the delegates. He hated to fly and had a clause in his Warner Brothers contract that he would travel only by rail or car. Yet the importance of the issue and the shortness of time outweighed his aviation aversion, and he joined the others on a flight from Los Angeles. Their mission was to ask the Wise Men in person what they had meant in their original decision and the clarification. "We wangled a meeting with them—three distinguished, sincere, and, I am positive, thoroughly honest men," Reagan recalled. By Reagan's account, the three said their authority as arbitrators had ceased, but they were willing as private individuals to explain the principles behind their decision. Their explanation was simple, if unsatisfactory. They had been unable to apply jurisdictional rules from the rest of the AFL to the Hollywood case, given the peculiar craft-crossing history of the IATSE. They had rejected suggestions to dissolve the disputing unions and create a new, comprehensive body, because that would violate the AFL's own history and traditions. So the best they could do was go forward with the current structure, resolving jurisdictional disputes in Hollywood on a case-by-case basis.

Reagan and the others tried to get the three to elaborate on this decision as it applied to the issue that was currently the crux of the dispute: whether stage sets should be built by carpenters represented by the CSU or by the stagehands of the IATSE. The Wise Men at first declined, saying they had said enough on the matter. Yet they eventually allowed that set construction ought to go to the stagehands. But they noted that this part of the decision had been unacceptable to William Hutcheson, head of the brotherhood of carpenters that served as the CSU's link to the AFL. They added, according to Reagan's version of the meeting, that Hutcheson had applied great pressure to have the decision overturned or suspended.

Reagan professed astonishment. "Do you mean that the first vice-president of the AFL"—Hutcheson—"is deliberately and willfully flouting the principles of arbitration by blocking the award?" he remembered saying.

The three nodded.

Reagan and the others shook their heads in dismay. "We were beginning to get wiser, if a little sadder," he recalled. Yet they refused to give up. They took their case to William Green, the AFL president, to register their protest at Hutcheson's obstruction. "We said that if something was not done about this one-man block in the AFL, the Screen Actors Guild was prepared to fly stars to every key city in the United States to make personal appearances and show films of the violence outside the studio gates, and to tell people that one man—the first vice-president of the AFL, Bill Hutcheson—was responsible."

In Reagan's recounting, Green broke down in tears of frustration. "What can I do?" he said. "We are a federation of independent unions. I have no power to do anything."

The threat of the adverse publicity, however, got Hutcheson's attention. He agreed to see the SAG delegation. The meeting began with Hutcheson in good humor but adamant that construction of sets belonged to the carpenters of the CSU. When Reagan and the others demanded that he abide by the decision of the arbitrators, he grew angry. "Those three blockheads of arbitrators don't know anything about construction!" he said, in Reagan's telling.

"In this country," Reagan responded, "if you decide to play ball and use an umpire, you obey his decisions."

Hutcheson turned to Reagan. "Look," he said, "thirty years ago the AFL ruled against my men in a dispute with the machinists. I haven't obeyed that for thirty years. Because of that the IAM"—the machinists—"got out of the AFL and I've kept them out."

Reagan and his SAG associates tried to change Hutcheson's mind, but he refused to budge. "It was apparent we were getting nowhere," Reagan recalled. "This was a roadblock in labor consisting of one arrogant man completely wrapped in the cloak of his own power. No one, he was convinced, could tell him what to do." Finally the actors gave up. But as they left, Hutcheson delivered a parting message: "Tell Walsh"—Richard Walsh, the head of the IATSE—"that if he'll give in on the August directive, I'll run Sorrell"—of the CSU—"out of Hollywood and break up the CSU in five minutes." He added, "I'll do the same to the Commies." Reagan thought the addendum significant, in that Hutcheson until then had denied that there were communists in the CSU.

On the way out of Hutcheson's hotel, the actors ran into Herb Sorrell. They told him what Hutcheson had said. Sorrell responded defiantly. "It doesn't matter a damn what Hutcheson says," he declared. "This is going on, no matter what he does! When it ends up, there'll be only one man running labor in Hollywood, and that man will be me!"

8

H AD THE LABOR troubles been confined to Hollywood, much
of the country would hardly have noticed. The studios kept
cranking out movies, and viewers kept filling the theaters. As
things happened, though, the two years after the war witnessed a tsunami
of strikes. Hundreds of work stoppages in scores of industries affected
millions of workers as unions large and small sought pay hikes to match
the increased productivity their members had delivered since the start
of the war but been unable to collect because of wartime wage controls.
Railroad workers walked off the job in the spring of 1946, paralyzing
the nation's transportation network and prompting Harry Truman, who
had succeeded to the presidency on Franklin Roosevelt's sudden death
in April 1945 and whom the rail workers supposed to be sympathetic, to
threaten to draft the strikers into the army, where they would be subject
to his orders as commander in chief. The rail union declined to test Truman's resolve, instead settling the strike. But the experience left the country edgy and willing to heed assertions that radical unionists were seeking
to undermine the American economy.

Meanwhile, a coal strike sent hundreds of thousands of miners out of
the pits and shafts. The coal strike forced steelmakers and other manufacturers to trim production; if it persisted until winter, millions of Americans would be without fuel to heat their homes. John L. Lewis, the mine
workers' chief, had refused during the war to join the leaders of other
major unions in a no-strike pledge, and he had been roundly condemned
as an unpatriotic radical; now he was denounced by Truman as a danger
to America's health and safety. *Time* magazine depicted him on its cover
as a volcano about to erupt.

THE RAIL AND coal strikes, and the Hollywood strike, took place amid a fundamental rethinking of reform in American life. Compared with Europe, the United States had long been politically conservative. From the onset of industrialization in the mid-nineteenth century through the first three decades of the twentieth century, socialism never caught on in America the way it did in Europe, and communism, the militant form of socialism espoused by Marx, Lenin, and other European radicals, won almost no following. But things changed during the 1930s. The left wing of the Democratic Party advocated anti-depression measures that verged on socialism, and even communism acquired a certain intellectual respectability. The principal alternative to socialism and communism, capitalism, had gone bust, and there was little compelling reason to think it would revive. During the sixty years or so since capitalism had taken industrial root in the American economy, it had lurched from crisis to panic to depression. The panic of 1873 produced the country's first nationwide depression, which featured bloody labor battles between striking workers and the hired guns of management. The panic of 1893 triggered a depression that was broader and deeper and included more strikes. The panic of 1907 jolted Congress into taking control of the nation's money supply out of the hands of J. P. Morgan and the money trust and giving it to the new Federal Reserve. The panic of 1929, the stock market crash, was followed by the worst banking crisis in the nation's history and the longest and most painful depression. By then it was easy to believe that Marx had been right and that the contradictions of capitalism impelled the system to excess and self-destruction. After each crisis so far, the system had recovered, but the crises kept getting worse, and as the Great Depression dragged on, the radical critique of capitalism grew ever more persuasive.

Communism looked good by comparison. This was partly because, until very recently, it had not been tested. Only after the Russian Revolution of 1917 were the theories of Marx made the basis for policy in any sizable country. The early results were promising, from what those in the West could see. The Soviet Union largely escaped the depression of the 1930s, and to those few Westerners who trekked east to observe the communist regime there, it appeared to be making steady economic progress, if from a poverty-stricken start. The violence and famine that accompanied Stalin's collectivization campaign remained invisible to most outsiders. To the extent the suffering in the countryside was known, it was often explained as a vestige of historical Russian practice, not a consequence of communism. The czars hadn't required Marx to teach them to mistreat peasants.

Communism acquired moral cachet as well. At a time when the capitalist countries of the West conspicuously avoided confronting fascism, the Soviet Union consistently and vehemently denounced Hitler and Mussolini. Moscow sent weapons and men to Spain to fight the Spanish fascists, who were aided by the German and Italian governments, after the civil war broke out in that country. The antifascist side ultimately lost, but the communists got credit for courageous and worthy intentions.

As a result of all this, communism during the 1930s enjoyed a vogue in the United States unlike anything it had experienced before or would experience after. Membership in the American Communist Party grew significantly, and many who didn't join the party sympathized with its views. Party members meanwhile soft-pedaled talk of world revolution, in favor of a popular front against fascism. Communists joined liberal organizations and in many cases were welcomed. The communists and their fellow travelers suffered a jolt when Stalin signed a 1939 nonaggression pact with Hitler, clearing the way for Germany to launch World War II by invading Poland (and allowing the Soviet Union to seize the eastern part of that luckless country). But Stalin's reversal could be interpreted as the desperate act of a government that could no longer resist Germany alone. Anyway, Hitler's 1941 betrayal of Stalin set things right once more. After Pearl Harbor drove the American government into an alliance with the Soviet Union, the American communists and their friends boasted that they had got there first.

The American alliance of communists and liberals lasted until the end of the war. And it fell apart for the same reason the alliance of the Soviet Union and the United States was falling apart at the same time: an essential incompatibility of purposes. A shared aversion to Hitler had been the cement holding the Soviet-American alliance together; on Hitler's death the cement swiftly dissolved. Washington and Moscow remembered that they weren't just antifascist; the former was also anticommunist, the latter anticapitalist and antidemocratic. Each embraced an ideology that had universal application: the United States aimed to make the world more capitalist and democratic, the Soviet Union to make it more communist.

Whether the clash of ideologies would produce a clash of arms was the question that seized the world from the moment the smoke of World

War II dissipated. Given the penchant for violence the world had manifested during the previous three decades, the outlook wasn't good.

And it was this grim outlook—the possibility, even likelihood, of armed conflict between the United States and the Soviet Union—that shattered the alliance between liberals and communists in America. The former put their faith in democracy and thus in their own country; the latter stuck with communism, which meant opting for the Soviet side. Before 1945 liberalism and communism had been merely different locations on the spectrum of American reform; after 1945 they became antagonists in a struggle for world dominance.

HARRY TRUMAN GOT caught in the cross fire. Truman wasn't on the ballot in 1946, but Democrats in Congress were, and after sixteen years as the majority party they faced a backlog of voter grievances. The result was a Republican sweep of both houses, which rendered Truman's iffy position as an accidental president even more precarious.

During their long exile the Republicans had nursed numerous grudges against the Democrats. Most Republicans had never become reconciled to the New Deal, with its novel constraints on business and its unprecedented social welfare programs; many hoped to roll back the federal government to something resembling its size and scope during the 1920s. But Social Security, the signature public welfare program, was gaining a constituency that grew stronger by the month as more workers retired and began receiving pension checks, and many businesses preferred the regulations they knew to the uncertainty that would accompany efforts at repeal. Besides, though the Republicans controlled Congress, they didn't hold the White House, and Truman could veto any anti–New Deal legislation.

Even so, the labor turmoil of the postwar period provided the Republicans with an opening for attack. Until the 1930s, American law and political practice had typically favored employers over employees, capital over labor. Federal courts issued injunctions against strikes; federal troops were deployed against strikers. Things changed with the New Deal, in particular Section 7(a) of the National Industrial Recovery Act, which shifted the ground sharply in favor of organized labor. The Supreme Court had overturned the Recovery Act, thereby voiding Section 7(a), but the Democratic Congress had passed a substitute, the Wagner Act, which guaranteed unions the right to organize and specified various unfair practices by management. Under the auspices of the Wagner Act, labor had won signal victories in strikes against General Motors and other large employers.

The onset of the war froze the new labor status quo in place without convincing Republicans and conservatives that it was permanent or ought to be. And when the postwar period brought its epidemic of strikes, which alienated voters and contributed to the Republicans' big victory in 1946, the new congressional majority was eager to launch its counteroffensive.

The spearhead of the assault was a 1947 bill sponsored in the Senate by Republican Robert Taft of Ohio and in the House by Republican Fred Hartley of New Jersey. The measure aimed to turn back the clock on labor relations to a more management-friendly time, identifying unfair practices by labor, outlawing the closed shop (which required employers to hire only union members), banning jurisdictional strikes and secondary boycotts, and authorizing the government to break strikes by means of injunctions when the strikes were determined to endanger the national welfare.

Union leaders condemned the Taft-Hartley bill as restoring the shackles the Wagner Act had chiseled off the limbs of American labor. But the Republicans, with the support of conservative southern Democrats who had never liked unions, possessed the votes and passed the bill. Truman vetoed the measure, calling it a "shocking piece of legislation," yet the anti-union coalition mustered an overriding two-thirds majority and rammed it down the president's throat.

WILLIAM HUTCHESON AND the Wise Men remembered their meeting with Reagan and the SAG delegation differently than Reagan did. The AFL leaders denied that any untoward pressure had been applied or experienced in their efforts to resolve the strike. Reagan defended his account in testimony before a congressional committee investigating the strike; he observed that as an actor he had honed his skills at remembering dialogue. Besides, he and the others had been sent to Chicago expressly to listen and remember. "We went into that meeting, knowing in advance of the fact that every word said to us in Chicago—every single thing that happened to us—must be reported factually to our membership; that is why we were sent there. We went in with the definite knowledge we were going to remember everything that was said."

Regardless of who said what, it quickly became clear that the strike wasn't ending. Reagan and other members of the SAG board continued to try to mediate. They persuaded more than forty local unions to come to an October meeting at the Knickerbocker Hotel in Los Angeles. Reagan revisited the origins and evolution of the strike and reiterated his desire for a settlement. But Herb Sorrell and the CSU remained intransigent.

Reagan then went public with his belief that it was the CSU that was the intransigent party. "I am no longer neutral," he declared. "The CSU has proved itself unreliable. Its leadership does not want a settlement of the strike. It stands to gain by continued disorder and disruption in Hollywood."

Reagan's open opposition to the CSU provoked opposition to him within SAG. The dissenters demanded a meeting of the full membership to determine if the board's bias against the CSU reflected the wishes of the guild as a whole. Reagan reluctantly agreed. "We were scared to death," he said later, referring to the possibility that the dissenters would stampede the meeting. But he couldn't well deny the dissenters their right to be heard.

The meeting was rowdy, and Reagan became the object of vituperation. The leftists lashed him for opposing worker democracy and siding with the studios. Reagan presented his and the board's position again, his voice rising and accelerating amid the excitement. "Reagan spoke very fast," observed Alexander Knox, a character actor who had worked with Reagan but didn't like his politics. "He always did, so that he could talk out of both sides of his mouth at once."

The dissenters proved to be a small minority. A motion was offered that the assembled body should vote confidence in the board's leadership. Under the circumstances this equated to opposition to the CSU strike. The motion passed by an overwhelming majority of those present, who evidently agreed with Reagan that working and collecting paychecks outweighed whatever arguments the CSU made for its vision of worker representation.

The studio chiefs were no less pleased with Reagan's performance. "Ronnie Reagan has turned out to be a tower of strength, not only for the actors but for the whole industry," Jack Warner told his son.

The strike went on for months, but without the support of the actors it weakened. The strikers wandered back to their jobs and then out of the union, which expired for lack of interest. Reagan was happy for the part he had played in killing it. The SAG board seemed equally happy, for in March 1947 it made him the guild president.

The dissidents despised him more than ever. "Eddie Arnold and I were crossing an intersection one night on our way to a board meeting," Reagan wrote later. "Coming toward us were two actors we both knew. My smile was already forming and I had just started to greet them when one of the two thrust his face close to mine, his eyes burning with hatred. 'Fascist!' he hissed, literally spitting the word at me."

9

A LESSER CLAUSE OF the Taft-Hartley Act required union officers to affirm that they were not communists. This provision was comparatively uncontroversial, in that the big unions were as eager to rid themselves of communists as conservatives and Republicans were to see the communists rid. But the consequences of the provision, and the mind-set it manifested, contributed to one of the most controversial chapters of modern American history, a chapter in which Reagan played a crucial part.

Congress had been conducting investigations since the eighteenth century. The first congressional investigation probed the 1791 defeat by Indians in Ohio of an army force under General Arthur St. Clair. Congress investigated Abraham Lincoln's conduct of the Civil War. It investigated corruption in the construction of the transcontinental railroad. It investigated the financial power of J. P. Morgan in the early twentieth century. It retrospectively investigated the "merchants of death" who were said to have manipulated America into World War I and battened on the profits therefrom.

The purposes of the congressional investigations were twofold. The avowed aim was to gather information necessary for effective legislation. The unstated purpose was to put or keep the elected investigators in the public eye. Members of Congress relished their role as guardians of the commonweal; it provided them a platform denied to nonincumbent rivals.

Conduct of war was a favorite topic; every armed conflict produced at least one major investigation. Suspected subversion ran a close, related second, as it touched similar chords of anxiety. Fear of sedition inspired by the French Revolution had prompted a close look at foreign aliens in the 1790s; fear of Southern sympathizers exercised Congress during the Civil War. In some respects subversion made a better target for congressional investigators than the overt conduct of war. Challenging the conduct of war entailed taking on the president, a politically risky thing to do during wartime. This helped explain why various of the war investigations occurred after their wars were over. Unmasking subversives, by contrast, was politically safe. The subversives, if they actually existed, were marginal types with few defenders. Congress could wax wroth against them with little worry about political repercussions.

The modern search for subversion began near the end of World War I, when the Senate Judiciary Committee created a special subcommittee to track down German influence in the United States. The defeat of Germany largely mooted that issue, but the committee found a new target: radical Russian Bolsheviks and their sympathizers. The findings of the committee contributed to the antiradical crackdown known to its critics as the red scare. The search for subversives continued when the House of Representatives in 1930 established a special committee to ferret out domestic communist influences, which appeared to be growing as millions of Americans considered alternatives to capitalism. A reconfigured committee was given a broadened mandate that brought fascism as well as communism into its purview, under the rubric of "un-American activities."

The House Committee on Un-American Activities, acronymed imprecisely but universally as HUAC, conducted its first hearings in 1938. Chairman Martin Dies of Texas tried to link the labor movement, in particular the CIO, and the New Deal to communism. The CIO deflected Dies's assault, but the New Deal's Federal Theatre Project fell victim to the hostile investigators, partly because it was federally funded and therefore could be federally *un*funded, and partly because the artistic and intellectual types involved in the theater project made easy political targets. They worked in words and ideas, which might be insidiously twisted to warp the minds of unsuspecting audiences.

This point wasn't lost on the members of Congress who took charge of HUAC after the war. Many Republicans and conservative Democrats had been silently incensed by America's reliance on the Soviet Union in the victory over fascism; the necessity of backing the communists was what had kept them silent, but it didn't make them happy. The end of the war freed them to speak their minds against the communists, and against Franklin Roosevelt, whom many despised, even after his death, almost as much as they hated the communists. They discovered that they could swipe both objects of their animus by attacking certain wartime films produced at the behest of the Roosevelt White House and designed to paint the Soviet Union as a worthy ally. Warner Brothers' *Mission to Moscow* was exhibit A in the double indictment; other evidence included MGM's *Song of Russia* and RKO's *North Star.* The films had accomplished their wartime purpose of rendering American assistance to Russia politically palatable, but after the war they left the responsible studios and writers vulnerable to anticommunist criticism.

The criticism was swift in coming and alarmist in tone. A confidential report produced for HUAC in 1945, and later leaked, asserted that Hollywood was infested with communists. "It is estimated that 514 writers in the motion picture industry either belong to the Communist Party or follow the party line to the letter," the report asserted. "If the industry itself continues to do nothing about it, the great majority of the persons in the industry performing work of a creative nature will, within the not distant future, be either Communist Party members or close sympathizers following the party line. The industry will then be dependent upon this radical group for its output." The charge of communist subversion became a powerful weapon against the Democrats in the 1946 congressional elections, and after the Republicans swept to victory in both houses, they swung into action against the communists, against the Truman administration, and against Hollywood.

THE HOUSE COMMITTEE launched a new investigation in the spring of 1947. Members traveled to California to assess conditions on the ground in the alleged nest of the reds. Studio executives were asked about the influence exerted by the Roosevelt administration in the production of wartime movies. The hearings were closed to the public, but a HUAC subcommittee subsequently reported, "Some of the most flagrant Communist propaganda films were produced as a result of White House pressure."

The spring operation served as a prelude for a major autumn offensive. The committee called dozens of Hollywood producers, directors, writers, and actors to Washington to testify. This time the hearings were open to the public and the press; they were broadcast by radio and recorded by cameras for distribution as newsreels. The HUAC chairman, J. Parnell Thomas, Republican of New Jersey, dismissed criticism already raised that the hearings would undermine the Constitution and stifle free speech. The hearings were for informational purposes only, Thomas said. "Our committee's job is to spotlight the Communists." What private individuals and groups did with the information was up to them. "The movie industry and the American people will take care of the rest." Thomas helpfully estimated that the number of "dues-paying Communists" in the United States was 100,000; these were supported by a roughly equal number who followed the party line without being members.

An added benefit of investigating Hollywood became apparent as the hearings opened. The typical witness at an ordinary congressional hearing was someone most Americans had never heard of. But the film industry hearings involved some of the most famous people in the country. The press and radio treated the hearings with fanfare ordinarily reserved for Hollywood premieres. More than a hundred reporters crowded into the old House caucus room, where the hearings were held. They wedged themselves between and behind loudspeakers, radio microphones, and newsreel cameras. Klieg lights glared upon witnesses and questioners; smaller floodlights dangled from the chandeliers. Special police fought to control the throng of spectators that battled for the three hundred seats reserved to them. When big stars appeared to testify, the cops served as a flying wedge to open the way through the massed bodies.

Chairman Thomas gaveled the hearings to order. "The committee is well aware of the magnitude of the subject which it is investigating," he declared. "The motion-picture business represents an investment of billions of dollars. It represents employment for thousands of workers, ranging from unskilled laborers to high-salaried actors and executives. And even more important, the motion-picture industry represents what is probably the largest single vehicle of entertainment for the American public—over 85 million persons attend the movies each week." It was precisely the importance of movies in American life that made oversight of the industry so necessary. "We all recognize, certainly, the tremendous effect which moving pictures have on their mass audiences, far removed from the Hollywood sets. We all recognize that what the citizen sees and hears in his neighborhood movie house carries a powerful impact on his thoughts and behavior. With such vast influence over the lives of American citizens as the motion-picture industry exerts, it is not unnatural—in fact it is very logical—that subversive and undemocratic forces should attempt to use this medium for un-American purposes." Thomas took pains to assert his confidence in the loyalty of the great majority of men and women who worked in movies. But the danger posed by the minority was so dire as to make a thorough investigation of the industry imperative. "There is no question that there are communists in Hollywood. We cannot minimize their importance there, and that their influence has already made itself felt has been evidenced by internal turmoil in the industry." But the full magnitude and pernicious nature of communist activities and influence remained to be determined. "The question before this committee, therefore, and the scope of its present inquiry, will be to determine the extent of communist infiltration in the Hollywood motion-picture industry."

The committee first called studio executives. Jack Warner yielded to no one in his loathing of communists and other subversives, which were a problem not for the movie business alone. "Ideological termites have burrowed into many American industries, organizations, and societies," he said. "Wherever they may be, I say let us dig them out and get rid of them. My brothers and I will be happy to subscribe generously to a pest-removal fund. We are willing to establish such a fund to ship to Russia the people who don't like our American system of government and prefer the communistic system to ours." In earlier testimony before the committee, in May, Warner had been asked to identify individuals in the movie industry he thought to be communists or associated with communists. That testimony had been kept secret, but it was now read back to Warner so he could publicly confirm his identifications. The committee, the spectators, and the radio audience listened as the names were read off: Alvah Bessie, Gordon Kahn, Guy Endore, Howard Koch, Ring Lardner Jr., Emmet Lavery, John Howard Lawson, Albert Maltz, Robert Rosson, Irwin Shaw, Dalton Trumbo, John Wexley, Julius and Philip Epstein, Sheridan Gibney, Clifford Odets. When the reading of his testimony was completed, Warner was asked whether he stood by the identifications. "Yes, I do," he said.

Producer and director Sam Wood, who had directed Reagan in *Kings Row*, added names to Warner's list: John Cromwell, Irving Pichel, Edward Dmytryk, Frank Tuttle. Wood wanted nothing to do with censorship of the movies. "I think you should tell all things in pictures. I think that if a story has a good point to it—I mean, *Grapes of Wrath*—things happen in America, and we ought to show it." But the reds had put themselves beyond the pale of artistic acceptability. "I think communism is treason and should be treated as such." Wood noted that many people, including some prominent men in the movie industry, did not want to see the Communist Party outlawed, if only because it would then go underground. He disagreed. "I think you have to awaken the public to the fact that they are here and what they are doing." The reds masqueraded as friends of labor and the downtrodden. And anyone, especially in Hollywood, who called them out found himself labeled antilabor, anti-Semitic, anti-Negro. But their actions revealed their true identity. "If you wanted to drop their rompers you would find the hammer and sickle on their rear ends."

Louis B. Mayer thanked the committee for its outstanding work and volunteered to do his part. "Communism is so completely opposed to the principles of democratic government that I welcome the opportunity provided by this committee to be of any service possible to bring out the true facts concerning reported infiltration of un-American ideology into motion pictures," Mayer said. Yet he thought the facts would reveal that the industry was doing a good job on its own keeping the subversives at bay. "I am proud of the motion-picture industry, proud of its record in war and peace. With press and radio, it shares today a solemn trust: to preserve our sacred freedom of speech and fight with our every energy any attempt to use that freedom as a cloak for subversive assassins of liberty." Mayer declared that he and others in the industry had maintained a "relentless vigilance" against subversive influences. "If, as has been alleged, communists have attempted to use the screen for subversive purposes, I am proud of our success in circumventing them."

The executives walked a thin line. They didn't want Congress to dictate content for their films, but neither did they wish to be seen as obstructing an investigation that appeared to be popular with Americans at large—that is, with the people they hoped to continue to bring into the movie theaters. Warner, Mayer, and the others were no less sensitive, in their profit-seeking way, to the public psychology of the moment than Thomas and the elected officials on the committee were from a political standpoint. A boycott, organized or informal, of the films of a studio seen as soft on communism could be fatal to the bottom line. Warner and Mayer had special reason for avowing their anticommunist bona fides, having been responsible for two of the wartime films—*Mission to Moscow* and *Song of Russia*—now lambasted as communist propaganda.

A final consideration was unspoken but never absent from the executives' thinking. They remained vulnerable to the charges of oligopoly in their control of the theaters that distributed their films. The system reeked of restraint of trade, and the victims of the oligopoly were again petitioning Congress to break up the studio system. Warner, Mayer, and the other executives wished to avoid anything that upset the legislators.

Chairman Thomas evinced pleasure at the start of the hearings. "You really lay it on the line," he told Sam Wood. "If the great, great majority of persons in industry, labor, and education showed the same amount of courage that you show, we would not have to worry about communism or fascism in this country. In other words, you've got guts."

AFTER THREE DAYS with the producers and executives, the committee brought out the stars. Robert Taylor told the committee that in his work with the Screen Actors Guild he had often detected communist influences. "At meetings, especially meetings of the general membership of the guild, there is always a certain group of actors and actresses whose every action would indicate to me that if they are not communists they are working very hard to be communists," Taylor said. He thought the studios should take decisive action against the reds. "If I were given the responsibility of getting rid of them I would love nothing better than to fire every last one of them and never let them work in a studio or in Hollywood again." Congress had a role as well. Taylor said he thought the Communist Party should be outlawed and its members banished. "If I had my way about it they would all be sent back to Russia or some other unpleasant place."

Robert Montgomery asserted that communists and other subversives were a small minority in Hollywood. But they were dangerous nonetheless. "They are well organized, they are well disciplined," he said. "They appear at public meetings tremendously well organized and with a complete program." Montgomery was willing to support whatever steps were necessary, including war, to defeat the ideology the communists stood for. "Mr. Chairman, in common with millions of other men in this country in 1939 and 1940, I gave up my job to fight against a totalitarianism which was called fascism. I am quite willing to give it up again to fight against a totalitarianism called communism."

George Murphy agreed that American communists were agents of the Soviet Union, and he believed they had infiltrated Hollywood, but not Hollywood uniquely. "I think there is communism in the motion-picture industry, as there is in practically every other industry in our nation today," Murphy said. He joined Jack Warner in contending that Hollywood was holding its own against the reds. "I think that the screen has been very successful in keeping any attempts to propagandize off the screen."

REAGAN FOLLOWED MURPHY. The lead investigator for the committee, Robert Stripling, inquired about Reagan's background in films. Reagan replied that he had been in the movie business since June 1937—"with a brief interlude of three and a half years," he added nonchalantly.

What period was that? Stripling asked.

"That was during the late war," Reagan replied. The committee members and many in the audience nodded approvingly.

Was Mr. Reagan a member of the Screen Actors Guild? If so, how long had he been a member?

"Since June 1937."

He was president of the guild, was he not?

"Yes, sir."

Had he held any other positions?

"Yes, sir. Just prior to the war I was a member of the board of directors, and just after the war, prior to my being elected president, I was a member of the board of directors."

Stripling posed his first substantive question: "As a member of the board of directors, as president of the Screen Actors Guild, and as an active member, have you at any time observed or noted within the organization a clique of either communists or fascists who were attempting to exert influence or pressure on the guild?"

Reagan had expected the question, which was essentially that asked of each previous witness. He answered forthrightly: "There has been a small group within the Screen Actors Guild which has consistently opposed the policy of the guild board and officers of the guild, as evidenced by the vote on various issues. That small clique referred to has been suspected of more or less following the tactics that we associate with the Communist Party."

Had this clique been a disruptive influence within the guild?

"At times they have attempted to be a disruptive influence."

Did Mr. Reagan know whether they were members of the Communist Party?

"I have no investigative force, or anything, and I do not know."

Had he ever heard that they were members of the Communist Party?

"I have heard different discussions and some of them tagged as communists."

Had they attempted to dominate the guild?

Yes, they had, Reagan said. But like the studio executives, he thought Hollywood could police itself. "I guess in regard to that you would have to say that our side was attempting to dominate, too, because we were fighting just as hard to put over our views." And his side was winning. "An average of 90 percent or better of the Screen Actors Guild voted in favor of those matters now guild policy."

Previous witnesses had testified that communist-front organizations had been established in Hollywood. Had Mr. Reagan ever been solicited by these?

"Well, sir, I have received literature from an organization called the Committee for a Far-Eastern Democratic Policy. I don't know whether it is communist or not. I only know that I didn't like their views and as a result I didn't want to have anything to do with them."

Had he ever been asked to contribute to the Joint Anti-Fascist Refugee Committee?

"I was never solicited to do that, but I found myself misled into being a sponsor on another occasion for a function that was held under the auspices of the Joint Anti-Fascist Refugee Committee."

Could he explain?

"I was called several weeks ago. There happened at the time in Hollywood to be a financial drive on to raise money to build a badly needed hospital in a certain section of town, called the All Nations Hospital. I think the purpose of the building is so obvious by the title that it has the support of most of the people of Hollywood—or, of Los Angeles, I should say. Certainly of most of the doctors, because it is very badly needed. Some time ago I was called to the telephone. A woman introduced herself by name. Knowing that I didn't know her I didn't make any particular note of her name and I couldn't give it now. She told me that there would be a recital held at which Paul Robeson would sing and she said that all the money for the tickets would go to the hospital, and asked if she could use my name as one of the sponsors. I hesitated for a moment, because I don't think that Mr. Robeson's and my political views coincide at all; and then I thought I was being a little stupid because, I thought, here is an occasion where Mr. Robeson is perhaps appearing as an artist, and certainly the object, raising money, is above any political consideration: it is a hospital supported by everyone. I have contributed money myself. So I felt a little bit as if I had been stuffy for a minute, and I said, certainly, you can use my name. I left town for a couple of weeks and when I returned I was handed a newspaper story that said that this recital was held at the Shrine Auditorium in Los Angeles under the auspices of the Joint Anti-Fascist Refugee Committee." Leftist politics had dominated the event. "I did not in the newspaper story see one word about the hospital. I called the newspaper and said I am not accustomed to writing to editors but would like to explain my position, and he laughed and said, 'You needn't bother, you are about the fiftieth person that has called with the same idea, including most of the legitimate doctors who had also been listed as sponsors of that affair.'"

Did he find this to be typical of the tactics of the communists?

"I think it is in keeping with their tactics—yes, sir."

Mr. Reagan was a leading figure in the film industry, Stripling said. What was his judgment about appropriate steps to rid the industry of communist influence?

Reagan reiterated that the industry could handle its own affairs. "Ninety-nine percent of us are pretty well aware of what is going on, and I think within the bounds of our democratic rights and never once stepping over the rights given us by democracy, we have done a pretty good job in our business of keeping those people's activities curtailed. After all, we must recognize them at present as a political party. On that basis we have exposed their lies when we came across them, we have opposed their propaganda, and I can certainly testify that in the case of the Screen Actors Guild we have been eminently successful in preventing them from, with their usual tactics, trying to run a majority of an organization with a well organized minority. So that fundamentally I would say in opposing those people that the best thing to do is make democracy work. In the Screen Actors Guild we make it work by insuring everyone a vote and by keeping everyone informed. I believe that, as Thomas Jefferson put it, if all the American people know all of the facts they will never make a mistake. Whether the party should be outlawed, I agree with the gentlemen that preceded me that that is a matter for the government to decide. As a citizen I would hesitate, or not like to see, any political party outlawed on the basis of its political ideology. We have spent 170 years in this country on the basis that democracy is strong enough to stand up and fight against the inroads of any ideology. However, if it is proven that an organization is an agent of a power, a foreign power, or in any way not a legitimate political party—and I think the government is capable of proving that, if the proof is there—then that is another matter." Meanwhile, Hollywood would deal with the challenge. "I happen to be very proud of the industry in which I work; I happen to be very proud of the way in which we conducted the fight. I do not believe the communists have ever at any time been able to use the motion-picture screen as a sounding board for their philosophy or ideology. I think that will continue as long as the people in Hollywood continue as they are, which is alert, conscious of it, and fighting."

Reagan was asked whether he knew of communist infiltration of the Screen Writers Guild, as opposed to his own Screen Actors Guild.

"I must say that that is hearsay," he responded. "I have heard discussions concerning it." But he offered nothing specific and no names.

Chairman Thomas tendered the committee's thanks to Reagan for appearing. Picking up on the witness's mention of Thomas Jefferson and the self-correcting power of democracy, he predicted, "Once the American people are acquainted with the facts there is no question but what the American people will do a job, the kind of job that they want done, that is, to make America just as pure as we can possibly make it."

"Sir," Reagan interjected, "if I might, in regard to that, say that what I was trying to express, and didn't do very well, was also this other fear. I detest, I abhor their philosophy, but I detest more than that their tactics, which are those of the fifth column, and are dishonest, but at the same time I never as a citizen want to see our country become urged, by either fear or resentment of this group, that we ever compromise with any of our democratic principles through that fear or resentment. I still think that democracy can do it."

"We agree with that," Chairman Thomas said. "Thank you very much."

10

THE SESSION WAS unlike anything Reagan had ever experienced. Such an openly political stage, with a national audience, was new to him. He realized he liked it. And he was good at it. He was quick on his feet. He could feel the room and sense its mood. The camera had always been kind to him, and he knew how to flatter it back. He struck just the right balance between cooperation with the investigation and defense of his industry.

Reagan's reviewers thought so. The movie press emphasized his earnest and determined appearance. Regular papers liked his appeal to Jefferson and the principles of democracy. Most looked forward to seeing more of this articulate, photogenic spokesman for the actors.

Other witnesses were dealt with more harshly. John Howard Lawson was one of those identified to the committee by Jack Warner and others as a subversive; he was summoned to explain himself. Trouble started at the outset of his testimony when he began to read an opening statement. Chairman Thomas demanded to see a copy. After a glance he tossed it down. "I don't care to read any more of the statement," he said. "The statement will not be read."

"You have spent one week vilifying me before the American public—" Lawson objected.

"Just a minute—" Thomas said.

"—and you refuse to allow me to make a statement on my rights as an American citizen."

"I refuse you to make the statement because of the first sentence in your statement. That statement is not pertinent to the inquiry. Now, this is a congressional committee—a congressional committee set up by law.

We must have orderly procedure, and we are going to have orderly procedure. Mr. Stripling, identify the witness."

"The rights of American citizens are important in this room here," Lawson insisted. "And I intend to stand up for those rights, Congressman Thomas."

"Mr. Lawson, will you state your full name, please?" Stripling asked.

"I wish to protest against the unwillingness of this committee to read a statement," Lawson continued, "when you permitted Mr. Warner, Mr. Mayer, and others to read statements in this room. My name is John Howard Lawson."

Things calmed down until Stripling asked whether Lawson was a member of the Screen Writers Guild.

"The raising of any question here in regard to membership, political beliefs, or affiliation—" Lawson replied.

"Mr. Chairman—" Stripling appealed.

"—is absolutely beyond the powers of this committee," Lawson continued.

"Mr. Chairman—" Stripling said again.

"But—" Lawson attempted.

Thomas pounded his gavel.

"It is a matter of public record that I am a member of the Screen Writers Guild," Lawson acknowledged.

Several audience members applauded.

Thomas glowered. "I want to caution the people in the audience: You are the guests of this committee and you will have to maintain order at all times. I do not care for any applause or any demonstrations of one kind or another."

Stripling asked the chairman to require the witness to be responsive to the questions.

"I think the witness will be more responsive," Thomas said, frowning at Lawson.

Lawson resisted. "Mr. Chairman, you permitted—"

Thomas pounded his gavel to make Lawson stop.

Lawson continued: "—witnesses in this room to make answers of three or four or five hundred words to questions here."

"Mr. Lawson," Thomas said, "will you please be responsive to these questions and not continue to try to disrupt these hearings."

"I am not on trial here, Mr. Chairman. This committee is on trial here before the American people. Let us get that straight."

Stripling proceeded with the questioning. "Mr. Lawson, how long have you been a member of the Screen Writers Guild?"

"Since it was founded in its present form, in 1933."

"Have you ever held any office in the guild?"

"The question of whether I have held office is also a question which is beyond the purview of this committee."

Thomas pounded his gavel again.

Lawson ignored him. "It is an invasion of the right of association under the Bill of Rights of this country. It is also a matter—"

Thomas pounded his gavel yet again. "You asked to be heard," he told Lawson. "Through your attorney, you asked to be heard, and we want you to be heard. And if you don't want to be heard, then we will excuse you and we will put the record in without your answers."

"I wish to frame my own answers to your questions, Mr. Chairman, and I intend to do so."

"You will be responsive to the questions or you will be excused from the witness stand."

There was more jousting, more interrupting, more gaveling. Finally, Stripling asked the question everyone in the room had been waiting for: "Mr. Lawson, are you now or have you ever been a member of the Communist Party of the United States?"

"In framing my answer to that question I must emphasize the points that I have raised before," Lawson replied. "The question of communism is in no way related to this inquiry, which is an attempt to get control of the screen and to invade the basic rights of American citizens in all fields."

"Mr. Chairman—" Stripling said.

Another set of gavel blows.

Lawson continued over the interruption and the gaveling: "The question here relates not only to the question of my membership in any political organization, but this committee is attempting to establish the right—"

More gaveling.

"—which has been historically denied to any committee of this sort, to invade the rights and privileges and immunity of American citizens, whether they be Protestant, Methodist, Jewish, or Catholic, whether they be Republicans or Democrats or anything else."

More gaveling, and an order from Thomas: "Mr. Lawson, just quiet down again. Mr. Lawson, the most pertinent question that we can ask is whether or not you have ever been a member of the Communist Party. Now, do you care to answer that question?"

"You are using the old technique, which was used in Hitler's Germany, in order to create a scare here—"

More gavel blows.

"—in order to create an entirely false atmosphere in which this hearing is conducted—"

More gavels.

"—in order that you can then smear the motion-picture industry, and you can proceed to the press, to any form of communication in this country."

Thomas: "You have learned—"

"The Bill of Rights was established precisely to prevent the operation of any committee which could invade the basic rights of Americans. Now, if you want to know—"

Stripling: "Mr. Chairman, the witness is not answering the question."

"If you want to know—"

Gavel after gavel.

"—about the perjury that has been committed here and the perjury that is planned—"

Thomas: "Mr. Lawson—"

"—you will permit me and my attorneys to bring in here the witnesses that testified last week and you will permit us to cross-examine these witnesses, and we will show up the whole tissue of lies—"

Thomas pounded the gavel and declared, "We are going to get the answer to that question if we have to stay here for a week. Are you a member of the Communist Party, or have you ever been a member of the Communist Party?"

"It is unfortunate and tragic that I have to teach this committee the basic principles of American—"

More gaveling. "That is not the question. That is not the question. The question is: Have you ever been a member of the Communist Party?"

"I am framing my answer in the only way in which any American citizen can frame his answer to a question which absolutely invades his rights."

"Then you refuse to answer that question—is that correct?"

"I have told you that I will offer my beliefs, affiliations, and everything else to the American public, and they will know where I stand—"

Thomas had heard enough. Pounding his gavel more definitively than ever, he directed the security officers present, "Excuse the witness."

"—as they do from what I have written."

More gavel blows. "Stand away from the stand," he ordered Lawson.

"I have written Americanism for many years, and I shall continue to fight for the Bill of Rights, which you are trying to destroy."

"Officers, take this man away from the stand."

Applause and boos filled the hearing room as Lawson was led away.

Thomas pounded the gavel at the audience. "There will be no demonstrations. No demonstrations, for or against."

LAWSON'S PERFORMANCE AND experience were repeated, in essence if not in detail, by nine other witnesses: writers and directors. All refused to answer the crucial question put by the committee: whether they were or had ever been members of the Communist Party. The Hollywood Ten, as they soon came to be called, held that the committee lacked authority to require what amounted, in the fervid anticommunist mood of the time, to self-incrimination. They stood on the First and Fifth Amendments, which trumped, they contended, the authorizing statutes of the Committee on Un-American Activities.

The committee responded by unanimously charging the ten with contempt of Congress. The full House supported the contempt charge by the margin of 346 to 17.

The Hollywood Ten became heroes and pariahs simultaneously. Leftists and many liberals hailed them as defenders of freedom of speech and association, artists who placed their calling and convictions above their personal interests. Conservatives condemned them as foreign agents or misguided dupes.

The movie industry itself split along slightly different lines. Studio executives and producers were initially ambivalent. They hesitated to impose a loyalty test on writers and directors, fearing lawsuits, negative publicity, and loss of creative talent. Eric Johnston, the president of the Motion Picture Association of America, summarized the drawbacks of any politically inspired ban or blacklist: "With no vested right to be heard and no vested right to challenge accusations against him, the innocent citizen is helpless. He can be indicted and convicted in the public mind on the unchallenged say-so of a witness who may be completely sincere but can be either misinformed or riddled with prejudice."

Yet when public opinion sided with the House and against the Hollywood Ten, the executives shifted their position. They countered the free-speech argument by arguing that the crux of the matter wasn't speech but employment. The First Amendment guaranteed free speech to the Hollywood Ten, but it didn't guarantee them jobs. The studios were entirely within their rights in withholding employment from those who damaged the studios' business by alienating customers. The executives gathered hastily at New York's Waldorf Astoria hotel in November 1947 to consider their course; the meeting produced a statement delineating their policy: "Members of the Association of Motion Picture Producers deplore the action of the ten Hollywood men who have been cited for contempt. We do not desire to prejudge their legal rights, but their actions have been a disservice to their employers and have impaired their usefulness to the industry. We will forthwith discharge or suspend without compensation those in our employ and will not re-employ any of the ten until such time as he is acquitted or has purged himself of contempt and declares under oath that he is not a Communist." Nor would this policy be confined to the Hollywood Ten. "We will not knowingly employ a Communist or a member of any party or group which advocates the overthrow of the Government of the United States by force or by illegal or unconstitutional methods." The producers acknowledged that their policy entailed hazards. "There is the danger of hurting innocent people. There is the risk of creating an atmosphere of fear." Creative work suffered when fear ruled. But the risk was worth taking, for the good of the country.

T HE HUAC HEARINGS on Hollywood changed Reagan's life. Beyond exposing him to the allure of politics and premiering him on a new stage, the hearings placed him at the bank of an ideological chasm, which he leaped right over. He sided with the studios on the communist question with scarcely a second thought. He would have had greater difficulty had the Hollywood Ten included actors, his constituents as guild president. But writers and directors weren't his responsibility. What *was* his responsibility was to keep the actors working, and in this regard his and the guild's interest coincided with that of the producers.

Not long after the release of the Waldorf Declaration, as the producers' policy statement came to be called, Reagan and other representatives of the movie guilds met with the industry executives. Louis Mayer explained that the motive behind the declaration was economic rather than political; the producers' primary obligation, he said, was "to protect the industry and to draw the greatest possible number of people into the theaters."

Reagan saw his responsibility in similar terms. He quizzed Mayer and the other producers on the terms of the declaration. How would they know who was a communist and who wasn't? Would the word of the person in question suffice? Mayer responded that no formal screening procedure had been established. The producers would use their discretion. Reagan asked what would happen if the congressional investigators charged someone with being a communist and that person denied it? Nicholas Schenck of Loew's, the corporate parent of MGM, answered that the industry would not abdicate decisions on hiring to Congress, but if a congressional committee called a studio employee to testify and that employee refused to say whether he was a communist, he would be terminated. Reagan didn't object.

Though Mayer and the other producers, and Reagan with them, cast the communist question as an economic issue, in the anxious atmosphere of the emerging Cold War it had undeniable political ramifications. It would have had them even if the Hollywood Ten had not taken their stand precisely on the politics of the HUAC probe. After they did so, no one could deny that politics was at the heart of the matter. By siding with the producers against the Hollywood Ten, Reagan proclaimed his anti-communist politics to the world. He didn't know it yet, but he had found the issue on which he would build a political career.

PARNELL THOMAS WASN'T the only one investigating communists in Hollywood, nor was his committee the only group to whom Reagan spoke. J. Edgar Hoover and the FBI had tracked subversives since before the war. They initially focused on German sympathizers, and in this context agents of the bureau interviewed Reagan in 1943. He reported having encountered a man they were trailing, and he said he had nearly punched him for anti-Semitic remarks at a party. After the war Hoover's men shifted their aim to communists, and they renewed their acquaintance with Reagan. They visited him at his and Jane's home in Hollywood amid the stagehands' strike. By Reagan's recollection he initially rebuffed them. "I don't go in for red-baiting," he said. They replied that they didn't either. They were looking for spies and saboteurs. They added that they thought Reagan would want to help them, in light of the fact that the communists hated him so much. He asked what they meant. They described a meeting at which some radicals had posed the question: "What are we going to do about that sonofabitching bastard Reagan?" Reagan decided to cooperate. "We exchanged information for a few hours," he recalled. "The whole interview was an eye-opener."

Reagan received another visit from FBI agents in the spring of 1947. He spoke of the politics of the Screen Actors Guild. Most members were loyal and true, he said, but a small faction always seemed to "follow the Communist Party line." Reagan gave the names of several of the offenders, including Anne Revere, the guild treasurer and an Academy Award winner.

Reagan didn't publicize his contacts with the FBI. The bureau cultivated various informants in Hollywood. There were at least eighteen; Reagan was "T-10." For obvious reasons the bureau preferred that the informants' identities remain secret. Reagan was happy to oblige. He didn't think he was doing anything wrong. He supported the effort to root out subversives. And he judged he would be more effective if the subversives didn't know he was reporting on them.

Yet in at least one instance he went beyond silence about his FBI contacts to misrepresentation. His first memoir, published in 1965, included the assertion: "In all the battles over the weary months the Screen Actors Guild never used the word Communist except in general terms, nor did we point a finger at any individual." Yet finger-pointing was precisely what Reagan did in his 1947 meeting with the FBI.

REAGAN'S INCREASING POLITICIZATION distracted him from his marriage. This did the marriage no good, but the marriage was having trouble already. He and Jane had never grown close. Part of the problem was temperamental and historical. Neither he nor she had a childhood model of a happy, fulfilling marriage to pattern their own after; they had to invent the institution for themselves. And neither opened to the other without difficulty. Both had learned in childhood to fend for themselves emotionally; to let another inside the wall risked repeating the pain and disappointment they so often felt when young.

The circumstances of their lives made avoidance of emotional intimacy easy. They had their jobs and careers, and even the children they shared did little to bring them together. They hired help to manage Maureen and Michael, who saw more of the help than of their parents. "I think we both measured the attention we received from our parents, because there wasn't all that much of it to go around," Maureen recalled later. "More often than not, they were working six days a week. Like many children of famous people, Michael and I were left to the daily care of people like Nanny Banner"—their principal caregiver. Children often anchor families emotionally; as the parents bond with the children, they become closer to each other. Not in the Reagan household.

Economics has frequently served as marital glue, especially in that mid-century era when most American wives depended on their husbands for material support. But, again, not in the Reagan household. During the war Jane earned far more than Reagan, and she grew accustomed to the feeling of independence it afforded her. After the war the scales rebalanced, but she remained entirely capable of supporting herself, if it came to that.

She seems to have lost respect for him professionally. When they married, they both had bright careers ahead of them. For the first couple of years they advanced commensurately. But during and after the war his acting arc flattened and tipped down, while hers continued to rise. She was simply a better actor than he was, able to convey complex emotions in a way he never could. Her roles and performances kept getting better, leading to a part as a deaf-mute rape victim in the 1948 *Johnny Belinda*, for which she won an Academy Award without speaking a single line of dialogue.

As Reagan's movie prospects drooped, he doubtless seemed less the stalwart than she had thought him. Meanwhile, she grew bored with the politics of the industry, which fascinated him. She found the labor troubles tedious when they weren't downright distasteful. And the politics of the nation, which were claiming more of his interest, were even worse. Years later Reagan was asked whether Jane Wyman was a Republican or a Democrat. He said he didn't know; she had never shown sufficient interest in politics for her views to register with him.

In early 1947, Jane became pregnant. Possibly the pregnancy was planned; quite likely it was inadvertent. Perhaps another child would have drawn the family together; probably not. In any event, the child, a girl, was born prematurely and died the next day. The experience was understandably difficult for Jane, and Reagan had no chance to comfort her, for at that moment he was battling a severe case of pneumonia and was in another hospital miles away. Doubtless Jane felt very alone.

Maybe she realized she didn't mind being alone, for during the months that followed they grew further and further apart. She retreated into herself and into the character she would play in *Johnny Belinda*. She stuffed her ears with wax to simulate deafness, and possibly to shut out his voice. He grew busier than ever with the work of the guild, the hearings of the House committee, and the fallout from the Hollywood Ten.

The film press caught wind of their troubles. He denied that anything was wrong; she didn't. The difference in their reactions drove them still further apart.

Did he see the end approaching? Likely not. Things had been much worse between his parents, and Nelle had never left Jack. Neither Catholics nor Disciples divorced; nor, for that matter, did most Dixonians of other denominations. Even Hollywood remained committed to marriage as an institution, at any rate by comparison with a later day.

And so he was stunned when she told him, in the autumn of 1947, that she wanted out of the marriage. More immediately, she wanted him out of the house.

He didn't know what to do. He had to leave, of course; he was too much the gentleman to force his presence on a reluctant woman, even if she was his wife. But where to go? How to live from one day to the next? His home had been his harbor—an imperfect harbor, to be sure, but a harbor nonetheless. He had thought it could provide the security he had never felt in his childhood home. But now, without warning, he was cast adrift, as vulnerable as he had been as a child, when he never knew when the next eviction notice would arrive and the family would have to move again, never knew whether his father would be the happy Jack of the rollicking stories or the drunken Jack passed out in the snow.

The rootless childhood had taught him how to fit in but not how to make friends. A smile and a story gave him entrée to new settings, made people see him as sunny and optimistic, caused people to want to be around him. But he never let people get close. He had learned to protect himself by holding back.

His marriage to Jane had made him think, for a time, that he didn't have to hold back. She would provide the security he had never had. She would be his wife forever. He would let himself lean on her as he had leaned on no one before.

But he didn't know how. His mother and father had coexisted because his mother couldn't see an alternative. Jack wasn't much of a breadwinner, but he brought in something. And in their straits every little bit counted. Yet they hadn't really loved, not in a way Reagan could imitate. He had no map for intimacy, no guideposts or landmarks. He was traveling blind.

Jane's own issues made intimacy still harder. She too sought intimacy without knowing how to give or receive it. But unlike him, she could see alternatives to remaining married. She had divorced before and survived. She would survive this time.

And so the marriage ended. Jane officially filed for divorce in June 1948. California laws required her to show cause; she unconvincingly but satisfactorily cited mental cruelty. Reagan didn't contest the suit. The divorce was granted.

12

HARRY TRUMAN HAD never expected, before Franklin Roosevelt died, to be president, and afterward he often wondered why anyone wanted the job. The Republican majorities in Congress stymied him in domestic affairs, blocking any extension of the New Deal and rolling back, by the Taft-Hartley labor law and other measures, some of the New Deal's gains. The rest of the world wasn't much more cooperative. Nearly everyone had assumed that the Allied victory in the war would be followed by an Allied-dominated peace conference, much as World War I had been followed by the Paris Peace Conference of 1919. But American and Soviet leaders couldn't agree on the terms of a conference, and a status quo of distrustful military occupation congealed in the heart of Europe. American and Soviet soldiers glowered at each other in Berlin and on the border of the German zones their armies had captured from the Nazis in 1945.

Elsewhere on the continent the rivalry between democracy and communism took other forms. Communist parties flourished in France and Italy, threatening to win control of those countries by democratic means. In Greece communist insurgents battled a conservative government and raised the specter of a Marxist-Leninist beachhead in the Balkans. Throughout Europe national economies struggled amid the wreckage of the war; millions wondered if they would survive the next week, the next month, the next winter. Under the circumstances they seemed susceptible to the blandishments of those groups—here the communists conspicuously identified themselves—who hadn't caused either the war or the depression that triggered it.

American leaders and their democratic counterparts in Britain and

France recalled how Hitler had gradually gathered power to his noxious regime; they swore not to repeat the appeasing mistakes of their predecessors. But the British and the French lacked the funds to conduct the kinds of policies anti-appeasement appeared to demand. In early 1947, London's envoys told the Truman administration that Britain could no longer play its traditional stabilizing role in the Balkans. American officials responded with an alarm that combined concern for the region's future with fear of the broader consequences of the fall of Greece or its neighbors to communism. The State Department prepared a rescue plan for the conservative regime in Greece, balanced by funds for rival Turkey, which had lesser leftist problems of its own. Truman went to Congress to sell the package. He delineated the threat to the Balkans and placed it in a sweeping ideological and moral context. "At the present moment in world history nearly every nation must choose between alternative ways of life," Truman said. "The choice is too often not a free one. One way of life is based upon the will of the majority, and is distinguished by free institutions, representative government, free elections, guarantees of individual liberty, freedom of speech and religion, and freedom from political oppression. The second way of life is based upon the will of a minority forcibly imposed upon the majority. It relies upon terror and oppression, a controlled press and radio, fixed elections, and the suppression of personal freedoms." For America to stand idle while brutal minorities crushed the liberties of majorities would be unconscionable folly. "I believe that it must be the policy of the United States to support free peoples who are resisting attempted subjugation by armed minorities or by outside pressures. I believe that we must assist free peoples to work out their own destinies in their own way."

Truman got what he wanted in the near term: a package of aid to Greece and Turkey that kept those countries friendly to the United States. He got perhaps more than he wanted in the longer term. His statement of principle, soon called the Truman Doctrine after the model of the Monroe Doctrine of the nineteenth century, apparently committed the United States to a policy of opposing whatever looked like communist expansion almost anywhere on earth. Having rhetorically separated humanity into the sheep and the goats, Truman had committed the United States to acting as global shepherd.

The Truman Doctrine was merely the start. Two years after the end of the war Europe still couldn't get its economy going. French and Italian communists capitalized on capitalism's distress, making political gains that perhaps augured their imminent takeover of the French and Italian governments. American leaders couldn't imagine anything more calamitous, and they mobilized to prevent it. Secretary of State George Marshall proposed a reconstruction plan for Europe, underwritten by American taxpayers. The sums required were many multiples of those Truman had requested for Greece and Turkey, yet Congress went along, in part because the money would yield benefits to American producers, contractors, and shippers even as it reconstructed Europe.

Truman's emerging strategy in the evolving Cold War would become the basis for forty years of American foreign policy. Eight presidents after Truman, including Ronald Reagan, would applaud his foresight and follow his lead. But he got precious little support from his contemporaries. Republican conservatives complained that the Truman Doctrine and the Marshall Plan were simply more of what they had hated about the New Deal: big government growing bigger and bleeding the American people. Other Republicans opposed Truman merely for being a Democrat and sought to prevent this accidental occupant of the White House from signing a new lease in his own name. The 1948 election looked unpromising for Truman, with voters seeming restive after sixteen years of Democrats in the presidency, and it grew even less promising when a significant wing of southern Democrats defected over the issue of civil rights. Truman had ordered the military to desegregate, and though the desegregation went slowly, it boded ill for the future of Jim Crow in Dixie.

Yet Truman survived the election, barely. Reagan, out of habit, remained loyal to the Democrats, endorsing the president and raising money for his campaign. Just enough other voters developed a grudging admiration for the feisty Missourian to push him over the top against Thomas Dewey of New York.

Truman celebrated by affronting the conservatives even more. He rejected the advice of America's founders and overturned a cardinal principle of American foreign policy by negotiating a treaty of peacetime alliance. The North Atlantic Treaty committed the United States, in advance of any conflict, to defend Britain, France, Italy, and eight other countries of the North Atlantic region against external attack. The Soviet Union wasn't mentioned in the treaty, but everyone understood that it was the only country the allies were seriously worried about.

The North Atlantic Treaty completed the edifice of "containment," as Truman's anti-Soviet policy was summarized. It angered conservatives who judged George Washington smarter than Harry Truman and who objected to what they considered power grabbing by the executive. The

Atlantic treaty evidently took war-making authority out of the hands of Congress and gave it to the president, who would determine when an attack triggered the treaty's required response. Robert Taft of Ohio, Truman's Senate bête noire on the labor issue, again wrung his hands and shook his finger at the president. He warned that the Atlantic treaty would produce a permanent American occupation of Europe and an overweening American defense establishment.

Yet Taft took the road less traveled. The treaty compelled conservatives to make a fateful choice: between their devotion to small government and their aversion to communism. Many supposed that Taft was right in predicting that the Atlantic alliance and the rest of containment would inevitably swell American government. But with varying degrees of difficulty, most decided that the threat to American liberty from foreign communists was greater than that from domestic liberals. They approved the treaty and endorsed Truman's Cold War agenda.

13

Actress Patricia Neal encountered Reagan at a Hollywood gathering and thought she had never seen a man so glum. "His wife, Jane Wyman, had just announced their separation," Neal said. "And it was sad because he did not want a divorce. I remember he went outside. An older woman went with him. He cried."

Reagan continued working, not knowing what else to do. Eddie Bracken appeared with him in *The Girl from Jones Beach*, a forgettable film about the search for the perfect female figure. "Reagan was a lonely guy," Bracken said. He thought it striking that Reagan ignored the beautiful women all around him. "He was never for the sexpots," Bracken said. "He was never a guy looking for the bed. He was a guy looking for companionship more than anything else."

Work took him unexpectedly overseas. The Marshall Plan would help right Britain's listing economy, but in the autumn of 1948 the stabilizing effect remained mostly in the future. The British needed every bit of cash they could lay hands on, and so the British government had forbidden the export of profits by foreign companies operating in Britain. For Warner Brothers and other Hollywood studios that owned and operated theaters in Britain, this meant that the profits their British theaters earned could be spent only in Britain. Warner decided to use its "frozen dollars," as such funds were called, to make a film in England. Reagan, Patricia Neal, and other cast members sailed for England in November 1948 to shoot *The Hasty Heart*.

The project tried the patience and endurance of all involved. The weather was cold, and persisting shortages of fuel compelled the British to spend even less on heating their buildings than usual. The setting of the film, Burma at the end of the war, aggravated the discomfort, requiring the cast to traipse around in tropical clothing.

Reagan put on a good front for the cameras and the public. He and Pat Neal stayed at London's Savoy hotel, prompting the mandatory speculation in the movie press about a romance. But the relationship was purely professional. "We got along well enough to choose each other's company even when we were not working," Neal remarked later. "We would have dinner and even go dancing at some of the local dance halls." Yet the desire wasn't there, not on his part and apparently not on hers.

Reagan deflected his forlornness in various ways. He wrote a long, joking letter to Jack Warner describing the plight of the cast and crew in their distant island outpost. "To the finder: Please see this letter reaches J. L. Warner, Burbank, California," the letter began. It continued: "Dear J.L.: I am putting this letter in a bottle and throwing it on the tide with the hope that somehow it may reach you. Perhaps my report of life here in this dismal wilderness will be of help to future expeditions. You will recall with what light hearts we set out such a long time ago—optimistic about an ability to find and thaw the 'frozen dollar.' If we could have known then what lay ('lay'—there's a word I no longer experience or understand) before us how different would have been our mood. Our first glimpse of this forbidding land was almost as frightening as a look at *The Horn Blows at Midnight*. There seems to be a heavy fog but it had the odor of cow dung and coal soot—fearing an explosion of this gaseous stuff, I ordered 'no smoking.' Better I should have ordered 'no breathing.' The natives were friendly in a sort of 'below freezing' way but were won over by gifts— mostly cash. We were quite generous in this inasmuch as it was *your* cash. They speak a strange jargon similar in many ways to our language but *different* enough to cause confusion. For example—to be 'knocked up' here refers in no way to those delights for which 'Leander swam the Hellespont.' It merely means to be awakened from a sound sleep by a native device somewhat like our telephone. Another instance of this language difference is the word 'bloody.' You could see a native cut stem to stern but to describe the spectacle as 'bloody' would get you thrown out of a saloon in London. Mentioning a pain in my 'fanny' (which is easy to get here) I was distressed to learn that even this standard American term has an opposite meaning. If I had what they call a 'fanny' I could be Queen of England . . . There is a cleared space near the center of the native capital called Piccadilly Circus. I have gone there many times and have yet to see an elephant or an acrobat. In fairness I must admit how even there are some characters (mostly female) who seem to be selling tickets to something. They keep pulling my sleeve and saying 'two bob, Governor.' One of the most interesting customs of the higher-class natives is something of a sport. They all wear red coats to chase some dogs which in turn are chasing a fox. I should add the natives are mounted on horses. This affair is mistakenly called 'a fox hunt.' I say mistakenly because the red object has nothing to do with the fox; they actually are doing this to muscle up the horses which are then served for dinner. I have been very lucky so far in that I have been able to avoid the horse and eat only the saddle and harness. In connection with this let me write a word about English cooking. What they do to food we did to the American Indian . . . Cheerio! (that is the native word for good by. It is spoken without moving the upper lip while looking down the nose)."

Reagan did what he could to make England seem more like home. He ordered a cargo of steaks from New York's 21 Club. But several fewer than he paid for reached his table. The hotel staff said the others had spoiled en route; Reagan suspected they had been pilfered by meat-hungry locals.

Filming practices in England differed from those in America. The English took full weekends off. On one such weekend Reagan and Neal were driven about the countryside by an Englishman who was courting one of Neal's friends. Conversation turned to what each would like to be more than anything else in the world. Reagan answered, with a wry laugh, "The president of the United States."

MAYBE HE MEANT it. More likely it was another joke, something to lift the gloom of the English winter, the gloom on his soul.

He returned to America amid the debate over the North Atlantic Treaty, and he reached Hollywood just weeks after the arrival in the film capital of a young woman from Illinois who, as he had done the previous decade, traveled west to try her luck in the movies. Nancy Davis had been born Anne Frances Robbins in New York in 1921. Her parents were Edith Luckett and Kenneth Robbins, whose marriage foundered before their daughter was old enough to remember. She followed her mother, an actress, from theater to theater, until Edith decided the trouping life wasn't good for a little girl and handed Nancy, as she was always called, to an aunt who lived in Maryland. After six years of separation mother and daughter were reunited when Edith married Loyal Davis, a Chicago physician. Edith abandoned the stage but took parts in radio dramas produced in Chicago.

She kept in touch with former colleagues, and when the likes of Spencer Tracy, Mary Martin, and Lillian Gish passed through Chicago, they often stayed at the family's Lake Shore Drive apartment. "Spence was the most charming man I have ever known," Nancy recalled later. "He suffered from insomnia, and when I came home late from a date or a night out with friends, he would be up, eager to have a long talk." With multiple role models in the business, Nancy eventually considered an acting career for herself. She mentioned the idea to Tracy, who offered simple advice: "Know your lines and don't bump into the furniture." Katharine Hepburn, another visitor, offered a warning. She said Nancy had met only stars, people who had succeeded in the business beyond ordinary expectations. She needed to be aware that most hopefuls did much less well, requiring regular work as waitresses and secretaries to round out their meager pay from acting.

Nancy nonetheless went ahead, moving from Chicago to New York to try her luck on the stage. She had acted in college, at Smith, and in summer stock, but the reality of the professional theater was daunting. Casting call after casting call left her unchosen. Eventually, she landed a small part in *Lute Song*, at the insistence of Mary Martin, the female lead. The play ran for four months, which turned out to constitute her whole Broadway career.

Yet she made new contacts. Clark Gable was between wives and past his prime, but he was handsome, charming, and, after an introduction by Spencer Tracy, apparently interested in Nancy. They spent much of a week together in New York, inspiring speculation in the movie magazines about the new young thing in the leading man's life. But when he went back to California, she stayed behind.

Not for long, though. Edith decided Nancy might have better luck in movies than on the stage, and she called Tracy to see what he could do. He arranged a screen test at MGM with the studio's best director, cameraman, and technicians. The test yielded the desired result, and MGM offered her a contract. She packed her few belongings and, in the spring of 1949, headed for Hollywood.

She had more in mind than a movie career. Or perhaps she was simply hedging her bets. She had always imagined getting married, to someone as successful as her stepfather. Her sole serious love affair had ended tragically when her sweetheart was killed by a train. Now, at nearly twenty-eight, she had to consider how much time she had left. New York hadn't turned up anyone marriageable, but Hollywood might.

By at least one account she took pains to identify the most eligible men in the movie industry. An acquaintance at MGM recalled her sharing a list she had made, with unattached males listed by professional category: producers, directors, agents, lawyers, actors. At the top of Nancy's list in the actor category was Ronald Reagan, perhaps Hollywood's most conspicuously eligible bachelor following his divorce from Jane Wyman.

Dore Schary, who knew Reagan through the Screen Actors Guild, had just become head of production at MGM. He learned of the studio's new hire and that she wanted to meet Reagan. He and his wife hosted a small dinner that brought them together. "There was a lot of political talk and some arguments," recalled Schary's daughter, who took part in the dinner. "Reagan made his views very clear. He was terribly articulate. Nancy listened to him attentively. She was sitting opposite him at the dinner table and she kept smiling at him in agreement."

Reagan wasn't smitten. He pleaded an early departure to New York the next day and left the dinner before the other guests. His SAG work kept him busy during the following weeks. Conceivably, he forgot about the dinner, for he subsequently claimed that the first time he met Nancy Davis was several months later, in the autumn of 1949. Nancy contacted him indirectly to express her worry that she was being mistaken for another Nancy Davis, who was associated with certain leftist causes. Reagan looked into the matter and assured the intermediary that all was well; the studios would keep the two Nancy Davises straight. But Nancy wanted to hear the message from the SAG president himself. Reagan reluctantly agreed.

They met for dinner. He told her he had an early shooting session the next morning and couldn't stay out late. She did too, she said. ("I didn't, but a girl has her pride," she admitted later.) He greeted her on a pair of canes, which he needed to help him walk following a leg fracture in a celebrity softball game. They dined at a restaurant on Sunset Strip, beginning their conversation with the identity problem that had ostensibly brought them together. As Nancy seemed to lack confidence that he had solved it, he offered a simple remedy: a name change.

"I can't do that," she said matter-of-factly. "Nancy Davis is my *name.*"

Plenty of actors and actresses worked under stage names, he countered.

She wouldn't think of it.

The discussion moved on. He gradually warmed to her and said he might have time, after all, to take in the first show of a musical act that was opening down the street. Would her schedule permit it?

"Just for the first show," she said.

They stayed for both shows.

"I don't know if it was exactly love at first sight," she remembered, "but it was pretty close."

Closer for her than for him. They began dating but not as regularly as she wanted. "I wish I could report that we saw each other exclusively, and that we couldn't wait to get married," she recounted. "But Ronnie was in no hurry to make a commitment. He had been burned in his first marriage, and the pain went deep. Although we saw each other regularly, he also dated other women." He described the circumstances of his divorce and in the process revealed much about himself. "He was totally unprepared for it," she recalled. "He also had nobody to confide in when it happened." She came to understand that he didn't make friends easily or well. "It's hard to make close friends or to put down roots when you're always moving, and I think this—plus the fact that everybody knew his father was an alcoholic—explains why Ronnie became a loner." The better she got to know him, the more she realized how difficult it was for him to let people near. "Although he loves people, he often seems remote, and he doesn't let anybody get too close. There's a wall around him. He lets me come closer than anyone else, but there are times when even I feel that barrier."

Reagan afterward acknowledged that he wasn't the model suitor. "The truth is, I did everything wrong, dating her off and on, continuing to volunteer for every Guild trip to New York—in short, doing everything which could have lost her if Someone up there hadn't been looking out for me. In spite of my determination to remain foot-loose, in spite of my belief that the pattern of my life was all set and would continue without change, nature was trying to tell me something very important."

Maybe it was nature, or maybe it was Nancy. His determination to be footloose was no greater than her determination not to let him get away. She abided his travels and his seeing other women, although not without jealousy. She overheard another actress tell of a gift he had given her. "That hurt," she remembered decades later. He invited her to a ranch he had purchased in the Santa Monica Mountains above Malibu, after owning a smaller ranch near Northridge; she gamely helped paint fences and do other chores around the place. One day he said, "You know, you really should buy a house. It would be a terrific investment." She had been thinking about living in *his* house as his wife, and she was stunned by the comment. "I just about died!" she said.

She hung on, though, and he decided he liked having her around. "Gradually I came out of a deep-freeze and discovered a wonderful world of warmth and deep contentment," he remembered. He invited her to spend time with Maureen and Michael on the weekends they were with him. Her goal eventually seemed within sight. "I began to believe that we really would get married," she said.

At this point the previous Mrs. Reagan became a problem. "Jane was perfectly nice to me," Nancy recalled of occasions when he would visit the children at their mother's house and take her along. "But these visits were awkward. Not only had she been married to Ronnie, but she was very much The Star, and it was her house and her children. I felt out of place, and I was a little in awe of her." She was also miffed. "I could see that Jane knew how to play on Ronnie's good nature. She had convinced him that he shouldn't get married again until she did."

Yet Nancy knew what she wanted, and she wouldn't let a mere star stand in her way. "It took me a little time, but I managed to unconvince him."

REAGAN'S NEW ROMANCE caused him to reconsider other things he thought he knew. An old friend from Dixon had written saying she had lost her husband and was reconciled to never finding another love; Reagan responded with uncharacteristic reflectiveness. "Your letter led me to believe you are embarked on a course which can only lead to unhappiness and a barren future," he wrote. "This is all wrong. You are young and very attractive and have a great deal to offer some worthwhile man and both you and your son need a man in your life or lives. You spoke of your aunt and the 'ideals' she gave you. It is high time you reviewed those teachings in the light not of modern living but of *modern knowledge*. I too was raised in a home where 'ideals' similar I'm sure to yours were taught, by my Mother. Now I have the highest regard for her and for her teachings but I have had to go on from there and find a 'code for living' in keeping with my conscience and knowledge of right and wrong. This does not mean casting her principles aside but rather it is building to meet my present needs on a foundation I learned from her. At the same time I have learned painfully that some 'idealism' is in effect a flight from reality. You say you believe there is *one* love in life for each of us—this is just *not* true. Can you believe that God means for millions of really young people to go on through life alone because a war robbed them of their first loves? Maybe you'll resent this, Florence, but I must say it—you have to look into your own heart and ask yourself if you really believe in *one love* now lost to you or if this is a shield behind which you hide because your past experience did not measure up to your girlhood dreams and now you *fear* men."

Reagan shared his own experience of love and sex and marriage. "I will grant you that all of us grow up with a 'moonlight and roses' outlook on romantic relationships and sometimes it comes hard to reconcile this dream with the actualities of *physical* contact. To show you how 'over idealistic' my training was—I awoke to the realization (almost too late) that even in marriage I had a little guilty feeling about sex, as though the whole thing was tinged with evil. A very fine old gentleman started me out on the right track by interesting me in the practices of, or I should say moral standards of, the primitive peoples never exposed to our civilization—such as the Polynesians. These people who are truly children of nature and thus of God, accept physical desire as a natural, normal appetite to be satisfied honestly and fearlessly with no surrounding aura of sin and sly whispers in the dark. By our standards they are heathens but they are heathens without degeneracy, sex crimes, psycho-neurosis and divorce. I guess what I am trying to say is that I oppose the dogmas of some organized religions who accept marital relationship only as a 'tolerated' sin for the purpose of conceiving children and who believe all children to be born in sin. My personal belief is that God couldn't create evil so the desires he planted in us are good and the physical relationship between a man and woman is the *highest form of companionship*."

Reagan spoke of what he would tell his daughter when she came of age, but he spoke as well of what he had discovered for himself. "I want her to know that nothing between her and the man she loves can be wrong or obscene, that *desire* in itself is normal and right. There is one other thing I think she should know. If some man she finds attractive or likable feels desire for her, like any parent I hope she'll have the common sense and good taste not to be promiscuous or involve herself in casual affairs but (and this is equally important) I don't want her to be disgusted and convinced that his desire is an indication of moral decay and vulgarity. Of course a man feels desire for an attractive woman—nature intended that he should and something would be amiss if he didn't. A girl's judgment of this man should be based *only* on *his* respect for *her wishes* but don't ask him not to feel an instinct as much a part of him as hunger and thirst."

Second loves were perfectly possible and entirely respectable, he said. "The world is full of lonely people, people capable of happiness and of giving happiness, and love is *not* a magic touch of cosmic dust that preordains two people and two people *only* for each other. Love can grow *slowly* out of warmth and companionship and none of us should be afraid to seek it." He concluded, "Now I am going to seal this letter very quickly and mail it because if I read it over I won't have the nerve to send it."

HE DID SEND it, and he likewise summoned the nerve to ask Nancy to marry him. His timing might have been influenced by the fact that Nancy evidently was pregnant ("Go ahead and count," she wrote in her memoir, referring to the birth of their first child, Patti, seven and a half months after the wedding). Reagan was quite satisfied with a small ceremony for his second try. But Nancy would surely have insisted on something larger had decorum not caused her to want to tie the knot as quickly as possible.

And so the hastily arranged service, held on March 4, 1952, at the Little Brown Church in the San Fernando Valley, included only the bride and groom, the minister, and William Holden and his wife, Ardis, who served as best man and matron of honor. Nancy didn't notice that the Holdens, who were having marital troubles, sat on opposite sides of the small church. "I spent the entire day in a happy daze," she recalled.

14

Nancy's acting career essentially ceased upon her marriage to Reagan. Having landed her man, she focused her ambitions on *his* career, which continued to evolve. Warner Brothers had basically written him off as an actor. Jack Warner remained friendly, but this only complicated Reagan's position. Reagan's agent, Lew Wasserman, headed the Music Corporation of America, which was tussling with Warner Brothers. Wasserman told Reagan he could employ the William Morris Agency in dealing with Warner, to avoid a potential conflict of interest. Reagan declined. "I don't feel that strangers can suddenly take over and represent my best interests," he explained to Warner. He said he wanted to deal with Warner on a more personal basis. And he had a bone to pick. "I know you will recall our discussion some time ago with regard to *That Hagen Girl*"—in which Reagan played the much older suitor of Shirley Temple. "You agreed that the script and role were very weak but asked me to do the picture as a personal favor which I gladly did. At that time you encouraged me to bring in a suitable outdoor script which you agreed to buy as a starring vehicle for me. I found such a property in *Ghost Mountain* and the studio purchased it." Reagan had heard nothing more about the studio's plans for the film until recently, and what he was now hearing wasn't promising. "There have been 'gossip items' indicating you intend to star someone else in this story. Naturally I put no stock in these rumors—I know you too well to ever think you'd break your word. However, I am anxious to know something of production plans—starting date, etc., in order to better schedule my own plans. Frankly I hope it is soon, as I have every confidence in this story."

In fact it *was* soon, but it wasn't with Reagan. Warner Brothers cast

Errol Flynn in the part Reagan wanted, leaving Reagan to mutter against Jack Warner and the ingratitude of the studio system.

The fault wasn't entirely with the studios, for the film industry was laboring under unprecedented burdens. Despite the producers' best efforts to curry popular and political favor, the Supreme Court in 1948 ruled against the major studios on the control of theaters. The studios were compelled to sell their outlets, a development that eroded the rationale for the B movies that had been pushed upon the public by the captive theaters, whose revenue supported the studios' oligopoly. Forced for the first time to compete, the studios slashed costs wherever they could. The stars survived, but marginal actors like Reagan found less and less work.

A second blow to old Hollywood was the advent of television. Experimental broadcasts of live moving images began in the 1920s, but not until the late 1930s did regular programming commence. World War II diverted the talent and resources of the infant industry, but soon after the war the small screen of television revealed itself to be a worthy and disruptive competitor to the big screen of movies. In 1945 television receivers were almost unheard of in American homes; by 1950 nearly four million homes boasted the new devices. By 1955 thirty million homes, or more than half the residences in America, had sets; by 1960 the number of sets approached sixty million and the proportion nine out of ten.

The challenge to movies was obvious and immense. The millions of television owners and their families could now experience the emotional escape movies had provided, but without leaving their homes. Their individual decisions summed to a disaster for Hollywood: movie attendance plunged by three-quarters between 1945 and 1960.

Reagan first encountered television professionally in his role as SAG president. The new medium posed novel challenges to the existing structure of labor relations. The most important questions for Reagan were whether television actors were screen actors and whether screen actors became television actors when their films were shown on television. Reagan and SAG had no pressing desire to extend the guild's jurisdiction to actors in live television shows, as they seemed more like stage actors (who had their own union, Actors' Equity) or radio performers (who belonged to the American Federation of Radio Artists). But some on the radio side sought to recruit not only television actors but all actors and performers and amalgamate them into a single comprehensive union. They linked arms in a committee called the Television Authority, or TVA.

Reagan resisted. The screen actors were the moneyed elite of the acting and performing corps, and they would lose ground by joining with the others. Moreover, screen actors typically lived and worked in Hollywood, whereas most stage actors and television performers were in New York. But the critical element, in Reagan's view, was political. The big union the radio men advocated struck him as a stalking horse for the radical politics he had been battling in SAG and before Congress. "Let me make one thing plain," he wrote afterward. "I am not suggesting the TVA movement was a Communist plot, but just that a controversy of this kind was catnip to a kitten where the little Red brothers were concerned. They had to latch on and do what they could to cause trouble—particularly for SAG and also because 'one big union' is right down their alley. The party line will always back anything that simplifies and centralizes. It's easier to subvert one organization where policy decisions are far removed from the rank and file than it is to take over a dozen groups."

Reagan spent much of two years fighting the single-unionists. The work required endless meetings at which the amalgamationists would raise point of order after point of privilege after point of information, only to be voted down overwhelmingly by the general membership of SAG, who knew they had a good deal as things stood. Ultimately, Reagan and the other SAG leaders preserved the independence of the screen actors, leaving the television actors to join the radio folks in the American Federation of Television and Radio Artists.

AMERICAN POLITICIANS HAVE always been early adopters of new communication technologies; they have seized with alacrity on whatever enables them to reach voters. Theodore Roosevelt exploited the mass-circulation newspaper press to make himself the center of America's attention and the first president to be a national celebrity. Franklin Roosevelt turned radio to his New Deal purposes, conducting intimate seminars in democratic philosophy and Democratic policies with audiences of fifty million in his Fireside Chats.

Ronald Reagan would become to television what Franklin Roosevelt was to radio, but he and the rest of his generation took first political lessons in the new medium from Joseph McCarthy. The Wisconsin Republican had ridden into the Senate on the anti–New Deal wave of 1946 but for three years had done little to distinguish himself. At the beginning of 1950 he hit upon the theme of communist infiltration of the federal government. It was hardly original, as anyone from Harry Truman, who had launched his own loyalty probe in 1947, to Ronald Reagan and the other witnesses at the Hollywood Ten hearings could have told him. But his timing turned out to be inspired. The Soviet Union had just shocked Americans and much of the world by detonating an atomic bomb; given that credible experts had predicted a much later date for Moscow's acquisition of the ultimate weapon, the conclusion that spies must have revealed the atomic secret was nearly unavoidable. In truth spies *had* been at work, as the world discovered when Klaus Fuchs was convicted in a British court for passing information about the British and American atomic programs to the Soviets. Julius and Ethel Rosenberg were subsequently convicted in an American court on similar charges and executed. Three months before McCarthy's epiphany China's communist People's Liberation Army had completed its conquest of the world's most populous nation. No one accused the Chinese communists of infiltrating the American government, but the mere fact of their victory seemed to raise the stakes in the struggle between democracy and communism. And not long after McCarthy asserted the presence of communists in the federal government, the communists of North Korea attacked South Korea, triggering the first armed conflict of the escalating Cold War.

McCarthy's discovery of communism, and the popular reaction to it, gave the Republican Party a powerful weapon to use against Truman and the Democrats. The Republicans had soft-pedaled their criticism of Truman's containment policy in the 1948 election, not wishing to appear unpatriotic or spoil their own chances of directing that policy, with which most of them agreed. Truman's surprise victory over Dewey stunned and angered them, and they abandoned all respect for his office and all concern for appearances and declared political war on everything he did. McCarthy struck some of the Republican leadership as uncouth and perhaps unprincipled, but he appeared just the kind of bashi-bazouk to lead the charge.

McCarthy assailed the State Department, which he described as infested with communists. He blasted Truman for harboring said communists, and after Truman fired General Douglas MacArthur for insubordination amid the Korean War, he declared that the president should be impeached. He castigated George Marshall—George Marshall!—for being at the center of a "conspiracy so immense and an infamy so black as to dwarf any previous venture in the history of man."

McCarthy's attacks sealed the fate of the Truman administration. Truman was eligible to run again in 1952 but became patently unelectable and didn't even seek the Democratic nomination. Dwight Eisenhower, the commander of Allied forces in Europe in World War II and a strong advocate of Truman's containment policy despite being a Republican, handily defeated Democrat Adlai Stevenson, giving the Republicans the White House for the first time since Herbert Hoover.

McCarthy briefly reconsidered his tactics, now that his party held the high ground of policy. But only briefly: he soon slammed Eisenhower for insufficient alarm at the insidiousness of the communist threat. Eisenhower despised McCarthy, but the senator's Republican colleagues in the Senate still considered him useful and gave him control of the Committee on Government Operations.

McCarthy employed the committee as a platform for his signal contribution to the history of congressional investigations: the use of live television in national coverage of committee hearings. The U.S. Army had bristled at the allegations by McCarthy against Marshall, Eisenhower, and other members of the service, and it looked for means to retaliate. When a McCarthy aide sought favored treatment for an assistant who had been drafted, the army detected an opening and denounced the senator. McCarthy convened hearings, which two television networks—ABC and DuMont—aired from start to finish and two others—NBC and CBS— covered in part. The hearings attracted twenty million viewers, lasted thirty-six days, and filled 188 hours of broadcast time.

They did nothing good for McCarthy, who turned out to lack the persona for television and who appeared nonplussed when questioned by the counsel for the army. "Have you no sense of decency, sir, at long last?" Joseph Welch demanded. "Have you left no sense of decency?" McCarthy lacked a rejoinder, let alone decency. His approval rating plunged, and his hold on the public imagination vanished.

Yet his defeat demonstrated the power of television to shape political perceptions. Should someone else emerge, someone with an attractive camera presence and a message of hope rather than fear, television would deliver the audience.

Top left: Ronald Reagan got his good looks and his knack for telling stories from his father, Jack Reagan. But Jack was an alcoholic and utterly unreliable.

Top right: Little "Dutch" (in the eponymous haircut) is smiling in this Christmas photo, with Jack; elder brother Neil; and mother, Nelle. But he learned to dread the holidays, because that was when Jack fell off the wagon.

Bottom: As a teenager he was a lifeguard in Dixon, Illinois. He took pride in the number of rescues he made, although some observers suspected that the pretty girls weren't really drowning.

Top: Reagan's fondest hope at Eureka College was to become a football hero. He would have succeeded, if determination had sufficed. But at least he looked the part.

Bottom: Radio was his first career, one that capitalized on his pleasing voice but didn't do justice to his face.

Top: This was more like it: a promo still from Warner Brothers, where he realized his dream of acting in movies.

Bottom: World War II gave Reagan new roles to play. Here he is a flier in a training film.

Top: His first family seemed happy enough for ABC to feature it in a story about home lives of Hollywood stars. Daughter Maureen is between the reporter and her mother, Jane Wyman, who is holding son Michael. Jane appears distracted; perhaps she is reflecting that things are not what they seem.

Bottom left: As audiences found other favorites, Reagan turned to the politics of the film industry. In 1947 he testified at the HUAC hearings on communists in Hollywood.

Bottom right: It took him a while to realize that Nancy was his true love, but she gradually convinced him, and their wedding ensued. The love affair lasted the rest of his life.

Top: A secret of his success was his persistent optimism. He should have been disappointed at being demoted from film to television, but he appears delighted to be host of *The General Electric Theater*.

Bottom: Reagan's GE job required meeting company employees. The female workers usually outnumbered the males in the get-to-know-you sessions.

Top: His breakthrough to the political world occurred when he campaigned for Barry Goldwater in 1964. Goldwater lost the election, but Reagan won conservative hearts.

Bottom: He proved a natural, easily winning his first race, for California governor. Nancy joins him at the inaugural ball.

His children sometimes felt forgotten amid their father's celebrity, but they knew how to smile for the camera. From left: Patti, Nancy, Reagan, Michael, Maureen, Ron.

On January 20, 1981, Reagan stepped onto his largest stage. Here he is about to address the world for the first time as president of the United States.

15

THE PUBLICISTS AT General Electric weren't thinking of politics when they proposed that Ronald Reagan switch from film to television. They saw in Reagan something movie audiences didn't see. Television's small screen portrays actors differently than film's big screen, and a persona that doesn't fill the big screen can serve quite well in television's miniature.

Reagan definitely wasn't filling the big screen. His film career had fizzled almost completely. He blamed not himself but the industry. "A star doesn't slip," he told movie columnist Hedda Hopper. "He's ruined by bad stories and worse casting." Reagan was speaking of a generation of actors, but his own experience clearly colored his remarks. "The present system of casting is bad for pictures and death on actors. A man, for instance, may do an outstanding bit as a cop. A producer, seeing the picture, says, 'That guy certainly knows how to play a cop.' So he casts him as a cop in his next picture. The fellow plays a cop in fifteen films, and then he's through." Reagan further faulted the producers for believing audiences constantly demanded fresh faces on the screen. "Don't get me wrong. I'm thoroughly in favor of new faces. They're the lifeblood of this business, as most of us know. I think you'll find that actors, more than any other class in our profession, discover and push new talent." And the eight thousand members of the Screen Actors Guild, he said, constituted the greatest pool of talent anywhere. "But the present custom in Hollywood seems to be not to use talent, but to exploit it." This was woefully shortsighted. "Did you know there are 65 million people who don't go to the movies with any degree of regularity?" Reagan asked Hopper. "Most of them are over thirty years of age. That's the group we need to bring back into the theaters."

Warner Brothers wasn't listening, and when the studio made plain it wasn't going to promote his work, Reagan negotiated the right to accept work from other studios. Yet little materialized. He portrayed an alcoholic baseball pitcher in *The Winning Team* and was cast opposite a chimpanzee in *Bedtime for Bonzo*. And these were his best roles. The harsh fact was that audiences didn't want to watch him and so producers didn't want to work with him.

His immersion in the politics of the actors' guild gave him something else to do, but even that option ran out when he relinquished the SAG presidency to Walter Pidgeon at the end of 1952. He had already served longer than any president in the guild's history, and more than a few in the guild sought a change at the top. Besides, Nancy was pregnant, and he didn't wish to travel as much as the office required.

"I sat down and looked myself in the career," he said afterward. "One of the first signs of Hollywood chill is not only who doesn't call—it's who does. Producers complete with shoestring have a great script you ought to read. A short time before they wouldn't have called you because you were out of their reach. Now, having them on the line gives you the same feeling a fellow lost in the desert must have when he looks up and sees the buzzards starting to gather."

But he needed to work. He had a house in Hollywood and the Malibu ranch to pay for; he had a wife and a child on the way, not to mention the two children he shared with Jane Wyman. He had been making a handsome salary since the war, but the marginal tax rate on high earners was over 90 percent, and he hadn't managed to shelter much of his income.

Television beckoned, but Reagan, like most film actors, considered it déclassé. It didn't pay nearly as well as movies, and it marked actors as has-beens or never-weres. He rejected the offers. He tried his hand at emceeing in Las Vegas, the gambling town that was rising from the rock and sand of the Nevada desert just beyond the reach of California's less lenient laws. He couldn't get comfortable in the role, and his discomfort showed. He liked the pay but couldn't see himself as a floor-show fixture.

At this point his agent approached him with a novel idea. General Electric wanted to sponsor a television show, a weekly series of short dramas. These would be quality productions, with top actors in guest appearances. The series needed a host, an introducer who would become the face of the program. And there was something else. The host would double as a spokesman for General Electric, traveling the country and speaking on behalf of the company's management to its far-flung workforce and to other groups in the cities and towns where GE had plants. The company's thinking was that the two functions, television host and company spokesman, would reinforce each other. The hundreds of thousands of employees would furnish the core of a television audience that would multiply into the millions when family members and friends also watched.

The offer appealed to Reagan. It entailed a regular paycheck and would keep his face in front of the public. The traveling was a drawback, but a person in his position couldn't have everything he wanted. Reagan had always liked the personal appearance tours he had done to promote his films; he enjoyed the crowds and the celebrity treatment. He wasn't the celebrity he had been or had hoped to become, but he would be a star to the GE workforce. He would have to preach the virtues of GE and capitalism, but this was no problem as he believed in capitalism and presumed he could come to believe in GE.

And so *The General Electric Theater* was launched, with Ronald Reagan as host. His contract was "the fattest TV deal ever signed," Hedda Hopper reported. This wasn't saying much, given television's youth. But Reagan could portray it as a forward step. "Best part of the deal: I can have my cake and eat it too," he told Hopper. "My contract allows me to make motion pictures—all of them I want. So I can be a week-end TV actor and carry on my screen work too."

HE WAS TALKING fantasy about screen work. He made one film in 1955 and another in 1957. The latter, *Hellcats of the Navy*, included Nancy Reagan in her sole screen appearance after her marriage to Reagan. But beyond these, a couple of voice roles, and a small part in one last hurrah in 1964, Reagan's film career ended when he signed with General Electric.

He put the best face on his premature retirement from films. "In the old days I used to feel that Ronald Reagan was constantly on the soapbox, trying to change the world and doing his best to solve the problems of this complex motion picture industry," Louella Parsons wrote in the spring of 1955. "Today, he is more fun and less serious about the world in general." Reagan had sought out columnist Parsons, his old friend from Dixon, to tout the GE series. She inquired as to the source of his easier mien. "I suppose TV has done this for me," he replied. "You know, I used to be president of the Screen Actors Guild, not only off the screen but on. I was never cast in a picture in which this position didn't influence the producers. I was always given the role of a sedate, solid citizen, and if I was put in a Western I was sure to play an Eastern lawyer!" He hadn't closed the door forever to movie roles. "If a good part comes along in either medium I'm going to grab it if I can," he said. "But the beautiful thing about television is that you can pick and choose your stories, because you're in a financial position to wait for what you want." He granted that things weren't what they once had been, and not for him alone. "Do you realize how this industry is changing? There are very few stars under contract these days. Many of the big ones free lance and are on television, too."

Several of those big ones landed on Reagan's show. "We have Fred Astaire, Jimmy Stewart, Tony Curtis, Alan Ladd, Charles Laughton, Audie Murphy, Art Linkletter, Jeannie Carson and many others already on film or committed to do at least a half-hour episode for our series this season," Reagan told journalist Walter Ames in 1957. Ames inquired how Reagan did it: How did he and General Electric entice such talent to television's small screen? "Good stories, top direction, production quality," Reagan answered. "An actor's primary desire, and a necessary requisite in our industry, is to entertain to the best of his ability. *General Electric Theater* gives him, or her, that opportunity." Reagan added that the program often cast actors against type, and that this appealed to them. Fred Astaire would perform in a nondancing role. Heartthrob Tony Curtis would battle bulls. Jimmy Stewart was going to star in Dickens's *Christmas Carol* reimagined as a Western. Charles Laughton would become the coach of a Little League team.

The General Electric Theater was more than an innovation in the new medium of television; it was also an experiment in the developing art of public relations. Since the dawn of American industrialism in the nineteenth century, corporations had pondered how to portray themselves to the individuals and groups who shaped their world. Customers and clients formed one important constituency, employees another, government officials and the voters who chose them still others. Customers were typically wooed, by advertising and commercial promotions. Employees might be coddled and patronized in company towns, or threatened and intimidated by wage cuts and private security forces when the employees went on strike. Government officials could be bribed, as in several scandals of the Gilded Age, or funded in election campaigns, until Congress outlawed most corporate contributions in the early twentieth century.

The techniques of public relations grew more sophisticated during the 1920s, when a whole industry arose around the enterprise. Bruce Barton became the face of the field, and his firm of Barton, Durstine & Osborn gave guidance to such emerging powers as General Motors and General Electric. (Barton meanwhile won a following as a guru of self-improvement and the author of *The Man Nobody Knows*, which portrayed Jesus as the founder not merely of Christianity but of the culture of modern success.) The sell was softer but no less insistent than in the Gilded Age, and it made use of the modern media, especially radio. The private sector taught government a thing or two: Franklin Roosevelt manipulated radio in a manner to make Barton proud (though not happy: Barton was a Republican). During World War II the government's campaign to promote the war effort employed both personnel and ideas from the public relations industry.

General Electric's hiring of Reagan represented another step forward for the industry. GE was one of the largest corporations in America, with manufacturing plants and research laboratories in dozens of states and a workforce that numbered more than 200,000. Its chief of public relations was Lemuel Boulware, who had devoted decades to the study of corporate communications and devised a theory of the subject he intended for Reagan to put into practice. The theory operated at several levels. *The General Electric Theater* presented the company as a patron of the arts, not elitist arts like opera, but popular arts enjoyed by the company's millions of current and prospective customers. Reagan's handsome face, warm smile, and soothing voice made him just the person Boulware wanted those millions to see and hear every Sunday evening.

But Boulware had other audiences in mind as well. Like most corporations, GE disliked labor unions and sought to diminish their influence. Boulware believed that one way to accomplish this was to encourage the men and women who worked for the company to feel part of a community that shared the values of management. Reagan's contract made him the point man of the company's community building. He visited the plants and walked the factory floors; he shook hands with all who approached him and told stories of Hollywood. And he articulated the values of personal liberty and individual responsibility that Boulware hoped would inoculate the workers against the expansion of union influence.

There was risk and some irony in Boulware's approach. Reagan was a union man, of course, the recent president of an AFL affiliate, no less.

Might he be emotionally tempted to side with the workers against management? If he did, would Boulware be able to dump him without embarrassing the company?

But Boulware, like every master of public relations, was a student of personality. He understood that Reagan wasn't the typical unionist. His union, the actors' guild, wasn't like the International Union of Electrical, Radio, and Machine Workers, the principal group GE had to deal with. Reagan's guild was more like a company union, one of those corporate-sponsored organizations established to fend off the real unions. Reagan had more often been a partner of the producers than their antagonist. And the political views he had revealed in congressional testimony and speeches to SAG members and other industry audiences made clear that he stood solidly behind the pro-business principles Boulware wanted him to espouse.

Reagan later boasted that every speech he gave for GE consisted of his words alone. The company's leaders "never suggested in any way what I should talk about," he said. "Nor did they ever indicate I was singing the wrong song and should switch tunes." They didn't have to, for Reagan's views reflected the company line as closely as Boulware could wish. And they grew closer the longer he took the company's money. "As the years went on, my speeches underwent a kind of evolution, reflecting not only my changing philosophy but also the swiftly rising tide of collectivism that threatens to inundate what remains of our free economy," he wrote in the mid-1960s. The Republican presidency of Dwight Eisenhower did not produce the dismantling of the New Deal conservatives hoped for; instead, Eisenhower's Republicans endorsed and extended Social Security, lavished federal money on highways, launched an expensive space program, and generally looked to conservatives like clones of the Democrats. When the Democrats retook the White House after the 1960 election, conservatives expected still worse. "I don't believe it was all just a case of my becoming belatedly aware of something that already existed," Reagan wrote. "The last decade has seen a quickening of tempo in our government's race toward a controlled society."

At times, however, Reagan carried his warnings against government too far. General Electric's largest customer was the federal government, which purchased instruments for warplanes and other weapons systems, equipment for government labs, and especially generators for the power plants of the Tennessee Valley Authority and other electrical installations. Reagan's jeremiads against encroaching government cited the TVA as a case in point—until he got wind that TVA executives were listening and wondering to General Electric's boss, Ralph Cordiner, why they shouldn't shift their purchases to a more appreciative company.

Cordiner said he wouldn't censor Reagan—a move that caused Reagan to censor himself. "Suddenly, realization dawned," Reagan recalled. "There wouldn't be a word. Ralph Cordiner meant what he said and was prepared to back those words with $50,000,000 of business. Now the responsibility was mine. How free was I to embarrass or hurt the company, just because I had carte blanche to speak my mind?"

Reagan called Cordiner. "I understand you have a problem and it concerns me," he said.

"I'm sorry you found out about that," Cordiner answered. "It's my problem and I've taken it on."

Reagan said he appreciated the support and freedom the company gave him. But he couldn't abuse that freedom by making comments that might cost thousands of GE workers their jobs. "Mr. Cordiner, what would you say if I could make my speech just as effectively without mentioning TVA."

Reagan recalled the reaction: "There was a long pause. Then a very human voice said, 'Well, it would make my job easier.'"

Reagan concluded the story: "Dropping TVA from my speech was no problem. You can reach out blindfolded and grab a hundred examples of overgrown government. The whole attempt only served to illustrate how late it is if we are to save freedom."

REAGAN'S WORK FOR General Electric lasted eight years, interrupted once and briefly, at the end of the 1950s, by a pinch-hit reappearance with the actors' guild. Reagan's time with GE transformed him from a Hollywood figure into a national spokesman for conservative views. "Looking back now, I realize it wasn't a bad apprenticeship for someone who'd someday enter public life—although believe me, that was the farthest thing from my mind in those days," he wrote much later. "For eight years I hopscotched around the country by train and automobile for GE and visited every one of its 139 plants, some of them several times. Along the way I met more than 250,000 employees of GE—not just shaking their hands, but talking to them and listening to what was on their minds." He met business leaders in the towns he visited, and he found that his tales of government meddling in the movie industry struck sympathetic notes. "No matter where I was, I'd find people from the audience waiting to talk to me after a speech and they'd all say, 'Hey, if you think things are bad in your business, let me tell you what is happening in my business.' I'd listen and they'd cite examples of government interference and snafus and complain how bureaucrats, through overregulation, were telling them how to run their businesses. Those GE tours became almost a postgraduate course in political science for me. I was seeing how government really operated and affected people in America, not how it was taught in school."

Earl Dunckel served as Reagan's assistant and travel planner. He recalled how Reagan learned retail politics on the GE tours. At a typical plant, the women employees would gather around Reagan first, eager to meet the famous actor. Their male counterparts were less easily charmed. "The men would all stand over here, all together, looking at him, obviously saying something very derogatory—'I bet he's a fag,' or something like that," Dunckel recounted. "He would carry on a conversation with the girls just so long. He knew what was going on. Then he would leave them and walk over to these fellows and start talking to them. When he left them ten minutes later, they were all slapping him on the back saying, 'That's the way, Ron.'" Occasionally the women, or some of them, were the tougher sell. Dunckel remembered a large, formidable woman who heckled Reagan. "Buster, I'd like to back you up in a corner sometime," she said. Reagan smiled and responded, "Well, it would have to be a pretty big corner."

The tours kept him busy but nonetheless afforded time for reflection and reading. He continued to avoid airplanes and so had many days in compartments and parlor cars of cross-country trains. "I still can't think of a more comfortable way of travel than taking the Super Chief from Los Angeles to Chicago," he reminisced. On the Super Chief and its counterparts he read materials Lem Boulware supplied on the meaning and purpose of General Electric and American capitalism. Earl Dunckel recalled him as an apt pupil. "He was interested very much in our employee relations philosophy, Boulwarism, because we were out there talking to the people who were affected by it," Dunckel said. Reagan read the *General Electric News*, which covered company happenings that management wanted to publicize, including Reagan's tours. He read the *Supervisor's Guide to General Electric Job Information*. He read the numerous "Blue Books" in which Ralph Cordiner expounded the company's philosophy. He read various titles Boulware recommended for GE employee book clubs; selections included Lewis Haney's *How You Really Earn Your Living* and Henry Hazlitt's *Economics in One Lesson*. The consistent theme was less government and more commercial and personal freedom.

And he read a miscellany of books and articles he found on his own. He had a magpie's eye for the glittering tidbit and a storyteller's memory for material he could weave into his speeches. "Ron had the dope on just about everything," a Hollywood acquaintance recalled: "this quarter's up-or-down figures on GNP growth, V. I. Lenin's grandfather's occupation, all history's baseball pitchers' ERAs, the optimistic outlook for sugar beet production in the year 2000, the recent diminution of the rainfall level causing everything to go to hell in summer in Kansas and so on. One could not help but be impressed."

The more he read, and the more he traveled and spoke, the more he recognized that his formal political affiliation no longer suited his evolving beliefs. "One day I came home and said to Nancy, 'You know, something just dawned on me,'" he recalled later. "'All these things I've been saying about government in my speeches (I wasn't just making speeches—I was preaching a sermon), all these things I've been criticizing about government getting too big, well, it just dawned on me that every four years when an election comes along, I go out and support the people who are responsible for the things I'm criticizing.'"

This wasn't quite true. Reagan had joined some other Democrats in urging Dwight Eisenhower to run for president in 1952 as a Democrat; when the previously unpartied general opted for the Republicans, Reagan still thought he was the best man for the job and voted for him over Democrat Adlai Stevenson. He voted for Eisenhower over Stevenson again in 1956.

Yet he remained a registered Democrat. In 1960, John Kennedy ran for president on the Democratic ticket. Kennedy's father, Boston tycoon and Democratic donor Joseph Kennedy, had produced movies, among other ventures, and he pressured Hollywood to get behind his son. He appealed to Reagan on grounds of shared Irishness as well. Reagan refused, having decided that the Democrats were the party of egregious government, and he endorsed Richard Nixon instead. He didn't campaign actively for Nixon, as that would have undermined the nonpartisan face he and General Electric presented to the country. Nixon meanwhile discouraged Reagan and other anti-Kennedy Democrats from switching parties, reckoning that a strong contingent of "Democrats for Nixon" would more effectively undermine Kennedy than a bolt of the disaffected to the Republicans.

If it did, it didn't undermine Kennedy enough, for Joe Kennedy's boy beat Nixon in a close contest. Yet Reagan still admired Nixon sufficiently to endorse him in 1962 when he ran for California governor. Amid that race Reagan was saying nice things about Nixon and his Republican views when a woman in his audience stood up and asked if he had registered as a Republican.

"Well, no, I haven't," he replied. "But I intend to."

The woman announced to the crowd, "I'm a registrar." She strode to the platform where Reagan was speaking and thrust out a registration form.

"I signed it and became a Republican," Reagan later recounted.

PART THREE

A TIME FOR CHOOSING

1962–1980

16

SOME PEOPLE ENTER politics seeking power; Reagan wanted attention. The political dynamo of the 1960s was Lyndon Johnson, whose hunger for power had been evident from the moment he set foot in Congress in the 1930s. Johnson was hell-bent to make his mark on the world, and he spared no effort or principle in his drive to do so. Reagan wasn't like that. Reagan wanted an audience. He wanted the notice and the applause he had learned to crave as a youth. He wanted a stage. He always wanted a stage.

He might have been happy remaining with General Electric if GE had been happy remaining with him. But by the early 1960s the hold of *The General Electric Theater* on the Sunday evening television audience was slipping. The format seemed creaky, and the country had new small-screen favorites, including the four male stars of the top-rated Sunday show, *Bonanza*.

There was a broader issue. In 1961 the Justice Department launched a probe into price-fixing in the electrical equipment industry. General Electric was a prime target. Corporate management decided prudence lay in avoiding anything that raised the company's profile needlessly. Reagan's attacks on big government did just that. His message hadn't changed since the Eisenhower era, but the country had. John Kennedy's election signaled a shift in the political tides, which again flowed in a liberal direction. Reagan bucked the tide, creating turbulence GE didn't need.

The company offered to keep him on pitching commercial products if he would stop talking politics. He weighed the offer, not knowing what else he would do for a living. But he decided the reduced stage was too small. He rejected the offer. In 1962 the company canceled *The General Electric Theater* and severed its relationship with Reagan.

REAGAN'S UNEMPLOYMENT OCCURRED at the direst moment of the Cold War. The North Atlantic Treaty had given rise to the North Atlantic Treaty Organization, or NATO, under which American troops garrisoned West Germany against potential Soviet attack. The creation of NATO prompted Moscow to create a mirror alliance, the Warsaw Pact, equally ready for war. Tension was chronic and occasionally acute, as in 1961, when communist East Germany unexpectedly built a wall around West Berlin, the portion of the old German capital politically attached to democratic West Germany. But the tension never reached the breaking point, and the overarching story of the Cold War's European theater was that nothing much happened there.

This left the superpowers to wrangle over the rest of the world. The Korean War ended equivocally, with a 1953 armistice rather than a peace treaty. Concern shifted south as communists in Indochina forced France to abandon its pretensions of empire there and built a communist regime in northern Vietnam that claimed authority over all of Vietnam. The Eisenhower administration rejected the claim and furnished assistance to an anticommunist regime in southern Vietnam. By the early 1960s this regime was calling itself the government of South Vietnam, and the United States accepted the characterization. American arms and soldiers underscored the acceptance and underpinned the government, whose legitimacy was denied by the communists in North Vietnam and undermined by insurgents in the south.

The Cold War expanded to Africa and Latin America. The European powers were shedding their African colonies with tardy haste; successor regimes struggled to gain footing and then retain it, amid enticements and less positive forms of motivation from Washington, Moscow, and Beijing. The Chinese added a twist to the competition between West and East by declaring the Soviets insufficiently devoted to the ideals of world revolution. The Kremlin often found itself more vexed by Chinese communists than by American capitalists. The African regimes attempted to negotiate the crosscurrents, with varying success. Patrice Lumumba, prime minister of the new Congo republic, leaned too far left for Washington's taste; the Eisenhower administration authorized attempts to assassinate him. Lumumba wound up dead, although at the hands of his

Congolese enemies rather than American agents. Congo gravitated into the American orbit, but the Sino-Soviet-American struggle for political and ideological influence in Africa continued.

The Cold War reached Latin America after Fidel Castro seized power in Cuba in 1959. The Eisenhower administration declared an economic embargo against Castro's leftist regime and plotted methods for murdering Castro. Nothing came of the plots before Eisenhower left office, but an operation to topple him militarily was set in motion. The operation envisioned the arming of anti-Castro Cuban exiles who, with American help, would land in Cuba and provide a nucleus for anti-Castro groups within the country. John Kennedy approved the invasion, which quickly became a fiasco. Castro had infiltrated the exiles and knew all about the landing; the invasion was crushed. Kennedy was badly embarrassed; Castro was comparably heartened.

But the Cuban leader wasn't so heartened that he didn't seek protection against a second assault. The obvious place to look was Moscow, which spied a chance to rectify a strategic imbalance vis-à-vis the Americans. The state of the Armageddon art was nuclear-tipped missiles, of which the United States had many more than the Soviet Union. Some of the American missiles were based in Turkey, minutes in flight time from the Kremlin. A Soviet deal with Cuba could enable Moscow to put missiles in America's backyard and give American leaders a sobering taste of what Soviet leaders had been drinking alone until now.

The deal was struck. The Russians would get missile bases a hundred miles from American shores; Castro would receive protection against another American assault. Secrecy was essential: if Washington discovered the plan before the missiles were activated, it would be *more* tempted, rather than less, to invade.

Construction on the missile sites began, but it hadn't progressed far before the Americans, who had their own informants, as well as reconnaissance satellites and U-2 spy planes, learned of it. Kennedy pondered possible responses: invasion, air strike, blockade, diplomacy. He held off on invading or bombing, noting that the United States wasn't at war with Cuba and that Soviet military aid to Cuba was perfectly legal under international law. Yet he left open the possibility of invasion or bombing when he issued a public ultimatum to Nikita Khrushchev to halt the construction and remove any missiles from Cuba. Meanwhile, he imposed a blockade on Soviet shipping to Cuba.

The world held its breath awaiting Khrushchev's response. For the

Soviet leader to accept Kennedy's demand would be humiliating, but to reject it might be suicidal for the Soviets and homicidal for millions caught in the cross fire of a nuclear war between the superpowers. After what seemed forever but was actually six days, Khrushchev consented to remove the missiles.

Kennedy's advocates claimed a decisive victory. A back-channel bargain that pulled the American missiles from Turkey was not made public. Kennedy's popular approval rating spiked upward. Looking forward to 1964, when he would run for reelection, Kennedy's advisers were the heartened ones now.

But Kennedy didn't survive until 1964. In November 1963 he was murdered by Lee Harvey Oswald. No one but Oswald knew why he did it, and he took his reasons to the grave after he was fatally shot while in police custody, on television, by a nightclub owner, Jack Ruby, whose motives were equally opaque. The tragically bizarre sequence of events inspired conspiracy theories that long outlived everyone involved.

AND THEY GAVE Reagan the opportunity to publicize his conversion to Republicanism. Since World War II the Republicans had experienced their own version of the kind of internecine squabbling that had split world communism. Republican purists contended that the party had lost its way under Dwight Eisenhower, accommodating Social Security and other aspects of the New Deal and endorsing containment with its ever-growing global and governmental footprint. Republican pragmatists countered that Social Security was too entrenched in the expectations of millions of Americans to be uprooted and that containing communism was essential to American security. The pragmatists pointed to Eisenhower as evidence that moderation won elections. The purists rejoined that moderation might win elections but would cost the party its soul and the nation its future.

Barry Goldwater wasn't the purest of the pure, but the Arizona senator was the most politically credible of the comparatively pure. Goldwater's paternal grandfather had fled Russian Poland in the belief that a Jew without wealth had little future under the czars; he wound up in Phoenix, Arizona, where his son built the region's largest department store. Barry was born in 1909 and was baptized in the Episcopalian Church of his mother; he identified as Christian his whole life without denying his Jewish antecedents. He worked in the family store until World War

II, which opened his eyes to public affairs. He entered politics at the city level before audaciously challenging an incumbent Democrat for one of Arizona's Senate seats in 1952 and then riding Eisenhower's Republican coattails to victory. His gratitude didn't extend to Eisenhower's pragmatism, and after Goldwater called Eisenhower's domestic policies a "dime store New Deal," the president barely spoke to him.

But Goldwater's forthrightness endeared him to his constituents, who reelected him in 1958, and to the millions of Americans who purchased and read his political manifesto, *The Conscience of a Conservative.* Goldwater's conscience accepted the Cold War, for while he lamented the growth of government he made an exception for big defense, which he considered necessary to meet the communist threat. In fact he thought the United States should take a firmer line against the Russians and their proxies, using nuclear weapons if necessary. Goldwater judged that the real America resided in the rugged West; he remarked, "Sometimes I think this country would be better off if we could just saw off the Eastern Seaboard and let it float out to sea." He favored equality for blacks and other minorities, but he opposed federal civil rights legislation on the ground that it intruded unconstitutionally on the prerogatives of the states.

Goldwater supported Nixon in 1960 out of party loyalty rather than conviction; upon Nixon's defeat he predicted that conservatives would soon reclaim the party. They did, but not without a fight. Nelson Rockefeller inherited Eisenhower's moderate mantle as well as family millions that made the New York governor a formidable opponent. Goldwater and Rockefeller squared off during the 1964 primary season, with each winning multiple states. Yet when Goldwater narrowly captured delegate-rich California, the nomination seemed his.

The moderates nonetheless struggled to stop him. The Republican convention, held at San Francisco's Cow Palace, was the ugliest anyone in the party could remember. The West Coast venue seemed to favor Goldwater, and it inspired western conservatives who heckled and howled when Rockefeller attempted to address the convention. The nastiness grew personal when the conservatives loudly held Rockefeller's divorce and remarriage against him; the nation had never elected a divorced man president, and the conservatives didn't intend for it to start. An eleventh-hour movement to block Goldwater foundered when Governor William Scranton of Pennsylvania failed to find traction among the delegates; Scranton's public complaint to Goldwater that "you have too often casually prescribed nuclear war as a solution to a troubled world" merely inflamed the conservatives the more.

Goldwater fanned the fire himself in his acceptance speech. The nominee assailed the Democrats for failing to stem the communist tide. "I needn't remind you, but I will," he said: "It has been during Democratic years that a billion persons were cast into Communist captivity and their fate cynically sealed." A Republican administration, a Goldwater administration, would halt the communists in their tracks. "I want to make this abundantly clear: I don't intend to let peace or freedom be torn from our grasp because of lack of strength or lack of will." He had been labeled an extremist; coming, as it did, from self-proclaimed moderates, the label was one he welcomed. "I would remind you that extremism in the defense of liberty is no vice. And let me remind you also that moderation in the pursuit of justice is no virtue."

The conservatives bellowed their approval and stormed out of the convention hall to take on the Democrats and the world. But they soon discovered what the moderates had been saying all along: the conservatives could nominate a candidate but couldn't elect him. Within weeks opinion polls showed Goldwater trailing Lyndon Johnson badly, and the Republican candidate's prospects didn't improve as the election neared. Johnson was no pushover on defense, as his policy in Vietnam was beginning to demonstrate, and Goldwater's embrace of the extremist tag frightened voters who were still edgy after the Cuban missile crisis. The Johnson side ran a television spot showing a little girl counting daisy petals; an ominous male voice took over the counting and worked it backward to zero, when the mushroom cloud from a nuclear explosion filled the screen. Viewers were urged, by a calmer voice, to vote for Johnson. "The stakes are too high to stay home."

17

A S A RECENT Democrat, Reagan was well positioned to woo other Democrats to the Republican cause. He spoke on Goldwater's behalf in California, appealing to the same antigovernment sentiments that had won fellow westerner Goldwater the nomination. But there weren't enough conservative western Democrats to narrow Johnson's lead materially. The largest pool of restive Democrats was in the South, where conservatives resented Johnson's championing of civil rights. A hope to reach these distant Democrats was what lay behind the decision of the Goldwater campaign to broadcast Reagan's "Time for Choosing" speech nationally.

The speech was a huge success—for Reagan. It might have done more than it did for Goldwater had the Goldwater campaign been better prepared. The campaign appended an appeal for donations to Reagan's remarks, and viewers responded by contributing $1 million, a large amount at the time. The Goldwater camp wasn't expecting it and didn't know what to do with it. Much of the money remained in the campaign's account when Goldwater received his drubbing—he garnered less than 39 percent of the popular vote and carried just six states—a week later.

In American political history, no speech ever did more than Reagan's to launch a national political career. Lincoln's 1860 Cooper Union address earned the Illinoisan credibility in the East; William Jennings Bryan's "Cross of Gold" speech won him the 1896 Democratic nomination. But both Lincoln and Bryan had been in politics, been members of Congress. Reagan was a tyro. He had never held political office, never even run for office. He had been a member of his new party barely two years. And with one speech he became the most attractive Republican in America.

No one realized at the time that Reagan had identified beliefs that would carry him to the highest office in the land and survive a quarter century's hard use essentially unchanged. Reagan supporters would come to call his October 1964 performance "The Speech," and its twin themes of smaller government at home and stronger defense abroad would provide the template for the most successful political career of the second half of America's twentieth century.

What contemporary viewers *did* realize was that the former actor made a far more compelling political candidate than the actual candidate. And if Goldwater's performance at the polls dispirited conservatives, Reagan's speech gave them something to cheer about. They buried him in fan mail of a new sort. "I've never had a mail reaction like this in all my years in show business," he told a reporter. The consensus among his correspondents was that the Republicans should have nominated him. If Reagan had been on the ballot, the party and the conservative position might have fared better. And he *should* be on the ballot sometime soon, the writers said.

Conservatives in Michigan formed a Reagan-for-president committee; Republicans in other states began talking similarly. But a more realistic first race was for California governor. The second term of the incumbent, Democrat Pat Brown, would expire in 1966, giving the Republicans what they considered a reasonable shot at replacing him. The handicapping had already begun, and Reagan's stirring speech propelled him to the front of the small group of perceived hopefuls. "It's 14 months away from filing time, but already two prominent Republicans are beginning to think seriously about running for governor," political analyst Richard Bergholz wrote for the *Los Angeles Times* shortly after the Goldwater debacle. "One is Ronald Reagan, 53, actor and dyed-in-the-wool believer in Sen. Barry Goldwater's brand of political conservatism." The other was George Christopher, formerly mayor of San Francisco and a Republican moderate. "Reagan is the hottest—and the newest—prospect," Bergholz said. "Articulate, handsome, well-identified, the native of the little Illinois community of Tampico came on big toward the end of the recent presidential campaign . . . The response: tremendous."

Bergholz acknowledged the challenges Reagan would face. George Murphy, the actor, had gone into politics and just been elected to the Senate; some voters might think his victory eased Reagan's way, but Bergholz judged that it could instead inspire a feeling that one actor in politics was enough. Another handicap was Reagan's background as a Roosevelt

Democrat. "Some of his detractors say his career as a Democrat was 'pretty liberal,' to the point where it might prove embarrassing." And then there was his lack of experience. Would voters select someone who had never held public office? Perhaps he was too conservative for California, a state that had gone very heavily against Goldwater. "Some political 'pros' now are wondering whether Reagan could or would modify his views enough to reach the vast bulk of the Republican voters in California who have demonstrated they don't want political extremes." Finally, Reagan didn't travel by plane. "In a state like this, and in a fast-moving gubernatorial campaign, that's a severe problem."

But Reagan had certain advantages, Bergholz said. His speech had been a huge hit and won him an instant following. His likely Republican opponent, George Christopher, suffered from being from Northern California. "Reagan is a Southlander," Bergholz said. "And this is where the votes are." It was also the home of television, which Reagan used so well. "He would be expected to have his greatest pull where his televised image would have the greatest impact. And Southern California yields to no other area when it comes to taking its politics through the electronic tube."

Reagan read the columns about him but was canny enough to be noncommittal. He spoke of principles rather than politics. The Goldwater defeat reinforced his conviction that conservatives must stand fast. "The conservative philosophy was not repudiated," he told a Los Angeles gathering of Young Republicans. These were the zealots of the Republican right, and Reagan gave them what they wanted to hear. He laid the blame for Goldwater's loss not on the conservatives but on party moderates. Calling the moderates "traitors" to the party, he declared, "We will have no more of those candidates who are pledged to the same socialist goals of our opposition and who seek our support. If after the California presidential primary our opponents had then joined Barry Goldwater at the national convention and pledged their support, we could very well be celebrating a complete victory tonight." Reagan described the letters and calls he had been receiving from across the country; he said they told him and other conservatives, "Stay together and keep on working."

He dodged questions as to whether he would run for governor. A reporter told him a movement was afoot to place his name on the ballot for 1966; if the movement gained strength and the Republicans made him an offer of the nomination, how would he react? Reagan replied, "I hope I could turn it down."

But he decided this sounded too negative, and when the enthusiasm persisted, he rephrased his response. He still disclaimed a desire for office but said he couldn't ignore the will of the people or the call of duty. "I have some other thoughts about where an individual's responsibility lies despite his tastes and personal desires."

THE 1960S WERE the worst of times for conservatives, and the best. Conservatives value tradition and stability, and during the 1960s a confluence of forces challenged tradition and stability in America as rarely before. A century after the Civil War, African Americans demanded that the nation honor the pledges of the Thirteenth, Fourteenth, and Fifteenth Amendments. The Supreme Court had knocked several bricks from the wall of the Jim Crow system in 1954, when its decision in the case of *Brown v. Board of Education of Topeka* outlawed segregation in schools. Congress loosened a couple more with the Civil Rights Act of 1957. But as the 1960s began, American blacks, especially in the South, remained largely segregated and disenfranchised.

They took measures into their own hands. A bus boycott in Montgomery, Alabama, had vaulted a young minister named Martin Luther King Jr. into the national spotlight. Handsome, articulate, and charismatic, King became the face of the civil rights movement. Thousands of blacks, many of them students, rallied in protest of Jim Crow provisions in state laws, municipal codes, and corporate practices. They sat down at segregated lunch counters and refused to leave until arrested. They marched to state capitals and county courthouses to demand to be registered to vote. They endured taunts, threats, and physical violence that ranged from cuffs with fists and blasts from fire hoses to bullets and bombs.

Their movement would not have succeeded without the modern media, especially television. Americans in the North had long read about Jim Crow in newspapers, magazines, and books, but words on a page, and even photographs, had limited emotional impact. Television dramatically reduced the felt distance between the South and the rest of the country, and it brought the violence visited upon the black protesters into living rooms throughout the land.

Television never operated more effectively in favor of civil rights than during the summer of 1963. For decades black leaders had tried to organize a protest march to Washington to highlight discrimination in the workplace, in public accommodations, in education, and elsewhere in American life. One thing and then another had postponed the march, but in the centennial year of the 1863 Emancipation Proclamation, several civil rights groups collaborated to bring it about. The event drew some 200,000 to the National Mall; the highlight was a riveting address by Martin Luther King. "I have a dream," King said, "that one day this nation will rise up and live out the true meaning of its creed: 'We hold these truths to be self-evident, that all men are created equal.' I have a dream that one day on the red hills of Georgia, the sons of former slaves and the sons of former slave owners will be able to sit down together at the table of brotherhood. I have a dream that one day even the state of Mississippi, a state sweltering with the heat of injustice, sweltering with the heat of oppression, will be transformed into an oasis of freedom and justice. I have a dream that my four little children will one day live in a nation where they will not be judged by the color of their skin but by the content of their character." The crowd, silent at first, fell into King's rhythm; millions watching on television were mesmerized and then moved to tears as he riffed on "America the Beautiful" in calling for freedom to ring out across the country. "And when this happens," he concluded, "when we allow freedom ring, when we let it ring from every village and every hamlet, from every state and every city, we will be able to speed up that day when *all* of God's children, black men and white men, Jews and Gentiles, Protestants and Catholics, will be able to join hands and sing in the words of the old Negro spiritual: 'Free at last! Free at last! Thank *God* Almighty, we are free at last!'"

King's speech lit a fire under the Kennedy administration, which had hesitated to make civil rights a priority lest the president lose the support of white southerners, who had formed a critical element of the Democratic coalition since the Civil War. Kennedy's allies in Congress advanced a civil rights bill in the autumn of 1963, but the measure had far to go when Kennedy was assassinated that November. Lyndon Johnson inherited the bill, and he brought to civil rights both a passion and a credibility Kennedy had lacked. Johnson's passion arose from experience teaching Mexican American children in the small town of Cotulla, Texas, where he saw how racial prejudice stunted his pupils' opportunities and sapped their self-confidence. His credibility came from his southern roots, which let him speak to southerners on their own terms and in their own language.

It didn't hurt that Johnson was a master legislator. As Senate majority leader in the 1950s he had perfected the arts of persuasion and coercion essential to successful lawmaking; as president he employed those arts along with the powers of the presidency on behalf of the civil rights bill. Victory came within months, when Johnson signed the Civil Rights Act of 1964. The new law barred most forms of public racial discrimination, opening restaurants, hotels, theaters, and stores to patrons of all races and reinforcing existing laws and rulings mandating equal treatment in schools and the military and at the ballot box. Bolstered by the Voting Rights Act of 1965, the new law kicked the props from under the Jim Crow system and guaranteed its rapid dismantling.

In so doing, it simultaneously laid the groundwork for the resurgence of the party that would make Ronald Reagan president. Hours after signing the civil rights law, Johnson seemed less elated than aide Bill Moyers thought he ought to be. Moyers asked him why. "Because, Bill," Johnson said, "I think we just delivered the South to the Republican party for a long time to come."

OTHER EVENTS DELIVERED California to the Republicans. The civil rights reforms of the Johnson administration moved too slowly for many blacks who lived in America's large cities, and their frustration and anger at continuing inequality burst into violence. The first wave hit Harlem in the summer of 1964, just days after Johnson signed the Civil Rights Act. A white policeman fatally shot a black teenager, touching off rioting that lasted five days and caused hundreds of injuries and one death. In the following weeks similar eruptions occurred in Philadelphia, Rochester, and Jersey City.

The violence leaped to the West Coast, to Reagan's backyard, the next year. In August 1965 the black neighborhood of Watts in Los Angeles exploded after police arrested a black motorist for drunk driving. City and state officials hoped to forestall anything like the eastern violence by flooding the neighborhood with police and national guard troops, but the show of force simply elevated the tension. Many thousands of blacks took to the streets; whole blocks went up in flames as arsonists torched white-owned buildings. The local press hesitated to send white reporters into the battle zone, but the *Los Angeles Times* pulled a black man from its advertising department to cover the story. He quickly realized he needed to act like one of the rioters. "I, too, learned to shout, 'Burn, baby, burn'"—the slogan of the rioters—"after several shots were fired at me," he wrote. "Luckily none of the bullets hit my car, and luckier still, none hit me." The destruction was as mystifying as it was appalling. "The rioters were burning their city now, as the insane sometimes mutilate themselves. A great section of Los Angeles was burning, and anyone who didn't return the crazy password was in danger." He could gather impressions from his car, but filing his story required him to phone the paper. "I had to do all of my telephoning from street-corner booths in gas stations," he explained. "You have no idea how naked you can feel in an exposed, lighted telephone booth. But I was hep by that time. Whenever a group of Negroes approached to look me over I knew what to do. You open the door, stick your head out, and shout, 'Burn, baby, burn.' Then you are safe." Many locals who didn't participate in the violence, which ultimately exacted 34 deaths and more than a thousand injuries, not to mention tens of millions of dollars in property damage, professed to understand the feelings of the rioters and sympathized. "That's the hate that hate produced, white man," a black service station owner told a white reporter. "This ain't hurting us none. We have nothing to lose. Negroes don't own the buildings. You never did a decent thing in your life for us, white man." Another black man said, "This is a grass roots thing, white devil. Negro leaders can't stop this. The U.S. Army can't stop this. It just has to run its course."

Until the mid-1960s the principal complaint of conservatives against government was that it was growing too large; the riots in Harlem, Watts, and the other cities made them think it was sometimes too small. They demanded stricter enforcement of laws and an increase in the number and power of the police, augmented if necessary by state and federal troops. Meanwhile, they interpreted the riots as another manifestation of the bleeding-heart liberalism that blamed bad behavior not on the misbehavers but on social conditions, in this case poverty and inequality. The conservatives had long alleged that liberalism corroded the American character; they interpreted the riots as confirming evidence.

OTHER CHALLENGES TO the status quo evoked a similar conservative response. For generations colleges and universities had acted in loco parentis—as surrogate parents—toward their students. But when the children born after World War II began arriving on campuses during the 1960s, they demanded greater autonomy than their elders had enjoyed. They protested restrictions on speech, contending that the First Amendment applied to them as fully as to independent adults. The University of California at Berkeley was the initial hotbed of the protests; leaders and members of the Free Speech Movement there demanded the right to speak

their minds even when their speech irked or infuriated those individuals
and groups who professed to run the state and the country. The student
protesters were fully as arrogant as youth often is; they were often obscene
and occasionally violent. They indicted the "establishment" for its complicity in racism; they condemned the "military-industrial complex"—a
term they gleefully stole from Dwight Eisenhower—for America's deepening involvement in Vietnam.

The antiwar protests particularly irked the conservatives, whose model
war was World War II, when the country had been united in the all-out
struggle against fascism. Many conservatives branded resistance to the
draft as sedition; they judged obstruction of operations at military bases
and depots as treason. The conservatives couldn't decide who was more
culpable, the protesters or the government officials who allowed the protests. Many couldn't fathom why the Johnson administration didn't insist
on a war declaration from Congress and mobilize the country against
Asian communism the way Franklin Roosevelt had mobilized the country
against fascism—unless Johnson was as foolish or venal as liberals typically were.

While the protests outraged most conservatives, some concluded that
they would be good for conservatism and the country in the long run.
Liberals were a lost cause, these political strategists reasoned, but voters
would respond to the riots and the student unrest by demanding a return
to the verities that had made America great. The political tide would shift
in a conservative direction. With the right candidate, conservatism would
rule once more.

18

RUNNING FOR GOVERNOR— or not running for governor—was not a paying job, and Reagan needed to work. Finding a new gig took time, but eventually he landed another hosting role. *Death Valley Days* was a rare series with roots in radio that had successfully leaped the media divide into television. Stanley Andrews, playing the part of the "Old Ranger," had hosted the show since its television debut, but after thirteen years the producers wanted a fresher face. In 1965, Reagan got the part.

The job kept him in front of the viewing public while he tested the waters for a political run. He tramped about California and occasionally, but significantly, beyond the state speaking to the same kinds of councils, committees, chambers, and boards he had addressed under the General Electric label, but this time in the service of his own brand. He told the Inglewood Chamber of Commerce that the philosophy behind the New Deal and every other attempt at social engineering was morally bankrupt. "Each individual has inalienable rights," he said. "The acceptance of the statement 'the greatest good for the greatest number' will not bear up under examination. Our country was founded on the belief in the individual." He told the Republican Associates of Orange County, meeting at the Disneyland Hotel, that a proposal to withhold state income taxes from California paychecks was designed to lull voters into complacency. "I don't believe in painless taxes. Everyone should know exactly when he is paying his taxes and how much he is paying." Lyndon Johnson's War on Poverty was hopeless. "It's just a new pork barrel and a rehash of old ideas that do not work." The Civil Rights Act was misguided and illegitimate. Reagan didn't oppose equal treatment for people of different races.

"I'm all for it and have been all my life," he said. But the federal law was "badly written" and trampled the rights of individuals and the states. He condemned Medicare, approved by Congress and signed by Johnson in the summer of 1965, as "socialized medicine." It was another step down the road to collectivism. "If you can socialize the doctor, you can then socialize the patient."

Public opinion polls showed him far ahead of George Christopher and other potential Republican candidates, and the national press began to take notice. "The most startling fact on the listless Republican horizon today is the emergence of Hollywood actor Ronald Reagan as the new messiah of the Goldwater movement," columnists Rowland Evans and Robert Novak declared after a Reagan address in Cincinnati. "Indeed, many militant conservative Republicans who paid $100 a plate to swelter at the Cincinnati Gardens and hear Reagan excoriate the welfare state have all but forgotten Barry Goldwater. They talked to us quite seriously of Ronald Reagan running for President in 1968 (though some would prefer Richard M. Nixon as a sacrificial lamb against President Johnson in 1968, saving Reagan for 1972). Preposterous? Not completely." Evans and Novak explained that though Reagan hadn't announced for California governor, he was widely expected to do so and to win the Republican nomination. Governor Brown's fortunes were declining on account of an eighth-year itch in voters exacerbated by popular distress over the demonstrations on the state's college campuses and especially the Watts riot. Consequently, Reagan appeared, to Evans and Novak at any rate, a cinch to beat Brown in November 1966. And that might be just the start. "As governor of the nation's most populous state and with the loyalty of the fanatical Goldwater movement behind him, Reagan would be a formidable figure in the Republican Party. This tends to prove that not nearly so much was settled last Nov. 3 as liberal Republicans once thought. Far from admitting that Goldwater-style conservatism spells disaster at the polls, the conservatives now contend all they need is a candidate to package the doctrine in more appetizing fashion. That candidate is Reagan."

Evans and Novak profiled the former actor for their readers. "Reagan (though shaky in dealing personally with the press) is an absolute master of the banquet dais. Immaculately groomed and in superb physical condition, the 54-year-old movie hero could pass for 34 from a distance. But his greatest asset is his carefully polished basic speech. It amounts to Barry Goldwater's doctrine with John F. Kennedy's technique. Rather than coaxing applause in the time-honored manner, Reagan follows the JFK system of spewing out a profusion of statistics, wit and literary allusions (including one quote from Hilaire Belloc). The audience is too fascinated to clap." His celebrity power was obvious. "Reagan has captured the same starry-eyed devotion from female Republicans that Goldwater enjoyed. One trim young Cincinnati matron confided that she sat entranced through the Reagan TV speech three times last year. A state government official revealed: 'My wife says she's going to vote for him for President whether he's nominated or not.'" Yet the road to the top wouldn't be completely smooth. "Inherent in Reagan's meteoric rise are the same immutable factors that destroyed Goldwater. In a rambling press conference at Cincinnati, Reagan stumbled into the same ideological traps that undid Goldwater. He equivocated on the John Birch Society, refused to say 'yes' or 'no' about a voluntary approach to Social Security and declared his opposition to the most important provisions of the 1964 Civil Rights Act . . . Reagan's major goal in the California primary campaign will be to keep his devoted right wing militants happy without scaring the wits out of everybody else (a feat Goldwater never managed). For this reason, the coming struggle in California takes on national implications for the Republican Party."

William F. Buckley Jr. thought so too. Buckley in the 1950s had laid the intellectual foundations for the modern conservative movement in America; his combative *National Review* lambasted liberals and provided a home for libertarians, McCarthyites, reformed leftists, and others convinced that America was headed toward collectivist perdition. As a result, he was inclined to approve of Reagan, whose performance during 1965 confirmed the inclination. "He is developing a political know-how which astounds the professionals, who believe that it is immoral that an actor, as distinguished from a haberdasher, should be a good politician," Buckley pronounced, referencing Harry Truman's pre-political occupation. Buckley noted that Jesse Unruh, the Democratic speaker of the California state assembly, was paying Reagan sufficient respect to have developed a plan for neutralizing him. "The Unruh strategy is to provoke Ronald Reagan so as to cause him to reveal his 'mean streak,'" Buckley said. "The theory is that if a professionally good man like Ronald Reagan could be got to snarl, c-rrr-ack would go the image built up by 20 years of good-guying on the screen, and the public disillusion would be bitter and purposive." Buckley was skeptical. "The difficulty with Unruh's strategy is that if there is a mean streak in Ronald Reagan's character, it is deeply buried. I have not gone spelunking into his depths, and I would suppose there is a certain amount of bile in his system, as I suppose there was bile in the system of St. Francis of Assisi. But I should think it very unlikely that it would surface under even the severest political provocations." Unruh and Reagan's Republican opponents, notably George Christopher, were painting him as an extremist, Buckley observed. Perhaps in the wake of the Goldwater defeat Reagan had spoken harshly of moderates in the party, but now he was the soul of discretion. "He has gone around the state uttering nothing but kindnesses concerning his Republican competitors, denying himself even the pleasure of flirtatious animadversions on the tactics of some of his Republican opponents who preach the necessity of Republican unity by blasting everyone to the right of their impeccable selves. Reagan smiles, continues to speak vigorously his dissent from the wild spending policies of Gov. Brown, and the creeping anarchy whose manifestations at Berkeley and Watts are the big issue in California this year."

BY THE BEGINNING of 1966, Reagan was sufficiently confident of his chances to announce formally. He did so in a thirty-minute video recording released simultaneously to fifteen television stations around California. He identified himself as a "citizen politician," distinct from the professional politicians he would face in the primary and general elections. He reiterated his belief in the rights of individuals and warned against the growth of "big brother, paternalistic government." He pointed to the uproar at Berkeley as evidence that Brown and the Democrats were failing in their obligation to protect individual rights and preserve public order. "Will we allow a great university to be brought to its knees by a noisy, dissident minority? Will we meet their neurotic vulgarities with vacillation and weakness, or will we tell those entrusted with administering the university we expect them to enforce a code based on decency, common sense and dedication to the high and noble purpose of the university?" He opposed acceptance of federal aid to state education. "With federal aid goes federal control, and as the administration in Sacramento relinquishes state sovereignty to Washington, at the same time it takes more power from those who have been elected to run our towns and cities." He lamented the politics of hyphenated Americanism, accusing the Democrats of pandering to "Negro-Americans," "Mexican-Americans," and other special groups whose interests were promoted for "political expediency so cynical men could make cynical promises in a hunt for votes." He promised to run a clean campaign adhering to the "Eleventh Commandment" promoted by the Republican state chairman, Gaylord Parkinson, which forbade Republicans to attack fellow Republicans.

Lyn Nofziger, a journalist who joined the Reagan campaign as press secretary, recalled the Parkinson commandment as specially favoring Reagan. "Of course, the chairman is supposed to be neutral, but they came up with this thing mainly to keep the other candidates from attacking Reagan for being ignorant and for not having any political experience and that sort of thing," Nofziger said. "It worked very well because we'd say, 'You can't pick on Reagan because he's a fellow Republican.'" Reagan was happy to play along. "I will have no word of criticism for any Republican," he said.

He didn't quite live up to his promise. George Christopher and other moderate Republicans tried to rattle Reagan, pressing him to disavow endorsement by the John Birch Society, the neo-McCarthyist group that revered the Tenth Amendment and rejected every advance of federal authority since the eighteenth century. This conspicuously included federal laws intended to secure civil rights to minorities; as a result the Birchers were often branded racists by their many opponents. Some *were* racists, which made the charge plausible and required political candidates to keep their distance.

Reagan recognized that the Birchers would vote for him if they voted for any candidate not on the unelectable fringe, and he didn't want to alienate them. For months he dodged questions about the society, which naturally encouraged Christopher and the moderates to call him a fellow traveler and suggest that he was a closet racist. Still he resisted disavowal, saying he rejected "blanket indictments" of people for the company they kept. When the pressure increased, he issued a statement declaring himself in "great disagreement" with some of the words and actions of Birch founder Robert Welch. "I am not a member," he added of the society. "I have no intention of becoming a member. I am not going to solicit their support."

This wasn't good enough, and the needling from his left continued. In March 1966 he attended a forum of black Republicans at the Miramar Hotel in Santa Monica. George Christopher and a couple of lesser candidates also attended, and someone said something that was too quiet for the audience and reporters to hear but that Reagan took sorely amiss. "I resent the implication that there is any bigotry in my nature," he responded angrily in a voice all present *could* hear. "Don't anyone ever imply I lack integrity. I will not stand silent and let anyone imply that, in this or in any other group." He stalked out of the ballroom, pounding one fist into the palm of the other hand. More than one reporter heard him say, "I'll get that SOB," but none of them could tell which SOB he was referring to.

At once he realized he had misstepped. He returned to the meeting room and finished the session calmly. He released a statement clarifying his position on the Civil Rights Act and on civil rights generally. "I believe it was not as well written as it could have been," he said of the act. For this reason he had opposed it. "But I've been, heart and soul all my life, active in promoting goals of that act. I regret the great bitterness that exists. I have repeatedly said that where the constitutional rights of citizens are violated for any reason, it is the responsibility of government, at bayonet point if necessary, to enforce those rights." He said he would not patronize a business that discriminated. But he didn't think the Constitution allowed the federal government to force a shop owner to stop discriminating on his own property. Nor did he think state governments should infringe upon the rights of property owners. He opposed a Democratically inspired and recently adopted California fair-housing law. "Freedom can't survive in a nation that tolerates prejudice or bigotry," he said. But neither could it survive ever-expanding government. Basic rights like those attached to ownership of property "cannot be submitted to majority rule," he said. If they were, there would be no limit to government's grasp. "Eventually it will be dangerous to all of us."

REAGAN'S EXPLANATION APPARENTLY satisfied Republican primary voters, who handed him a two-to-one victory over Christopher. The size of the win and the enthusiasm of Reagan's supporters caused many California Republicans, discouraged after the party's poor showing in 1964, to think there was hope for the GOP after all. "I was not a big fan of Reagan's," Michael Deaver remembered of his first impressions of the former actor. "I was a young guy in the Republican party in California, and I had worked in Santa Clara County as executive director of the party. I was a northern Californian in my politics, although I'd been a big Goldwater young person. But always being a pragmatist, when I woke up the morning after the Goldwater election and realized that we had carried five, six states, or whatever it was, I decided I was never going to do that again. I wanted to win elections." Something about Goldwater's version of conservatism brought out the mean streak in people, Deaver thought. "We had four or five Goldwater organizations that wouldn't speak to each other in California. It was just terrible, and the whole Goldwater organization, you talk about right wing. These were scary people, when I look back on it now. It was the John Birch Society, and it was get us out of the U.N., and don't let them fluoridate our water, and all that kind of stuff. Those were the people who were involved in it. So I just didn't want to have anything more to do with that."

Deaver assumed Reagan was cut from the same off-putting cloth, until he encountered him personally. "I met him at a dinner when he had decided to go around the state and allegedly test the waters," Deaver said. "He was coming into every town and meeting with the Republican leaders. At that time I was working for the Republican State Committee in Santa Barbara, and about thirty of us got together for dinner at the Talk of the Town restaurant there in Santa Barbara. He was very impressive because here you could ask him anything, and you could see how his mind worked. And he certainly was an agreeable guy. Because of his size, he was imposing in a room, but then when he spoke, he was even more unforgettable because he was such a nice guy. He really was a nice guy, and he was very bright. So that left me with a pretty good impression."

The impression improved the more when Reagan trounced Christopher. Deaver detected the winner he had been looking for and joined the Reagan campaign. He was utterly charmed by the candidate. "You wanted to help Reagan to float through life," he said decades and several campaigns later. "You wanted to make it easy for him. You wanted to be sure that everything was taken care of. I can't tell you why that was; everybody who has ever worked for him felt that way. He never asked for it, but it was just instantly apparent that that was something that everybody was going to do. I think there are very few people around, certainly nobody in my life that I've ever met, whom you had this respect for. You wanted him to succeed, and you'd be willing to do whatever it took to take the load off him of all the shitty little things that normal people have to do."

Deaver was more smitten than most, but many observers saw in Reagan's big primary win a sign of a Republican revival, and not in California alone. "The California primary results may prove prophetic," political columnist David Lawrence wrote in the *Los Angeles Times*. "If a united Republican Party emerges in the state, and the bitterness of the 1964 campaign can be superseded by cooperation among the factions, California could become a strong Republican state." And California could be a harbinger for the country at large. The key was the candidate. "It is the character of the man, rather than the position he takes on public issues, which so often wins an election," Lawrence said. "In fact, there are many cases where the candidate who says less than his opponent on specific issues and sticks to general principles turns out to be the victor, very largely because of a winning personality."

Reagan possessed the winning personality, and Pat Brown didn't. The incumbent had never set hearts aflutter, and next to Reagan he looked stodgy and slow. He sometimes tripped over his own tongue. "Pat is a nice man, but the reporters looked upon him as a kind of buffoon," Lyn Nofziger recalled of Brown. Nofziger still chuckled, decades later, at a remark by Brown after he inspected the devastation to Crescent City from a tsunami: "This is the worst disaster since I was elected governor." Nor did Brown win the confidence of baseball fans when he spoke hopefully of the Los Angeles Dodgers and the San Francisco Giants: "I am looking forward to the day when these two teams meet in the World Series." Both teams were in the National League, making a meeting in the World Series impossible.

A June 1966 poll showed Reagan with an eleven-point lead over the governor, and in the five months of the general race Brown never closed the gap. Reagan evaded an ambush in Sacramento by Democrat Alan Cranston, the state controller, who confronted him physically and demanded a response to a report asserting that the John Birch Society was anti-Semitic, among its other sins. Reagan refused to take the report Cranston thrust in his face, and kept walking. He encountered labor-union hecklers in Oakland who shouted him down. "Boy, I dream of the day when I'm not a candidate and can answer these guys," he muttered, loudly enough for reporters to hear. Subsequently asked his feelings about the heckling, he replied, "It didn't bother me. This was the labor hierarchy. I don't have them and frankly I don't want them." He received the endorsement of former president Eisenhower and of Pennsylvania's William Scranton, who said Reagan could be in the running for the Republican nomination for president in 1968 if he won big in California. "He's put on a very good campaign and is an attractive personality," Scranton said. "The Republicans could use attractive personalities and I'm glad we have one."

The attractive personality triumphed in November. Reagan crushed Brown, piling up a million-vote margin while leading the Republicans to a near sweep of statewide offices. Republicans advanced throughout the country, benefitting from the typical sixth-year reaction against the party that holds the White House, from unease over the turbulence on campuses and in the cities, and from worries about the war in Vietnam. The Republicans gained eight governorships, three seats in the U.S. Senate, and forty-seven seats in the House.

19

R EAGAN'S HUGE WIN made him the talk of the nation. Political analyst Warren Weaver Jr. of the *New York Times* projected the 1968 presidential race and put Reagan in the top four of Republican likelies, along with Richard Nixon, who had toured the country touting the virtues of Republican candidates in many states; Governor George Romney of Michigan, who had been reelected almost as handsomely as Reagan had been elected; and Illinois industrialist Charles Percy, who had just defeated a Democratic warhorse to claim a Senate seat from the state of that greatest of Republicans, Abraham Lincoln.

Reagan dismissed the presidency talk. "I am honored and flattered that anyone would even link my name with the presidency," he said on the ABC interview program *Issues and Answers*. "But I have a four-year contract with the people of California."

Yet he didn't avoid topics more appropriate to a president than a governor. He urged an escalation of the war in Vietnam. "Once the killing starts and we send young American boys over there to die, the nation has a moral obligation to impose its full resources to end it as soon as possible," he said. He wanted more bombing of North Vietnam, especially depots of weapons. "Knock them out where you get them in the biggest bunches, not just coming down some jungle trail on a coolie's back." He thought the army ought to be returned to volunteers. "I question this whole business of the draft," he said. "Why can't we evolve a program of voluntary service? I don't want the uniform to become a symbol of servitude." He called for complete revamping of federal welfare and poverty programs, which were full of "graft and outright misuse of funds." He predicted that the national civil rights movement was entering a quieter, more peaceful phase. Black Power advocate Stokely Carmichael would be left "more and more behind by his own people, who will determine there is a better way of achieving equality than friction and violence."

ALL THE SAME, he was eager to start work as governor. So eager, in fact, that he jumped the gun. His term was set to begin on Monday, January 2, the first workday of 1967. But he signed and orally swore the oath of office several days early. The California secretary of state subsequently claimed a paperwork mix-up and said it was his own fault. Yet the assistant secretary of state, who administered the oath and certified the signing, remembered telling Reagan, "This is the document that will officially make you governor." The assistant secretary later fudged his recollection, in Reagan's favor. "To be fair to Governor Reagan," he amended, "I can quite understand in retrospect that it was not entirely made clear."

The kerfuffle was forgotten in the rush of the Republican takeover of California's executive branch. Reagan was sworn in again a moment past midnight on the morning of January 2. He uttered some modest remarks about the need to reduce the size of government, and then the few people present went home to bed. He saved his energy and dramatic effort for the public inaugural ceremony, which took place three days later. "Government is the people's business, and every man, woman and child becomes a shareholder with the first penny of tax paid," he declared. Those taxes were too high and must come down; the ambitions of government must be curtailed. "The path we will chart is not an easy one. It demands much of those chosen to govern, but also from those who did the choosing. And let there be no mistake about this: we have come to a crossroad—a time of decision—and the path we follow turns away from any idea that government and those who serve it are omnipotent."

Certain functions of government were necessary, Reagan allowed. The government must keep the peace against people who would disrupt it. "Those with a grievance can seek redress in the courts or Legislature, but not in the streets. Lawlessness by the mob, as with the individual, will not be tolerated. We will act firmly and quickly to put down riot or insurrection wherever and whenever the situation requires."

Government should assist people who could not help themselves. But it must not coddle idlers and freeloaders. "We are a humane and generous people and we accept without reservation our obligation to help the aged, disabled and those unfortunates who, through no fault of their own, must depend on their fellow men. But we are not going to perpetuate poverty by substituting a permanent dole for a pay check. There is no humanity or charity in destroying self-reliance, dignity and self-respect, the very substance of moral fiber."

The colleges must shape up or their students must ship out. "Hundreds of thousands of young men and women will receive an education in our state colleges and universities. We are proud of our ability to provide this opportunity for our youth and we believe it is no denial of academic freedom to provide this education within a framework of reasonable rules and expectations. Nor is it a violation of individual rights to require obedience to these rules and regulations or to insist that those unwilling to abide by them should get their education elsewhere. It does not constitute political interference with intellectual freedom for the tax-paying citizens, who support the college and university systems, to ask that, in addition to teaching, they build character on accepted moral and ethical standards."

Reagan was formal, even stern, to this point in his speech. His lighter side emerged as he described the budget. "Our fiscal situation has a sorry similarity to the situation of a jet liner out over the North Atlantic, Paris bound. The pilot announced he had news—some good, some bad—and he would give the bad news first. They had lost radio contact; their compass and altimeter were not working; they didn't know their altitude, direction or where they were headed. Then he gave the good news: they had a 100-mile-an-hour tail wind and they were ahead of schedule."

The sternness resumed as he described the fiscal hole the previous administration and legislature had dug and what must be done for California to climb out. Drastic cuts were necessary and would be made. "For many years now, you and I have been shushed like children and told there are no simple answers to the complex problems which are beyond our comprehensions. Well, the truth is, there *are* simple answers; there just are not easy ones." The culture of taxing and spending had to be changed. "The time has come to match outgo to income, instead of always doing it the other way around . . . We are going to squeeze and cut and trim until we reduce the cost of government. It won't be easy, nor will it be pleasant, and it will involve every department of government . . . We will put our fiscal house in order. And as we do, we will build those things we need to make our state a better place in which to live and we will enjoy them more, knowing we can afford them and they are paid for."

He closed with another anecdote, more touching than the one about the wayward plane. He pointed to the state flag flying over the gathering and observed that it was smaller than the flag that usually flew there. "There is an explanation. That flag was carried into battle in Vietnam by young men of California. Many will not be coming home." One young man, Sergeant Robert Howell, did come home, but badly wounded. "He brought that flag back. I thought we would be proud to have it fly over the Capitol today. It might even serve to put our problems in better perspective. It might remind us of the need to give our sons and daughters a cause to believe in and banners to follow. If this is a dream, it is a good dream, worthy of our generation and worth passing on to the next. Let this day mark the beginning."

DETAILS OF GOVERNING would rarely interest Reagan. He was an idea man, a purveyor of big principles. Details he left to others. William Clark, who jumped from the campaign to the governor's office as chief of staff, put it charitably when he said of his boss and the issues that confronted him, "He had the underlying philosophy and the vision in approaching these issues, but he had to rely on expertise." Reagan's philosophy and vision would prove his strength; his reliance on others would prove his weakness. Both became apparent in the first big job he faced as governor: balancing the state budget.

California, like most states, had constitutionally prohibited itself from running a deficit. But its elected officials hadn't eliminated the temptations that afflict their class when it comes to spending the people's money. Pat Brown's parting gift to Reagan was a budget that was balanced only by dint of an egregious fiction: a onetime shift to accounting methods that allowed the state to tally revenues at the time they were levied rather than at the time they were collected. By this means Brown's last budget was able to claim fifteen months of revenues to cover twelve months of spending. Reagan had criticized the gimmick during the election, and the criticism contributed to Brown's defeat. But now Reagan had to deal with the consequences, starting with a budget that was impossibly out of balance.

He tackled the problem by proposing a 10 percent reduction in state spending across the board. This had the merit of simplicity, and it reflected Reagan's long-standing assertion that government as a whole was bloated. He left to others to defend this program or that; he aimed to slash them all.

The problem with Reagan's approach was that it antagonized everyone who looked to any government program for assistance, patronage, or votes. His budget produced no winners, only losers. California's lawmakers, like lawmakers everywhere, used government spending to build networks of support; Reagan's plan threatened every such network.

The new governor didn't help his cause by refusing to adjust his habits to the political culture of the California capital. Reagan wasn't a natural socializer. "My father was a very private person," Ron Reagan observed later. But the governor was expected to socialize. Michael Deaver, who joined William Clark in the governor's office, explained, "All of those guys who went to Sacramento loved Sacramento, to get to Sacramento, to get away from their wives—it was allegedly a part-time legislature—and go to Frank Fats and Posey's every night and sit around and chase young staffers and drink. And Reagan went home at six o'clock every night and had a TV tray with Nancy or the kids or whoever was at home and never did that. They were always bitching about that. Why doesn't he ever do like the governors are supposed to? He's supposed to have us down to his office at six o'clock at night, pull out a couple of bottles, and we put our feet up on his desk, and that's how we get things done." The complaining prompted Reagan to make a modest effort to accommodate. "We finally tried to have the legislators over to the house once a week," Deaver continued. "We'd pick five or six of them. I don't think we had the wives. I think we just had the legislators. They would have dinner. Nancy would be there. Then they'd go down in the basement, and they had a pool table down there. It was just awful. It just didn't work. I mean, he could be charming, and he would have a good time. But it just wasn't what they— they didn't want to be at somebody's house with a wife there."

The simpatico gap became apparent as soon as Reagan's budget was sent to the legislature. The majority Democrats, led by assembly speaker Jesse Unruh, declared it utterly unacceptable. Unruh believed budget writing was the responsibility of the legislative branch of the state government, not the executive branch, and anyway he was happy to cross swords with Reagan, whom he intended to challenge for governor in 1970. Unruh argued that the governor's budget blindly cut essential programs as well as the wasteful. The Department of Mental Hygiene, for instance, would have to terminate thousands of staff who cared for the mentally impaired. Was the governor willing to accept responsibility for the suffering his cuts would impose on these most vulnerable members of society? Or for the harm the untreated patients might inflict on the rest of society?

There was a broader problem with Reagan's budget. Even with the 10 percent cuts it wouldn't come close to reaching balance. Unruh and the Democrats held that tax increases were unavoidable. The governor needed to acknowledge this before he could expect any cooperation from the legislature.

In the 1960s, American conservatives prided themselves on fiscal responsibility. They disliked taxes but disliked deficits even more. Reagan shared this set of priorities and consequently suffered no crisis of conscience in proposing a revised budget that included new taxes. All the same, he winced when he saw the headlines his proposal engendered. "RECORD TAX HIKE," the *Los Angeles Times* blared in a page-wide head just two months after the governor had inaugurally promised to "match outgo to income" rather than the other way around. The tax increases would total nearly $950 million. And state spending would top $5 billion, another record, and another reversal for the governor who had pledged to "squeeze and cut and trim."

The revised budget proposal furnished the basis for a deal with the legislature. Reagan and Unruh wrangled at the margins, with Unruh wanting state income taxes withheld from paychecks and Reagan resisting. Unruh argued that withholding would be fairer to honest taxpayers by making cheating harder; Reagan contended that withholding, by easing the pain of taxes, would simultaneously lessen demands to cut them. Reagan won this round, in part by promising future property tax relief, which Unruh wanted. But so did Reagan, which meant that on withholding he basically got something for nothing.

By the time the budget passed the legislature and received Reagan's signature, the tax hike topped $1 billion. Some conservatives complained that the governor had betrayed his principles. Reagan responded that compromise was inherent in democratic politics. "I'm willing to take what I can get," he told reporter Lou Cannon.

COMPROMISE CAME HARDER on another bill, but it came nonetheless. Opposition to abortion wasn't yet a litmus test for conservatives, not least because abortion was generally illegal and had been since the nineteenth century. But attitudes toward abortion changed along with attitudes toward women, and as women assumed greater legal and political freedom during the twentieth century, many began to demand greater control of their reproductive processes as well. The development of oral contraceptives during the 1950s triggered a debate about sexuality and who should speak for women; at about the same time, the birth of deformed babies to mothers who had taken thalidomide, a medication frequently prescribed for morning sickness, produced a desire to consider legal means for terminating high-risk pregnancies.

California wasn't the first state to liberalize its abortion laws, but a bill introduced during Reagan's first year in office was one of the most sweeping. The author, Democrat Anthony Beilenson, had previously cosponsored a bill in the state assembly to allow abortions to save the life of the mother. He and the bill's supporters heard testimony describing the gruesome deaths of women who had felt compelled to obtain illegal abortions from incompetent amateur surgeons. But the Catholic Church adamantly opposed the bill, and the measure failed.

Beilenson tried again in 1967 after moving from the assembly to the state senate. Attitudes toward women and sex continued to evolve, and Beilenson's new bill gained ground. The measure would allow abortion in cases of rape or incest, in pregnancies in which the physical or mental health of the mother was in danger, or where there was a substantial risk of deformation in the child. As the debate proceeded, the last clause was the one that attracted most of the negative attention. The Catholic Church still condemned abortion under any circumstances, but a growing number of Californians were willing to let women choose to end pregnancies that had been forced on them or that endangered their lives or well-being. Yet even among these, the idea of aborting a pregnancy simply because the infant might be malformed often seemed a step too far.

Reagan was among this group. He had no profound convictions about abortion, never having considered the matter carefully. If, as a boy, he had followed his father into the Catholic Church, he might have adopted the church's views without having to think too much. But he had not, and so he had more room to make up his own mind. He was pondering the matter while the Beilenson bill moved forward. "It is a very profound and deep issue," he told reporters at a capitol news conference. "There are legal questions that have not been resolved yet." He mentioned "loopholes" in the language regarding statutory rape. Yet the matter that gave him the greatest pause was the provision for abortion of deformed fetuses. "There is a very great question to me as to where we can actually stand, trying to judge in advance of a birth that someone is going to be born a cripple and whether we have the right to decide before birth what cripple would not be allowed to live. We have had some great contributions made to mankind who have been in the technical sense crippled." The logic behind this part of the bill could lead to infanticide, he said. "Would anyone here advocate that we should, after they are born, make a choice and line up which cripple should be destroyed and which should be saved?"

Reporters asked if he would veto the bill if it passed the legislature.

He hadn't decided. "I'm still waiting," he said. "I'm not going to make a comment until I see what the bill is."

A reporter commented that North Carolina had passed a law that required residency in that state before an abortion could be performed. Would the governor favor such a restriction?

Reagan said he hadn't thought about it. But it seemed a good idea. "I'd not want to create a kind of an attraction in the state for this kind of thing."

Reporters asked what the governor liked about the bill.

"Certainly the protection of the mother—the health, the life of the mother—and very frankly I think there is justice in not forcing someone who's been the victim of a forcible rape or incest to go through with this."

Again he was asked his overall verdict.

"This is not in my mind a clear-cut issue," he reiterated. "And I just can't give you a decision."

Reagan would have preferred that the bill expire in the legislature. He was no crusader for women's rights, but neither was he a defender at all costs of the unborn. And yet, as the bill moved forward, he gradually made his peace with most of it. "I am satisfied in my own mind we can morally and logically justify liberalized abortions to protect the health of a mother," he declared at another news conference. Yet he still had qualms about the deformity clause. "I cannot justify the taking of an unborn life simply on the supposition that the baby may be born less than a perfect human being." The dangerous next step would be deciding after birth that some had to die, and this, he said, "wouldn't be much different from what Hitler tried to do." He repeated himself as he thought aloud: "Where would you draw the line? We've had a great many contributions to humanity by persons who are crippled or deformed."

But would he veto a bill with the deformity provision? he was asked.

He still wouldn't commit. "Don't put my feet in concrete yet on this," he said. "I've laid my soul bare already."

He continued to hope not to have to decide. The bill narrowly passed the senate and moved to the assembly. Hours before the lower house was to vote, Reagan still refused to declare whether he would sign it or not. But when the assembly approved the measure by a surprising 48-to-30 margin, he realized he had to choose, and he decided that the sooner he chose, the better. He signed the bill, saying, "I am confident that the people of California recognize the need and will support the humanitarian goals of the measure." Yet his doubts surfaced once more in a caveat: "We must be extremely careful to assure that this legislation does not result in making California a haven for those who would come to this state solely for the purpose of taking advantage of California's new law."

20

UCH AS THE Watts riot helped the Republicans elect a governor in California, so disturbances in other cities made them think they could elect a president two years later. Summer became the riot season in America during the 1960s; as the temperature rose and tempers grew short, urban police forces braced for violence. The summer of 1967 brought an outburst in Newark in early July, and it was followed two weeks later in Detroit by what could only be called urban warfare. The Detroit violence started, like the violence elsewhere, when police responded to minor trouble and met resistance that then escalated. In the Detroit case the burning, looting, and shooting lasted five days, prompting Michigan governor Romney to dispatch state national guard troops and President Johnson to send U.S. Army forces. More than forty people died in the fighting, hundreds were injured, thousands were arrested, and scores of millions of dollars of property were destroyed. Detroit's survivors were shell-shocked; Americans elsewhere watched in disbelief and fear that what happened in Detroit might be coming to a city near them.

Things got worse. Martin Luther King had long preached peaceful resistance to injustice; the principal spokesman for the civil rights movement implored African Americans to eschew violence and exercise their hard-won political rights. King found himself competing with other, more militant voices, including those of Stokely Carmichael and H. Rap Brown. In California the militants coalesced behind the Black Panther Party, founded by Huey Newton and Bobby Seale. The Panthers rejected King's vision of a color-blind America; they preached black nationalism and self-defense. They staged a spectacular protest by storming, armed, into the California state capitol to protest what they called police brutality and the selective enforcement of weapons bans.

Yet King kept the nonviolent faith and held the respect and affection of millions of African Americans who wanted to believe that change was possible within the evolving framework of democracy. Then, in April 1968, King was assassinated in Memphis. The motives of the assassin weren't immediately clear, as he eluded capture for two months, but the reaction among the black community was anger and despair. If King, the apostle of nonviolence, could be gunned down, what hope was there for change within the existing system?

The King killing triggered the broadest violence to date. Rioting broke out in more than a hundred cities across the country. Anarchy seized Chicago; Washington and Baltimore burst into flames. Scores of people died and many thousands were injured in fires and clashes with police; property damage defied calculation.

THIS LATEST PHASE of rioting coincided with the season of presidential primaries. Richard Nixon had followed his 1960 loss to John Kennedy with a 1962 loss to Pat Brown in the race for California governor. Some imagined that he then retired from politics, not least because he said, following his loss to Brown, that he was calling it quits. But he unobtrusively gave counsel to Republican candidates, helped them raise money, and positioned himself as the moderate who could steer the party out of the conservative ditch into which Goldwater had driven it in 1964.

This position gained enormously in value when Johnson unexpectedly withdrew from the contest on the Democratic side. Johnson was thought to be the ultimate politico, the stubborn Texan who would defend his Alamo to the last breath. But Johnson was haunted by fears of impending mortality, having nearly died of a heart attack in 1955, and he knew enough political history to realize that second terms for presidents rarely end well. He had exhausted his political capital persuading Congress to pass his civil rights measures, Medicare, and the other reforms of the Great Society. There was liberal work yet to be done, but he doubted he was the one to do it. Besides, the war in Vietnam had been going badly, despite his cumulative decisions to send more than half a million troops and commensurate resources there. The Southeast Asian conflict took a particularly sobering turn in early 1968, when a communist offensive that started on the Tet holiday demonstrated unexpected strength. Johnson thereupon reversed his war policy and declared his desire for a negotiated settlement; he simultaneously threw in the political towel and said he wouldn't seek another term as president.

Suddenly Republicans could see a clear path to the White House, unimpeded by incumbency. The waters appeared to part still further when southern Democrats prepared to bolt in protest of the national party's embrace of civil rights.

REAGAN SUDDENLY BEGAN to fancy himself the one who would lead his party to the promised land. He had deflected queries about the presidency, saying he had too much to do in California. He permitted his name to be placed in nomination at the Republican convention, but only as a California favorite son; this pro forma gesture would enable the California delegation to draw together behind his candidacy and thereby mend the rift between conservatives and liberals that had vexed the state party since 1964.

But he started to think that the favorite son of California could become the party's favorite. Nixon lacked charisma; even his supporters admitted that. His two defeats branded him a loser. And his governing philosophy was suspect, indeed inscrutable. No one could say just where he stood on the moderate-to-conservative axis. Reagan was a loyal Republican, but he was also a conservative. He would back the party's nominee, but he hoped it would be a conservative. As he looked around, the only credible conservative he could see was himself. A candidate who had the support of the eighty-six-member California delegation, the convention's largest, would have a head start on everyone else. It wasn't delusional to think he might attract enough additional votes to boost him over the top.

In public he remained coy. He was a "noncandidate," he said. But he let his supporters establish a committee that prepared the groundwork for a campaign. When a pollster found significant support around the country for a Reagan candidacy, he began to qualify his disclaimers. "Naturally I was interested in hearing that," he said of the pollster's report. "I'm not going to run away and pretend it isn't happening. Obviously I'm going to evaluate it." Asked again if he would seek the presidency, he responded, "The job seeks the man." To inquiries whether he encouraged those who were working for his candidacy, he responded, "It's a free country." What would be his response if he attracted a large write-in vote in the primaries? "I'll wait till such a thing happens and make a decision then."

He undertook a several-state speaking tour that looked remarkably like what candidate Nixon was doing. When he spoke in Boise, Idaho, to a crowd that applauded and shouted with a passion conspicuously denied to Nixon by *his* audiences, he predicted that the race for the Republican nomination would not be decided in the primaries but would go to the convention, in Miami Beach. Tom Wicker, a columnist for the *New York Times*, followed Reagan in Idaho and thought he saw a contender. "At close range, Reagan looks and sounds formidable," Wicker wrote. "He comes on fast and smiling, rocking his audience with a battery of one-liners in the Bob Hope manner . . . He glides smoothly into a denunciation of big government, welfare, crime in the streets, American foreign policy, and politicians. Before he finishes touching all these exposed political nerves, his audiences are cheering his most innocuous remarks ('The times cry out for statesmanship,' he declared last night, to thunderous applause)." Wicker wasn't about to say that Idaho was the nation's bellwether. But he quoted a likely convention delegate who said, "The farther west you go, the closer you get to 1964." In his own words he limned a scenario that could cause the convention to turn to Reagan. "The expectation here is that a pro-Nixon but formally uncommitted delegation will be chosen by Idaho . . . But the expectation also is that most of the 14 delegates will be Republicans who supported Goldwater in 1964 and who will swing comfortably into the Reagan camp if and when the time comes—maybe on the second or third ballot at Miami Beach."

Reagan continued to campaign like a candidate. "The nation is totally out of control," he told the annual convention of the National Newspaper Association, conveniently meeting in Los Angeles. The current administration and the leading Democratic candidates, including New York senator Robert Kennedy, were encouraging people to expect something for nothing, he said, while proposing nothing to stem the violence in America's cities and the erosion of American credibility abroad. "Civilization simply cannot afford demagogues in this era of rising expectations. It cannot afford prophets who shout that the road to the promised land lies over the shards of burned and looted cities. It cannot afford politicians who demand that Social Security be tripled without coming up with any plans as to how this impossibility could be accomplished; that a national duty in Vietnam be discarded to provide huge make-work programs in the city slums with the money diverted from Vietnam; that no youth need honor the draft; that Negroes need not obey the law . . . It is a grand design for the Apocalypse."

THE APOCALYPSE CAME closer in June, though not in a way that benefited Reagan. Robert Kennedy was celebrating a crucial victory in the California Democratic primary when a stranger approached him at the Ambassador Hotel in Los Angeles and shot him. Kennedy died a day later. The killing seemed to underscore Reagan's complaint that the country was falling apart, but politics and simple discretion prevented him or anyone else from trying to turn it to personal advantage. If anyone benefited, it was the candidates closest to the political center, those who seemed least likely to evoke strong passions.

Nixon still didn't excite voters, but neither did he scare them. And now his work on behalf of other Republicans began to tell. He had scored one primary victory after another in small states, amassing almost enough delegates to claim the nomination on the convention's first ballot. Nelson Rockefeller ran second and Reagan third. Rockefeller naturally thought that if anyone should benefit from a Nixon failure, it should be him, not Reagan. In any event, the Rockefeller delegates preferred Nixon to Reagan, just as the Reagan delegates preferred Nixon to Rockefeller.

Nixon recognized this balance of ambivalence before Reagan did. Reagan looked more and more like a candidate as the convention drew near. "I do not believe the nomination is locked up for any candidate and I do believe it will be an open convention," he telegraphed the chairman of his unofficial campaign committee. "My name will be placed in nomination. Obviously at that time I can be considered a candidate by any delegate so inclined." Lest his availability be in any continuing doubt, he added, "I have never subscribed to the Sherman statement"—in which Civil War hero William T. Sherman had said that if nominated he would not run and if elected would not serve. "Indeed it is my belief that any citizen's response should be the direct opposite." Reagan's backers spread stories that Nixon's support in the South was soft and uncertain. "These delegates are still looking," one said. Another declared that if Nixon didn't win at the start of the convention, he wouldn't win at all. "The front runner cannot lose strength or he's dead."

Reagan nonetheless retained the formal pretense of noncandidacy. "I have not solicited and will not solicit," he said. Yet he traveled to the South in search of delegates. In Birmingham he met with some hundred delegates and alternates and tried to reassure them that defection from Nixon would not hand the nomination to Rockefeller. One delegate asked

Reagan if he would endorse Nixon if the race came down to a Nixon-Rockefeller contest. Reagan answered obliquely: "It is inconceivable to me that anyone who could support Dick or me could support Nelson Rockefeller." In Texas he was asked if he would run harder and more openly, should he receive the nomination, than he was running now. "I won't be a reluctant candidate," he said. "I'll run like hell." He met Strom Thurmond in South Carolina; the formerly Democratic and currently Republican senator took him aside and offered unwelcome encouragement. "Young man, you'll be president some day," Thurmond said. "But not this year."

Rockefeller's advisers took heart from Reagan's more open campaigning. They agreed that Nixon's southern support was soft, and they expected that Reagan would steal some Nixon delegates before the convention began. Nixon would fall short of victory on the first ballot, and his weakness would feed on itself in the second ballot. "At that point the convention will be wide open," a Rockefeller man predicted.

Reagan and Rockefeller both traveled to Miami to sap Nixon's strength. The Rockefeller group continued to lowball Nixon's committed delegate count, while Reagan's people, recalling his speech-making magic of 1964, tried to finagle an appearance in front of the convention as a whole.

But Nixon demonstrated the benefits of long experience in politics. He let southerners know he wouldn't select a liberal running mate, and he persuaded minor favorite sons not to throw their delegates to Rockefeller or Reagan. Most crucially, he kept Reagan off the stage.

Nixon's delegates held firm; the defections hoped for by the Reagan and Rockefeller camps failed to occur. Nixon won a majority on the first ballot.

Only at this point did he let Reagan in front of the cameras. He permitted Reagan to address the convention and recommend that the decision be made unanimous.

Reagan did what was expected of him. The party had chosen, he said, and now must unite behind its nominee. "This nation cannot survive four more years of the kind of policies that have been guiding us." The delegates bellowed their approval, although how many were approving the message and how many the speaker was impossible to say.

F OR A PERSON who remembered college with lyrical fondness, Reagan got great political mileage out of bashing the University of California. Probably, as in certain other areas of politics, he was compensating for the youthful liberalism he had abandoned with maturity. Likely the very fondness with which he remembered Eureka College made it impossible for any other institution to measure up. Possibly he resented the intellectual elitism of the University of California, which by the 1960s was sufficiently selective that a mediocre student like himself would have had difficulty gaining admission. The further irony that his first taste of politics had come in a student revolt against the administration of Eureka seems to have been lost on him entirely.

Reagan took special pleasure in attacking the California flagship campus in Berkeley. "The overwhelming majority of the young people at that university are seriously intent on getting an education," he had said while a candidate for governor. "But a vacillating administration has permitted a fractional minority of beatniks, filthy-speech advocates and malcontents to interfere with the purpose. This minority has brought shame on the university." The state needed a new governor if only to clean up the mess at Berkeley and restore honor to higher education.

The cleanup started sooner than he expected. Clark Kerr had been chancellor at Berkeley and was president of the several-campus University of California system; he naturally concluded that Reagan's criticisms were directed at him. Upon Reagan's inauguration as governor he asked the board of regents for a vote of confidence. Several members of the board, which now included Reagan ex officio, had their own doubts about Kerr's handling of the Berkeley turbulence, and they didn't like being put on the spot. To the surprise of both Kerr and Reagan, the latter's first meeting with the regents resulted in the dismissal of the former.

Few beyond the board believed Reagan's disclaimers of intent, which were accurate as to timing if not to eventual outcome. Liberals in California and around the country wrung their hands that the crown jewel of public higher education in America was being threatened by Reagan and the know-nothings. They lamented the more when Reagan's first budget projected sharp cuts to the university, and California liberals in particular assailed his proposal to begin charging tuition at the university. The no-tuition policy possessed greater significance as symbol than as substance; student fees of hundreds of dollars served much the purpose of tuition in other states. But the symbol mattered to those many Californians who boasted that the finest higher education in the country was available to even students of the most modest means. Reagan countered that honesty was the best policy in government as in life; if a fee was the equivalent of tuition, it ought to be called tuition. And in the current state of financial distress, it ought to go up.

Reagan's proposal ignited new protests, this time aimed directly at him. Ten thousand students and faculty descended on Sacramento. "Don't Loot the Colleges to Balance Your Budget," their signs read. "Impeach Ronnie Reagan." "Lousy, Just Like His Movies." Reagan's schedule had called for him to be in Oregon on this day, but he postponed his trip to meet the protesters. "I wouldn't miss this for anything," he told William Clark. He let the demonstration form outside his office, then he headed out to meet the protesters. Clark accompanied him. "We walked through the double doors to the steps where this man was carrying on, I think he was a student leader," Clark recalled. "He couldn't see us approach—his back was to us as we went out the doors—but this vast crowd suddenly spotted the governor and their shocked faces told the speaker that something was going on behind him. He turned around and saw the governor and in shock just handed him the mike as a matter of courtesy."

"A funny thing happened to me on the way to Oregon," Reagan said to the students, who didn't think it funny at all. They had read his schedule and were counting on his absence. "Hey, hey, what do you say? Ronald Reagan ran away!" they were chanting before he showed up. They booed and tried to shout him down when he explained his change of plans. "I don't think any group of citizens should come to the capitol with the expressed purpose of delivering any message to the governor and have the governor be absent," he said. When the booing persisted, he remarked, "I believe nothing I can say would create an open mind in some of you." He asserted his desire to keep politics out of education, but he added, "The people of California, who have contributed willingly and happily to educational growth, do have some right to have a voice in the philosophy and principles that will go along with the education they provide. As governor, I will never inject politics into the board of regents, but as governor I am going to represent the people of this state."

THE COMPROMISE BUDGET Reagan and Jesse Unruh worked out spared the universities the worst of the cuts and postponed a decision on tuition. But higher education remained a polarizing issue. African American students at San Francisco State College had established the Black Student Union, which in 1968 led a strike against the college administration, against Reagan and the state government, against the Vietnam War, and against the exploitation of the masses by the capitalist system. The strike and surrounding violence produced damage to property, arrests of perpetrators and passersby, the resignation of the college's president, and his replacement by S. I. Hayakawa, a faculty semanticist who wore a tam-o'-shanter to work and promised to bring the militants into line. "You are a hero to some," he said of himself, "and a son of a bitch to others."

The strike in San Francisco challenged radicals across the bay at Berkeley to match it. In February 1969 a group calling itself the Third World Liberation Front attempted to close the Berkeley campus; students walking to their classes were threatened and in some cases assaulted.

Reagan responded vigorously. He declared a state of "extreme emergency" in Berkeley and dispatched state troopers to assist the local police. "We are winning the ball game at San Francisco," he said, a bit prematurely; "they had to try someplace else." Asked how long the troopers would remain on campus and in the neighborhood, he replied, "As long as may be necessary." He elaborated: "The lives and safety of students and faculty, and the property of the university, must be protected. The campus must be free of violence, threats and intimidation."

The property of the university became the flash point several weeks later. The Berkeley administration had acquired a piece of property south of campus for future expansion, but in the spring of 1969 it lay fallow. An alliance of hippies—the countercultural dropouts who preached love, peace, and drugs—and political radicals determined to put the site to use. The hippies wanted to plant flowers and vegetables, the radicals to sow seeds of confrontation. Together they christened the block "People's Park" and proclaimed it a brave experiment in a new form of property relations.

Reagan didn't care much about the hippies, but he was as eager to accept the radicals' challenge as they were to pose it. His diffident campaign for president had cost him credibility as a decisive leader, and like the radicals he was looking for a chance to show he mattered. Over the heads of the university administrators, who didn't want a confrontation they could avoid, he ordered the property cleared of unauthorized persons and a fence erected to keep additional intruders out.

Both Reagan and the radicals got what they wanted and then some. Before dawn on May 15 some 250 California state police arrived and ordered all those sleeping or loitering in the park to leave. All did, except for a few who were too drugged to know what was happening and had to be hauled away. The police sealed off several blocks around the park to prevent other people from getting close. A bulldozer arrived a short while later and began scraping the perimeter of the property for the fence. By noon the fence was completed and the site secured.

But only briefly, for at the same time a large crowd was gathering in Sproul Plaza, the epicenter of campus protests. Student leaders denounced the seizure of People's Park as in keeping with the fascist policies that had produced the imperialist war in Vietnam and were crushing individual rights in America. One speaker concluded with a call to reclaim the park. The crowd began chanting, "Take the park! Take the park!" They marched down Telegraph Avenue toward the park.

Blocks before they got there, they encountered the police cordon. Some protesters threw rocks, others pieces of concrete and metal. One person with obvious protest experience employed an oversized wrench to open a fire hydrant that flooded the street with water. The police responded with tear gas and then shotgun fire. Whether most of the guns were loaded with bird shot—light pellets that caused pain but not much damage unless they hit their targets in the eyes and face—or heavier and more lethal buckshot was a matter of subsequent dispute. In fact one crowd member was blinded and another killed. Dozens were wounded. As word of the fighting reached Sacramento, Reagan ordered troops of the state's national guard to the scene. By the time they arrived, the fighting had ended, but the troops remained and clamped a curfew on the neighborhood.

———————

REAGAN DEFENDED HIS own actions and those of the local authorities. Recounting at a press conference the series of events leading up to the riot, he said, "After the property was cleared, mob violence erupted and additional police were called to the scene. On that day, police took a tremendous and unprovoked beating from a well prepared and well armed mass of people who had stockpiled all kinds of weapons and missiles. They included pieces of steel rods as well as bricks, large rocks, chunks of cement, iron pipes, etc. Dissidents stood on fire escapes and roof tops and showered officers with steel bars, rocks and chunks of cement. One officer was stabbed in the chest with a thrown dagger." Police responded appropriately with tear gas and bird shot, Reagan said. "This was done only to protect life and property and in response to felonious assaults with deadly weapons." He regretted the injuries sustained by the demonstrators and especially the death of the one young man, a twenty-five-year-old named James Rector. Yet the blame lay not with the authorities but with the "street gangs" and "campus radicals" who had organized "this entire attempt at revolution." The people of California needed to understand that demonstrations like this weren't innocent pranks. "How much farther do we have to go to realize this is not just another panty raid?"

Reagan's words did nothing to calm the situation. More protests broke out in Berkeley, prompting the police, with Reagan's approval, to deploy a helicopter that sprayed tear gas on the heads of the protesters. An angry delegation of Berkeley faculty traveled to Sacramento and demanded to see the governor; when Reagan invited them into his office, they denounced him for the military occupation of their city and insisted on its lifting.

Reagan stood fast. He defended his actions to the professors and to anyone else who would listen. A live audience of a thousand heard him address the Commonwealth Club of San Francisco; many more watched the speech on television. "In the past eleven months four major riots have erupted in Berkeley," he explained. "All of them involve militants from the south campus area"—Telegraph Avenue and People's Park. "In these eleven months there have been eight major bombings or attempted bombings, nearly 1100 drug arrests, 750 in the south campus area alone." The police and national guardsmen, he said, had confiscated numerous explosives and hundreds of firearms. They hadn't always acted soon enough. "There have been dozens of arson attempts resulting in more than $800,000 damage . . . One policeman has been ambushed and shot and a dozen others fired upon." The big riot on May 15 was part of the broader pattern. "This was no spontaneous eruption. The rooftops had been stockpiled with rocks and other missiles." Only after the riot got out of control of the police on hand did the Alameda County sheriff send in deputies with shotguns. "When they arrived, they literally had to step over the bodies of injured officers who couldn't be helped or moved because the few left standing were under severe assault and literally fighting for their lives."

Reagan distinguished between the motives of the leaders of the protest and those of the followers. "The leaders of this property takeover have made it plain their only purpose was political," he said. "They were challenging the right of private ownership of land in this country." The followers were mostly well-meaning students alienated by the culture and practices of a large university. They wanted to learn from the great minds of the age but found themselves in oversized courses conducted by teaching assistants. "The feeling comes that they are nameless, faceless numbers on an assembly line—green cap at one end and cap, gown and automated diploma at the other. They want someone to know they are there—they aren't even missed and recorded as absent when they aren't there. The majority of faculty are scholars too busy with their own research and writing." Reagan sympathized with the students against both the radicals and the faculty. "This generation of students—better informed, more aware—deserves much more." If they didn't get it, the entire state would suffer. "The challenge to us is to establish contact with these frustrated young people and to join in finding answers before they fall to the mob by default. At this moment in California, the danger of this happening is very real."

Reagan typically enjoyed taking on protesters: trading verbal blows with hecklers, giving as good as he got. But one experience disturbed him. He told reporters of visiting a campus for a regents meeting. "I remember one very nice looking little girl, who stood in the crowd of students as I walked to my car and who kept shouting, 'Fuck you. Fuck you.' She practically spit at me. I walked over to her and asked her if she didn't think that when she was a few years older she would be ashamed of what she was doing. She just looked at me and spit another 'Fuck you.'"

22

SUMMER AND THE departure of most students eased the troubles at Berkeley, but renewed protests provided the backdrop to Reagan's reelection campaign in 1970. The hot spot this time was the University of California at Santa Barbara, a campus better known for parties than for protests. Militants rejected the surfer image and battled police over university policies; they then carried their fight to the neighborhood of Isla Vista, where they besieged a branch of the Bank of America, the most convenient symbol of the military-corporate complex.

Reagan again reacted quickly. He flew to Santa Barbara to confront the protesters. Branding them "cowardly little bums," he declared another state of emergency and called in the national guard.

His action contained the violence without alleviating its underlying cause. Reagan thought he knew what that cause was: the desire of a small group of revolutionaries to radicalize the rest of the campus community by provoking the police and state authorities to violence. Some on campus agreed and said his use of force was playing into the militants' hands. But Reagan refused to be deterred. "Appeasement is not the answer," he declared. The radicals didn't want solutions; they wanted disruption. If they weren't careful, they would get what they wanted and more. "If it's to be a bloodbath, let it be now."

Reagan at once regretted the "bloodbath" remark. Later that day he qualified his comment. "There comes a time when we must bite the bullet, so to speak, or take action when we know it is necessary to do so," he said. "I certainly don't think there should be a bloodbath on campus or anywhere else."

"Biting the bullet" wasn't a big improvement, and the comment came back to haunt him. Violence erupted again in Isla Vista, and in the violence a student, Kevin Moran, was killed, apparently by a policeman who was aiming elsewhere.

The killing shook Reagan badly. He fought back tears as he addressed reporters. "It isn't very important where the bullet came from," he said. "The bullet was sent on its way several years ago when a certain element in our society decided they could take the law into their own hands. And every person that has aided and abetted them is equally guilty." He renewed his call for an end to the violence, appealing to the memory of Kevin Moran. "If his death is not to be totally in vain, I hope this will bring some sober reflection and some common sense to the so-called silent majority of students, faculty and administrators to where they themselves will take a stand and say, 'This is the end. No more attending rallies, no more even supporting with an expression of sympathy those who have resorted to this kind of violence.'"

THE TROUBLES IN Santa Barbara didn't end right away, but they were overshadowed by much larger protests elsewhere that spring. Campuses around the country erupted when Richard Nixon ordered the invasion of Cambodia. The president's strategic purpose was to deny the North Vietnamese sanctuary in Vietnam's neutral neighbor; his political achievement was to mobilize broader domestic protests than ever. At Kent State University in Ohio, troops of the national guard fired on demonstrators, killing four students and wounding several others. At Jackson State in Mississippi, police shot and killed two students and wounded a dozen.

The campus violence in California might have complicated Reagan's reelection had the Democrats run a more compelling candidate. Jesse Unruh tried to make the leap from the assembly to the governorship, but he had difficulty escaping his unsavory reputation as the "Big Daddy" of the legislature. His campaign stumbled and failed to raise the money he needed to challenge the incumbent effectively.

Reagan ran on his record as a budget balancer and a defender of law and order against radical challenge. The latter role lost some of its luster after the killings at Berkeley and Isla Vista; more than a few voters asked if the authorities hadn't gone too far. But others shared Reagan's view that blame for the deaths lay with the radicals, not the authorities.

He also ran as a pragmatist who got things done. The University of California regents, after clawing back some of the revenues Reagan had proposed to cut, accepted his demand that students start paying tuition. When a new budget stalled in the legislature, Reagan was the one who compromised, dropping his opposition to the withholding of state income taxes. Acknowledging that he had previously said his feet were set in concrete on the withholding issue, he joked, "That sound you hear is the concrete cracking around my feet."

Voters liked Reagan's principles; they also liked his pragmatism. But they weren't nearly as enthusiastic as they had been four years earlier. His 53 percent of the vote fell substantially shy of the 58 percent he had polled then, and his margin of victory over Unruh was half his margin over Pat Brown. Yet a win was a win, and Reagan was happy to accept it.

23

REAGAN'S SLIPPAGE AT the polls took some of the shine off his national appeal. The Republican Party wouldn't be looking for presidential candidates until 1976, given Nixon's certainty of renomination in 1972. And when the party did start looking, there was no guarantee it would be seeking conservatives. Nixon confused constituents and pundits by talking like a conservative but acting like a liberal. The law-and-order theme of his 1968 campaign appealed to conservatives and others distraught by the wave of big-city riots and the permissiveness of the counterculture, and the showpiece of his domestic policy, an approach he called the New Federalism, appeared to reverse the centralizing tendencies of Lyndon Johnson's Great Society. But appearances deceived in this case, as in much Nixon did, for the essence of the New Federalism was the money Washington bestowed on the states for them to spend. What Washington gave, Washington could take away.

In certain areas Nixon didn't even pretend to be conservative. He pushed environmental reforms harder than any president since Theodore Roosevelt. The Clean Air Act of 1970 dramatically expanded the power of the federal government to regulate emissions from vehicles and industrial plants. The Environmental Protection Agency, created the same year, enforced the air act and comparable legislation covering water, land, and other resources, besides issuing binders full of regulations on its own authority. The Occupational Safety and Health Administration, established in 1971, stuck the federal government's nose into the affairs of nearly every employer in the country. Nixon's was the first administration to push affirmative action as a federal policy on race. His Labor Department applied a plan devised to remedy racial discrimination in Philadelphia to cities across the country. Contractors doing work for the federal government were required to hire minimum numbers of black workers. Nixon boosted funding of the Equal Employment Opportunity Commission, and he furnished federal money to school districts striving to ensure compliance with court orders to desegregate.

Nixon's most audacious initiative was also his most liberal. Or perhaps it was his most conservative. It certainly was his most confusing, receiving endorsements from both liberals and conservatives, as well as condemnations from both groups. The Family Assistance Plan was designed to make federal aid to the poor more efficient and less costly. This aspect appealed to conservatives, including economist Milton Friedman, who helped design it. But it would do so by means of a "negative income tax"—a federal payment to families with incomes below a poverty threshold—without the onerous and often embarrassing investigations long required for welfare payments. This part appealed to liberals, as did the fact that the efficiencies of the new program would allow its coverage to be expanded to millions of people, especially children, previously uncovered.

REAGAN WOULD HAVE saved himself a great deal of trouble had he followed Nixon's lead and endorsed the Family Assistance Plan. Reagan made welfare reform a focus of his second term as governor, chiefly because California's ballooning welfare rolls threatened to undo the progress he had made toward balancing the state's budget. Reagan had railed against welfare cheats who lounged on the largesse of honest taxpayers and, he took pains to point out, deprived the truly needy of the help he thought they should receive. He launched his second administration with a promise to reform the welfare system. "Mandated by statute and federal regulation," he said, "welfare has proliferated and grown into a Leviathan of unsupportable dimensions. We have economized and even stripped essential public services to feed its appetite." Liberals wanted to raise taxes to cover the shortfall. This path had no end, Reagan said. "Unless and until we face up to and effect complete reform of welfare, we will face a tax increase next year, the year after that, and the year after that—on into the future as far as we can see."

The national economy had tipped into a mild recession after the Federal Reserve raised interest rates to curb inflation; Reagan acknowledged the recession's deleterious effect on California's state budget. But he rejected the pessimism many Americans felt as a result of the downturn and the disturbing events of the previous several years. "Those who whine of a sick society aren't talking about *us*," he declared for California. "Our young people seek a cause in which they can invest their idealism, their youth and their strength . . . As Mark Twain once said, 'The easy and slothful didn't come to California. They stayed home.'" With the optimism that was becoming his trademark in politics, Reagan perorated, "It is time to ignore those who are obsessed with what is wrong. Concentrate our attention on what is right—on how great is our power and potential and how little we have to fear. As I told a group of your fellow citizens who visited this capitol last fall, if California's problems and California's people were put in a ring together, it would have to be declared a mismatch."

Reagan sent the legislature a detailed proposal for revamping the welfare system. The twin goals of the plan were to boot unworthy recipients off the welfare rolls and to increase payments to people who really couldn't fend for themselves. Critics accused him of being hard-hearted and of overreacting to the recession; the Democratic leadership in the legislature preferred handing the welfare problem to the federal government, under the terms of Nixon's Family Assistance Plan.

Nixon's offer was tempting, but Reagan refused. A guaranteed income epitomized all that was wrong about the liberal approach to governing, he said. "I believe that the government is supposed to promote the general welfare," he quipped. "I don't believe it is supposed to *provide* it."

Reagan's opposition didn't endear him to Nixon, but it did get the president's attention. "Nixon sent several people out to sit down with Reagan to shut him up on welfare reform," Michael Deaver recalled. They failed, so Nixon took matters into his own hands. The president kept a house in California, at San Clemente, where he sometimes vacationed. On one trip west he invited Reagan to drop by. Nixon apparently offered Reagan a deal: the governor would moderate his criticism of the Family Assistance Plan, and the president would relax federal welfare regulations sufficiently to allow California to experiment with work requirements for capable recipients of welfare checks.

Reagan evidently accepted the deal, for his criticism diminished and the experiment went forward. Meanwhile, he wrestled with the legislature, in the person of Bob Moretti, the Democratic speaker of the assembly, over broader welfare reform. Moretti one day asked to see the governor. "I remember he was sitting at his desk and there was a chair right off to the right where I sat," Moretti later remarked of the visit. "And he said, 'Yeah, what do you want to talk to me about?' And I said, 'Look, governor, I don't like you particularly and I know you don't like me, but we don't have to be in love to work together. If you're serious about doing some things, then let's sit down and start doing it.'"

And so they did. Both men took their task seriously; each understood he needed the other. Moretti could deliver the Democrats who controlled the legislature; Reagan could bring the Republicans and possessed a veto. Each was principled, but neither was ideological. For a week they met daily; for another week Reagan's aides met with Moretti's lieutenants and his allies in the legislature.

The result was a measure that reflected democratic politics at its best, which was to say welfare reform that made neither side ecstatic but that substantially improved on the status quo. Eligibility requirements were stiffened, reducing the number of recipients by hundreds of thousands. Payments to those remaining on the rolls were increased, to reflect more accurately the cost of California living. Taxpayers saved billions.

A SECOND MEASURE of his second term made Reagan almost equally proud. Real estate values had been rising in California for years, pushing up property taxes, which became a heavy burden on pensioners and other owners whose incomes didn't rise commensurately. Reagan wanted to provide relief. Meanwhile, he and the rest of the state's elected officials found themselves under court order to make more equitable the state's education spending, most of which came from property taxes. The desire for property tax relief and the need for equalization seemed at first to work at cross-purposes, but after some false starts Reagan and Moretti managed to produce another compromise. The measure reduced property taxes while boosting state support for schools, especially those in poorer districts.

NIXON'S WELFARE PLAN fared less well than Reagan's, struggling in Congress for two years before the president set it aside ahead of the 1972 election. Nixon, anyway, had other priorities, starting with the most audacious restructuring of international affairs since the beginning of the Cold War. Even casual observers of communist-bloc politics noted during the 1960s that the bloc wasn't what it once had been. The Chinese increasingly condemned what they called the Kremlin's "revisionism": its unwillingness to push world revolution in all places at any cost. By the decade's end the acrimony had grown so virulent that Chinese and Soviet troops exchanged fire across the border their countries shared in northeast Asia. American and allied leaders didn't have to be unduly Machiavellian to wonder if the Eastern troubles might be turned to Western benefit.

In fact Richard Nixon *was* Machiavellian, and turning those troubles to America's benefit was precisely what he had in mind. Nixon understood that the enemy of an enemy can be, if not necessarily a friend, at least a useful associate. He proposed playing the Chinese against the Russians, and the Russians against the Chinese, to America's advantage. He hoped the two communist powers could be persuaded to reduce their support for the communists of Vietnam, thereby easing an end to the war there. More broadly, he looked to augment America's usable leverage in world affairs.

But it was tricky business. Americans like to believe that their country's policies are rooted in principle. For a quarter century they had been told, and had been telling themselves, that America's enemy in the Cold War was communism—godless, authoritarian communism. Neither Russia nor China had abandoned communism; neither had embraced God or democracy. But Nixon wanted to work with them nonetheless.

He moved stealthily. He sent Henry Kissinger, his national security adviser, to Pakistan on a seemingly innocuous diplomatic mission. While in Karachi, Kissinger complained of stomach troubles of the sort travelers are prone to. He encouraged the reporters traveling with him to take a few days off while he recovered; they wouldn't be missing anything. And then he slipped across the Himalayas in a Pakistani plane and surfaced in Beijing, where he met with Mao Zedong and Zhou Enlai, respectively the reddest of the "Red Chinese" and the ablest of China's diplomats. He delivered American greetings and wishes for constructive relations. They responded in kind.

Nixon and Kissinger reveled in their coup. Nixon called the opening to China "the most significant foreign policy achievement in this century." Kissinger arranged a visit to China by Nixon himself. "We have laid the groundwork for you and Mao to turn a page in history," Kissinger told the president after returning to Washington. "The process we have now started will send enormous shock waves around the world."

The shock waves rolled most powerfully to Moscow, as Nixon intended. The Kremlin would have to be cooperative lest America get too chummy with China, Nixon reckoned. And this was just how things developed.

The president traveled to Beijing in February 1972 and professed Americans' friendship for the Chinese people. He urged rapid progress toward goals the two nations shared. "Seize the day, seize the hour," he quoted from the canon of Mao's wisdom. In his own words he declared, "This is the day, this is the hour for our two peoples to rise to the heights of greatness which can build a new and better world."

The Kremlin was listening, as became evident three months later when Nixon arrived in Moscow. Soviet general secretary Leonid Brezhnev couldn't let Mao and Zhou get all the love from the Americans; Brezhnev consented to the first major arms-control accord of the Cold War, the Strategic Arms Limitation Treaty, or SALT. As part of the deal, the two sides agreed to forgo a weapons race in anti-ballistic missile defenses; the ABM Treaty placed strict limits on missile defense. Brezhnev also put his signature to what amounted to an armistice in the Cold War. The dozen basic principles of détente, as the armistice was called, began with an affirmation that in the nuclear age there was no alternative to peaceful coexistence. Despite their different belief systems, the United States and the Soviet Union would pursue normal relations based on "sovereignty, equality, non-interference in internal affairs and mutual advantage." The subsequent principles wordily reinforced this live-and-let-live approach.

EVERY REVOLUTION HAS to cope with the forces of reaction, and the revolution in global affairs Nixon attempted with détente was no exception. But before reaction could mobilize, Nixon cruised through the election of 1972. The Democrats had difficulty attracting strong candidates into the primaries, so formidable did Nixon seem on account of his shrewd maneuvering between liberals and conservatives and his clever conduct of American diplomacy. Yet even taking that into account, the Democrats outdid themselves in nominating the weakest candidate in their party's modern history. Nobody thought George McGovern was anything less than an honorable man, but South Dakota has never grown much presidential timber, and McGovern's positions on crucial issues placed him considerably to the left of the middle ground that always decides presidential races. The Republicans scorned him as the "triple-A candidate," the spokesman for "acid, amnesty, and abortion," referring to the hippies he was said to attract, the pardons he advocated for some Vietnam War resisters, and the support he promised to advocates of abortion rights. McGovern had scarcely been nominated before he appeared certain to become for the Democrats in 1972 what Barry Goldwater had been for the Republicans in 1964: a principled disaster.

Yet Nixon wanted more than a victory; he wanted a landslide. Hubris had set in, and he countenanced a campaign of dirty tricks against the Democrats. He later claimed that he feared for national security after the leaking and publication of the Pentagon Papers, a classified history of the Vietnam War. But the political espionage set in motion by the Nixon White House went far beyond trying to plug leaks, and when five administration operatives were arrested at the Watergate office complex in Washington in June 1972, their target was the headquarters of the Democratic National Committee. Nixon denied advance knowledge of the affair, and his denial held long enough for him to win an enormous victory over McGovern. He garnered 61 percent of the popular vote and carried forty-nine states.

The landslide seemed an irrefutable endorsement of moderation in politics. In 1964, American voters had rejected Goldwater's rigid conservatism; in 1972 they refuted McGovern's bleeding-heart liberalism. Nixon appeared to have found the magic middle ground. Americans looked to government to ensure that they didn't suffer old-age poverty and untreated illness, they counted on government to clean the air and water and safeguard the workplace, and they insisted that government protect minorities against public discrimination. Yet they didn't want government to do everything for them, preferring to do for themselves what they reasonably could. Government wasn't their enemy, but neither was it their best friend. Most of all, Americans rejected passionate appeals from either left or right for any drastic altering of the status quo. And judging by their embrace of the uncharming Nixon, they put little store in charisma.

And then, almost before he was reinaugurated, Nixon's presidency began to unravel. A federal judge in the District of Columbia refused to accept the Watergate burglars' guilty plea, and they started to talk. The trail of evidence led back to the White House and, under congressional investigation, into the Oval Office itself. The charisma-less moderation that had been Nixon's trademark became his undoing, for no zealous admirers rallied to his defense. One by one Republicans abandoned the president, until he stood almost alone against the Supreme Court, which heard his plea to retain crucial recordings of White House conversations. When the high court ruled against him, the House of Representatives moved toward impeachment. In August 1974, Nixon resigned the presidency, handing the White House to Gerald Ford.

24

O N THAT DAY Reagan gained hope for life after the governorship. As pragmatic as he proved to be as California's chief executive, he would never have been mistaken for a Nixonian moderate. The California constitution didn't bar a run for a third term, but he didn't want to be seen as a professional politician, let alone a permanent occupant of the governor's office. If there was a public role for Reagan after Sacramento, it was in Washington or nowhere. Until Nixon imploded, nowhere seemed the likelier option.

Reagan would turn sixty-four a month after leaving the governor's mansion. He would be old enough to retire from full-time work, and with the money he could earn from speeches and service on corporate boards, he and Nancy would be able to live in all the comfort they could wish. But he still wanted a stage. And the only one that appealed to him at this point in his career was the presidency.

He understood at once what Nixon's resignation meant. The road from Sacramento to Washington was suddenly wide open. Nixon was no longer around to anoint a moderate successor. Gerald Ford would be the favorite for the Republican nomination, but Ford wounded himself badly by preemptively pardoning Nixon weeks after taking office. Democrats and not a few Republicans muttered about a backroom bargain: the presidency for the pardon. Those who knew Ford didn't believe the charge. But that didn't lessen the damage it did him.

IN JANUARY 1975, Reagan handed the California governorship to Pat Brown's son. The succession suggested that Reagan's mark on the state might be fleeting, for Jerry Brown was cut from considerably more liberal cloth than Reagan. Or perhaps Brown's election simply reminded those paying close attention that Reagan's style of governing had always been more pragmatic than his style of speaking.

Once again Reagan had to figure out how to fill his time. Of course he would run for president in 1976, but he mustn't appear overeager. He needed to seem gainfully occupied. Ranch life beckoned, and he answered the call. He had sold his Malibu ranch about the time he was elected governor; as he prepared to leave office, he and Nancy purchased another ranch, in the Santa Ynez Mountains above Santa Barbara. They called it Rancho del Cielo—Ranch in the Sky, or Heavenly Ranch—and Reagan devoted hours and days to renovating the house and improving the nearly seven hundred acres.

His service as governor had eaten dramatically into his income, but eight years as chief executive of the nation's most populous state simply made him more appealing on the lecture circuit. Vacating the governor's office also allowed him to resume his broadcast career. He received offers to become a television commentator but opted instead for radio. Michael Deaver was stunned. "Walter Cronkite had called me, which impressed me, and said that he would like to have Reagan do a twice-weekly five-minute commentary on the CBS Evening News," Deaver recalled. "Well, I thought this was incredible. The CBS Evening News, at that point, was 30 or 40 million people a day. Then, this old guy from Hollywood named Harry O'Connor, who was a radio producer who didn't have any active clients at the moment, had come in and seen Reagan and told him he could get him on the radio, a five-minute radio show a day. So, the hour of decision came, and I thought this was going to be a slam-dunk. And Reagan said, 'I'm going to do the radio show.' I said, 'What? You're not going to do the CBS?' 'No, I'm not going to do the CBS Evening News.' I said, 'I don't believe this. I can't believe this.' He said, 'Mike, people will tire of me on television . . . They won't tire of me on the radio.'"

Deaver later acknowledged that Reagan had been right. "At the end of that, when we finally had to give it up"—in 1980—"we were speaking to about 50 million people a day on the radio. In the key cities, New York, L.A., we were speaking to them twice a day, both commute times, morning and evening." Deaver recalled being asked a question by Walter Mondale, by then the former vice president (and the Democratic nominee in 1984): "Do you really think that radio show had any impact on Reagan getting the nomination?" Deaver replied, "I think it had everything to do with it." Mondale said, "Well, I'm thinking about doing that myself, a radio show." Deaver said, "Well, good. Mr. Vice President, let me just tell you one thing. Ronald Reagan wrote every radio show himself." Mondale said, "You're putting me on." Deaver said, "No. He wouldn't let anybody write them. He'd let Pete"—Hannaford, a staffer—"write his newspaper column, but he always said, I think I can write the spoken word better."

When Reagan predicted that people would tire of him on television, he might have been indulging the vanity of the aging actor worried about his appearance. His hair remained black—naturally so, he told anyone who inquired, and his barber never contradicted him. But his face and neck showed the inevitable lines and creases. He understood that his age would be an issue in a run for the presidency, and he had no desire to imprint an old face on the public mind.

He could indeed be vain about the way he looked. As a person in the public eye, he couldn't avoid cameras, but he kept still photographs to a minimum. Michael Deaver noticed that he always grew tense when a still photographer approached him. "Finally, one day I said to him, 'I don't get it,'" Deaver recalled. "'How come when I bring a still camera in here, I can see the back of your neck stiffen?' He smiled at me and said, 'You're the first person who ever said that to me.' He said, 'Mike, I can never recover from a still photographer.'" Television pictures were fleeting; an unflattering image was gone in an instant. But not so with a still shot. "I can't recover from a still," Reagan said.

Vanity wasn't the only issue, though. Reagan understood that radio was a more intimate medium than television. It was far more suited to the personal stories and anecdotes that had long been his greatest strength in touching the heartstrings of his audiences. On television, if he told an uplifting story about a soldier home from Vietnam or a cautionary tale about a welfare queen on Chicago's South Side, the medium would almost require him to show pictures. And the pictures would diminish the impact of his words. On radio the words were everything, spoken in his wonderful voice, which, if anything, grew more seductive with the throatiness of age. Reagan remembered the effect of Franklin Roosevelt's Fireside Chats; he recalled the mental images Roosevelt had conjured with spoken words and the feelings he elicited. Roosevelt hadn't had an alternative to radio in that pretelevision age; Reagan did have one but declined to use it. He judged that he couldn't do better than his political hero in trying to reach and touch his fellow Americans.

HE HAD NO policy agenda beyond basic conservative principles. He expected events to furnish direction. They obliged from the start. Three months after he left Sacramento, the final chapter of America's Vietnam War came to a disillusioning end. The army of North Vietnam, flouting a 1973 agreement under which the United States had withdrawn its troops, overran South Vietnam and captured Saigon. Two decades of American effort to prevent the conquest had failed.

Reagan blamed a failure of leadership in Washington. "When we withdrew our forces from the long bloodletting in Vietnam," he told his radio audience, "we did so with the understanding that we would provide weapons and ammunition to enable South Vietnam and Cambodia to resist if the North Vietnamese violated the negotiated ceasefire." Reagan wasn't surprised that the cease-fire had failed. "Violating agreements is standard operating procedure for communists. They violated this one 72,000 times in the first twelve months." But Washington, or rather the Democrats who controlled the legislative branch, had let them get away with it. "We do nothing because the Congress has taken from the commander-in-chief the authority to take any action at all to enforce the terms of the treaty. Now that same Congress, with unprecedented irresponsibility, has refused to authorize the money that would permit this great nation to keep its pledged word."

Reagan recalled for his listeners the domino theory of the 1950s, which asserted that the fall of any country to communism would risk the fate of an entire region. And he reminded them how the domino theory had followed from the failure of appeasement before World War II. "Those who ridicule the domino theory believed it when Hitler was picking off small nations in Europe thirty-seven years ago," he said. "They just don't believe it applies when the enemy is communist and the countries losing their freedom are Asian." But it *did* apply, he said, as much as ever. "The term domino theory very simply describes what happens to our allies if we back down and let one ally be taken over by the communists because we don't want to be bothered. The enemy decides it's safe to go after others—that we represent no threat to his aggression. But even worse, our allies, no longer able to trust us, start making deals."

The deal making had already begun in Asia, Reagan said. Thailand was turning its back on the United States and negotiating with China. The Philippines were seeking accommodation. Japan had commenced discussions with Hanoi. Nor was the damage confined to one region or continent. "The dominoes are worldwide." Turkey was drawing away from NATO. Greece snubbed visits by the American Sixth Fleet. Portugal was tilting dangerously left. "Secretary of State Henry Kissinger returns empty-handed from the Middle East. A few months ago the power and reliability of the United States had brought the Israeli-Arab conflict closer to peace than at any time in fifty years. Now there is talk of war by summer. The press described Kissinger's eyes as wet with tears of frustration. Our one-time power and reliability are no longer believable because of our failure to stand by an ally in far-off Indochina."

The failure in Indochina was symptomatic of a larger misreading of the world, Reagan thought. He remained a loyal enough Republican not to attack the policies of Republican administrations directly, but he began to question the philosophical underpinnings of détente. Nixon's opening to Moscow had permitted a grain sale that sent millions of tons of American wheat and corn to Russia at below-market prices. Critics called it the "Great Grain Robbery," but their ranks didn't include the midwestern farmers who were delighted at the boost the sale gave to prices for the rest of their crops. Gerald Ford extended the deal in 1975, following a new shortfall in the Soviet harvest.

The extension prompted Reagan to express doubts about détente. "The Russians want to buy American wheat and American farmers want to sell their wheat," he told his radio audience. The transaction sounded reasonable on its face. "If we believe in a free market, shouldn't our farmers be allowed to sell their produce anywhere in the world for the best price they can get?" But there were other considerations, starting with the nature of the country doing the buying. "If we believe the Soviet Union is hostile to the free world—and we must or we wouldn't be maintaining a nuclear defense and continuing in NATO—then are we not adding to our own danger by helping the troubled Soviet economy?" Beyond this was the moral issue. "Are we not helping a Godless tyranny maintain its hold on millions of helpless people? Wouldn't those helpless victims have a better chance of becoming free if their slave masters' regime collapsed economically? One thing is certain, the threat of hunger to the Russian people is due to the Soviet obsession with military power."

It was also due to the fundamental wrongheadedness of socialist economics. "Nothing proves the failure of Marxism more than the Soviet Union's inability to produce weapons for its military ambitions and at the same time provide for their people's everyday needs," Reagan said. America required but 2 percent of its workforce to feed the American people and much of the world besides. "A full one-third of Russia's workers are in agriculture and still they'd starve without our wheat. And the failure is not Russian; it is communist, for every other country that has collectivized its agriculture has gone downhill in farm production."

Whether because he was sincerely ambivalent or because he didn't want to come down too hard on a Republican administration, Reagan judged the grain question a close call. "The wheat deal is beneficial to us economically. Right now in our time of economic dislocation and imbalance of trade *maybe* it benefits us enough to outweigh the strategic factor. In other words it strengthens us more than we'd be benefitted by weakening them." But the morality of the sale still troubled him. "The moral question in the long run won't go away. The Soviet Union is an aggressor and a threat to world peace. It can remain so only by denying its people freedom and the basic commodities that make life worth living, which we take for granted." Morality in the long run aligned with strategy. "The Russians have told us over and over again their goal is to impose their incompetent and ridiculous system on the world. We invest in armaments to hold them off, but what do we envision as the eventual outcome? Either that they will see the fallacy of their way and give up their goal, or their system will collapse—or (and we don't let ourselves think of this) we'll have to use our weapons one day."

Reagan's dilemma prompted him to float a solution that hadn't occurred to many others in this context and that sounded odd coming from a conservative, because it entailed a major government intrusion into the private market. "Maybe there is an answer," he concluded. "We simply do what's morally right. Stop doing business with them. Let their system collapse. But in the meantime buy our farmers' wheat ourselves and have it on hand to feed the Russian people when they finally become free."

REAGAN'S VIEW OF détente was that of an outsider. He wasn't privy to the confidential discussions of foreign policy that took place within the Ford administration. In another area of policy, however, the curtain parted a little. Watergate inspired the media to dig deeper into the affairs of government, and what they found included evidence that the Central Intelligence Agency had exceeded the terms of its charter. Reports indicated that the CIA, which was supposed to confine its activities to foreign countries, had engaged in domestic operations, including the tapping of telephones, the opening of mail, and the infiltration of dissident political groups. Gerald Ford felt obliged to respond to the reports; he did so by appointing a commission to investigate them and other matters relating to the CIA. Vice President Nelson Rockefeller headed the commission, and various individuals of standing and distinction formed the membership. Reagan, newly released from the California governorship, took a seat on the Rockefeller Commission.

But he did so only intermittently. He informed Rockefeller at the outset that existing commitments would prevent his attending all the meetings, and he found little in the meetings to make him want to break those commitments. (He ultimately attended fewer than half of the twenty-six meetings.) The commission's makeup revealed the Ford administration's lack of interest in a searching analysis of CIA activities during the Cold War. The members included no outspoken critics of the CIA; most, like Reagan, sympathized with the difficulties confronting American intelligence officers in identifying and combating threats to American national security. The commission concentrated on domestic activities by the CIA, which, while forbidden by the CIA's charter, often fell within the realm of what Reagan and the others considered reasonable precautions.

Ford got what he wanted from the Rockefeller Commission. Its report, which Reagan signed, chided the CIA for "some activities that should be criticized and not be permitted to happen again," and it recommended closer oversight of the agency's operations. But it stopped far short of the kind of overhaul CIA critics were demanding.

The critics were happier with another committee, organized by congressional Democrats and headed by Senator Frank Church of Idaho. The Church Committee dug deep and uncovered much that Reagan, among other conservatives, thought should have stayed secret. The committee documented the CIA's role in the overthrow of the Iranian government in 1953 and the Guatemalan government in 1954, in the Bay of Pigs fiasco in 1961, and in the attempted assassination of various foreign leaders in the early 1960s.

Reagan was more upset with the Church Committee than with the CIA. "In any bureaucracy of about 16,000 people," he told his radio listeners, "there are going to be individuals who make mistakes and do things they shouldn't do." But the intelligence agency as a whole had honorably and effectively defended America against mortal threats. And it must be allowed to continue to do so. "We are being spied upon beyond anything that the American people can possibly conceive, not internally, not by our own people, but by potential enemies."

25

ONSERVATIVES IN MODERN America face a chronic problem in running for office. Often believing government to be the enemy, they have to explain to themselves and others why they want to join that enemy. Some seem to agonize; others exhibit only mild compunction. But eventually most arrive at the lesser-evil theory: that if they don't run and get elected, liberals will, to the further detriment of the national interest.

Gerald Ford wasn't a liberal, but Reagan decided he wasn't conservative enough to remain in the White House. That's what he told himself, at any rate. And had he been younger, that might have been the whole truth. But Reagan was already very old by American political practice. Only William Henry Harrison had been older at election than Reagan would be in November 1976, and Harrison died a month after inauguration. Reagan assumed he couldn't wait until Ford stepped aside; if he would achieve the presidency, it was 1976 or never.

So he ran. It was a desperate move rather than a smart one. The odds were against him, and the hazards were large. Presidents, even unelected presidents like Ford, have power. They command the attention of the national media without having to strain or pay for the coverage. They can make appointments that please allies and constituents. They can arrange appropriations that secure the loyalty of influential members of their party. As a result they typically control the machinery of the party, which writes rules for primaries and conventions. They can rely on the patriotic reflex of most Americans when the national interest is threatened and, if adept, can convert that reflex into political support.

For Reagan to defeat Ford would require him to overcome these incumbent advantages. For Reagan merely to *challenge* Ford risked split-ting the party. Rarely had a sitting president faced a challenge from within his party, and in nearly every case that party had lost the presidency. If Reagan challenged Ford, and if the Republicans lost, Reagan would be blamed.

But he went ahead nonetheless. He tacitly approved the formation of an exploratory committee in the summer of 1975. Paul Laxalt, a Repub-lican senator from Nevada who shared Reagan's brand of western conser-vatism as well as his relaxed personal style, headed the group. John Sears, who had helped elect Nixon in 1968 and now wanted to do the same for Reagan, provided ideas and energy. Reagan himself stood off. Until he formally announced his candidacy, he could keep his radio show, his newspaper column, and his paid speaking engagements. Once he became a formal candidate, those revenue streams would stop.

The exploratory committee discovered intense interest in a Reagan candidacy. Conservatives in the Republican Party had distrusted Nixon, and many delighted in his downfall. Watergate accomplished something the conservatives had been vainly attempting for more than a decade: to discredit moderation in the party. Conservatives remained a minority among Republicans, and until Nixon self-destructed, they seemed to be losing ground rather than gaining it. Watergate came as a gift, something they couldn't have foreseen, and they itched to take advantage.

Reagan was their man. His rhetoric remained as conservative as ever, and now that he was out of office, he could put aside the pragmatism that awkwardly undercut his words. He stumped California and the country during the early autumn of 1975 recycling the speech that had launched his political career in 1964. It was as satisfyingly unspecific as ever, and it allowed him to blame America's ills on the federal government without detailing which parts of government he would shrink or eliminate.

Yet he still refused to commit formally to the race. Michael Deaver wondered what sign he was looking for, until it appeared. "We were on a plane," Deaver said of a November 1975 commuter flight from San Fran-cisco to Los Angeles. Reagan's ambition by now had long since defeated his aerophobia. Deaver continued: "Everybody had the same class on there. The only thing they would do for us is that the security people would put us on in the first two seats as you got on the plane. So we'd get on first. Reagan would sit by the window. I'd sit on the aisle. Then, 126 people would get on, and everybody would either say hello or stop and say something to him. There had been hundreds of thousands of people who had said practically the same words. But this one woman stopped and said to him, 'You have to run.'"

For some reason this woman's words hit home. The rest of the passengers boarded, the crew did its preflight check, and the plane began taxiing down the runway. Reagan turned to Deaver. "You know, she's right," he said.

Deaver wasn't sure which passenger Reagan was referring to. "What are you talking about?" he asked.

"That woman who said I have to run. I have to run."

Deaver agreed, but he didn't know why Reagan suddenly did. "You do?" he said.

"Yes, I just don't think Jerry can do it," Reagan said. "And if I don't do it, I'm going to be the player who's always been on the bench who never got into the game."

On November 20 he got into the game. At the National Press Club in Washington he declared that he was challenging Ford for the Republican nomination in 1976. "Our nation's capital has become the seat of a buddy system that functions for its own benefits, increasingly insensitive to the needs of the American worker who supports it with his taxes," he said. "Today it is difficult to find leaders who are independent of the forces that have brought us our problems: the Congress, the bureaucracy, the lobbyists, big business, and big labor." The inclusion of big business in Reagan's rogues' gallery raised eyebrows among those who remembered him as a longtime front man for one of America's biggest businesses, General Electric. He would soon abandon this aspect of his critique, finding in government ample targets for indignation. He called for swift and stringent cuts in federal spending. "We have no choice," he said. "This government must get back as quickly as possible to a balanced budget." Responding to questions whether his unmoderated embrace of conservatism risked a repeat of the Republicans' debacle with Goldwater in 1964, he asserted that Goldwater had simply been ahead of his time. "The only thing wrong in 1964 was that the voters of this country were still in something of a New Deal syndrome. They still believed that federal help was free and that federal programs did solve problems. Now the change has come, and the people no longer have to be convinced that the federal government is too big, too costly and hasn't really solved any problems."

He denied, against the evidence, that his candidacy was directed against Gerald Ford, and he wrapped himself in the Republican Eleventh Commandment. Lyn Nofziger, his press secretary, said the former governor had spoken by phone with the president and that each had expressed a wish to avoid splitting the party. Reagan's aides characterized a conversation between the candidate and Ford's vice president, Nelson Rockefeller, as "very cordial."

John Sears, Nofziger, and others on Reagan's staff had arranged for the announcement of his candidacy to take place in Washington, rather than California, to mesh more neatly with the news cycles of the major television networks and to allow Reagan time to jet to Florida for another appearance that afternoon. In Miami he addressed a crowd that seemed uniformly delighted that he was taking on the establishment. One young man, however, was out of place, as became apparent when he pointed a pistol in Reagan's direction. Security personnel instantly wrestled the man to the ground, discovering in the process that the weapon was a toy. Reagan brushed off the incident; the news media mentioned it in passing.

But Nancy Reagan, at her husband's side, was badly upset. "I was trembling, and Ronnie had to calm me down," she recalled.

26

ICHAEL REAGAN WANTED to be part of his father's campaign. Reagan's elder son had spent much of his life wanting
to be a larger part of his father's life, but circumstances and
the personalities of those involved worked against it. His mother and his
stepmother never got along. "For thirty-five years I feel as if I have been
in the middle of a battle between Mom and Nancy," Michael wrote later.
Jane Wyman didn't like her son growing close to Nancy, not least because
Nancy obviously made Reagan happier than she ever had. Nancy, for her
part, didn't appreciate being reminded that her husband had loved someone before he had met her. She knew that the split between Jane and
Reagan hadn't been his idea; if matters had been left to him, he and Jane
would still have been married.

The tension between Nancy and Jane affected Maureen Reagan, too.
But she had been older than Michael when her parents divorced and older
when she acquired a stepmother. More tellingly, perhaps, she didn't face
the questions adopted children often face: about why their birth parents
gave them up, about whether they are really part of their adoptive families.
By his own testimony Michael required constant reassurance that he was
loved. And he often didn't get it. Jane was too busy with her film career,
and Reagan with the Screen Actors Guild and then politics. Michael
bounced from one boarding school to the next, wondering why neither
of his parents seemed to want him. He craved affection that his father
couldn't demonstrate. "He can give his heart to the country, but he just
finds it difficult to hug his own children," Michael wrote.

Much later Michael revealed that he had been plagued with guilt
since being sexually molested by a camp counselor at the age of seven.

When his father entered politics, Michael feared that reporters or Reagan's opponents would uncover what he considered his shameful secret. His dread increased with each victory his father won. And simply being the son of a famous man, and a famous woman, was burden enough. He concluded that people pretended to like him to get close to his father or mother.

Reagan's distraction hardly helped matters. Michael attended a boarding academy in Arizona for his last two years of high school; as graduation day approached, he understood that he would not be allowed to participate in commencement exercises on account of previous misbehavior. But a member of the faculty suggested that if he could prevail on his father to speak at commencement, his indiscretion would be overlooked. Reagan might or might not have understood the linkage, but he was happy to do anything that would help Michael get his diploma.

Reagan arrived on graduation day and greeted the graduates. "As the others passed in front of him one by one," Michael recalled, "I heard Dad introduce himself and then ask for the graduate's name. My grin was as wide as a cavern when I came before him.

"'My name is Ronald Reagan,' Dad said. 'What's yours?'"

Michael was badly hurt but not wholly surprised. "I took off my mortar board. 'Remember me?' I said. 'I'm your son Mike.'

"'Oh,' said Dad. 'I didn't recognize you.'"

MICHAEL CONTINUED TO seek his father's approval. He was again wounded, but again not surprised, when his father, then governor, failed to attend his wedding, in 1971 in Hawaii. "Dad and Nancy were conspicuously absent," Michael wrote. "To my chagrin, they attended Tricia Nixon's wedding in Washington that same day. That hurt me deeply. As surely as acting had deprived me of my mother, it now seemed clear that politics had deprived me of my father."

In lieu of attending, Reagan sent Michael a letter—"the first I had ever received from him," Michael recounted. Reagan had watched from a distance as Michael acted the Lothario as a young man, and now he sent him fatherly advice of the sort he couldn't bring himself to deliver face-to-face. "You have entered into the most meaningful relationship there is in all human life," Reagan wrote. "It can be whatever you decide to make it. Some men feel their masculinity can only be proven if they play out in their own life all the locker room stories, smugly confident that what a wife doesn't know won't hurt her. The truth is, somehow, way down inside, without her ever finding lipstick on the collar or catching a man in the flimsy excuse of where he was till three A.M., a wife does know, and with that knowing, some of the magic of this relationship disappears. There are more men griping about marriage who kicked the whole thing away themselves than there can ever be wives deserving of blame. There is an old law of physics that you can only get out of a thing as much as you put in it. The man who puts into the marriage only half of what he owns will get that out. Sure, there will be moments when you will see someone or think back on an earlier time and you will be challenged to see if you can still make the grade, but let me tell you how really great is the challenge of proving your masculinity and charm with one woman for the rest of your life. Any man can find a twerp here and there who will go along with cheating, and it doesn't take all that much manhood. It does take quite a man to remain attractive and to be loved by a woman who has heard him snore, seen him unshaven, tended him while he was sick and washed his dirty underwear. Do that and keep her still feeling a warm glow and you will know some very beautiful music. If you truly love a girl, you shouldn't ever want her to feel, when she sees you greet a secretary or a girl you both know, that humiliation of wondering if she was someone who caused you to be late coming home, nor should you want any other woman to be able to meet your wife and know she was smiling behind her eyes as she looked at her, the woman you love, remembering this was the woman you rejected even momentarily for her favors."

Reagan acknowledged that his son had faced challenges growing up. "Mike, you know better than many what an unhappy home is and what it can do to others." This was all the more reason for him to do whatever he could to ensure that his new home was a happy one. "Now you have a chance to make it come out the way it should. There is no greater happiness for a man than approaching a door at the end of a day knowing someone on the other side is waiting for the sound of his footsteps."

Reagan signed the letter "Love, Dad." He added a postscript: "You'll never get in trouble if you say 'I love you' at least once a day."

Michael appreciated the sentiments, even if he had wished to hear them in person. "The letter was just like Dad," he wrote. "It was straight from the heart and full of square, honest, old-fashioned sentiments. I was so touched when I read it that I cried."

REAGAN'S ADVICE DIDN'T prevent Michael's marriage from ending as Reagan's first marriage had, in divorce. But Michael didn't stop seeking his father's approval. As Reagan decided to run for the presidency, Michael said he hoped the campaign would bring the family close together. "He looked at me quizzically," Michael recalled. "'But the family *is* close,' he said." Michael mentioned the same hope to Nancy. "I wouldn't count on it," she said.

Michael and Maureen both wanted to help with the campaign. Maureen had inherited her father's penchant for politics, while Michael simply wanted to be part of his father's life. But they hit a wall. Maureen saw it coming, for she had been made to feel the pariah before. Early in Reagan's first campaign for governor, one of his advisers, Bill Roberts, paid her a visit. He explained that he and Stuart Spencer believed that the divorce issue had cost Nelson Rockefeller dearly in 1964. "The consultants were very nervous about Dad's previous marriage," Maureen remembered. "And the very clear message I was getting was that Michael and I were not to be involved in any way in the campaign. In fact, Stu Spencer later suggested to my husband that I dig a hole and pull the dirt in over me until after the election."

Years later Maureen still felt the pain of that moment. "I was crushed by Bill Roberts' visit," she said. "How dare he see me as a liability to Dad's campaign? Of course I understood the reasoning from his perspective, even if I disagreed with it, but I couldn't shake the feeling of being kicked in the stomach. It was bad enough that I'd grown up feeling removed from my family, but on top of that I was all of a sudden being told by this so-called expert that for the good of the campaign I should pretend that I didn't even exist."

She called her father hoping for sympathy but not really expecting it. "His reaction was predictable. 'If you pay someone to manage a campaign,' he said, 'then you've got to give them the authority to do it as they see fit.'" And that was that. "Michael and I were 'rubbed out' by the Spencer/Roberts plan," she said.

In 1975 they got the cold shoulder again. This time their age was the complaint of the campaign staff. Maureen was thirty-four and Michael thirty. "They felt we made Dad look too old," Michael said. Reagan's handlers much preferred the candidate to be seen with his second set of children. Patti had been born in 1952; Ron in 1958. When Reagan stood with them—a twenty-three-year-old and a teenager—he seemed almost young.

Nancy much preferred that the campaign showcase Patti and Ron, too. To Michael and Maureen this was ironic, besides being hurtful. The irony reflected the fact that Patti and Ron wanted nothing to do with their father's politics or campaigns. The hurt was the same old stepmother story. "We were invariably identified as 'the adopted son and the daughter of Ronald Reagan and Jane Wyman,' thus reminding Nancy of a marriage that had ended twenty-eight years earlier," Michael reflected.

Only later was he able to sympathize with Nancy, at least a little. "Those constant references to a past marriage must have hurt Nancy every time she heard or read them, but I didn't understand that then. All I knew was that we felt as though Nancy was pushing us out of the family circle and trying to bring Ron and Patti in."

27

R EAGAN'S FORMAL ANNOUNCEMENT produced the excitement
he and his team hoped for. A Gallup survey in early December
put him ahead of Ford among Republicans by 40 percent to 32.
Among independents, key to victory in the general election, he led Ford
by 27 percent to 25.

But polls were simply polls. The first real test would come in New
Hampshire in February 1976. Reagan braved the New England chill day
after day, courting voters at diners and factory gates. He won the endorsement of William Loeb, the cranky publisher of the state's largest newspaper, the *Manchester Union Leader.* The campaign proceeded so smoothly
that Reagan's handlers sent him out of the state two days before the primary so that the local team, which had been dealing with the logistics of
his appearances, could concentrate on getting voters to the polls.

The decision proved a tactical blunder. While Reagan wooed voters
in the Midwest, Ford gained ground in New Hampshire. Mild weather
on primary day boded well for the moderates, and Ford wound up beating
Reagan by a bit more than 1 percent of the votes cast.

John Sears wanted to spin the result as a victory. "We've got to go out
there as if we had really won this," he told the campaign team. The argument wasn't implausible. To push a sitting president so hard was a feat. A
close call in New Hampshire had brought down Lyndon Johnson in 1968;
Ford would be the next to topple.

Still, the disappointment was hard to hide. "The press could see it in
our faces, and it was all about impression," Michael Deaver remembered.
Reagan had fallen short. He had been the front-runner, and Ford had

caught him and won. Ford's side claimed the momentum of victory and the mantle of the new favorite.

"That was the start of a very disastrous period," Lyn Nofziger recalled. Reagan lost the next five primaries. Each loss eroded Reagan's credibility. Republicans of assorted persuasions began asking when he was going to drop out of the race, when he would fall in line behind the president like a loyal member of the party. He responded that he hadn't entered the race lightly and wouldn't leave it so. He would battle all the way to the convention in Kansas City.

His quest seemed increasingly quixotic after he lost the Florida primary in March. Ford's team beat the drums more loudly for party unity. If Reagan really believed in the Eleventh Commandment, they said, he would step aside, for his continued campaign did more damage to the party than any speeches against the president could have.

Even Nancy concluded he ought to get out, although she was thinking of him rather than the party. "Nancy was most unhappy," Nofziger remembered. She took Nofziger aside in a hotel room. "Lyn, you know you've got to get Ronnie out of this race," she said. "We can't embarrass him any further."

At this moment Reagan entered the room. "He thought that I was going to go along with her," Nofziger remembered. "And he said, 'Lynwood'—which is not my name, but it's what he calls me—he says, 'I am not going to get out of this race. I am going to stay in this through Texas. I am going to stay in it all the way.'"

Nofziger finished the story, which he considered characteristic of Reagan and his relationship with Nancy. "She accepted that okay. People who thought that Nancy ran Reagan—no. She ran Reagan when he didn't care. When he cared, she didn't. I mean, I've been there on a number of occasions where she wanted her way, and he got his way."

So Reagan stayed in the race, reiterating that he would fight through to the convention. Yet brave words were no substitute for hard dollars, and as his chances of victory grew slimmer, so did his campaign coffers. The primary contest moved across the South, with Reagan desperate for funds to continue the campaign. Then a supporter in North Carolina, recalling the effect of Reagan's 1964 televised speech for Goldwater, suggested airing something similar on stations in the Tar Heel State. Nofziger found a half-hour clip of a speech Reagan had given in Florida, and, slightly edited, it went out to North Carolina viewers.

The effect was less dramatic than that of the 1964 national speech, but it showcased Reagan for southern voters. The message had hardly changed in a dozen years, yet it was what southern conservatives wanted to hear.

They liked something else Reagan said. So far in the campaign he had trod lightly in the realm of foreign policy, in part because attacking the commander in chief on matters of national security carried the greatest risk of a political backlash, and in part because he could claim no expertise or experience on the subject. But Jesse Helms, a conservative Republican who represented North Carolina in the Senate, had been railing against détente and other aspects of the Nixon-Kissinger-Ford foreign policy, and he was getting a good response. Reagan decided to chime in.

He criticized arms control as controlling only American arms; the Soviets continued their buildup, he said. Before long the United States would find itself vulnerable to Russian blackmail, if not wholesale annihilation. He blamed Ford and Kissinger for ignoring the activities of Soviet proxies and communist agents in Central America, Africa, and Southeast Asia. And in a line he borrowed from Helms, he accused the Ford administration of trying to give away the Panama Canal.

This last count of the indictment was puzzling. Negotiations over the future of the Panama Canal had been under way since the 1960s. They had never sparked much interest among Americans, and North Carolinians had even less stake in the canal than residents of several other states.

But for some reason they responded. Reagan's recycled television speech and his dark warning about a canal giveaway, combined with the conservative disposition of most North Carolina Republicans, resulted in a stunning victory in the North Carolina primary. Reagan beat Ford by 52 percent to 46. North Carolina's Republican rules specified proportional division of the delegates, so the effect on the delegate count was modest, with Reagan winning 28 delegates to Ford's 26. But North Carolina allowed Reagan to fight on. The pressure to abandon the race didn't end; if anything, the jolt prompted the Ford side to intensify its efforts to cast Reagan as a wrecker. Yet Reagan could now dismiss the efforts as evidence that his message was boring home. And the money flowed in, not in gushers, but in a steady stream.

He scored victories elsewhere in the South during May. He captured Indiana and Nebraska and predictably thrashed Ford in California in early June.

Ford countered with victories in the industrial Midwest and the Northeast. And the president's team enlisted the services of James Baker, a Houston lawyer with an uncanny ability to work the political system in his candidate's favor. Baker hunted down delegates in states with conventions and caucuses, employing the charm of his southern upbringing, the guile of his years in law, and the leverage of the White House.

By the time the primaries, conventions, and caucuses had been completed, Ford held a modest lead in delegates over Reagan. The numbers were imprecise, given the diversity of rules determining whom the delegates were bound to, if bound at all. Each side publicly interpreted the imprecision in its favor. Each spoke of covert supporters who would surface at the decisive moment of the convention. But impartial estimates gave Ford around 1,090 delegates and Reagan about 1,030. Ford needed roughly 40 delegates to claim the convention's majority; Reagan some 100. In the scrapping for those last delegates, the president's institutional heft would surely work in his favor.

Reagan resorted to novelty. At the instigation of John Sears he announced his running mate ahead of the vote on the presidential nomination. Richard Schweiker was a moderate Republican senator from Pennsylvania. "What Sears thought was that if he picked Schweiker, we could peel off the Pennsylvania delegation, and that would help us get some of these other delegations," Lyn Nofziger recalled.

The announcement intrigued the media but backfired among the delegates. "The Southern Reagan thing just fell apart overnight because of Schweiker," Michael Deaver remembered. "We go down to Mississippi and we start meeting with all of the delegations, and it was just a total disaster. The whole point of picking Dick Schweiker was to cut into the Northeast, and to see if we could get Pennsylvania. Then maybe we could get a little bit of New Jersey, New York, and then it would all start to unravel for Ford. Of course, Schweiker couldn't even deliver Pennsylvania. So then we had to go defend our base, which was in the South. We'd had these delegations into this Marriott or Ramada Inn, or wherever it was, in Jackson, Mississippi. The Alabama delegation, there were four of them, I think. We're in this room that's about four times the size of this, with these four little people sitting out there. Schweiker, and Mrs. Claire Schweiker, and Ronald Reagan are up at this head table. They go through this whole thing, and this man from Alabama stands up. He's got a bow tie on, perfectly dressed. 'Governor,' he said, 'I am not a drinking man. But when I heard that you picked Dick Schweiker to be your running mate, I went home and drank a pitcher of whiskey sours.' And he said, 'I would rather have had my doctor call me at home and tell me that my wife had a venereal disease.'"

The Schweiker gambit sealed Reagan's defeat. The delegates gathered and did the usual convention business until the roll call, when, in the predawn hours of August 19, they gave Ford the nomination by 1,187 votes to Reagan's 1,070.

Some conservatives refused to yield even in defeat. Jesse Helms thundered his undying opposition to détente and to those responsible for it. A Reagan campaign worker from Missouri, buttonholed after the balloting, hoped for Ford's November defeat. "The Republican party needs to lose soundly, and that's the inevitability of the Ford candidacy," he said.

But the candidates moved quickly to close ranks. Ford gestured toward making Reagan his running mate. Reagan responded diffidently, or perhaps coyly. James Baker, who later worked closely with Reagan, thought a Ford-Reagan ticket would have been appealing to voters and could have happened had either side been a bit more forthcoming. "You know, Mr. President," he told Reagan afterward, "if President Ford had asked you to run with him, he would have won." Baker added, thinking of what happened in the next four years, "And you might never have been president."

"You're right," Reagan responded. "If he had asked, I'd have felt duty-bound to run."

Baker continued: "President Ford didn't ask you because we received word from your campaign that you would join him for a unity meeting only on condition that he *wouldn't* offer you the vice presidency. And besides that, you very publicly shut down the movement by your supporters in Kansas City to draft you for the vice presidential nomination."

"Look, I really did not want to be vice president, and I said so at the time," Reagan responded. "But I don't have any recollection of telling anyone to pass a message to President Ford not to offer me the spot. If he had asked, I would have felt duty-bound to say yes."

Baker could hardly believe what he was hearing. "I was shocked," he recalled. "How different history might have been. Given the intensity of their primary battle, Ford really didn't want Reagan as his running mate, but the president might have asked if he had thought Reagan would accept. And with a Ford-Reagan ticket in 1976, I think two portraits might be missing from the White House walls today—those of Jimmy Carter and Ronald Reagan."

Ford did not ask Reagan to join the ticket, but he did invite him to join the victory celebration on the convention stage. Their clasped hands conveyed at least the appearance that unity prevailed among the Republicans. Reagan's supporters demanded a speech from their man; his remarks caused their hearts to flutter anew and some to consider demanding a recount. But he understood that the moment wasn't his, and he stepped aside before provoking a stampede, but not before receiving an ovation louder and more heartfelt than Ford got.

The next day Reagan bade his supporters thanks and farewell. At least one journalist spotted him dabbing a tear; many observers assumed, given the candidate's age, that this was his last convention. Reagan's words revealed little of his plans. "Sure, there's disappointment in what happened," he said. "But the cause, the cause goes on . . . It's just one battle in a long war, and it's going to go on as long as we all live . . . You just stay in there, and you stay there with the same belief and the same faith to do what you're doing here. The individuals on the stage may change, but the cause is there. The cause will prevail because it's right."

James Baker left the convention with the winner but deeply respectful of the loser. "He damn near took us down," he said of Reagan's challenge to Ford. "It was really close."

THE BLOW OF defeat was softened for Reagan by the common perception that the Republican nomination wasn't worth much that season. The Republicans were still answering for Watergate, which the Democrats milked for every vote. Several prominent Democrats made a run for their party's nomination, but the best known suffered from the taint of government experience, especially in Washington, the home of the corruption voters extrapolated from Watergate to politicians at large. Jimmy Carter had been governor of Georgia, but he soft-pedaled this part of his résumé in favor of his background as a plainspoken peanut farmer from Plains, Georgia. His persistence and evident candor, which included an interview with *Playboy* magazine in which he admitted to lustful feelings about women not his wife, impressed enough primary-season Democrats for him to secure the nomination a month ahead of the July convention. The result was that while Ford and Reagan were still wrestling their way to Kansas City, Carter was catching his breath and building his campaign reserves. Polls gave him a big lead over either Republican.

The campaign for the general election inspired almost no one. Ford was damaged goods following the Nixon pardon and his close call with Reagan; though the race tightened after Labor Day, as presidential campaigns often do, flubs by Ford in debates with Carter recalled the cutting comment by Lyndon Johnson that Ford had played too many football games without his helmet (at the University of Michigan, where he was the sort of lineman Reagan had aspired to be at Eureka College).

Reagan did little to help the Republican cause. He gave enough speeches on Ford's behalf to deflect charges of sulking in his tent, but his enthusiasm for the moderate president was conspicuous by its absence. Reagan never wholly mastered the partisan mind-set: the psychological frame that puts the interest of the party ahead of that of the country. He could and did say that Ford was preferable to Carter, but he barely believed it. He wasn't immune to the conservative argument that the best thing for the country would be Ford's defeat and the final discrediting of Republican moderation. The conservatives could then seize the party and spearhead an American renaissance.

They got the first part of what they wanted. Ford continued to gain ground but finally fell short of Carter by a popular vote of 50 percent to 48. Many in the Ford camp blamed Reagan for weakening the president in the long battle for the nomination. "We might never have lost to Carter without that challenge," James Baker said. The result was a less resounding repudiation of Republican moderation than the most zealous conservatives desired, but at least it meant that the next GOP nomination would be wide open. And nearly all the conservatives assumed that Carter would so mishandle the presidency that voters would be happy to give the Republicans another try.

"ONCE UPON A time there was a little red hen who scratched about the barnyard until she uncovered some grains of wheat," Reagan told radio listeners two weeks after the election. He was glad to be back on the air, happy for the opportunity to tell his stories, and appreciative again of the discipline required to distill complicated questions of policy into a few minutes of airtime. In this installment he borrowed from an old fable to make a modern point. His little red hen calls her neighbors and asks who will help her plant the wheat, that they all might have bread. The cow, the duck, the pig, and the goose beg off. So the hen plants the wheat herself. It grows tall and bears ripe grain. She asks who will help harvest the wheat.

"Not I," says the duck.

"Out of my classification," says the pig.

"I'd lose my seniority," says the cow.

"I'd lose my unemployment compensation," says the goose.

So the hen harvests the wheat herself. In time she asks who will help her bake the bread.

"That would be overtime for me," says the cow.

"I'd lose my welfare benefits," says the duck.

"I'm a dropout and never learned how," says the pig.

"If I'm to be the only helper, that's discrimination," says the goose.

The hen bakes the loaves herself. She shows them to her neighbors. They each demand a share. But the hen won't give them any. She keeps the bread for herself.

"Excess profits!" cries the cow.

"Capitalist leech!" screams the duck.

"I demand equal rights," yells the goose.

The pig grunts, and the four complain to the government, whose agent tells the hen she must share.

"But I earned the bread," says the hen.

"Exactly," says the agent. "That is the wonderful free enterprise system. Anyone in the barnyard can earn as much as he wants. But under our modern government regulations, the productive workers must divide their product with the idle."

The irony in Reagan's tone was lighthearted but unmistakable as he concluded: "And they lived happily ever after, including the little red hen, who smiled and clucked, 'I am grateful, I am grateful.' But her neighbors wondered why she never again baked any more bread."

The performance was vintage Reagan. It engaged the listener; it delivered a conservative message without the anger that infused so much rhetoric on the right. Barry Goldwater could never have managed the trick. Franklin Roosevelt could have, though Roosevelt's Fireside Chats were in fact less chatty than Reagan's show. Not being president, Reagan wasn't burdened with the dignity of the high office. But there was that same link to an invisible audience, that same meeting of imaginations in the ether. And Reagan's voice was better than Roosevelt's: soothing, warm, serious but with an undercurrent of humor.

How many voters Reagan won over by radio is impossible to know. Like other pundits he often preached to the converted. But with these he cemented his reputation as the most attractive conservative in the country. He doubtless pulled in some fence-sitters, perhaps wanderers across the radio dial who heard his voice and stopped to listen to the story. And he alienated almost no one. Critics might complain that his messages were oversimplified, but the honest among them attributed this to the genre as much as to Reagan. People could disagree with Reagan, but rarely did they find him disagreeable.

However the performances played with listeners, their greater importance was to Reagan's political and intellectual development. The radio show required him to learn about topics he had hardly considered before; he had to find something to talk about every day. He read more broadly than he ever had, mining newspapers and magazines for information, for stories, for hooks.

He spoke about health care, warning of the advance of socialized medicine. "The campaign goes on to bring health care in America out of the free market system and into the protective custody of government," he said. "Those who brought us the postal service and Amtrak"—two other regular targets—"are anxious to provide medical service of the same high caliber." Some in Congress were promoting a measure that would require employers to offer medical insurance to their employees. Reagan cited Britain's national health service as a cautionary tale of where such meddling in the market might lead. A woman in England—"attractive except for some facial scars"—had boasted to a visiting American that all her medical treatment was free. She acknowledged that it was sometimes slow. "I had to wait eight years for an appointment with a dermatologist about my face." And she had to wait another year before the treatment started. "But it *is* free." Except that it wasn't, Reagan pointed out. "They are taxed far more heavily than we are," he said of the British. "And their health service takes a big bite of those taxes."

He talked about education. A St. Louis television station had aired a story that seemed to summarize the deficiencies of public education. "They interviewed a product of the St. Louis public school system," Reagan said, "a young man twenty years of age who had gone from kindergarten through grade twelve and had his high school diploma to prove it. He is a functional illiterate, unable to read or write who is presently enrolled in an adult remedial reading program." Reagan assured his listeners there was nothing wrong with the young man. "He is not mentally retarded. Neither is he stupid. He's just plain untaught." Reagan blamed the liberal theorists of the education graduate schools who emphasized reasoning processes rather than the retention of facts. And behind the theorists was the muscle of the National Education Association, which like all big unions put the interests of its members and especially its leaders ahead of the people it ostensibly served, in this case young people like the St. Louis illiterate.

He chided the environmental movement. Poking fun at efforts to save endangered species, he asked his listeners, "How much do you miss dinosaurs? Would your life be richer if those giant prehistoric flying lizards occasionally settled on your front lawn?" He called for renewed use of DDT, contending that its discontinuance in America was based on fear rather than on evidence. "The EPA back in 1972 said that DDT was harmless to human beings and that properly used it posed no threat to animal, bird or marine life. Yet it is banned by the EPA on the theoretical grounds that it might, under some circumstances, someday harm someone or something." He said recent hand-wringing over the clubbing deaths of northern harp seal pups by fur hunters had gotten out of control. "The harp seal is not in danger of extinction. It is one of the most abundant seal species in the world, and the herd is growing, not shrinking. Elimination of the seal pup harvest would have a disastrous effect on the already depleted Atlantic fishing grounds. The seals consume each year a half million tons of small fish that are a vital link in the food chain for cod, sea birds and whales." The campaign for the harp seal, he said, was make-work for the environmentalists. "There is an international organization which stays in business year round primarily to raise money to protect against the seal harvest. A $40,000-a-year executive rides around in the organization's own helicopter."

He criticized public transit. Washington, D.C., was building a new subway system, with a cost originally projected at $2.5 billion. "That cost figure has already doubled," Reagan said. And the work was far from finished. "It is years behind schedule and only four-and-a-half miles of track are open for use at a loss of $55,000 a day." People preferred the freedom of cars. "Most cities, including those of modest size, once had rapid transit. The clang of the trolley car's bell was a familiar sound until people abandoned public transportation for their own set of wheels. The automobile gave man more freedom, the freedom to choose his own time table and route of travel on a portal to portal basis. He has shown he does not intend to give up that freedom, and government has no right to take it from him."

Reagan's broadcasts were overwhelmingly negative. Negativity, of course, had been the posture of American conservatives since the New Deal. And opposition is expected of minority parties and factions. Republican conservatives were a double minority during the late 1970s. Their party was a minority in national politics; not since the 1940s had the Republicans commanded a majority in the House, and not since the early 1950s in the Senate. With Carter in the White House, the Republicans were exiles from the executive branch as well. Meanwhile, within the

Republican Party, conservatives had been a minority since the Goldwater season of 1964. If Reagan sounded negative, like the embattled outsider, he had reason.

Even so, his listeners might have wondered what he stood *for*. Smaller government, presumably, but despite his incessant complaints about government waste and inefficiency, he carefully avoided calling for the elimination of specific programs. He lamented the growth of Social Security but didn't advocate its dismantling. He railed against "socialized medicine" but left seniors to enjoy their Medicare.

He sounded negative, certainly. But he also sounded like a candidate.

29

NEARLY EVERY SUCCESSFUL presidential candidate treats his election as a mandate to pursue the policies he espoused during the campaign, whether voters actually favored those policies or not. Jimmy Carter was elected primarily because he had been farthest from the scene of the Watergate crimes, but he interpreted his election as cause to re-chart the path of American foreign policy. He explained his new approach in the spring of 1977 to an audience at the University of Notre Dame. The setting suited his theme, in that Notre Dame's president, Theodore Hesburgh, had often spoken on behalf of human rights, which Carter emphasized this day. Carter contended that during the Cold War the United States wandered from its traditional values. "For too many years, we've been willing to adopt the flawed and erroneous principles and tactics of our adversaries, sometimes abandoning our own values for theirs," he said. "We've fought fire with fire, never thinking that fire is better quenched with water. This approach failed, with Vietnam the best example of its intellectual and moral poverty." Carter took his own election, on a platform stressing human rights, as evidence that Americans had learned from their country's failure. "We have now found our way back to our own principles and values."

The world had changed dramatically since the 1940s, Carter continued. The bipolar model on which America's containment policy had been based no longer described reality. New nations in Asia and Africa and newly assertive nations in Latin America demanded their place at the international table. And they refused to accept the priorities of the superpowers. "We can no longer expect that the other 150 nations will follow the dictates of the powerful," Carter said. This was all to the good, for it played to America's fundamental moral strength. "The great democracies are not free because we are strong and prosperous," Carter asserted. "We are strong and influential and prosperous because we are free." Freedom must guide the United States in international affairs. "Our policy must reflect our belief that the world can hope for more than simple survival and our belief that dignity and freedom are fundamental spiritual requirements." Carter reiterated that the transition had already begun. "We are now free of that inordinate fear of communism which once led us to embrace any dictator who joined us in that fear. I'm glad that that's being changed."

Some Americans found the new international order threatening, Carter acknowledged. It need not be. "It is a new world, but America should not fear it. It is a new world, and we should help to shape it. It is a new world that calls for a new American foreign policy—a policy based on constant decency in its values and on optimism in our historical vision." This vision should lead America and the world into the new era. "Our policy is rooted in our moral values, which never change," he said. "Our policy is designed to serve mankind. And it is a policy that I hope will make you proud to be Americans."

Carter took steps to institutionalize his vision. He established a special position in the State Department for monitoring human rights, and he appointed civil rights activist Patricia Derian to head it. He tapped Andrew Young, another veteran of the civil rights movement, to be American ambassador to the United Nations. Derian and Young made human rights a touchstone of American foreign policy, lecturing foreign despots and urging the withholding of assistance from dictators on the American dole. Carter himself corresponded publicly with Andrei Sakharov, the most visible of Soviet dissidents. He signed United Nations covenants on civil, political, economic, social, and cultural rights, and he cut aid to oppressive regimes in Argentina, Chile, and Nicaragua. He imposed sanctions against the white-supremacist governments of Rhodesia and South Africa and the brutal tyranny of Idi Amin in Uganda.

CARTER'S NEW POLICY indeed made some Americans proud, but it made most conservatives ill. Jeane Kirkpatrick was an academic who crossed over into polemics to join the ranks of the neoconservatives, a group of intellectuals who had trekked from the left to the right of the political spectrum without losing the certitude that infuriated their critics.

The neoconservatives cared about domestic issues but about foreign policy much more. They despised détente and assailed it at every turn. They embraced ideals but prided themselves on their hard-eyed realism.

It was as a realist that Kirkpatrick attacked Carter. In a 1979 article titled "Dictatorships and Double Standards," published in *Commentary*, the house organ of neoconservatism, she blasted the president for willful naïveté and consequent malpractice of office. She contended that Carter used human rights as a stick to beat America's authoritarian friends while ignoring the far larger crimes of the real tyrants of the planet, the totalitarian leaders of the Soviet Union, China, and the other communist states. She saw a crucial distinction between conservative dictatorships of the right and socialist dictatorships of the left. The former allowed personal autonomy the latter denied. The rightists, moreover, were redeemable. "Although there is no instance of a revolutionary 'socialist' or Communist society being democratized," Kirkpatrick wrote, "right-wing autocracies do sometimes evolve into democracies—given time, propitious economic, social, and political circumstances, talented leaders, and a strong indigenous demand for representative government." Carter ignored this possibility and in doing so rendered reform less likely. Meanwhile, by treating foreign policy as a morality play, he undermined American strength and credibility. "What makes the inconsistencies of the Carter administration noteworthy are, first, the administration's moralism, which renders it especially vulnerable to charges of hypocrisy; and, second, the administration's predilection for policies that violate the strategic and economic interests of the United States. The administration's conception of national interest borders on doublethink: it finds friendly powers to be guilty representatives of the status quo and views the triumph of unfriendly groups as beneficial to America's 'true interests.'"

CERTAIN EVENTS OF the late 1970s seemed to support Kirkpatrick's view. Nicaragua had been badly ruled for decades by the Somoza family and their cronies, who grew increasingly distasteful to various elements of Nicaraguan society. During the 1970s the dissidents aligned in the leftist Sandinista National Liberation Front, which included elements ranging from moderate reformers to committed communists. Carter had to decide whether the Somoza regime was preferable to the Sandinistas and, if it was, whether it was salvageable. Neither question allowed a definitive answer. Had Anastasio Somoza, the current jefe, so alienated Nicaraguans as to have lost all credibility? If the Sandinistas won, would the moderates or the radicals among them take charge? Would keeping Somoza in power require the use of American troops? Would the American people stand for this in the wake of Vietnam?

Carter tried to split the difference. He jawboned Somoza to clean up his act and allow moderates to participate in Nicaraguan politics. He cut back on military assistance without terminating it entirely.

Somoza responded not as Carter hoped. Gunmen presumed to be associated with the regime murdered the most visible moderate, editor Pedro Chamorro. The killing strengthened the radical elements of the insurgency, who attacked the capital and briefly captured the national palace, along with a thousand hostages. Somoza's hold on power slipped.

But not until a Sandinista victory was all but assured did Carter openly call for Somoza's ouster. By then, Carter had lost whatever leverage he might have had in Nicaraguan affairs. The Sandinistas gave him no credit for assisting their revolution, which swept to victory. Conservatives in the United States blamed him for not defending Somoza and defeating the leftists.

Carter's Iranian problem was similar. The shah of Iran, Mohammad Reza Pahlavi, owed his position partly to the United States, which in 1953 had joined forces with Britain to help overthrow the populist prime minister, Muhammad Mussadiq, in favor of the shah. Yet the shah showed scant gratitude. He led the price hawks in OPEC, the international oil cartel, as they hiked prices fourfold during the 1970s, and he ignored American warnings that he was losing touch with the Iranian people. Carter confronted another dilemma. Should he insist that the shah reform and accept the inevitability of change? Or should he stand by the shah for fear that change might jeopardize America's position in the Middle East? As with Nicaragua, it was impossible to know which part of the insurgency carried the most weight. Moderates in the anti-shah movement promised an improvement over the shah, both for Iranians and for the United States. But Islamic radicals damned the United States and the West with every second breath.

Again Carter waffled. He lectured the shah on human rights but declined to cut off military aid. He brought the shah to Washington on a visit that provoked demonstrations by anti-shah Iranians in the American capital, counterdemonstrations by pro-shah Iranians, and scuffling between the two groups. Washington police fired tear gas to break up the crowd; the gas drifted onto the White House grounds and into the eyes of Carter, the shah, and their entourages. Carter recalled the moment as an augury. "The tear gas had created the semblance of grief. Almost two years later, and for fourteen months afterward, there would be real grief in our country because of Iran."

Carter felt the grief personally and politically. The shah's grip on power diminished, as did his health. He was dying of cancer and grew increasingly detached from everyday events. In early 1978 police fired on theology students in the holy city of Qom and killed two dozen. The incident caused the unrest to spread, eventually driving the shah into exile and delivering power to a small group of Islamists led by Ruhollah Khomeini, the principal ayatollah, or Shiite religious leader. As on Nicaragua, Carter was condemned from both sides. Khomeini and the new rulers of Iran blasted America as the "Great Satan," while American conservatives blamed the president for losing another ally to forces hostile to American interests.

Carter's credibility sank further when a crowd in Tehran stormed the American embassy and seized several dozen diplomats and staff. Some were shortly released, but fifty-two remained in captivity. Carter vowed to stay in Washington and labor night and day until the fifty-two hostages were freed. Yet his very vow worked against him. The Iranian regime realized the hostages were a valuable bargaining chip and held on to them. Carter himself became a hostage, imprisoned in the Oval Office, the symbol of good intentions gone fecklessly awry.

30

R EAGAN COULDN'T RESIST such an easy target and saw no reason to try. The only thing that might have prevented his running for president again would have been faltering health. But he avoided the heavy drinking that took his father young, and he inherited good genes from his mother, who lived almost a full eight decades before dying in California in 1962 at the age of seventy-nine. He got plenty of exercise and fresh air at his ranch. He felt as strong as he ever had. He had no reason to think he didn't have many years of solid health ahead.

So his formal announcement of candidacy in November 1979 surprised no one. He personally addressed a ballroom full of well-heeled Republicans in New York, and he spoke to the nation at large in a recorded, televised version of the same speech. He again raided Franklin Roosevelt's rhetorical library, giving Roosevelt's famous phrase a conservative spin: "A troubled and afflicted mankind looks to us, pleading for us to keep our rendezvous with destiny: that we will support the principles of self-reliance, self-discipline, morality and, above all, responsible liberty for every individual." As ever, he called for a reduction in the size of the federal government. He promised tax cuts, which would force Washington to shrink. He decried regulations. He proposed to increase defense spending. He reiterated his earlier criticisms of Carter as weak in foreign policy and misguided at home. Referring to what was widely dubbed the "malaise speech," in which Carter had asked Americans to look within to find the source of the country's unhappiness, Reagan declared, "Leaders in our government have told us that we, the people, have lost confidence in ourselves; that we must regain our spirit and our will to achieve our national goals. Well, it is true there is a lack of confidence, an unease with things the way they are. But the confidence we have lost is confidence in our government's policies."

HIS TIMING COULDN'T have been better. Polls revealed that barely three out of ten Americans approved of Carter's performance. Yet Reagan stumbled out of the gate. Hoping to preempt questions about his age, he observed in an interview with NBC that he was younger than most world leaders. Tom Brokaw countered, "Giscard d'Estaing of France is younger than you."

"Who?" Reagan responded.

"Giscard d'Estaing of France," Brokaw said again.

Reagan clearly didn't know who Giscard was. His staff later claimed that Reagan hadn't heard the question, but they dropped this line when they realized that Reagan would suffer less from voters concluding he didn't know who the president of France was than from their discovering he was partly deaf.

The initial miscues might have damaged Reagan more had he not received, during the second month of his campaign, an incredible gift from, of all places, the Kremlin. Americans weren't the only ones alarmed by the Iranian revolution; Soviet leaders feared that radical Islamism would leap into the largely Muslim Soviet republics of central Asia. Moscow had been building a barrier against the Islamists by supplying support to the Afghan government of Muhammad Daoud Khan, but Daoud suffered credibility and likability problems comparable to those of Somoza in Nicaragua and the shah in Iran. His end was similar, too, for he was overthrown in 1978. (In his case he and his family were slaughtered.) His successors, Nur Muhammad Taraki and Hafizullah Amin, battled increasingly confident Islamist militants and then each other, with Amin arranging Taraki's murder in September 1979. Moscow gave Amin a chance to suppress the Islamist uprising, but it grew only stronger, inspired in part by the Islamist triumph in Iran. Desperate to keep the Islamists at a distance, the Kremlin in December 1979 airlifted troops over the mountains into Afghanistan. Soviet leaders contended that Amin had invited the intervention, which therefore didn't qualify as an invasion. Amin's sudden death cast doubt on this explanation, which few in Afghanistan or the outside world had credited anyway. The Soviets installed a new regime and commenced a bloody campaign against the Islamists.

The Soviet invasion of Afghanistan knocked the scales from the eyes of Jimmy Carter. Such, at least, was Carter's explanation of the change in policy he immediately ordered. "My opinion of the Russians has changed more drastically in the last week than in the two and one-half years before that," he told a reporter on the final day of 1979. "The action of the Soviets has made a more dramatic change in my opinion of what the Soviets' ultimate goals are than anything they've done in the previous time that I've been in office."

Carter proceeded to act on his epiphany. In his State of the Union address in January 1980 he described the Soviet invasion of Afghanistan as "the most serious threat to the peace since the Second World War," and in unmistakable terms he warned the Russians against moving any closer to the warm waters and oil fields of the Persian Gulf. "An attempt by any outside force to gain control of the Persian Gulf region will be regarded as an assault on the vital interests of the United States of America, and such an assault will be repelled by any means necessary, including military force."

Carter's reversal could hardly have been more dramatic. And it played into the hands of Reagan and other critics of détente. In explaining how wrong he had been about the Soviets, the president conceded that Reagan and the others had been right. And in threatening war should the Red Army move farther south, he was doing precisely what they would have done, or said they would have done.

Carter showed his seriousness by asking Congress for a big increase in military spending, which Congress approved. He canceled grain sales and other commercial aspects of détente. He withdrew permits to Soviet vessels to fish in American waters. He effectively ordered the U.S. Olympic team to stay home from the 1980 Summer Games in Moscow. And he never uttered the word "détente" in public again.

Carter's capitulation on détente, combined with the continuing ordeal of the American hostages in Iran, might have guaranteed his defeat for reelection by any credible Republican. Or it might not have. Americans have rarely cast their ballots for president with international issues foremost in mind. Domestic questions, starting with the state of the economy, have mattered far more. Do I have a job? Will I keep it? Can I afford what I need to buy? These questions demand answers from nearly every voter every day. Foreign policy questions arise less often and almost always less pressingly.

It was the economic questions with which Reagan most effectively skewered Carter. The American economy had performed quite satisfactorily during the two decades after 1945, lifting standards of living and supporting the government activities Americans desired and voted for. But during the 1960s the economy began to wobble. Revived Germany and Japan sent more and more goods to America, creating an imbalance of trade and putting pressure on the dollar. Meanwhile, heavy federal spending on the Great Society and the war in Vietnam caused inflation to creep upward, adding to the pressure on the dollar as foreign dollar-holders divested themselves of their depreciating asset. The strains eventually forced the Nixon administration to pull the plug on the international monetary system that had been in place since the war. The fixed links of other currencies to the dollar and of the dollar to gold disappeared; the greenback became just one currency among many floating on a shifting sea of money traders' hopes and fears.

The sea grew stormy when the OPEC oil producers took advantage of growing demand in the early 1970s to quadruple prices. The 1973 war between Israel and its Arab neighbors added a political element to the oil question as Arab producers proclaimed an embargo against shipments to the United States for its support of Israel. The embargo lasted only months, but the price increases persisted, adding to the troubles of the American economy.

The result was a state of economic affairs Americans had never experienced. Inflation bred unemployment, a development that puzzled many economists. In standard economic theory inflation and unemployment were thought to be inversely related. Rising unemployment forced workers to accept lower pay and depressed consumer demand, thereby limiting producers' ability to raise prices. But the standard theory no longer seemed to apply. Unemployment and inflation rose simultaneously, prompting the coinage of a new term, "stagflation," to denote the novel and discouraging situation. And Republicans popularized a new metric, the "misery index," the sum of the inflation and unemployment rates, to measure it.

Reagan appeared best placed to benefit politically from the economic troubles, which the Republicans naturally imputed to Carter. Of the plausible Republican candidates, he was the only one with a national reputation and a national following. Yet George Bush, who had served in the House of Representatives before accepting a series of appointive positions, decided to challenge Reagan for the nomination. Bush was a New Englander who had migrated to Texas and raised a family there without becoming a Texan (his eldest son, by contrast, also called George, would be Texan through and through). Bush began the pre-primary season far behind Reagan, but he hoped to raise doubts in voters' minds regarding Reagan's age and overall fitness for the presidency. Senator Howard Baker of Tennessee and Representative John Anderson of Illinois put their names forward on the chance Reagan and Bush both would falter. Gerald Ford amused himself dropping hints that he might run again, but he amused himself even more playing golf in Palm Springs and ultimately abandoned the charade.

Reagan initially underestimated Bush. The Texas transplant pitched a tent in Iowa ahead of that state's quirky caucuses and shook hands and kissed babies all around the state. Reagan's people discounted Iowa, believing the race wouldn't start until the New Hampshire primary. In previous seasons they might have been right, but Iowa got more attention than usual because Edward Kennedy, senator from Massachusetts, was challenging Carter for the Democratic nomination. Reporters in Iowa for the Democratic fireworks couldn't avoid covering the Republican contest as well. And in that contest Bush beat Reagan by a small margin but one large enough to knock the crown off the head of the nominee apparent. "It was a big surprise," James Baker admitted afterward. Baker, having opposed Reagan on Gerald Ford's behalf in 1976, now opposed him on behalf of Bush, a personal friend from Houston. He ran the Bush campaign. "It gave us a lot of momentum," he said.

The upset and shift of momentum surprised Reagan as much as anyone else, and it prompted him to campaign harder than before. The vigor of his campaigning, in the New England winter, went far toward allaying concerns about his age. He joined several other candidates for a debate in Manchester the week before the primary, and although he didn't particularly distinguish himself, neither did Bush, who thereby lost some of that "Big Mo," as he called the trend in his direction.

A second debate was the event that stuck in the minds of those following the campaign. The Bush camp wanted a one-on-one with Reagan, the better to gather the moderate stop-Reagan vote. Reagan's side was split. Some of his advisers thought a head-to-head would allow Reagan to finish Bush off with a single blow. Others preferred a Reagan-against-the-rest, which would diminish Bush by lumping him with the rest. The two campaigns eventually agreed to a one-on-one. But then they began arguing about who would pay for the debate. The Bush team shortsightedly balked, and when Reagan's handlers agreed to pick up the tab, they realized it gave them control over crucial details and terms of the event.

Reagan himself wasn't privy to the haggling, but his instinct was to include the other candidates, who were complaining at their exclusion. Word went out to them to show up at the gymnasium in Nashua where the debate was to be held. They arrived at the appointed hour and engaged Reagan in discussion while Bush's managers complained to moderator Jon Breen of the *Nashua Telegraph* that their man had been deceived. Breen agreed and refused to let the four extras—Howard Baker, John Anderson, Bob Dole of Kansas, and Phil Crane of Illinois—participate. Bush walked onto the stage and took his chair. Reagan did the same, but he was followed by the extras, who, lacking chairs, stood on the stage behind Breen.

Bush didn't know what to do, so he stared straight ahead and said nothing. Reagan argued that the four ought to be allowed to speak. Breen, guided by what he thought were the ground rules, rejected Reagan's request. When Reagan, encouraged by the capacity crowd of two thousand, continued to argue for the broader inclusion, Breen directed the sound technician to turn off Reagan's microphone.

Reagan had always been able to play some emotions better than others. One of his best was righteous indignation, which he exhibited now. "I'm paying for this microphone!" he declared. The other candidates should have their turn at it.

Breen refused and the room dissolved in chaos. Many shouted for Reagan, very few for Bush. The excluded four mugged for the crowd, pointing favorably at Reagan and dismissively at Bush. They ultimately left the stage, and the one-on-one debate proceeded. But it was anticlimactic and got little coverage in the next day's news, which was all about how Reagan had taken charge and shown his personal ascendancy over Bush. As Bush press aide Pete Teeley told his candidate afterward, "The bad news is that the media are playing up the confrontation. The good news is that they're ignoring the debate, and you lost that, too."

31

THE RESULTS OF the New Hampshire primary corroborated the media judgment of Reagan's ascendancy. He swamped Bush by more than two to one, with the other candidates even further behind. Bush never recovered, though he kept fighting. Reagan rolled through the subsequent primaries until his nomination became irresistible. The minor candidates dropped out, leaving only Bush, who continued to rebuff the counsel of party elders to concede and fall in behind Reagan. "Bush is very competitive," James Baker observed later, by way of explanation. "He didn't want to drop out." Bush himself credited his deceased father, the former senator Prescott Bush. "Every time I weighed my options, I could hear my dad's voice saying, 'You have to see this through,'" Bush remembered. "He taught all of his children not to be quitters. Maybe that advice did not necessarily apply to campaigns, but I couldn't help but think it did, and I should not quit."

Yet reality eventually set in, and Bush too acknowledged defeat. His doggedness, however, had won him respect among Republican voters who thought that though Reagan was the party's first choice, Bush might not be a bad number two.

Reagan reached the same conclusion more slowly. He didn't like Bush at this point, and he thought Bush had weakened the party by prolonging the primary season. He flirted with Gerald Ford after a Palm Springs visit that was intended to demonstrate party unity turned into a lovefest. The two agreed that Carter must be defeated at all costs. Reagan apparently broached the idea of a Reagan-Ford ticket. Ford waved the gesture aside but didn't forget it.

The Republican convention, held in Detroit, was a coronation. The only issue that provided any drama was Reagan's choice of a running mate. Reporters got wind of what Reagan had said to Ford, who remembered he liked the limelight. Erstwhile members of the Ford administration perked up. "All the old Ford guys wanted to make it happen," James Baker recollected. "They wanted their old jobs back." Ford was invited to open the convention, and he did so in a speech that startled observers with its energy and its promise that Jerry Ford was ready to take the field again.

Reagan again offered Ford the vice presidential slot. Ford again declined, but less decisively than before. Reagan grew optimistic about what reporters were calling the "dream ticket." Several of his advisers, however, thought it was a terrible idea. How would a former president adjust to being the nonentity vice presidents were supposed to be? What if he resisted?

Ford suggested he might resist. He told Walter Cronkite of CBS News he would not be a mere "figurehead" as vice president. "I have to go there with the belief that I will play a meaningful role across the board in the basic and the crucial and the important decisions that have to be made in a four-year period," Ford said.

Reagan and Michael Deaver watched the Ford interview together. "As I had done so many times in the years (now fourteen of them) that had brought us there," Deaver recalled, "I studied the face of the man next to me." Ford's remarks snapped Reagan out of his fantasy about a dream ticket. "He was stunned. His eyes sparked. He said, 'This has gone too far.'" Reagan knew he couldn't give away some of the responsibilities of the presidency without running afoul of the Constitution; more to the point, after all the effort he had expended getting this far, he wasn't about to share the presidency. The great stage of American politics was going to be his alone.

He realized the Ford interview might be interpreted as indicating that Ford had the number-two slot wrapped up. He didn't want to embarrass Ford, but in a hastily arranged private meeting he made clear that he couldn't agree to Ford's terms. Ford understood, and the almost-agreement was off.

Reagan turned at once to Bush. He had to hurry lest the media dwell on the deal that fell through. He called Bush and asked him two questions, one broad and the other specific. "Can you support my policy positions?" Bush said he could. "Can you support my position on abortion?" Reagan had come to regret his role in liberalizing California's abortion law, and he now took a conservative, restrictive line. He wanted to be sure

Bush did too. Bush again said yes. Reagan thereupon offered Bush the vice presidential nomination. Bush accepted.

Reagan went to the convention hall. Nearly all the delegates expected him to announce that he had chosen Ford, and so they were flummoxed when he explained that this was not the case. "He and I have come to the conclusion, and he believes deeply, that he can be of more value as the former president campaigning his heart out, as he has promised to do, and not as a member of the ticket," Reagan said. Before the delegates could react, Reagan went on to say that instead of Ford he had chosen "a man we all know and a man who was a candidate, a man who has great experience in government, and a man who has told me that he can enthusiastically support the platform across the board." By the end of this description he hardly needed to add the name: George Bush.

The vice presidential candidate took the stage. "If anyone wants to know why Ronald Reagan is a winner," Bush said, "you can refer him to me. I'm an expert on the subject. He's a winner because he's our leader, because he has traveled the country and understands its people. His message is clear. His message is understood."

The next night Reagan reiterated that message. He hammered Carter and the Democrats for failing the people of America domestically and in foreign affairs. "The major issue of this campaign is the direct political, personal and moral responsibility of Democratic Party leadership—in the White House and in Congress—for this unprecedented calamity which has befallen us," Reagan said. "They tell us they have done the most that humanly could be done. They say that the United States has had its day in the sun; that our nation has passed its zenith. They expect you to tell your children that the American people no longer have the will to cope with their problems; that the future will be one of sacrifice and few opportunities. My fellow citizens, I utterly reject that view. The American people, the most generous on earth, who created the highest standard of living, are not going to accept the notion that we can only make a better world for others by moving backwards ourselves." Those who believed this lie should have no role in governing the nation. "I will not stand by and watch this great country destroy itself under mediocre leadership that drifts from one crisis to the next, eroding our national will and purpose."

Reagan painted an alternative vision. "I ask you to trust that American spirit which knows no ethnic, religious, social, political, regional or economic boundaries; the spirit that burned with zeal in the hearts of millions of immigrants from every corner of the earth who came here in search of freedom. Some say that spirit no longer exists. But I have seen it—I have felt it—all across the land; in the big cities, the small towns and in rural America. The American spirit is still there, ready to blaze into life if you and I are willing to do what has to be done." He pointed to the Pilgrims as examples of the American spirit. He cited the founding fathers and Abraham Lincoln. And he again drew on Franklin Roosevelt. "I believe that this generation of Americans has a rendezvous with destiny," he said. "The time is now, my fellow Americans, to recapture our destiny, to take it into our hands."

He concluded with a carefully considered ad-lib. "I have thought of something that is not part of my speech and I'm worried over whether I should do it," he said, gazing out over his audience. But he went ahead and brought God into the conversation. "Can we doubt that only a divine Providence placed this land, this island of freedom, here as a refuge for all those people in the world who yearn to breathe freely: Jews and Christians enduring persecution behind the Iron Curtain, the boat people of Southeast Asia, of Cuba and Haiti, the victims of drought and famine in Africa, the freedom fighters of Afghanistan and our own countrymen held in savage captivity." He paused and again looked out across the convention hall. "I'll confess that I've been a little afraid to suggest what I'm going to suggest—I'm more afraid not to—that we begin our crusade joined together in a moment of silent prayer." The hall fell duly silent. Then Reagan dismissed them with the sign-off that would become his trademark: "God bless America."

REAGAN REMEMBERED THAT Franklin Roosevelt had won the presidency in 1932 chiefly because he wasn't Herbert Hoover. He guessed that he himself would similarly benefit from not being Jimmy Carter. By mid-1980, Carter's position had become politically unsustainable. The misery index of unemployment plus inflation topped 21 percent in May and June and remained above 20 percent through the election. Considering that this was nearly as high as it had been in 1932 (when unemployment was higher than in 1980 but inflation was inconsequential—in fact, negative), Carter was doomed on economic grounds alone. The international situation merely made things worse. Soviet troops and aircraft brutalized Afghanistan, reinforcing the Republican message of Carter's early naïveté about the communists. The American hostages still languished in Tehran. Carter had authorized a rescue attempt during the spring, but the operation went badly awry, killing several U.S. servicemen and marking Carter as more inept than ever.

Yet Reagan wasn't good at playing to protect a lead. He overthought things and lost his spontaneity. And precisely because he was ahead, his slips received more scrutiny than they would have in an underdog. Addressing a convention of the Veterans of Foreign Wars, he described the American effort in Vietnam as a "noble cause." The veterans applauded, but Reagan's managers grimaced. They didn't disagree with the sentiment, but the comment led to a debate over the Vietnam War that distracted the media from Reagan's central message: that the economy was in shambles and that fixing it required a change in the White House. On another day some ill-considered words by Reagan appeared to link Carter to the Ku Klux Klan. Carter's side naturally protested, and Reagan was forced to apologize. At a convention of Christian evangelicals, Reagan was asked for his views on creationism, as opposed to evolution. He knew what the audience wanted to hear, and he said creationism should be taught in the schools. Again his handlers shuddered, although one put the incident in context. "The only good news for us at this time was that we were making so many blunders that reporters had to pick and choose which ones they would write about," this staffer said afterward. "'Creationism' made Reagan look like an idiot, but he got away with it."

POST–LABOR DAY OPINION polls showed the typical tightening of the race. By some tallies Carter pulled even with Reagan. But the polls were misleading, for Reagan retained his advantage in the states that would give him the electoral votes he required.

The two sides jockeyed for position regarding debates. John Anderson had bolted the Republican Party to run an independent campaign; potential voters unsatisfied with Carter but unattracted by Reagan gave Anderson just enough support to make his campaign viable. Carter's managers didn't want a three-way debate, for they believed that Anderson would siphon more votes from Carter than from Reagan. Reagan was canny enough to realize that his boffo performance in the Nashua debate couldn't be repeated; he consented to debate Anderson without Carter. Anderson was more articulate than Reagan, but Reagan didn't embarrass himself. And the experience afforded him sufficient confidence to accept Carter's one-on-one terms.

The Reagan-Carter debate occurred the week before the election.

Carter, as expected, showed himself to be a master of detail but deficient in personal appeal. Reagan was just the opposite. And where Carter had to defend the past, Reagan could promise the future. Carter had prepared for the debate by immersing himself in the issues, Reagan by considering one-liners and bons mots he might drop on his opponent. Reagan received an unexpected boost by the mysterious acquisition of a Carter briefing book. James Baker had been brought into the Reagan campaign along with Bush; the Californians around Reagan realized they needed the experience Baker commanded. "I was the only Republican who had run a presidential campaign and not gone to jail," Baker commented later, referring to the Watergate woes of the Nixon team. Baker's chief task was preparing Reagan for the debates; he later said he got the briefing book from William Casey, who had taken over as Reagan's campaign manager when John Sears alienated the rest of the team and was fired. Casey said he had no recollection of the book. "Casey was not telling the truth," Baker asserted in the aftermath. Baker nonetheless resisted taking a polygraph test to resolve the matter, as the media helpfully suggested. Casey had become director of the CIA and had a reputation for skulduggery. "I was scared," Baker admitted. "He could game the lie detector and I couldn't." No one was strapped to a machine, and neither party ever proved the other wrong, not least because the briefing book was not very important. Mostly news clippings, it revealed nothing crucial of Carter's strategy. "It wasn't worth the paper it was written on," Baker said.

Reagan had a more important advantage in the debate. "All you have to do is hold your own in these things, because nobody wins or loses these debates on points," Lyn Nofziger explained later. "They do it on perception. Since the press always thinks that Reagan is dumber than the other guy, just by holding his own, Reagan wins."

Reagan held his own on points, and he won on perception. The highlight of the evening came as Carter was chiding Reagan for being against national health insurance, as he had been against such worthy programs as Social Security and Medicare. One camera focused on Carter; another showed Reagan readying his reply. When Reagan's turn came, he smiled indulgently at the president and said, "There you go again." The remark didn't rebut Carter logically, but the audience in the Cleveland music hall laughed, and millions in the television audience concluded that Reagan was a much more appealing fellow than the humorless Carter.

Reagan rode the approval into his closing remarks. "Are you better off than you were four years ago?" he asked. "Is it easier for you to go and buy things in the stores than it was four years ago? Is there more or less unemployment in the country than there was four years ago? Is America as respected throughout the world as it was? Do you feel that our security is as safe, that we're as strong as we were four years ago?" The questions needed only to be asked for the answers to be plain. The appropriate response for voters was equally plain.

32

ONE THING ALONE worried Reagan's team as the election approached. William Casey and others feared that Carter would spring an "October surprise" by arranging the release of the Iran hostages. Casey established what the campaign's chief of staff, Edwin Meese, later called the "October surprise watch" to keep a lookout for signs of a breakthrough in the administration's negotiations with Tehran. Richard Allen, who headed the group, explained, "Our business was to react to what happened as the result of a resolution, a successful resolution of the hostage crisis."

The watch team spared no effort in imagining possible scenarios for a release and devising appropriate responses. On October 19 the team produced a confidential memo for Ed Meese declaring, "The Iranians know that the race is very close and that Carter will be susceptible to pressure in the next two weeks"—until the election. On the assumption that Carter might yield to the pressure, the team advised that Reagan be ready. "It is recommended that beginning now, up to the time the hostages are released, Governor Reagan's posture be to emphasize the following: 1) note that there are increasing signs that the hostages' release may be imminent. Greet this news cautiously, but favorably. Ronald Reagan should express his hopes and prayers that the hostages will be coming home soon, even if it is the day before the election. 2) Insist, though, that the U.S. not complete any deals or trades until all our people are home, and the conditions are made public. Add that we must be mindful of the long-range consequences of any arrangement we make." Such a posture would have two positive effects for the Reagan side. "1) If the hostages are actually released, it does not come as such a surprise. By generating the expectation that this will occur, we could dull somewhat the outpouring of enthusiasm to be expected from the hostages' return. 2) If the hostages are not released before the election, Carter faces a heightened credibility problem because of the greater expectation of their release."

But the negotiations stalled, and as the election drew nearer, the Reagan team breathed more easily. Bill Casey urged the candidate to keep quiet about the hostages. Speaking of Carter, Casey wrote to Reagan and Meese two days before the election, "I believe he will be widely perceived as having engaged in a desperate last attempt to manipulate the hostages again for political benefit and to have once more bungled it. If this analysis is correct, we should say very little and leave it that way." Upon the rest of the campaign staff, Casey imposed a gag order. "Precautions must be taken to make sure nothing is attributed to our campaign organization that could in any way be said to jeopardize the possibility of securing the release of the hostages," he wrote. "That means that nobody, except those who are specifically authorized, express opinions to the media from now until Election Day."

Casey might have had particular reason for his sensitivity to allegations that the campaign was trying to delay the release of the hostages. He soon acquired a reputation for letting little stand in the way of accomplishing ends he deemed worthy and for taking an activist, no-holds-barred approach to covert operations. With others on the Reagan side, Casey considered Carter a disaster as president. It would not have been out of character for him to seek to stall the release of the hostages until after the election so that Carter would be retired to Georgia.

This was precisely what certain Carter supporters later alleged, most pointedly after the Iran-contra scandal revealed that the modus operandi of Reagan's administration included methods that couldn't stand public scrutiny. The strongest indictment came from Gary Sick, a member of Carter's National Security Council staff who was closely involved in the hostage negotiations. In a 1991 book Sick asserted that Casey had met with persons with ties to the Iranian government and offered arms aid if the hostages were held until after the election.

The assertion was explosive, suggesting violations of the Logan Act, the eighteenth-century law that forbids private citizens to engage in diplomacy, as well as the prolonging of the misery and jeopardy of the American hostages. Several of the hostages demanded a congressional investigation, and though most Republicans denounced the charges as baseless and politically driven, the Senate and the House conducted inquiries.

The Senate went first. Its investigation was hampered by the inability of the appointed special counsel to question Casey, who had died by then, or Reagan, who in retirement declined to testify. It was also hindered by the counsel's limited subpoena power and the reluctance of Senate Republicans and the presidential administration of George Bush to cooperate.

Even so, the investigation uncovered evidence, albeit circumstantial, that lent plausibility to the allegations. The counsel sought records from Casey's widow and daughter that appeared likely to bear on the subject. The two women produced some documents, but others that appeared to be critical were missing, including a file labeled "Hostages," a schedule book for 1980, and some loose-leaf calendar pages for the period when Casey's alleged meeting, in Madrid, with the Iranian middlemen was said to have occurred. Casey's passport, which should have recorded his travels, was also missing. Eventually, the schedule book surfaced along with some of the loose-leaf pages, but other pages remained unaccounted for.

The investigation's authority and money ran out with many questions still unanswered. Yet the investigators concluded that the existing evidence did not support the allegation that the Reagan campaign had struck a deal with the Iranian government to delay the release of the hostages. In fact, the existing evidence pointed in the opposite direction. "The great weight of the evidence is that there was no such deal," the report of the Senate committee declared. The report labeled as "wholly unreliable" the testimony of the principal witnesses to the bargain. "Their claims regarding alleged secret meetings are riddled with inconsistencies, and have been contradicted by irrefutable documentary evidence as well as by the testimony of vastly more credible witnesses."

But the report didn't let Casey off the hook. "The totality of the evidence does suggest that Casey was 'fishing in troubled waters'"—the report here quoted a witness—"and that he conducted informal, clandestine, and potentially dangerous efforts on behalf of the Reagan campaign to gather intelligence on the volatile and unpredictable course of the hostage negotiations between the Carter Administration and Iran." The report also chided Casey's heirs, saying that their refusal to cooperate with the investigation suggested "a willful effort to prevent Special Counsel from getting timely access to the materials."

A House task force examining what had come to be called the "October Surprise" question—despite the absence of such a surprise—drew the same general conclusion the Senate panel did. Chairman Lee Hamilton, a Democrat of Indiana, reiterated the gravity of the allegations against Casey and the Reagan campaign: "If true, these extraordinarily serious claims would have cast doubt on the legitimacy of the Reagan Presidency." He added, "If false, it would have been unfair to allow this cloud to linger over the reputations of those accused of being involved." Hamilton reported that the task force he headed had concluded that the claims were not true. "There was virtually no credible evidence to support the accusation. Specifically, we found little or no credible evidence of communications between the 1980 Reagan campaign and the Government of Iran and no credible evidence that the campaign tried to delay the hostages' release." Hamilton acknowledged that some important evidence remained missing. "The task force did not locate Mr. Casey's 1980 passport, and one of the three Casey 1980 calendars the task force did obtain—a loose-leaf version—was missing a few crucial pages." But the lacuna was not fatal to the investigation. "The absence of these materials did not prevent us from determining the whereabouts of Mr. Casey and others on dates when meetings were claimed to have occurred." Hamilton declared the case closed: "The overwhelming weight of the evidence should put the controversy to rest after all."

The controversy did rest for a time, but it didn't die. New evidence sporadically rekindled interest. In 1996 author Douglas Brinkley, at work on a book about Jimmy Carter as former president, told a conference of diplomatic historians about a comment made to Carter by Yasser Arafat earlier that year. Carter had traveled to Gaza City to meet with Arafat; Brinkley tagged along. "Mr. President, there is something I want to tell you," Arafat said, according to Brinkley. "You should know that in 1980 the Republicans approached me with an arms deal if I could arrange to keep the hostages in Iran until after the election." Arafat looked for a reaction from Carter, but Carter merely listened. "I want you to know that I turned them down," Arafat said. Brinkley, speaking in his own voice to the historians' group, added, "Arafat kept detailed records, which should soon be made public."

The records Brinkley referred to never became public. Nor did Carter display interest in seeing them. Asked later about Arafat's statement, Brinkley said Carter seemed not to want to hear more. Brinkley attributed the lack of interest to Carter's desire to focus on Middle East peace in 1996 and not on what had happened in 1980.

Other records, however, did become public. In 2011 the presidential library of George (H. W.) Bush, responding to Freedom of Information

Act requests, released documents relating to the earlier Senate and House investigations of the October Surprise affair. The documents reflected a debate within the Bush administration as to how fully it should cooperate with the investigations. The Bush team worried that the mere raising of the October Surprise issue would damage Bush's 1992 reelection chances, in that some of the allegations asserted a Bush role in contacts with the Iranians, in particular at a meeting in Paris in October 1980. The administration preferred that the investigations be kept small and short. But it couldn't stonewall entirely. Bush indignantly denied the allegations that touched him. "I can categorically assure you that I never was in Paris as claimed by the rumormongers," he wrote to one of the former hostages. "I can also categorically assure you that I have no information direct or indirect of any contact with Iranians relating to this hostage question." He said the same thing to reporters. And the administration turned over to the investigators materials corroborating Bush's denial.

But the administration declined to share evidence indicating that William Casey had been in Madrid at the time of the alleged meeting between Casey and the Iranian contacts. A memorandum for the record by White House associate counsel Paul Beach recounted a conversation between Beach and Edwin Williamson of the State Department. Williamson explained that the State Department was gathering relevant materials and deciding what to turn over to the investigators. "In this regard," Beach wrote, "Ed mentioned only a cable from the Madrid embassy indicating that Bill Casey was in town, for purposes unknown."

The Beach memorandum, when released, surprised Lee Hamilton, by then retired. Hamilton condemned the Bush White House for withholding the evidence. "If the White House knew that Casey was there, they certainly should have shared it with us." Hamilton stopped short of saying that the new evidence proved the October Surprise allegations, but he reiterated the importance of Casey's whereabouts to the task force's dismissal of the charges. "We found no evidence to confirm Casey's trip to Madrid," he told journalist Robert Parry. "We couldn't show that." And one reason they couldn't was that the Bush White House was withholding evidence. "The White House did not notify us that he did make the trip. Should they have passed that on to us? They should have because they knew we were interested in that."

Other evidence continued to surface. In 2013, Ben Barnes, a former lieutenant governor of Texas, told the present author he had accompanied former Texas governor John Connally on a trip to the Middle East in the summer of 1980. Connally had made a run for the Republican nomination that year, but after a slow start he dropped out of the race, endorsing Reagan over Connally's Texas rival George Bush. Barnes had handled fund-raising for the Connally campaign. Connally, who had served as Treasury secretary under Richard Nixon and was clearly hoping for an important post in a Reagan administration, was then associated with the Houston-based law firm of Vinson & Elkins, and the purpose of the trip was described for the firm's records as "personal business for private interests." But public business was in prospect. Recommendations by Nixon preceded Connally to the Middle East. "I am sure that you will find a talk with him most interesting in view of his enormous experience in government and the likelihood (I hope!) that he will play a major role in the Reagan administration," Nixon wrote to one foreign interlocutor.

Early in the journey, Connally seems to have spoken by phone with Reagan. A memo to Connally by an aide bore the subject line "Governor Reagan" and read, "Nancy Reagan called—they are at ranch. He wants to talk to you about being in on strategy meetings." Connally would certainly have returned the call, but just what was said in the conversation is unknown.

Barnes volunteered to the author that the trip had a connection to the American hostages in Iran. Barnes said Connally passed word to the government officials he met with in Israel and several Arab countries that the release of the hostages before the November election would "not be helpful" to the Reagan campaign. When asked by the author whether this message had come from William Casey, Barnes said he wasn't told and hadn't inquired.

More than three decades after the fact, the October Surprise story remained puzzling. The evidence demonstrated conclusively that Casey and the campaign team were very worried that Carter would secure the release of the hostages ahead of the election. The evidence demonstrated with equal clarity that the campaign was preparing to make a release politically more difficult by intimating that Carter was opportunistically cutting a deal with the hostage holders. The evidence indicated that Casey was dropping hints, perhaps even making promises, that a Reagan administration would look favorably on those governments and individuals who had helped Reagan win election. And the evidence suggested (in the case of the missing passport and calendar pages) and demonstrated (in the case of the Bush White House memo) that interested parties had consciously covered up pertinent information.

What none of the evidence, with the possible exception of a Reagan-Connally phone call, indicated or even hinted was that Reagan himself had anything directly to do with the efforts made on his behalf. He flatly denied having been involved, calling the allegations "absolute fiction." By the time the story emerged, Reagan's detached style of management had become famous—notorious, as it related to the Iran-contra affair. And Casey's obsession with secrecy was just as well-known. Between Reagan's detachment and Casey's secrecy, Reagan's denial was entirely believable.

All the same, Reagan was responsible for what was done by his campaign to get him elected. If his campaign took measures that offended ethics and even the law, any blame ultimately rested with him.

But his wouldn't have been the first campaign to stray, if stray it did. And in any event, the efforts to prevent an October surprise were almost certainly superfluous. The Iranians liked Jimmy Carter less in October 1980 than ever. Iraq had just invaded Iran, and Iranian leaders thought Carter was behind the invasion. They had no reason to give him the satisfaction of winning the hostages' freedom, especially if it meant he might thereby win the American election. To the Iranian leaders, Carter was a known and detested quantity. Reagan was an unknown quantity, but he couldn't be worse than Carter. Whether or not Reagan's campaign had promised weapons in exchange for hostages, the Iranians determined to wait Carter out.

IN THE ABSENCE of an October surprise, November was predictable. Americans cast their ballots on November 4 and awarded Reagan an overwhelming victory. He beat Carter by more than eight million votes, winning 51 percent of the popular vote to Carter's 41 percent (and Anderson's 7 percent). Reagan carried forty-four states to Carter's six and tallied 489 electoral votes to Carter's 49.

Reagan watched the returns in the house he and Nancy had purchased in Pacific Palisades. Carter telephoned him there to concede the election. Reagan drove to the Century Plaza Hotel to address his supporters. "You know," he said, "Abe Lincoln, the day after his election to the presidency, gathered in his office the newsmen who had been covering his campaign, and he said to them, 'Well, boys, your troubles are over now, but mine have just begun.'" Reagan said he thought he knew how Lincoln felt. "Lincoln may have been concerned in the troubled times in which he became president, but I don't think he was afraid. He was ready to confront the problems and the troubles of a still youthful country, determined to seize the historic opportunity to change things." Reagan said he shared the feeling and the hope. "I am not frightened by what lies ahead, and I don't believe the American people are frightened by what lies ahead. Together, we're going to do what has to be done."

PART FOUR

HEROIC DREAMS

1980–1983

33

Ames Baker was nothing if not flexible. Having led two campaigns to deny Reagan the Republican nomination, he had jumped to the winning side after the failure of the second and helped Reagan become president. And two days after Reagan beat Carter, Baker was tapped to run Reagan's White House.

Baker's appointment as chief of staff vexed some of those who had battled longer at Reagan's side. Edwin Meese thought he should have the job. Meese had been with Reagan since the 1960s, serving variously as legal adviser to the governor, executive secretary, and chief of staff. Meese was smart, hardworking, and astute on policy, and he was a committed conservative. But he wasn't much for organization. "He's got a briefcase that has never been emptied," Lyn Nofziger suggested decades later. "I suppose you go to the bottom of it, and you can find stuff back in 1967–8." Nor was he as stern as a chief of staff often had to be. "It's a good thing Ed was not born a woman because he can't say no," Nofziger continued. "I mean that in the nicest way. Ed will do anything in the world for you. He is one of the sweetest, nicest men in the whole damn world. But when you can't say no, you take on more things than you can handle." And he simply liked to do things himself. "He's not a very good distributor of jobs and missions." Stuart Spencer agreed. Spencer was a pioneer of political consulting, one of the first professional campaign managers. No one besides Reagan was more responsible for Reagan's victories. Spencer knew Meese well. "There was absolutely nothing wrong with Ed Meese except he couldn't organize a two-car funeral," he said. "You went in his desk and the papers were here, there, down on the floor, across the room. One of the jobs of a chief of staff is to make the paper move in the White House and go to the right corners and the right boxes. It's a terrible job. We knew that Ed couldn't do that."

He might have gotten the job anyway. Reagan didn't like to disappoint people, especially those who had worked their hearts out for him. And he felt more comfortable philosophically with Meese than with anyone else. "If you were sitting in this room and you asked Ed about an issue," Spencer later told an interviewer, "he could give you the precise answer that Ronald Reagan would give you. He totally understood Ronald Reagan ideologically, because they're so much alike ideologically."

But Michael Deaver, who was closer to the Reagans personally than anyone else, and Spencer thought Meese would serve the president better in another position. For chief of staff they wanted someone sterner and better organized. They also wanted someone better versed in the ways of Washington. None of the longtime Reagan loyalists qualified; they were Californians through and through. Some of them saw this as their strength: they hadn't been infected by the capital's liberal culture. But Deaver and Spencer relied on Reagan's own resistance to the noxious airs off the Potomac, and they urged the president-elect to choose Baker as chief of staff. Deaver broached the subject with Reagan, who expressed surprise that the question of who should be chief of staff even came up. "I've always assumed Ed Meese would fill that," Reagan said. Deaver nodded that he understood, before observing, "Ed may be more valuable in another role. As chief of staff, you need to think about someone who knows Washington, knows the way the town works. We're about to embark on something, Governor, that we don't know a lot about." Reagan asked him if he had anyone in mind. "Yes," Deaver responded, "Jim Baker." Reagan repeated the name. "Jim Baker," he said. "That's an interesting thought."

Spencer remembered things differently. According to him, he and Deaver agreed that Spencer should raise the matter of staff chief with Reagan and Nancy. "Everyone assumed that Ed Meese was going to be chief of staff," Spencer recalled. "I thought, 'This can't be. I'll give it my shot.'" He went to speak to the Reagans. "I brought up Ed Meese. Before I said one word, both the Reagans said, 'Oh no, not Ed.' They understood. They wanted Ed around, and they wanted Ed to do something, but they understood this single organizational problem that he had."

Baker himself credited the appointment to Nancy Reagan. "She was the reason I was there," Baker said. Nancy knew Meese's strengths and liabilities; more important, she knew her husband's. She had utter faith in Reagan's ability to steer a true course philosophically, but she judged he needed help avoiding the shoals of Washington. Baker was just the man for the job.

Whoever first raised the subject, Reagan agreed that Baker made the most sense. But the appointment didn't sit well with the loyalists. Lyn Nofziger distrusted Baker from the start. "The President is elected to do certain things," Nofziger said later. "He has made certain promises, certain commitments. He has a certain philosophy of government. If you hire people who don't believe that, and who at best are not going to work very hard for it and at worst are going to work against it, then you're hurting. You're hurting the guy you came to serve." Baker was no conservative, as his preference for Ford and then Bush over Reagan had demonstrated. How could he serve a president committed to conservative change? Nofziger considered Baker an unreliable opportunist. "Jim Baker was there for Jim Baker," Nofziger said. He added, "Jim is a very competent individual. I would never say that he's dumb or anything else. But I just think he's basically dishonest."

Baker recognized the animus against him. But he considered it foolish and counterproductive to the new administration's goals. And it didn't bother him, because it wasn't shared at the top. "President Reagan understood what many of his followers did not: that it's more important for the chief of staff to be competent and loyal than to be a so-called true believer," he said, adding parenthetically, "I had more faith in his ideas than I was given credit for, and that faith grew stronger over the years." Reagan had another insight, Baker said. "He also understood that one of the most important tasks of a White House chief of staff is to look at policy questions through a political prism. After watching me at work in 1976 and 1980, he apparently believed I could do this."

BAKER'S DEPUTY WAS Deaver, chosen for his loyalty to Reagan and, no less important, to Nancy. "Of all the advisers who have worked for my husband over the years, I was closest of all to Mike, who was my link to the West Wing," Nancy wrote. "Ronnie and I go way back with Mike, who served as Ronnie's deputy executive secretary during the Sacramento years. From the very start, the three of us hit it off. By the time he came into the White House, he really knew Ronnie and understood when to approach him, and how. Mike was never afraid to bring Ronnie the bad news, or to tell him when he thought he was wrong."

Mostly Deaver thought Reagan was right, if not necessarily simple to fathom. "At times, Ronald Reagan has been very much a puzzle to me," he wrote later. "I had never known anyone so unable to deal with close personal conflict. When problems arose related to the family, or with the personnel in his office, Nancy had to carry the load. Literally, it was through working with Nancy that I came to know her husband." Deaver took charge of what he and others on the staff called the "Mommy watch." He remarked, "I probably found the phrase more amusing than Nancy did. She might have been upset, if she thought it was true, this suggestion that anyone needed to be assigned the job of humoring her."

Yet humoring Nancy was the way to handle her husband. "Ronnie Reagan had sort of glided through life, and Nancy's role was to protect him," Deaver said. "She accepted almost total responsibility for their family and home, and at the same time remained his closest adviser in public life." Deaver had watched other wives of famous and powerful men, but Nancy was something special. "It's not just that she knows or understands her husband as no one else does. Most wives do, or think they do. She has made him her career, and the White House did not change or enlarge her methods or motives. For as long as I have known them, she has used her persuasion with care, knowing when and how hard to apply the pressure. If he resists, she will back off and return to that issue at another moment."

Nancy's agenda was her husband, not politics or policy. But protecting and promoting her husband often had political and policy implications. "She has not gotten involved at all, it should be noted, unless there is a controversy around him, or he needs to be convinced that an action is unavoidable," Deaver said. "She knows you cannot barge in and tell him he has to fire Dick Allen or James Watt or Don Regan; that someone he likes has lost his effectiveness or has ill served him. She will wage a quiet campaign, planting a thought, recruiting others of us to push it along, making a case: Foreign policy will be hurt, our allies will be let down." In her quiet manner she weighed in on some major issues. "She lobbied the president to soften his line on the Soviet Union; to reduce military spending and not to push Star Wars at the expense of the poor and dispossessed. She favored a diplomatic solution in Nicaragua and opposed his trip to Bitburg." Her methods didn't always work, but they often did—and for good reason, Deaver said. "Nancy wins most of the time. When she does, it is not by wearing him down but by usually being on the right side of an issue."

ED MEESE HAD to settle for the post of counselor to the president. He wasn't at all happy. "Ed reacted as I would have expected Ed to react," Stuart Spencer observed. "He was in a little bit of shock about this decision." The job of White House counsel let Meese weigh in on matters of policy, and Reagan eased the blow by promoting that job to cabinet rank, giving Meese a seat at the administration's head table. But a seat at the table wasn't the same as an office next door to the Oval Office. Meese resented James Baker's sudden importance, and he immediately challenged the chief of staff. "I don't know what the term is: fight back," Spencer remarked. "He was going to protect his property."

Baker took his cue from Reagan. "I want you to make it right with Ed," Reagan told Baker. Baker tried to do so but without yielding any ground. Being a lawyer, and knowing that Meese was a lawyer, he drafted what amounted to a contract delineating their responsibilities. Tactfully, or tactically, he listed Meese's first: "Counselor to the President for Policy (with cabinet rank). Member Super Cabinet Executive Committee (in absence of the President and Vice President preside over meetings). Participate as a principal in all meetings of full Cabinet. Coordination and supervision of responsibilities of the Secretary to the Cabinet. Coordination and supervision of work of the Domestic Policy Staff and the National Security Council. With Baker coordination and supervision of work of OMB, CEA, Trade Rep and S&T. Participation as a principal in all policy group meetings."

Baker's responsibilities, per this memo, were seemingly more modest. He claimed nothing on the foreign policy side, leaving that large part of the president's portfolio to Meese and the National Security Council. Yet he insisted on "hiring and firing authority over all elements of White House staff" and "coordination and control of all in and out paper flow to the President and of presidential schedule and appointments." And he would "operate from office customarily utilized by Chief of Staff."

Meese was suspicious. He feared that Baker's proximity to the Oval Office would work to his—Meese's—disadvantage. He insisted that Baker write in a clause at the bottom of his side of the memo: "Attend any meeting which President attends—with his consent." Baker agreed—and wrote the same clause on his own side.

Baker was pleased with the pact. "You've got the policy; I'll just make the trains run on time," he told Meese. But he knew that running the trains was a prerequisite of implementing policy. The memo of understanding didn't exactly amount to a schedule of departures, but it might prevent wrecks. "It was a good, lawyerly way to mark our territory at the beginning," Baker recalled. "That way, we could spend our time working together for the president, each on his own portfolio, rather than quarreling over who was on first."

To reporters Baker spun the arrangement as best for the president. "Who's boss?" one reporter asked. "You or Meese?"

"Ronald Reagan is the boss," Baker answered. "Ed Meese and I are to serve him in complementary capacities."

Meese adopted the same line, less happily. "The president liked the issues brought before him," Meese later recalled. The divergent opinions among the "troika," as the Baker-Deaver-Meese arrangement was called, ensured that the president heard all sides of important arguments. Meese acknowledged that the differences gave rise to friction. But he attributed these to honest disagreements over policy. "At the outset, I think, the President was well served by such differences."

Others close to Reagan thought the friction was personal. "It was primarily because Baker wanted to be *numero uno*," Lyn Nofziger declared. "Anything he could do to move Meese to one side or cut him down, he would do. I don't think there was much in the way of policy. I think it was just Jim Baker wanting to control the place, and Meese was there as the guy who'd been closest to Reagan."

Baker agreed with Meese that the troika formula served its purpose— that is, Reagan's purpose. "It really worked well for the president," Baker remembered. "He got the benefit of all sides." But the division of responsibilities took a toll on the dividers. "It was tough. It was very difficult."

BEYOND THE WHITE House troika, Reagan had to construct a cabinet. The secretary of state is the senior cabinet member and has often been the most important of a president's picks. It was not so important under Reagan, who had spent a decade decrying the diplomacy of détente and had no desire to restore the State Department to the influence it wielded under détente architect Henry Kissinger. Reagan's choice for secretary of state was Alexander Haig, the holder of perhaps the most impressive résumé in American government at the time. Haig was an army man; he had served with Douglas MacArthur in the Korean War and been decorated for valor in Vietnam. He worked in the Nixon White House, rising to chief of staff amid the chaos of Watergate. Returning to the army, he headed NATO forces in Europe. Reagan intended a muscular form of diplomacy; having General Haig at State sent the right flexing signals.

More important than State, in Reagan's estimate, was the Defense Department. Jimmy Carter had stolen some of Reagan's thunder by requesting and receiving a large boost in defense spending during his last year in office, but Reagan intended to continue and accelerate the expansion. He did *not* intend to start any wars; hence substantial military experience, such as Haig's, was not a requirement at Defense. More essential was facility with numbers and budgets. Reagan knew just the person. Caspar—"Cap"—Weinberger had been Reagan's budget director in Sacramento before heading Nixon's Office of Management and Budget and then the Department of Health, Education, and Welfare. At HEW he acquired the sobriquet "Cap the Knife" for his willingness to slice social spending. In Reagan's Pentagon his mission was just the opposite: to spend more money, a great deal more. But his reputation for wielding a sharp pencil provided preemptive cover against allegations of wastefulness in what would be the biggest defense buildup in American history.

Reagan hoped to make cuts in most other areas of government besides defense, and he aimed to start by cutting taxes. The Treasury Department oversees federal taxes, and Reagan wanted someone reliable there. Nixon recommended William Simon, who had held the post under him and then Ford. But Simon wasn't thrilled about a second tour unless he received more authority than Reagan wanted to give him. So Reagan turned to Wall Street, in the belief that no one knew more about money than the masters of finance. Donald Regan headed Merrill Lynch, and though Reagan knew him not at all, he seemed a good bet for the job initially held by Alexander Hamilton, the founder of Wall Street's oldest bank and every Republican's model of what a Treasury secretary ought to be.

The Office of Management and Budget resided below the cabinet departments in seniority, but its director had more influence on the course of government than most cabinet secretaries. To head OMB, Reagan took a chance on a whiz kid half his age. David Stockman was a congressman from Michigan, an ardent fiscal conservative, and conspicuously brilliant. "He was one of the smartest people I've ever known," said Phil Gramm, a Stockman colleague from Congress and his partner in the budget wars of the Reagan years. James Baker agreed. "He was extraordinarily talented,"

Baker said of Stockman. Stockman had stood in for Jimmy Carter in Reagan's debate preparations, and he had given Reagan all he could handle. Reagan now reasoned that Stockman would be equally effective battling the opponents of smaller government. He waved aside worries that Stockman was too young and full of himself, and he named him head of OMB.

34

OST DEPARTMENTS AND agencies of the federal government anticipated the approach of Ronald Reagan with trepi-
dation. For decades Reagan had railed against the bloated
federal bureaucracy, and after his landslide victory at the polls, the bureaucrats had cause for concern.

A few parts of the government, however, hoped to benefit. The
Defense Department anticipated bigger budgets and all the leverage and
perks more money entailed. But it was the CIA that breathed the largest
sigh of relief at the election results. After the Church Committee had
chastised the agency for its illegal, unsavory, and embarrassing activities, Jimmy Carter took the opportunity to clean house. He appointed
Stansfield Turner, a former admiral and no enthusiast of the clandestine
service, to head the agency. In what came to be called the "Halloween
massacre," Turner fired hundreds of senior officers and put the fear of
termination into the rest. The Turner regime coincided with additional
revelations, some by disaffected former agents, of CIA misdeeds. Frank
Snepp detailed the dismal last days of America's involvement in Vietnam,
in the process baring secrets even Turner wanted to keep. The agency
tried to silence Snepp, but its efforts merely stirred media interest in what
he had to say. The CIA, the celebrity child of the early Cold War, became
an object of popular horror and derision: horror for the assassination plots
and the dirty tricks against Americans, derision for its inability to succeed in those plots and to keep its own secrets. Morale at the agency's
headquarters in Langley, Virginia, plumbed depths never touched before.

Reagan's election promised to reverse the trend. Agency officials
knew he had defended them against the Church Committee; some of the

older ones recalled his cooperation with the FBI and the House Committee on Un-American Activities against communists in Hollywood in the
1940s and 1950s. They gained additional reason to expect greater sympathy for their mission when Reagan chose one of their own, or at least one
after their own hearts, to head the agency. William Casey had worked
with the OSS, the CIA's predecessor, running spies in Europe during
World War II, and he believed, as Reagan did, that intelligence operations were essential to the conduct of war and diplomacy. He was clearly
smart, having built a successful New York law practice and chaired the
Securities and Exchange Commission. But no one could tell *how* smart
he was, for his habit of mumbling made it impossible for most people to
figure out what he was saying. As the manager of Reagan's successful
campaign, Casey was in a position to get almost any office he requested.
He wanted the State Department. "It would cap off an extraordinary,
illustrious career," Martin Anderson observed. Anderson had worked in
the Nixon White House before concluding that Reagan was the future
of the Republican Party; he advised candidate Reagan on policy during
the 1976 and 1980 campaigns and President Reagan on policy starting in
January 1981. Anderson knew Casey from work in government and on the
campaign, and he thought him well suited to being secretary of state. "His
background and experience, his demonstrated ability to manage, and his
brilliant, crafty mind easily qualified him for the job." But others around
Reagan thought Casey's mumbling and general demeanor and appearance made him a poor choice to be America's top diplomat. "He was tall,
somewhat stoop-shouldered, bald with wisps of white hair on the sides
and back," wrote Robert Gates, who would serve as Casey's deputy at the
CIA. "He had a receding chin, large lips, a crooked smile, and piercing
eyes. He dressed expensively and formally. Even on weekends, when he
would come in to the office, he almost always wore a jacket and tie. His
shoes were always well-polished. With all that, he usually looked as if he
had just concluded an all-night plane trip. When he walked, it looked
like a committee of bones and muscles all trying to amble more or less in
the same direction." Casey elicited a negative reaction in many of those
he met, including legislators. Senator Howard Baker of Tennessee sat in
on a Casey briefing marked by the usual mumbling. Reagan turned to
the senator and said, "You know, I've never been able to understand Bill."
"Mr. President," Howard Baker replied, "that's the scariest thing I've ever
heard."

So the State Department went to Al Haig, whose mien was as impressive as his résumé, and Casey had to settle for the CIA. "God, he must have been bitter," Martin Anderson remarked. "Most people seemed to view Casey's appointment to the CIA as a juicy political plum"—a chance for the aging Wall Streeter to relive his youth by playing spy once again. Casey didn't interpret his appointment this way at all, Anderson said. He saw the CIA as a consolation prize. "It was a bitter, vengeful old man who grudgingly accepted the job as the best he could get at the time."

Casey determined to make the most of his job. "Bill Casey came to CIA primarily to wage war against the Soviet Union," Robert Gates remarked. Casey viewed the 1980s through his experience during the 1940s, with Russia replacing Germany as America's mortal foe. "Casey wanted information and analysis that provoked action," Gates observed. "Not for him assessments that were simply 'interesting' or educational. He wanted information that would help target clandestine operations better, or be useful for U.S. propaganda, or assist military operations, or put ammunition in the hands of negotiators. For Casey, the United States and CIA were at war, just like when he was young and in the OSS."

WARS REQUIRE WAR plans. The CIA readied Reagan for overseeing intelligence and foreign affairs by bringing the president-elect up to speed on the state of the world. Just days after the election, agency officials inquired of Reagan's staff as to his preferences in intelligence. Stansfield Turner invited Casey and Ed Meese, along with Richard Allen, Reagan's choice for national security adviser, to his office in downtown Washington. Turner said the agency wished to tailor the president's daily briefing (PDB, in CIA-speak) to make it most useful to President Reagan. "The DCI"—Director of Central Intelligence Turner—"showed our visitors the PDB and described its function, making the point that the PDB is done to the President's specifications and we would hope to use the period between now and inauguration to determine how the President-elect would like it done," the note taker for the meeting recorded. "The only comment made"—by the Reagan team—"was that a larger typeface would probably be in order."

Turner offered to brief Reagan during the coming weeks on the world's trouble spots, both when the president-elect was in Washington and when he was in California. The latter location presented certain difficulties, as there were no secure communications facilities near the Reagan ranch, and the PDB had to be very carefully guarded. But the agency would work something out.

Turner broached the issue of funding for the CIA. Meese and the others were receptive. "Meese asked that we prepare our 'wish list' for the new Administration," the note taker wrote. Turner responded by inviting the Reagan team to Langley to meet with the rest of the agency leadership. They said they would be happy to do so, time permitting.

Agency officials spent the next week preparing for their first session with Reagan, which took place in a meeting room across the street from the White House. George Bush accompanied Reagan, to the delight of the CIA officials, who remembered Bush fondly for his stint as agency director in the mid-1970s. Meese, Allen, and Casey were also present, as was James Baker. Turner opened the meeting with a mission description of the CIA and the other branches of the intelligence community. He segued to conditions in the parts of the world that posed current challenges to American policy: the two-month-old war between Iraq and Iran, the year-old Soviet war in Afghanistan, the ongoing Iranian revolution. He spoke on possible ramifications of these developments for Saudi Arabia, Israel, and the rest of the Middle East.

A second meeting was convened the next day. At this session Turner and his aides briefed Reagan, Bush, and the others on Poland, where the Solidarity trade union movement had launched a surprisingly successful campaign of opposition to the Polish government; Nicaragua, where the ruling Sandinistas were driving the country toward the left; and El Salvador, where a conservative government was struggling to forestall a Sandinista-style revolution. Turner also discussed the military balance between NATO and the Warsaw Pact countries. He intended to talk about the condition of the Soviet economy, but demands on Reagan's time cut the meeting short.

Turner was pleased with the sessions. "The briefings in general went well," his assistant recorded. "There were a number of questions, mostly from Ambassador Bush and Mr. Allen. Governor Reagan's questions went largely in the direction of 'what can we do about it?'"

Reagan received another briefing in December. Turner again conducted the session. Meese, Casey, and Allen once more accompanied Reagan, though Bush did not. The lead topic this time was the Soviet economy. For decades the CIA had been monitoring the economic performance of the Soviet Union. During the 1950s the communist model appeared to be working reasonably well, at least in terms of delivering overall economic growth. Soviet growth outstripped American and made plausible the Kremlin's claims to newly independent countries that the communist road was the one that led to the future. Lately, however, the Soviet economy had faltered and its growth curve flattened. "Economic prospects are gloomier and policy choices more difficult than at any time since Stalin's death," agency analysts wrote in a report that informed the briefing Reagan received. Industry was lagging, and agriculture had suffered consecutive failures. "Moscow's basic problem is that the formula for growth used over the past 25 years—maximum inputs of labor and investment—no longer works."

The CIA's chief interest in this was that the stagnant Soviet economy constrained Moscow's choices in foreign policy. The Soviet hold on Eastern Europe was only partly military; Soviet economic aid played a large role as well. Aid would come harder for the Kremlin in the future, and Soviet influence might diminish. Of greater direct importance to the United States, the economic troubles limited Moscow's ability to keep up with America in the arms race. Soviet leaders might devote a larger share of national production to defense, but they would have to steal from the consumer sector to do so. This would antagonize ordinary citizens. Soviet citizens couldn't vote, at least not meaningfully, but they could register their unhappiness in other ways. "Worker morale and productivity could drop sharply, further jeopardizing Moscow's efforts to maintain even low rates of economic growth."

The CIA analysts predicted no major policy shifts by the Kremlin during the next few years. But in the longer term the status quo was unsustainable. "Soviet economic problems are too severe." By the mid- to late 1980s the Kremlin would be forced to choose between two alternatives. The first was more of the painful same. "Moscow could impose more austerity at home to support military spending. Consumption would suffer greatly." The Kremlin would probably claim new danger from the West or China in order to justify this course. The other path was toward reform. "A new generation of leaders, less committed to the status quo, might come to power and view a change in resource allocation policy in favor of consumers as a more viable way of maintaining 'superpower' status." The change of leadership might come soon. "Brezhnev is in poor health and most of those who hold key positions are in their seventies."

The record of Reagan's briefing did not describe his reaction to the CIA's assessment of Soviet prospects. He apparently listened and kept his thoughts to himself. But he couldn't help taking heart from the troubles the communists were experiencing. "My theory of the Cold War is: We win and they lose," he had said to Richard Allen earlier. At that time he had been able only to guess how broken the Soviet economy was. Now he knew, and he had reason to hope victory might be closer than he had imagined.

35

REAGAN AND NANCY awoke on January 20, 1981, at Blair House, across Pennsylvania Avenue from the White House. At nine thirty they attended a brief service at St. John's Episcopal Church, around the corner on the north side of Lafayette Square. "We sat in George Washington's pew," Nancy remembered, "and I couldn't help feeling history closing in on us that morning."

Jimmy Carter had the same feeling, amplified. Carter considered himself far more competent to be president than Reagan, and he still resented his loss in the election. His attitude didn't improve amid final round-the-clock efforts to free the hostages in Iran. A deal was near, but the Iranians appeared determined to deny him the victory of winning their freedom while he was still president. Nancy Reagan sympathized with the departing chief executive. "President Carter had been up all night working on the Iran hostage situation—and it showed," she observed. "It was impossible not to feel for him."

Reagan was less charitable. He described the ride to the Capitol: "The atmosphere in the limousine was as chilly as it had been at the White House a few days before when Nancy and I had gone there to see for the first time the rooms where we would be living. We'd expected the Carters to give us a tour of the family quarters, but they had made a quick exit and turned us over to the White House staff. At the time, Nancy and I took this as an affront. It seemed rude." Retrospect softened Reagan's conclusion. "Eight years later I think we could sense a little of how President Carter must have felt that day—to have served as president, to have been through the intense highs and lows of the job, to have tried to do what he thought was right, to have had all the farewells and good-bye parties, and then be forced out of the White House by a vote of the people. It must have been very hard on him."

THE LIMOUSINE ARRIVED at the Capitol, and Reagan stepped onto the largest stage in America. Half a million people had come to see the new president inaugurated. Their approach clogged the streets and overwhelmed the Washington subway system, compelling the attendants to throw open the turnstiles and let riders in free lest the system break down entirely. Even then they threatened its structural integrity; at the stop nearest the Capitol, passengers reported a shaking that felt like an earthquake.

As the noontime ceremony neared, the throngs crowded onto the National Mall, west of the Capitol. Since the nineteenth century presidents had been inaugurated on the Capitol's east side, but Senator Mark Hatfield of Oregon, the chairman of the congressional committee on the inauguration and, like Reagan, a westerner, decided that the time had come for the new president to take his oath on the opposite side, the side facing the direction that had always signified the American future. Reagan happily endorsed the innovation, which allowed him to speak to an audience larger by far than any he had ever addressed in person, larger than any addressed by more than a handful of speakers in all of human history.

He couldn't have scripted a better setting, nor cued the lighting more dramatically. The warmth of the morning had broken records for the date in Washington, but clouds covered the sky until the moment Reagan stepped forward, when the sun burst through in cinematic glory. He took his oath from Chief Justice Warren Burger; Nancy held Nelle Reagan's Bible as Nelle's son laid his hand on it and swore to preserve, protect, and defend the Constitution.

Reagan turned to deliver his inaugural address. He paused to absorb the moment. Perhaps he remembered when Nelle had first put him onstage. Perhaps he recalled the music he had heard when his first audience applauded. This crowd was immensely larger, and the music far more powerful. He couldn't see Illinois from where he stood, but he *could* see where his fellow Illinoisan, Lincoln, sat in marble splendor two miles down the Mall. Between them spired the monument to George Washington. In the foreground were the hundreds of thousands of ordinary

Americans who had come this day not to see Lincoln or Washington but to see *him*. They waved American flags; they shouted his name. Their hopeful faces looked upward at him as he began to speak.

He offered a grace note. He cited America's long tradition of peaceful transfers of power from one party to the other, even amid grave trials. He nodded to Carter with greater warmth than he felt, and he thanked his predecessor for his cooperation during the transition.

He returned to the themes of the campaign, the themes that had brought him to this time and place, the themes that had summoned this tremendous audience. The economy was in shambles, he said. He shook his head and frowned slightly. Inflation roared out of control. "It distorts our economic decisions, penalizes thrift, and crushes the struggling young and the fixed-income elderly alike. It threatens to shatter the lives of millions of our people." Unemployment robbed millions of honest Americans of their dignity and hope. Government punished the rest with rising taxes. Yet the tax take couldn't keep up with government's appetites. "For decades we have piled deficit upon deficit, mortgaging our future and our children's future for the temporary convenience of the present." This destructive, demoralizing trend could not continue; the deficit must be tamed.

Reagan knew a sound bite when he spoke it, and he could envision himself on the evening news when he declared, "In the present crisis, government is not the solution to our problem; government *is* the problem." He let his audience ponder the meaning of his sentence: the just-inaugurated head of the American government was declaring war on that government.

He went on to explain that special interest groups had captured the government and turned it to their own ends. He said he spoke for a broader interest group: the American people. He promised to do the American people justice by restraining government. He added that he would be more respectful of the rights of the states. "All of us need to be reminded that the federal government did not create the states; the states created the federal government."

Some of the new president's listeners doubtless wondered at this last assertion, especially coming from a former governor of California, which had indisputably been created by the federal government. But Reagan rolled on. He derided those who said America's best days were past. On the contrary, national renewal required only a summoning of the valiant spirit that had built the country. "We have every right to dream heroic dreams," he said. Heroism was in America's genetic code, the inheritance as fully of ordinary Americans as of the great figures of American history.

He looked again across the Mall. He gestured toward Lincoln and Washington. He lifted his gaze. "Beyond those monuments to heroism is the Potomac River," he said, "and on the far shore the sloping hills of Arlington National Cemetery, with its row upon row of simple white markers bearing crosses or Stars of David." Each marker signified exemplary service to America. "Under one such marker lies a young man, Martin Treptow, who left his job in a small town barbershop in 1917 to go to France with the famed Rainbow Division. There, on the western front, he was killed trying to carry a message between battalions under heavy artillery fire. We're told that on his body was found a diary. On the flyleaf, under the heading 'My Pledge,' he had written these words: 'America must win this war. Therefore I will work, I will save, I will sacrifice, I will endure, I will fight cheerfully and do my utmost, as if the issue of the whole struggle depended on me alone.'"

The crisis now facing America did not require the degree of sacrifice made by Martin Treptow, Reagan said. "It does require, however, our best effort and our willingness to believe in ourselves and to believe in our capacity to perform great deeds, to believe that together with God's help we can and will resolve the problems which now confront us. And, after all, why shouldn't we believe that? We are Americans."

36

David Stockman hadn't expected to join the shock troops of the Reagan revolution. "Ronald Reagan?!" he spluttered when his political mentor Jack Kemp, Republican congressman from New York, said he was not going to run for president in 1980 but instead was joining the Reagan team. "Jack, I can't believe you're hooking up with Reagan." Stockman later explained his astonishment: "The man was more ancient ideologically than he was in years. I considered him a cranky obscurantist whose political base was barnacled with every kook and fringe group that inhabited the vasty deep of American politics."

Stockman, like many other neoconservatives, had commenced public life in the tall grass on the radical left of American politics; like them he cared little for the social issues that inspired much of the Republican right. "I didn't give two hoots for the Moral Majority, the threat of unisex toilets, the school prayer amendment, and the rest of the New Right litany," he said. These distracted from the overriding dual issue of the time: "How do you get a prosperous economy and hold off the Russians?" In fact, the social issues were worse than a distraction; they were a contradiction. "I didn't believe in economic regulation and I didn't believe in moral regulation."

Neither did Kemp, Stockman knew. This was what made his association with Reagan so shocking. "He was aligning himself with Jerry Falwell, the anti–gun control nuts, the Bible-thumping creationists, the anti-Communist witch-hunters, and the small-minded Hollywood millionaires to whom 'supply side' meant one more Mercedes. So there I was, thinking, 'How is this antediluvian going to help us? He's *exactly* what the establishment needs to discredit our ideas.'"

The establishment, the nexus of Washington insiders and crony capital, was, to Stockman and his fellow supply-side theorists, the enemy of America's regeneration. Supply-side economics defined itself in opposition to the demand-side economics of John Maynard Keynes and of the American government during much of the period since the 1930s. The demand-siders contended that ensuring sufficient demand would keep the economy growing and the country prosperous. When private demand fell short, as during the Great Depression, the government should step in with public demand. The supply-siders said this approach was bound to fail, for the country inevitably became addicted to government spending. As with other addictions, they asserted, government spending had to be administered in ever larger doses to prevent withdrawal. The supply-siders' evidence was the economy's recent and present abysmal performance, with its record inflation and almost unprecedented unemployment.

The solution, the supply-siders said, was to focus on the other half of the supply-demand equation. The supply-siders rejected the Keynesian contention that capitalist economies inherently experience booms and busts; they blamed depressions and other ills on the meddling of government. The answer was not to create artificial demand but to ensure soundness on the supply side. As Stockman delineated the supply-side agenda, "The establishment had to be taught that you couldn't stop inflation with wage and price controls; you had to stop printing money. It had to be taught that you couldn't create economic growth by expanding the welfare state; you needed to start dismantling it and cutting taxes."

Stockman knew Reagan merely by reputation, and he couldn't imagine that the former actor grasped the essentials of supply-side economics. But Kemp said he did. "Reagan had been successfully 'converted,'" Stockman recounted. "There had been a powwow out in California on the eve of the day-to-day primary campaigning. Ed Meese decided the governor should be drilled on supply side—so he'd get the basic message down." Kemp arranged for Reagan to meet supply-siders Jude Wanniski and Art Laffer. "According to Jack, they'd spent days out there with Reagan, discussing the gold standard, the tax cut, supply-side theory, economic growth, the whole enchilada. And Governor Reagan had responded enthusiastically. Kemp said he had an intuitive 'feel' for the Laffer curve"—a theoretical graph showing that reducing tax rates could increase tax revenues by stimulating economic activity. "'He's ninety percent with us,' Kemp enthused."

This wouldn't have been such a revelation had Stockman or Kemp bothered to read what Reagan had been saying and writing for decades.

Reagan wasn't a goldbug, but he had long preached the virtues of smaller government and lower tax rates, not simply for individual liberty, but also for economic growth.

Whether or not he should have been surprised at Reagan's endorsement of ideas held by the supply-siders, Stockman was thrilled when Reagan, after the election, invited him to head the Office of Management and Budget. Kemp, who had recommended Stockman to the president-elect, told him that a telephone call would be coming. "I'd worked out a little script with some clever lines," Stockman recounted. But the call was delayed, and his wit vanished. "When the phone finally rang, my hands were trembling. It was the first time I had ever spoken to a president. All that came out was a flat midwestern 'Haallo?'" Reagan didn't notice. "As I would learn again and again, Ronald Reagan had the gift of setting you utterly at ease. 'Dave, I've been thinking,' he said in a relaxed, melodious voice, 'about how to get even with you for that thrashing you gave me in the debate rehearsals. So I'm going to send you to OMB.'"

DONALD REGAN WAS less starstruck than David Stockman at the opportunity to shape the economic policy of the new administration. And he was definitely less taken with supply-side economics. Regan was a Harvard graduate, which impressed Reagan a little; a former marine, which impressed him more; head of Wall Street's Merrill Lynch, which seemed good training for the Treasury Department; and a fellow Irishman, which prompted Reagan to affect an affinity for Regan the latter never entirely reciprocated. Reagan was certain they shared ancestry, despite the difference in pronunciation of their names (Regan was *Ree*gan). Reagan liked to tell a story on himself that almost made him part of Regan's branch of the extended tree. In the story Reagan was to be the guest of honor at a luncheon in Los Angeles shortly after his election as governor. The master of ceremonies had seen Reagan's name printed but unaccountably had never heard it pronounced. He didn't know if it was *Ray*gan or *Ree*gan. Amid his perplexity he took a walk through Beverly Hills and met a man walking a dog. Thinking the man might know the answer, the emcee asked him how the new governor pronounced his name. The man said, "It's *Ray*gan." The emcee asked him if he was sure. "Believe me, it's *Ray*gan," the man repeated. "I've known the guy for years." The emcee expressed relief and thanked the man for solving his problem. "By the way," he said, "that's a nice dog. What breed is it?" "A bagel," the man replied.

Regan had met Reagan a couple of times before the campaign of 1980. He encountered him again after William Casey suggested that Regan, as a good Republican and well-connected Wall Streeter, organize a fundraiser. Regan did so, and he spent a few minutes discussing the economy with the candidate after the event. "He said nothing remarkable, but he seemed to have had sound economic advice," Regan recalled.

Regan heard rumors after the election that he was being considered for Treasury secretary. Yet he discounted the rumors because William Simon was said to be the first choice. Then Simon declined, and Reagan called to offer him the job. "Thank you very much," Regan replied. "I accept." Reagan seemed surprised. Didn't Regan have to think it over, perhaps talk to his wife? "Mr. President, what is there to think over?" Regan answered. "How could any American say no when asked to serve by the president-elect? If you've selected me, it's my duty to say yes." Reagan expressed satisfaction. Regan would be hearing from members of the White House staff. "I'll see you in Washington," Reagan said.

In fact Reagan did *not* see Regan in Washington, at least not very often. Eight weeks into the president's first term, Regan jotted a memo to himself. "To this day I have never had so much as one minute alone with Ronald Reagan!" he wrote, mystified. "Never has he, or anyone else, sat down in private to explain what is expected of me, what goals he would like to see me accomplish, what results he wants." Regan's experience of the business world had caused him to embrace written, measurable objectives. He found their absence in Washington—under Reagan, at any rate—disconcerting. "How can one do a job if the job is not defined? I have been struggling to do what I consider the job to be, and let others tell me if I'm wrong, or not doing the right thing." So far no one had. He couldn't help thinking this absence of guidance was fraught with peril.

REGAN'S IMMEDIATE CONCERN involved the budget the president was supposed to deliver to Congress soon. In the infancy and youth of the American republic the federal budget originated in Congress, as the framers of the Constitution intended. But during the twentieth century the initiative on the budget, as on many other aspects of national governance, shifted to the executive branch. The federal budget became the vehicle by which presidential promises were transmuted into public policy. In Reagan's case, his budget proposal to Congress would indicate how his general calls for tax cuts and smaller government would take specific shape.

Two weeks into his presidency, Reagan launched his campaign for economic reform. He and his advisers had considered a formal State of the Union but opted instead for what he called "a report on the state of our nation's economy." The economy's state was not good, he said for the thousandth time. "We're in the worst economic mess since the Great Depression." Government was, as he had declared in his inaugural address, the heart of the problem. "The federal budget is out of control." The deficit for the current fiscal year would be nearly $80 billion. This was more than the entire federal budget a generation earlier. The federal payroll had quintupled in twenty years. Interest rates were higher than at any time since World War I. The unemployed numbered seven million. "If they stood in a line, allowing three feet for each person, the line would reach from the coast of Maine to California."

On the stump Reagan had often blamed malign intent, a bureaucratic will to power, for the growth of government. He took a different tack this evening. He pointed at the American people collectively. "We all had a hand in looking to government for benefits," he said. For a time the benefits had appeared inexpensive. The nation's income doubled in the generation after World War II, and the economy sustained the burden of growing government without obvious difficulty. Inflation had risen, but not to alarming levels.

Yet Americans should have been paying closer attention, Reagan said. Some *had* been, though he didn't identify himself by name. "If we look back at those golden years, we recall that even then voices had been raised, warning that inflation, like radioactivity, was cumulative, and that once started it could get out of control." And so it had gotten out of control. Now it was ravaging the country, and it would continue to do so until the federal deficit was tamed.

The question was how. One way would be to raise taxes. But this had been tried and had failed utterly. "Prior to World War II, taxes were such that on the average we only had to work just a little over 1 month each year to pay our total federal, state, and local tax bill. Today we have to work 4 months to pay that bill." Taxes had grown, but government had grown faster.

The solution was not to raise taxes but to cut them. This sounded paradoxical, for it appeared to aggravate the deficit problem. Yet it was the only way to get a grip on spending, the source of the problem. "Over the past decades we've talked of curtailing government spending so that we can then lower the tax burden. Sometimes we've even taken a run at doing that. But there were always those who told us that taxes couldn't be cut until spending was reduced. Well, you know, we can lecture our children about extravagance until we run out of voice and breath. Or we can cure their extravagance by simply reducing their allowance."

Likely no one in Reagan's audience recognized the significance of that last sentence. Reagan himself did not recognize it. But by putting tax cuts ahead of spending cuts, he proposed to lead America across an economic Rubicon. Republicans and conservatives had hitherto made balanced budgets the touchstone of their fiscal philosophy. They sought to cut taxes, but not at the cost of increasing debt. They knew that cutting taxes is politically easy, because it makes constituents happy. Cutting spending is the hard part, for it causes constituents pain. Reagan proposed doing the easy part first. The hard part could wait.

Not that he ignored spending cuts. He explained that he had placed a freeze on federal hiring, ordered reductions in government travel, trimmed the number of consultants hired by the federal government, and canceled orders for new office equipment. This was just the beginning. More must be done. His administration would have a blueprint soon. "It will propose budget cuts in virtually every department of government."

Yet against this unspecific promise of spending reductions, Reagan proposed very specific, and substantial, tax cuts. "I shall ask for a 10 percent reduction across the board in personal income tax rates for each of the next three years."

Reagan pitched his package as the country's last chance to reclaim prosperity and restore freedom from overweening government. "Over the years we've let negative economic forces run out of control. We stalled the judgment day, but we no longer have that luxury. We're out of time." Future generations would thank this one or condemn it. "We can leave our children with an unrepayable massive debt and a shattered economy, or we can leave them liberty in a land where every individual has the opportunity to be whatever God intended us to be."

37

W HEN DAVID STOCKMAN arrived in his office in the Executive Office Building, just west of the White House, he noticed two things. The office was huge—"about the size of my junior high school gymnasium," he said. And it was filthy. "When I picked up my phone, it almost slipped out of my hand it was so greasy." Stockman was willing to ascribe the condition to laudable thrift in housekeeping on the part of his Carter administration predecessors at OMB, but one of his deputies declared, "The reason it's greasy is they spent the last four months of the campaign handing out pork."

Stockman cleaned up the office and set to work on eliminating the pork. Reagan's promise to Congress of an economic blueprint compelled long days and sleepless nights by the president's economic team. Stockman tried to assert control of the process by proposing deep cuts for most cabinet departments. He assumed that because the cabinet secretaries had been chosen by Reagan, they shared the president's passion for reducing the size of government. In theory they did—theory being when the cuts targeted other departments. In practice—when Stockman's scalpel came their own departments' way—they objected. James Edwards, whose Department of Energy Reagan had promised to eliminate entirely, resisted Stockman's proposal to unfund the office that allocated oil supplies and end the allocation program. Stockman was astonished. "It was so central to our free market approach," he said of deregulation, "that I hadn't imagined anyone would object." Edwards wasn't alone. Secretary of Transportation Drew Lewis accused Stockman of seeking power for himself by means of deregulation. "What kind of bureaucracy are you building up over at OMB?" Lewis demanded. Again Stockman couldn't believe what he was hearing. "I was flabbergasted," he said. He wasn't building a bureaucracy but dismantling it. "He had the equation upside down," Stockman said of Lewis.

Donald Regan thought Stockman was the one who misunderstood matters. Regan didn't buy the boy-wonder reputation of Stockman, and he wasn't going to accept Stockman's seizure of economic policy. "Stockman was possessed of one simple idea," Regan wrote. "He believed that the federal budget should run the economy and thereby shape social policy. This was a philosophical position designed to be executed by bureaucratic means. His plan of action was correspondingly simple: by controlling the flow of money into the cabinet departments, the director of the Office of Management and Budget would starve certain programs (for instance, welfare) and feed others that were more productive in economic terms."

Regan was no politician, but he thought Stockman's approach profoundly arrogant and dismissive of the democratic process. "Stockman had things backward," he said. "What the country needed—and what Reagan had promised it—was not more centralization, but less. Surely, I said to the group"—the interagency group arguing over the budget—"we wanted to discuss the economy first, adopt a policy to avert recession and institute growth, and *then* decide what the budget would be."

Regan's problem, and Stockman's, was that the budgeters were receiving little guidance from Reagan. Regan still couldn't get a meeting with the president outside the crowded cabinet sessions, and neither could Stockman. Stockman blamed the blockade on the White House troika, especially Ed Meese. "By now it was clear that Ed Meese was protecting the president from having to choose sides among his cabinet members," Stockman recalled. "He was seeing to it that Reagan never had to make a disagreeable choice among contending factions. That certainly kept Reagan above the fray, but presidents have to make unpleasant decisions. Whenever there was an argument, Meese would step in and tell us to take our arguments to some other ad hoc forum. The president would smile and say, 'Okay, you fellas work it out.'"

CASPAR WEINBERGER SMILED too. His Defense Department, almost alone among the executive agencies, counted not merely on avoiding budget cuts but on receiving major increases in funding. During the decade of détente conservatives and especially neoconservatives had made an article of faith of the assertion that the American military was being starved of funding. They wrote articles and printed graphics claiming that the Soviets had built a dangerous lead over the United States in nuclear and conventional weaponry, and though they never found an active or retired general or admiral willing to swap America's arsenal for Russia's, they painted Armageddon as alarmingly nigh. Reagan adopted this view and, as a candidate, promised to restore American arms to their previous condition of unquestioned primacy.

Weinberger became Reagan's point man for the Pentagon buildup. Weinberger's hero was Winston Churchill; he remembered reading Churchill as a boy in the 1920s and then following Churchill's political fortunes during the 1930s, when in opposition in Parliament he warned his compatriots about Hitler and the need to gird for war. Weinberger tried to enlist in the British Royal Air Force in 1940, as Churchill was rallying the British against the Nazi onslaught, but was rejected on account of poor vision. Pearl Harbor pleased him for putting the United States into the war beside Britain; as an American infantryman he listened on the radio when Churchill addressed a joint session of Congress and called for Anglo-American solidarity against fascism. Meanwhile, he grumbled and fretted at the old equipment he was forced to train with and even carry into battle in the Pacific, on account of years of stinginess in Congress regarding defense appropriations. "I would not forget how long it took us to get proper equipment, and how inexperienced we were, and how completely unready to fight in jungles against opponents who knew all about jungles and were remarkably well equipped and trained," Weinberger recalled. "Thus, when forty years later I was placed in a position to have some ability to help influence events, and I saw what I believed then to be the dangerous downward spiral of our military strength and our national will in the 1970s, I determined to do all I could to prevent America from continuing down that path of drift and self-disparagement and weakness that I was sure could lead to another war."

WEINBERGER'S INSISTENCE ON rebuilding the American military, when enthusiastically endorsed by Reagan, made David Stockman's job immensely more difficult. Stockman didn't object, exactly. "I had become a big-budget proponent on defense," he later said. "Some of my hawkishness had to do with the zeal of the convert. More of it came from watching the grim footage of the charred remains of the U.S. servicemen being desecrated by the Iranian mullahs at the site known as Desert One"—where the hostage-rescue attempt had failed. But at a time when Stockman and the other budgeters were projecting 30 percent reductions in tax rates, giving the Pentagon what Weinberger wanted made it impossible to forecast a balanced budget in the conceivable future with anything like a straight face. Stockman programmed his calculator to tally the bill for what Weinberger was demanding. "I nearly had a heart attack," he said. "We'd laid out a plan for a five-year defense budget of *1.46 trillion dollars!*"

Weinberger didn't like or trust Stockman. "I became a little troubled by the quickness and positiveness with which he would take positions and make his points," Weinberger said. "Particularly troubling was that he was most positive when he did not yet quite have his facts straight." Weinberger later accused Stockman of lying; referring to a Pentagon meeting at which defense spending was the focus, Weinberger said that Stockman's account of the session was "most politely described as fanciful."

Weinberger could simply have stared Stockman down. He knew that building up defense meant more to Reagan than balancing the budget. Yet Weinberger was canny as well as forceful. He knew that the administration would take heat for expanding defense while slashing social programs. So he arranged for the Pentagon to accept cuts, too. The cuts were notional. Weinberger wrote even bigger increases into the defense budget, then gave them back and called the givebacks cuts. Reagan recognized the ruse but appreciated the political cover it provided the administration.

38

THERE COMES A moment near the beginning of every presidency when the president feels in a personal way that this new job is unlike any he has held before. The president of the United States has *power*—power greater than that of any other person on earth. The power of a governor, a senator, a corporate CEO, is puny compared with what a president can unleash. By a word he can send armies into combat, launch air strikes, conceivably commence a nuclear war. Candidates for president envision that power, imagine the moment when it will become theirs. Those who have lusted for power look forward to grasping it; the ordinarily ambitious accept it as part of the president's job.

But they typically misapprehend it. The great majority of presidents have sought the position for reasons of domestic politics. Only a few, as seekers of the office, have put foreign affairs first. Yet it is almost solely in foreign affairs that the president exercises his singular power. In domestic politics presidents are constrained by the Constitution, with its separation of powers; by the habits of Congress, which dictate procedures for the passage of legislation; by the political parties, which inject their own interests into policy considerations; by innumerable interest groups, each with its own agenda; and by the American people, who hold opinions on domestic affairs far stronger than those they have on foreign affairs.

Presidents have *influence* in domestic matters rather than power. Patronage provides one form of influence; favors for friends and allies help grease the gears of government. But the most important form of influence, for those able to exercise it, comes from a president's monopoly of what Theodore Roosevelt called the bully pulpit. Presidents command the attention of the country merely by being president; those who can communicate their views in compelling fashion have an advantage over everyone else in the legislative loop.

Reagan was the most compelling communicator in American politics since Franklin Roosevelt, and he knew it. His mastery of the rhetorical art reflected his long experience as an actor and public speaker. His years with General Electric taught him to read a room; his time before the camera trained him to see an audience beyond the camera. He mixed humor and pathos, philosophy and anecdote.

But his greatest strength was the focus he brought to his task. His message never changed. Details varied according to context, but the basic pitch was always the same: smaller government and lower taxes.

ON FEBRUARY 18, Reagan mounted the pulpit to pitch his budget proposal. He spoke in the House of Representatives to a joint session with the Senate, but he aimed equally at the millions watching on television. He summarized the grim state of the economy by citing a midwestern worker who had told him, "I'm bringing home more dollars than I ever believed I could possibly earn, but I seem to be getting worse off." He reiterated that the country had reached its moment of truth. "We can no longer procrastinate and hope that things will get better. They will not. Unless we act forcefully—and now—the economy will get worse."

He challenged Congress to enact a four-part plan. Part one targeted government spending. He called for $49 billion in cuts, although he immediately qualified this. The Democrats had preemptively criticized Reagan for eviscerating programs on which millions of Americans depended; he rebutted the criticism by pointing out that the spending reductions were reductions in projected *increases*. "We're only reducing the rate of increase," he said. The $49 billion decrease for 1982 would still allow an absolute increase of $41 billion over 1981.

If this weakened the thrust of his argument, he weakened it further when he explained what he was exempting from cuts. "We will continue to fulfill the obligations that spring from our national conscience," he said. "Those who, through no fault of their own, must depend on the rest of us—the poverty stricken, the disabled, the elderly, all those with true need—can rest assured that the social safety net of programs they depend on are exempt from any cuts." Social Security and Medicare, along with veterans' pensions and programs for the disabled, would be spared.

Then there was the Defense Department. "It's the only department in our entire program that will actually be increased over the present bud-geted figure," Reagan announced. The increase was necessary because America faced unprecedented challenges to its security. "Since 1970 the Soviet Union has invested $300 billion more in its military forces than we have." Reagan didn't mention that this figure was disputed, reflect-ing problematic estimates of wages and prices in the Soviet Union and conversions of rubles to dollars. Instead, he stressed what he took to be the figure's significance for American security and consequently for the American defense budget. "To allow this imbalance to continue is a threat to our national security."

Having exempted such big-ticket programs as Social Security, Medi-care, and defense from cuts, Reagan explained where his ax would fall. Federal aid to education would be reduced, as would federal support for the arts. But there was a silver lining here, Reagan said, for reduced aid to schools would reduce federal control over schools and restore it to the states and local school boards, where it belonged. Cuts in aid to the arts would encourage the charitable giving that had historically supported the arts in America.

Reagan ticked off other cuts. The Department of Energy's synthetic fuels program would be terminated; private industry could do a better job developing the fuels of the future. The Export-Import Bank would lose a third of its funding; again Reagan relied on the private sector. The Economic Development Administration would be zeroed out, for similar reasons. The Trade Adjustment Assistance program duplicated existing unemployment benefits; it would go. Recipients of food stamps would be more rigorously scrutinized to eliminate those who didn't genuinely need the nutritional help. Federal rules for welfare would be tightened and work requirements increased to ensure that the program served those who needed it and not those who didn't. School breakfast and lunch programs would be means-tested. Medicaid payments to states would be capped. The Postal Service would learn to live on a smaller subsidy. NASA and the space program must become more cost-effective.

Part two of Reagan's program was tax cuts. "Our proposal is for a 10-percent across-the-board cut every year for three years in the tax rates for all individual income taxpayers, making a total cut in the tax-cut rates of 30 percent," he said. He realized that conventional wisdom among economists said that cutting taxes at a time of high inflation would simply drive inflation higher, by fueling demand. He disagreed. For one thing, like the spending cuts, the tax cuts were cuts only in projected increases.

Taxes would continue to rise from current levels. For another, the conventional Keynesians were wrong, Reagan judged. Without uttering the phrase "supply side" or mentioning any supply-siders by name, he referred to "a solid body of economic experts" who contended that tax cuts would *reduce* inflation by expanding output. "I've had advice that in 1985 our real production in goods and services will grow by 20 percent and be $300 billion higher than it is today. The average worker's wage will rise in real purchasing power 8 percent, and this is in after-tax dollars."

Beyond the across-the-board tax cuts, Reagan proposed to accelerate depreciation of business expenses, to encourage investment. He wanted to index tax brackets to adjust for inflation, but this worthy reform would have to await another day. He didn't state explicitly that indexing would dramatically increase the projected federal deficit; experts understood this, and others didn't know what they were missing. For similar reasons, other reforms—of the marriage penalty, of inheritance taxes—would also have to wait.

Part three of Reagan's plan was deregulation. Reagan agreed with conservative economists who likened government regulations to hidden taxes, and he believed regulations should be cut along with other taxes. He disavowed any intention of removing regulations essential to the health and safety of Americans. But many others could be dispensed with and should be. He said he had declared a moratorium on new regulations by the executive branch and was convening a cabinet-level task force, headed by Vice President Bush, to undertake a comprehensive review of existing regulations.

The fourth and final part of Reagan's economic plan dealt with monetary policy. "In order to curb inflation we need to slow the growth in our money supply," Reagan said. He acknowledged that monetary policy wasn't, strictly speaking, within the purview of the president. "We fully recognize the independence of the Federal Reserve System and will do nothing to interfere with or undermine that independence." But he wanted to let the Fed chairman, Paul Volcker, and the rest of the Fed board know the White House was watching and expected cooperation in reforming the economy.

REAGAN PAUSED TO let his listeners catch their breath. He realized that no economic program so sweeping had been presented to the legislature since the New Deal. It was *his* plan, but it required the lawmakers' assent.

"I'm here tonight to ask you to join me in making it *our* plan," he said. "Together we can embark on this road." The room burst into applause, loudest from the Republican side but with many Democrats joining in. Reagan ad-libbed: "Thank you very much. I should have arranged to quit right here." The lawmakers laughed.

But he had a bit more to say. "Together we can embark on this road, not to make things easy, but to make things better. Our social, political, and cultural, as well as our economic institutions, can no longer absorb the repeated shocks that have been dealt them over the past decades. Can we do the job? The answer is yes. But we must begin now." There was nothing wrong with the American economy that Americans, acting together, couldn't fix. Government must do its part. Yet the results would rest with the American people, once they were freed to do what they did best.

Reagan repeated his stock theme of the greatness of the American people. "The substance and prosperity of our nation is built by wages brought home from the factories and the mills, the farms, and the shops," he said. "They are the services provided in ten thousand corners of America—the interest on the thrift of our people and the returns for their risk-taking. The production of America is the possession of those who build, serve, create, and produce." Government must simply get out of the people's way. And it must do so at once. "The people are watching and waiting," he told the lawmakers.

39

ARGARET THATCHER HAD had had her eye on Reagan for years. "I had met Governor Reagan shortly after my becoming Conservative Leader in 1975," the British prime minister later wrote. "Even before then, I knew something about him because Denis"—her husband—"had returned home one evening in the late 1960s full of praise for a remarkable speech Ronald Reagan had just delivered." Thatcher got a copy of the text and was equally impressed. She arranged to meet Reagan at first chance. "I was immediately won over by his charm, sense of humour and directness." She followed his rise in American politics and kept reading his speeches. "I agreed with them all."

British voters were quicker to appreciate Margaret Thatcher's virtues than American voters were to reward Reagan's; she became prime minister in the spring of 1979, eighteen months before he was elected president. British Conservatives, or Tories, shared the small-government predilections of American Republicans, and Thatcher was the most forthright, indeed combative, of the Tories. She tackled the British welfare state, slashing spending and reducing red tape. She challenged British labor unions, provoking strikes that caused the entire economy to shudder. But she held her ground until the strikes collapsed and the unions' power was broken. She privatized public utilities, undoing decades of growth of the government's hold on the British economy.

Her stern policies took a toll on her popularity. In late 1980 her job approval rating sank to depths not visited by any prime minister before her. Number 10 Downing Street, the prime minister's residence, became a lonely place. Her convictions never wavered, yet she valued her steadfast supporters more than ever, and she welcomed the ascendance of a kindred spirit across the Atlantic.

She sent congratulations on Reagan's election and laid plans to visit Washington as soon as possible, consistent with the dignity of her office. Inquiries were made, and she was delighted to learn that she was the first foreign leader the president-elect wished to see after assuming office. Travel arrangements were made and diplomatic briefings held. She grew expectant and somewhat anxious as the time neared. "Mrs. T told me that she was a little worried by her forthcoming visit to Washington," Nicholas Henderson, the British ambassador to Washington, recalled. "She did not quite see how it would go. She admitted to being nervous about it. She looked drawn—pale and rather distinguished. I did my best to reassure her, telling her how welcoming Reagan would be and how much he was looking forward to her arrival. I told her about the Californian gang who had come to Washington. We went through the programme. She was somewhat taken aback when I said that her after-dinner toasts would be televised. 'Then I shall have to think about them very carefully,' she said, adding, 'I shall want all the best historical advice I can get so as to get the allusions just right.'"

She asked about gifts: What would the Reagans like? They decided on Halcyon boxes. "As we became more and more involved in the plans of the visit, the worries seemed to flow off her and she became less taut," Henderson said. He grew aware that Thatcher saw the American visit as a break from the labor and political troubles at home; in Washington, at least at the White House, her conservative views would be valued and shared. "It was noticeable how little we talked about the substance of her discussions with Reagan. She was rather clear that she wanted to see him alone for a few moments, and then in a restricted meeting—the fewer the better, but she did not give me the impression that she had decided upon what subjects she wished to focus."

She flew to Washington at the end of February. Reagan greeted her on the White House lawn. A color guard provided pageantry; both leaders gave speeches extolling the special relationship that existed between America and Britain. They adjourned to the Oval Office, where they spoke privately for half an hour. They were then joined by their foreign ministers, Alexander Haig and Lord Carrington, and things grew more formal again. Larger entourages surrounded them in the Cabinet Room. Thatcher noticed the jelly beans on the table; Reagan said they came in thirty flavors, including peanut. "'We haven't yet had time to take them out,' he quipped, referring of course to Carter's background as a producer of peanuts," Henderson commented.

Thatcher talked of relations between the democratic world and the communist sphere. The evolving crisis in Poland was one point of contention, turmoil in Central and South America another. Reagan responded, "The villain in Central and South America is the same as confronts the world at large." Thatcher nodded. Henderson observed of Reagan, "He went on, his head shaking slightly, his voice quite deep and with a frequent smile, very charming and very unBismarckian: 'The U.S. has tried a variety of programmes that were and look like our plan. But we looked like the Colossus of the north. We will now try a new approach to bring the continents together.' I didn't really know what he meant."

REAGAN'S PLAN FOR Central America would unfold over time; for now the two leaders concentrated on getting to know each other better. The president and Nancy Reagan hosted a dinner at the White House; the Thatchers reciprocated with a dinner at the British embassy. "Rather to my disappointment the President did not ask Mrs. T to dance, though we had provided plenty of what we thought was appropriate music, such as 'Dancing Cheek to Cheek' and 'Smoke Gets in Your Eyes,'" Henderson remarked after the British dinner. "I am not sure why. It is possible that he may not have known in advance that dancing would be going to take place and did not therefore know whether it would have been in order to have started. Oddly, at the White House party the previous evening, he had accompanied the Thatchers to the door to say goodbye and had then returned to the party to dance with Mrs. Reagan."

Thatcher was disappointed too. "After the Reagans had left the embassy party a number of guests departed but Mrs. Thatcher stayed chatting and watching the dancing," Henderson said. "She had said to me in London beforehand that she hoped people would not rush away, which was why we had arranged to have a band. Nobody asked her to dance. So I went up to her and said, 'Prime Minister, would you like to dance?'" His gallantry was appreciated. "Mrs. T accepted my offer without complication or inhibition, and, once we were well launched on the floor, confessed to me that that was what she had been wanting to do all the evening. She loved dancing, something, so I found out, that she did extremely well. Long afterwards I read that one of the few frivolous things she did as an undergraduate at Oxford was to learn ballroom dancing. The band showed great brio, and I think Mrs. T was happy."

Other than the dancing, Henderson thought the dinner went well. Reagan seemed relaxed and engaging. "He shook hands and had a friendly remark for everyone. How excellent he is at that." At their table the president and the prime minister exchanged toasts. "Mrs. T used most of the text I had prepared for her, including the jokes, but interjected a long passage about the courage needed at two o'clock in the morning when you woke up aware of all the problems confronting you," Henderson said. Reagan laughed at the jokes but especially appreciated the personal reflection. "Later, Michael Deaver, who works in the White House and is close to the Reagans, vouchsafed to me, without any prompting, that the president had been moved by Mrs. T's embassy speech, especially the passage about two o'clock courage."

The visit, as a whole, was a rousing success. "Despite the UK's economic difficulties, the visit resulted in great exposure for Mrs. T, even more than planned, and in more favourable media coverage for her and the UK than the circumstances really warranted," Henderson observed. "She returned to a very different type of reception in the UK where unemployment and bankruptcies accumulate, and there are widespread doubts within her cabinet and party about her policies. I think that her acclaim in the USA may have helped to restore her."

A parting personal touch by Reagan confirmed the bond that was developing between the two leaders. "On the last morning the Reagans invited the Thatchers to go to the White House for a farewell cup of coffee on their way to the helicopter," Henderson said. "This was intended, I am sure, as a gesture of friendship because they had already had plenty of opportunity for chitchat at the successive dinners." Henderson was pleased to note that Reagan's spokesman seconded his opinion of the affinity between the two leaders. "Brady, the White House press secretary, said after the visit was over that it had been 'difficult to prise them apart.'"

40

REAGAN ENJOYED HOLDING news conferences. He liked dealing with reporters, whose names he took care to learn, and he valued the opportunity to show that an actor needn't be a dummy. If his mastery of policy minutiae was less than Jimmy Carter's, his camera presence was far greater. And he understood that presence mattered more to television viewers, the audience he cared about, than the details of his answers.

Reagan held his first news conference a week after his inauguration. He gave a brief statement reiterating the economic themes of the campaign and his inaugural address, and then he opened himself to questions. The American hostages in Iran had been released almost at the moment of his taking office; Helen Thomas of United Press International asked whether his policy toward Iran would be one of revenge or reconciliation. "I'm certainly not thinking of revenge," Reagan replied, while adding, "I don't know whether reconciliation would be possible with the present government."

Sam Donaldson of ABC News inquired what the president thought the long-range goals of the Soviet Union were. Was the Kremlin bent on world domination, or was détente possible? Donaldson patently wanted to see if Reagan as president espoused the same hard line he had taken as a candidate. Reagan made plain he did. "So far détente's been a one-way street that the Soviet Union has used to pursue its own aims," he said. "I don't have to think of an answer as to what I think their intentions are; they have repeated it. I know of no leader of the Soviet Union since the revolution, and including the present leadership, that has not more than once repeated in the various Communist congresses they hold their determination that their goal must be the promotion of world revolution and a one-world socialist or communist state, whichever word you want to use. Now, as long as they do that and as long as they, at the same time, have openly and publicly declared that the only morality they recognize is what will further their cause, meaning they reserve unto themselves the right to commit any crime, to lie, to cheat, in order to attain that, and that is moral, not immoral, and we operate on a different set of standards—I think when you do business with them, even at a détente, you keep that in mind."

Another reporter wondered what the president's remarks implied for the grain embargo imposed by the Carter administration against the Soviets after the invasion of Afghanistan. As a candidate, Reagan had criticized the embargo; did he now intend to lift it? Reagan replied, "With the grain embargo, my quarrel with it from the first was that I thought it was asking only one group of Americans to participate, the farmers. You only have two choices with an embargo: you either lift it or you broaden it." He hadn't decided which to do. But he tipped his hand slightly. "As I say, it was asking one group of Americans to bear the burden and, I have always thought, was more of a kind of gesture than it was something real."

REAGAN RETURNED TO the topic of relations with the Soviets in an interview with Walter Cronkite in early March. Cronkite was days from retiring as anchor of *CBS Evening News*; his exclusive with Reagan was a last hurrah. "Your hard line toward the Soviet Union is in keeping with your campaign statements, your promises," Cronkite said. "But there are some who, while applauding that stance, feel that you might have overdone the rhetoric a little bit in laying into the Soviet leadership as being liars and thieves, et cetera."

"Well, now, let's recap," Reagan replied. "I am aware that what I said received a great deal of news attention, and I can't criticize the news media for that. I said it. But the thing that seems to have been ignored—well, two things—one, I did not volunteer that statement. This was not a statement that I went in and called a press conference and said, 'Here, I want to say the following.' I was asked a question. And the question was, what did I think were Soviet aims? Where did I think the Soviet Union was going?" Reagan reiterated to Cronkite what he had said to Sam Donaldson about the immorality of Soviet behavior. He added, "Remember, their ideology is without God, without our idea of morality in the religious sense." And he noted, "They have never denied the truth of what I said."

Cronkite pressed Reagan. "You don't think that name-calling, if you could call it that, makes it more difficult when you do finally, whenever that is, sit down across the table from Mr. Brezhnev and his cohorts?" he asked.

"No," Reagan responded. "I've been interested to see that he has suggested having a summit meeting since I said that."

Cronkite noted that Reagan's State Department had rescinded a privilege accorded the Soviet ambassador, of parking in the basement garage of the building. Anatoly Dobrynin's car had been conspicuously turned away, and he had been told to use the street door like other diplomats. "It was obviously tipped to the press that this was going to happen," Cronkite observed. "What advantage is there in embarrassing the Soviet ambassador like that? A phone call would have said, 'Hey, you can't use that door any longer.' Was that just a macho thing for domestic consumption?"

"I have to tell you, I didn't know anything about it until I read it in the paper, saw it on television myself," Reagan rejoined. "I don't know actually how that came about or what the decision was, whether it was just one of those bureaucratic things."

"You didn't ask Secretary Haig about it?" Cronkite said.

"No, and I just don't know."

"Don't you think the Russians kind of think we're childish when we pull something like that?"

"I don't know; I don't know," Reagan said. With a slight smile he added, "Or maybe they got the message."

Cronkite asked what Reagan would require of the Soviets before he agreed to a summit with Brezhnev.

Reagan indicated he was in no hurry. "A summit meeting of that kind takes a lot of preparation. And the first preparation from our standpoint is the pledge that we've made to our allies, that we won't take unilateral steps. We'll only do things after full consultation with them." Reagan wanted to shore up support in the alliance so he could present a united front to Brezhnev. Answering Cronkite's question, the president said, "It would help bring about such a meeting if the Soviet Union revealed it is willing to moderate its imperialism, its aggression—Afghanistan would be an example. We could talk a lot better if there was some indication that they truly wanted to be a member of the peace-loving nations of the world, the free world."

"Isn't that really what you have to negotiate?" Cronkite asked. "I mean, is it really conceivable that you're going to get such a change of heart, a change of statement that you could believe on the part of the Soviet Union before you ever sit down to talk with President Brezhnev?"

Reagan cited Franklin Roosevelt. "I remember when Hitler was arming and had built himself up," Reagan said. "Franklin Delano Roosevelt made a speech at the dedication of a bridge over the Chicago River. And in that speech he called on the free world to quarantine Nazi Germany, to stop all communication, all relations with them until they gave up that militaristic course and agreed to join with the free nations of the world in a search for peace."

Cronkite didn't point out, if he knew, that Roosevelt hadn't been so specific and that the quarantine speech had been prompted by Japanese aggression in Asia rather than German aggression in Europe. In any event, Cronkite said ironically, "That did a whale of a lot of good."

"Oh, but the funny thing was he was attacked so here in our own country for having said such a thing," Reagan continued. "Can we honestly look back now and say that World War II would have taken place if we had done what he wanted us to do?" Returning to the present, he reiterated, "As I say, some evidence from the Soviet Union, I think, would be very helpful in bringing about a meeting."

"It sounds as if, sir," Cronkite observed, "you are saying that there isn't going to be any summit meeting with Brezhnev."

"No, I haven't put that as a hard and fast condition," Reagan said. But he repeated that a summit would come more readily if the Russians improved their behavior.

Cronkite noted that many in Europe wanted the United States and the Soviet Union to negotiate an arms-control treaty. The Europeans feared a new arms race and hoped to halt the Soviet and American build-ups before it was too late.

"Too late for what, is the question," Reagan countered. "I don't know, but I do believe this, that it is rather foolish to have unilaterally disarmed, you might say, as we did by letting our defensive, our margin of safety, deteriorate. And then you sit down with the fellow who's got all the arms. What do you have to negotiate with? You're asking him to come down to where you are, or you build up to where he is." The latter was more realistic. And rebuilding America's strength was what the administration intended to do. Once the Kremlin got the message, maybe then there could be negotiations.

41

PEOPLE OFTEN ASK me what it was like to live in the White House, and what routines we followed there," Nancy Reagan recalled. She proceeded to explain. "Our day normally began at seven-thirty, when a White House operator called on the telephone on my side of the bed and said, 'Good morning, it's seven-thirty.'" Her husband was usually awake by then, Nancy noted. She would push a button that signaled to the White House butler that it was time to bring in the newspapers and throw open the curtains.

She and Reagan remained in bed with the papers and breakfast. Reagan read the *Washington Post* and the *New York Times*; on Mondays he glanced through the fresh weeklies: *Time*, *Newsweek*, and *U.S. News & World Report*. Nancy started with *USA Today* and the *Washington Times*. The television was tuned to ABC's *Good Morning America*. Breakfast consisted of juice, cereal, coffee, toast, and, about once a week, an egg.

Around 8:30, Reagan rose and dressed for work. He kissed Nancy and took the elevator downstairs. His personal assistant, Jim Kuhn, greeted him. A Secret Service agent accompanied him to the West Wing and the Oval Office. His physician, John Hutton, made a point of meeting him in the hallway to say good morning and assess him visually.

His first meeting, with Jim Baker and often George Bush, began at nine. Meetings filled the rest of the morning and led to lunch, which he took at his desk or in the small study off the Oval Office. He read briefing papers or made telephone calls while having soup and fruit. On Thursdays he lunched with the vice president.

Afternoon was given to more office work, broken up as necessary or advisable by meetings and photo sessions with members of Congress, dignitaries from abroad, schoolchildren, firefighters, championship sports teams, and the like. He left the office by five and returned upstairs to the residence. At six he exercised in a bedroom converted to a private gym, on a treadmill and with resistance devices. A shower was followed by dinner, often on tray tables in the study, with the evening news on the television. The food was delivered by another butler. "Everybody who served us was from the White House staff," Nancy remarked. She added, democratically but inaccurately, "Apparently, we were one of the very few presidential families to arrive without any personal servants." State dinners and other public events occurred several times a month. After dinner Reagan and Nancy read; on Sunday evenings they watched television: *60 Minutes* and *Murder, She Wrote.*

Both Reagan and Nancy found the White House confining; most weeks they fled to Camp David on Friday afternoon. They traveled by helicopter unless the weather grounded them, in which case they went by car. "Thank God for Camp David!" Nancy wrote. The presidential retreat in the Maryland mountains gave them room to walk and ride horses, the latter more comfortably after Reagan ordered the paths Richard Nixon had had paved, to facilitate touring by golf cart, restored to their natural surfaces. Reagan's work followed him, but his staff did not, except for the Secret Service. Friends and family came to Camp David, as well as foreign visitors Reagan especially wanted to impress. Fridays and Saturdays were movie nights at Camp David; Reagan and Nancy screened films from their days in Hollywood and, with less regularity and enthusiasm, more modern pictures. On Sunday mornings they watched the news shows, particularly *This Week with David Brinkley*. Sunday lunch was followed by departure for the White House. "Coming back was always a slight letdown," Nancy wrote after Reagan left the presidency. "And even now, when Ronnie looks at pictures from Camp David, he feels a pang."

As restful as Camp David was, Reagan and Nancy's own retreat, Rancho del Cielo, was more soothing still. Every few months Air Force One would whisk them to California for a respite at the ranch. Reporters and cameras were usually barred. Reagan could roam afoot or on horseback; he repaired fences and chopped firewood. He was able to remember what life had been like before he became president—until the telephone rang and he had to deal with a crisis or other matter that couldn't wait until he returned to Washington.

NEVER HAS A First Couple found each other's company more congenial and comforting than the Reagans did. Except during his work hours they spent nearly all their time together. And when he was at work, he wasn't far from her thoughts, nor she from his. She called him Ronnie; he called her Mommy.

His pet name for her might have reflected nothing more than the fact that she was the mother of two of his children. But it suggests something else: that he found in Nancy's love and devotion some of the security he had relied on from his own mother in childhood. When he was with Nancy, he felt strong and confident; on the rare occasions when they were apart, he fretted and counted the hours until they would be reunited. Reagan's heart, perhaps because of its bruising by his alcoholic father, had limited capacity. He gave all of it to Nancy, as his children discovered on various occasions, to their disappointment. Nancy was everything to him emotionally. And in his view, she was enough.

Nancy, in her own way, depended on him as much as he did on her, and she was just as uneasy when the demands of their lives took them in opposite directions. She was as protective of him as his own mother had ever been; if anything, she guarded him *more* fiercely than Nelle had. If he had not gone into politics, she would have paid little attention to the subject. As it was, her political agenda consisted solely of promoting him and fostering his success. Michael Deaver was her liaison; he took her calls and discreetly translated her wishes, whenever possible, into action.

She witnessed all of her husband's major speeches and many of his minor ones. But she didn't see him address the leaders of the Building and Construction Trades Department of the AFL-CIO at the Washington Hilton, just up Connecticut Avenue from the White House, on March 30, 1981. Organized labor was not a natural constituency for Republicans, but some unions—the Teamsters, for instance—had endorsed Reagan over Carter, and blue-collar conservatives swelled the ranks of the so-called Reagan Democrats.

On this day the president appealed to the work ethic he said he shared with union members. He reminded them of his life membership in the AFL-CIO, and he cited Samuel Gompers, the founder of the AFL, on the subject of individual initiative. "Doing for people what they can and ought to do for themselves is a dangerous experiment," Reagan quoted Gompers. "In the last analysis the welfare of the workers depends upon their own initiative. Whatever is done under the guise of philanthropy or social morality which in any way lessens initiative is the greatest crime that can be committed against the toilers." Reagan noted that Gompers was speaking against socialism, but he believed the same might be said of the welfare state. "America depends on the work of labor, and the economy we build should reward and encourage that labor as our hope for the future," he said. "We've strayed far from the path that was charted by this man who believed so much in the freedom and dignity of the worker." The goal of the administration's economic reforms was to reengage the American spirit of enterprise, Reagan said. "The idea is to unleash the American worker, encourage the American investor, and let each of us produce more to make a better life for all." He hoped he could count on the unionists. "You and your forebears built this nation. Now please help us rebuild it."

The union leaders listened respectfully but skeptically. One of their chiefs had already warned the president that labor must not be made a scapegoat in the administration's efforts to reform the economy. After Reagan's speech several delegates interviewed by reporters expressed disappointment that the president had refused to endorse federal funding for mass transit and energy projects that might provide employment for some of the nation's 660,000 idle construction workers. They gave him credit for coming to address them, but if he wanted their support, he would have to do more to earn it.

NANCY REAGAN HAD a lunch engagement of her own that day, and she had just arrived back at the White House when the head of her Secret Service detail, George Opfer, drew her aside. "There's been a shooting at the hotel," he said. "Some people were wounded, but your husband wasn't hit. Everybody's at the hospital."

Nancy at once declared that she was going to the hospital. Opfer said it wasn't necessary or desirable. The place was chaotic enough without the addition of the First Lady. She insisted, saying she would go even if she had to walk. He grudgingly ordered a car.

Their approach to the George Washington University Hospital was blocked by police cars, emergency vehicles, reporters, and a crowd of curious onlookers. Nancy became increasingly agitated. "I was frantic," she recalled. She told Opfer, "If this traffic doesn't open up, I'm going to run the rest of the way."

Opfer kept her in the car, and eventually they reached the hospital. Mike Deaver, who had been informed by the Secret Service that she was on the way, met her at the door. "He's been hit," he said.

"But they told me he *wasn't* hit," she objected, growing more fearful by the moment.

Deaver and others recounted the events of the previous hour. On leaving the Washington Hilton, Reagan was about to enter his car. Several shots were fired. Reagan later said they sounded like firecrackers, but the Secret Service and the police on the scene immediately recognized them as pistol shots.

One bullet hit James Brady, Reagan's press secretary, in the head. He fell to the ground, grievously wounded. A second bullet struck police officer Thomas Delahanty in the back. A third hit Secret Service agent Tim McCarthy in the chest. Three other bullets seemingly did no damage other than to the president's limousine and the pavement.

Immediately on hearing the first shot, Secret Service agent Jerry Parr pushed Reagan unceremoniously into the limousine, shoving him onto the floor of the back part of the car. Another agent shoved Parr in on top of the president and slammed the door behind them. Parr ordered the driver to get out of the area as quickly as possible. Meanwhile, he reported that the president had not been hit. "Rawhide is okay," he radioed to the Secret Service command post, using Reagan's code name. He repeated: "Rawhide is okay."

Reagan did not feel okay. "I felt a blow in my upper back that was unbelievably painful," he wrote several days later. "I was sure he'd broken my rib." As the car sped away from the hotel toward the White House, Reagan tried to find a more comfortable position, to no avail. "I sat up on the edge of the seat almost paralyzed by pain," he recalled. "Then I began coughing up blood which made both of us think, yes, I had a broken rib and it had punctured a lung."

Parr ordered the driver to change course, to the hospital at George Washington University, several blocks northwest of the White House. The drive took just a few minutes, but during that time Reagan's condition worsened. "I was having great trouble getting enough air," he recalled. Even so, he insisted on walking from the car to the emergency room. But just inside the double doors he passed out and collapsed. He might have hit his head on the floor, but Parr and another Secret Service agent caught him. They and some hospital attendants carried him the rest of the way to the emergency room and laid him on a gurney.

The hospital staff initially thought Reagan was having a heart attack. They cut off his clothes and prepared to insert intravenous lines.

Reagan regained consciousness. "I'm having a hard time breathing," he said haltingly.

An intern placed an oxygen mask over his nose and mouth.

"Am I dying?" Reagan asked.

"No, you're going to be fine," the intern said.

The oxygen did little good. "I can't breathe," Reagan repeated. "My chest hurts."

The senior surgeon present listened to Reagan's lungs with a stethoscope. The right lung sounded normal but the left wasn't inflating. The surgeon instructed the attendants to roll Reagan onto his right side.

When they did, the surgeon noticed a small, bloody slit in the skin beneath Reagan's left armpit. Emergency rooms in Washington received their share of gunshot victims, and the surgeon recognized this as a bullet wound, despite the odd shape. He didn't take time to consider how the bullet had hit Reagan there, but what apparently happened was that one of the bullets had ricocheted off the bulletproof glass or armor of the limousine, flattening in the impact, and then sliced into Reagan. The wicked disk evidently remained within the president's body, for there was no exit wound.

Discovering the cause of Reagan's distress cued the trauma team as to how to alleviate it. A chest tube began draining the blood that had filled the chest cavity and was hampering Reagan's breathing. Intravenous fluids helped restore his blood pressure.

As the blood drained from around his lung, Reagan breathed more easily. The trouper's spirit in him revived. Noting the people hovering around him, he quipped to Jerry Parr, "I hope they are all Republicans."

An X-ray was taken to find the bullet. The image was imprecise, but the bullet appeared close to the heart. Conceivably, it had grazed the aorta, which might be near rupture.

Sometimes bullets are left inside shooting victims. Surgery is always risky, and a bullet can remain inside a person's body for years without incident. One of Reagan's predecessors, Andrew Jackson, carried souvenirs from a duel and a separate gunfight encysted within his body. But surgery's survival rate had improved since the nineteenth century, and the chief surgeon, on reflection, decided not to leave a bullet lying next to the heart of the leader of the Free World.

NANCY REAGAN PACED and worried in the waiting room while the trauma team was stabilizing her husband. At length they let her see him. "I walked in on a horrible scene—discarded bandages, tubes, blood," she recalled. "In the corner were the remains of Ronnie's new blue pin-stripe suit, which he had worn that day for the first time. I had seen emergency rooms before, but I had never seen one like this—with my husband in it."

Reagan, ashen and weary, brightened on seeing her. He pulled his oxygen mask to the side and said, "Honey, I forgot to duck." She fought back the tears and tried to smile. She kissed him and said, "Please don't try to talk."

She walked beside the cart as they wheeled him to the operating room. The crowd in the hallway included Jim Baker, Ed Meese, and Mike Deaver. Reagan, recognizing his troika, asked Baker, with what passed for a smile beneath the oxygen mask, "Who's minding the store?" At the entrance to the operating room, Nancy and the others had to stay behind. She kissed him and said, "I love you."

Inside the room Reagan was transferred from the cart to the operating table. The operating team gathered around him, and the anesthesiologist prepared to put him under. Realizing he had a fresh audience, Reagan recycled his earlier line. "I hope you are all Republicans," he said.

The head of the team responded, "Today, Mr. President, we are all Republicans."

42

THE FIRST NEWS of the shooting had thrown the White House into confusion as Jim Baker and the others there attempted to learn what was happening. Baker had declined to join Reagan at the Washington Hilton, pleading the press of work. He was in his office when he heard of the shooting; Ed Meese soon joined him there. For several minutes they couldn't tell who had been shot or how badly. Mike Deaver called from the hospital, saying that Jim Brady had been badly wounded and Reagan had taken a bullet in the side. One of the doctors joined Deaver's call and said the president had lost a great deal of blood. His condition was very serious.

Baker and Meese decided to join Deaver at the hospital. Just before Baker left his office, he got a call from Al Haig. The secretary of state was alarmed that the president was incapacitated, if perhaps only temporarily, while the vice president was out of the city, in Texas. Haig's military training kicked in, and he stressed the need to ensure the chain of command. He told Baker he would gather the cabinet members most crucial to national security: Weinberger from Defense, Regan from Treasury, Casey from the CIA, William French Smith from Justice, Dick Allen from the NSC. Haig said he would get in touch with George Bush.

To Baker as chief of staff fell the initiative in determining whether to invoke the Twenty-Fifth Amendment, which provides for a transfer of authority to the vice president in case of presidential incapacity. By the time he had sufficient facts to make a reasoned decision, the doctors had stabilized Reagan. The only question was whether his sedation during surgery would constitute sufficient incapacity to warrant invoking the amendment.

He decided it did not. It would be temporary, for one thing. For another, it would make Bush acting president. Baker had no qualms about Bush, but he knew that many of Reagan's supporters still doubted Bush's conservative bona fides. And those supporters were leery of Baker as Bush's best friend and former campaign manager. "They might view the transfer as something just short of a Bush-Baker *coup d'etat*," Baker remembered.

Baker's diffidence wasn't matched back at the White House. Jim Brady's injury compelled Larry Speakes, his assistant, to be the administration's chief liaison to the media. The reporters clamored for more information than Speakes had received, and under the glare of the television lights he inadvertently gave the impression that the president's condition left no one in charge of the government.

Al Haig and Dick Allen were watching Speakes's performance. They agreed that he was struggling, and they worried that this would send the wrong impression to the world. They had no reason to think that the shooter—by this time identified by Washington police as John Hinckley Jr., who would turn out to be an emotionally unbalanced fan of actress Jodie Foster, whom he hoped to impress by assassinating the president— was part of a conspiracy. But they couldn't be sure he was *not* part of a conspiracy, perhaps one with Soviet connections, and they didn't want to take any chances.

"This is very bad," Allen said to Haig. "We have to do something." Haig agreed. "We've got to get him off," he said, referring to Speakes. As Haig explained later, "It was essential to reassure the country and the world that we had an effective government." He asked Allen to join him. "Together, Allen and I dashed out of the Situation Room and ran headlong up the narrow stairs. Then we hurried along the jigsaw passageways of the West Wing and into the press room."

They arrived flushed and out of breath. Haig commandeered the podium to update the reporters on Reagan's condition. One reporter asked who was making the decisions for the executive branch.

"Constitutionally, gentlemen, you have the president, the vice president and the secretary of state, in that order," Haig replied. "Should the president decide he wants to transfer the helm, he will do so. He has not done that. As of now, I am in control here, in the White House, pending return of the vice president and in close touch with him. If something came up, I would check with him, of course."

Haig had intended to calm the country and reassure the world, but his red face, his breathlessness, and his words had just the opposite effect. The secretary of state was not third in line for the presidency; the speaker of the House and the president pro tem of the Senate came before him. Haig's proclamation "I am in control here" was too easily excerpted for the news networks to resist, and it made him look like a power grabber. "Perhaps the camera and microphone magnified the effects of my sprint up the stairs," he reflected later. "Possibly I should have washed my face or taken half a dozen deep breaths before going on camera . . . Certainly I was guilty of a poor choice of words." But he defended the point he was trying to make about the chain of command at the White House, awaiting the return of the vice president. "I was the senior cabinet officer present."

REAGAN'S SURGERY BEGAN smoothly. Fresh blood replaced the large quantity he had lost, a breathing tube kept him oxygenated, and his vital signs were stable. The surgeons on his team had extracted many bullets in their various practices, and this bullet seemed unlikely to be more elusive than most of those. The X-rays told them where to look, if not precisely where the bullet was located.

But the bullet seemed not to want to be found. The lead surgeon probed around the president's left lung and discovered nothing solid. He tried again and then again. He turned to his assistant and asked her to try. She had no better luck. The lead surgeon, puzzled, ordered a new X-ray while wondering whether he might have to leave the bullet in the president after all.

The X-ray showed the slug, about where it had appeared to be earlier and where the surgeon had been looking. He concluded that his probing fingers were causing it to move, always just out of his reach. Now, taking precautions to prevent the motion, he finally located it. A scalpel cut it free, and it was extracted.

The rest of the surgery was straightforward, though not free from risk. A damaged artery, the one that had caused most of the bleeding, was repaired. The wound to the lung was sutured, as were the incisions produced by the surgery. The patient was cleaned up and sent to recovery.

RON REAGAN WAS the first of the children to arrive. He had been in Nebraska when he heard of the shooting. No scheduled flights east were leaving soon, so he chartered a plane for himself and his wife, Doria. He got to the hospital while his father was still in surgery. His mother was nearly in shock. "I'm so frightened," she said, reaching out to him. "I know, Mom," he replied. "But hold on."

At about seven thirty in the evening, five hours after the shooting, Nancy and Ron were allowed into the recovery room. Reagan looked like many patients after major trauma and surgery: drained of color and energy, tubes down his throat and in his arms, wires connecting him to monitors. Nancy began crying at the sight. "I love you," she told him through her tears.

He groggily returned her gaze, but fear crept into his eyes. He fumbled for a pad and pencil. "I can't breathe," he wrote.

"He can't *breathe*!" she shouted to the room.

A doctor told her not to worry. The respirator took some getting used to, but it supplied the president all the air he needed.

"It's okay, Dad," Ron Reagan told his father. "You've got a tube in your throat. It's like scuba diving. Just let the machine breathe for you." Afterward Ron wondered why he had employed this analogy. "Dad had never been diving; I had barely been diving myself. And having a plastic hose lodged in your throat is probably entirely different and quite a bit more unpleasant than breathing pressurized oxygen from a tank while communing with brightly colored fish. Nevertheless, this non sequitur seemed to calm everyone who needed calming—except, perhaps, my father, though I doubt it did him any harm."

The visit was brief. Reagan drifted in and out of consciousness. The doctor told them to go and let him rest.

As they drove from the hospital to the White House, they passed crowds of people standing vigil and holding signs conveying encouragement. "Get Well Soon" and "Tonight We Are All Republicans," the signs said.

At the White House, Nancy couldn't sleep. "Nothing can happen to my Ronnie," she wrote in her diary. "My life would be over."

REAGAN RECOVERED, BUT Nancy never did. Four days after the shooting he developed a fever. The doctors couldn't discern its cause, but they put him on antibiotics in case it signaled an infection. The fever gradually subsided.

The list of his visitors expanded from family members to staff. Eight days after the shooting Tip O'Neill, the Democratic speaker of the House, was allowed in. "God bless you, Mr. President," O'Neill said. He began reciting the Twenty-Third Psalm: "The Lord is my shepherd; I shall not want. He maketh me to lie down in green pastures." Reagan joined him in a voice a bit above a whisper.

As he gained strength, Reagan reflected on the meaning of his near-death experience. "It heightened his sense of mission," Ron Reagan said later. "He thought God had saved his life and so he had a greater responsibility." Reagan himself wrote in his diary, "Whatever happens now I owe my life to God and will try to serve him in every way I can."

After thirteen days Reagan was released from the hospital. Knowing there would be cameras, he refused the wheelchair required of most non-presidential patients and insisted on walking out. He managed a smile and a wave.

He recuperated at the White House during the next two weeks. Nancy arranged the solarium so he could spend his days there in the spring sunshine. On the warmest afternoons they sat outside on the terrace. Soon he began to laugh off his ordeal. "I don't know what you're worried about," he told Nancy, who still fretted. "I knew all along that I'd be fine."

But she couldn't stop worrying. "I was devastated after the shooting," she recalled. "Ronnie recovered, but I'm a worrier, and now I really had something to worry about: that it might happen again, and that this time I would lose him forever." She thought time might ease her distress, but it didn't. "I continued to be haunted by what had happened, as well as by what had almost happened," she said. "For the rest of Ronnie's presidency—almost eight more years—every time he left home, especially to go on a trip, it was as if my heart stopped until he got back."

Subsequent events increased her foreboding. Six weeks after the attempt on Reagan's life, a gunman shot and wounded the pope in Rome. Five months later, Egyptian president Anwar Sadat was murdered in Cairo.

"Everyone said it was just a coincidence," Nancy recounted. "And yet I worried. How could any public figure be protected from acts of violence? And what if these three events were somehow connected in a way that would become known only at some future time?"

Nancy knew of the fatal pattern that had long afflicted presidents elected in years divisible by twenty. Since 1840 every chief executive so elected had died in office: William Henry Harrison, Lincoln, Garfield,

McKinley, Harding, Franklin Roosevelt, Kennedy. Lincoln, Garfield, McKinley, and Kennedy had been assassinated. Now her husband had nearly been assassinated. Did death in office still await him?

The specter wouldn't leave her. She couldn't sleep. She couldn't eat. Her thin frame grew gaunt. She prayed, to no lasting avail. "When Ronnie wasn't around, I cried," she remembered. "Sometimes I also cried when he *was* around, but I would usually manage to slip away into the bedroom or the bathroom so he wouldn't see me."

She sought the advice of friends she could trust. Some she saw in person; others she consulted by phone. "One afternoon I was on the phone with Merv Griffin, an old friend from my Hollywood days," she recalled. "He mentioned that he had recently talked with Joan Quigley, a San Francisco astrologer. I had seen her years ago on Merv's television show, where she was part of a panel of astrologers. Later, Merv had apparently introduced us, although I don't remember meeting her. Joan had then volunteered her advice during Ronnie's 1980 campaign, and had called me several times to talk about 'good' and 'bad' times for Ronnie. I was interested in what she had to say, and I was pleased when she told me that Ronnie was going to win—that it was in his chart and in mine."

Griffin said that he and Quigley had spoken about the attempt on Reagan's life. "I remember as if it were yesterday my reaction to what Merv told me on the phone," she said eight years later. "He had talked to Joan, who had said she could have warned me about March 30. According to Merv, Joan had said, 'The president should have stayed home. I could see from my charts that this was going to be a dangerous day for him.'"

Nancy recalled her response to Griffin: "Oh, my God! I could have stopped it!"

She immediately hung up on Griffin and called Quigley. "Merv tells me you knew about March 30," she said.

"Yes, I could see it was a very bad day for the president," Quigley replied.

"I'm so scared," Nancy said. "I'm scared every time he leaves the house, and I don't think I breathe until he gets home. I cringe every time we step out of a car or leave a building. I'm afraid that one of these days somebody is going to shoot at him again."

Quigley responded with sympathy. Nancy subsequently called her again, and again. She shared her fears and concerns not simply about her husband but about her children and her parents. "On all these matters, Joan was helpful and comforting," Nancy said. "We had a professional relationship, but I came to view her as a friend. I now see that she was also a kind of therapist."

Quigley suggested that she could help Nancy by identifying days that were good or bad for her husband.

"Well, I thought, what's the harm in that?" Nancy remembered. "And so once or twice a month I would talk with Joan (sometimes by appointment, sometimes not). I would have Ronnie's schedule in front of me, and what I wanted to know was very simple: Were specific dates safe or dangerous? If, for example, Ronnie was scheduled to give a speech in Chicago on May 3, should he leave Washington that morning, or was he better off flying out on the previous afternoon?" Quigley would listen and take notes. She would consult the stars and whatever other sources she used, and she would call Nancy back with her recommendations. "I would, if necessary, call Michael Deaver, who was in charge of Ronnie's schedule," Nancy said. "Sometimes a small change was made." After Deaver left the White House and Don Regan became chief of staff with control of the schedule, Nancy worked through Regan.

"I knew, of course, that if this ever came out, it could prove embarrassing to Ronnie," she observed. "But as long as I worked with Mike Deaver, I knew my secret was safe. Mike was discreet. He had known Ronnie and me for years and was one of my closest friends. I never even thought of asking him to keep a confidence. I just knew he would."

43

FOUR WEEKS AND a day after the shooting, Reagan returned to the political arena. He requested permission to address Congress and duly received an invitation. When he entered the House chamber, the senators and representatives leaped to their feet in a politically mandatory but no less heartfelt expression of relief that democracy had not been derailed by a madman. Reagan had to fight his way through the arms and hands that reached out for his; like the celebrity he had been for half a century, he reveled in and reciprocated the good feeling. When he mounted the dais, the applause and cheers kept on and on. He smiled and waved and nodded, and smiled and waved and nodded again and again. The applause continued. Finally he quipped, in obvious reference to his close brush with death, "You wouldn't want to talk me into an encore, would you?"

He had come to speak about the business of government. But he had a personal message first. "I'd like to say a few words directly to all of you and to those who are watching and listening tonight, because this is the only way I know to express to all of you on behalf of Nancy and myself our appreciation for your messages and flowers and, most of all, your prayers, not only for me but for those others who fell beside me. The warmth of your words, the expression of friendship and, yes, love, meant more to us than you can ever know. You have given us a memory that we'll treasure forever."

Reagan's audience was as moved as he himself obviously was. Applause again poured from both sides of the aisle. He told of the cards and letters he had received. He drew one such letter from his lapel pocket. The writer was a second grader in Rockville Centre, New York. "I hope you get well quick," Reagan read, "or you might have to make a speech in your pajamas." Reagan's words and delivery lifted the somberness that had infused the applause; all remembered what a funny fellow he was and were delighted to have him back. Reagan let the laughter flow and slowly ebb. He finished the story with his young correspondent's closing line: "P.S. If you *have* to make a speech in your pajamas, I warned you." The legislators roared again, the Democrats despite themselves.

He wasn't finished with his prologue. Referring, as in the campaign, to Jimmy Carter's lament at the malaise that afflicted Americans, augmented now by comments that only a sick society could produce a deranged gunman like John Hinckley, Reagan repeated what he himself had said, that there was nothing wrong or sick about America at all. He cited his own recent experience. "Sick societies don't produce young men like Secret Service agent Tim McCarthy, who placed his body between mine and the man with the gun simply because he felt that's what his duty called for him to do." The audience applauded, loudly and long. "Sick societies don't produce dedicated police officers like Tom Delahanty." More applause. "Or able and devoted public servants like Jim Brady." Even more applause, and the eyes of the legislators turned, with the television cameras, to Brady's wife, Sarah, seated in the gallery. "Sick societies don't make people like us so proud to be Americans and so very proud of our fellow citizens."

REAGAN ALWAYS KNEW when he had an audience where he wanted it, and he knew he had this one. He launched into the job at hand. "Let's talk about getting spending and inflation under control and cutting your tax rates," he said. "Thanks to some very fine people, my health is much improved. I'd like to be able to say that with regard to the health of the economy." But he could not. Six months after the election, an election in which voters had clearly registered their desire for a change of course, the economy remained on life support. Inflation had scarcely abated; interest rates were still punishingly high. Nearly eight million Americans were still unemployed. Real wages had fallen. "Six months is long enough. The American people now want us to act and not in half measures. They demand and they've earned a full and comprehensive effort to clean up our economic mess."

The effort must begin with the budget. Reagan reiterated the message of the election: "Our government is too big, and it spends too much." He was pleased to report that the Senate Budget Committee had just that day approved a bipartisan budget resolution consistent with the recom-mendations the administration had issued. Unfortunately, the House was lagging. The House Budget Committee, controlled by Democrats, had presented a bill that was woefully deficient. It cut social programs too lit-tle and shortchanged defense. And rather than reduce taxes, it would raise them. "It adheres to the failed policy of trying to balance the budget on the taxpayer's back," Reagan said. The Democratic measure was conser-vative in the worst sense of the word: it would entrench the failed policies of the past. "High taxes and excess spending growth created our present economic mess; more of the same will not cure the hardship, anxiety, and discouragement it has imposed on the American people."

Reagan responded to expressed concerns that the administration's program of cuts in spending and taxes would produce large deficits. Poll-sters had asked Americans whether they placed greater importance on lower taxes or a balanced budget, and most chose the balanced budget. Reagan asserted that the question had been wrongly framed. He repeated that his proposed tax cut was really a refusal to raise taxes in the future. "A gigantic tax increase has been built into the system," he said, referring to the effects of inflation in boosting people into higher tax brackets. "We propose nothing more than a reduction of that increase." The pollsters should make this clear. "Our choice is not between a balanced budget and a tax cut. Properly asked, the question is, 'Do you want a great big raise in your taxes this coming year or, at the worst, a very little increase with the prospect of tax reduction and a balanced budget down the road a ways?' . . . I'm sure we all know what the answer to that question would be."

Reagan reiterated that the Democratic bill from the House was unsat-isfactory. Fortunately, there was an alternative. Conservative Democratic congressman Phil Gramm of Texas had worked closely with the adminis-tration from the start. As Gramm put it later, "Stockman and I wrote the Reagan budget." Gramm had enlisted Republican Del Latta of Ohio, and the two sponsored a measure that Reagan now endorsed. "We embrace and fully support that bipartisan substitute," the president said. It would accomplish the crucial goals of cutting spending, reducing taxes, and bol-stering defense. And it would foster economic growth.

Two weeks earlier NASA had completed a successful mission by the space shuttle, returning America to space after a hiatus of six years. The timing couldn't have been better for Reagan, who cited the mission as an example of America at its best. "With the space shuttle we tested our ingenuity once again, moving beyond the accomplishments of the past into the promise and uncertainty of the future," he said. "The space shuttle did more than prove our technological abilities. It raised our expectations once more. It started us dreaming again."

He quoted Carl Sandburg on American dreams: "The republic is a dream. Nothing happens unless first a dream." Resuming his own words, Reagan continued, "That's what makes us, as Americans, different. We've always reached for a new spirit and aimed at a higher goal." He challenged Congress to dream with him. "We have much greatness before us. We can restore our economic strength and build opportunities like none we've ever had before . . . All we need to have is faith, and that dream will come true."

44

T HE SHOCK OF the shooting, Reagan's grace at death's door, and his dramatic return made him politically irresistible. He knew his speech was a hit when scores of Democrats joined the cheering. Overnight calls to the White House registered the same enthusiasm. Reagan's job approval rating, as measured by Gallup, bounced upward to 68 percent, higher than it had yet been and as high as it would ever go.

The Senate, under the guidance of the Republicans and Majority Leader Howard Baker of Tennessee, accepted Reagan's direction on the budget easily. In the House, Tip O'Neill and the Democrats made a show of resistance. But as letters and calls supporting the president clogged the mailboxes and phone lines of House members, O'Neill found himself losing ground. "Am I lobbying people?" he asked reporters rhetorically. "The answer is yes. Am I getting commitments? The answer is no." Reagan was simply overwhelming, the speaker explained. "We're facing a popularity issue. That's what we're facing out there." And Reagan was too popular. "He's done the greatest selling job I've ever seen."

On May 7, nine days after the president's appeal to the people, Reagan defeated O'Neill. Sixty-three Democrats joined the Republican minority to approve the Gramm-Latta bill by a broad margin. "We never anticipated such a landslide," Reagan remarked privately. "It's been a long time since Republicans have had a victory like this." The administration celebrated and prepared to seal the triumph in the reconciliation of the Senate and House bills.

———

"THEN WE SHOT ourselves in the foot," James Baker recollected. The bullet was Social Security. In the half century since Franklin Roosevelt had made it the signature program of the American welfare state, Social Security had developed an enormous and powerful constituency. Retired people and those approaching retirement were poorly positioned to replace lost income, including income lost to Social Security cuts; they believed, with reason, that society had made them solemn promises and that cuts to Social Security represented the worst kind of promise breaking. Moreover, the pensioners and near pensioners voted in proportions that put younger Americans to shame. Reagan understood this, which was why he had exempted Social Security from the initial round of budget reductions. But the system was becoming financially unsound as the ranks of the retired grew. Payments would soon exceed workers' contributions, and the problem would get worse over time.

How to reform the system evoked bitter fights within the administration. Richard Schweiker, the secretary of Health and Human Services and a former member of Congress, advocated broadening the base of Social Security by extending it to currently exempt government workers and employees of nonprofit organizations. Doing so would increase revenues without immediately expanding outlays and would buy years, perhaps decades, of relief.

David Stockman judged this exactly the wrong approach. "Schweiker and I might as well have been standing on different planets," Stockman wrote. Calling Social Security a "Ponzi scheme," he said that bringing in more contributors would compound the deception. "Our job is to shrink the Social Security monster, not indenture millions more workers to a system that's already unsound."

Stockman swayed most of his administration peers with supply-side logic and some tactical compromises that ultimately brought even Schweiker around. He presented his program of benefit cuts at an Oval Office meeting where he wrapped his argument in budget arcana no one in the room could rebut. Reagan, as a candidate, had often complained about Democrats' faux fixes of Social Security; at this meeting he again berated the Carter administration. "They gave us the largest tax increase in history and said it would be sound until 2030," he said. "Now we're here four years later and it's already bankrupt. It just proves what we've always said."

Stockman nodded vigorous agreement and praised the president's insight. Reagan accepted Stockman's proposal, delighted at the thought of finally making Social Security sound. Stockman ally Martin Anderson congratulated the president on a genuine breakthrough. "You'll be the first president in history to honestly and permanently fix Social Security," Anderson said. "No one else had the courage to do it."

James Baker hadn't been prepared for the supply-siders' blitz. "I was apoplectic," he remarked afterward. Baker was certain there would be a backlash against the Social Security cuts, and he believed the president hadn't been warned. "Our success on the budget resolution may have encouraged him to shoot for the moon on this issue, which he had talked about for years."

Baker didn't think he could change Reagan's mind directly, given the president's pleasure at having saved Social Security. So he worked to deflect the criticism away from the White House. He called a meeting of the Legislative Strategy Group. "Look," he said, "we've all agreed around here that the economic program is number one, top of the list. So let's be a little concerned about whether we screw up the agenda." He decreed that the Social Security plan be presented to the media and the public as a Health and Human Services project, not something from the White House. "To be precise," he emphasized, "this isn't Ronald Reagan's plan. It's Dick Schweiker's. Has everybody got that?"

David Stockman objected. "This isn't extraneous to the president's economic plan," he declared. "It's integral to it, because it"—the overall plan—"doesn't add up without it."

Schweiker said Baker was sabotaging the Social Security proposal. "If there's *any* doubt as to where the president stands, this'll be dead on arrival when it gets to the Hill." Schweiker wondered where Baker got the idea he could dictate political strategy. "By damn, I've spent twenty years on the Hill, and I know when something will fly. So let's not start on the defensive. This is a plan we can be proud of."

Baker refused to reconsider. Reagan's fingerprints must not be on the Social Security plan, he said. It was Schweiker's responsibility.

"I was furious," Stockman recalled. "But there was nothing I could do. Baker was chief of staff."

Baker's misgivings proved accurate. "Within two days I knew we were in deep trouble," Stockman remembered. The budget director met with congressional Republicans to explain the Social Security reforms. "No sooner had I finished the final sentence of my opening remarks than Congressman Carroll Campbell of South Carolina lit into me like a junkyard dog. 'You absolutely blind-sided us with this Social Security plan,' he seethed. 'My phones are ringing off the hook. I've got thousands of sixty-year-old textile workers who think it's the end of the world. What the hell am I supposed to tell them?'" House speaker O'Neill happily piled on, calling the plan "despicable" and a "rotten thing to do" to seniors. Massachusetts Democrat James Shannon of the House Ways and Means Committee pinned the blame on Reagan. "He has gone too far," Shannon said. "It's time we stood up."

The Senate, in fact, stood up first. Without waiting for the administration's Social Security plan to arrive, the upper house preemptively buried it by a unanimous vote.

"And that was that," Baker remarked later. The administration dropped the Stockman plan and said no more about it. "Social Security was off the front pages, but at a significant cost to our legislative momentum," Baker reflected.

45

T HE SOCIAL SECURITY debacle cost the administration weeks and cast doubt on the entire project of tax and budget reform. Reagan rolled with the reverse but refused to retreat. Springtime brought invitations to college commencements; Reagan accepted an offer of an honorary degree at the institution with which he had long been identified in the public mind. Notre Dame had given degrees to other presidents, but none of them had played George Gipp. After warming the crowd with one-liners even he admitted were hoary—"A university like this is a storehouse of knowledge because the freshmen bring so much in and the seniors take so little away"—he riffed on his famous role. "Today I hear very often, 'Win one for the Gipper,' spoken in a humorous vein," he said. "I've been hearing it by congressmen who are supportive of the programs that I've introduced." He pointed out that the story was more complicated than was commonly known, and he said it might serve as a parable for the present. "Rockne could have used Gipp's dying words to win a game any time. But eight years went by following the death of George Gipp before Rock revealed those dying words, his deathbed wish. And then he told the story at halftime to a team that was losing, and one of the only teams he had ever coached that was torn by dissension and jealousy and factionalism . . . It was to this team that Rockne told the story and so inspired them that they rose above their personal animosities." Congress should take the lesson and pass the administration's tax and budget bills.

Congress wasn't listening, not yet. The House and Senate bills went to the largest reconciliation committee in American history, comprising 72 senators and 183 representatives. The discussions there recapitulated the arguments made in the separate houses, with the added wrinkle that the expectations and sensitivities of the participants confusingly reflected the traditions of the two houses simultaneously instead of each separately. The Democrats dragged out the process, hoping for distraction from the public and perhaps more missteps by the administration.

Reagan got to know Tip O'Neill better. O'Neill could swap Irish stories with Reagan, but he was all business when it came to politics. "Tip O'Neill is getting rough," Reagan observed in his diary. "Saw him on TV telling the United Steel Workers union I am going to destroy the nation." On another day O'Neill took his complaint to Reagan directly. "Tip was bluster on the phone and accused me of not understanding the Constitution—separation of powers etc." At issue on this occasion was Reagan's proposal to expand state control of programs funded by the federal government. O'Neill opposed it, arguing that Congress had the obligation to oversee spending of money federal taxes raised. "Claims Congress would be abdicating its responsibility," Reagan jotted. The president disagreed. "In truth, Washington has no business trying to dictate how states and local governments will operate these programs." But Reagan expected nothing different from O'Neill. "Tip is a solid New Dealer and still believes in reducing the states to administrative districts of the federal government. He's trying to gut our program because he believes in big spending."

O'Neill's bluster wasn't without effect. The Democrats held up the tax bill long enough that Reagan felt compelled to bargain. They wanted a smaller tax cut in the first year; in exchange they would accept a reduction in the top tax rate on unearned income, from 70 percent to 50 percent, which Reagan wanted but hadn't proposed. "I'll reluctantly give in," the president noted to himself, "provided they'll accept the 3-year across the board cut which will be 5-10-10 instead of the 10-10-10 we originally proposed." The old negotiator in Reagan quietly smiled. "I'll hail it as a great bipartisan solution. H--l! It's more than I thought we would get. I'm delighted to get the 70 down to 50. All we give up is the 1st year 10 percent beginning last January to 5 percent beginning this October. Instead of 30 percent over 3 years (36 months), it will be 25 percent over 27 months."

Yet even with this compromise, the tax and budget bills moved slowly. "Jim Wright is playing games," Reagan observed of the House majority leader from Texas. Wright was revisiting the Social Security issue, condemning the administration for wanting to eliminate the floor under payments to individuals, which remained in both the House and the Senate versions of the budget bill. "It is a political trick aimed solely at creating a 1982 election year issue for the Democrats," Reagan remarked. Senate leaders were throwing the issue back to the White House. "Sen. Baker said I could fight or retreat—he's not sure we can win either on the floor or in the conference committee." Reagan vowed to fight it out. "If I retreat, the gains we've made in lowering inflation will be lost. It will be taken as a test of my determination and looked upon as a sign that I'll back down on the tough decisions. Well, I have no intention of retreating; I've sent a letter to our leaders on the hill informing them that early in August I'll go on TV to discuss the Social Security problem. I think this will shake Jim Wright more than a little."

In fact he didn't wait until August. Reagan appreciated his own gifts, and he recognized that his ability to reach voters, to speak to them in terms they understood and felt, was his administration's most potent weapon. Each time he had spoken on the economic package, he had moved the measure forward; one more blow and the logjam should be broken.

"I'd intended to make some remarks about the problem of Social Security tonight," he told a national audience in the final week of July. "But the immediacy of congressional action on the tax program, a key component of our economic package, has to take priority." This bit of rhetorical indirection—he had intended all along to speak about the economic package—allowed him to rebut an argument involving Social Security that was being made by opponents of the economic package. "I've been deeply disturbed by the way those of you who are dependent on Social Security have been needlessly frightened by some of the inaccuracies which have been given wide circulation." Reagan sought to allay the fears with a straightforward promise. "I will not stand by and see those of you who are dependent on Social Security deprived of the benefits you've worked so hard to earn. I make that pledge to you as your president. You have no reason to be frightened. You will continue to receive your checks in the full amount due you."

Tip O'Neill and other Democrats doubtless bridled at Reagan's misrepresentation of their position. Their complaint was not that current recipients of Social Security would be shortchanged but that *future* recipients would receive less than they were slated at present to receive. But the Democrats had to admire Reagan's rhetorical sleight of hand; he had the audience and they didn't.

Reagan went on to lampoon the substitute tax bill promoted by the

House Democratic leaders. "If I could paraphrase a well-known statement by Will Rogers that he had never met a man he didn't like," he said, "I'm afraid we have some people around here who never met a tax they didn't hike." The Democratic bill claimed to cut taxes, but the cuts were ephemeral, Reagan said. He produced a chart showing two paths for future taxes. The path produced by the Democrats' bill was lower than the path of the bipartisan bill favored by the administration, but only for two years. After that, because of inflationary bracket creep and an increase in Social Security taxes, it soared $100 billion above the bipartisan track. "The majority leadership claims theirs gives a greater break to the worker than ours," Reagan said, with a sly smile. "And it does—that is, if you're only planning to live two more years."

Reagan called on the American people to hold their elected officials accountable. "Contact your senators and congressmen," he said. "Tell them of your support for this bipartisan proposal. Tell them you believe this is an unequalled opportunity to help return America to prosperity and make government again the servant of the people."

AGAIN REAGAN'S APPEAL worked its magic. The response from voters was overwhelming and positive. The next day Reagan met with members of Congress, urging their support. "All of them told the same story," he noted afterward. "Their phones in their districts and in the Capitol were ringing off the wall . . . There is no doubt the people are with us."

Where the people—and the president—led, Congress followed. The reconciliation deadlock on the budget finally broke; Howard Baker phoned the White House: "The bill is done." The bargain called for cuts from projected spending of 3 percent for fiscal 1982, 4 percent for 1983, and 4.5 percent for 1984. The cuts ranged widely across the waterfront of federal activity. Schools took a 20 percent hit. Food-stamp funding fell 15 percent. School lunches lost a third, Medicaid a round $1 billion. The Job Corps gave up a fifth of its budget, the CETA program of apprenticeships its whole tab. Support for public housing fell 40 percent, for the arts and humanities 30 percent.

Reagan praised the budget bill as entailing "the most sweeping cutbacks in the history of the federal budget." He thanked and congratulated all who had made it possible. Then he waited for word on the tax bill.

It arrived the next day. The House debated for seven hours on July 29; at the end of the debate the members cast their votes. Forty-eight Demo-

crats joined 190 Republicans to give Reagan a solid 238 to 195 victory
on the key roll call. The Senate's favorable decision came as no surprise,
though the overwhelming margin, 89 to 11, hadn't been foreseen. The tax
law accomplished nearly all of what Reagan expected and some things he
had only hoped for. It cut personal income tax rates by 5 percent in the
first year and 10 percent in each of the next two years. The top rate fell
from 70 percent to 50 percent on both earned and unearned income. The
lowest rate declined from 14 percent to 11 percent. The tax rate on capital
gains was reduced from 28 percent to 20 percent. Business depreciation
was accelerated, and the marriage penalty for two-income couples was
diminished. The exclusion for estate taxes was increased, exempting all
but the very wealthy. The biggest bonus for the administration was the
indexing of tax rates to eliminate bracket creep.

Members of the administration clapped themselves on the back for
their brilliant triumph. "I cannot imagine anything that will help the
economy more," Caspar Weinberger told Donald Regan, who fully concurred. Reagan, in his diary, called the outcome of the tax and budget
battle "the greatest political win in half a century."

In the moment of victory such self-congratulation was in order. Reagan and his team had indeed won a great battle. Yet there was another
battle ahead, and if candor had informed the mood, Reagan would have
been required to admit that the coming battle would be harder than the
one just finished. Metaphorically speaking, while the tax cuts were written in the political equivalent of stone, the spending cuts were written on
paper, in ink that might readily evaporate. A congressional promise to cut
taxes can be taken, almost literally, to the bank; a congressional promise
to cut spending has to fight its way through committee after hostile committee.

But this was Reagan's day to celebrate. At a session with reporters at
his California ranch, the president said of the new measures: "They represent a turnaround of almost half a century of a course this country's been
on and mark an end to the excessive growth in government bureaucracy,
government spending, government taxing." He praised the Republican
leadership in Congress and the Democrats who provided crucial support.
The elected officials, though, had simply heeded the popular will. "The
real credit goes to the people of the United States, who finally made it
plain that they wanted a change."

46

A REPORTER AT THIS session asked Reagan a question unrelated to taxes or the budget. "Mr. President," he said, "on the air controllers' strike, the International Association of Air Controllers has called on you to negotiate with PATCO. Why do you continue to believe that you should not negotiate with them?"

The Professional Air Traffic Controllers Organization, or PATCO, represented the men and women who guided commercial planes through American skies. The union had responded to the rampant inflation of the later 1970s and early 1980s as other labor organizations had done: by demanding higher pay. But its position was different from that of many other unions in that the controllers' employer was not a private corporation but the federal government. The union, in talks with the Department of Transportation during the spring of 1981, sought annual pay increases of $10,000 across the board and a reduction of the workweek from forty hours to thirty-two. The reduction in hours was to acknowledge the peculiar stress of the controllers' job. But PATCO president Robert Poli and Transportation secretary Drew Lewis agreed, just three hours before the union's June 22 strike deadline, to a much smaller deal, giving the controllers a $4,000 raise for their existing forty-hour week. Poli endorsed the deal as reasonable, if not everything the union wanted, and he referred it to his members. They took a very different view and rejected the pact by a margin of twenty to one.

Lewis and Poli resumed their talks but got nowhere. "We're still miles apart and there hasn't been much bargaining," the federal mediator reported a month later. Lewis called the union's latest demands, which were considerably closer to its original position, "nothing short of outrageous." The union meanwhile set another strike deadline, August 3. As it approached, Poli declared, "The outlook now isn't good." Lewis rejoined that a strike by the controllers, as federal employees, would be illegal. "We're going to bring the full force of the Justice Department down on the traffic controllers," he warned. "It will probably be both civil and criminal penalties, and the penalties will start immediately."

Lewis's position had Reagan's full backing. The president had followed the talks closely from the start. "Negotiations are still going on to try and head off tomorrow's illegal strike by the air controllers," he wrote in his diary just before the first deadline. "I told Drew L. to tell their union chief I was the best friend his people ever had in the White House but I would not countenance an illegal strike nor would I permit negotiations while such a strike was in process."

When the second deadline passed and the union made good on its strike threat, Reagan took swift and decisive action. "This morning at 7 a.m. the union representing those who man America's air traffic control facilities called a strike," Reagan read to reporters on August 3. "This was the culmination of seven months of negotiations between the Federal Aviation Administration and the union. At one point in these negotiations agreement was reached and signed by both sides, granting a $40 million increase in salaries and benefits. This is twice what other government employees can expect. It was granted in recognition of the difficulties inherent in the work these people perform. Now, however, the union demands are seventeen times what had been agreed to—$681 million. This would impose a tax burden on their fellow citizens which is unacceptable."

Reagan explained that the nation's air-traffic system continued to operate despite the strike. Supervisors had pitched in and were filling the roles ordinarily occupied by the controllers. "In the New York area, for example, four supervisors were scheduled to report for work, and seventeen additionally volunteered." Some controllers had resigned from the union to cross the picket lines. Reagan commended these brave individuals' public spirit, which was exemplified by the comment of one of them: "How can I ask my kids to obey the law if I don't?"

Reagan emphasized this man's point. "Let me make one thing plain," he said. "I respect the right of workers in the private sector to strike. Indeed, as president of my own union I led the first strike ever called by that union. I guess I'm maybe the first one to ever hold this office"—the presidency—"who is a lifetime member of an AFL-CIO union. But we cannot compare labor-management relations in the private sector with government. Government cannot close down the assembly line. It has to provide without interruption the protective services which are government's reason for being."

The distinction between the public and the private sectors was crucial, and it explained the sanction Reagan held over the heads of the striking controllers. He had long admired Calvin Coolidge for his modesty and small-government views; he knew that Coolidge had come to national prominence as Massachusetts governor when he declared, during a Boston police strike, "There is no right to strike against the public safety by anyone, anywhere, any time." Such was the attitude Reagan adopted toward the controllers, and it was one he shared with Congress, which had passed various laws forbidding strikes by federal employees. The controllers, moreover, as a condition of employment had signed an oath not to strike. "It is for this reason," Reagan said, emphasizing the personal pledge, "that I must tell those who fail to report for duty this morning they are in violation of the law, and if they do not report for work within 48 hours, they have forfeited their jobs and will be terminated."

MANY OF THE controllers didn't believe him. Skilled workers have always had leverage over employers in contract negotiations, as their skills are difficult to replace quickly. The controllers assumed that a strike would paralyze air travel and compel the government to improve its current offer.

On the other hand, the administration had the leverage of the law, as well as that of a monopoly employer. The private market for air controllers is very small; if the PATCO members lost their federal jobs, most would have to find new careers.

Reagan hoped the controllers' economic self-interest, their commitment to their sworn word, and their fear of prosecution would bring them back to the control towers of the nation's airports. Many responded as he wished. About a quarter of the PATCO members defied the strike call and reported to work. These controllers, together with the supervisors, kept about half the country's flights in the air.

But that meant that half were grounded. The airlines hemorrhaged revenue from the lost business; they reported losing $10 million a day from canceled flights and customer alienation. The controllers consequently considered the airlines their allies and hoped that if the Republican administration didn't heed labor officials, it might listen to corporate boards.

Yet Reagan stood firm. The administration moved to decertify PATCO as the bargaining agent for the controllers. The Justice Department brought suit against Robert Poli, and a federal court found him in contempt. The court set a fine of $1,000 per day if the union chief didn't call off the strike. The union as an organization faced fines of $1 million per day. Drew Lewis asserted that the president was quite serious about the August 5 deadline. "I don't care whether it's 9,000 or 12,000 or 100,000," he said. "Whoever is not at work will be fired." No less to the point, Lewis declared that the government was readying replacements for the strikers. "We will be advertising. We have a number of applicants right now. There's a waiting list in terms of people that want to be controllers."

The deadline came and went, with most controllers still out. The firings began. Dismissal notices were sent to the strikers; several strike leaders were jailed. "I'm sorry, and I'm sorry for them," Reagan told reporters. "I certainly take no joy out of this." But the strikers had brought it on themselves, and he had no intention of changing his mind.

Five days into the strike, the Federal Aviation Administration and the airlines had managed to get three-quarters of the planes back into the air. "United Airlines is still flying. So you can keep flying, too," United advertised. "Delta is ready when you are," Delta chimed. The FAA allowed the airlines to decide which flights to cancel, letting them focus on their best-performing routes. "We cancel those flights that have the fewest number of people on them, those with the least demand," a spokesman for American Airlines explained. The companies' profits per flight accordingly increased, though total revenues were still down.

After a week it was clear that Reagan had won. Columnists Rowland Evans and Robert Novak called the strike a "crisis made in heaven" for the president, as it played at once to his principles and to his political convenience. The president had demonstrated his resolve and his willingness to inflict pain on those who doubted or opposed him.

YET REAGAN GAVE no victory speeches. If anything, he made an effort not to gloat. A Mrs. Browning sent a letter to the White House complaining that her son, a military veteran, had been among the controllers fired. Reagan responded sympathetically. "I can understand your concern and heartache," he wrote back. Then he took the time to explain his position. "I can only hope that you will understand why it isn't possible for me to reinstate all those who went on strike. The law specifically prohibits public employees from striking. As you say, striking 'is an inalienable right'— but not for government employees." Strikes in the public sector were very different from those in the private sector. "A strike is an economic contest between labor and management when negotiations have failed to resolve an issue. But governments can't shut down the assembly line. The services provided to the people, who in this case are the employers of all of us in government, must be continued." Reagan asked his correspondent to consider the consequences of her request, however well-intentioned. "Mrs. Browning, there are more than two million federal employees. What message would we be sending to all of them if we allowed a strike by one group or gave amnesty to them if they did strike? Believe me, there is no thought of punishment in what we are doing. There just is no way I can avoid enforcing the law." Even so, he was weighing means to ease the plight of the fired controllers. Law prohibited fired federal employees from reapplying for federal work for a period of three years. "I am trying to arrange a waiver of that law so that all the 12,000 can apply for whatever government jobs are available without waiting." Reagan reiterated the concern he had for Mrs. Browning's son. "I do feel a very real sorrow for those who followed the union leadership at such sacrifice. This is especially true of someone like your son who served our country in uniform."

His stronger sympathies, though, were with the controllers who crossed the picket lines to honor their commitment to the public welfare. This was Reagan's message to another correspondent, one of the faithful controllers. "I am more grateful than I can say to all of you who are undergoing the hardships of added hours and added days of the week to keep our planes in the air," he wrote to Jerry McMillan of Atlanta. McMillan had urged the president to hold fast, and Reagan said he would. "Our obligation is to you, and I certainly have no intention of weakening in the stand I have taken with regard to those who chose to ignore their pledge."

REAGAN KNEW THERE was another budget battle coming, but he didn't realize it would be so soon. Nor that it would be fought under such adverse conditions. Only days after his Capitol Hill victory, the president met with David Stockman and the rest of the administration's economic team. Stockman had recognized he was playing loose with projections for the economy four and five years out, yet, faced with the need to enlist votes in Congress, he had kept his qualms to himself. Now that the bills had passed, he ran his numbers again and discovered that his projections were more troubling than ever. Balancing the budget would require drastic cuts beyond those already included in the budget. At this meeting Stockman handed out black binders detailing the grim news. "The scent of victory is still in the air," he said, "but I'm not going to mince words. We're heading for a crash landing on the budget. We're facing potential deficit numbers so big that they could wreck the president's entire economic program. It's going to be harder than hell to get to a balanced budget even by 1986. On the margin, every single number in the budget is going in the wrong direction." Stockman reminded the group that the budget bill contained numerous and large unspecified savings; these would have to be specified, at political cost. More worrisome were the economic assumptions on which the budget bill was premised. Stockman had assumed rapid economic growth in response to the tax cuts, but even he knew he was pushing the bounds of the plausible. Now, behind the closed doors of the Cabinet Room, he spoke more candidly. The federal deficit seemed likely to top $80 billion by fiscal 1983 and $110 billion by 1986.

"The president was stunned," Stockman recalled later. "His response was an irritated stammer: 'Dave, if what you are saying is true, then Tip O'Neill was right all along.'"

Ed Meese objected that Stockman wasn't reckoning with the new tax revenues the cut in tax rates would yield. "Meese was referring, of course, to the Laffer curve," Stockman noted. Stockman had never believed in the Laffer curve, and he was irritated that anyone in the administration did. "The whole California gang had taken it literally (and primitively)," he recounted. "The way they talked, they seemed to expect that once the supply-side tax cut was in effect, additional revenue would start to fall, manna-like, from the heavens." They were wrong, he proceeded to tell Meese and the others at the meeting. "Higher real GNP and employment growth will not increase projected revenues by a dime," he said. "Remember, we're putting the squeeze on inflation at the same time. That will bring down the growth rate of money GNP *and* federal revenue."

Stockman's lecture had little effect. "As I looked around the table, it was evident I had accomplished nothing," he recounted. The few who understood nodded their heads but kept silent. "The others were puzzled, bored, or annoyed." Stockman pressed on. He said the benefit of the anticipated recovery had already been factored into the projections. "So the only way to reduce these red ink projections is by cutting more spending or raising some new revenue. That is the strategic choice we face." On the other hand, the administration could simply live with the deficit and abandon its promise of a balanced budget.

Reagan refused to countenance such defeatism. "No, we can't give up on the balanced budget," he said. "Deficit spending is how we got into this mess."

Stockman pointed to another option. The Pentagon was scheduled to gain nearly 10 percent annually; if this was pared to 7 percent, the savings would add up fast.

Again Reagan refused. "There must be no perception by anyone in the world that we're backing down an inch on the defense buildup," he said. "When I was asked during the campaign about what I would do if it came down to a choice between defense and deficits, I always said national security had to come first, and people applauded every time." He wouldn't go back on his word, he said, and he wouldn't betray the people who supported him.

———

BUT SOMETHING HAD to give, Stockman insisted. Perhaps the administration should consider modest increases in excise taxes—on tobacco, alcohol, and imported oil, for example—and user fees.

Donald Regan now spoke up. "I strongly object to that kind of tax increase talk," the Treasury secretary said. "We've just worked our fanny off to give the American people a tax *cut*." Employing an analogy he liked, he continued, "You can raise the bridge or lower the water level. Our job is to do the latter—to cut the spending."

Regan had been working on Reagan—working to gain access to the president, despite the barriers imposed by the Baker-Deaver-Meese troika, and working to educate the president on the details of the budget and government finance. "My job was to establish an atmosphere of frank give-and-take with the president that would permit him to know about and approve the policies and actions Treasury proposed to undertake," Regan recalled. "I would have preferred to speak my mind in private, but as I have said, I never saw the president in private. Therefore I had to make my points in the presence of the sizable group that crowded into the Oval Office or any other room in which the president happened to be receiving one of his advisers." Regan, an informal sort by temperament, found it hard to break through the formality that inevitably invested these large affairs.

On one occasion, though, he found a way to reach Reagan emotionally. For years the Treasury had been selling Series E bonds, the successors to the war bonds that had been marketed to patriotic citizens during the Civil War and the two world wars. The Treasury still relied on patriotism in pitching the bonds, for the E series paid a mere 5 percent, far below the market rate for bonds and substantially below the inflation rate. The purchasers were losing money on each bond they bought. Regan's conscience bothered him, and he decided to broach the issue with Reagan.

"Mr. President," he said, "I don't know how you expect me to sell these goddamn things when I know in my heart that the buyer is getting ripped off. The government doesn't put out a prospectus on Series E bonds, but if it did, we'd all deserve to go to jail. Five percent with a thirteen percent rate of inflation? It's a fraud and we're perpetrating it on the very people who trust us most and know the least about money."

Reagan responded as Regan hoped. "I can't believe what I'm hearing," the president said. "We can't do that to people. I take it you want to change the situation?"

"I certainly do," Regan said.

"Then go to it," Reagan replied.

Regan felt doubly good about the session. He had rectified an indefensible policy, and he had connected with Reagan. "That was the first hammer-and-nails discussion I had with the president," he remarked.

HE HOPED TO have more as the looming deficit threatened to derail Reagan's economic program. Events confirmed his skepticism about Stockman's budget-driven approach to government reform. Congressional promises to cut spending were one thing; actual cutting was wholly another. Not even the offices of the executive branch could be relied on. "The cabinet departments and other agencies had resisted the Office of Management and Budget's efforts to manage their programs and dictate their priorities by manipulating their budgets, and in so doing had found effective allies on Capitol Hill," Regan recalled. Democrats and more than a few Republicans, guessing that the president wouldn't be able to repeat his appeals to the people indefinitely, reembraced the spending that pleased their constituents and generally helped reelect them. The economy meanwhile tipped into recession, which reduced tax revenues and increased outlays for unemployment compensation and other relief, making the bad deficit situation worse.

Regan, with many others, blamed the Federal Reserve for the recession. The administration had gotten off to an unpromising start with Paul Volcker, who refused the president's invitation to come to the White House to talk about monetary policy. Accepting the invitation would compromise the Fed's independence, Volcker said. He likewise refused Reagan's offer of a presidential visit to the Fed. Eventually, though, he consented to eat lunch with the president on the comparatively neutral ground of the Treasury Building. Reagan walked the quarter mile from the White House, alarming the Secret Service and stopping traffic on Pennsylvania Avenue. And he flabbergasted Volcker at the start of the lunch meeting by saying, "I was wondering if you could help me with a question that's often put to me. I've had several letters from people who raise the question of why we need any Federal Reserve at all. They seem to feel that it is the Fed that causes much of our monetary problems and that we would be better off if we abolished it. Why do we need the Federal Reserve?"

"The president was serious," Martin Anderson recollected. Anderson knew Reagan well enough not to be surprised. Reagan's question reflected his characteristic combination of innocence and self-confidence: innocence in that he really wondered just what the Fed did and why, self-confidence in that he was not afraid to ask. Phil Gramm of Texas, an economist by training, later characterized the president's mind-set simply: "He knew what he knew." He also knew what he didn't know. And he was willing to be educated.

But Volcker did not know Reagan. "I was sitting across the table from Volcker and the view was priceless," Anderson wrote. "His face muscles went slack and his lower jaw literally sagged a half-inch or so as his mouth fell open. For several seconds he just looked at Reagan, stunned and speechless. It is a good thing Volcker had not had time to light one of his long cigars, because he might have swallowed it. My God, he must have thought, here I am the head of the largest, most powerful banking system in the world and the very first thing this guy—who is going to be president of the United States for at least the next four years—says to me is to justify my existence."

Volcker recovered sufficiently to give the president a primer on the Fed and its functions. Reagan seemed satisfied, and the lunch proceeded uneventfully. But Volcker became a thorn in the administration's side, for he was determined to wring the inflation out of the economy regardless of the pain he inflicted. Volcker was a behaviorist as well as a monetarist, and he believed that public expectations drove wages and prices higher and caused them to resist restraint even when the money supply stopped growing. The only solution, he concluded, was shock therapy: tight money for as long as necessary to change the minds and expectations of markets and individuals. Volcker's policy produced howls across the economy as the high interest rates strangled demand and pitched the country into recession.

Don Regan thought he knew as much about money as Volcker did, and he judged that the Fed chief was carrying things too far. "Volcker, possessed of an almost messianic desire to drive inflation out of the economy, pursued restrictive policies that created large, unpredictable swings in the money supply," Regan wrote. When Congress continued to spend, Volcker squeezed still harder. "Thus Congress was stomping on the accelerator of the economy while Volcker was simultaneously slamming on the brakes. The administration, given the scary job of holding the steering wheel of the skidding jalopy, was sorely tempted to throw up its hands and cover its eyes."

Regan tried to moderate Volcker's policy. Acknowledging the institutional independence of the Fed, Regan nonetheless worked on its boss. Every Thursday he ate breakfast with Volcker, at the Treasury one week, at the Fed the next. "I argued with Volcker for a steady, predictable monetary policy that would assure an adequate and dependable supply of money for the private sector," he recalled. Volcker responded that the past decade of inflation had rendered his rigorous policy essential. Regan asked him to consider the cost. "Volcker is a brilliant and dedicated man, and there is no doubt that his actions did, indeed, cauterize inflation," Regan wrote afterward. "But the burn cost the patient the use of his right arm for nearly two decades."

Regan thought Volcker sometimes chastened the bankers simply because he thought they needed chastening. "'Paul, you're a nanny!' I used to say to him after he had given the bankers another spoonful of medicine." Yet the bankers took their medicine, believing that they, as creditors, would ultimately benefit from a sounder dollar. "The bankers liked him," Regan observed. "So did the press." Regan supposed that the Volcker vogue owed something to the fact that the Fed chief was the only person in the capital who could withstand President Reagan's popularity. "Whatever the reason, Volcker enjoyed a remarkably good press—a fact that did not escape the notice of the public relations experts in the White House."

To the dismay of the administration, Volcker engineered the sharpest recession since World War II. Unemployment topped 8 percent in early 1982, on its way to nearly 11 percent. Not since the Great Depression had so many Americans been out of work. And the federal deficit grew larger than ever.

A NOTHER BOMB," REAGAN wrote in his diary after meeting again with his economic team. "The latest figures on deficit projections, bad."

The president had expected pain during the adjustment to the new era of smaller government, but he hadn't anticipated anything like this. Inflation was falling, but so were projected tax revenues, which had counted on inflation pushing taxpayers into higher brackets until indexing took effect. "We face the prospect of low inflation and lower interest rates, all of which is good, but gigantic deficits, and that's bad," Reagan wrote. "A very dark picture economically."

In early November the administration suffered an acute embarrassment. David Stockman had been meeting secretly with William Greider, an editor at the *Washington Post* and an occasional contributor to the *Atlantic Monthly*. Stockman later explained that Greider was a friend and a smart fellow on whom he liked to sharpen his thinking. He also said that he misunderstood the ground rules of their conversations. Greider agreed not to publish anything until after the budget bill passed or failed; evidently, he did *not* agree not to quote Stockman by name. An article by Greider appeared in the December 1981 issue of the *Atlantic*, which hit the newsstands in early November. Titled "The Education of David Stockman," it portrayed Stockman sympathetically but evinced skepticism toward supply-side economics. And it included quotations that weren't shocking in the context of the long article but made damaging sound bites when excerpted. "Kemp-Roth was always a Trojan horse to bring down the top rate," Greider's Stockman said of the broad-based tax cuts, making the administration seem a shill for the wealthy. "Supply side is 'trickle-down' theory."

Administration officials were slow to react to the article, in part because it was very long and they were very busy. James Baker and the administration's Legislative Strategy Group shared a chuckle over Stockman's discomfiture and presented him with a framed copy of the magazine cover. "We even autographed the darn thing," Baker remembered.

But Democrats seized on the "Trojan horse" and "trickle-down" language as revealing a basic dishonesty at the core of Reaganomics. Senator Gary Hart of Colorado charged Stockman with "one of the most cynical pieces of performance by a public official since the Vietnam era." Senator Ernest Hollings of South Carolina called Stockman's act the "best off-Broadway show we've ever had." The media played the story for all it was worth. "The networks hammered us for two straight nights, less about what the article said (in my opinion) than what the Democrats said it said," Baker remarked.

Ed Meese and Mike Deaver wanted Stockman fired at once. The president had no choice, they declared. Baker disagreed. The administration needed Stockman's skill with numbers, he judged. "I don't know who the hell else we could have put in there at that time," Baker recalled.

But Stockman needed to be taught a lesson. Baker summoned him for a chat. Stockman had frequented Baker's office during the nine months of Reagan's presidency, until it had become familiar to him, even comfortable. "Today was different," Stockman recounted. "A different James Baker was now sitting two feet away. He had just plunked himself down in his chair without saying a word. His whole patented opening ritual had been completely dispensed with. No off-color joke. No casual waltz around his big office before he sat down. No jump shot that resulted in the arched flight of a paperwad across the room and without fail into the wastebasket. This time it was all business, and his eyes were steely cold."

Stockman knew Baker had been hearing from Meese, Deaver, and others in the administration. Baker's words indicated as much. "My friend," he said, "I want you to listen up good. Your ass is in a sling. All of the rest of them want you shit-canned right now. Immediately. This afternoon. If it weren't for me, you'd be a goner already. But I got you one last chance to save yourself. So you're going to do it precisely and exactly like I tell you. Otherwise you're finished around here . . . You're going to have lunch with the president. The menu is humble pie. You're going to eat every last mother-f'ing spoonful of it. You're going to be the most contrite sonofabitch this world has ever seen."

Stockman absorbed the lecture. Baker asked him if he understood. Stockman nodded. Baker stood up to let him know the session was over. Stockman headed for the door. Baker fixed him again with his cold eyes. "Let me repeat something, just in case you didn't get the point," he said. "When you go through the Oval Office door, I want to see that sorry ass of yours dragging on the carpet."

BAKER'S PERFORMANCE WAS primarily for effect. He distrusted Stockman. "He was disloyal," he later said. But Stockman was smart, and now that he had become a lightning rod, he could draw criticism that might otherwise have hit Reagan. He could be fired later if necessary. Meanwhile he had to learn to keep his mouth shut. He had to be whipped into better behavior.

Baker knew *he* had to do the whipping because the president wouldn't. Reagan was known to his staff as a softy, unable to blame anyone he considered to be on his side. "I'm reading an article about Dave Stockman supposedly telling all to a reporter in the Atlantic Monthly," Reagan wrote in his diary. "If true, Dave is a turncoat—but in reality he was victimized by what he'd always thought was a good friend."

Reagan shared this sympathy with Stockman at their noon session in the Oval Office. Stockman arrived suitably chagrined and expecting a dressing-down. "I had lunch," Reagan recorded in his diary. "He couldn't eat. He stood up to it"—admitted speaking out of school—"and then tendered his resignation. I got him to tell the whole thing about his supposed friend who betrayed him; then refused to accept his resignation. Told him he should do a 'mea culpa' before the press and clear the misconception that had been created by the story."

Stockman remembered the session more vividly. "The president's eyes were moist," he wrote. "It was unmistakable—they glistened." Stockman had expected anger; what he got was closer to sorrow. "Dave, how do you explain this?" the president asked. "You have hurt me. Why?"

Stockman stumblingly told his story. But nothing came out right. Finally he gave up. "Sir, none of that matters now," he said. "One slip and I've ruined it all." He offered to resign.

"The president responded by putting his hand on mine," Stockman recalled. "He said, 'No, Dave, that isn't what I want. I read the whole article. It's not what they are saying. I know, the quotes and all make it look different. I wish you hadn't said them. But you're a victim of sabotage by the press. They're trying to bring you down because of what you have helped us accomplish.'"

Reagan stood and offered Stockman his hand. "Dave, I want you to stay on," he said. "I need your help." He started toward his desk. But then he turned back. "Oh," he said, "the fellas think this is getting out of control. They want you to write up a statement explaining all this and go before the press this afternoon. Would you do that?"

WILLIAM CASEY SWALLOWED his bitterness at being deprived of the State Department, but the dose didn't suit his stomach, and the CIA felt his dyspepsia. "He was frustrated by its ponderous bureaucratic ways, the amount of time it took to accomplish straightforward tasks, its reluctance to look outward, its timidity, its lack of diversity," Robert Gates said of his new boss. "The veteran of OSS arrived at CIA to wage war and found, instead of a clandestine dagger, a stifling bureaucracy." Casey started a shake-up at once. "I would like to tell you about some personnel, organizational and conceptual changes I've made or am in the progress of making at the CIA," he wrote to Reagan in May 1981. "It is a good outfit, composed of dedicated people with good spirit, but it has been permitted to run down and get too thin in top level people and capabilities." Casey blamed Stansfield Turner for hamstringing the agency and the media for scapegoating it, but a more systemic problem was the pay cap applied to CIA personnel (and other federal officials). Able people could make far more outside the government than they could in the CIA; the result was that many left the agency just when they were reaching the prime of their careers.

Casey couldn't do anything about the pay situation, so he concentrated on other matters. He explained to Reagan that the CIA comprised four major units: analysis, operations, technology, and administration. "As I size things up, the Analytical and Operations units are most in need of improvement and rebuilding," he wrote. "The analysis has been academic, soft, not sufficiently relevant and realistic." Casey said he was remedying the situation by switching the director of the operations unit to analysis. "I have frequently found that I get better intelligence judgments from the streetwise, on-the-ground Operations staff than I get from the more academic Analytical staff."

As for operations: "I spent most of the last three weeks talking to all the operational people and carefully sizing up all the activities of the Operations unit. It quickly became clear to me that there were too many components for any one man to manage adequately." Consequently, Casey had divided the operations unit into two parts. Beneath a single operations chief would sit two deputies, one who would run the "worldwide clandestine service," the other who would organize support activities. Casey described his thinking about the appropriate director of operations. "I had a tough bullet to bite," he said. "The only one around of whom I had personal knowledge and experience which made me confident that he could impart the kind of thrust and drive that the necessary rebuilding will require is Max Hugel." Casey reminded Reagan that Hugel had worked on the 1980 campaign. He had a previous background in military intelligence and a career in the corporate sector. He lacked experience in intelligence operations and was being criticized on that account, but Casey was willing to defend him. "Once I concluded appointing Hugel was the best thing to do, I felt I had to bite the bullet and take the flak. I'm confident it was the right thing to do."

Casey's campaign to resurrect the CIA would define much of Reagan's foreign policy, for good and ill. His appointment of Max Hugel proved part of the ill, at once. "It was the appointment from hell," Robert Gates recalled. Gates agreed that the agency was ingrown and required outside ideas and energy. But he thought the operations division was a bad place to put such an extreme novice. Gates wasn't alone, and the veterans of the division deliberately made Hugel's life difficult. "Leaks to the press about Hugel's mistakes, mannerisms, and faux pas began nearly immediately," Gates said. Hugel didn't help himself by his ignorance. "Everyone was embarrassed to have him go to the Hill to testify or to the White House for meetings, and all kinds of stratagems were employed to keep him out of sight." Casey eventually agreed that the appointment was counterproductive, and a minor scandal involving allegations of earlier insider trading gave him an excuse to let Hugel go. The allegations proved to be inaccurate, but Casey had no desire to bring him back.

Casey learned a lesson from the affair, Gates observed, but the wrong one. "It was the first and last time Casey would challenge the DO"— Directorate of Operations—"institutionally. Badly burned, from then on he would work around the operations bureaucracy rather than try to change it. This would have dreadful consequences. Now he would indulge his instincts and play Donovan"—William Donovan, the legendary chief of the wartime OSS. "He would reach down into the clandestine service to kindred spirits and work directly with them." And he would keep his own people in the dark, treating them as though they were the enemy. Bobby Ray Inman, Casey's first deputy director, put it bluntly: "He customarily lied."

REAGAN LET CASEY play Donovan. But he insisted that his intelligence director meanwhile provide information on the Soviet Union. Reagan's foreign policy, from the beginning of his administration, was dedicated to combating Soviet communism. Whatever contributed to the fight, he encouraged, though he didn't always supervise it. What did not contribute, he rejected or ignored. Reagan instructed Casey and the CIA to compile the best estimates of the American intelligence community on the actions and motives of Soviet foreign policy. The exercise took several months; in the summer of 1981, Casey delivered his report.

"We believe that Soviet military leaders regard military strength as the foundation of the USSR's status as a global superpower and as the most critical factor underlying Soviet foreign policy," the secret report asserted. "As it enters the 1980s, the current Soviet leadership sees the heavy military investments made during the last two decades paying off in the form of unprecedentedly favorable advances across the military spectrum, and over the long term in political gains where military power or military assistance has been the actual instrument of policy or the decisive complement to Soviet diplomacy." The Soviets had been especially active in the nonaligned world, supporting leftists in Angola and Ethiopia since the mid-1970s and invading Afghanistan in 1979. "This more assertive Soviet international behavior is likely to persist as long as the USSR perceives that Western strength is declining and as it further explores the utility of increased military power as a means of realizing its global ambitions." The Kremlin's ambitions might provoke a confrontation with the United States. "Moscow still views such a prospect as extremely hazardous. However, in light of the change in the strategic balance and continued expansion of general purpose forces, the Soviets are now more prepared and may be more willing to accept the risks of confrontation in a serious crisis, particularly in an area where they have military or geopolitical advantages."

Yet Moscow was not uninterested in better relations with the West.

"The Soviets will continue to stress the importance of the arms control dialogue with Washington as the key to bilateral relations," the intelligence report declared. "And they will seek to resuscitate détente as the most promising way of constraining US military policies, of advancing their military and political objectives, and of controlling the costs and risks of heightened international tensions." If their overtures succeeded, they would continue on this path. If not, they would alter course. "If they conclude that there is no prospect in the near term for meaningful results from renewed SALT, they may decide to go beyond the SALT II constraints, seeking to place the onus for failure on the United States and to exploit the breakdown to widen cleavages in the Atlantic Alliance."

The Kremlin perceived an opening in Europe, the intelligence paper said. "The Soviets see a lack of Western consensus—for example, in implementing NATO's program to modernize its long-range theater nuclear forces (LRTNF). They seek to exploit these differences with a dual purpose: to pursue certain economic and political interests with the Europeans even if Soviet relations with the United States deteriorate, and to generate pressures on West European governments to influence Washington toward greater flexibility in its dealings with the USSR."

Yet the troubles in Poland surrounding the rise of the Solidarity movement offset some of the Soviet advantage farther west. "Poland presents the USSR with the most threatening and complex challenge to its vital interests to emerge in Eastern Europe in the postwar period. Soviet leaders are prepared to use military force to preserve Soviet domination if they become convinced that changes taking place in Poland jeopardize the USSR's hegemony over Eastern Europe. However, because they know that the political, military and economic costs of intervention would be extremely high, they may bring themselves, so long as Poland's commitment to the Warsaw Pact is assured, to live with a much-modified Communist system in Poland."

50

MUCH OF BEING a big-state governor prepares a person to be president: staffing, budgets, relations with the legislature and the media. But governors get no preparation in the crucial realm of foreign policy. The occasional senator who finds his way to the White House has an edge on the governors, as the Senate ratifies treaties and joins the House in funding foreign policy. Governors who become president have to learn foreign policy on the job.

Reagan had an advantage over some other governors elevated to the White House, in that he had to run three times before being elected president. His first race, in 1968, being tardy and timid, gave him little grounding in foreign policy. But he studied, thought, and spoke a great deal about international affairs in preparing for and conducting his campaigns in 1976 and 1980.

Even so, making decisions on foreign policy was a different matter from making promises or critiquing the decisions of others. Reagan's on-the-job training took place primarily in meetings of the National Security Council and the smaller, more focused National Security Planning Group. Reagan was an apt pupil, though not uniformly attentive. Bobby Ray Inman recalled that Reagan often sat silently through the first fifty minutes or so of an hour-long meeting. The president would nod occasionally, but Inman noticed that the nods didn't always follow comments calling for assent or disagreement. His mind was clearly wandering. Yet several minutes from the end, he would perk up as Ed Meese began asking a series of short, sharp questions designed to elicit the views of the participants. Reagan would take this in, then adeptly summarize the meeting on the basis of the questions and answers.

At the start of his foreign policy training, however, Reagan was fully engaged. His first NSC meeting involved the Caribbean basin. "There are 33 states in the region, 19 independent and 14 self-governing," Richard Allen said by way of introduction. "They are small, beset by problems, and vulnerable to outside force." The national security adviser proposed a comprehensive approach to the region. "The wisdom of a comprehensive policy is that we would thereby recognize that any action taken with respect to one country or one issue will have an impact on others in the area."

Al Haig jumped in. "This area is our third border," the secretary of state said. "There is no question that it is in turmoil. The middle class in the region is demanding a greater stake in societies which can't easily cope with the need for change. Yet these countries could manage if it were not for Cuba. Cuba exploits internal difficulties in these states by exporting arms and subversion." El Salvador was Cuba's principal target. "Six hundred tons of arms are going into El Salvador in various ways." Nicaragua was Cuba's accomplice, and because it still received some American aid, it was susceptible to American pressure. "The first order of business is to show the Nicaraguans that we will not tolerate violations"—of regional agreements not to interfere in other countries' affairs—"as did the past administration."

Reagan spoke up. "My own feeling, and one about which I have talked at length, is that we are way behind, perhaps decades, in establishing good relations with the two Americas," he said. The previous administration had gone about things just backward. "We must change the attitude of our diplomatic corps so that we don't bring down governments in the name of human rights. None of them is as guilty of human rights violations as Cuba and the U.S.S.R. We don't throw out our friends just because they can't pass the saliva test on human rights. I want to see that stopped. We need people who recognize that philosophy."

Caspar Weinberger argued for action. "The problem stems from Cuba," the defense secretary said. "With some covert aid, we could disrupt Cuban activities." The covert route was necessary because the American people didn't understand the threat to American interests from Cuba's actions. But while the covert operations proceeded, so should an educational effort. "We need to explain to people that this is a dangerous situation for the U.S. and that we may have to move strongly."

Reagan thought El Salvador was the place to make a stand and a statement. "El Salvador is a good starting point," he said. "A victory there could set an example."

William Casey suggested that time wasn't on America's side. The British were pulling out of Belize; the longtime colony was slated to achieve independence in a few months. This had serious implications for regional security, the CIA director said.

Reagan repeated that El Salvador was the key. "We can't afford a defeat," he said. "El Salvador is the place for a victory."

CENTRAL AMERICA AND the Caribbean remained the focus in subsequent discussions of foreign policy. Al Haig brought home the American ambassador in Nicaragua to speak to the president and the NSC. Lawrence Pezzullo was unimpressed by the Sandinista leadership. "They are not men of great stature," he said. "They fell into power after a general insurrection against Somoza was started with all sectors of Nicaraguan society participating." The Sandinistas had no experience in government and were doing a dismal job directing the country. As for their Salvadoran connection: "The Sandinistas were grabbed by the romance of the revolutionary process as they saw it in Central America and were swept along into helping in El Salvador. They also saw a revolutionary El Salvador being a forward defense position for their own revolution, and were probably convinced by Castro to get involved."

Pezzullo identified essential questions for the Reagan administration: "Can we get the Sandinistas to back off in El Salvador? Can we impress on them the high cost of continuing their efforts? Can we drive a wedge between them and the Cubans?" Pezzullo didn't deny that strong measures might become necessary, but he thought they hadn't yet. The administration should move carefully. "Avoid any precipitous act," he said. "Don't cut off aid for the moment. The evidence is there for such an action, but a sudden action on our part would lead to a very negative reaction in Managua and have a cascading effect that would cool or terminate relations."

Haig suggested giving the Sandinistas thirty days. They should be told that if they didn't lay off in El Salvador, the United States would suspend all assistance and perhaps take further steps.

At this meeting Reagan pondered going to the regional source of the Central American troubles. "What can we do specifically about Cuba?" he asked the group.

William Clark, Haig's deputy at State, said the State Department was planning to show the leaders of Congress evidence of Cuban complicity in El Salvador's troubles.

Reagan wanted more. "What specific pressures can be placed on Cuba?" he demanded.

Caspar Weinberger replied that clandestine operations were one possibility. Economic pressure was another. The United States was already embargoing trade with Cuba, but the administration could try to persuade America's allies to join the embargo.

Reagan asked for military options.

Haig evidently responded forthrightly to the president's question, but his remarks were excised when the minutes of this top secret meeting were declassified.

Weinberger pointed out a problem with the military option, one not shared by clandestine operations. "The problem with military action is that as it escalates, congressional checks come into play," the defense secretary said.

Reagan didn't respond to Weinberger's objection. Instead, he returned to El Salvador. "If the junta falls in El Salvador, it will be seen as an American defeat," he said. He endorsed the thirty-day warning to Nicaragua, but he was prepared to consider escalation. "We must not let Central America become another Cuba on the mainland. It cannot happen."

R EAGAN HAD NEVER been an impulsive person. His career steps had been deliberate: planned and executed with care. It took him years to make the leap from radio to films. He required a decade to shift from films to politics. He was slow even to conclude that Nancy was the love of his life.

His decisions as president were, for the most part, equally deliberate. As determined as he was to prevent Central America from becoming another Cuba, he refused to rush into anything.

Sometimes, though, he was tempted to move more swiftly. Poland had been restive under communist rule for decades. During the 1950s, Polish workers walked off their jobs to protest dismal and dangerous conditions in factories and corruption in government. In 1970 shipyard workers in Gdańsk marched and rioted against rising food prices; the government's feckless response inspired workers in other cities and intellectuals to join the antigovernment demonstrations. The 1978 elevation of Polish cardinal Karol Wojtyła to the papacy, as Pope John Paul II, afforded the Polish protesters additional confidence; a papal visit the following year pulled hundreds of thousands of Poles into the streets in an unsubtle rebuke of the regime. During the summer of 1980 a hike in meat prices provoked the largest protests to date and the establishment at Gdańsk of Solidarity, led by the charismatic Lech Wałesa. Strikes spread across the country, paralyzing the economy and presenting the communist rulers with a stark choice: to order the army against the strikers or to grant some of their demands. The government chose the latter, which convinced Wałesa and the workers that events were moving their way and spurred them to demand still more.

The Soviet government of Leonid Brezhnev observed developments in Poland with mounting concern, as the CIA noted. The Kremlin cared little about Polish meat prices, but it cared much about who governed the country. Since World War II the overriding objective of Soviet policy toward the countries to Russia's immediate west had been to prevent their falling under hostile influence. What this meant was that any government in Warsaw had to suit Moscow. Thrice previously—in East Germany in 1953, in Hungary in 1956, in Czechoslovakia in 1968—the Kremlin had dispatched Soviet troops and armor to crush insurgencies that threatened pro-Soviet regimes. When the Kremlin in the autumn of 1980 spoke ominously about "antisocialist elements" in Poland and moved troops to the Polish frontier, it appeared to be setting the stage for another armed intervention.

Reagan inherited the Polish problem along with the presidency. And he inherited an American policy that was stouter than he liked to give Jimmy Carter credit for. "The United States is watching with growing concern the unprecedented building of Soviet forces along the Polish border," Carter had declared in December 1980. "The Polish people and authorities should be free to work out their internal difficulties without outside interference." Carter offered economic assistance to Poland to ease the country's debt and overall distress; at the same time he issued a sharply worded warning: "The attitude and future policies of the United States toward the Soviet Union would be directly and very adversely affected by any Soviet use of force in Poland."

Reagan could do no less than Carter, having campaigned against the weakness he ascribed to the Democrats' foreign policy. He echoed Carter's admonitions. "The Polish people must be allowed to work out their own solutions to their problems," he said shortly after inauguration. "Outside intervention there would affect profoundly and in the long term the entire range of East-West ties."

Whether the Soviets would intervene or not preoccupied American intelligence analysts during the first year of Reagan's presidency. A crucial conduit of information was a Polish colonel, Ryszard Kukliński, who had been cooperating with the CIA for years. "We waited eagerly for each of his reports," recalled the CIA's Robert Gates. The administration prepared for two scenarios: "the worst case: a Soviet invasion, resistance, and significant bloodshed," as Gates put it, and internal repression by the Polish regime, perhaps to forestall Soviet intervention. The menu of American responses included recalling the American ambassador in Poland, curtailing economic aid, and imposing stiffer credit conditions on loans to the Polish government. Significantly, nothing stronger was contemplated, even in the worst case. "For all the tough talk," Gates recalled, speaking of the remarks by Reagan and other administration officials, "the conservative new team was wholly focused on stern warnings and possible economic sanctions in the event the Soviets acted in Poland. More dramatic measures weren't even discussed."

The tension in Poland mounted as the months passed. Colonel Kukliński sent word that the Polish regime, headed by General Wojciech Jaruzelski, was consulting with the Kremlin on imposing martial law in Poland. Whether this would serve as a prelude to Soviet intervention was impossible to say. But Gates and the CIA, assuming it might, prepared a statement Reagan could issue in response. The plan was for the president to proclaim a "Polish Patriots Day" and ask Americans to "stand with our Polish brothers and sisters" by wearing ribbons of the Polish national colors, white and red.

Yet the CIA thought Soviet intervention remained unlikely, at least in the near term. The Soviets were in a "desperate dilemma," William Casey wrote to Reagan. "If they go, they will get economic chaos arising from the debt, a slowdown of the whole Polish work force and millions of Poles conducting a guerrilla war against them. If they don't, they are open to the West and a political force which could unravel their entire system." It was a decision the Soviet leadership didn't want to have to make. "Before sending divisions in," Casey predicted, "they will move heaven and earth to get the Poles to crack down themselves."

Reagan realized he faced a dilemma, too. "Now we must take on the problem of what to do or if to do something to help the Polish people," he wrote in his diary. "Their economy is going bust. Here is the first major break in the Red dike—Poland's disenchantment with Soviet Communism. Can we afford to let Poland collapse? But in the state of our present economy, can we afford to help in a meaningful way?"

The strains in Poland eased slightly during the summer of 1981. Polish cardinal Stefan Wyszyński implored Wałesa and Solidarity not to carry out a threatened general strike, contending that massive violence would be the inevitable result. When Wałesa at first refused, the elderly and ailing cardinal knelt down before the Solidarity leader and said he would remain on his knees until death unless Wałesa canceled the strike. Wałesa gave in.

BUT CONDITIONS AGAIN grew fraught during the autumn. The slow pace of reform prompted Solidarity once more to threaten a general strike. The Polish government warned against such action, and the Soviets sent advisers, including Marshal Viktor Kulikov, the military commander of the Warsaw Pact, to Warsaw to stiffen the government's resolve.

In December the Polish government imposed martial law. The government arrested Wałesa and other Solidarity leaders. The union itself was outlawed. Travel and communications were curtailed; universities were closed; Poland's borders were sealed; a curfew was imposed. In the crackdown at least a dozen people, perhaps scores, were killed.

The CIA had lost its chief asset in Poland when Colonel Kukliński concluded that his cover had been compromised and fled the country. Yet his warning about the possibility of martial law had prepared the administration for the moment Jaruzelski made the move. Reagan responded with a call to the pope. "Your Holiness, I want you to know how deeply we feel about the situation in your homeland," he said, according to a transcript released to the media. "Our sympathies are with the people, not the government." Reagan praised John Paul for making Poland's struggle part of the struggle for freedom across the globe. "Our country was inspired when you visited Poland, and to see their commitment to religion and belief in God. It was an inspiration to the whole world to watch on television. All of us were very thrilled."

The president opened other avenues to the Vatican and, through the Vatican, to Poland. "Lunched with Cardinal Casaroli, Secretary of State to the Vatican," he wrote in his diary for December 15. "Most of the talk was on Poland. This thing going on there was no sudden reaction as the Communist government would have us believe. The operation is so smooth it must have taken weeks for planning. Solidarity was going to demand a vote by the people as to whether they wanted to continue under Communism. That the Commies can never permit."

Reagan spoke to reporters about Poland. "All the information that we have confirms that the imposition of martial law in Poland has led to the arrest and confinement, in prisons and detention camps, of thousands of Polish trade union leaders and intellectuals," he said in a prepared statement ahead of a news conference. "Factories are being seized by security forces and workers beaten." For eighteen months Poland had been moving toward greater freedom and personal liberty; this progress had been abruptly and brutally reversed. "Coercion and violation of human rights on a massive scale have taken the place of negotiation and compromise." The hand of the Kremlin was clear. "It would be naive to think this could happen without the full knowledge and the support of the Soviet Union. We're not naive."

Confidentially the president considered his options. At a long and contentious meeting of the National Security Council on December 21, Reagan heard, made, and weighed arguments for and against strong action against the Soviets and their Polish protégés. Al Haig described the current situation in Poland, as American intelligence understood it. "There is widespread resentment among the people against the Polish government but no major, overt challenge to it," Haig said. Church leaders, including Józef Glemp, archbishop of Warsaw, were taking a cautious line. "Archbishop Glemp has 'walked the cat back,'" Haig said. "He has shifted from a position of strong condemnation of the military law that has been imposed to a plea for moderation and for no bloodshed." The Polish military had warned parish priests against denouncing martial law, and most of the priests appeared to be complying.

Haig said the State Department had received a detailed analysis of the Soviet position from the embassy in Moscow. "The theme of this message is that the Soviets are 'cooling it,'" Haig said. "They are not preparing for intervention and, significantly, they are not preparing the Soviet people for intervention." The embassy had concluded that the Kremlin didn't have the stomach for intervention. "The Soviets are afraid to intervene because they know they can't hack it," Haig said. They would go to great lengths to keep the Jaruzelski government afloat. "The Soviets are preparing food for shipment to Poland and preparing for a massive bailout of the Polish economy."

Offering his own recommendation, Haig urged caution. "I am not one who espouses the devil theory that all is lost, that the Soviets are in charge, that Solidarity is dead, that all this is the case with or without Soviet intervention. I don't think we should proceed on these assumptions." Instead, the administration should watch carefully and respond accordingly. "We should husband our leverage and use it as the assessment changes."

Reagan sought a stronger response. "This is the first time in sixty years that we have had this kind of opportunity," he said, referring to the cracks Solidarity had made in the wall of communist rule. "There may not be another in our lifetime. Can we afford not to go all out? I'm talking about a total quarantine on the Soviet Union. No détente! We know, and the world knows, that they are behind this. We have backed away so many times! After World War II we offered Poland the Marshall Plan. They accepted, but the Soviets said no." Reagan talked of suspending licenses that allowed American companies to trade with Poland. He noted that Lane Kirkland and the AFL-CIO had taken a forceful position in support of Solidarity. "Kirkland said in a conversation that our unions might refuse to load ships," Reagan told the NSC. "How will it look if we say yes"—let U.S. exports to the Soviet Union proceed—"while our unions, our own 'Solidarity,' won't load the ships?" Reagan acknowledged that big companies doing business with Poland would suffer from an embargo. "I recognize that this is a great problem for International Harvester and for Caterpillar. It may mean thousands of layoffs." But what was the alternative? "Can we allow a go-ahead?" He didn't think so, though he suggested examining means for softening the blow to Americans. "Perhaps we can find a way to compensate the companies if we say no. Perhaps put the items in inventory and use them by some other means." But the administration had to do something. "Can we do less now than tell our allies, 'This is the big casino'? There may never be another chance!" Reagan likened Solidarity and the Polish dissidents to America's founding fathers. "It is like the opening lines in our own Declaration of Independence: 'When in the course of human events.' This is exactly what they are doing now."

George Bush echoed Reagan's remarks. "I have thought a lot about this problem over the weekend," the vice president said. "I agree with the president that we are at a real turning point." Bush urged Reagan to sound the call for Poland. "The president should really identify, in a speech, with Walesa and the Polish ambassador. I really feel that—particularly at this Christmas time—the country is waiting for a more forward position. This is not a political matter but one of world leadership."

Caspar Weinberger endorsed Bush's recommendation. "I suggest that you talk to the world," the defense secretary told Reagan. "This is not a time for prudence or caution. The world needs to be told that it has a leader." Weinberger wanted Reagan to fix the blame squarely on the Kremlin. "Let's not be mistaken," he said. "What Poland has now in Jaruzelski is a Russian general in Polish uniform. The Soviets are getting what they want." Weinberger pressed for action. "This is a chance to seize the initiative. It is the time to do it."

Bill Casey chimed in. "We lose credibility if we fail to follow through now on this situation," the CIA chief asserted. "We are seeing an unraveling of the communist economic system." Casey warned that America's European allies wouldn't support an embargo, but he didn't think their timidity should deter the president from doing what needed to be done. "We should go with across-the-board sanctions."

John Block, the secretary of agriculture, tried to slow things down. Block had to deal with farmers, who would suffer the brunt of an embargo, but he framed his case for caution more broadly. "The Soviet communist system is collapsing of its own weight," he said. "I believe there should be a presidential message, but we must be careful. If we play our trump card—total economic sanctions—at this time, what else can we then do? We must wait for the time to play that card, not do it prematurely."

Reagan spoke again. "Let me tell you what I have in mind," he said. "We are the leaders of the Western world. We haven't been for years, several years, except in name, but we accept that role now. I am talking about action that addresses the allies, and solicits—not begs—them to join in a complete quarantine of the Soviet Union. Cancel all licenses. Tell the allies that if they don't go along with us, we let them know—but not in a threatening fashion—that we may have to review our alliances." The president cited Franklin Roosevelt. "I am thinking back to 1938 when there was a great united effort opportunity. In a speech in Chicago, FDR asked the free world to join in a quarantine of Germany. On that request his brains were kicked out all over." No one in the room commented that Reagan (again) had confused crucial details about the quarantine speech. Instead, they listened to him tell a story from Hollywood, about how Warner Brothers had made a movie, *Confessions of a Nazi Spy*, that irritated studios seeking to continue to show movies in Hitler's Germany. The studios tried to suppress the film, but Warner stuck to its guns. "The film was run and had as much impact as anything" in alerting the world to Hitler's evil designs, Reagan said.

Historical analogies apart, the United States needed to stand up for its principles, Reagan said. "If we show this kind of strength, and we have labor and the people with us, if we demand that Solidarity get its rights—if that happens"—if Solidarity got its rights—"nothing will be done. But if not, then we invoke sanctions. And those who do not go along with us will be boycotted, too, and will be considered to be against us." Reagan scoffed at the sanctions imposed by the Carter administration against Moscow after the invasion of Afghanistan. "The wheat and Olympic actions were ridiculous," he said. "It is time to speak to the world."

Don Regan joined John Block and Al Haig in trying to soften the stridency at this meeting. "We want to send some message," he said. "But we do not want to incite street fighting." Regan thought allied support essential for effective sanctions, if things came to that. "Al has to have time to get our allies on board without bullying them. Show them where we stand and where we are heading. This takes time."

Haig seconded Block's concern about going all in at once. The Soviets were still uncertain about what they might do on Poland, the secretary of state said. "If you now slap on a full court press, then they can say to themselves they have nothing left to lose."

"That doesn't bother me at all," Reagan replied. The president clearly wanted to move decisively. "If we don't take action now, three or four years from now we'll have another situation and we'll wonder why didn't we go for it when we had the whole country with us? I'm tired of looking backward."

George Bush shifted toward the middle ground. "I agree with Don and Al," he said. "We should take the time to consult, but giving a speech now is essential. What is missing is moral leadership." Bush urged Reagan to do what he did best. "You should state how strongly you feel about Walesa, about Solidarity, about the Polish ambassador and about the Polish people. You can speak in generalities without spelling out details." Bush rephrased Reagan's position, saying, "We are at an emotional turning point."

Weinberger pushed forward again. "My worry is that we will wait too long because a single ally can hold us back," the Pentagon chief said. "If there is moderation in the Soviet position, the way to find out is not to hold back, but to make the speech, then if there are no results, spell out the specifics of what we will do."

Haig didn't like making even veiled threats unless a decision had been made to follow through if the Russians didn't respond. "We are not dealing with giving a speech but with setting policy," he said. "I would never give a speech unless we are prepared to act. From my viewpoint, I don't think we are in such a bad position now."

"No, no litany of items is to be recited," Reagan replied. "But what we should say is an overall expression that what we will do is an absolute quarantine of all trade as President Roosevelt had proposed in 1938."

"To warn them again is an empty threat," Haig rejoined. "When you speak, it should be to inform them that you have decided to do something."

Jeane Kirkpatrick jumped in. Reagan had made the Georgetown professor ambassador to the United Nations, where she lectured almost as regularly as she had on campus. "Mr. President, you must tell the truth," she said. "You must stand by the central core of this administration." Kirkpatrick noted that conservative pundits, starting with columnist George Will, were complaining that the president had been silent and inactive. Reagan needed to correct this impression. "One of our objectives is to prevent our own demoralization by inactivity," Kirkpatrick said. "It made me ill this morning to read a *Post* article on Afghanistan where the Afghans are still fighting Soviet tanks with ancient rifles. Perhaps one of the things we can do is more effective aid to Afghanistan. We don't have to talk about it—just do it."

Ed Meese wanted the group, and the president especially, to consider the range of measures an embargo or quarantine should entail. "Are we going to cut off all trade?" Meese asked. "Part of trade? All communications, including flights and telephones? Are we going to cut diplomatic and political contacts? Are we going to recall our ambassador?"

"We have all these things we can do," Reagan responded. "We don't have to let them out." He drew the line at closing the embassy, however. "We would have to give back the seven Christians that are there," he explained, referring to dissidents who had taken refuge in the embassy. "We should also keep arms limitation negotiations going for the time being," he added, "but be prepared to walk out."

Haig agreed that the embassy should stay open. "We don't want to close our embassy or break diplomatic contact," he said. "We don't want to get into a World War III scenario." Haig reminded the group how important Poland was to Moscow. "Let us make no mistake. This is a matter of life and death for the Soviet Union. They would go to war over this."

Caspar Weinberger thought Haig was being melodramatic. "The Soviets may take military actions against Poland," the defense secretary said, "but this is not world war."

The president said he wanted to write a letter to Leonid Brezhnev. The letter would remind the Soviet leader of what was at stake in the event of sanctions. "It could address the fact that they haven't been able to provide their people the living standard they would like and that they would be in an even worse plight without trade," Reagan said. "We could say that we cannot continue trade and that we will press our allies to follow us unless the Polish situation is alleviated. But again holding out our hand. Can he envision what it would be like if trade with the West were open? It would be a different, much better world. He can have that one, giving up nothing, or the one that will result if we are forced to take trade-cutting sanctions."

Reagan rarely made decisions in large meetings like this. He hadn't made a decision on Poland when Ed Meese informed him that he was fifteen minutes late for a session with a visiting women's group. Reagan rose to go, joking on his way out: "Remember, everyone, stock up on vodka!"

THE NEXT DAY Reagan met with the Polish ambassador and his wife, who had defected following the imposition of martial law. The ambassador praised the U.S. government for the moral support it had offered over the years; he specifically mentioned Radio Free Europe and said he hoped it would continue broadcasting for many more years. He then asked a favor. "Mr. President," he said, "would you light a candle and put it in the window tonight for the people of Poland?"

Michael Deaver, who was present at the meeting, recounted the response. "Right then, Ronald Reagan got up and went to the second floor, lighted a candle, and put it in the window of the dining room. Later, in what I still recall as the most human picture of the Reagan presidency, he escorted his guests through the walkway and out to the circular drive on the South Lawn of the White House. In a persistent rain, he escorted them to their car, past the C-9 Secret Service post, holding an umbrella over the head of the wife of the Polish ambassador, as she wept on his shoulder."

The following evening the president made Poland the centerpiece of his Christmas address to the American people. "As I speak to you tonight, the fate of a proud and ancient nation hangs in the balance," he said. "For a thousand years, Christmas has been celebrated in Poland, a land of deep religious faith. But this Christmas brings little joy to the courageous Polish people. They have been betrayed by their own government." The violence and mass arrests under martial law made a mockery of the Polish government's pledges in the United Nations charter, the Helsinki Accords on human rights, and even its own Gdańsk agreement of the previous year. As before, Reagan blamed the Soviets. "It is no coincidence that Soviet Marshal Kulikov, chief of the Warsaw Pact forces, and other senior Red Army officers were in Poland while these outrages were being initiated. And it is no coincidence that the martial law proclamations imposed in December by the Polish government were being printed in the Soviet Union in September." The Jaruzelski regime targeted Solidarity but in doing so assaulted the entire country. "By persecuting Solidarity the Polish government wages war against its own people."

Reagan, like Carter a year earlier, offered the carrot of economic aid, should the Polish government rescind martial law and release the arrested, and the stick of sanctions. He emphasized the latter. "If the outrages in Poland do not cease, we cannot and will not conduct business as usual with the perpetrators and those who aid and abet them," he said. "Make no mistake, their crime will cost them dearly in their future dealings with America and free peoples everywhere. I do not make this statement lightly or without serious reflection." Some sanctions were being imposed already, Reagan said. Shipments of agricultural products to the Polish government were being suspended, though food aid could continue through private humanitarian organizations. Credit insurance through the Export-Import Bank was being terminated. Landing privileges for Polish planes at American airports and fishing privileges for Polish ships in American waters were being canceled. The administration was working with America's allies to curtail technology exports to Poland. "These actions are not directed against the Polish people," Reagan explained. "They are a warning to the government of Poland that free men cannot and will not stand idly by in the face of brutal repression."

The president revealed that he had written to Jaruzelski urging him to withdraw the martial law order. Reiterating that Moscow bore a "major share of blame" for the events in Poland, he said he had sent a letter to Brezhnev as well. "In it, I informed him that if this repression continues, the United States will have no choice but to take further concrete political and economic measures affecting our relationship."

Reagan asked the American people to join him in expressing support for the Polish people. "Yesterday, I met in this very room with Romuald Spasowski, the distinguished former Polish Ambassador who has sought asylum in our country in protest of the suppression of his native land. He told me that one of the ways the Polish people have demonstrated their solidarity in the face of martial law is by placing lighted candles in their windows to show that the light of liberty still glows in their hearts." Reagan told of the candle he had placed in the window. "I urge all of you to do the same tomorrow night, on Christmas Eve, as a personal statement of your commitment to the steps we're taking to support the brave people of Poland in their time of troubles."

POLAND'S TROUBLES SERVED as Reagan's first real test on foreign policy. They gave him an opportunity to move boldly against the Soviets, and they sorely tempted him to do so. But ultimately the caution that marked most of his decisions set in here as well. He recognized, on second and third thought, that his leverage with the Kremlin on Poland was sharply limited. He couldn't take stern action without doing more harm to Americans and Poles than to the Soviets. He certainly wasn't going to risk war over the jailing of Polish dissidents. In the end, his substantive response to the martial law declaration didn't go beyond the measures he described in his Christmas speech. And the Polish government, with Soviet backing, persisted in its suppression of Solidarity.

Yet the crisis in Poland enabled Reagan to do what he always did best: state the case for freedom against those who would suppress it. His words didn't free any prisoners, but the Poles and others heard Reagan's call for Polish self-determination, and many took heart from his support.

A T HOME THE battle of the budget continued. December brought little holiday cheer. David Stockman's projections grew more dire by the week. And Reagan grew more dismayed. "We who were going to balance the budget face the biggest budget deficits ever," he wrote in his diary for December 8. The mounting tsunami of red ink frightened fiscal faint hearts, but Reagan refused to retreat from his tax cuts. For the moment most of his administration agreed with him. He met with his Council of Economic Advisers on December 10. "While one or two spoke of possible tax increases after 1982, the others (majority) said no," he noted. "Tax increases don't eliminate deficits; they increase government spending."

Reagan, like Don Regan, blamed the recession on the tight money decreed by Paul Volcker and the Federal Reserve. Reagan met with Volcker and tried to get him to loosen up. He failed. "I'm not sure he sees the need to let the increase in money supply go forward," he wrote after the meeting. "This recession is because they slammed the door in April and kept it closed until September—almost October." He hoped Volcker would change his mind. "Our plan will get the economy moving only if the Fed allows."

As the deficit projections continued to swell, Reagan encountered increasing pressure from traditional conservatives to raise taxes. "Met with Senate leaders who are beginning to panic on taxes," he wrote. "They want us to raise or impose new ones. I'm resisting. D--n it, our program will work, and it's based on reduced taxes."

Reagan worked his team harder than ever to reduce spending, to ease the tax-hike pressure. But Congress refused to trim much of anything except defense. "They're so used to spending (for votes)," he observed, "they're getting edgy with '82 being an election year."

One by one Reagan's own advisers concluded that new taxes were unavoidable, given the daunting deficit and the uncooperativeness of Congress. "The recession has worsened, throwing our earlier figures off," Reagan wrote in late December. "Now my team is pushing for a tax increase to help hold down the deficits." Yet Reagan dug in his heels the harder. "I'm being stubborn," he wrote. "I think our tax cuts will produce more revenue by stimulating the economy. I intend to wait and see some results."

He grew lonelier as the calendar turned. He met with Republican House leaders in the second week of January. "Except for Jack Kemp they are h--l bent on new taxes and cutting the defense budget," Reagan observed after the meeting. "Looks like a heavy year ahead."

DON REGAN STOOD by Reagan longer than anyone else. The Treasury secretary listened impatiently as Bob Dole, the Republican chairman of the Senate Finance Committee, explained that Congress would insist on new revenues to reduce the deficit. Dole was spouting the same line the legislature always used, Regan concluded. "In other words, Capitol Hill, which in fiscal year 1982 had mandated spending $128 billion more than Treasury was receiving in taxes and other revenues, claimed it wanted more money so that it could balance the books and start over again with a clean slate. This Orwellian argument did not make sense to me in practical terms or in terms of the president's promises to bring government spending under control and cut taxes." To acquiesce in new taxes would destroy the positive effect of the hard-won tax cut, Regan believed. "It meant sacrificing not only the tangible benefits of this measure, but also its symbolic meaning." Nor would a tax increase have the effect its advocates predicted. "Suppose the president could somehow renege on his promise to reduce taxes without inflicting mortal damage on his political credibility, what then? I was convinced that an increase in taxes, coupled to a monetary policy that was already starving business of capital, would make our economic troubles worse. An economy could not expand if it was burdened by new taxes at the moment when it was already all but overwhelmed by high interest rates that devastated profits and eliminated millions of jobs."

This last point was the critical element, Regan contended. "In my judgment, having 8 or 9 million unemployed was worse than having a deficit of $128 billion"—the current Stockman estimate. Regan thought an obsession with deficits could hamstring the administration and sabotage the economy. "I did and do believe that deficits did not matter in the short run," he said, "if in the long run the economy generates sufficient revenues to pay off the deficits, and the rate of government spending is controlled in such a way that it is consistently less than the real growth of the economy." The key was consistency over the long term—and help from the Fed. "The deficit could be reduced and confidence could be restored if a slow, steady increase in the money supply"—which he continued to work on Volcker about—"was accompanied by a controlled rate of federal spending." A resort to new taxes would spoil everything. It would eliminate the pressure on Congress to agree to spending limits, the sine qua non of a long-term balanced budget. And it would undermine such progress as had been painfully made toward ending the recession.

Regan urged the president to stick to his tax cuts and ignore the deficit until the economy recovered. "It was better to borrow money to finance the deficit while the economy recovered and people went back to work than to impose taxes that would cripple the recovery or prevent it altogether. I never have believed, and never will believe, that increasing taxes is a cure for recession."

REGAN'S RECOMMENDATION TO ignore the deficit carried the administration further across the Rubicon that guarded the Italy of fiscal responsibility from the Gaul of unconditioned tax cuts. Regan was a money man, and if he gave permission to set budget balance aside, who was the president to contradict him?

Jim Baker wasn't ready to go as far as Regan. The chief of staff agreed that an obsession with the deficit could be counterproductive. "Downplay deficits and avoid specific deficit numbers," he wrote in a memo of tactical guidance to the president. Yet Baker appreciated the revolutionary nature of Regan's advice, and he realized that revolutions evoke resistance. Baker knew that the looming deficit terrified many Republicans and that Congress was going to act on the deficit whether the White House liked it or not. Baker still preferred spending cuts to tax increases, but he realized the cuts wouldn't happen. "Both parties in Congress had simply lost their appetite for major spending cuts," Baker recalled later. "So had a lot of cabinet officers." The administration was forced to face political facts.

"We could be proud of the budget cuts of 1981, but we would never again repeat that success."

New taxes were the only option, Baker judged. He got Meese and Deaver to agree. He found another ally in Nancy Reagan. The First Lady was pained by the criticism of her husband as insensitive in demanding more cuts in social programs at a time of high unemployment and a growing defense budget, and she quietly added her voice to those in favor of new taxes.

Her husband remained stubborn. "I told our guys I couldn't go for tax increases," he wrote on January 22. "If I have to be criticized I'd rather be criticized for a deficit than for backing away from our economic program."

Reagan thought he should appeal to the public again. He blamed the media for exaggerating and misinterpreting the recession. "The press has done a job on us, and the polls show its effect," he observed. "The people are confused about the economic program. They've been told it has failed, and it's just started."

Baker declined to schedule a presidential speech, believing it would merely postpone the inevitable. Through the end of winter and into spring the economic numbers kept getting worse, and so did Reagan's job ratings. In April, Gallup showed that only 43 percent of Americans approved of his handling of the presidency. Reagan again blamed the media. "It reflects the constant media drumbeat of biased reporting against what we're trying to do," he said.

At Baker's urging, Reagan reluctantly consented to negotiations between the White House and Congress. The Senate sent five delegates, the House seven, and the administration five. The "Gang of Seventeen" met almost constantly for weeks. "We met at Blair House, in the family theater in the White House, in the Roosevelt Room, at the Vice President's residence," Don Regan recalled. The talks weren't exactly secret, but neither did the participants want them publicized—hence the changing venues. Progress came slowly. "Innumerable sets of numbers were discussed, innumerable formulas were proposed, but no obvious compromise emerged," Regan said. "We could not even agree on the size of the deficit." At this point Regan was willing to grant the sincerity of all concerned. Yet the difference between the two sides seemed intractable. "The administration wanted to cut spending in domestic programs and control it more closely in defense programs; Congress wanted to increase revenues and slash defense spending so as to maintain high levels of domestic spending.

We thought that Congress was running up the bills with no thought for the consequences; they thought that the administration was letting untold billions in revenue slip through its fingers as a result of its unprecedented tax cuts."

Reagan grew impatient at the slow pace of the talks and again threatened to go to the people. He proposed to tell the country that the Democrats were putting party interest above the national interest. "There will be blood on the floor," he vowed.

Baker thought blood would make matters worse, and he again put the president off. Reagan grew more frustrated. "The D's are playing games," he growled of Tip O'Neill's crew. The Democrats were demanding that Reagan rescind the third year of the tax cuts. "Not in a million years!" Reagan swore.

Reagan called O'Neill and suggested a personal conversation. The House speaker agreed, and Reagan rode to the Capitol. The president had originally proposed $100 billion in spending cuts; O'Neill and the Democrats had countered with $35 billion. During the course of the Gang of Seventeen discussions, the administration had come down to $60 billion. The Democrats hadn't budged. Reagan hoped to induce movement during his meeting with O'Neill. In three hours he got nowhere. He made a last offer—to split the difference between the administration's $60 billion and the Democrats' $35 billion. O'Neill again refused. Reagan gathered his papers and left.

The next day he finally took his case to the people. He explained the concessions the administration had been willing to make, and he denounced the intransigence of the Democrats. With charts he asserted that the Democrats' policies would lead to unsustainable spending and taxes. "The philosophical difference between us is that they want more and more spending and more and more taxes," Reagan said. "I believe we should have less spending, less taxes, and more prosperity." He pledged to continue working with "responsible members" of the Democratic Party to find a solution to the fiscal impasse. And he once again called on Americans to support him. "Make your voice heard. Let your representatives know that you support the kind of fair, effective approach I have outlined for you tonight. Let them know you stand behind our recovery program. You did it once, you can do it again."

THIS TIME THE Reagan magic failed. The public declined to rally to the president. His approval numbers slipped further. He continued to deny that anything was wrong with his policies. "People are confused on the whole budget issue," he said.

O'Neill and the Democrats read the polls and grew more determined to hold their ground. Baker urged Reagan to cut a deal before he lost the public entirely. Baker gathered Ed Meese and Mike Deaver, and the troika made a united pitch for a bargain that included higher taxes.

Reagan didn't like the idea any more than he had from the start. But he realized he was out of options. "The president listened," Baker recalled, "then took off his reading glasses and threw them down on the Oval Office desk. 'All right, goddammit,' he said. 'I'm gonna do it, but it's wrong.'" Decades later, Baker remembered the president's vehemence. "I thought they were going to break," he said of the flung spectacles.

What Reagan agreed to was increases in business and excise taxes, to yield the Treasury almost $100 billion over three years. The 1981 personal income tax cuts remained in place. Reagan wasn't happy, but he understood that politics rarely made anyone really happy. "A compromise is never to anyone's liking," he observed. "It's just the best you can get and contains enough of what you want to justify what you give up."

Reagan hoped that by yielding on taxes, he would win on spending. "The tax increase is the price we have to pay to get the budget cuts."

53

THE QUESTION FOR any administration is not whether scandal will strike but when. The executive branch comprises many thousands of men and women, subject to the same temptations to sin and opportunities for error humans are always prone to. The closer the individuals are to the center of power, the greater the temptations and opportunities, and the sharper the scrutiny by the media and the public.

The first scandal of the Reagan administration was small beer as scandals go, but it nonetheless rocked Reagan's inner circle. In September 1981, $1,000 was discovered in the office safe of Richard Allen. The national security adviser had shifted quarters in the West Wing, and the money was left behind. Allen explained to Reagan that a Japanese magazine that had interviewed Nancy Reagan had tried to pay her for the interview. Allen had intercepted the money to avert embarrassment to Nancy or to the magazine. His secretary put the money in his office safe, and he forgot about it until its recent discovery. Reagan accepted Allen's explanation. But the FBI had to investigate, and the investigation leaked, embarrassing the president.

Reagan interpreted the leak politically. "I suspect bureaucratic sabotage," he wrote. "Our administration and not Dick Allen is the target." The FBI found nothing against Allen, who wanted to keep his job.

But Reagan, usually a forgiving boss, decided to get rid of him. Reagan's foreign policy team wasn't working smoothly; Allen was often at odds with Al Haig or Caspar Weinberger or both. Reagan judged Allen the most expendable of the three. "The press is not going to let up if he's in that job," the president wrote.

WILLIAM CLARK MOVED over from the State Department to take Allen's post. Reagan knew Clark from California, where he had served on the state supreme court. He also owned a ranch near Reagan's and shared an outdoorsy sensibility. Clark's quiet style promised fewer distractions from the substance of foreign policy, which remained focused on the Caribbean. "We are now at a watershed in U.S. foreign policy," Clark told a meeting of the NSC in February 1982. "The greater Caribbean is to us what the Mediterranean is to Europe. It is our front yard—not our back yard, a metaphor which suggests an area of marginal concern." American interest in the Caribbean dated to the nineteenth century; by World War II the region had become a secure part of the American sphere. "This is no longer the case entirely," Clark said. "In the region today we are faced with a combination of threats." Weak economies and fragile political institutions invited subversion by anti-American forces. "The chief instigators are Cuba and its patron, the Soviet Union." Leftists in Nicaragua and Grenada aggravated the turmoil. "It is a formidable political, military, economic, propaganda apparatus facing us with new targets of opportunity being developed all the time." Clark didn't mind sounding alarmist. "The threat to the Caribbean is unprecedented in severity and proximity and complexity. By contrast, the Nazi threat in the 1930s and 1940s and the Castro threat in the 1960s were more limited in scope, with fewer resources being expended. The strategies were of a less sophisticated nature and were employed for a shorter period of time."

Clark yielded the floor to William Casey, who detailed the activities of the Cubans in the region. Cuba was projecting its influence around the region in part as a way of employing the young men who formed a demographic bulge in the country's population and couldn't find work in Cuba's floundering economy, Casey said. The Cuban troops were well armed and provisioned. "The Soviets gave Cuba some 66,000 tons of military equipment last year—more than $1 billion in arms including SA-6s, MIG-23s, T-62 tanks, MI-24 helicopters, etc. Cuba has a modern army with substantial reserves plus 200 MIG aircraft. It receives $8 million a day in aid in the form of cheap oil and a subsidized price for Cuba's exports: nickel and sugar." Castro had developed a strategy for destabilizing conservative and moderate governments in the region. "Cuba and Castro bring together the various guerrilla factions within the target countries and after they are unified Havana supplies them with arms, training, etc. in order to make the guerrillas more effective."

The Sandinista government of Nicaragua was copying the Cuban model of subversion, Casey said. "Nicaragua continues to build up its military capabilities. MIGs are expected soon. Nicaragua's build-up in military strength will intimidate its neighbors and tip the balance in El Salvador in favor of the guerrillas against the government forces because, quite frankly, people join what appears to be the winning side."

Casey concluded that the United States found itself at an increasing disadvantage to Moscow and its Caribbean-basin allies. "The Soviets are in a no-lose situation," the CIA chief said. "If we don't act, we lose credibility and the Soviets gain an increasing number of allies within our own hemisphere. If we react strongly, the Soviets will be able to say the United States is no better than the Soviets are in Poland."

Thomas Enders, the assistant secretary of state for inter-American affairs, reported that an interagency group had been working on the Caribbean basin. It had produced a detailed plan for countering Cuban and Soviet influence. Enders summarized the plan as consisting of three prongs. "First of all, we have to win on the ground in El Salvador and deal with the source of the arms problem in Nicaragua and Cuba," Enders said. "Secondly, we need to obtain the support of the American people as well as the United States Congress. And thirdly, we need to mobilize support in the region—that is, the hemisphere."

Mobilizing support, particularly among the American people, was Reagan's specialty. Bill Clark had called this meeting to obtain a decision on a presidential speech on the Caribbean. Robert—"Bud"—McFarlane, Clark's deputy, made the pitch to Reagan. "While we can propose solutions, we cannot carry out the solutions to these problems without the support of the American people," he said. "The American public must understand the nature of the threat because for most Americans this hemisphere has always seemed to be a quiet, even a docile area, and extremely non-threatening." The president's communications skills were crucial in changing this impression—though not changing the impression too much. "It is essential that we do not come on as alarmists," McFarlane said. "This morning, Mr. President, we have been alarmists." But the president would know how to explain the threat more calmly. "This is a process that is going to take time. We must elevate the public awareness of what is going on, and that means three things: why the area is important, how it is threatened, and what we can do in economic, political and military terms. And military would be the last of the terms, but all of these must be understood by the American people."

JIM BAKER DIDN'T want Reagan to give anything like the speech Clark and McFarlane sought. Baker doubted that conditions were as dire as Casey portrayed them, and he feared that a Caribbean adventure would derail the administration's domestic agenda. Moreover, he didn't want Reagan getting out front on any half-baked initiative. "The speech alone won't solve the problem, won't give us the consensus, and may risk a revival of our Vietnam problem," Baker told the NSC. "The president should and can address the economic situation at an appropriate time, but a speech that deals with the security problem will add to our serious domestic political problem. We must go to the Congress first. We cannot put the president out in front until we have an answer and until we have a strategy under way."

Ed Meese sided with Baker. The Caribbean Basin Initiative, as Clark was calling the recommended program, made sense as an economic assistance package, Meese allowed. "The CBI is one of the best initiatives that we have in this administration. Let's press on this." But to entangle it with military and security issues was unwise. "Let's not mix in El Salvador with the CBI because that will kill it. If we try to do both economic and security at the same time, we will lose both."

Don Regan joined the skeptics. "First we must ask ourselves, who is this speech for?" he said. "Is it for Havana and Moscow, or is it for Duluth? With our internal economic problems, it would be very difficult to get people's attention on a region outside the United States. Furthermore, by raising the question of security you are upping the ante by dwelling on the threat."

William Casey fought back. "Unless you alert the country, you won't get the support from the Congress or the country on the Caribbean Basin Initiative," the CIA chief said. "You must go and outline the whole problem as it is."

"How?" Baker demanded.

"We must spell out the CBI," Casey said. "The CBI itself cannot be justified without a sense of threat."

"We must do what we need to do," Baker granted. But the president didn't have to be the one to do it. "Don't put the president up front until public opinion and the Congress begin to understand the problem better than they do now."

REAGAN LISTENED DURING the first ninety minutes of the meeting, content to let Clark, McFarlane, and Casey battle Baker, Meese, and Regan. On another subject his silence might have signaled lack of interest. But Central America stirred his anticommunist passions, and he followed the arguments closely. He now engaged. He said he appreciated the need to organize and focus America's efforts in the Caribbean basin. "If the president fails to mobilize those efforts, how much further behind will we be?" he mused aloud. Yet he didn't want to frighten anyone. His critics were already calling him a warmonger. "Many people believe we will be in a war soon." He preferred not to add to this impression. "If I do make a speech, how do I avoid an I-told-you-so reaction among the public?" But he couldn't remain silent. "If we look further down the road, I would not want history to record that there was a time when we could have headed off this hemisphere becoming an extension of the Warsaw Pact. Lenin may then turn out to have been right when he said that someday the Western Hemisphere would be ripe fruit after Europe."

Reagan agreed that the American people needed to be reminded that the Caribbean was America's southern border. "What a bastion of strength it would be if North and South America had bonds like those between the U.S. and Canada. No Kremlin would want to take on that." He reflected again on the difficulty of dealing forthrightly with the danger without provoking the antiwar left. "How do we frame a speech that keeps the protesters out of the snow?" He elaborated on Baker's Vietnam analogy. "We never explained Vietnam, did we? Eisenhower told Kennedy that more troops would be needed. We tried to fight a war pretending there was none."

As to the Caribbean speech, it required further thinking. "We need concepts of what the speech would say. Shouldn't we say that there is too much misinformation, that we did not discover El Salvador in this administration, that we are trying to address the economic problems of El Salvador, that we want to be a friend, that the CBI is our way of helping countries to achieve self-sustaining growth, that we will continue our close friendship with Canada and Mexico, that in the end we are all Americans? Can we do a speech without making it sound like war? We are seeking to offer the advantages of our economic system to others. We have had good neighbor policies before. None of them succeeded. We forget our size and our strength. We tried to impose our way. We should go to the Caribbean and say we are all neighbors. Let's hear your ideas and together bring about the things you are interested in."

Stepping back, the president commented on what the American people thought of him. "The problem is how I am perceived. I was a hawk in Vietnam because I believe if you ask people to die you should give them a chance to win. The best way to prevent war is to get to the problem early. Can I do something without adding to the perception of me as a hawk?"

Reagan closed the meeting by returning to the subject of Cuba, albeit obliquely. "Let's talk about others, not Cuba," he said of the speech he might give. "Let's isolate them. It's the only state that is not American. Let's give Cuba a chance to rejoin the Western Hemisphere." He said this topic wasn't for the speech in question but for a broader venue, with a larger aim. "North and South America together equals China, a pretty big colossus if we were all buddies."

R EAGAN ESCHEWED ALARMISM, but he was plenty concerned.
"Central America is really the world's next hotspot," he wrote in
his diary. "Nicaragua is an armed camp supplied by Cuba and
threatening a communist takeover of all of Central America." A short
while later he reiterated: "There is no question but that all of Central
America is targeted for a communist takeover."

To prevent the takeover, Reagan launched a campaign of covert operations. The Caribbean Basin Initiative was the public face of the administration's policy; its funding required congressional approval, which would
take time. To prevent the communists from capturing Central America
before Congress acted, Reagan turned to his shadow warriors. "We have
decided on a plan of covert actions, etc., to block the Cuban aid to Nicaragua and El Salvador," he wrote in his diary in November 1981. The
covert measures included arming anti-Sandinista Nicaraguans known as
contras; the contras were supposed to keep the Sandinistas occupied at
home and thereby hinder their aiding leftist rebels in El Salvador. Progress came slowly. "We have problems with El Salvador," Reagan wrote in
February 1982. "The rebels seem to be winning." This was bad news for
the region. "Guatemala could go any day," he said. "And of course Nicaragua is another Cuba."

The president took a briefing by the CIA on El Salvador. "The guerrillas have a really sophisticated set-up," he noted afterward. "I'd never
suspected their organization and communications. They have divided the
country into sections with a separate command group for each section and
a network of permanent camps, well fortified." He added, "Now we must
find a way to counter it." American critics of the administration's policy

weren't helping. "Ed Asner and some performers show up in Washington with $25,000 they've raised for the guerrillas."

REAGAN UNDERSTOOD THAT in foreign policy "covert" and "secret" aren't synonyms. He knew that the targets of America's shadow campaign would learn about it; in fact he intended that they learn about it. The purpose of the campaign was to get the Sandinistas and other regional leftists to change their ways. The covert campaign—which was covert only as to details and in being unacknowledged—would cease when they had done so.

Fidel Castro was the ultimate target of Reagan's campaign, and to assess how it was working upon the Cuban leader, the president dispatched Vernon Walters, a veteran American troubleshooter, to Havana. Walters had orders to discuss three topics: Cuban arms aid to the government of Nicaragua, Cuban support for antigovernment guerrillas in El Salvador, and the possible repatriation of Cuban criminals and mental patients included in the mass exodus of Cuban refugees from Mariel harbor in 1980. The subtext of the message Walters was to convey was that the American government was newly serious about cleaning up the Caribbean.

Reagan didn't expect miracles. He appreciated that Castro hadn't remained in power in Cuba for two decades accidentally. But the president judged a shot across the Cuban bow long overdue. And he could hope for movement on the Mariel problem. "Maybe we'll be sending Castro back his jailbirds and maniacs," he wrote in his diary.

In the event, nothing of substance came of the Walters mission. Cuba continued to support its allies in Central America, and the Mariel refugees remained in the United States. But Reagan thought the effort wasn't wasted. "They are uptight thinking we may be planning an invasion," he wrote of Castro and his comrades. "We aren't but we'll let them sweat."

In late February 1982, Reagan decided the time was ripe for the speech the NSC had argued about. He ventured the few blocks from the White House to the headquarters of the Organization of American States and addressed a gathering of the group's permanent council, along with other persons interested in Latin America. The first part of his speech was as innocuous as Jim Baker wanted it to be. "In the commitment to freedom and independence, the peoples of this hemisphere are one," Reagan said. "In this profound sense we are all Americans." He proposed economic reforms to encourage prosperity among the countries of the

Caribbean basin, starting with the elimination of tariffs on imports to the United States from the countries of the region. To this he would add tax incentives for American firms to invest in the Caribbean basin and $350 million of new economic aid. "It is an integrated program that helps our neighbors help themselves, a program that will create conditions under which creativity and private enterprise and self-help can flourish," Reagan said.

The second part of the speech invoked the sterner themes Bill Clark and Bill Casey wanted. "A new kind of colonialism stalks the world today and threatens our independence," Reagan asserted. "It is brutal and totalitarian. It is not of our hemisphere, but it threatens our hemisphere and has established footholds on American soil for the expansion of its colonialist ambitions." The Caribbean was at a crossroads. One route led toward a bright future of democracy, already embraced by two-thirds of the region's countries. The other went a very different way. "The dark future is foreshadowed by the poverty and repression of Castro's Cuba, the tightening grip of the totalitarian left in Grenada and Nicaragua, and the expansion of Soviet-backed, Cuban-managed support for violent revolution in Central America."

Reagan asserted that the economic reforms he proposed could take place only in a political and military framework that addressed the region's security threats. "Our economic and social program cannot work if our neighbors cannot pursue their own economic and political future in peace, but must divert their resources, instead, to fight imported terrorism and armed attack. Economic progress cannot be made while guerrillas systematically burn, bomb, and destroy bridges, farms, and power and transportation systems—all with the deliberate intention of worsening economic and social problems in hopes of radicalizing already suffering people." He shared some of the intelligence Casey had presented at the NSC meeting. "Last year, Cuba received 66,000 tons of war supplies from the Soviet Union—more than in any year since the 1962 missile crisis. Last month, the arrival of additional high performance MIG-23 Floggers gave Cuba an arsenal of more than 200 Soviet warplanes—far more than the military aircraft inventories of all other Caribbean Basin countries combined." The Nicaraguan Sandinistas assisted the Cubans in their terrorist purposes. "For almost two years, Nicaragua has served as a platform for covert military action. Through Nicaragua, arms are being smuggled to guerrillas in El Salvador and Guatemala."

El Salvador was in grave peril, Reagan said. "Very simply, guerrillas armed and supported by and through Cuba are attempting to impose a Marxist-Leninist dictatorship on the people of El Salvador as part of a larger imperialistic plan." The Salvadoran guerrillas, purporting to speak for the people of the country, opposed an election empowering the people. "More than that, they now threaten violence and death to those who participate in such an election," Reagan said. "Can anything make more clear the nature of those who pretend to be supporters of so-called wars of liberation?"

The United States had no choice but to move decisively against the agents of subversion. "If we do not act promptly and decisively in defense of freedom, new Cubas will arise from the ruins of today's conflicts. We will face more totalitarian regimes tied militarily to the Soviet Union." Listeners familiar with the origins of America's Cold War containment policy heard echoes of the Truman Doctrine when Reagan declared, "I believe free and peaceful development of our hemisphere requires us to help governments confronted with aggression from outside their borders to defend themselves. For this reason, I will ask the Congress to provide increased security assistance to help friendly countries hold off those who would destroy their chances for economic and social progress and political democracy." This might be just the beginning. "Let our friends and our adversaries understand that we will do whatever is prudent and necessary to ensure the peace and security of the Caribbean area."

REAGAN'S CRITICS RECOILED at his bellicose rhetoric. "If he had just given the first half of the speech, I would have left the hall with a different feeling," the Reverend Joseph Eldridge said. Eldridge spoke for the Washington Office on Latin America, one of many groups that had been protesting the administration's Central American policy. Eldridge and the other critics, including the Reverend J. Bryan Hehir of the United States Catholic Conference, thought Reagan grossly misrepresented the causes of unrest in the region. "The conflict in El Salvador is rooted in longstanding patterns of injustice and denial of fundamental rights for the majority of the population," Hehir said.

Senator Christopher Dodd, Democrat of Connecticut, deemed Reagan's remarks uninformed and unhelpful. "To blame the Cubans for everything that happened since 1960 is ridiculous," Dodd said. "I'm willing to agree that Cubans have not been shy about exploiting the situation, but to say they caused it is ridiculous. If the president really wanted bipartisan support, he should have gotten away from that kind of thing." Democratic congresswoman Mary Rose Oakar represented Cleveland, the home of two of four American churchwomen murdered in El Salvador by persons alleged, and later proven, to be linked to the government of José Napoleon Duarte. Oakar resented even the economic side of Reagan's initiative, asserting that it would encourage additional killings. "I wish he would send that $350 million in economic aid to Cleveland." Columnist Anthony Lewis likened El Salvador to Vietnam, declaring, "As in Vietnam, our policy is based on ignorance of history. Washington sees in El Salvador a sudden threat, mounted from outside, that is susceptible to instant military remedies. But what is happening is a response to decades of oppressive history in El Salvador, and no American policy can neatly determine the result."

Reagan chalked up the complaints to misguided liberalism and concentrated on the reaction of most of those in the hall where he gave the speech. "It was extremely well received, and remarks from the ambassador relayed to me afterward were to the effect that it was the most impressive presentation ever made to the OAS," he wrote in his diary. He added that initial soundings of Congress were positive as well. "I think we may have support on this," he noted after meeting with the leaders of both parties. "Jim Wright"—the Democratic majority leader in the House—"seemed darn right enthused."

THE PROTRACTED BUDGET negotiations delayed congressional action on the Caribbean initiative but didn't deter the administration from moving forward on the covert side. "Met with National Security Council Planning Group re a former Nicaraguan rebel leader who has left the government there and wants to head up a counter revolution," Reagan wrote in his diary in early April. The counterrevolutionary was Edén Pastora, the flamboyant "Comandante Cero" of the Sandinista revolution, who had grown disillusioned with corruption in the new regime. The CIA began assisting him and his contra army, which included former members of the Nicaraguan national guard and Miskito Indians and initially operated from camps in Honduras and Costa Rica.

The contra campaign appeared promising in the summer and early autumn of 1982. "Within a relatively short period of time the Moskitos will have comparatively free rein throughout the underpopulated eastern portion of Nicaragua," the CIA's Central America specialist, Duane Clarridge, told Reagan and the NSC at a November meeting. "Two columns of Pastora elements will have moved into Nicaragua from the south, and 1200 Nicaraguans who have been in the Honduran camps will be operating in Nicaragua." Pastora's units in northern Nicaragua would soon join the struggle. "This group is small but politically very important as it is hoped that Pastora's presence will lead to the defection of both individuals and units to his cause." At Bill Casey's prompting, Clarridge provided additional details on the numerical strength of the insurgency. Some 1,200 armed contras were operating inside Nicaragua; 200 to 300 were being sent out of the country to Honduras for training. Between 4,000 and 6,000 peasants who lived in the coffee regions in the mountains of northern Nicaragua were thought to be likely recruits. The Honduran camps contained 1,700 Miskitos awaiting arms. "When fully deployed we can anticipate that the Moskito troop level will rise to 4800," Clarridge said.

THE WORLD HAS a habit of springing surprises on presidents. This was less so before the 1940s, when Americans and their chief executives often ignored what happened beyond the Atlantic and the Pacific. But after Pearl Harbor discredited hemispheric isolationism and the country adopted a global approach to national security, presidents frequently found themselves having to respond to sudden events in distant countries, whether they wanted to or not.

By contrast to Central America, which Reagan considered a central theater in the struggle against communism, the Middle East meant little to him when he assumed the presidency. To be sure, it had oil, necessary for the smooth operation of Western economies. And it was the home of Israel, America's special partner and responsibility since the 1960s. But Reagan was an ideologist, not a geopolitician, and so the battle of organizing philosophies meant more to him than any contest for natural resources. And though his theology occasionally made him wonder if Armageddon was nigh and might start where Zion had regathered, he wasn't holding his breath.

Yet the Middle East came to mean a great deal to Reagan. His reeducation began in his first year in office when he wrestled with the Israeli government over the sale to Saudi Arabia of American military hardware, especially AWACS aircraft, equipped with enhanced radar and air control capabilities, and upgrades for F-15 fighter planes. Reagan intended for the weaponry to bolster Saudi Arabia as an ally against communism, but Israeli officials complained that it strengthened the Arab anti-Israel front. Israel's supporters in the American media and on Capitol Hill took up the cudgels and battered the administration for endangering the security of America's only true friend in the Middle East.

The vehemence of the response caught Reagan by surprise. "I'm disturbed by the reaction and the opposition of so many groups in the Jewish community," he wrote to himself. "It must be plain to them they've never had a better friend of Israel in the White House than they have now." The president thought his critics misconstrued his purposes. "We are striving to bring stability to the Middle East and reduce the threat of a Soviet move in that direction. The basis for such stability must be peace between Israel and the Arab nations. The Saudis are a key to this. If they can follow the counsel of Egypt the rest might fall in place. The AWACS won't be theirs until 1985. In the meantime much can be accomplished toward furthering the Camp David format. We have assured the Israelis we will do whatever is needed to see that any help to the Arab states does not change the balance of power between them and the Arabs."

The uproar caused the president to postpone sending the Saudi aid package to Congress. He didn't want to distract the legislators from his tax and budget proposals, and he hoped the fuss would dissipate. Yet he considered the arms sales important, and hardly had the economic measures cleared their hurdles on the Hill when he informed Congress that he was pushing forward with the AWACS and the F-15 parts. "I am convinced that providing Saudi Arabia with this equipment will improve the security of our friends, strengthen our own posture in the region, and make it clear both to local governments and to the Soviet leadership that the United States is determined to assist in preserving security and stability in Southwest Asia," he declared in a cover letter to the aid proposal. "I am aware that information from a variety of sources has been circulating on Capitol Hill regarding this sale and that many members have been under some pressure to take an early position against it. I hope that no one will prejudge our proposal before it is presented. We will make a strong case to the Congress that it is in the interest of our country, the Western Alliance and stability in the Middle East."

Reagan did make his case, repeatedly. "I have proposed this sale because it significantly enhances our own vital national security interests in the Middle East," he told a gathering of reporters. "By building confidence in the United States as a reliable security partner, the sale will greatly improve the chances of our working constructively with Saudi Arabia and other states of the Middle East toward our common goal—a just and lasting peace. It poses no threat to Israel, now or in the future. Indeed, by contributing to the security and stability of the region, it serves Israel's long-range interests. Further, this sale will significantly improve the capability of Saudi Arabia and the United States to defend the oil fields on which the security of the free world depends."

The president warned Israel to step back. "As president, it's my duty to define and defend our broad national security objectives. The Congress, of course, plays an important role in this process. And while we must always take into account the vital interests of our allies, American security interests must remain our internal responsibility. It is not the business of other nations to make American foreign policy."

But Israel did not back off. Prime Minister Menachem Begin came for a visit. Reagan employed his charm. "We did some getting acquainted and surprisingly it was very easy," he remarked that night. Begin broached the subject of the AWACS. "He of course objects to the sale," Reagan noted. The president reiterated his desire to bring the Saudis into the peace process. He assured Begin of America's commitment to Israel, at present and in the future. He thought his argument had a positive effect. "While he didn't give up his objection, he mellowed," Reagan said of Begin. The president was pleased at how he had handled the sometimes prickly prime minister. "I think we're off to a good start."

He soon discovered he was wrong. Begin went from the White House to Capitol Hill, where he lobbied hard against the AWACS sale. Reagan felt double-crossed. "He told me he wouldn't."

Begin's lobbying initially proved more effective than Reagan's. The Senate Foreign Relations Committee sent the administration's request to the full Senate but with a narrowly negative recommendation. Reagan spun the defeat as positively as he could. "Frankly, I'm gratified that it was that close," he told reporters. "I, of course, would have wished that it would have been the other way. If one of them had a headache and had to go home early or something, it might have." He refused to be disheartened. "I still am going to continue believing that we can get it in the Senate vote on the floor."

He redoubled his efforts on behalf of the sale. He met personally or spoke by phone with most of the senators. He solicited and received endorsements from secretaries of state and defense in previous administrations. He sent a letter to Howard Baker, the majority leader, putting on paper the assurances he had made orally regarding his concern for the security of Israel.

This time his efforts succeeded. The crucial vote in the full Senate favored the administration, 52 to 48. At a joint news conference, Howard Baker lauded the president's efforts on behalf of the sale. "The president was our chief negotiator," Baker said. "And at one time or the other I expect the president saw, virtually, maybe every member of the Senate or almost every member of the Senate. And with some of them he met more than once. I sometimes got ashamed of myself for calling down here and asking him if he would meet with so-and-so. And sometimes the president would say, 'Well, I already did that.' I'd say, 'Well, I know, but you've got to do it again.'" Baker described one holdout whose mind had been changed by the president at the eleventh hour. "He said, 'You know, that man down at the White House could sell refrigerators to an Eskimo.' I said, 'Well, I'm glad he could sell AWACS to you.'"

REAGAN'S VICTORY ON AWACS simply increased the testiness of the Israeli government. Begin berated the administration for acting more like an enemy than a friend. Three times in the past several months Reagan had punished Israel for actions taken in Israel's self-defense, Begin said. The Israelis had destroyed an Iraqi nuclear reactor, and the administration had suspended deliveries of aircraft. Israel had retaliated for the murder of Israeli civilians by attacking the Beirut headquarters of the Palestine Liberation Organization, and again the administration had stopped arms deliveries. Most recently, Israel had announced the annexation of the Golan Heights, and the administration had suspended a military cooperation agreement. All this came on top of the administration's obsession with selling warplanes to Saudi Arabia.

Begin blasted Reagan in language no Israeli prime minister had ever employed toward an American president. "Are we a vassal state of yours?" he demanded. "Are we a banana republic? Are we fourteen-year-olds who, if we misbehave, we get our wrists slapped?" Begin accused the administration of waging or condoning "an ugly anti-Semitic campaign" in the effort to win Senate approval of the AWACS sale. "First we heard the slogan, 'Begin or Reagan,' and then it followed that anyone who opposed the deal with Saudi Arabia supported a foreign head of state and was not loyal to the United States . . . Afterward we heard the slogan, 'We will not let the Jews determine the foreign policy of the United States.'" Begin played a Jewish card of his own by promising that the Jews of America would support not the government of their own country but the government of

Israel. "No one will frighten the large and free Jewish community of the United States. No one will succeed in deterring them with anti-Semitic propaganda. They will stand by our side. This is the land of their fore-fathers, and they have a right and a duty to support it."

Reagan thought Begin was way out-of-bounds, and he was severely tempted to say so. But he pragmatically bit his tongue and sought to calm the situation. He brushed aside a reporter's question whether the rising tension foreshadowed a reconsideration of American policy toward Israel. "No, it's just friends sometimes have some arguments, and I guess this is one of them," he said. He was asked if he objected to Begin's choice of words. "There was a little harsh tone to that," he admitted. But he reaf-firmed America's commitment to Israel's security.

Yet he didn't retreat from his decisions. He intended for the Arabs to understand that the United States hadn't forgotten them. "We want them to know that we want fairness for them," he said. He added, "I think we've made great progress."

At the same time, he dispatched Al Haig to Israel. The secretary of state got an earful, less from Begin, who was nursing a recently broken hip, than from Ariel Sharon, the Israeli defense minister. "Sharon is a brawny man who uses his bulk, his extremely loud voice, and a flagrantly aggressive manner, which I suspect he has cultivated for effect, to over-whelm opposition," Haig recalled. "'We are your ally and friend and should be treated as such!' he shouted, pounding on the table so that the dishes jumped." Haig could get loud himself, but on this occasion he held back. "If you act like an ally, General, you'll be treated like one," he told Sharon.

Haig reported mixed results to Reagan on his return to Washington. Begin and Sharon seemed somewhat reassured, he said. But the Israeli leaders remained touchy about the situation with the PLO in Lebanon. "He fears they may—on slightest provocation—war on Lebanon," Reagan wrote.

THE TOUCHINESS ONLY increased. William Clark called Reagan a week later to report that Israel was on the verge of invading southern Leb-anon to clear out the PLO. Reagan once more sought to talk the Israelis back. "We are trying to persuade them they must not move unless there is a provocation of such a nature the world will recognize Israel's right to retaliate," he wrote to himself. "Right now Israel has lost a lot of world sympathy."

Israel won back a little sympathy when it completed its long-scheduled withdrawal from the Sinai that spring. Reagan telephoned Begin to congratulate him on making a statesmanlike but difficult decision. "Many of his people resisted leaving the Sinai, and his army had to physically eject them," Reagan wrote. "The army went in unarmed and did a magnificent job."

As matters turned out, the withdrawal from Sinai cleared Israeli decks for action in Lebanon. Six years of civil war had created a political and military vacuum in Lebanon that was filled by battling militias linked to various sects within Lebanon and certain of the neighboring countries. Syria sent regular troops into Lebanon to stake its claim to at least a portion of the apparently disintegrating country. The PLO operated in southern Lebanon, from which its fighters launched attacks against Israel. The Israelis responded with air strikes and threats of ground action. In June 1982, Palestinian terrorists in London shot and gravely wounded the Israeli ambassador to Britain. The PLO denied responsibility, blaming it on a dissident faction, but the Israeli government declined to distinguish among its enemies. Begin and Sharon sent the Israeli army into Lebanon.

"I'm afraid we are faced with a real crisis," Reagan wrote.

CRISES CAME IN clusters that season. Before Reagan could respond to Israel's invasion of Lebanon, he had to deal with a war in the South Atlantic over some islands most Americans hardly knew existed. The Falklands conflict was a throwback to the age of empire, yet it had resonance for the Cold War. For four hundred years Britain had claimed dominion over the Falklands, by virtue of discovery of the then-uninhabited archipelago off the coast of southern South America. For almost as long, Spain and then independent Argentina had disputed the British claim to the islands, which they called the Malvinas, citing the archipelago's distance from Britain (nearly eight thousand miles) and its proximity to Argentina (about three hundred miles). Britain and Argentina eventually opened negotiations on the future of the islands, but the talks moved very slowly and, at the start of 1982, showed no signs of speeding up.

At this point a recently self-installed government in Argentina decided to make an issue of the Falklands. The new president, General Leopoldo Galtieri, evidently hoped to confer retrospective respectability on his coup by a bold stroke in foreign affairs. In March 1982, Argentine marines in mufti landed on South Georgia, a British possession six hundred miles east of the Falklands. The purpose, apparently, was to test the British response; the civilian garb would allow the Argentine government to disavow the operation if it went badly.

London protested the landing but lacked the local muscle to evict the Argentines. Encouraged, the Galtieri government readied ships, planes, helicopters, and troops for an assault on the Falklands.

American intelligence caught wind of the preparations. Reagan had reversed Jimmy Carter's policy of shunning the Argentine government for human rights violations, instead cultivating Buenos Aires as an ally in the battle against Latin American leftism. When the Falklands crisis began, the Argentine regime was funding a small army of contras against the Nicaraguan government. American attachés and diplomats nonetheless kept watch on Argentina, and they reported the ship and troop movements to Washington.

Margaret Thatcher received similar news from her own sources. The British prime minister was determined to retain the Falklands, and she prepared to fight to defend them. Yet she hoped not to have to. Britain would certainly lose the first round of a South Atlantic war, because an adequate task group would require weeks to reach the islands. At that point British marines would have to root out the Argentines by bloody force. "Our only hope now lay with the Americans," Thatcher recalled. The Americans were friends of Britain and sponsors of Galtieri and his colleagues; surely the Argentines would heed the counsel of President Reagan. Thatcher called Reagan and urged him to talk sense into them.

Reagan hoped he could. The last thing he wanted was a war between two of America's allies. In such a conflict he would come under pressure to choose sides. If he did, he would certainly antagonize the party he opted against. If he declined to choose, he might antagonize both.

He called Galtieri on April 2. "Talked for forty minutes trying to persuade him not to invade," he wrote in his diary. "I got nowhere." Galtieri insisted that Argentina's claim to the Falklands could not be surrendered or compromised. A new twist complicated the historic tangle. "Now we learn there is a possibility of oil there," Reagan wrote.

THE ARGENTINE OCCUPATION of the Falklands commenced even while Reagan was trying to talk Galtieri out of it. Argentine marines landed at Port Stanley, the capital of the colony, and seized the town's airport and harbor. The small garrison of British marines resisted ineffectually. The islands' population of two thousand stood by as observers.

The news of the landing required hours to reach London and Washington, as unsettled atmospheric conditions in the Southern Hemisphere disrupted radio communications. By the time Thatcher got the word, she was already organizing the naval force she vowed would retake the islands. The British media sizzled with anticipation of war. The national stiff upper lip appeared when readers learned that Prince Andrew was serving on the *Invincible*, one of the ships that would take part in the assault. "There could be no question of a member of the royal family being treated differently from other servicemen," Thatcher remarked unremarkably.

The time required by the task force to reach the Falklands allowed Reagan to dispatch Al Haig to mediate between the British and the Argentines. Haig discovered that Thatcher was in no mood for mediation. She conspicuously kept him waiting for an interview. "The United States Secretary of State, Mr. Haig, wished to visit London that day," the minutes of Thatcher's cabinet meeting on April 7 recorded, paraphrasing the prime minister. "It should be explained to him that Ministerial preoccupation with the Parliamentary debate made this impossible but that he would be very welcome the following day, on the basis that he would not come as a potential mediator but as a friend and ally of the United Kingdom."

When Thatcher did see Haig, she let him know Britain would brook no compromise with Argentine aggression. "She rapped sharply on the tabletop," Haig wrote later, "and recalled that this was the table at which Neville Chamberlain sat in 1938 and spoke of the Czechs as a faraway people about whom we know so little and with whom we have so little in common. A world war and the death of over 45 million people followed." Her government would not repeat Chamberlain's mistake, Thatcher said. She rejected Haig's proposal, approved by Reagan, of an international peace force that would administer the islands and oversee a transition to self-determination. Britain would make no bargains under duress, she said.

Haig hoped for better luck in Buenos Aires. A large crowd shouting nationalist slogans greeted him after a long flight. He assumed the reception had been orchestrated for his benefit, but he thought it significant nonetheless. Galtieri proved as determined as Thatcher. The Malvinas were Argentine, Galtieri said; on this there could be no compromise. "We cannot sacrifice our honor." Like Thatcher, Galtieri placed the current events in a larger context. "Our crisis today can easily result in the destabilization of South America and thereby weaken the defense of the West," he said. He added, with deliberate significance, "I cannot fail to express to you that I have received offers of aircraft, pilots and armaments from countries not of the West."

Haig didn't know how to read this remark. The Soviets might well be trolling in the troubled waters of the South Atlantic, but the Argentine government would have to do an ideological backflip to accept aid from the headquarters of communism. Yet Argentina could count on the support of nearly all of Latin America, even if Galtieri's hint of a Soviet connection came to nothing.

Reagan continued to resist choosing between London and Buenos Aires. "Both sides want our help," he noted. "We have to find some way to get them to back off." The president adopted a public position midway between the disputants. "We're friends with both of the countries engaged in this dispute," he told reporters. "And we stand ready to do anything we can to help them. And what we hope for and would like to help in doing is have a peaceful resolution of this with no forceful action or no bloodshed."

Media reports, however, cast doubt on the president's assertion of evenhandedness. *ABC News* and the *Washington Post* related that the administration was allowing the British navy to use a channel on an American communications satellite and that American intelligence agencies were sharing information with London on Argentine military activity.

Reagan bristled on reading the reports, all the more because they were said to be confirmed by sources the *Post* identified as "senior administration officials." The president didn't know who the leakers were, but he blamed the media for the story's dissemination, which he privately called "a most irresponsible act," not to mention a dangerous distortion of the truth. "We are providing England with a communications channel via satellite but that is part of a regular routine that existed before the dispute. To have cancelled it would have been taken as supporting the Argentines." In public he kept still. Asked point-blank about the reports of American intelligence aid to Britain, he said he couldn't respond without endangering efforts to achieve a diplomatic resolution. "The safest thing is to not comment."

Eventually, though, he tipped his hand. Thatcher's resolve convinced Haig that the only way to avoid a war was for Argentina to compromise. When Galtieri stood firm, Haig remarked to reporters that if fighting commenced, the United States would supply military assistance to Britain. Reagan wished the secretary hadn't said so much, but he chose to explain rather than disavow the comment. "That would only be in keeping with our treaties, bilateral treaties that we have with England by way of the North Atlantic alliance," he said. "At this moment we've had no request for any such help from the United Kingdom. But I think what the secretary was saying is, we must remember that the aggression was on the part of Argentina in this dispute over the sovereignty of that little ice-cold bunch of land down there, and they finally just resorted to armed aggression, and there was bloodshed. And I think the principle that all of us must abide by is, armed aggression of that kind must not be allowed to succeed."

Reagan again tried to talk the Argentines away from the brink. "Spent half an hour on the phone with President Galtieri," he wrote in his diary. "He sounded a little panicky and repeated several times they want a peaceful settlement." But Galtieri wouldn't remove his troops from the islands, and he wouldn't retreat from his claim of Argentine sovereignty.

Thatcher remained as adamant as before. "It was not Britain who broke the peace but Argentina," she wrote to the president. "Any suggestion that conflict can be avoided by a device that leaves the aggressor in occupation is surely gravely misguided. The implication for other potential areas of tension and for small countries everywhere would be of extreme seriousness. The fundamental principles for which the free world stands would be shattered."

Reagan agreed, though he declined to speak as forcefully as Thatcher. He concluded that there was little he could do. "As of noon things looked hopeless," he wrote on April 17. He increasingly blamed the Argentines as the days passed. "The shooting could start," he wrote on April 23. "It would be a war mainly because an Argentine general-president (result of a coup) needed to lift his sagging political fortunes."

The shooting did start a week later. The British task force reached the vicinity of the Falklands at the end of April. On May 1, British aircraft bombed the airport at Port Stanley to deprive the Argentines of its use. On May 2 a British submarine sank the Argentine light cruiser *General Belgrano*, with the loss of more than three hundred officers and crew.

The sinking eliminated any hope for a diplomatic solution. Britain smelled victory; the Argentines sought revenge or at least a salvaging of honor. They got some of both two days later when an air-launched Argentine missile blasted the British destroyer *Sheffield*, killing a score of British sailors and setting fires that ravaged and eventually sank the ship.

REAGAN WAS COMPELLED to respond to the outbreak of fighting. He called no news conference but let himself be drawn into an exchange with reporters who shouted questions as he departed the White House for a brief trip out of Washington. "Mr. President, was the British attack on the Falklands expected?" one reporter asked. Another demanded, "What are we going to do about the Falklands attack?" A third yelled, "Mr. President, did you have any advance warning at all that this attack by the British was coming this morning, or was it a complete surprise?"

Reagan's aides groaned at these drive-by video shootings, believing they caught the president off guard. Sometimes they did. But they also gave Reagan a chance to choose the questions he wanted to answer. The others blew away in the draft from the helicopter blades.

In this case he answered the third question. "Complete surprise," he said. This wasn't exactly true, but it was close enough for the moment. Neither Reagan nor Haig had asked to be apprised of the details of British planning, and the president hadn't been informed as to when the British assault was going to occur. Yet he was fairly certain it was going to happen, given Thatcher's obvious resolve.

Reporters soon tested the president's accuracy. They learned that the British planes involved in the initial bombing had taken off from Ascension Island in the Atlantic, where the United States operated an air base under a World War II–era lease from the British. The administration had debated whether to allow the British strike to originate there. Jeane Kirkpatrick argued against giving permission, saying it would antagonize Argentina and jeopardize hemispheric solidarity. Bobby Ray Inman, the deputy director of the CIA, sitting in for William Casey, responded sharply. "It was the only time I ever lost my temper in a meeting with the president," Inman recalled later. He branded hemispheric solidarity a "myth" and reminded the group that Britain had stood by the United States "since the War of 1812." Reagan accepted Inman's argument, and the British got the use of Ascension.

But this left Reagan with some explaining to do. "Mr. President, how could you have been surprised about the attack if they took off from Ascension Island while we control the air traffic?" a reporter asked at the next opportunity.

"Simply because there was no report of it to us," Reagan replied.

"Are they using our airstrips on Ascension Island to bomb the Falklands?"

"There is a joint-use base there."

"If there's a joint-use base, then how could we have been surprised?"

"Well, I've never told the British when *we* took some plane off from there."

The bombings and the battle at sea were clearly preparation for a British landing in the Falklands. Reagan feared that they might also presage an extension of the fighting to the Argentine mainland. Brazil's president was visiting Washington; he told Reagan that his diplomats had learned that the British were preparing to attack military bases in continental Argentina. "Our intelligence community confirmed that preparations for such attacks were under way," Reagan recalled. He phoned Thatcher and warned her against widening the war. She refused to rule it out with Reagan at this point, though she had no intention of taking on more than she had committed to. "Whether or not such attacks would have made any military sense," she wrote later, "we saw from the beginning that they would cause too much political damage to our position to be anything but counterproductive."

Reagan tried to postpone or prevent the collision of ground forces. He called Thatcher again. "I talked to Margaret but don't think I persuaded her against further action," he noted on May 13. Nor were the Argentines willing to back down. "Hundreds have been killed," Galtieri told Vernon Walters, whom Reagan had sent in a last-ditch effort to forestall further fighting. "What can I tell my people they have gained by their sacrifices?"

On May 21 the British went ashore, triggering a series of pitched battles. Reagan called Thatcher yet again. He spoke of a settlement by which Britain would stop short of total victory and the Argentine government would not fall. Thatcher was in no mood for compromise. "The prime minister is adamant," Reagan wrote. "She feels the loss of life so far can only be justified if they win."

She also felt that Reagan was on her side, despite his diplomatic efforts. The Pentagon quietly increased its assistance to Britain, supplying Sidewinder missiles and the matting for a temporary airstrip, among other items. The president himself endorsed the British position in a conversation with Thatcher in early June. He and she had separately traveled to Paris for a meeting of the Group of Seven, the major economic powers. They spent an hour together at the American embassy discussing South Atlantic affairs. "The Prime Minister said that she had opened the discussion by thanking President Reagan warmly for the material help which the United States had extended to us," the British account of the meeting recorded. "She regretted, but understood, that she could not make public the very valuable assistance which the Americans had given." She reiterated her determination to carry the conflict through to the end. Yet she hoped the effects of a British victory would not destabilize South America. "The Prime Minister had made it plain that she was not interested in humiliating Argentina nor was she at war with the mainland. No one was more anxious for an armistice than she."

Reagan picked up this thread. "President Reagan had expressed a keen wish to minimise the loss of life," the British memo recounted. "He wondered whether persistent bombardment, rather than a frontal assault, might not help to achieve this." Thatcher explained that bombardment, by lengthening the conflict, might actually increase casualties. Reagan replied that a long conflict would benefit no one. "He was worried about the situation in Argentina. He was not sure that Galtieri would fall, but if he did so it seemed likely that the Air Force commander would take over." Reagan went on to say that Galtieri was getting what he had brought on himself. "President Reagan volunteered the view that Galtieri had authorised the invasion because he otherwise would have fallen from power within days. Large-scale strikes, sympathetic to the Peronistas, had been envisaged."

Reagan met with Thatcher again in London a few days later. They spoke in private, each reiterating previous positions. The president then addressed Parliament. He talked broadly of the need for solidarity in the struggle against aggression, focusing on the Soviet Union and its communist allies and proxies. But he included the conflict in the Falklands as part of the necessary effort to maintain the rule of law. "On distant islands in the South Atlantic young men are fighting for Britain," he told his Westminster audience. "And, yes, voices have been raised protesting their sacrifice for lumps of rock and earth so far away. But those young men aren't fighting for mere real estate. They fight for a cause, for the belief that armed aggression must not be allowed to succeed." Borrowing from Thatcher, he added, "If there had been firmer support for that principle some forty-five years ago, perhaps our generation wouldn't have suffered the bloodletting of World War II."

The fighting continued until the middle of June, when the Argentine defenders of the Falklands suddenly lost heart and quit. "The speed with which the end came took all of us by surprise," Thatcher remembered. But the lesson she drew from the war endured. "We have ceased to be a nation in retreat," she told her compatriots. "Britain has rekindled that spirit which has fired her for generations past and which today has begun to burn as brightly as before. Britain found herself again in the South Atlantic and will not look back from the victory she has won."

THATCHER EMERGED FROM the Falklands War a hero, and to none more than Reagan. "She believed absolutely in the moral rightness of what she was doing," the president remarked. He liked to think of himself as similarly stout in defense of the right, and Thatcher's victory afforded a reminder that armed morality can indeed win.

Yet there was collateral damage. The collapse of the Galtieri regime just days after the Falklands defeat left the Reagan administration on the hook for the two thousand contras the Argentine government had been supporting against the Nicaraguan government. Reagan found himself deeper in Central America sooner than he had expected.

More obvious to the world was Reagan's loss of his secretary of state. Al Haig had always been an awkward fit in the administration. James Baker judged him pretentious. "He had grandiose ideas," Baker said. Bob Inman thought he lacked discretion. "He was a swashbuckler," Inman recalled. Martin Anderson believed that Haig never understood or appreciated the president's style of leadership. "He was somewhat contemptuous of the views of anyone who was not a certified, blue-ribbon foreign policy expert," Anderson said. Anderson lacked a blue ribbon but was included in preparations for a presidential trip abroad, to Haig's great annoyance. "He was baffled by Reagan's insistence on including these foreign policy amateurs in the inner circle of the summit planning," Anderson said. "The thing that seemed to annoy Haig the most was Reagan's habit of involving trusted advisers in policy discussions on issues in which they were not expert." When Anderson appeared at a final briefing before

Reagan's departure, Haig boiled over. "He straightened up, drew himself together like a small Charles de Gaulle, and bellowed, 'What the hell are you doing in *my* meeting, Anderson?'"

Anderson's sarcastic response typified the attitude of the Reagan loyalists to Haig. "Mr. Secretary," he said, "anytime I get the chance to brighten your day, I take it." The Reaganites lost few opportunities to vex Haig. His self-importance struck them not simply as arrogant but as demeaning to Reagan, whom they determined to protect. They kept Haig from seeing the president as often as Haig wanted, leaving him to wonder who was making the decisions. "To me, the White House was as mysterious as a ghost ship," he wrote later. "You heard the creak of the rigging and the groan of the timbers and sometimes even glimpsed the crew on deck. But which of the crew had the helm? Was it Meese, was it Baker, was it someone else? It was impossible to know for sure." When Haig complained to Richard Allen, the national security adviser replied, "Al, why don't you just worry about the State Department?" Meese and Baker often spoke for the administration, on foreign policy among other matters; when Haig objected that their words lacked the precision required of diplomacy and suggested they leave that realm to him, they brushed him aside. "Sometimes, after hanging up the phone, I would have the impression that they regarded me as some sort of naïf who did not understand that publicity is the engine of politics," Haig said.

Haig found himself defending his territory on an almost daily basis. Caspar Weinberger crossed the line most irritatingly. "It is not easy to convince other governments or the public that the minister of defense of a superpower is talking off the top of his head on issues of war and peace," Haig said. Yet that was the way of Weinberger, who knew budgets but not international affairs. "His tendency to blurt out locker-room opinions in the guise of policy was one that I prayed he might overcome. If God heard, He did not answer in any way understandable to me."

IT WAS THE leaks, however, that drove him crazy. "If I had some difficulty in wrenching opinions from the White House staff when I spoke to them in person, its members conversed with remarkable fluency through the press," Haig said. He learned in the *Washington Post* that William Clark's function at the State Department was not so much to be his deputy as to keep watch for the White House on his presidential ambitions.

The *New York Times* told him that his nickname among Reagan staffers was CINCWORLD—Commander in Chief, World—on account of his grandiose airs. He read direct quotations from his confidential reports to the president and from his remarks at supposedly secret meetings of the National Security Council.

"What it all meant, what it all served, who was turning the faucets, were questions that could not be answered with certainty," Haig reflected. His protests to Baker, Meese, and the other staffers yielded nothing. "Al, it's just newspaper talk," Meese told him. "Don't pay any attention." The leaks continued.

Reagan's practice was to ignore intra-administration squabbling. "Sit down and work it out" was his standard response. Yet he wondered why Haig, of all those in the administration, seemed so beset. Haig complained at discovering secondhand that George Bush was being named chairman of the administration's crisis council, a post that would normally have been held by Dick Allen as national security adviser. "Al thinks his turf is being invaded," Reagan remarked in his diary. "We chose George because Al is wary of Dick. He talked of resigning. Frankly I think he's seeing things that aren't there. He's secretary of state and no one is intruding on his turf. Foreign policy is his, but he has half the cabinet teed off."

Haig repeatedly threatened to resign, and Reagan repeatedly talked him out of it. But one thing and then another kept popping up. Reagan, for obvious reasons, didn't see Haig's overwrought performance on the day the president was shot, but he heard about it afterward. And he heard about it again, and again. In November 1981 he got a call from Haig, who had just found out that columnist Jack Anderson was going to report that the secretary of state would be fired shortly. Anderson's source was an unnamed White House official. Reagan assured Haig that there was no truth to the story. He called Anderson and told him that Haig was the best secretary of state the country had had in years. Anderson killed his column and ran Reagan's endorsement instead. "Of course he wouldn't reveal the White House source," Reagan remarked in his diary.

Reagan didn't bother trying to discover the source. But he gradually concluded that something about Haig caused unresolvable friction. Amid the Falklands crisis Haig got into a carping match with Jeane Kirkpatrick, whose sympathy toward Argentina angered Margaret Thatcher and the British as well. Thatcher complained to Reagan that Kirkpatrick had attended a dinner hosted by the Argentine ambassador even as the Argentine invasion of the Falklands unfolded. From Haig's perspective,

Kirkpatrick's actions and statements cast doubt on his ability to speak for the president in his efforts to defuse the crisis.

Reagan tried to get Haig and Kirkpatrick to work together. He met separately with the two and urged them to display greater team spirit. He judged the meetings a success. "I think we can get a lid on it with no further damage," he remarked to himself.

He was wrong. Haig grew ever more convinced that the White House staff was conspiring to do him in. His shuttle diplomacy between Britain and Argentina began just as Reagan was to leave for some meetings with friendly Caribbean leaders. "I was startled to hear reports from the White House that I had undertaken the Falklands mission as a means of upstaging Ronald Reagan in his visits to Jamaica and Barbados," Haig recalled. "The White House term for my peace mission, I was told, was 'grandstanding.'" He read a report in the *New York Times* that he had refused an airplane from among those assigned to the administration and insisted on something fancier. In fact he had. But the issue wasn't style or comfort. "The issue was working space and communications." The plane he wanted was better equipped. Haig declined to level accusations regarding this leak, but one of his assistants told a reporter that the *Times* story must have been planted by Jim Baker.

The charge simply fed the fire. Unidentified White House officials told reporter Hedrick Smith that Haig's job depended on the success of his Falklands peace mission. "You can say Haig needs a win," one of them declared. When Haig didn't deliver, the secretary heard the knives being sharpened. "Shortly after my return," he recounted, "a lifelong friend who has never failed to tell me the truth, and who is in a position to know the truth, called to say that there had been a meeting in the White House at which my future had been discussed. 'Haig is going to go, and go quickly,' James Baker was quoted by my friend as saying. 'And we are going to make it happen.'"

BAKER DID WANT him to go, but chiefly because he had become a distraction and a burden to the president. "He was suspicious of everybody," Baker recalled of Haig. "He was fighting with everybody." Baker later granted that Haig had some cause for complaint. He told of a day when Michael Deaver dressed up in a gorilla costume and paraded outside a cabinet meeting, in a gibe at Haig's belief that the White House staff were out to get him. On a London visit Deaver deliberately assigned Haig a military helicopter that was noisy and windy, in contrast to the quiet civilian model the White House staff rode in. "I don't blame him for being pissed off," Baker said. But he added, "I had nothing to do with it."

Whoever was responsible, Haig's days were numbered. The Falklands War was just ending when Haig presented the president with a list of the slights he had suffered at the hands of White House staff and other cabinet secretaries. "Mr. President," Haig said, "I want you to understand what's going on around you. I simply can no longer operate in this atmosphere. It's too dangerous. It doesn't serve your purposes. It doesn't serve the American people." He again offered to resign but said his resignation would not take effect until after the November elections, to avoid embarrassment to the president.

"The Al H. situation is coming to a head," Reagan wrote. "I have to put an end to the turf battles we're having and his almost paranoid attitude." The president thought it a shame that things had grown so fractious. Describing a meeting of the NSC on the Lebanon crisis, he wrote, "Al H. made great good sense on this entire matter. It's amazing how sound he can be on complex international matters but how utterly paranoid with regard to the people he must work with."

Haig apparently expected Reagan to refuse his resignation, as he had done before. But the president decided he had had enough of the Haig problem. Haig was getting too much attention, for the wrong reasons. Reagan had no particular policy quarrels with Haig, but he didn't like being overshadowed. He told Haig he would read his bill of particulars and get back to him.

He called Haig into the Oval Office the next day. He handed him an unsealed envelope. Haig read the letter it contained. "Dear Al," it said, "It is with utmost regret that I accept your letter of resignation."

Haig was nonplussed. "The president was accepting a letter of resignation I had not submitted," he recalled. Haig realized that an immediate, unexplained resignation in the middle of a foreign policy crisis would not look good on his résumé, and he requested time to compose a letter. He explained that he would ascribe his departure to policy differences.

Reagan nodded. But while the secretary was finding the words to frame his departure, the president called George Shultz, formerly secretary of labor and secretary of the Treasury under Richard Nixon. Reagan had met Shultz in Sacramento when the then governor had some questions about the finances of government. The meeting lasted three hours. "He gave me the most intense grilling I ever had on the federal government,"

Shultz recalled later. Shultz had guessed that Reagan wanted to run for president. But Reagan's interrogation signaled something more substantive. "He wanted to *do* the job," Shultz said. Subsequently, Shultz invited Reagan to a gathering of academic and policy types at Shultz's home on the campus of Stanford University. "He was impressive," Shultz remembered. Reagan had strong views, which wasn't unusual in a politician. But Reagan's views were remarkably well-informed. "He understood why he had the views."

At the time of Haig's departure, Shultz was president of Bechtel Corporation, a global construction and engineering firm. Reagan's call reached him in a meeting in London. "Al Haig has resigned," Reagan said, "and I want you to be my secretary of state."

Shultz wasn't sure he had heard the president correctly. "Haig has already resigned?" he asked Reagan. "It has already happened?"

Reagan fudged. "He has resigned," he said. "It hasn't been announced, but it has happened. I have accepted his resignation, and I want you to replace him."

Shultz suddenly realized that Reagan expected an immediate answer. "Mr. President, are you asking me to accept this job now, over the phone?"

"Well, yes, I am, George," Reagan said. "It would help a lot because it's not a good idea to leave a post like this vacant. When we announce that Secretary Haig has resigned, we'd like to announce that I have nominated you."

Shultz thought a few seconds, then said, "Mr. President, I'm on board."

Reagan hung up and headed for the White House press room. While Haig was still composing his resignation letter, Reagan announced his successor. Then he flew off to Camp David.

Haig told his side of the story from the State Department later that day. Reagan was informed Haig would be holding a news conference, and he and Nancy turned on the television. Haig ascribed his resignation to a disagreement on foreign policy. Reagan shook his head. "The only disagreement was over whether I made policy or the secretary of state did," he wrote that evening.

58

REAGAN RARELY LOOKED backward. From boyhood he had always looked forward—beyond his father's drunken binges, beyond the emotional dislocations of moving from town to town, beyond the narrow confines of Dixon, beyond Illinois to Hollywood, beyond Hollywood to Sacramento and then Washington. Ambition had driven him to look forward, to the next level of achievement and renown, but so also had temperament. He preferred action to reflection, moving ahead to contemplating the past. He almost never admitted mistakes, partly because he didn't think he made many of them but also because admitting mistakes required the kind of retrospection he disliked. If his career had been less successful, he might have found his self-imposed amnesia untenable. He would have had to ask himself why his achievements had fallen short of his ambitions. But his career was astonishingly successful. So why worry about the past?

Reagan never admitted that choosing Al Haig for secretary of state had been a mistake. Nor did he admit that his detached style of leadership lent itself to the kind of bureaucratic guerrilla warfare that drove Haig to distraction before it drove him from office. Reagan simply blamed Haig for the troubles of the secretary's tenure and moved on.

George Shultz soon learned that the truth was more complicated than that. Shultz flew by supersonic Concorde across the Atlantic and by helicopter to Camp David. "President Reagan and I had lunch under a canopy of trees outside Aspen Cottage," he recalled. "Bill Clark, Jim Baker, and Ed Meese joined us. The shells were falling in Beirut, the press was howling, and pressure on the United States was mounting at the United Nations to take some kind of action against Israel. The president was calm and affable. But he and his aides, I could see, were also gripped with a sense of urgency, frustration, and crisis."

Reagan had felt the pressure since the Israelis crossed the border into Lebanon. "We're walking on a tightrope," he wrote in his diary. Elias Sarkis, the Lebanese president, seemed willing to let the Israelis neutralize the several thousand PLO fighters in southern Lebanon, but he couldn't say so in public. That put Reagan in a bind. "The world is waiting for us to use our muscle and order Israel out," he said. "We can't do this if we want to help Sarkis, but we can't explain the situation either. Some days are worse than others."

Reagan's days didn't get any better. The president understood the Israeli government's reasons for going into Lebanon, although he disbelieved their public declaration that they simply wanted to drive the PLO back from Israel's border. He guessed that Begin and Sharon intended to destroy the PLO or at least force it out of Lebanon. They made no secret of their desire to eject Syrian forces from the country. Reagan recognized that much of the world saw Israel as America's stalking horse and blamed the United States for the casualties Israeli forces were inflicting in Lebanon.

He declined to lecture Begin publicly, not least because he supposed that such a course would simply make the prime minister more intransigent. But behind the doors of the White House, when Begin again visited Washington, the president let him know he didn't have carte blanche from the United States. "I was pretty blunt," Reagan wrote after the meeting. Begin responded that Israel had to defend itself. Reagan said Israeli forces were taking too many casualties. Begin denied it. Reagan said it again. Yet to himself, in his diary, he admitted, "It's a complex problem. While we think his action was overkill, it still may turn out to be the best opportunity we've had to reconcile the warring factions in Lebanon and bring about peace after seven years."

Peace was what Reagan wanted, both for the sake of Lebanon and for the credibility of the United States in the Arab world. Yet he realized this was a tall order, and in the meantime he would settle for a ceasefire. He sent special envoy Philip Habib to mediate between the belligerents. Habib got an agreement, only to have each side violate the truce and blame the other. Habib's central problem was that the Israelis didn't intend to call off their offensive until they had accomplished the purpose of their invasion. But his task wasn't made easier by the long-standing refusal of the United States to negotiate directly with the PLO. Habib, the American mediator, had to employ mediators of his own—Lebanese go-betweens—to exchange messages with the Palestinian leadership. When, in the interest of efficiency, he edged physically closer to the Palestinians, the Israelis complained, and he had to step back.

He nonetheless got his messages across, thanks in part to a striking diplomatic style. "Habib never ceased to rave and rant and wave his arms in perpetual motion as he shouted imprecations at anyone in range," George Shultz recounted. "Habib's tantrums were at once theatrics and persuasively serious. Beneath the surface everyone discerned a just and good-natured gentleman ... Habib could convey unpleasant truths and stark realities in a manner that would often ultimately win agreement without resentment."

All the same, Habib's leverage was no greater than Reagan allowed him to apply. And Reagan, for all his impatience with Begin, refused to risk a rift with Israel, America's most important partner in the Middle East.

THE SITUATION GREW tenser when Israeli forces approached Beirut. Israel's occupation of rural Lebanon had angered Arabs and much of the rest of the world, but a takeover of an Arab capital would almost certainly produce an emotional and political explosion of far greater force. Yet from the Israeli view, Beirut was a legitimate target, for the PLO had retreated from southern Lebanon into the city.

Reagan tried to forestall the attack. Judging that private warnings had lost their force, the president came close to lecturing Israel openly. A reporter asked him, ahead of a meeting with Israeli foreign minister Yitzhak Shamir, if he was going to get tough with the Israeli government for violating the cease-fire. "Let me say I'll be firm," Reagan replied. "This must be resolved, and the bloodshed must stop." The reporter asked if he was losing patience with Israel. "I lost patience a long time ago," the president said.

On August 4, Reagan convened the National Security Council to assess the situation and devise a plan. He commenced the meeting by asking for the latest news from the front. He said he had been awakened that morning by an aide with a report that an "all out assault" on Beirut had begun. Was this true?

George Shultz said the Israeli activity fell short of a full assault. But the Israeli shelling made it impossible for Phil Habib to continue cease-fire talks. Shultz relayed Habib's request for "a very strong letter that would threaten sanctions if the Israelis did not provide him with the amount of time and quiet that he needed to conclude the negotiations." Shultz supported the request, adding that sanctions might include another suspension of arms sales and a resolution by the UN Security Council condemning the Israeli attacks.

Jeane Kirkpatrick objected to the anti-Israel tone of Shultz's remarks. "We should not lose sight of the fact that the PLO is not a bunch of agrarian reformers," the UN ambassador said. "They are international terrorists who are working against U.S. interests and committing acts of violence throughout the world supported by the Soviet Union." Israel's aim in Lebanon was America's, Kirkpatrick said. "The U.S. should not throw away the possibility of getting rid of the PLO by taking measures against Israel which will inhibit, if not eliminate, the prospects of achieving our objectives. Clearly, once we have removed the PLO from Lebanon we can make fast progress in the peace process."

Reagan agreed with Kirkpatrick and asked, "How do we inform the PLO of the situation and the need to get out?"

Caspar Weinberger didn't answer the president's question; instead, he returned to the issue of how to deal with Israel. The defense secretary concurred that the PLO should leave Lebanon, but he thought Israel was going too far. "The U.S. must let Israel know of the cost to Israel of its nightly activities," Weinberger said, referring to the bombardment of West Beirut, the Muslim section of the city, where the PLO had taken refuge.

Reagan preferred to pressure the Palestinians. "We have to let the PLO know that their games must stop," the president said. Thinking aloud, he suggested working through Saudi Arabia. "Perhaps the best way to do this would be to communicate something along the following lines to King Fahd: We have continued to hold back the Israelis, and I am again in communication with Prime Minister Begin. But the intransigence of the PLO, who all of us agreed should move out, is causing problems and leading the Israelis to resume their activities. It is time for the PLO to move out."

None of Reagan's advisers contradicted the president, but his suggestion received no second, and the matter was dropped. Discussion turned to what Reagan should say to Begin. Bill Clark had drafted a letter, which he presented to Reagan. The president studied the letter for several minutes. A frown creased his face as he read the final section, which he proceeded to revise on the spot. "Last night we were making significant progress toward a settlement that would result in the removal of the PLO from Beirut," the president wrote. "That progress was once again frustrated by the actions taken by your forces. There must be an end to the unnecessary bloodshed, particularly among innocent civilians. I insist that a ceasefire-in-place be reestablished and maintained until the PLO has left Beirut. The relationship between our two nations is at stake."

Reagan proposed to address Begin in the letter as "Menachem." But the consensus among the NSC members and staff was that this would vitiate the otherwise stern tone of the letter. Reagan reluctantly agreed to commence the letter "Dear Prime Minister."

STRONGER LANGUAGE PROVED necessary. The Israeli bombardment of Beirut intensified, prompting Reagan to telephone Begin. Geoffrey Kemp, the top Middle East expert on the NSC staff, silently monitored the call but nearly gasped aloud when Reagan dropped the rhetorical *h*-bomb on Begin. "Menachem, this is a holocaust," Reagan said.

"Begin bristled," Kemp remembered. "You could almost feel it on the telephone." The prime minister spoke slowly and bitterly: "Mr. President, I know all about a holocaust."

Reagan's call had the desired effect; the attacks on Beirut diminished. But it deeply offended Begin, whose parents and brother had died at the hands of the Nazis.

Habib worked out a deal. The principal points were a new cease-fire, the evacuation of the PLO from Lebanon, and the subsequent withdrawal of Israeli and Syrian forces from Lebanon. A multinational peacekeeping force would supervise the PLO withdrawal; American troops would be included. "Our purpose will be to assist the Lebanese armed forces in carrying out their responsibility for ensuring the departure of PLO leaders, officers, and combatants in Beirut from Lebanese territory under safe and orderly conditions," Reagan explained in a Rose Garden statement. "The presence of United States forces also will facilitate the restoration of the sovereignty and authority of the Lebanese government over the Beirut area. In no case will our troops stay longer than thirty days."

Reagan had told reporters before his statement that he would not answer questions. Secretary of State Shultz was about to convene a news conference, he explained. But reporters shouted at him anyway. "Mr.

President, how can you be sure that American troops will stay safe?" one asked.

"That will be covered," Reagan replied, referring to Shultz's news conference.

The reporter persisted. "If they're shot at, will they be withdrawn, sir, immediately?" he said.

"What?"

"If they're shot at, will they be withdrawn immediately?"

"Yes, yes," Reagan said.

Larry Speakes broke in. "We said no questions," he reminded the reporters. He hustled Reagan off.

THE PLO EVACUATION proceeded without major incident, allowing Reagan on September 1 to tell the American public, "Today has been a day that should make us proud. It marked the end of the successful evacuation of PLO from Beirut." The president congratulated Philip Habib for his tireless efforts, and he recognized the several hundred U.S. marines who had helped supervise the operation. "Our young men should be out of Lebanon within two weeks. They, too, have served the cause of peace with distinction, and we can all be very proud of them."

The president expressed hope that the Lebanese settlement could lead to a larger resolution of the Arab-Israeli conflict. Suggesting a framework for such a resolution, he issued three calls. "I call on Israel to make clear that the security for which she yearns can only be achieved through genuine peace, a peace requiring magnanimity, vision, and courage. I call on the Palestinian people to recognize that their own political aspirations are inextricably bound to recognition of Israel's right to a secure future. And I call on the Arab states to accept the reality of Israel—and the reality that peace and justice are to be gained only through hard, fair, direct negotiation."

Elaborating on his peace vision, Reagan explicitly rejected an independent Palestinian state in the West Bank and Gaza, but he also rejected permanent retention by Israel of those territories. He proposed Palestinian self-government in association with Jordan. He declared America's opposition to the construction of Israeli settlements in the occupied territories. And he embraced the concept of giving the Palestinians land in exchange for a peace treaty with Israel. "We base our approach squarely on the principle that the Arab-Israeli conflict should be resolved through negotiations involving an exchange of territory for peace," he said.

Reagan wasn't surprised when Begin rejected his proposal. The Israeli prime minister regularly proclaimed that the West Bank was Israeli and would forever remain Israeli. "What some call the West Bank, Mr. President, is Judea and Samaria," Begin wrote to Reagan. "Millennia ago there was a Jewish kingdom of Judea and Samaria where our kings knelt to God, where our prophets brought forth a vision of eternal peace, where we developed a rich civilization which we took with us in our hearts and in our minds on our long global trek over eighteen centuries, and with it we came back home." Though Jordan had governed Judea and Samaria after 1948, Israel's people never forgot them. "In a war of most legitimate self-defense in 1967 after having been attacked by King Hussein we liberated with God's help that portion of our homeland. Judea and Samaria will never again be the West Bank."

REAGAN WAS DISAPPOINTED at Begin's hard line, which the president feared would produce only more violence. His fears proved true sooner than he anticipated. On September 14 a bomb blast killed Lebanon's president-elect, Bashir Gemayel. The assassination alarmed the Israelis and prompted them to occupy West Beirut. Four days later, Lebanese militiamen entered two Palestinian refugee camps in the sector now controlled by the Israeli army and slaughtered hundreds of men, women, and children. The Israeli forces stood by.

Reagan was appalled and said so publicly. "I was horrified to learn this morning of the killing of Palestinians which has taken place in Beirut," the president declared. "All people of decency must share our outrage and revulsion over the murders, which included women and children." He didn't directly blame the Israelis for the killings, but he asserted their complicity. "During the negotiations leading to the PLO withdrawal from Beirut, we were assured that Israeli forces would not enter West Beirut. We also understood that following withdrawal, Lebanese Army units would establish control over the city. They were thwarted in this effort by the Israeli occupation that took place beginning on Wednesday. We strongly opposed Israel's move into West Beirut following the assassination of President-elect Gemayel, both because we believed it wrong in principle and for fear that it would provoke further fighting. Israel, by yesterday in military control of Beirut, claimed that its moves would prevent the kind of tragedy which has now occurred."

Reagan decided that the only way to get Israel out of Lebanon was to put America more firmly in. He convened the NSC for consideration of next steps. The discussion didn't move fast enough for him. "I finally told our group we should go for broke," he recorded that evening. He advocated sending the multinational force, including the American contingent, back into Lebanon to prevent further violence. The administration would pressure the Israelis to leave Lebanon and would rely on various Arab states to talk Syria into withdrawing. Meanwhile, the Lebanese government would build up its military to the point where it could defend the country. "No more half way gestures," Reagan wrote. "Clear the whole situation while the MNF is on hand to ensure order."

George Shultz and Jeane Kirkpatrick enthusiastically endorsed the president's proposal. No one at the meeting expressed opposition. Reagan was pleased. "The wheels are now in motion," he wrote.

THE STRENGTH OF Reagan's approach to foreign policy as a whole was his weakness in policy toward the Middle East. Reagan kept his eye on the big picture, meaning the struggle with Soviet communism, and in that realm he eventually succeeded beyond any other president. But his big-picture orientation diminished his ability to deal with smaller issues, such as the war in Lebanon. He lacked expertise in the personalities and prejudices that made that country one of the most complicated and vexed on earth. Success in Middle Eastern diplomacy required attention to detail Reagan was simply incapable of. It was no coincidence that the one president to make a lasting mark on the Middle East was Reagan's polar opposite in temperament and approach: Jimmy Carter. Carter was often derided, by Reagan among many others, for micromanaging policy. But without that attention to detail, Carter would never have achieved the breakthrough Camp David agreement between Egypt and Israel.

Reagan nonetheless hoped for something similar. And he hoped the return of American forces to Lebanon would make it possible. The landing and deployment went smoothly, encouraging Reagan to bring several Arab leaders to Washington. "The big day!" he wrote on October 22. King Hassan of Morocco led the delegation. Hassan knew that the American government had consistently said it would not deal directly with the PLO until the PLO acknowledged Israel's right to exist. Hassan thought he could get PLO head Yasser Arafat to utter the required words. "He offered a sample of what Arafat should say," Reagan noted. "And I agreed it was good enough. Then he indicated he thought he could deliver that in three weeks or a month."

The Israelis provided less encouragement. Begin refused to with-draw Israeli forces from Beirut, contending that the PLO would simply return. Reagan met with Phil Habib, who was growing more frustrated with Begin by the day. The Israeli occupation of Lebanon—now opposed by the government of Amine Gemayel, brother of the murdered Bashir Gemayel—confirmed Arab skepticism of Israel's intentions. And it played into the hands of Palestinian extremists. Reagan sent Habib back to the Middle East with a message for Israel's government: If Israel failed to leave Lebanon, it might lose America's support.

Reagan continued to be more favorably impressed by the Arabs than by the Israelis. King Hussein of Jordan arrived in Washington in late December. "I really like him," Reagan noted. "He is our hope to lead the Arab side and the PLO in negotiating with the Israelis." Reagan gave Hussein every encouragement. President Hosni Mubarak of Egypt followed Hussein. "We had good meetings and affirmed our solid relationship," Reagan wrote. Mubarak warned that Israel's intransigence in Lebanon could make any peace settlement impossible and that Israel and Syria, though enemies, seemed to have the common goal of dividing Lebanon between them. "I share his concern," Reagan observed.

REAGAN'S FRUSTRATION WITH Israel continued to mount during the first quarter of 1983. Ariel Sharon's resignation as defense minister following an investigative commission's finding of culpability in the massacres at the Palestinian refugee camps briefly gave Reagan reason to think things might improve. Yet while a March visit by Yitzhak Shamir, the Israeli foreign minister, included fewer angry words than Reagan's exchanges with Begin, it brought no greater progress. "Still Israel dragging their feet," Reagan muttered.

April yielded a new shock and further reason for discouragement. On April 18 a car bomb exploded outside the American embassy in Beirut. More than sixty people were killed, including seventeen Americans. Among the American dead were several State Department and CIA officials and a marine guard. Never had an American embassy suffered such intentional damage. A faction linked to Iran claimed responsibility for the bombing.

"D--n them," Reagan wrote in his diary. The next day, following an NSC meeting at which he learned more details, he added, "Lord forgive me for the hatred I feel for the humans who can do such a cruel but cow-ardly deed."

Four days later the president met the plane bringing home the bodies of the slain Americans. "There can be no sadder duty for one who holds the office I hold than to pay tribute to Americans who have given their lives in the service of their country," he told the families and the broader public. "These gallant Americans understood the danger they faced, and yet they went willingly to Beirut. And the dastardly deed, the act of unparalleled cowardice that took their lives, was an attack on all of us, on our way of life and on the values we hold dear." For this reason, Reagan said, the mission in Lebanon was more important than ever. "We would indeed fail them if we let that act deter us from carrying on their mission of brotherhood and peace . . . Let us here in their presence serve notice to the cowardly, skulking barbarians in the world that they will not have their way."

"MR. PRESIDENT," A reporter had asked at the outset of the intervention, "do you have a plan for getting the United States out of Lebanon if fighting should break out there. Or could the marine presence there lead to another long entanglement such as Vietnam?"

The specter of Vietnam hovered over every American intervention after the 1970s. Presidents routinely denied the analogy, and Reagan denied it now. "I don't see anything of that kind taking place there at all," he said. Yet the very need to deny it testified to its power in the American imagination. American voters learn lessons slowly in foreign policy, but they learn them well. The lesson of the 1930s, that appeasement must be shunned and aggression resisted, became the basis for forty years of policy toward the Soviet Union and its allies. The lesson of Vietnam, that other countries' wars could become quagmires for the United States, caused presidents from Jimmy Carter forward to deny that their interventions were anything like the intervention in Vietnam. Sometimes it led to decisions to let revolutions run their course, as Carter did in Nicaragua. Sometimes it led to covert warfare, like that Reagan waged in Central America by means of the contras. Always it produced a defensive reaction when reporters or other skeptics raised the Vietnam issue.

"The marines are going in there, into a situation with a definite understanding as to what we're supposed to do," Reagan elaborated. "I believe that we are going to be successful in seeing the other foreign forces leave Lebanon. And then at such time as Lebanon says that they have the situation well in hand, why, we'll depart."

The reporters weren't convinced. "Sir, if fighting should break out again, would you pull the marines out?" another asked.

"You're asking a hypothetical question, and I've found out that I never get in trouble if I don't answer one of those," Reagan said.

BUT THE BOMBING of the embassy wasn't hypothetical. It underscored the dangers to the United States of involvement in Lebanon's troubles, and it drove Reagan to intensify his efforts to find a solution. He sent George Shultz to the Middle East to spell the weary Habib and add the prestige of Shultz's office to the negotiations. Initial reports on the secretary's dealings with the Israelis were good. Shultz cabled Reagan saying the Israelis seemed close to an agreement to withdraw.

Suddenly Syria became the obstacle to a settlement. Oddly, this afforded Reagan a certain relief. Reagan's big picture of a world divided between democracy and communism had struggled with the local factionalism, sectarianism, and personalism of Lebanese politics. But Syria had ties to the Soviet Union, which made it part of the big picture. It also gave Reagan an opportunity to lecture Leonid Brezhnev, an exercise he found much more congenial than lecturing Menachem Begin. Brezhnev had blamed Israel for the violence in Lebanon. "Israel is pursuing a regular war against Lebanon," Brezhnev declared in a letter to Reagan. "Israel began this war with an act unprecedented in its impudence and contempt for the norms of the international community"—namely crossing lines established by United Nations forces. "Israel is continuing its large scale aggression against a sovereign country, a member of the UN. Blood is being shed, thousands of people are tragically perishing, the peaceful population of the country—Lebanese, Palestinians—are experiencing unbelievable suffering." Brezhnev held Reagan responsible—"in view of the well known fact that the United States has at its disposal major possibilities of influencing Israel." And he went on to warn the American president that the Kremlin would not stand idly by. "The Soviet Union watches with utmost attention developments of the situation in this region which is located in the immediate proximity of our southern borders and where we have no shortage of friends." The Soviet Union would act to protect its interests. "Unless the war of Israel against Lebanon and the UN is immediately stopped, the consequences may prove unpredictable."

Reagan liked feeling indignant as much as most people do, and Brezhnev's blaming gave him an opportunity. The president didn't take seriously the implied threat in Brezhnev's letter; Lebanon was hardly on the border of the Soviet Union, and Moscow in fact suffered from a shortage of friends in the region, especially after the Camp David accords caused Egypt to look to the United States rather than the Soviet Union for aid. Reagan ignored that part of Brezhnev's letter. Instead, he challenged Brezhnev's good faith and his assignment of blame. "Your expressions of concern for the suffering of the people of Lebanon cannot but appear ironic in view of the fact that the Soviet Union has provided immense quantities of weapons to elements which have actively worked to undermine the political stability of Lebanon and provoked Israeli retaliation by attacking Israel's northern territories." He told Brezhnev to cut the claptrap and get to work on a solution. "I will continue to use my personal influence to that end and expect that you will press a similar course on those forces with which the Soviet Union enjoys influence."

THE EXCHANGE WITH Brezhnev was satisfying for Reagan, but it didn't get at the root of the Lebanon problem, which was intensely local. And it was deep, far deeper than the comparatively recent struggle between democracy and communism. Sometimes Reagan sensed roots that ran to biblical times. At a moment of particular exasperation with Syria, he wrote in his diary, "Armageddon in the prophecies begins with the gates of Damascus being assailed."

Reagan didn't really think Armageddon was about to start, but he didn't want to take any chances. He ordered Shultz and Robert McFarlane, who replaced Habib as Reagan's special envoy to the Middle East, to step up their mediation efforts. For a time they reported progress.

But then the factional war in Lebanon heated up again, with the factions splintering into new factions and the Lebanese government becoming merely one contestant among the many. The United States still recognized the government and hoped to bolster it. Reagan met with President Gemayel and assured him he wouldn't be abandoned. Reagan promised Gemayel weapons that would help the government fend off its opponents.

Reagan considered himself an honest broker in the Lebanon conflict, but his aid to Gemayel, not to mention the much longer and broader American support for Israel, made American soldiers seem like combatants to those who opposed the government and the Israelis. In August 1983, Reagan received a cable informing him that American marines at the Beirut airport had come under artillery attack. The news reminded him, as if a reminder were necessary, what a hard problem the Middle East was. He remarked wistfully, "The world must have been simpler in the days of gunboat diplomacy."

PERHAPS THE WISH was father to the ensuing reality, for Reagan shortly authorized the use of American naval power in the Lebanon war. The president's military advisers insisted that the marines be defended. They advocated sending the battleship *New Jersey* to the Lebanese coast to shell the positions from which the attacks against the marines originated. Reagan had to think the matter through. "This could be seen as putting us in the war," he acknowledged. Yet he allowed himself to be persuaded. "This can be explained as protection of our marines," he reasoned. "If it doesn't work, then we'll have to decide between pulling out or going to the Congress and making a case for greater involvement."

The decision was indeed seen as putting the United States in the war. The *New Jersey* bombarded the heights above the Beirut airport with sixteen-inch shells that weighed over a ton. The destruction was immense, and it silenced the artillery attacks against the marines at the airport. But it was often indiscriminate, killing noncombatants, destroying their homes, and expanding the ranks of people who considered the Americans their enemies.

Those ranks included a suicide bomber who in late October crashed a truck filled with explosives into the airport building that served as a barracks for the marines. The blast leveled the concrete structure and killed 241 American servicemen. A second, almost simultaneous attack on a French barracks a few miles away killed 58 French soldiers.

"The president's face turned ashen when I told him the news," Robert McFarlane recalled. "He looked like a man, a 72-year-old man, who had just received a blow to the chest. All the air seemed to go out of him. 'How could this happen?' he asked disbelievingly."

Reagan recovered sufficiently to issue a statement to reporters. "There are no words to properly express our outrage," he said. He added his condolences to the families of the deceased. And he reaffirmed his commitment to the cause for which they had died. "We should all recognize that these deeds make so evident the bestial nature of those who would assume power if they could have their way and drive us out of that area. We must be more determined than ever."

60

OURS AFTER HEARING the terrible news from Beirut, Reagan launched a military operation that seemed to have nothing to do with the conflict in Lebanon. Most Americans had never heard of Grenada before Reagan became president; even American newscasters required time to get the pronunciation right (gre-NAY-da). The invasion of this tiny island country in the eastern Caribbean took the American public by such surprise that Reagan's critics hardly had time to react before the deed was done.

Reagan intended things that way. Since entering office, he had been looking for an opportunity to demonstrate his and America's decisiveness in foreign affairs, in particular to exorcise the ghost of Vietnam and dispel the impression that the United States would not act forcefully in defense of its interests. Latin America seemed a likely place for the kind of demonstration Reagan intended. Fidel Castro and his leftist allies in the region needed a chastening, Reagan judged, and in Latin America the United States enjoyed an overwhelming military advantage over any conceivable foe.

Suriname briefly caught his eye. In December 1982 soldiers in the service of military strongman Desi Bouterse killed fifteen political dissidents in that former Dutch colony. Bouterse then made statements that struck Reagan's ear as suggesting he was cozying up to Castro. "This must not be allowed," Reagan wrote confidentially. "We have to find a way to stop him." The president considered sending in the marines but decided against it. "We'd lose all we've gained with the other Latin American countries."

So instead he plotted covert warfare. In the spring of 1983, Reagan's national security team developed a plan for neutralizing or toppling Bou-terse. "Based on the President's directives at the NSPG meeting yesterday, we suggest the following possible actions," staffers Alfonso Sapia-Bosch and Oliver North wrote: "That a Presidential emissary travel to Venezuela and Brazil this week to meet with the respective presidents to brief them in detail on what is now taking place in Suriname and what the result is likely to be, e.g., the Cubanization of Surinamese society. Furthermore this will allow the establishment of a Cuban and Soviet base on the tip of South America that will give improved access to the South Caribbean and a base from which to extend their influence with South America. Northeastern Brazil will then be open to propaganda infiltration at the very least. Venezuela will have another unfriendly country near its border." Sapia-Bosch and North recommended briefing not only the president of Venezuela, Luis Herrera Campins, but also his probable successor, Jaime Lusinchi. "Herrera Campins feels very vulnerable because of ineptitude, financial problems, corruption, etc. By bringing Lusinchi into the loop, we would reduce pressure on Herrera Campins." In Brazil the approach should be straightforward. "President Figueiredo must be made to under-stand the threat that Cubans and Soviets will present when they are on his northern border. He is an army general and should recognize the problem."

Sapia-Bosch and North recommended other actions that were deemed too sensitive to reveal when their memo was declassified a quarter century later. But George Shultz, in his memoir, indicated what they had in mind. "The CIA sent briefers to me to outline a plan under which a force of 50 to 175 Korean commandos would stage out of Venezuela and run an assault into Paramaribo to overthrow Bouterse," Shultz wrote. The secretary of state could hardly believe what he was hearing. "It was a hare-brained idea, ill thought out, without any convincing likelihood of success and with no analysis of the political consequences at home or internationally." He added, "The whole thing depended on impossibly intricate timing and a presumption that the Koreans would be taken as members of the local population. That was crazy. I was shaken to find such a wild plan put forward seriously by the CIA."

Reagan nonetheless used the threat of invasion as leverage for diplo-macy. He named William Clark as his emissary to Venezuela and Bra-zil. The journey was secret, but its point was clear. "Our message," Clark recalled later, "was, 'Look, either you take care of the situation, of the Soviet foothold, the Cuban foothold . . . either you take care of it down here or we'll have no alternative but to do so ourselves.'" Clark laid out the

American invasion plan to Herrera Campins in Caracas. "He turned pale, and before I left his office, said, 'Talk to Brazil, they're closer. I don't want anything to do with it right now, I'm in enough political trouble.'" Clark proceeded to Brasília, where he met not with the Brazilian president but with the general who chaired the country's military chiefs of staff. "We parked at the end of the runway; it was after dark," Clark recalled. Again he delineated what an American-backed invasion of Suriname would look like. "The chairman ran to the men's room and threw up, he was so frightened," Clark said.

Perhaps Clark misunderstood the cause of the general's distress. Or perhaps the general did not convey that distress to his civilian bosses. In any event, the Clark mission failed to achieve what Reagan wanted. "Venezuela couldn't go along," Reagan noted after debriefing Clark. "President of Brazil had an idea somewhat different than ours." What that idea was, Reagan didn't say. But he added cryptically, "So operation 'Guiminish' is born. We'll know before the month is out whether it has succeeded."

WHATEVER THE NATURE of Operation Guiminish—named for a horse Reagan kept at his California ranch—it did not topple Bouterse, who remained in power for several years. Yet Suriname did not become a Soviet satellite or a base for Cuban operations in mainland Latin America. And so Reagan had to look elsewhere to make his statement of resolve against Latin leftism.

He didn't have to look far. Grenada was even more difficult for most Americans to find than Suriname, being a small island at the tag end of the Lesser Antilles. But unlike Suriname it actually touched the Caribbean, thus gaining in strategic value what it lacked in size. And it had a government, headed by Maurice Bishop, that was more obviously leftist than Bouterse's merely brutal regime. Reagan had been watching Grenada since the beginning of his administration and had been warning Americans for months about the worrisome things happening there. "On the small island of Grenada, at the southern end of the Caribbean chain, the Cubans, with Soviet financing and backing, are in the process of building an airfield with a 10,000-foot runway," the president declared in a March 1983 address on national security. "Grenada doesn't even have an air force. Who is it intended for?" As the television cameras panned to an aerial photograph of the suspicious runway, Reagan elaborated on Grenada's strategic importance and answered his own question: "The Caribbean is a very important passageway for our international commerce and military lines of communication. More than half of all American oil imports now pass through the Caribbean. The rapid buildup of Grenada's military potential is unrelated to any conceivable threat to this island country of under 110,000 people and totally at odds with the pattern of other eastern Caribbean states, most of which are unarmed. The Soviet-Cuban militarization of Grenada, in short, can only be seen as power projection into the region."

Yet Grenada remained merely a talking point for the administration until October 1983—until the weekend of the bombing of the U.S. marine barracks in Beirut. Maurice Bishop antagonized not only the American president but some of his own colleagues, who deposed, arrested, and executed him. The coup sent shudders through the eastern Caribbean, where the leaders of several small island states feared that the violence in Grenada might spread. They gathered hastily and sent a request to the American government for protection.

The request reached Reagan in Augusta, Georgia, where he was spending a golf weekend with George Shultz and Don Regan. Reagan wasn't much of a golfer, but he liked the getaway from Washington and the change of scenery from Camp David. Reagan and Nancy arrived on Friday afternoon; at four o'clock on Saturday morning he was awakened by a call from Robert McFarlane. McFarlane had just taken over as national security adviser from William Clark, after Clark alienated Nancy for being too visible as the orchestrator of administration foreign policy. "I had never really gotten along with him," Nancy later said of Clark. "He struck me as a user—especially when he traveled around the country claiming he represented Ronnie, which usually wasn't true. I spoke to Ronnie about him, but Ronnie liked him, so he stayed around longer than I would have liked." McFarlane now said the president needed to hear the latest from the Caribbean. Reagan put on a robe and met McFarlane and Shultz in the living room of the Augusta club's Eisenhower Cabin, where he and Nancy were staying. George Bush joined the group by phone from Washington.

McFarlane relayed the request from the Caribbean leaders for American intervention. He and Reagan's other advisers pointed out an American stake in Grenada apart from the island's strategic role. Several hundred American students attended a medical school in St. George's, the capital. Shultz had talked things over with Tony Motley, the American ambassador to Brazil and a military veteran. "We both had the searing memory of

Tehran and the sixty-six Americans seized from our embassy on November 4, 1979, and held hostage for well over a year," Shultz recalled. Shultz had no evidence that the new rulers of Grenada intended to seize any of the students, but with their Caribbean neighbors calling for American intervention, the Grenadians might have reasoned that taking hostages was a way to forestall such intervention.

Reagan remembered the Iran hostages even better than Shultz did, having won election partly because of them. He wasn't about to risk incurring a similar hostage problem of his own. "I asked McFarlane how long the Pentagon thought it would need to prepare a rescue mission," the president recalled, referring to a preemptive extraction of the students. McFarlane replied that the Joint Chiefs of Staff said the operation could begin within forty-eight hours.

"Do it," Reagan ordered.

The president later admitted to a larger agenda than either the American students or Grenada. He feared that the United States was becoming paralyzed by the memories of Vietnam. "I understood what Vietnam had meant for the country," he wrote in his post-presidential memoir, "but I believed the United States couldn't remain spooked forever by this experience." Reagan recognized that Grenada wasn't quite a dagger at America's heart, yet it *was* a place where he could make a statement that would keep other daggers away.

His statement-making purpose was bolstered just hours later by news of the Beirut bombing. The complexities of the Middle East prevented him from responding in Lebanon as forcefully as he wished he could, but these constraints simply rendered more necessary a demonstration of American power elsewhere.

PREPARATIONS FOR THE Grenada strike took place in secret. Reagan didn't want to alert the regime in Grenada, which might seize the students for self-defense, and he didn't wish to clue Congress, lest certain members blow the cover for political purposes. "I suspected that if we told the leaders of Congress about the operation, even under terms of strictest confidentiality, there would be some who would leak it to the press together with the prediction that Grenada was going to become 'another Vietnam,'" he said later.

Reagan kept the secret from Margaret Thatcher as well. Grenada was a member of the British Commonwealth, and the prime minister had let

Reagan know she thought the United States had no business meddling there. Reagan didn't agree, yet he didn't want to argue with her. "I believe Maggie Thatcher was the only person who could intimidate Ronald Reagan," Howard Baker asserted afterward. Baker spoke from personal knowledge of the two leaders and as one who overheard a Reagan-Thatcher conversation at a critical moment of the Grenada affair. The preparations for the invasion had proceeded smoothly, and the president had just given the order to launch. At this point he lifted the veil slightly, bringing Baker, his Democratic counterpart Robert Byrd, and House leaders Tip O'Neill and Jim Wright to the presidential living quarters for a confidential briefing. The briefing had hardly begun when the White House butler came in. "Mr. President, the Prime Minister is on the phone," he said. Reagan got up to take the call. "He went next door from the oval sitting room and closed the door," Baker recounted. "But as is typical of many people who don't hear very well, he spoke in a loud voice. I could hear him plain as day. He said, 'Margaret'—long pause. 'But Margaret'—and he went through that about three times, and he came back sort of sheepish and said, 'Mrs. Thatcher has strong reservations about this.'"

Yet Reagan refused to change his mind. The invasion went forward, as the president explained several hours later. "Early this morning, forces from six Caribbean democracies and the United States began a landing on the island of Grenada in the Eastern Caribbean," he said from the White House. The Caribbean forces were tokens, as the administration tacitly acknowledged. "We have taken this decisive action for three reasons," he continued. "First, and of overriding importance, to protect innocent lives, including up to a thousand Americans, whose personal safety is, of course, my paramount concern. Second, to forestall further chaos. And third, to assist in the restoration of conditions of law and order and of governmental institutions to the island of Grenada, where a brutal group of leftist thugs violently seized power."

Reagan's third point made clear that he wasn't content merely to extract the students. He would topple Grenada's government and replace it with one more to his liking. This suited the Caribbean countries that had requested the intervention. Eugenia Charles was prime minister of Dominica and chair of the Organisation of Eastern Caribbean States; she joined Reagan for the White House announcement. "We were all very horrified at the events which took place recently in Grenada," she said. "We, as part of the Organization of East Caribbean States, realizing that we are, of course, one region—we belong to each other, are kith and kin;

we all have members of our state living in Grenada—we're very concerned that this event should take place again." Charles said that the coup in Grenada had reversed that country's halting progress toward democracy. "It means that Grenadians have never been given the chance to choose for themselves the country that they want. And, therefore, it is necessary for us to see to it that they have the opportunity to do so."

A reporter asked Reagan if the Americans in Grenada were safe. He replied that they were, as far as he knew. Another reporter asked how long the American troops would remain in Grenada. "We don't know how long that will be," Reagan responded. "We want to be out as quickly as possible, because our purpose in being there is only for them to take over their own affairs."

A questioner raised the sovereignty issue. "Mr. President, do you think the United States has the right to invade another country to change its government?"

Eugenia Charles jumped in. "But I don't think it's an invasion," she said.

"What is it?" the reporter said.

"This is a question of our asking for support," Charles said. "We are one region. Grenada is part and parcel of us—"

"But you're sovereign nations, are you not?" the reporter interrupted.

"—and we don't have the capacity, ourselves, to see to it that Grenadians get the freedom that they are required to have to choose their own government."

Reagan supplied his own answer. "Once these nations, which were once British colonies, were freed, they, themselves, had a treaty. And their treaty was one of mutual support. And Grenada is one of the countries, signatories to that treaty." Grenada's government had been constitutional and democratic at the time the country ratified the treaty, which therefore had greater legitimacy than the dictates of the current unconstitutional regime. "So, this action that is being taken is being taken under the umbrella of an existing treaty."

The operation proceeded swiftly and smoothly. "I can't say enough in praise of our military—Army rangers and paratroopers, Navy, Marine, and Air Force personnel—those who planned a brilliant campaign and those who carried it out," Reagan told Americans two days later. The troops had captured Grenada's two airports and secured the campus where the students lived. They arrived without a moment to spare, Reagan said. American intelligence had assumed that some Cubans who worked at the main airport were military reservists. "Well, as it turned out, the number was much larger, and they were a military force. Six hundred of them have been taken prisoner, and we have discovered a complete base with weapons and communications equipment, which makes it clear a Cuban occupation of the island had been planned." Reagan described a warehouse that had been seized. "This warehouse contained weapons and ammunition stacked almost to the ceiling, enough to supply thousands of terrorists. Grenada, we were told, was a friendly island paradise for tourism. Well, it wasn't. It was a Soviet-Cuban colony, being readied as a major military bastion to export terror and undermine democracy. We got there just in time."

The invasion sparked international condemnation of the United States for trampling the sovereignty of Grenada. The UN General Assembly voted overwhelmingly to censure the American government. After-battle reports suggested that the American students had never been in danger and that the administration exaggerated the Cuban influence.

Reagan retreated not an inch. Reporter Helen Thomas inquired whether he was bothered by the heavy vote in the General Assembly. "It didn't upset my breakfast at all," Reagan answered. Another reporter asked him to explain how the American invasion of Grenada differed from the Soviet invasion of Afghanistan. "Oh, for heaven's sake!" Reagan replied. "This was a rescue mission. It was a successful rescue mission, and the people that have been rescued, and the Grenadians that have been liberated, are down there delighted with and giving every evidence of appreciation and gratitude to our men down there." Another reporter wanted to know whether the success of the Grenada operation inclined the president to use military force elsewhere. Reagan dodged the question, saying any other situation would be different. A third reporter said the Nicaraguan regime was asserting that Reagan was preparing to order the invasion of their country; was this true?

Reagan smiled, as if considering the matter. He had certainly intended that the Sandinistas take notice of what American power could accomplish. If they were worried, all the better. He didn't quite deny their assertion. "I haven't believed anything they've been saying since they got in charge," he said. "And you shouldn't either."

DURING REAGAN'S SECOND year in office, his father-in-law, Loyal Davis, became seriously ill. "Nancy is very depressed about her father's health and understandably so," Reagan wrote in his diary. Davis and Nancy's mother had retired to Scottsdale, Arizona, and his illness prompted repeated flights by Nancy across the country from Washington. Reagan liked and respected his father-in-law and was naturally concerned for his health. But he worried more about his spiritual health. "He's always been an Agnostic," Reagan wrote. "Now I think he knows fear for probably the first time in his life." Reagan couldn't take the time Nancy did to visit Davis, but he wished he could. "I want so much to speak to him about faith," he said. "I believe this is a moment when he should turn to God and I want so much to help him do that." Yet Reagan never found the time, and Davis died a few months later with Reagan's words unspoken.

This diffidence on religion was the rule with Reagan rather than the exception. Casual observers and even people close to him might sometimes have wondered whether he had any religion at all. Edwin Meese later asserted, "He got a lot of sustenance from his faith," but neither Nancy nor his children thought enough of Reagan's religious beliefs to remark more than passingly upon them in their memoirs. Ron Reagan recalled that his father subscribed to a sort of modern Manifest Destiny. "'I can't help feeling that the Lord put America here between two oceans for a purpose,' he used to say with a kind of unblinking innocence," the younger Reagan wrote. And Ron recorded that the family attended Sunday services at the Bel Air Presbyterian Church when he was growing up.

But beyond that, his father kept his religious beliefs largely to himself. "He was not a real Bible thumper," Ron said.

As president, Reagan sprinkled his speeches with religious references, making the closing tag "God bless America" mandatory for every president after him. In his diary and private letters he occasionally included a line about religion. Yet his faith was far less conspicuous than Jimmy Carter's, for example. On Sundays he preferred Camp David to church. He explained that his attendance disrupted the services, which was true enough. But his faith was internal rather than institutional, and he professed to perceive the divine as much in nature as in any building. "It bothers me not to be in church on Sunday but don't see how I can with the security problem," he wrote on a Camp David Sunday during his first year in office. "I'm a hazard to others. I hope God realizes how much I feel that I am in a temple when I'm out in his beautiful forest and countryside as we were this morning."

Now and then, however, Reagan spoke openly about religion. He had done so briefly at the Republican convention in 1980, and he did so at greater length in March 1983, when he traveled to Florida to address the annual convention of the National Association of Evangelicals. Conservative Christians had become a pillar of Republican politics about the time southern Democrats became Sunbelt Republicans; a Republican fundraiser featuring the president and including many of those in the audience was scheduled for the same hotel right after his address. Consequently, Reagan wasn't surprised at the warm welcome he received. The ovation that greeted him went on and on; when it finally ended, he thanked the members of the audience not only for their applause on this afternoon but for the more potent support they offered on other occasions. "Thank you for your prayers," he said. "Nancy and I have felt their presence many times in many ways. And believe me, for us they've made all the difference. The other day in the East Room of the White House at a meeting there, someone asked me whether I was aware of all the people out there who were praying for the President. And I had to say, 'Yes, I am. I've felt it. I believe in intercessionary prayer.'" He practiced what he believed, he said. "I couldn't help but say to that questioner after he'd asked the question that if sometimes when he was praying he got a busy signal, it was just me in there ahead of him." Reagan's audience laughed appreciatively.

He had another joke. "An evangelical minister and a politician arrived at heaven's gate one day together. And St. Peter, after doing all the necessary formalities, took them in hand to show them where their quarters would be. And he took them to a small, single room with a bed, a chair, and a table and said this was for the clergyman. And the politician was a little worried about what might be in store for him. And he couldn't believe it then when St. Peter stopped in front of a beautiful mansion with lovely grounds and many servants and told him that these would be his quarters. And he couldn't help but ask, 'But wait, there's something wrong. How do I get this mansion while that good and holy man only gets a single room?' And St. Peter said, 'You have to understand how things are up here. We've got thousands and thousands of clergy. You're the first politician who ever made it.'" Reagan's listeners roared laughter and shouted approval.

Yet Reagan didn't want the evangelicals to feel they and their religion had no place in politics. On the contrary, he asserted historic roots for the Christian religion in American politics and public life. He quoted William Penn: "If we will not be governed by God, we must be governed by tyrants." And Thomas Jefferson: "The God who gave us life, gave us liberty at the same time." And George Washington: "Of all the dispositions and habits which lead to political prosperity, religion and morality are indispensable supports." And finally Alexis de Tocqueville, the French conservative who had searched far and wide for the secret of American democracy: "Not until I went into the churches of America and heard her pulpits aflame with righteousness did I understand the greatness and the genius of America. America is good. And if America ever ceases to be good, America will cease to be great." More applause, serious this time, and many nods of approval.

Reagan thanked his audience for keeping America great by keeping it good. He explained that his administration supported their efforts to preserve the role of religion and faith in American life. It was no easy task. "I don't have to tell you that this puts us in opposition to, or at least out of step with, a prevailing attitude of many who have turned to a modern-day secularism, discarding the tried and time-tested values upon which our very civilization is based." Reagan didn't dispute the worthy intentions of the secularists, but he held that the results of their actions were pernicious. They arrogated to government what rightly belonged to individuals, and they substituted their godless values for the tested truths of religion.

He gave an example. "An organization of citizens, sincerely motivated

The new president disappointed Edwin Meese, here at his right hand, by giving the job of White House chief of staff to James Baker, at his immediate left. Meese grudgingly became counselor to the president. Michael Deaver, who had a special bond with both Reagan and Nancy, became Baker's deputy.

Secretary of State Alexander Haig, at the far left, is not sharing the laugh; he rarely did, for he often thought the laughs were at his expense. Secretary of Defense Caspar Weinberger is pointing to something the president likes. James Baker is closely monitoring what Weinberger is telling Reagan; he always did.

CIA director William Casey mumbled, and Reagan was hard of hearing. It was a wonder they communicated. Sometimes they didn't; Casey kept certain secrets to himself.

Top: David Stockman, who managed the budget, was smart, self-confident, and unable to hold his tongue. His conversations with one reporter reflected badly on the president. But Reagan, who found it hard to fire people, forgave him.

Bottom: White House relations with the State Department calmed down after George Shultz replaced Al Haig. Shultz had a thin skin but won and held the president's confidence.

Top: Nancy Reagan watched her husband's back; Michael Deaver kept Nancy's secrets, especially the one about Nancy's astrologer.

Bottom: Donald Regan and Nancy did not get along at all. They had few dealings during the first term, when Regan was Treasury secretary. But after Regan became chief of staff, they clashed constantly. She finally had him fired. He retaliated by telling the world about her astrologer.

Reagan exits a Washington hotel following a rare speech that left his audience cold. In seconds he will be shot and nearly killed. March 30, 1981.

He charmed almost everyone except Tip O'Neill, the Democratic speaker of the House. Vice President George Bush prepares to separate them if necessary.

Prime Minister Margaret Thatcher, Britain's "Iron Lady," was the only person who sometimes intimidated him. But he loved her politics and determination, and she reciprocated.

They should have been the oddest couple in world affairs: the American president who denounced the Soviet Union as an "evil empire," and Mikhail Gorbachev, the leader of that very empire. But they developed a close working relationship and a personal friendship. Here the much older Reagan, coatless and hatless in the Geneva cold, greets the bundled Gorbachev.

They came very close at Reykjavik to an agreement that might have led to the abolition of nuclear weapons. Their faces show their disappointment.

The Iran-contra scandal was the darkest blot on the Reagan administration's record. The president gets the embarrassing investigative report from Tower Commission chairman John Tower and member Edmund Muskie.

It wasn't the world-changing pact he and Gorbachev wanted, but the Intermediate-Range Nuclear Forces (INF) Treaty was still a big deal.

Reagan bids the American people farewell on his last day as president: January 20, 1989.

From the complexities of politics to the simple pleasures: at Rancho del Cielo.

and deeply concerned about the increase in illegitimate births and abortions involving girls well below the age of consent, sometime ago established a nationwide network of clinics to offer help to these girls and, hopefully, alleviate this situation." Reagan reiterated that he didn't fault the intentions of those involved. But their efforts undermined morality. "These clinics have decided to provide advice and birth control drugs and devices to underage girls without the knowledge of their parents." Reagan said he had ordered clinics receiving federal funds to notify the parents. And the secularists had cried foul. "One of the nation's leading newspapers has created the term 'squeal rule' in editorializing against us for doing this, and we're being criticized for violating the privacy of young people. A judge has recently granted an injunction against an enforcement of our rule." Reagan wondered aloud what the country was coming to. "I've watched TV panel shows discuss this issue, seen columnists pontificating on our error, but no one seems to mention morality as playing a part in the subject of sex. Is all of Judeo-Christian tradition wrong? Are we to believe that something so sacred can be looked upon as a purely physical thing with no potential for emotional and psychological harm? And isn't it the parents' right to give counsel and advice to keep their children from making mistakes that may affect their entire lives?" The evangelicals leaped to their feet for another ovation.

Reagan vowed to fight for parents' rights against the secular onslaught. He would fight on other fronts as well. He had sent Congress a constitutional amendment to put prayer back in the classroom. "There's growing bipartisan support for the amendment," he was pleased to report. "And I am calling on the Congress to act speedily to pass it and to let our children pray." His administration supported legislation guaranteeing student religious groups the same rights to use school facilities after hours as nonreligious groups.

He turned to an issue about which most of his audience cared passionately. "More than a decade ago, a Supreme Court decision literally wiped off the books of fifty states statutes protecting the rights of unborn children," he said, referring to the 1973 case of *Roe v. Wade*. "Abortion on demand now takes the lives of up to one and a half million unborn children a year. Human life legislation ending this tragedy will some day pass the Congress, and you and I must never rest until it does. Unless and until it can be proven that the unborn child is not a living entity, then its right to life, liberty, and the pursuit of happiness must be protected." Enthusiastic applause.

Reagan knew his audience felt embattled; more than a few *liked* feeling embattled. Yet he reminded them of the signs of progress on matters dear to their hearts. "There's a great spiritual awakening in America, a renewal of the traditional values that have been the bedrock of America's goodness and greatness," he said. He cited survey results showing that Americans were far more religious than people elsewhere. Nineteen of twenty Americans believed in God, and a very large majority took the Ten Commandments quite seriously. "Another study has found that an overwhelming majority of Americans disapprove of adultery, teenage sex, pornography, abortion, and hard drugs. And this same study showed a deep reverence for the importance of family ties and religious belief." America was far from perfect. "There is sin and evil in the world," Reagan said. "Our nation, too, has a legacy of evil with which it must deal." But America had dealt with evil, and it would continue to do so. "The glory of this land has been its capacity for transcending the moral evils of our past. For example, the long struggle of minority citizens for equal rights, once a source of disunity and civil war, is now a point of pride for all Americans. We must never go back. There is no room for racism, anti-Semitism, or other forms of ethnic and racial hatred in this country." Reagan enjoined his listeners to speak out against those who would take the country back to those old ways. "I know that you've been horrified, as have I, by the resurgence of some hate groups preaching bigotry and prejudice. Use the mighty voice of your pulpits and the powerful standing of your churches to denounce and isolate these hate groups in our midst. The commandment given us is clear and simple: 'Thou shalt love thy neighbor as thyself.'"

AMERICA REMAINED THE best hope of mankind, the torchbearer of human freedom, Reagan said. This brought him to his closing point, touching on the nation's struggle for right in the world. "During my first press conference as president, in answer to a direct question, I pointed out that, as good Marxist-Leninists, the Soviet leaders have openly and publicly declared that the only morality they recognize is that which will further their cause, which is world revolution. I think I should point out I was only quoting Lenin, their guiding spirit, who said in 1920 that they repudiate all morality that proceeds from supernatural ideas—that's their name for religion—or ideas that are outside class conceptions. Morality is entirely subordinate to the interests of class war. And everything is moral that is necessary for the annihilation of the old, exploiting social order and for uniting the proletariat."

The communists' subordination of morality to the needs of the state put them in fundamental conflict with Americans and others who placed morality first. And it complicated negotiations with them. "This doesn't mean we should isolate ourselves and refuse to seek an understanding with them," Reagan said. "I intend to do everything I can to persuade them of our peaceful intent, to remind them that it was the West that refused to use its nuclear monopoly in the '40s and '50s for territorial gain."

But it did mean that Americans must be clear about the kinds of people and regimes they were dealing with. "Yes, let us pray for the salvation of all of those who live in that totalitarian darkness—pray they will discover the joy of knowing God. But until they do, let us be aware that while they preach the supremacy of the state, declare its omnipotence over individual man, and predict its eventual domination of all peoples on the Earth, they are the focus of evil in the modern world."

A widespread refusal to acknowledge this fact was vexing his efforts to counter Soviet power and curtail the arms race, Reagan said. The refusal lately took the form of calls for a "nuclear freeze"—a halt to new weapons systems. Reagan explained that a freeze would reward the past Soviet buildup, prevent the United States from rectifying the resulting imbalance, and thereby actually hinder arms control, which the freeze advocates claimed to favor. The president granted that discussions of nuclear policy could get arcane, tempting nonspecialists to wash their hands of it. He cautioned his listeners against such a mistake. "I urge you to beware the temptation of pride—the temptation of blithely declaring yourselves above it all and label both sides equally at fault, to ignore the facts of history and the aggressive impulses of an evil empire, to simply call the arms race a giant misunderstanding and thereby remove yourself from the struggle between right and wrong and good and evil."

No one was above the struggle. "While America's military strength is important, let me add here that I've always maintained that the struggle now going on for the world will never be decided by bombs or rockets, by armies or military might. The real crisis we face today is a spiritual one; at root, it is a test of moral will and faith."

A s Reagan's audience leaped to its feet to applaud his conclusion, reporters scanned their notes for the hook that would lead the coverage that evening and the next day. "Evil empire" was the phrase that caught on, with "focus of evil in the modern world" elaborating where space allowed. Most of Reagan's conservative supporters joined the evangelicals in applauding the president's forthrightness in calling the communists evil. His liberal critics groaned at his moralizing and contended that name-calling would yield nothing good.

Many on both sides missed Reagan's point. Communism was evil, the president believed, but that didn't absolve Americans from having to deal with it. In this respect Reagan wasn't very different from Richard Nixon, the architect of détente. Nixon never declared himself an agnostic between democracy and communism; he simply contended that American security required normalizing relations with the communists lest the two sides eventually destroy the world. Reagan came to the same conclusion, which was why he cautioned the evangelicals against thinking they were above the politics of superpower relations.

As much time as Reagan devoted to policy toward other areas of the world—Central America, the Caribbean, Poland, the Middle East—he never lost sight of the Soviet Union. The Soviet nuclear arsenal threatened the United States in a way none of the other challenges to American interests even approached. From the beginning of his presidency, Reagan pondered and calculated how to reduce the threat from Soviet arms, for the benefit of the United States and of the world. Reagan's "evil empire" characterization of the Soviet Union fairly captured his judgment of communism as a guiding philosophy, but it didn't prevent him from pursuing policy toward the communists that was pragmatic and surprisingly nonjudgmental. As in other areas of policy, Reagan showed himself quite capable of saying one thing and doing something else.

BUT FIRST HE had to give the Soviets an incentive to negotiate arms reductions. And that required persuading Congress to fund critical parts of his defense buildup. Congressional Democrats as a group had never liked Reagan's defense plan, and with each round of budget negotiations they chipped away at programs they considered extravagant or expendable. The MX missile fit both criteria in the minds of its critics. The MX (for "missile experimental") was a proposed solution to the twin problems facing America's existing arsenal of land-based intercontinental missiles: their increasing age and the growing accuracy of Soviet missiles. Improvements in miniaturization and guidance made it possible for American arms builders to pack multiple, independently targetable warheads onto a single rocket, giving one launcher many times the destructive power of existing missiles. This offset the improved accuracy of the Soviet missiles, in that if even a small portion of the MXs survived a Soviet first strike, they could still obliterate most of the important targets in the Soviet Union. Soviet leaders, doing the apocalyptic arithmetic, would presumably be deterred from attacking.

On the other hand, given the paradoxes implicit in nuclear strategy, the Soviets might draw the opposite conclusion. *Because* the MXs packed so much punch, taking out even a few of them would be very tempting. One Soviet missile could save as many as ten Soviet cities. Reckoned this way, the MXs might *undermine* deterrence.

They might, that is, unless their vulnerability could be reduced. The missiles could be placed in hardened—reinforced—silos designed to withstand anything but a direct hit by a Soviet missile. Or they could be made stealthily mobile. Stealth and mobility were central to the potency of another leg of America's nuclear triad, submarine-launched missiles, which were hidden beneath the waves and constantly on the move. (The third leg of the triad, bombs and cruise missiles launched from aircraft, were mobile but at this time less stealthy.) Both versions of vulnerability reduction—hardening and mobility—were pursued by the Pentagon's weapon designers as they developed the MX.

But both were costly and so elicited resistance from Democrats and others who continued to complain that Reagan gorged the Pentagon while starving social programs. Some of the critics asked why the United States needed a nuclear triad; would two legs or even one not suffice? Others took up the argument that the MX was destabilizing. Many cited Eisenhower's lament about the military-industrial complex having imperatives separate from national security.

Yet Reagan considered the MX indispensable. "Back to Washington and what I've been told may be the most momentous decision any president has had to make," he wrote in his diary after a day trip to New Orleans midway through his first year in office. "It was to OK the strategic missile and bomber buildup for our future defense needs." Reagan approved funding for a hundred MX missiles to get the program started.

Putting the new weapons in the budget was one thing, though; keeping them there was another. During the budget battles within the administration in 1982, the MX posed a tempting target for David Stockman and the other deficit hawks. They didn't try to kill the program, merely to delay it. Reagan and his MX allies, most notably Caspar Weinberger, had to fight to keep it front and center. In May 1982 the president approved a National Security Decision Directive stressing the importance to American security of moving forward on the MX. "It is absolutely essential that we maintain the momentum of the MX program and that we achieve Initial Operational Capability in 1986," the directive declared. Getting specific, the directive added, "Development of MX will be completed and sufficient units produced to support 100 operational missiles."

The Democrats in Congress still objected. They campaigned against the MX and other examples of what they considered Pentagon excess, and though their victories in the 1982 congressional elections—the Democrats gained twenty-six seats in the House while holding their ground in the Senate—owed more to the recession, they interpreted their success as a mandate to block the MX. "We're going to have trouble," Reagan predicted. "The Dems will try to cancel out the whole system. It will take a full court press to get it. If we don't I shudder to think what it will do to our arms reduction negotiations in Geneva."

Reagan's shudder underlined the dual purpose of the MX in his national security strategy. He accepted the arguments of the MX proponents that Soviet progress in nuclear arms put America's existing arsenal of land-based missiles at risk. He concluded that the MX was vital for its own sake. But he also saw the system in the light of his negotiating position with respect to the Russians. Congressional approval of the MX would demonstrate America's resolve to match the Russians missile for missile. Moscow, realizing it couldn't outspend the Americans, would come to the negotiating table to talk seriously about arms reductions. Perhaps those reductions would include some of the proposed MX missiles; if so, the missiles would have served a purpose without ever being built.

Negotiators typically keep their cards close to the vest. Reagan had done so as head of the actors' guild when bargaining with the studios. Yet he was quite open with his nuclear strategy of bulking up for the purpose of slimming down. "The United States wants deep cuts in the world's arsenal of weapons, but unless we demonstrate the will to rebuild our strength and restore the military balance, the Soviets, since they're so far ahead, have little incentive to negotiate with us," he told the American people in a televised address. "Let me repeat that point because it goes to the heart of our policies. Unless we demonstrate the will to rebuild our strength, the Soviets have little incentive to negotiate. If we hadn't begun to modernize, the Soviet negotiators would know we had nothing to bargain with except talk."

The Democrats weren't buying. They continued to oppose Reagan's strategic missile upgrade. "Tip O'Neill has mounted an all out campaign to kill the MX," Reagan complained privately. It was one more thing he held against the House speaker, and it was perhaps the most damning of all, for it went beyond politics to the heart of national security.

63

EVEN WHILE BATTLING for the MX, Reagan opened a breathtaking new front in the arms race. In March 1983, two weeks after his speech to the evangelicals in Florida, the president addressed the nation on national security. His tone was decidedly different; his sole claim to the moral high ground was his assertion: "The United States does not start fights; we will never be an aggressor." America's defense policy was *defensive*, he said. Yet it had to be robust. Reagan repeated that American arms had failed to keep pace with Soviet arms, hence the need for the current buildup. A nuclear freeze would dangerously lock into place the Soviet advantage. The MX missile was essential to the parity at which American policy was aimed. Members of Congress must stay the course, and American voters must make them do it. "We must continue to restore our military strength. If we stop in midstream, we will send a signal of decline, of lessened will, to friends and adversaries alike."

Much of this was boilerplate by now. The novel part came toward the end. Reagan reminded his viewers that America's nuclear defense policy was based on deterrence through the threat of retaliation. The Soviet Union would not attack the United States, because it knew it would be destroyed in response, perhaps along with much of the rest of the world. Deterrence had worked so far. Or at least it had not failed. Yet Reagan found it fundamentally wanting. "I've become more and more deeply convinced that the human spirit must be capable of rising above dealing with other nations and human beings by threatening their existence." There must be another way. An obvious alternative was arms control, to which the administration remained committed. But arms control within the existing framework of deterrence would leave the world's billions in the crosshairs. "That's a sad commentary on the human condition," Reagan said. "Wouldn't it be better to save lives than to avenge them? Are we not capable of demonstrating our peaceful intentions by applying all our abilities and our ingenuity to achieving a truly lasting stability? I think we are. Indeed, we must."

What Reagan proposed were defensive technologies that would shield the United States from nuclear attack. Such technologies could produce a transformation in human hopes and expectations, he said. "What if free people could live secure in the knowledge that their security did not rest upon the threat of instant U.S. retaliation to deter a Soviet attack, that we could intercept and destroy strategic ballistic missiles before they reached our own soil or that of our allies?"

Reagan granted that constructing the defensive system he envisioned was not possible at present. "I know this is a formidable, technical task, one that may not be accomplished before the end of this century." Yet current technology permitted making a start. "Isn't it worth every investment necessary to free the world from the threat of nuclear war?" He answered his own question. "We know it is."

And so he was taking the crucial first step. "I am directing a comprehensive and intensive effort to define a long-term research and development program to begin to achieve our ultimate goal of eliminating the threat posed by strategic nuclear missiles. This could pave the way for arms control measures to eliminate the weapons themselves." A world beyond nuclear weapons, beyond nuclear fear, was the objective. The quest for this new world began at once. "Tonight we're launching an effort which holds the promise of changing the course of human history."

REAGAN ARRIVED LATE at his own revolution in some respects; the key concepts associated with the "Reagan revolution"—smaller government, lower taxes—had been embraced by conservatives for decades before he came along. But with his articulation of a vision of a world beyond nuclear weapons, Reagan took the lead in a revolution that was far more audacious than anything else he ever attempted.

What he and the administration would call the Strategic Defense Initiative, or SDI, marked the first step in this revolution. The idea had been percolating in Reagan's mind for years. "When he was governor of California," Caspar Weinberger recalled, "he had expressed to me the not surprising view that we would be better advised to rest our defenses on military strength not only of an offensive character, such as the missiles themselves, but also on means of protecting against the missiles of the other side."

Reagan wasn't alone; many nonspecialists thought defenses against nuclear missiles would be a grand idea. But no one could figure out how to make such defenses work. Ballistic missiles—the kind that blasted up into space and then hurtled back down into the atmosphere—approached their targets at many thousands of miles per hour, far faster than any interceptor in existence or planning. Moreover, because potential targets for enemy missiles were scattered across the breadth of the United States, it was impossible to know where to place the interceptors. Finally, no defensive system ever created had been wholly effective; a certain percentage of incoming fire—whether crossbow shafts, musket balls, or bombs dropped from airplanes—always managed to get through. In the pre-nuclear era, this was a problem but usually not a disqualifying one. In the nuclear age, even a few missiles that penetrated a defensive shield could kill millions.

For these reasons, nuclear strategists pinned their hopes for deterrence on the concept of "mutual assured destruction," acronymed as MAD. The MAD concept never made anyone very happy. It required constant rationality in those with their fingers on the nuclear triggers, and rationality had failed innumerable times in humanity's past. It also required that Soviet leaders perceive crises in roughly the same terms American leaders did. The MAD approach invited nuclear bluffing—"brinkmanship," in the vernacular—with one side or the other hinting or openly threatening nuclear war. Dwight Eisenhower had rattled his nuclear saber during crises in East Asia in the 1950s; John Kennedy had pushed to the brink of nuclear war over Soviet missiles in Cuba in 1962. The Soviets had declined to test the American resolve in these cases. But skeptics wondered whether this was simply dumb luck, and almost no one believed it was indefinitely repeatable.

The best that could be said of MAD was that it was the least bad of the feasible options. The worst that could be said of it was that it was morally bankrupt, holding billions of innocent people hostage to the failure of world leaders to find an alternative; that it blighted the lives of all who dwelled under the nuclear shadow; and that it was bound to fail eventually, humans being the imperfect and unpredictable creatures they are. Meanwhile, it compelled the two sides in the Cold War to accept the grotesque paradox that the most dangerous thing either side could do was to develop a defensive system. If Soviet leaders, for example, learned that the United States was about to deploy a defensive shield that would repel Soviet missiles, they would be tempted to attack before the system became operational. And they would feel this temptation even if their sentiments were otherwise peaceable, for they would have to allow that the Americans might soon experience the euphoria of invulnerability and act on their delirium.

Reagan was no student of nuclear strategy, and he had never immersed himself in the soul-warping arcana of the craft. But his instincts told him MAD was wrong, and he hated the position it put him in. Reagan's son Ron recalled discussing the grim subject with his father. "Several years earlier, prior to my father's announcement of SDI, I had spoken with him about the possibility of some sort of umbrella defense against nuclear attack," Ron said. "Dad's greatest horror as president—and one hopes he's not alone in this—was the thought that through misunderstanding, unforeseen circumstance, or some bizarre technical glitch, he would be compelled to launch our nuclear missiles on warning. 'I have to believe the Russian people are no different from Americans,' he would tell me. 'Hell, they're victims of their own government. Why should millions of them have to die, along with millions of our people, because leaders on both sides couldn't work things out?'" Reagan hoped that one day leaders *would* work things out and eliminate nuclear weapons; until then, strategic defense held the best hope of averting disaster.

The president's military advisers were willing to oblige his quest for an escape from MAD, albeit with various motives. Caspar Weinberger shared Reagan's philosophical dissatisfaction with existing strategy, and he especially scorned the experts who had made it the touchstone of their professional lives. "To those who traipse from resort to resort reading each other's papers on security and strategy," Weinberger said, "the idea that any country might try to defend itself against the nuclear missiles of any other country was not only revolutionary; it was sacrilegious." The Joint Chiefs of Staff agreed to pursue alternatives to MAD after assuring themselves that for the foreseeable future strategic defense would complement, rather than replace, strategic offense. Almost never during the Cold War had America's generals and admirals rejected new spending on the military, and Reagan's chiefs didn't reject it now.

The consensus within the administration informed a National Security Decision Directive signed by the president in May 1982. The directive ordered continued research and development of the MX and added, "R&D on Ballistic Missile Defense will also continue to hedge against

Soviet ABM breakout, to assist us in evaluating Soviet BMD activity, and
to provide an option for increasing M-X survivability."

The turgid language of the decision directive left much to be desired
in terms of mobilizing public opinion. Admiral James Watkins, the chief
of naval operations, gave the president the formula he was looking for.
"Would it not be better," Watkins asked the president rhetorically, "if we
could develop a system that would protect, rather than avenge, our people?" Reagan nodded emphatically. "Exactly," he said.

REAGAN DEVOTED MORE effort to the wording of his SDI speech than
he gave to almost any other address. "Much of it was to change bureaucratic talk into people talk," he remarked to himself as he finished the
draft. He invited a special group of diplomats, scientists, military officers,
and national security experts to the White House to hear him deliver the
speech. He met with them afterward. "I guess it was O.K.," he wrote later
that evening. "They all praised it to the sky and seemed to think it would
be the source of debate for some time to come."

The president's guests were right in predicting that his strategic
defense proposal would produce debate. Critics immediately labeled it
"Star Wars," after the George Lucas film franchise, and contended that it
was no more realistic than that cosmic fantasy. Pentagon-phobes perceived
an excuse for astronomical new spending at a time when the administration was trying to cut nearly everything else. Serious students of nuclear
strategy predicted that Soviet countermeasures—chiefly more offensive
missiles—would be less expensive than the American defenses, with the
result that the United States would have spent a great deal of money to no
lasting avail. The specialists also cited the destabilizing aspects of defensive deployments, at least in the transition period between MAD and
SDI. Margaret Thatcher echoed this concern, telling Reagan, "Ron, it
will make you look like you are going to launch a first strike."

Reagan rarely let criticism deflect him from goals he believed in. He
refused to let the criticism deflect him now. Instead, he listened to the
praise served up by the White House staff. "The reports are in on last
night's speech," he wrote in his diary the day after the SDI unveiling.
"The biggest return—phone calls, wires, etc., on any speech so far and
running heavily in my favor."

64

R EAGAN WAS PERFECTLY serious about strategic defense, as
events would prove. But he was also quite aware that it would
get the attention of the Soviet leadership at a time when that
leadership was in flux. Leonid Brezhnev had died four months earlier, in
November 1982. The longtime Soviet leader had been ill for months, preventing any progress on arms control, and Reagan hoped his death might
move matters forward. The president and his national security team
debated whether he should attend Brezhnev's funeral and meet his successor, whoever that might be. They ultimately decided against, unsure
what he would be getting himself in for. Reagan sent George Bush and
George Shultz in his place. After the ceremony the vice president and the
secretary of state met Yuri Andropov, the Kremlin's new chief and formerly head of the Soviet intelligence agency, the KGB. Bush joked that
the two had something in common, each having been their country's top
spy. Andropov didn't laugh. Shultz judged Andropov a figure to contend
with. "He looked more like a cadaver than did the just-interred Brezhnev,
but his mental powers filled the room," Shultz recalled. "He reminded
me of Sherlock Holmes's deadly enemy, Professor Moriarty, all brain in
a disregarded body." Andropov's background, if nothing else, suggested
toughness. "I knew that Andropov, as head of the KGB for so long, must
have a capacity for brutality as well as for skill in propaganda," Shultz said.
"I put him down as a formidable adversary."

Reagan soon seconded Shultz's view. The president tried to forge a
personal connection with Andropov. He invited Soviet ambassador Anatoly Dobrynin to the White House and said he wanted a direct line of

communication to Andropov: "No bureaucracy involved." Dobrynin was impressed. "This could be an historic moment," he said.

Reagan followed up with a handwritten note to Andropov. "We both share an enormous responsibility for the preservation of stability in the world," he said. "I believe we can fulfill that mandate, but in order to do so, it will require a more active level of exchange than we have heretofore been able to establish." The president repeated his wish to bypass normal channels. "Our predecessors have made better progress when they communicated privately and candidly."

Andropov thanked Reagan for the note. "I have considered its contents with all seriousness," he said. But the American government needed to demonstrate its good intentions if it sincerely sought an arms agreement. A starting point would be the cancellation of American plans to install intermediate-range missiles in Europe. "So long as the United States has not begun deploying its missiles in Europe, an agreement is still possible," Andropov said. Once deployment began, a deal would be out of the question. Reagan had suggested discussing the affairs of Central America and Eastern Europe. "What is there to be said?" Andropov responded. Soviet policy would be guided, as it always had, by the principle of sovereignty: "Every people, every country, wherever they may be located, should be masters of their fate."

Reagan realized he wouldn't get far if Andropov insisted on statements like this. Sovereignty of Poland? Yet he pressed on. He sent a reply defending his policy on the intermediate-range missiles. "Their only function would be to balance Soviet systems potentially threatening to Europe, and to ensure that no one in the future could doubt that the security of Western Europe and North America are one and the same," he said. "Try to see our point of view. What would be the Soviet reaction if we deployed a new, highly threatening weapon against its allies, and then insisted that you should not balance this with something comparable?" He didn't expect immediate agreement, but he reaffirmed his desire for direct communications. "I think that we must find a way either to discuss these problems frankly, or at the very least, to give greater weight to the attitudes of the other party when making fateful decisions."

SUCH SLIM HOPES as Reagan held for progress with Andropov suffered a grievous blow in September 1983. A Korean Air Lines flight, KAL 007, strayed off course on a journey from New York to Seoul via Anchorage.

The plane mistakenly entered Soviet airspace over the Kamchatka Peninsula and again over Sakhalin Island. The pilot, crew, and passengers apparently never realized that they were off course or that they were flying near Soviet missile sites. They didn't know that an American electronic surveillance plane had been in the area and had put Soviet air defense on hair-trigger alert. The coincidence of error, ignorance, and suspicion resulted in the shooting down of KAL 007 by a Soviet fighter plane, with the deaths of all 269 persons aboard. These included 62 Americans, among them a U.S. congressman, Larry McDonald of Georgia.

Reagan responded with outrage. "I speak for all Americans and for the people everywhere who cherish civilized values in protesting the Soviet attack on an unarmed civilian passenger plane," he declared. "Words can scarcely express our revulsion at this horrifying act of violence."

In subsequent days Reagan elaborated on what the attack revealed about the Soviet system. "Our first emotions are anger, disbelief and profound sadness," he told reporters. The war in Afghanistan had shown the Kremlin's continuing capacity for violence. "But this event shocks the sensibilities of people everywhere." The despicable Soviet action made meaningful dialogue with Moscow nearly impossible. "What can we think of a regime that so broadly trumpets its vision of peace and global disarmament and yet so callously and quickly commits a terrorist act to sacrifice the lives of innocent human beings?"

Reagan's outrage was genuine, but his response was calculated. The CIA and military intelligence soon concluded that the shoot-down was probably a case of mistaken identity: the Soviets confusing the Korean airliner with the American spy plane. Yet the president continued to treat it as deliberate. He convened top members of the executive branch to formulate the American reaction. The State and Defense Departments were represented, naturally, and the CIA and the Joint Chiefs of Staff, but so were the Treasury and Transportation Departments, the United States Information Agency, and the Federal Aviation Administration. The deliberations resulted in a National Security Decision Directive signed by the president and crafted to maximize the damage to Soviet prestige and the corresponding benefit to the United States. "This Soviet attack underscores once again the refusal of the USSR to abide by normal standards of civilized behavior and thus confirms the basis of our existing policy of realism and strength," the directive declared. Three objectives were defined as paramount. "Seek justice" was the first. "We must consult with, and help to lead, the international community in calling for justice,"

the directive explained. "Civilized societies demand punishment and res-
titution to deter, and raise the costs of, future egregious acts." The United
States would lobby its allies and protégés to insist on a full accounting of
what had happened, an official apology, and punishment of those responsible.

The second objective was to "demonstrate resistance to intimidation." Here the aim was to "bolster the confidence of our Asian friends,
and others, and demonstrate that Soviet intimidation will not achieve its
intended end of discouraging our friends from cooperating with us, particularly on mutual security concerns."

The third objective was to "advance understanding of the contrast
between Soviet words and deeds." The directive elaborated: "Soviet brutality in this incident presents an opportunity to reverse the false moral
and political 'peacemaker' perception that their regime has been cultivating. This image has complicated the efforts of the Free World to illuminate the USSR's true objectives."

A sixteen-point checklist specified how these three large aims would
be pursued and implemented. Some items combined diplomacy and public relations: "Seek maximum condemnation of the Soviet Union in the
U.N. Security Council and provide wide dissemination of statements
made in these sessions." Others were economic and commercial: "Seek
immediate agreement by as many countries as possible to stop Aeroflot
flights into their countries, to cancel interline ticketing arrangements,
and to take other possible measures to inhibit Aeroflot operations." Still
others endorsed actions the United States was already taking: "Reaffirm
the existing U.S. sanctions against Aeroflot that predate the Soviet attack
on KAL."

Reagan led the way with a televised address to the American people in which he blasted the fumbling cover stories the Soviets concocted.
"Despite the savagery of their crime, the universal reaction against it, and
the evidence of their complicity, the Soviets still refuse to tell the truth,"
he said. "They have persistently refused to admit that their pilot fired on
the Korean aircraft. Indeed, they've not even told their own people that a
plane was shot down. They have spun a confused tale of tracking the plane
by radar until it just mysteriously disappeared from their radar screens, but
no one fired a shot of any kind. But then they coupled this with charges
that it was a spy plane sent by us and that their planes fired tracer bullets
past the plane as a warning that it was in Soviet airspace." Reagan provided evidence of the Kremlin's duplicity, including recordings of radio

transmissions from the Soviet pilot who fired the fatal missile. The president explained that the silhouette of the KAL plane, a Boeing 747, could not have been mistaken for the American RC-135 that had been in the area earlier—"on a routine mission," he said. Reagan reasserted the heinousness of the Soviet action. "Make no mistake about it, this attack was not just against ourselves or the Republic of Korea. This was the Soviet Union against the world and the moral precepts which guide human relations among people everywhere. It was an act of barbarism, born of a society which wantonly disregards individual rights and the value of human life and seeks constantly to expand and dominate other nations."

If Reagan had been a more calculating statesman—a Metternich or even a Kissinger—he might have said less on the inherent evil of the system that produced the KAL tragedy. He was, after all, trying to coax the leader of that system to the bargaining table, and insults—as they must have seemed to the Kremlin—could only complicate the task. Moreover, if the president did succeed in negotiating an arms agreement with the Soviets, he would have to persuade the Senate to ratify it and the American people to accept it. Americans have never liked bargaining with the devil, and by demonizing the Soviets, Reagan rendered a bargain more distasteful than ever.

Reagan wasn't calculating, but he was canny. He was, in his own way, sincere, but he understood the difference between words and actions. Other administrations have played the bad-cop, good-cop routine by assigning the separate roles to different actors. The brooding John Foster Dulles was the heavy in Eisenhower's administration; smiling Ike was the one the people liked. Zbigniew Brzezinski tried to stiffen Jimmy Carter's spine; Cyrus Vance sought to make it flexible. Reagan played both roles himself: one in words, the other in deeds. He thundered against Soviet perfidy for the television camera, and he meant everything he said. But the substantive measures he took against the Soviets were remarkably modest. He suspended American landing privileges for Aeroflot, and he postponed negotiations toward some bilateral Soviet-American agreements. But otherwise it was business almost as usual.

The result was scarcely short of brilliant. Reagan credibly reiterated America's claim to the moral high ground vis-à-vis the Soviets, benefiting himself politically and America in the eyes of the part of the world he cared about. But to Soviet leaders, who, he always contended, paid more attention to deeds than to words, he left open the door for future negotiations.

Reagan's frequent references to Franklin Roosevelt revealed a felt affinity for his Democratic predecessor, but that affinity was deeper than Reagan acknowledged or probably realized. Both presidents entered office in times of economic turmoil and national discouragement; each sought to strike the optimal balance between the public and the private sectors in American life. Roosevelt, the eastern Democrat, approached the problem from the left, building up the public sector in response to the collapse of the private sector in the Great Depression of the 1930s. Reagan, the western Republican, tackled the problem from the right, promoting the private sector in response to the floundering of the Great Society during the 1970s. Both Roosevelt and Reagan recognized the difference between rhetoric and action, between inspiration and achievement. Roosevelt's stump speeches and Fireside Chats stirred the hearts of liberals, but his policies reflected a shrewd assessment of what the politics of his party and of the nation would bear. Reagan never departed, in his live remarks and televised addresses, from the core values that had made him the darling of conservatives in the 1960s, but as president he cut deals with Democrats and liberals when necessary to advance his cause. Roosevelt and Reagan were at once idealists and pragmatists. Each understood that a successful president provides a compelling vision for the long term while making concrete progress in the short term. Each understood that presidents are not czars; they must deliver what the people want, even as they try to make people want something different and better.

Reagan didn't ponder the parallels with Roosevelt; he was an intuitive student of history and politics rather than an analytical one. (Roosevelt wouldn't have pondered the parallels either, had he lived to observe Reagan. He was as much the intuitionist as Reagan.) Yet Reagan certainly reflected on the fact that one of the major chores of his first term was the stabilization and extension of the signal accomplishment of Roosevelt's first term. The Social Security system had for half a century defied every effort to rein it in; it was reformed several times between the 1930s and the 1970s, but each reform simply expanded coverage and payments. The reason for this was Social Security's overwhelming popularity and deceptively modest cost. As long as working contributors greatly outnumbered retired recipients, the system suffered no serious cash flow problems. But in the mid-1970s payments began to exceed revenues, and analysts reckoned that before the end of 1983 the system's pension checks might start to bounce.

Reagan in his early political career had opposed Social Security on principle, contending that people should plan for their own retirements without government compulsion. As he advanced in politics and discovered the popularity of the program, he shifted his objection from philosophical grounds to tactical ones, and he spoke of saving Social Security rather than eliminating it. The spectacular failure of his first reform attempt in 1981 suggested the need for a new approach, and he adopted a favorite method of presidents facing controversial issues: he appointed a commission. The National Commission on Social Security Reform comprised fifteen members, five chosen by the president, five by the majority leader of the Senate, and five by the speaker of the House. Republican control of the Senate and Democratic control of the House, along with the provision that in each of the five-person groups no more than three members could be of the same party, ensured the bipartisan character of the commission. The commission was charged with making recommendations that would secure the financial integrity of Social Security over the long term, even as it provided appropriate benefits to participants. The commission was to deliver its report by December 31, 1982, safely after the midterm elections.

Reagan appointed Alan Greenspan, an economist and chairman of Gerald Ford's Council of Economic Advisers, to chair the commission. The president's other appointees were the chief executive of the Prudential Insurance Company, the head of the National Association of Manufacturers, and two business consultants. Howard Baker's appointees were four senators and AFL-CIO president Lane Kirkland. Tip O'Neill tapped three members of the House, a former commissioner of Social Security, and a recent assistant secretary of health and human services. The commissioners were eight Republicans and seven Democrats.

The commission met nine times during 1982. It held no public hearings, lest they become a circus for lobbyists, but it interviewed numerous experts and consulted the dozens of reports on Social Security and related matters that had been produced during the previous decade.

Reagan kept hands off the commission while it deliberated. He was not especially surprised when it missed its deadline by two weeks; if anything, he was gratified that it came so close. And he was more gratified that the commission's report arrived with the approval of both Republican Baker and Democrat O'Neill. "Each of us recognizes that this is a compromise solution," Reagan said of the report. "As such, it includes elements which each of us could not support if they were not part of a bipartisan compromise. However, in the interest of solving the Social Security problem promptly, equitably, and on a bipartisan basis, we have agreed to support and work for this bipartisan solution."

The solution disappointed those who, like the earlier Reagan, wanted to dismantle or privatize Social Security. "The National Commission considered, but rejected, proposals to make the Social Security program a voluntary one," the report declared. It also refused to condition payments on need or to limit payments to what the individuals in question had themselves contributed. The essential structure of Social Security would remain as Franklin Roosevelt had designed it.

Nonetheless, the commission advocated substantial reform. The contributory base of the program would be broadened by including previously exempt federal and nonprofit employees. Receipts would be augmented by accelerating scheduled increases in Social Security tax rates, by raising the ceiling on income subject to Social Security taxes, by increasing taxes on the self-employed, and by taxing some Social Security benefits. Payments would be reduced by delaying cost-of-living increases and perhaps recalculating those increases.

Reagan began stumping for the Social Security package with his State of the Union address ten days later. "After months of debate and deadlock, the bipartisan Commission on Social Security accomplished the seemingly impossible," he told Congress and the American people. Cynics had predicted that the commission would end in deadlock, as so many Washington projects did. "Well, sometimes, even here in Washington, the cynics are wrong," Reagan said. "Through compromise and cooperation, the members of the commission overcame their differences and achieved a fair, workable plan. They proved that, when it comes to the national welfare, Americans can still pull together for the common good."

Reagan quoted Franklin Roosevelt: "Throughout the world, change is the order of the day. In every nation economic problems long in the making have brought crises of many kinds for which the masters of old practice and theory were unprepared." He quoted Roosevelt again: "The future lies with those wise political leaders who realize that the great public is interested more in government than in politics." Roosevelt had established Social Security a half century past, Reagan said; Americans of the current generation must render it sound for at least another half century.

Reagan's listeners in the Capitol took heed of his words, which he repeated to influential lawmakers singly and in groups. And with a swiftness that demonstrated the power of bipartisanship when supported at both ends of Pennsylvania Avenue, the commission's proposals sailed through Congress, with an added provision that incrementally increased the retirement age.

Reagan signed the resulting measure in April 1983. He saluted his hero once more, saying, "Today we reaffirm Franklin Roosevelt's commitment that Social Security must always provide a secure and stable base so that older Americans may live in dignity."

PART FIVE

A WORTHY ADVERSARY

1984–1986

66

EAGAN'S HUMOR WAS rarely sly. His jokes were the kind anyone could appreciate; his delivery, perfected in decades of speaking to actors' groups, General Electric workers, Rotary Clubs, chambers of commerce, trade associations, political donors, and myriad diverse others, relied on no special knowledge or shared background. Yet in a key passage in the first speech of his reelection campaign, he allowed himself an oblique reference that almost eluded his listeners. The occasion was the January 1984 State of the Union address. Presidents had long kicked off reelection campaigns with the quadrennial-year annual message, and Reagan saw no reason to deny himself the incomparable platform. To the gathered legislators and the television audience beyond the House chamber he touted the progress his administration had made since his election. The economy was again on track, with the terrible inflation of the 1970s vanquished. Punishing tax rates had been slashed and suffocating regulation reduced. America had reasserted itself in foreign affairs, regaining its self-respect and the respect of the world. "There is renewed energy and optimism throughout the land," Reagan said. "America is back, standing tall."

Of course, more needed to be done. "We've journeyed far, but we have much farther to go," Reagan said. "Franklin Roosevelt told us fifty years ago this month: 'Civilization cannot go back; civilization must not stand still. We have undertaken new methods. It is our task to perfect, to improve, to alter when necessary, but in all cases to go forward.'" Spending on government was still too high; Reagan called for constitutional amendments mandating a balanced budget and granting the president a line-item veto.

And the tax code had to be overhauled. "Let us go forward with an historic reform for fairness, simplicity, and incentives for growth," Reagan said. "I am asking Secretary Don Regan for a plan for action to simplify the entire tax code, so all taxpayers, big and small, are treated more fairly." Alluding unspecifically to people who weren't paying their fair share, the president suggested that tax reform could capture the lost revenue. "And it could make the tax base broader, so personal tax rates could come down, not go up." Reagan looked about the House and then into the camera. "I've asked that specific recommendations, consistent with those objectives, be presented to me by December 1984."

Reagan smiled ever so slightly as he spoke the date. Yet the lawmakers didn't catch on until he was halfway into his next sentence. "Our second great goal is to build on America's pioneer spirit . . ." Hesitant laughter interrupted him, slowly gathering strength. "I said something funny?" he asked innocently. The laughter swelled, rolling across the room in two intersecting waves, one of Republican relief and the other of Democratic derision. The Republicans were relieved to hear that tax reform was being postponed until after the November balloting; the Democrats hooted at Reagan's unwillingness to specify whose oxen would be gored while the voters could still act on the information.

Don Regan had a thin skin and selective sight and hearing. The Treasury secretary had battled within the administration for tax reform and apparently won; now he hardly noticed the Republican support on account of the Democratic gibes. "From my seat just below the rostrum where the president stood, I could see the faces of many congressmen and senators," he recalled. "Their features shone with mirth. They shot knowing glances at one another. They were laughing at the president and at me. I suppose that some of them thought that the president's proposal was an election-year gambit designed to get votes. Even as my blood rose, I realized that most of them were laughing because, like the men in the White House, they thought that true tax reform was a pipe dream. They may even have believed that the president thought so too, or else that he was a true naïf—for who else would believe that a measure that engaged the most selfish concerns of the most powerful interests in the nation could be accomplished by the deadline he had set, only eleven months in the future? The laughter swelled to a louder pitch. My anger rose. I said to myself, Just wait. I'll show you guys."

————

NEAR THE END of his speech Reagan departed from the usual annual-message script by addressing not simply Congress and the American people but a particular audience abroad. "I want to speak to the people of the Soviet Union," he said, "to tell them it's true that our governments have had serious differences, but our sons and daughters have never fought each other in war. And if we Americans have our way, they never will." Avoidance of war, however, to be enduring required the active pursuit of peace. "People of the Soviet Union, there is only one sane policy, for your country and mine, to preserve our civilization in this modern age: A nuclear war cannot be won and must never be fought."

He paused to let this message sink in. He had been accused of wanting war, of believing the United States could win a nuclear war. He had never believed this, but neither had he stated his disbelief so clearly. Now it was on the record for all to hear and read.

He drew the corollary. "The only value in our two nations possessing nuclear weapons is to make sure they will never be used," he said. "But then would it not be better to do away with them entirely?" The answer, he said, lay with the Soviet people and their government. "Americans are a people of peace. If your government wants peace, there will be peace. We can come together in faith and friendship to build a safer and far better world for our children and our children's children."

Reagan addressed the Soviet people, rather than the Soviet leadership, partly for rhetorical effect. The American people wanted peace, he said; the Soviet people presumably wanted the same thing. Governments should give their people what they wanted. But Reagan reached out to the Soviet people for another reason, more practical: he couldn't tell, at this point, who the Soviet leadership was. In the wake of the Korean Air shoot-down, Yuri Andropov had disappeared. Illness was rumored, reported, then confirmed. Communications between the White House and the Kremlin languished. Finally, in February 1984, came word he had died.

As Reagan awaited news of the succession, he reflected on a dawning revelation. "Three years had taught me something surprising about the Russians. Many people at the top of the Soviet hierarchy were genuinely afraid of America and Americans. Perhaps this shouldn't have surprised me, but it did. In fact, I had difficulty accepting my own conclusion at first. I'd always felt that from our deeds it must be clear to anyone that Americans were a moral people who starting at the birth of our nation had always used our power only as a force of good in the world. After World

War II, for example, when we alone had the atomic bomb, we didn't use it for conquest or domination; instead, with the Marshall Plan and General MacArthur's democratic stewardship of Japan, we generously rebuilt the economies of our former enemies." By contrast, the Soviet Union had seemed bent on conquest. "We had limitless reasons to be wary of the Red Bear, because from the day it was born on the streets of Russia it was dedicated to consuming the democracies of the world."

Reagan's preconceptions had accompanied him to the presidency. "During my first years in Washington, I think many of us in the administration took it for granted that the Russians, like ourselves, considered it unthinkable that the United States would launch a first strike against them. But the more experience I had with Soviet leaders and other heads of state who knew them, the more I began to realize that many Soviet officials feared us not only as adversaries but as potential aggressors who might hurl nuclear weapons at them in a first strike; because of this, and perhaps because of a sense of insecurity and paranoia with roots reaching back to the invasions of Russia by Napoleon and Hitler, they had aimed a huge arsenal of nuclear weapons at us."

Reagan had belatedly recognized what political scientists dubbed the "security dilemma": the paradoxical circumstance, especially acute in the nuclear age, that measures one side considers defensive are often seen as threatening by the other. America's nuclear arsenal was originally designed to deter a Soviet conventional attack in Europe, but the Soviets deemed it threatening. To defend themselves they built their own arsenal, which the Americans considered threatening. And so on, to second-strike arsenals and Reagan's projected Strategic Defense Initiative.

His discovery of the security dilemma prompted Reagan's reassurance to the Soviet people—and to his American and Western European critics—that he believed a nuclear war could never be won and therefore must never be fought. It also prompted him to pursue arms control with Andropov's successor, Konstantin Chernenko.

George Bush met Chernenko at Andropov's funeral. The vice president returned with the impression that Chernenko might be easier to work with than Andropov had been. He said as much to Reagan, who hoped he was right. "I'd like to talk to him about our problems man to man and see if I could convince him there would be a material benefit to the Soviets if they'd join the family of nations etc.," Reagan wrote in his diary. Yet he didn't want to move too fast. "We don't want to appear anxious, which would tempt them to play games and possibly snub us."

Chernenko wasn't interested. He proved as adamant as Andropov had been, first lecturing Reagan on America's provocations and then announcing that the Soviet Union would boycott the Los Angeles Olympics, as the United States had boycotted the Moscow Olympics in 1980. "They are utterly stonewalling us," Reagan grumbled.

He couldn't really blame them. Reagan's discovery of the security dilemma came wrapped in a newfound ability to imagine the world from Moscow's perspective. Or perhaps the ability was simply newly exercised. To this point in his political career Reagan had been content to hurl imprecations at the Soviet Union, with the goal of affirming American rectitude and steeling American resolve for the defense buildup he deemed necessary. But now that he sought to engage the Soviet leadership in meaningful dialogue, it behooved him to put himself in their shoes. The Democrats in Congress continued to reject full funding for the MX missile, while antinuclear groups in Europe were pressing their governments to drop plans to allow the deployment of American intermediate-range missiles—Pershing IIs and cruise missiles—to counter recently deployed Soviet missiles. Reagan had proposed to forgo deployment of the American intermediate missiles if the Soviets would agree to dismantle their existing missiles, but Moscow rejected this so-called "zero option" as unacceptably asymmetric. The antinuclear activists denounced it as a sham, designed to be rejected. Reagan recognized the political difficulties he faced on the arms front, and he realized that Chernenko did too. "What would I think, I asked myself," he wrote, "if I were a Soviet leader and saw this kind of fractiousness among the leaders of the United States and the Western alliance? I'd try to exploit it."

Which was just what the Kremlin did. Moscow continued to brand the Americans as warmongers, hoping to increase the antinuclear pressure in Europe and perhaps in the American Congress. When reports indicated that Chernenko was sick and might prove to have an even shorter tenure than Andropov, Reagan set aside hope of progress with the Soviets before the 1984 election.

R EAGAN'S NEW APPRECIATION for the fear the Soviets might feel toward America was an insight he kept to himself. For public consumption he dwelled on the reasons Americans should fear the Soviets. "In the last fifteen years, the growth of Soviet military power has meant a radical change in the nature of the world we live in," he told a national audience in May 1984. This didn't mean that a nuclear war was imminent; it was not, as long as America kept its arsenal strong. But the communists were a threat nonetheless. "They are presently challenging us with a different kind of weapon: subversion and the use of surrogate forces." In one developing country after another—Vietnam, Laos, Cambodia, Angola, Ethiopia, South Yemen, Afghanistan, Nicaragua, El Salvador—Soviet proxies had either seized power or were sapping the strength of those who held power.

Reagan focused this evening on Nicaragua, El Salvador, and their neighbors. Congress had funded the president's Caribbean Basin Initiative but not at the level he desired, as Democrats in the House registered deep suspicion of the government of El Salvador and especially the Nicaraguan contras. Edward Boland of Massachusetts, the Democratic chairman of the House Intelligence Committee, sponsored amendments to defense appropriations bills forbidding the CIA, which was directing the contra war, to spend money for the purpose of overthrowing the Nicaraguan government. The administration and its allies responded that they weren't trying to overthrow the Sandinistas, merely to get the Sandinistas to stop subverting the government of El Salvador. But the contras themselves were less discreet, and Congress approved the Boland amendments and slashed the administration's request for Central America funding.

Reagan judged the Boland amendments unwise and possibly unconstitutional. But rather than challenge the restrictions frontally, he reiterated that the objective of the contra war was merely to tame the Sandinistas, not to overthrow them. He asked Congress for new funding and directed the CIA to proceed as before. He approved a more vigorous anti-Sandinista offensive, which included planting mines in Nicaraguan harbors to disrupt supplies from the Soviet Union and Cuba and generally weaken the Nicaraguan economy.

Reagan was pleased with the covert war until, in the spring of 1984, the mining operation burst into public view. At this point even some of the president's staunchest backers expressed alarm. Barry Goldwater, chairman of the Senate Intelligence Committee, sent a scathing letter to William Casey, simultaneously releasing it to the press. "Dear Bill," Goldwater wrote, "All this past weekend, I've been trying to figure out how I can most easily tell you my feelings about the discovery of the President having approved mining some of the harbors of Central America. It gets down to one, little, simple phrase: I am pissed!" Goldwater felt personally betrayed. "During the important debate we had all last week and the week before, on whether we would increase funds for the Nicaragua program, we were doing all right until a member of the committee charged that the President had approved the mining. I strongly denied that because I had never heard of it. I found out the next day that the CIA had, with the written approval of the President, engaged in such mining, and the approval came in February! Bill, this is no way to run a railroad and I find myself in a hell of a quandary. I am forced to apologize to the members of the intelligence committee because I did not know the facts on this." The administration had done itself grave damage. "The President has asked us to back his foreign policy. Bill, how can we back his foreign policy when we don't know what the hell he is doing? Lebanon, yes, we all knew that he sent troops over there. But mine the harbors in Nicaragua? This is an act violating international law. It is an act of war. For the life of me, I don't see how we are going to explain it." Goldwater predicted that the president would lose his battle with Congress for new funding for the contras. "My simple guess is that the House is going to defeat this supplemental and we will not be in any position to put up much of an argument after we were not given the information we were entitled to receive; particularly, if my memory serves me correctly, when you briefed us on Central America just a couple of weeks ago. And the order was signed before that. I don't like this. I don't like it one bit from the President or from you. I don't think we need a lot of lengthy explanations. The deed has been done and, in the future, if anything like this happens, I'm going to raise one hell of a lot of fuss about it in public."

Reagan resented Goldwater's public airing of grievance and disputed the senator's assertions. "Says he was never briefed," the president grumbled privately. "He was briefed on March 8 and 13." Yet Reagan didn't specify what Goldwater was told in the briefings, which obviously didn't satisfy him. Nor could Reagan deny the underlying facts of the mining or the damage the affair was doing in Congress to the administration's Central American policy. "There is a rebellion which will probably lead to their shutting aid off to the Nicaraguan Contras—which will bring joy to the Soviets and Cubans."

Reagan thought his Central American policy was right, and he thought the American public would agree if he explained it to them satisfactorily. "Central America is a region of great importance to the United States," he declared from the Oval Office, looking sincerely into the television camera. "And it is so close: San Salvador is closer to Houston, Texas, than Houston is to Washington, D.C. Central America is America. It's at our doorstep." And it was in mortal danger. "It's become the stage for a bold attempt by the Soviet Union, Cuba, and Nicaragua to install communism by force throughout the hemisphere." The war for Central America had already begun. "Right now in El Salvador, Cuban-supported aggression has forced more than 400,000 men, women, and children to flee their homes. And in all of Central America, more than 800,000 have fled—many, if not most, living in unbelievable hardship." Some of those refugees had found their way to the United States; more would certainly follow.

The stakes could not be higher, Reagan said. "If we do nothing, if we continue to provide too little help, our choice will be a communist Central America with additional communist military bases on the mainland of this hemisphere and communist subversion spreading southward and northward." There might be no stopping the red tide. "A hundred million people from Panama to the open border of our South could come under the control of pro-Soviet regimes."

But it wasn't yet too late. "We can and must help Central America. It's in our national interest to do so, and morally, it's the only right thing to do." Helping Central America meant standing up to the communists who sought to destroy freedom and democracy there. Congress had voted assistance to El Salvador, but more was needed. "We've provided just enough aid to avoid outright disaster, but not enough to resolve the crisis, so El Salvador is being left to slowly bleed to death."

Most Americans didn't appreciate the gravity of the Central American crisis, Reagan said. Some still thought the Sandinistas of Nicaragua were honest reformers; this view couldn't be more wrong. "The Sandinista rule is a communist reign of terror." The Sandinistas had started showing their true colors almost as soon as they seized power. "The internal repression of democratic groups, trade unions, and civic groups began. Right to dissent was denied. Freedom of the press and freedom of assembly became virtually nonexistent." Groups that defied the regime experienced brutal repression. "There has been an attempt to wipe out an entire culture, the Miskito Indians, thousands of whom have been slaughtered or herded into detention camps, where they have been starved and abused. Their villages, churches, and crops have been burned." The Sandinistas had alienated even former supporters. "Many of those who fought alongside the Sandinistas saw their revolution betrayed. They were denied power in the new government. Some were imprisoned, others exiled. Thousands who fought with the Sandinistas have taken up arms against them and are now called the contras. They are freedom fighters."

The United States must assist the freedom fighters. "The simple questions are: Will we support freedom in this hemisphere or not? Will we defend our vital interests in this hemisphere or not? Will we stop the spread of communism in this hemisphere or not?"

REAGAN WAS DETERMINED to keep the contra war going whether Congress funded it or not. Robert McFarlane later recalled giving the president a paper describing the bleak prospects for the contras as appropriated funding dwindled and Congress refused to provide more. Reagan read the paper and handed it back. "We've got to find a way to keep doing this, Bud," he told McFarlane. "I want you to do whatever you have to do to help these people keep body and soul together. Do everything you can."

McFarlane set to work. In June 1984 he summoned the National Security Planning Group to the Situation Room. "The purpose of this meeting," he explained to the president and the others, "is to focus on the political, economic, and military situation in Central America—to offer a status report and to discuss next steps needed to keep our friends together while continuing to make progress toward our overall political goals." McFarlane offered good news and bad news. The good news was that Congress had approved $62 million in additional money for military assistance to El Salvador. The bad news was that the legislature was refusing to fund the Nicaraguan contras. On the most recent House vote the administration's contra proposal had lost by sixty-four votes, and while that margin might be whittled down, a reversal of the decision appeared unlikely.

William Casey described the progress and prospects of the contras. "The FDN in the north remains strong," Casey said, referring to the largest anti-Sandinista group. "The ARDE"—a more recently formed alliance— "in the south is on the run under pressure." The CIA had $250,000 in cash left from previous appropriations; this would soon be gone. Weapons were dwindling as well. "Our warehouses have arms and ammunition which can hold till August." When the money ran out, the contras would be on their own. "Many of the anti-Sandinistas will stay in place within the country in order to feed themselves," Casey said. "We estimate that about half will retreat into Honduras and Costa Rica in some disarray." The United States could not turn its back on the refugees. "We have to provide humanitarian assistance to help these individuals and those they bring out with them when they come into Honduras and Costa Rica."

Casey hoped Congress would heed the administration's appeal for contra funding. But if it didn't, there were alternatives. "The legal position is that the CIA is authorized to seek support from third countries," he said. "In fact, the finding"—the statement of the president's authority— "encourages third country participation and support in this entire effort." Casey said he was looking into support from the governments of El Salvador, Guatemala, and Honduras (as well as a "South American country" whose identity was deleted when the minutes of this meeting were declassified). "If we notify the oversight committees"—in Congress—"we can provide direct assistance to help the FDN get the money they need from third countries. There will be some criticism, but senior members of the oversight committees recognize that we need to do this." Looking toward the president, Casey said, "We need a decision to authorize our permitting the FDN to obtain third country support."

Reagan didn't respond at once to Casey's appeal. "It all hangs on support for the anti-Sandinistas," he said. "How can we get that support in Congress? We have to be more active."

George Shultz urged that the administration continue to engage the Sandinistas in negotiations, if only to deflect charges that the United

States was ignoring diplomacy in favor of a military solution to the Central American unrest.

Reagan took the secretary's point. "If we are just talking about negotiations with Nicaragua, that is so far-fetched to imagine that a communist government like that would make any reasonable deal with us," the president said. "But if it is to get Congress to support the anti-Sandinistas, then that can be helpful."

Jeane Kirkpatrick agreed that diplomacy had its place. But it might fail, and it shouldn't obscure the absolute necessity of funding the contras. "If we don't find the money to support the contras, it will be perceived in the region and the world as our having abandoned them," Kirkpatrick asserted. "And this will lead to an increase in refugees in the region and it will permit Nicaragua to infiltrate thousands of Nicaraguan trained forces into El Salvador. And this will be an infiltration we could not stop." She urged the president to appeal again to Congress and the American people. But if the Democrats in the House continued to ignore the national interest, the administration should take other measures. "We should make the maximum effort to find the money elsewhere."

Shultz offered a caution. Congress had voted on the contra funding and rejected it. The decision was on the record, and the administration couldn't simply pretend it hadn't been made. Bill Casey had said the presidential finding allowed raising money from third countries; Shultz relayed a different opinion. "I would like to get money for the contras also," he said, "but another lawyer, Jim Baker, said that if we go out and try to get money from third countries, it is an impeachable offense."

Casey cut in. "I am entitled to complete the record," he said. "Jim Baker said that if we tried to get the money from third countries without notifying the oversight committees, it could be a problem. He was informed that the finding does provide for the participation and cooperation of third countries. Once he learned that the finding does encourage cooperation from third countries, Jim Baker immediately dropped his view that this could be an 'impeachable offense.' And you heard him say that, George."

Shultz held his ground. "Jim Baker's argument is that the U.S. government may raise and spend funds only through an appropriation of the Congress."

Caspar Weinberger jumped in. "I am another lawyer who isn't practicing law, but Jim Baker should realize that the United States would not be spending the money for the anti-Sandinista program. It is merely help-ing the anti-Sandinistas obtain money from other sources. Therefore the United States is not, as a government, spending money obtained from other sources."

Shultz appealed to a lawyer who *was* practicing—on behalf of the United States. "I think we need to get an opinion from the attorney gen-eral on whether we can help the contras obtain money from third sources," he said. "It would be the prudent thing to do."

Ed Meese didn't object to going to the attorney general, William French Smith, but he thought the question needed to be framed appropri-ately. "As another non-practicing lawyer," Meese said, "I want to empha-size that it's important to tell the Department of Justice that we want them to find the proper and legal basis which will permit the United States to assist in obtaining third party resources for the anti-Sandinistas. You have to give lawyers guidance when you ask them a question."

Bill Casey returned to the fate of the contras. "It is essential that we tell the Congress what will happen if they fail to provide the funding for the anti-Sandinistas. At the same time, we can go ahead in trying to help obtain funding for the anti-Sandinistas from other sources. The finding does say explicitly 'the United States should cooperate with other govern-ments and seek support of other governments.'" He added, "We have met no resistance from senior members of the intelligence committees to the idea of getting third country funding."

Reagan remained noncommittal on third-party funding. He hadn't given up on Congress. "I am behind an all-out push in Congress," he said. "We must obtain the funds to help these freedom fighters." Congressional funding would send a message to the Sandinistas. "It is what will keep the pressure on."

The meeting had run overtime. Robert McFarlane realized that a consensus was lacking. "I propose that there be no authority for anyone to seek third party support for the anti-Sandinistas until we have the infor-mation we need"—from the attorney general. He added, "I certainly hope none of this discussion will be made public in any way."

Reagan closed the session with a caution cloaked in a smile. "If such a story gets out," he said, "we'll all be hanging by our thumbs in front of the White House until we find out who did it."

68

R EAGAN WARMED TO world travel only slowly. His postwar journey to England to shoot *The Hasty Heart* satisfied his modest pre-political wanderlust, which his aversion to flying did nothing to inflame. Ambition for office eventually prodded him into the air, but even after he became California's governor his transoceanic miles mounted slowly. He visited several American allies at the behest of Richard Nixon, who wished to assure them that Washington was keeping them in mind. He met Chiang Kai-shek of Taiwan (the Republic of China, formally), Francisco Franco of Spain, Ferdinand Marcos of the Philippines, and Lee Kuan Yew of Singapore. After leaving Sacramento and while readying runs for the White House, he traveled to Europe and Asia. The travel still didn't thrill him, but a former governor who sought to become the nation's diplomat in chief and commander in chief could stand the international exposure.

As president he finally discovered the joys of travel. Air Force One, of course, made the journeys themselves much more comfortable. And the White House staff handled all the logistics. He simply had to step out his door, board his helicopter for the short hop to Andrews Air Force Base, climb the steps of his personal Boeing 707, and be off.

Yet the effortlessness of travel was only part of what made foreign trips attractive. Reagan's Hollywood career had accustomed him to the perquisites of celebrity, but these were nothing next to the treatment a president received. Everywhere he went, he was the biggest story in that week's news, and American allies and protégés who sought to make a good impression turned out crowds that put to shame anything a mere actor could have commanded. Moreover, though the cliché that American politics stops at the water's edge has been honored more in the breach than in the observance, Reagan discovered that criticism of his actions was often muted when he was abroad. Even Tip O'Neill understood that it was bad form to blast America's head of state when he was representing the country to the world.

Reagan traveled to Canada in July 1981 for a meeting in Ottawa of the Group of Seven economic powers and to Mexico that October for a conference in Cancún on economic development. In June 1982 he took a ten-day trip to Europe, starting with France for a G7 meeting in Paris, continuing to Italy, where he had an audience with Pope John Paul, then to Britain to address Parliament and see Margaret Thatcher in her native environment, and finally to West Germany for a meeting of the NATO council and a look at the Berlin Wall. In late November and early December 1982, Reagan visited Central and South America, with stops in Honduras, Costa Rica, Colombia, and Brazil. The following year he crossed the Pacific to Japan and South Korea; in the former country he addressed the Diet, or parliament, while in the latter he visited the demilitarized zone that buffered South Korea from North Korea.

Presidential travel is good for a president's reelection prospects, or at least so most candidates for reelection conclude. Incumbents attempt to highlight the difference between themselves and their challengers, and no differences are starker than those between the pomp that surrounds presidential travel and the grind that candidates in the opposing party's primaries are subjected to. Reagan's handlers understood this perfectly, and while the Democrats in the early months of 1984 were traipsing through the snows of New Hampshire and the bayous of Louisiana, the White House laid plans for a pair of foreign spectaculars.

The first took Reagan to China in April. Reagan's schedulers, embarrassed that the president had nodded off while meeting with the pope on his 1982 European trip, made sure to space his events to give him plenty of rest. He laid over in Hawaii for two days and in Guam for one on the trip west and reset his eating and sleeping schedule to Chinese time well ahead of his arrival in the People's Republic. In Hawaii he met Barry Goldwater, who was returning from Taiwan. Reagan had been briefed by Richard Nixon by memo and phone before leaving; Nixon stressed the importance of China in American and international affairs. Goldwater, by contrast, clung to the Cold War view that Taiwan was the real China and registered displeasure that Reagan was going to Beijing. "Barry is upset about my trip and can't hide it," Reagan wrote in his diary. "He seems to think I'm selling out our friends on Taiwan." Reagan reassured him but without obvious success. "He should know better," Reagan wrote. "I've made it very plain to the leaders of the PRC that we will not forsake old friends in order to make new ones."

Nixon had told Reagan what to expect by way of banquets and the like, and a few hours after arriving, the president sat down with Chinese president Li Xiannian. "Our first go at a 12-course Chinese dinner," Reagan wrote afterward, speaking for himself and Nancy. "We heeded Dick Nixon's advice and didn't ask what things were. We just swallowed them. There were a few items I managed to stir around on my plate and leave."

The next day Reagan met with Premier Zhao Ziyang. They discussed world affairs generally and Asia in particular. The tone was formal, but Reagan felt a connection. "We get along very well," he wrote. "I like him and I think he reciprocates."

Hu Yaobang, the general secretary of the Chinese Communist Party, was a different sort. "He's a feisty little man and more doctrinaire than anyone I met," Reagan remarked. "He lectured me about removing our troops from South Korea. I gave it right back to him that there was no way we'd do that. If North Korea wants better relations, let them stop digging tunnels under the DMZ etc." Reagan spontaneously invited Hu to visit the United States. "He might learn something by seeing the outside world."

Reagan awoke the next morning with anticipation. "This was Big Casino day—my meeting with Chairman Deng," he wrote. Nixon and Reagan's own team had prepped him for Deng Xiaoping, the architect of China's unfolding economic reforms. Reagan discovered a mischievous wit. "Nancy went with me for the informal opening," he wrote. "Deng, who has a sense of humor, invited her to come back to China without me." But Deng was all business when he turned to international affairs. "He really waded in critical of our Mid-east policy, our treatment of the developing nations etc. and our disarmament failure." Reagan took the criticism personally and responded accordingly. "He touched a nerve. When it was my turn I corrected him with facts and figures and I meant it." Reagan was pleased with the result. "Funny thing happened—he warmed up although he did bring up Taiwan (the only one who did). I told him it was their problem to be worked out—but it must be worked out peacefully."

That afternoon Reagan's group visited the Great Wall. "We waved our arms off at the crowds lining the streets to see us," he wrote of the drive there. The wall itself took his breath away. "The Wall has an amazing effect even though you've seen photos and movies of it," he recorded. "There is a feeling I can't describe when you stand on it and see it disappear over the mountains in both directions."

After a visit to the ancient capital of Xi'an and a tour of the site where archaeologists had unearthed hundreds of life-sized statues of warriors, Reagan flew to Shanghai. He was shown a factory where Chinese workers assembled electronics products. He visited Fudan University, where he conversed with students and gave a formal speech. His words were aired on state television, and he made the most of the opportunity to describe America and its values to Chinese viewers. "We believe in the dignity of each man, woman, and child," he said. "Our entire system is founded on an appreciation of the special genius of each individual, and of his special right to make his own decisions and lead his own life." Americans chose their own rulers. "We elect our government by the vote of the people." Americans cherished freedom, for others as much as for themselves. "When the armies of fascism swept Europe four decades ago, the American people fought at great cost to defend the countries under assault. When the armies of fascism swept Asia, we fought with you to stop them." Americans were a compassionate people. "When the war ended we helped rebuild our allies, and our enemies as well." Americans were a peace-loving people. "We hate war. We think, and always have, that war is a great sin, a woeful waste." Reagan acknowledged that America's ways were not China's ways, yet the two nations could cooperate to their mutual benefit.

Reagan was never a harsh critic of his own performances, but he thought he had done particularly well this day. "It was a darn good speech," he jotted to himself. "The students ate it up." To reporters on Air Force One en route home, he said he thought he had made a good impression on China's leaders and people. "I think they have an understanding and a confidence in us."

FROM THE STANDPOINT of making Reagan appear a statesman, and hence deserving of reelection, the China trip was hard to beat. The Great Wall was the ultimate backdrop, and his thoroughly photographed sessions with the leaders of one of the world's oldest civilizations elevated him far above any challengers.

But Beijing was just the warm-up. Reagan mounted an even more compelling stage a month later. Preparations for the fortieth anniversary of the D-Day landings at Normandy had been in the works for years, and as the day itself approached, Reagan's handlers took pains with every detail. Timing, lighting, framing—nothing was left to chance.

The president stopped in Ireland on his way to France. He embraced his Irish roots by visiting Ballyporeen, the village that had sent his great-grandfather to America. He hopped to London, where he lunched with Queen Elizabeth and Prince Philip before meeting with Margaret Thatcher at 10 Downing Street.

On the big day he awoke at Winfield House, the home of the American ambassador. He was transported by helicopter across southern England to the English Channel, where the USS *Eisenhower* and other warships plowed the waters furrowed four decades earlier by the thousands of craft of the Allied armada.

He landed on the Normandy coast near Pointe du Hoc, the knife-like promontory between Omaha Beach to the east and Utah Beach to the west. The point had appealed to the German army, whose engineers placed an artillery battery on the summit to prevent attackers from achieving a foothold on the neighboring beaches. For precisely this reason Pointe du Hoc figured centrally in the invasion plans, and a battalion of U.S. Army Rangers was assigned the task of scaling the cliff and capturing the battery.

Reagan told their story in remarks delivered at the memorial atop the cliff. The French government had wanted President François Mitterrand to greet Reagan in the afternoon, before Reagan spoke at Pointe du Hoc, but that would have delayed the American president's remarks past the end of the morning news shows in the United States. Michael Deaver reminded the French ambassador in Washington how accommodating Reagan had been on a visit by Mitterrand to America; the ambassador relayed the message to Paris, and the schedule was rewritten to give Reagan live access to America's breakfast tables.

"We stand on a lonely, windswept point on the northern shore of France," he said to the audience of dignitaries, veterans, and distant television viewers. "The air is soft, but forty years ago at this moment, the air was dense with smoke and the cries of men, and the air was filled with the crack of rifle fire and the roar of cannon. At dawn, on the morning of the 6th of June, 1944, 225 rangers jumped off the British landing craft and ran to the bottom of these cliffs. Their mission was one of the most difficult and daring of the invasion: to climb these sheer and desolate cliffs and take out the enemy guns. The Allies had been told that some of the mightiest of these guns were here and they would be trained on the beaches to stop the Allied advance."

The president nodded to the veterans present as he recounted their heroism. "The rangers looked up and saw the enemy soldiers on the edge of the cliffs shooting down at them with machine-guns and throwing grenades. And the American rangers began to climb. They shot rope ladders over the face of these cliffs and began to pull themselves up. When one ranger fell, another would take his place. When one rope was cut, a ranger would grab another and begin his climb again. They climbed, shot back, and held their footing. Soon, one by one, the rangers pulled themselves over the top, and in seizing the firm land at the top of these cliffs, they began to seize back the continent of Europe. Two hundred and twenty-five came here. After two days of fighting, only ninety could still bear arms."

Reagan glanced over his shoulder at the memorial behind him, a chiseled shard of stone that gashed the air above the beaches. The sculpture, he said, symbolized the daggers the rangers thrust into the cliffs to help them up. "And before me are the men who put them there," he said, looking again to the veterans. "These are the boys of Pointe du Hoc. These are the men who took the cliffs. These are the champions who helped free a continent. These are the heroes who helped end a war."

Reagan inquired rhetorically into their motives. "You were young the day you took these cliffs; some of you were hardly more than boys, with the deepest joys of life before you. Yet you risked everything here. Why? Why did you do it? What impelled you to put aside the instinct for self-preservation and risk your lives to take these cliffs? What inspired all the men of the armies that met here?"

He offered the answer: "It was faith and belief; it was loyalty and love. The men of Normandy had faith that what they were doing was right, faith that they fought for all humanity, faith that a just God would grant them mercy on this beachhead or on the next. It was the deep knowledge—and pray God we have not lost it—that there is a profound, moral difference between the use of force for liberation and the use of force for conquest. You were here to liberate, not to conquer, and so you and those others did not doubt your cause. And you were right not to doubt."

Reagan acknowledged the other heroes of D-Day: the British, the Canadians, the Poles, the Free French. He paid tribute as well to the contributions of the Soviets to the defeat of the Germans. But he distinguished between the Soviets and the other Allies as he described the denouement of D-Day and the war. "In spite of our great efforts and successes, not all that followed the end of the war was happy or planned. Some liberated countries were lost. The great sadness of this loss echoes down to our own time in the streets of Warsaw, Prague, and East Berlin. Soviet troops that came to the center of this continent did not leave when peace came. They're still there, uninvited, unwanted, unyielding, almost forty years after the war. Because of this, allied forces still stand on this continent."

Yet he made this point primarily to emphasize his broader theme of remembrance and reconciliation. "I tell you from my heart that we in the United States do not want war. We want to wipe from the face of the earth the terrible weapons that man now has in his hands. And I tell you, we are ready to seize that beachhead. We look for some sign from the Soviet Union that they are willing to move forward, that they share our desire and love for peace, and that they will give up the ways of conquest. There must be a changing there that will allow us to turn our hope into action. We will pray forever that some day that changing will come." He spoke to his larger audience but referred to the heroes present and missing as he concluded: "Strengthened by their courage, heartened by their valor, and borne by their memory, let us continue to stand for the ideals for which they lived and died."

Reagan shook hands and personally thanked the veterans. He proceeded to Omaha Beach, to the American cemetery above the sand. He stopped in the chapel for a moment of prayer, walked among the nine thousand graves of the American dead, and laid a wreath at the burial site of Theodore Roosevelt Jr., who as the only general officer accompanying the landing forces had won the Medal of Honor and then died of a heart attack. He quoted General Omar Bradley observing of his troops, "Every man who set foot on Omaha Beach that day was a hero."

He told of Private First Class Peter Robert Zanatta, who hit the beach with the first assault wave. Private Zanatta survived the battle to relate its story to his daughter, Lisa. "Someday, Lis, I'll go back," he said. "I'll go back, and I'll see it all again. I'll see the beach, the barricades, and the graves." But he hadn't gone back; he died too soon. Yet his daughter promised, as he was dying, "I'm going there, Dad, and I'll see the beaches and the barricades and the monuments. I'll see the graves, and I'll put flowers there just like you wanted to do. I'll feel all the things you made me feel through your stories and your eyes. I'll never forget what you went through, Dad, nor will I let anyone else forget. And, Dad, I'll always be proud." Reagan gestured to a young woman as he completed his story: "Through the words of his loving daughter, who is here with us today, a D-Day veteran has shown us the meaning of this day far better than any president can. It is enough for us to say about Private Zanatta and all the men of honor and courage who fought beside him four decades ago: We will always remember. We will always be proud. We will always be prepared, so we may always be free."

He continued to Utah Beach for a gathering of the heads of state of several allied countries. Only France's Mitterrand spoke, but American soldiers joined French, British, Canadian, and others in representing the combined forces that had freed Europe from the Nazi yoke. The *Eisenhower* and the other ships stood offshore, out of earshot but in full view of the television cameras.

Reagan returned to London by helicopter. He flew once more over the *Eisenhower*, whose five thousand crewmen assembled on the aircraft carrier's deck in a formation that spelled out "Ike." His helicopter circled the ship while he addressed the officers and men by radio-telephone. "Believe me, all of us up here are inspired by the sight of your magnificent ship and the battle group which accompanied you to the coast of Normandy," he said. "Today, as forty years ago, our navy and all of our armed forces are advancing the cause of peace and freedom." The helicopter circled one last time. "Admiral Flatley, Captain Clexton, officers and men of the 'Ike,'" Reagan said, "I salute you for your devoted service to the cause of freedom."

W ALTER MONDALE HAD emerged from the defeat of the Carter-Mondale ticket in 1980 with reputation intact, as losing vice presidential candidates often do. And the Democratic victories in the 1982 elections gave Mondale and other Democrats cause to think Reagan might be vulnerable in 1984. The recession grew worse past the election, with unemployment reaching nearly 11 percent in December 1982; many voters reasonably wondered if Reagan's recipe for recovery wasn't, in fact, a formula that aggravated the problem.

Other issues contributed to the Democratic hopes. The Reagan arms buildup, including SDI and the Pershing program for Europe, continued to energize the antinuclear left. Deregulation of industry pleased business but antagonized labor, which still smarted over the firing of the air-traffic controllers. Environmentalists decried the policies and pronouncements of James Watt, Reagan's interior secretary. Watt's policies featured opening more federal lands to commercial development; this made many westerners happy but caused large numbers in the rest of the country to fear that the national patrimony was being sold for a mess of corporate pottage. Yet it was Watt's words that sparked the greatest uproar. The interior secretary, a conservative Christian, suggested to a House committee that long-term conservation was a waste of time. "I do not know how many future generations we can count on before the Lord comes," he said. Watt lambasted his opponents as un-American. "I never use the words Democrats and Republicans," he declared. "It's liberals and Americans." He ridiculed affirmative action, saying of a coal advisory committee, "I have a black, I have a woman, two Jews and a cripple."

Reagan supported Watt as long as he could. Watt's policies were essentially the president's policies. Reagan considered himself an environmentalist, with stewardship of his ranch to prove it. But he opposed what he called "environmental extremism," as he said Jim Watt was doing. "He's not going to destroy the environment, but he is going to restore some common sense," Reagan told reporters.

Yet Watt's language eventually made him a liability. Reagan wearied of questions about Watt at news conferences, and Watt's derisive comment about the coal committee, with the 1984 campaign approaching, was a phrase too far. Tellingly for Reagan, the Democrats were coming to love Watt. "He's the best thing we've got going for us," a Democrat on Capitol Hill anonymously said of Watt. Reagan was starting to think so too. A reporter asked if Watt could possibly be effective after his latest remark. Reagan left Watt dangling. "I think that's a decision that he, himself, would have to make, whether he feels that he has made it questionable as to whether he can be effective or not." Watt got the message and resigned.

If Watt had been the best thing going for the Democrats, the worst thing, by the beginning of the 1984 election season, was the economy. The fever of the recession broke in early 1983, and during the next several months the important economic indicators turned in directions favorable to the country and therefore to an incumbent president. Unemployment and inflation fell; production and profits rose. Reagan had always asserted that the economy would revive once his program took hold; now that the economy was reviving, he could persuasively claim credit.

Walter Mondale entered the 1984 Democratic primary season as his party's front-runner. He fended off challenges by Gary Hart, a Colorado senator who struck voters as a bit light for the top job in American politics, and Jesse Jackson, an African American minister and activist who thrilled black audiences and carried three southern primaries but left majorities elsewhere tepid or cold. Mondale claimed the Democratic nomination with little drama.

He created a modest buzz of his own by choosing as his running mate Geraldine Ferraro, a New York member of Congress and the first woman on a major-party ticket in American history. The rest of his campaign was more traditional, focusing on the federal deficit and pledging to rein it in. "Here is the truth about the future," Mondale told the Democratic convention, meeting in San Francisco. "We are living on borrowed money and borrowed time. These deficits hike interest rates, clobber exports, stunt investment, kill jobs, undermine growth, cheat our kids, and shrink our future. Whoever is inaugurated in January, the American people will have to pay Mr. Reagan's bills. The budget will be squeezed. Taxes will go up. And anyone who says they won't is not telling the truth to the American people." Mondale was generally accounted a liberal, but on this central issue he took a stance that made him more conservative, in the received fiscal sense, than Reagan. "I mean business. By the end of my first term, I will reduce the Reagan budget deficit by two-thirds. Let's tell the truth. It must be done, it must be done. Mr. Reagan will raise taxes, and so will I. He won't tell you. I just did."

Mondale took this message into the autumn campaign. "One of the key tests of leadership is whether one sees clearly the nature of the problems confronted by our nation," he declared in the first of his two debates with Reagan, in Louisville. "And perhaps the dominant domestic issue of our times is what do we do about these enormous deficits." The president had promised to balance the budget but hadn't come close. "Every estimate by this administration about the size of the deficit has been off by billions and billions of dollars. As a matter of fact, over four years, they've missed the mark by nearly $600 billion. We were told we would have a balanced budget in 1983. It was $200 billion deficit instead." The current fiscal year looked even worse. "Virtually every economic analysis that I've heard of, including the distinguished Congressional Budget Office, which is respected by, I think, almost everyone, says that even with historically high levels of economic growth, we will suffer a $263 billion deficit."

Reagan shook his head while Mondale spoke. In reply he ignored Mondale's numbers and attacked his convention speech. "I don't believe that Mr. Mondale has a plan for balancing the budget," Reagan said. "He has a plan for raising taxes."

Mondale repeated what he had said in San Francisco. "Mr. Reagan, after the election, is going to have to propose a tax increase," he insisted. Mondale had been following Donald Regan's progress on tax reform, and he wanted Reagan to own up to what was being prepared in his name. "His secretary of the Treasury said he's studying a sales tax or a value-added tax. They're the same thing. They hit middle- and moderate-income Americans and leave wealthy Americans largely untouched."

One of the debate questioners posed the issue to Reagan directly. "Do you think middle-income Americans are overtaxed or undertaxed?"

Reagan put on his best sheepish smile. "You know, I wasn't going to say this at all, but I can't help it. There you go again." He paused for the laughter, which came perfunctorily, unlike the honest amusement and applause that had greeted his use of the line four years earlier. "I don't have a plan to raise taxes," he continued. "Our problem has not been that anybody in our country is undertaxed; it's that government is overfed."

Mondale was ready for Reagan's recycled humor. "Mr. President, you said, 'There you go again,' right?"

"Yes," Reagan responded.

"You remember the last time you said that?"

"Mm-hmm."

"You said it when President Carter said that you were going to cut Medicare, and you said, 'Oh no, there you go again, Mr. President.' And what did you do right after the election? You went out and tried to cut $20 billion out of Medicare. And so, when you say, 'There you go again'— people remember this, you know."

THE HO-HOS AND clapping that greeted Mondale's riposte suggested he had the better of this exchange. And the reviews in the media extrapolated his victory to the debate as a whole. Reagan knew he had done poorly. He wandered off topic; he cited too many statistics; he forgot his closing statement; he looked uncharacteristically flustered. In a rare negative self-review, he afterward admitted, "I have to say I lost." But he didn't blame himself. "I'd crammed so hard on facts and figures in view of the absolutely dishonest things he's been saying in the campaign, I guess I flattened out." He refused to concede defeat on the substance. "He was never able to rebut any of the facts I presented and kept repeating things that are absolute falsehoods." Yet Reagan of all people knew that politics is about more than substance, and in the court of perception the verdict was against him.

Reagan's disappointment was fleeting, as disappointment generally was with him. "We left Louisville not feeling too bad," he wrote the next day. "There was a rally at the hotel last night—1000's of people who had all seen the debate and they thought I'd won."

But the hotel crowd was a gift from the advance team, as Nancy Reagan knew. She took her husband's dismal showing harder than he did. "It was the worst night of Ronnie's political career," she recalled later. "Right from the start, he was tense, muddled, and off-stride. He lacked authority. He stumbled. This was a Ronald Reagan I had never seen before. It was painful to watch. There was no way around it; that debate was a nightmare." She rushed to the stage at the end of the debate. He was seriously upset. "I was terrible," she remembered him telling her. She offered comfort but not dissent. "We both knew he was right." She couldn't sleep the night after the debate. He said the hotel room was stuffy. She agreed. "But we both knew that the real reason was that the debate had been a disaster."

She looked for answers. "What have you done to my husband?" she demanded of Mike Deaver. "Whatever it is, don't do it again." She called for the firing of Richard Darman, who had led the debate preparations. Darman's boss, Jim Baker, refused. "I never had one difference of opinion with her but one," Baker remembered, the one being over the responsibility for Reagan's flop. Baker thought Reagan simply hadn't studied. This made Nancy even angrier. She complained to Paul Laxalt, who accompanied her on the return from Louisville to Washington. "Jesus, Nancy Reagan was so unhappy," Laxalt remembered. "I went back with Nancy and heard for two or three hours how this debate had been screwed up." She vowed that things would change. "By God, it's going to be different, the preparation is going to be different next time," Laxalt recalled her saying.

The unspoken fear driving Nancy's anger was stated aloud in the media. The consistently sympathetic *Wall Street Journal* headlined it starkly: "Fitness Issue—New Question in Race: Is Oldest U.S. President Now Showing His Age? Reagan Debate Performance Invites Open Speculation on His Ability to Serve." The article beneath the banner went on to say, "Until Sunday night's debate, age hadn't been much of an issue in the election campaign. That may now be changing. The president's rambling responses and occasional apparent confusion injected an unpredictable new element into the race." The article quoted a management expert who had voted for Reagan in 1980: "I am very concerned, as a psychologist, about his inability to think on his feet, the disjointedness of his sentences and his use of the security blanket of redundancy . . . I'd be concerned to put him in a corporate presidency. I'd be all the more concerned to put him in the U.S. presidency." The article cited two gerontologists who contended that Reagan should take a mental-impairment test of the kind used to measure senile dementia, with the results made public.

Other papers and reporters pursued the age question. Lou Cannon of the *Washington Post*, who had followed Reagan since the California days, interviewed various members of the campaign before writing, "The president's advisers, pressed to find an explanation for a performance they consider unusually ineffective, are trying to defend Reagan, 73, from the charge that he is showing his age." James Reston wrote in the *New York Times*, "Age may have been a factor in his faltering performance in Louisville. Usually he is at his best onstage, and the bigger the audience the better. But he forgot his lines, even in his memorized closing speech, and that did surprise and trouble even his most devoted aides."

The Reagan campaign team, beyond enlisting the crowds to boost the candidate's spirits, felt obliged to trot out one of his physicians to attest to his soundness of mind. "Mr. Reagan is a mentally alert, robust man who appears younger than his stated age," the doctor declared.

REAGAN REMAINED CALM. He had received bad reviews in Hollywood and survived them; he would survive these too. Polls still showed him ahead of Mondale, if by less than before. He listened to Jim Baker, who waved aside the age question as recycled irrelevance. "It was the same old stuff," Baker remarked afterward. Reagan studied harder, even as he indulged Nancy in her efforts to relax and rest him. "Let Ronnie be Ronnie," she told all who would listen. She arranged for Maureen and Ron and their spouses to join her and Reagan in Kansas City ahead of the second debate. Whether or not the children provided him the moral support she ascribed to them, they made her feel better.

Reagan later claimed that the line that silenced his critics was an ad-lib. The topic of the second debate was national security; Henry Trewhitt, diplomatic correspondent for the *Baltimore Sun*, was one of the panelists. Half an hour into the debate Trewhitt said, "Mr. President, I want to raise an issue that I think has been lurking out there for two or three weeks and cast it specifically in national security terms. You already are the oldest president in history. And some of your staff say you were tired after your most recent encounter with Mr. Mondale. I recall that President Kennedy had to go for days on end with very little sleep during the Cuban missile crisis. Is there any doubt in your mind that you would be able to function in such circumstances?"

Reagan knew the question was coming. His facial expression and body language indicated he was ready for it. His answer wasn't exactly respondent, but it served his purpose. "Not at all, Mr. Trewhitt," Reagan said. "And I want you to know that I will not make age an issue of this campaign. I am not going to exploit, for political purposes, my opponent's youth and inexperience." The audience laughed, many with relief. Even Mondale was forced to laugh. Reagan took a sip of water to let the effect register. Then he almost spoiled it with a sentence that eliminated any pretense of spontaneity in his answer: "If I still have time, I might add,

Mr. Trewhitt, I might add that it was Seneca or it was Cicero, I don't know which, that said, 'If it was not for the elders correcting the mistakes of the young, there would be no state.'"

Reagan's one-liner accomplished all he required. It didn't remove questions about his age, for he was still seventy-three. But it neutralized them. If Reagan could joke about his age—if he could get a laugh out of his audience and even out of his opponent—how serious could it be? His substantive performance in the second debate was just marginally better than in the first debate, but the only thing people remembered was the joke.

Reagan's campaign rolled forward. The television commercial that set the campaign's theme portrayed an America reawakening under the president's able and inspiring leadership. "It's morning again in America," a reassuring voice declared over images of Americans happily engaged in wholesome activities. "Today more men and women will go to work than ever before in our country's history. With interest rates at about half the record highs of 1980, nearly two thousand families today will buy new homes, more than at any time in the past four years. This afternoon sixty-five hundred young men and women will be married, and with inflation at less than half of what it was just four years ago, they can look forward with confidence to the future. It's morning again in America, and under the leadership of President Reagan, our country is prouder and stronger and better. Why would we ever want to return to where we were less than four short years ago?"

American voters quite evidently did not want to return to those bad old days. When they went to the polls in November, they handed Reagan a thunderous victory. The president carried forty-nine of the fifty states, losing only Mondale's home state of Minnesota and that by fewer than four thousand votes. His eighteen-point margin in the popular vote—59 percent to Mondale's 41 percent—showed how dramatically Americans had shifted their political preferences since Reagan had burst on the national scene in 1964. In that year the liberal candidate, Lyndon Johnson, had defeated the conservative, Barry Goldwater, by more than 20 percent of the popular vote. In 1984, Reagan, the conservative, crushed Mondale, the liberal, by a comparable margin.

Reagan remembered that after Goldwater's defeat many pundits had declared conservatism dead. Even within the Republican Party the movement struggled to avoid being read the last rites. But Reagan had never faltered. He refused to change his message. On the campaign trail in

1980 and again in 1984 he used the same images and even some of the same phrases he had employed in his 1964 speech. Through the wilderness years of American conservatism, during the 1960s and 1970s, Reagan's optimism that the country would see the wisdom in conservatism had frequently appeared naive, if not delusional. But as the magnitude of his reelection victory became evident, what had been dismissed as delusion won new appreciation as vision, and his naïveté was recognized as the clearest-sighted realism.

70

Reagan reasonably assumed his landslide victory would increase his credibility in negotiations at home and abroad. He thought the press was still biased against him—"The press is now trying to prove it wasn't a landslide, or should I say a mandate?" he grumbled after a postelection news conference—but he was pleased that the Democratic leadership paid attention to the election results. "Tip O'Neill told me privately he was very conscious of the fact that I had received 59 percent of the vote."

The Soviets were paying attention too. The Kremlin's envoys had broken off arms talks in Geneva to protest Reagan's insistence on deploying the Pershing and cruise missiles in Europe, but after the election they signaled a willingness to return to the table. Reagan thought this a good sign, one he intended to exploit. He called a meeting of the National Security Planning Group in late November. Douglas George of the CIA outlined Soviet capabilities and likely negotiating strategies. "The Soviets are afraid that U.S. gains will erode the advantages which they have achieved," he said. The Kremlin hoped Congress would derail the MX system and the Europeans would reject the Pershings and cruise missiles. But SDI was what really kept Soviet leaders awake nights, George said. "The Soviet Union recognizes that no amount of capital that it can invest would permit them to compete successfully with the United States in terms of SDI."

Caspar Weinberger asserted that this made SDI all the more important. "It is strategic defense that gives the United States its leverage on the Soviet Union," the defense secretary said.

General John Vessey, the chairman of the Joint Chiefs of Staff, didn't argue with Weinberger about SDI but stressed the role of the MX. "The Soviet Union gets a great amount of military leverage from its ICBM force, and it is important that we develop a counter to that," he said.

Reagan returned to Douglas George's point and broadened the conversation. He asked whether the Soviet Union feared America's economic capability.

General Vessey responded, "The Soviet Union has a greater military and industrial base, but we have the lead in high technology."

Weinberger added, "The key is SDI." But America needed to move quickly. "We don't have the time to mobilize an industrial base the way we did in World War II."

Reagan had a more technical question. He asked whether deterrence would be enhanced if the administration publicly adopted a launch-under-attack policy. Everyone at this meeting understood that the point of the MX program was to allow the United States to absorb a Soviet first strike and still retaliate devastatingly. But because the MX didn't yet exist, Reagan was asking if the United States should launch as soon as it detected a Soviet launch. By one line of thinking, such an American hair trigger would banish Soviet thoughts of a first strike. But by another, it would make the Soviets nervous and prone to miscalculation. Moreover, it required reliable detection measures by the United States. Reagan followed up by asking whether such measures existed.

Weinberger acknowledged that there were gaps in America's radar coverage. But Vessey said that those applied only to Soviet missiles launched from submarines.

Robert McFarlane thought Weinberger and Vessey understated the problem with a launch-under-attack policy. "We do not have the kind of attack assessment capability that we would need to rely on such a policy," he said. American radar could see the missiles coming in, but it couldn't tell whether they were aimed at American missiles or American cities.

Vessey agreed that the detection was unreliable and therefore that launch under attack was infeasible.

Paul Nitze, who headed the administration's delegation to the intermediate-force talks in Geneva, rejected the president's suggestion on political grounds. He called it a "policy of weakness."

But William Casey thought launch under attack might be useful in prodding Congress to fund strategic defense. Launch under attack, he said, "would make SDI look very good indeed."

Weinberger stated simply, "SDI is the best response to the Soviet threat."

REAGAN AGREED. THROUGH the end of 1984 and into 1985 he conducted a two-pronged offensive: pushing the Kremlin to engage in meaningful arms talks and pressing Congress to fund the new weapons systems, the MX and SDI, that would make the talks meaningful. He thought he could pull it off. "We and the Soviet Union may be coming together more than many people realize," he told the National Security Planning Group. The president reiterated his discovery that the Soviets honestly feared American capabilities and intentions. "We could build on the Soviet preoccupation with defending the homeland by making clear that we have no intention of starting a nuclear war," he said. The Kremlin's concern for defense could afford an opening for SDI. "We have no objections to their having defenses, but we have to look at defenses for ourselves." He conceded that this would be a tough sell. "They are afraid of SDI." The administration's job was to demonstrate that they needn't be. "We must show them how defenses are not threatening. We must make it clear that we are not seeking advantage, only defense."

American analysts had reported that the Soviet Union was ahead of the United States in antisatellite technology, or ASAT. The Soviets were likening ASAT to SDI, perhaps as a basis for a trade. Reagan rejected the comparison. "We are willing to negotiate the end of ASATs because they are offensive weapons," he said. But he wasn't going to bargain away strategic defense. And the fact that the Soviets were nervous about it was all the more reason to keep it. "SDI gives us a great deal of leverage," he said.

Robert McFarlane suggested that the Kremlin was hoping for help from the administration's critics in Congress and the media. "The Russians may bet that the United States cannot sell its SDI program. We need to get support for strategic defense."

Reagan joked, "We can start by canceling our subscriptions to the *Washington Post*." Yet the president took seriously the political opposition to the administration's weapons program. The complaints from liberals like those at the *Post* didn't surprise him, but conservative resistance caused him dismay. Barry Goldwater singled out the MX as a boondoggle. The Arizona senator thought the Pentagon was spending too much already; the MX was more of the wasteful same. Reagan feared that Goldwater's opposition would be contagious. "He could well be the kiss of death," the president wrote.

Reagan invited senators and representatives of both parties to the White House. He pitched the MX and SDI as necessary precursors to arms reductions. "I hope we're making them realize we can't unilaterally disarm and hope to persuade the Soviets," he wrote afterward. A few weeks later he brought David Boren and Sam Nunn, two leading Democrats in the Senate, to the White House for cocktails and discussion of the MX. "I believe we'll have their support," Reagan noted. "In fact they talked of how wrong it was for Congress to interfere with a president in foreign affairs and how both parties must come together at the water's edge."

Tip O'Neill was unsupportive but not obstructionist. "Tip surprised me," Reagan recorded after a lunch with the House speaker. "He won't make an issue of MX but will not personally vote for it. He says it's a matter of conscience; having the MX, he says, will provoke a Russian nuclear attack." Reagan gave O'Neill modest credit for integrity on this crucial issue but none for intelligence. "He can't respond when asked how we can remain defenseless and let the Soviets have thousands of missiles aimed at us."

O N MARCH 11, 1985, Reagan made an entry in his diary that marked the beginning of the end of an epoch in modern history, although he didn't realize it at the time. "Awakened at 4 A.M. to be told Chernenko is dead," he wrote. "Word has been received that Gorbachev has been named head man."

American analysts had been watching Mikhail Gorbachev for some time. "We knew a lot about him," Robert Gates recalled, speaking for the CIA, which had picked Gorbachev as a comer since the Andropov interlude. In fact the CIA had been rooting for Gorbachev, for a number of reasons. First, the gravity of the problems facing the Soviet Union required someone willing and able to grasp the nettle of reform. "The twin dangers of chaos and a possible desperate military lunge for an economic lifeline or diversion from problems at home were a concern," Gates said. "Accession at last of a leader who was prepared to make tough decisions to address that crisis was to be welcomed by the United States." Second, the CIA analysts believed that the crisis in the Soviet Union couldn't be remedied without significant cuts in Soviet military spending. "Many were persuaded that Gorbachev would eventually face up to this reality." Third, they hoped Gorbachev would help calm relations between the United States and the Soviet Union. "CIA professionals were no more immune than other Americans to the feeling that the U.S.-Soviet confrontation had gotten a bit too hot in recent years." Fourth, Gorbachev was simply more fun to study than his predecessors. "After long years of watching every move of a group of aging, colorless, uninteresting Soviet leaders, here was one of flesh and blood, of energy and action, of emotion, a man seemingly determined to change things."

Gates and the CIA had reported to Reagan that Gorbachev was the likely successor to Chernenko. "If Gorbachev is chosen, it could lead to the emergence of a more articulate, self-confident brand of Soviet leadership," Gates and the agency predicted. "He might push for more innovative solutions to Soviet economic problems and greater flexibility and initiative in dealing with opportunities and challenges abroad."

Reagan gave greater thought to attending Chernenko's funeral than he had given to going to Brezhnev's or Andropov's. But again he decided not to risk appearing too eager. He again sent George Bush, accompanied by George Shultz, in his place.

Bush was used to the routine by now. "I think it was Jim Baker who came up with the slogan for me, 'You die, I'll fly,'" Bush recounted later. He and Shultz attended Chernenko's funeral and then a state reception at which Gorbachev greeted them. Shultz was impressed at once. "Gorbachev started with a grace note, thanking us for 'paying our respects to General Secretary Chernenko,' and then launched into the most far-ranging statement on foreign policy that I had heard from a Soviet leader," Shultz recalled. "'It is natural,' he began, 'to wonder what might change with the departure of one general secretary and the appointment of a new one. The United States should proceed from the premise that there will be continuity in both the domestic and foreign policy of the U.S.S.R.' Then he noted the chimes of an antique clock in the room and said, with a smile, that the clock was old and was not intended to serve as any kind of signal."

Gorbachev had come to the meeting prepared. A thick sheaf of papers apparently outlined what he intended to say. But he put it aside. "He was articulate and spontaneous," Shultz said. "He seemed to be thinking out loud. Perhaps he was." Bush outranked Shultz, and the vice president did the initial talking for the American side, leaving Shultz to take mental notes. "I could listen intently and watch Gorbachev, trying to size up what kind of a person he was," Shultz recalled. "Gorbachev later told me he had noticed me watching him in this first meeting and wondered what I was thinking."

The general secretary toured the horizon of international affairs. He cited the emergence of scores of newly independent countries since the 1950s, each having its own interests and agenda. "No one, not even the U.S.S.R. and the United States, can fail to take this into account," he said. "We have to learn to base our relations on these realities." Gorbachev mentioned statements by persons he called "very highly placed U.S. officials" that seemed to ascribe all the problems of the emerging world to

Soviet mischief. "Moscow would seem to be almighty," he said ironically. He continued seriously, "The U.S.S.R. has no expansionist ambitions. It has all the resources it will need for centuries, be it in terms of manpower, natural resources, or territory." He added, with a lighter touch, "We have no territorial claims against the United States, not even with respect to Alaska or Russian Hill in San Francisco." He pointed to past cooperation, particularly during World War II—"a bright page in the history of Soviet-U.S. relations"—and again during the era of détente.

He looked directly at Bush to make a statement he obviously considered very important. "The U.S.S.R. has never intended to fight the United States and does not have such intentions now," he said. "There have never been such madmen within the Soviet leadership, and there are none now. The Soviets respect your right to run your country the way you see fit. In the same way, it is up to the Soviet people to make such decisions on behalf of the U.S.S.R. And the U.S.S.R. will never permit anyone to teach it how to govern itself." He paused. "As to the question of which is the better system, this is something for history to judge."

He turned to the arms race and arms control. "The two countries have now reached a point in their arms buildup when any new breakthroughs resulting from the scientific and technological revolution—not to mention shifting the arms race to space—could set in motion irreversible and uncontrollable processes." He questioned the seriousness of the American side, asking why people in the Reagan administration often sounded so skeptical about arms talks. "These negotiations are being depicted as requiring years and years. Is the U.S. side really interested in these negotiations? Is it interested in achieving results? Or does the United States find these negotiations necessary in order to pursue its programs for continuing the arms race, for developing ever new types of arms?"

Shultz was more impressed than ever. "Gorbachev's free-flowing monologue showed a mind working at high intensity, even at the end of a long, hard day," he wrote. "He displayed a breadth of view and vigor, I thought." All the same, the positions Gorbachev described were nothing new.

Bush answered for the United States and for Reagan. "We have no aspirations of dictating how to administer the Soviet Union," the vice president said. "This is the farthest thing from our thoughts." Yet he proceeded to explain that respect for human rights was central to America's view of the world. "This issue is extremely important to the president and the American people." Harsh treatment of Soviet political dissidents and the denial of exit visas to Soviet Jews were matters America could not overlook.

Gorbachev shot back that the United States was in no position to lecture the Soviet Union on human rights. "The United States violates human rights not only on its own territory but also beyond its border," he said. America oppressed its black population and supported dictators abroad. "It disregards the human rights not only of individuals but of entire nations and countries. It brutally represses human rights." He nonetheless agreed that the subject might be discussed by the diplomats. But then he backtracked, saying internal affairs were inappropriate for negotiations between the two governments. Americans seemed to raise them to stall or block meaningful negotiations. "Every time there is a meeting involving our two countries, the United States proceeds to raise these questions." He wasn't going to apologize for the accomplishments of socialism. "Thank God there is socialism, because with socialism the people of former capitalist countries have gained more rights."

REAGAN HAD WRITTEN a letter to Gorbachev for Bush and Shultz to deliver. "As you assume your new responsibilities, I would like to take this opportunity to underscore that we can in the months and years ahead develop a more stable and constructive relationship between our two countries," Reagan said. He didn't underestimate the challenge involved. "Our differences are many, and we will need to proceed in a way that takes both differences and common interests into account." But the two leaders bore heavy responsibility for maintaining the peace. "The international situation demands that we redouble our efforts to find political solutions to the problems we face." Reagan pledged his personal commitment to engage Gorbachev in serious negotiations. "In that spirit, I would like to invite you to visit me in Washington at your earliest convenient opportunity."

Shultz explained to Gorbachev that Reagan had briefed him before his departure on what to tell the general secretary as accompaniment to the president's letter. "President Reagan told me to look you squarely in the eyes and tell you: 'Ronald Reagan believes that this is a very special moment in the history of mankind,'" Shultz said. The secretary of state continued in his own voice but reciting Reagan's themes. "You are starting your term as general secretary. Ronald Reagan is starting his second term as president. Negotiations are beginning in Geneva. Over the past year we have found solutions to some problems, though not to the great problems, and if it is at all possible, we must establish a more constructive relation-ship between the United States and the U.S.S.R. President Reagan knows he personally must work on this hard, and he is ready to do so." Shultz said the president's invitation to Gorbachev to visit Washington was evidence of his commitment. And there was no time to waste. "If important agree-ments can be found, the sooner the better."

Gorbachev responded positively, though noncommittally. He agreed that the Soviet Union and the United States were at a "unique moment" that mustn't be wasted. "I am ready to return Soviet-U.S. relations to a normal channel," he said. "It is necessary to know each other, to find time for meetings to discuss outstanding problems, and to seek ways to bring the two countries closer together."

After the meeting, Bush cabled Reagan an account of the exchange and offered his assessment of the Kremlin's new leader. "Gorbachev will package the Soviet line for Western consumption much more effectively than any (I repeat any) of his predecessors," the vice president wrote. "He has a disarming smile, warm eyes, and an engaging way of making an unpleasant point and then bouncing back to establish real communication with his interlocutors. He can be very firm. Example: When I raised the human rights question with specificity, he interrupted my presentation to come back with the same rhetorical excess we have heard before. Quote 'Within the borders of the US you don't respect human rights' or (refer-ring to African-Americans), 'You brutally repress their rights.' But along with this the following: 'We will be prepared to think it over' and 'Let's appoint rapporteurs and discuss it.' The gist being as follows—'Don't lec-ture us on human rights, don't attack socialism but let's each take our case to discussion.'"

S ECOND-TERM PRESIDENTS BENEFIT from the credibility that
comes from having survived a referendum on their performance.
In Reagan's case the referendum was overwhelmingly positive, and
on the basis of his historic triumph he should have rolled into his second
term with powerful momentum. But second-term presidents labor under
peculiar difficulties that offset some of their credibility. Not the least of
the challenges is that second-term presidents typically lead second-string
teams. On first election, presidents have their pick of the best people their
party has to offer; they fill critical cabinet and White House positions
with the party's first-string team. But the first-stringers grow weary of the
work, of politics, and of the comparatively low pay, and they often leave
before a second term is well under way. Their replacements occasionally
turn out to be stellar, but more frequently they lack something of the
experience, the judgment, the temperament, or the talent that might have
got them chosen in the first round. Good help is hard to find, and never
harder than at the apex of government, where mistakes are scrutinized,
magnified, and publicized.

Don Regan was one of the first stringers who became worn down
by his job and all that went with it. The leaking and backbiting that had
driven Al Haig from office vexed him almost as much. During 1984 he
had followed the president's directive and developed a proposal for tax
reform. He tried as a tactical matter to keep the discussions secret, lest
opponents of change mobilize against attacks on their pet programs
before the proposal could be unveiled and defended as a whole. He was
pleased to hand the president a comprehensive plan three weeks after the
election. The plan wasn't perfect, but it was an improvement, he judged.

"I reflected, as I placed this weighty document in his hands on November 26, 1984, that our simplified plan was still far too long"—262 pages of text and 536 of appendixes—"but it was a hell of a lot shorter than the sixty-three feet of bookshelves required to accommodate the existing tax code and its concordances," he observed.

To remind the president of the imperative for reform, Regan asked him an irreverently personal question. Had he ever made as much as $1 million a year before becoming president?

Reagan registered surprise. Not by a long shot, he said.

"Six figures, then?" Regan insisted.

Reagan nodded.

"Okay, how much did you pay in taxes?" Regan asked.

Reagan realized Regan was driving at something. He said he had paid about half his income in taxes.

"Sucker!" Regan pronounced. "With the right lawyer and the right accountant and the right tax shelters, you needn't have paid a penny in taxes even if you made more than a million dollars a year—and it would have been perfectly legal and proper. The tax system we have now is designed to make the avoidance of taxes easy for the rich and has the effect of making it almost impossible for people who work for wages and salaries to do the same. As someone who has made a lot money and benefited from the system, I can tell you it's a great thing for people with high incomes and good tax advisers. But as your secretary of the Treasury, I'm telling you that it ain't fair and that it is undermining the morale of taxpayers and crippling the economy. Too many people are getting away with too much. You asked me for a plan to change all that, and that's what I've brought you today."

Regan proceeded to explain the plan at length. The briefing lasted an hour and forty minutes—"the longest encounter by far I had had with him to date," Regan recalled. The essence of the plan was simplification. The fourteen brackets for personal taxes were reduced to three, with marginal rates of 15, 25, and 35 percent. Special deductions and preferences—"loopholes" to those who didn't benefit from them—were sharply pared. The corporate tax rate was cut to 33 percent. Capital gains were no longer treated specially but were taxed as ordinary income.

Reagan liked what he heard and read, giving Regan hope that something might come of the exercise. "If the president acted on his principles, I was sanguine about the outcome," Regan recounted. "I was under no illusion that we had produced an irresistible document, but I knew that we were giving the president a powerful lever; if he stood his ground he might very well move this particular world."

YET STANDING HIS ground proved a challenge. The numerous interest groups whose preferences were targeted for elimination besieged Congress, and senators and representatives on pertinent committees began to shake their heads in disapproval.

But what really annoyed Regan was the sabotage by those close to the president. "The ship of state began leaking like a sieve," Regan wrote. "On the morning after I presented the plan to the president (and before I had given my own verbal summary to the press) the substance of that confidential briefing, issuing from anonymous presidential aides, appeared on the front pages of the *Wall Street Journal*, the *New York Times* and the *Washington Post*. Even the *Baltimore Sun* was able to discuss my program in detail before I revealed it in a press conference. Unnamed White House sources were quoted as saying that the president had decided to distance himself from the plan."

Regan couldn't really complain about the substance of the stories, which were accurate enough, including the part about the president keeping clear of the tax reform proposals. Regan himself had suggested that Reagan not rush to endorse them. "Don't embrace the whole plan right away," Regan said. "Be cool—watch what happens." The currently favored interests would fight to preserve their advantages, and if they proved too persuasive with Congress, the president could walk away and blame the fuss on Regan.

But Regan was irked to be preempted, and he thought the leaking undermined the chances that the program would be approved. The president's aides were too protective of his image, he thought. "Great risks were involved in pushing the plan, and risk-taking is not the language of image-makers." The resistance revealed their perception of the recent election. "The president had not run on a promise of tax reform but on a wave of good feeling that his advisers believed, with some justice, was a product of their manipulation of the media. Why should they subject the president and themselves to the bruising public battle that tax reform was certain to be? Their hearts simply weren't in it."

Regan thought the president was being ill served by such timid advisers. "The good fight for tax reform, like so many issues before it, was degenerating into a squabble in the media rather than becoming a grand debate on the future of our nation led by the president," he said. This was simply bad management. "It seemed to me, after four years of living in an environment in which policy seemed to be made on the basis of a belief in public opinion that amounted to superstition, that the presidency was in need of sound management advice. Willy-nilly, Ronald Reagan had achieved great things in four years. What might he do if his office were better organized and his ideas were more systematically transformed into policy?"

Regan's thinking reached a crucial point following a cabinet meeting as the report on taxes was being finalized. George Shultz shared Regan's distress at the problem of leaks and had suggested that Regan raise the matter with the president. Regan did so at the cabinet meeting. After he reported on the progress of the tax reform group, he argued strongly that administration staff needed to keep their mouths shut and that violators should be sternly disciplined. The president seemed sympathetic. But in the next morning's *Washington Post*, Regan read a detailed account of his cabinet comments on tax reform.

"I was infuriated by this treacherous insult to the president and to me," he recalled. "And at 7:50 A.M., with the *Post* still in my hand, I called Jim Baker and gave him the full benefit of my reaction in Marine Corps terminology. The conversation ended with my shouting something a lot stronger than Go to the devil, Jim Baker! and slamming down the receiver."

Regan immediately dictated a letter of resignation. He dispatched an assistant to deliver it to the president, with instructions that it not go through Richard Darman, Baker's assistant who managed paper flow and who was Regan's prime suspect in many of the leaks.

A few hours later he received a call from the president. "I got your letter and I'm calling to tell you that I can't accept your resignation," Reagan said. "In fact I'm tearing it up right now and burning it in the fireplace."

"I appreciate that, Mr. President," Regan replied. "But I meant what I wrote. This atmosphere of leaks and mistrust is simply intolerable, and I want to go."

"Well, you can't, Don, and that's final. You're the only friend I have around here. If you go, I'll have to get my hat and go with you."

Regan withdrew his resignation. "The man is not yet born who could resist words like these from the president of the United States," he remembered.

BAKER SOON ARRIVED in Regan's office. "It was obvious that he wanted to explain the leak and smooth things over," Regan said. "I asked him to stay for lunch. My anger cooled, and I was glad enough to have the opportunity of talking to Baker. He seemed tired, distracted. He dropped into a chair, sighed loudly, shook his head, gave a wry smile. I asked him what was bothering him. He spoke the several names of the Lord one after the other and then described some of his behind-the-scenes experiences with the leading figures of American politics and government." The fight for tax reform was only a small part of the picture, Baker said. The annual budget battle was raging; dozens of causes were being promoted by scores of people who had to be listened to if not agreed with; the media were always complaining; he was constantly having to patch over the mistakes of his staff and other members of the administration.

"You know what the trouble with you is, Baker?" Regan responded. "You're tired."

Baker looked at him for a moment. "You're right," he conceded. "I really am tired. I've got to get away from this."

"You'll never do that," Regan said. "You're a political junkie. You're hooked."

Baker didn't deny it. They talked a bit longer. Then Regan said, "You know what we should do, Jim? We should swap jobs."

Regan claimed afterward that he was half kidding. "I tossed out these words without thinking," he wrote. "But Baker bobbed his head like a man who has been hit with an idea."

"Do you mean that?" he asked.

Regan thought it over for a few moments. "I guess I do."

They sat silently. Then Baker rose to leave. "Watch out," he said. "I may take you up on that."

"Okay," Regan said. "When you're ready to talk, I'll be here."

Baker broached the matter with the group he called his own troika: Dick Darman, Margaret Tutwiler, and Susan Baker, his wife. Darman and Tutwiler would accompany him to Treasury if he decided to go. Darman worked with Baker to produce a one-page balance sheet of the costs and benefits of staying against those of moving. "Possible Secretary of State," the memo listed under the reasons to stay. Baker much preferred the senior cabinet post, and he thought he might get it if he held out for it. Referring to the Treasury job, the memo declared, "Not as good as State." George Shultz, like Regan and Al Haig, became frustrated with the leaks in the administration, and one day he might get fed up and resign. But, then again, maybe he wouldn't. And where would that leave Baker? The Baker-Darman memo observed, "Bird in hand vs. bush."

The handy bird won. Two weeks later Baker met with Regan again. They talked about tax reform, with Baker asking more questions than a chief of staff needed answered. Regan wasn't surprised when Baker ended the meeting by inquiring if he was still serious about switching jobs. Regan said he was.

"How would we approach the Man on this?" Baker asked.

"Hell, I'll talk to him," Regan replied.

Baker had a better idea. "We need to get Deaver involved," he said. "We could never do this without telling Mike." Baker thought Deaver deserved to know, as he had wanted to be chief of staff and was leaving the administration in part because he guessed he wouldn't be. No less important, Deaver would sound out Nancy Reagan, whose support for the switch would be crucial.

Baker enlisted Darman to help him write a memo to Deaver. "It's time for a change," the memo began. Baker and Regan were both tired of their current jobs and had spent down their political capital. The switch would reinvigorate them personally and rejuvenate the administration. Regan, the better financial mind, had done a good job developing the Treasury's tax reform plan; Baker, the better political tactician, would give it the best chance of winning legislative approval. Meanwhile, Regan, the budget hawk, would help hold the White House line on spending. Baker and Darman said they hoped Deaver liked the idea, which they urged him to take to the president and the First Lady but no one else. "Leaks could stimulate conflict, which could destroy one of the main benefits: infusion of momentum."

Baker and Regan met with Deaver personally. The three had lunch at Baker's house, away from the prying eyes of the media and their own staffs. Regan launched into an explanation and justification of the switch before realizing that Deaver had already made up his mind—after consulting Nancy. "In my innocence the thought that Deaver had cleared the plan with the First Lady before discussing it with me, or even with the president, did not occur to me," Regan recalled. Nancy accepted the idea, and so did Deaver. To Baker and Regan, Deaver observed that the beginning of the second term was the logical time for a change. He added that Regan had been loyal to the president and wasn't known for any personal agenda that would raise political problems. "This would be your terminal job, Don," Deaver said, tacitly inviting Regan, who was about to turn sixty-six, to correct him. Regan did not.

The three decided to wait until after the Reagans took their Christmas vacation at the ranch in California to approach the president. But early in the new year they met with Reagan in the Oval Office. Deaver smiled and said, "Mr. President, I've brought you someone your own age to play with."

Reagan smiled quizzically.

"Don has something he wants to discuss with you that he's talked to Jim and me about," Deaver said. "We think it's very interesting and we'd like to know what you think about it."

Regan made his pitch. "Reagan listened without any sign of surprise," Regan recalled. "He seemed equable, relaxed—almost incurious. This seemed odd under the circumstances. The change I was describing was significant in itself, but it was only the latest in a series of changes that involved the president's closest aides." Deaver was leaving, and Ed Meese was slated to be the next attorney general. Now Baker, the third member of the White House troika, would be going to Treasury, replaced by Regan, whom Reagan knew but not well. "In the president's place I would have put many questions to the applicant," Regan observed. "How will you be different from Jim Baker? How will you handle Congress? What do you know about defense and foreign affairs? Who will you bring with you and who will you get rid of? What practices will you want to change? How will you handle the press? Why do you want this job?" But the president did nothing of the kind. "Reagan made no inquiries. I did not know what to make of his passivity."

Regan suggested that he might want time to think the matter over.

Regan asked Regan to say a bit more. Regan did so, still uninterrupted by questions. "Reagan nodded affably," Regan recounted. "He looked at Baker and Deaver as if to check the expressions on their faces, but asked them no questions either." When Regan finished, the president said, "Yes, I'll go for it."

Regan couldn't get over the apparent lack of reflection in the president regarding such a major personnel change. "The president's easy acceptance of this wholly novel idea of switching his chief of staff and his secretary of the Treasury, and of the consequent changes in his own daily life and in his administration, surprised me," Regan wrote. "He seemed to be absorbing a fait accompli rather than making a decision. One might have thought that the matter had already been settled by some absent party."

Regan again urged the president to think it over. Again Reagan waved him off. "I don't see why we shouldn't just go ahead with it," he said.

T HE WORLD SOON learned that the president's chief of staff and Treasury secretary were switching jobs. And it discovered not much later that Don Regan was no Jim Baker as chief of staff. Baker relaxed in his new life at Treasury, where important decisions didn't have to be made every day and where, when such decisions *were* made, they often escaped the intense scrutiny the media focused on the White House. Regan, moving in the opposite direction, quickly appreciated why Baker had seemed so worn. A chief of staff had to juggle a dozen balls simultaneously, and despite the efforts of Baker to brief him on what was in the air, some of the balls inevitably slipped through Regan's inexperienced fingers.

The fumble that first got the world's attention had its roots in a meeting between Reagan and West German chancellor Helmut Kohl in November 1984. Kohl traveled to Washington to discuss alliance matters and to lay the groundwork for a meeting of the G7 in Bonn the following May. Kohl confessed that he and other Germans had been offended by their country's exclusion from the fortieth-anniversary commemorations of the D-Day landings, and he shared that a subsequent bury-the-hatchet meeting between himself and François Mitterrand of France at the World War I battlefield at Verdun had yielded good feeling between their two countries and for the Western alliance in general. The chancellor hoped President Reagan would join him in a similar ceremony, perhaps at a wartime cemetery, on his visit to Germany. Kohl was fully aware of Jewish sensitivities toward anything that looked like a forgetting of the Holocaust; he suggested that Reagan balance a cemetery visit with a commemoration at Dachau or another concentration camp.

Reagan accepted Kohl's invitation in principle and turned the matter over to the State Department and the White House staff to arrange the details. The State Department went to work on the briefing papers and other materials that would inform the substance of the president's German tour; the White House staff took responsibility for the theatrics.

Unluckily, the White House staff was in the middle of the transition from Baker to Regan, and some details didn't get the attention they deserved. In February 1985, Mike Deaver led an advance team to Germany to examine the sites the president would visit. By this time Kohl's people had specified a military cemetery in Bitburg, in the chancellor's home state and in a region of West Germany where a crucial election was about to be held. Deaver and the others visited the small cemetery, which looked inoffensive beneath a covering of snow. One of Deaver's assistants later claimed to have asked whether any members of the notorious Nazi SS were buried there and been told that there were not. But neither Deaver nor his assistants brushed the snow off the gravestones to see for themselves.

Meanwhile, it was the possibility of a presidential visit to Dachau that provoked the first objections. The German press suggested that Dachau had been Reagan's idea; the White House denied the report. George Shultz told Reagan that a Dachau visit would be symbolically important, but Reagan thought the symbolism would be counterproductive. He wanted to look forward rather than back.

The president was asked about this in a news conference, and he responded that America and Germany needed to move on. "I feel very strongly that this time in commemorating the end of that great war, that instead of reawakening the memories and so forth and the passions of the time, that maybe we should observe this day as the day when, forty years ago, peace began, and friendship. Because we now find ourselves allies and friends of the countries that we once fought against. And that it be almost a celebration of the end of an era and the coming into what has now been some forty years of peace for us. And I felt that since the German people—and very few alive that remember even the war, and certainly none of them who were adults and participating in any way— and they have a feeling, and a guilt feeling that's been imposed upon them, and I just think it's unnecessary. I think they should be recognized for the democracy that they've created and the democratic principles they now espouse."

Reagan's words evoked a passionate response. "President Reagan apparently believes that all Germans alive today are under 60 years old," Menachem Rosensaft of the International Network of Children of Jewish Holocaust Survivors wrote in the *New York Times*. "It would seem that a brief history lesson is in order. In 1943, when my parents arrived at Auschwitz, they were in their early 30s. Most of the German guards and doctors who tortured them and sent their families to the gas chambers were their age or younger. Similarly, many of the killers of Treblinka, Bergen-Belsen, Dachau and all the other death camps were in their 20s and 30s when they participated in the annihilation of six million European Jews." Few of these personnel, being guards and other noncombatants, died in battle, and only a small number were executed after the war for their crimes. "Thus, many of them are today in their 60s and 70s, still alive and well and living in Germany." Rosensaft thought Reagan, of all presidents, should be aware of how long people lived. Josef Mengele, the monstrous chief doctor at Auschwitz, was seventy-four years old, the same age as Reagan. "Somehow I think Mengele remembers the Third Reich," Rosensaft said. The president had traveled to Normandy to honor the soldiers who died there; he regularly paid tribute to America's war dead. But now he wouldn't take time to remember the Holocaust. "He has made it clear that for him, the dead of Dachau, symbolic of the dead of all the Nazi concentration camps, are less worthy of respect than the fallen soldiers of Normandy or the G.I.s who lie buried in Arlington National Cemetery," Rosensaft said. "In essence, he is telling the world that he cares more about German sensibilities than about the memory of Hitler's victims. As a son of Holocaust survivors, I am angry. As an American, I am ashamed."

Reagan's problems multiplied when the White House announced that the president would be visiting the military cemetery at Bitburg. He would lay a wreath "in a spirit of reconciliation, in a spirit of forty years of peace, in a spirit of economic and military compatibility," Larry Speakes explained. The announcement provoked new outcry from Jewish groups and protests from American veterans. Hundreds of members of Congress petitioned the president to reconsider.

Reagan dug in his heels instead. "All it would do is leave me looking as if I caved in in the face of some unfavorable attention," he told a gathering of editors and broadcasters. "I think that there's nothing wrong with visiting that cemetery, where those young men are victims of Nazism also, even though they were fighting in the German uniform, drafted into service to carry out the hateful wishes of the Nazis. They were victims, just as surely as the victims in the concentration camps."

The parallel Reagan seemed to be drawing between the Jewish victims of the Holocaust and the Nazi troops struck many in America as bizarrely ahistorical. "To equate the fate of members of the German army bent on world conquest with that of six million Jewish civilians, including one million innocent children, is a distortion of history, a perversion of language and a callous offense to the Jewish community," Rabbi Alexander Schindler of the Union of American Hebrew Congregations asserted. "The president has made a terrible statement that brings shame to the American people. It insults not only Jews and others who suffered and perished in the camps, but every American and Allied soldier who gave his life to liberate Europe from the Nazi death grip."

By this time reporters had visited the Bitburg cemetery and discovered that the dead buried there included members of the Waffen SS, the military wing of Hitler's elite guard. The discovery raised the controversy to a new level, for even forty years after the war the mere mention of the SS sent shudders through those who had suffered under Nazi rule. Further investigation linked the Bitburg dead to one of the worst single atrocities committed by an SS army division during the war: the massacre of more than six hundred civilian residents of a French village in 1944.

The administration tried to mitigate the damage by inviting Holocaust survivor Elie Wiesel to the White House, where he received a medal for his work on behalf of human rights. Wiesel thanked the president and America for defeating the Nazis and liberating the death camps. "But, Mr. President," he continued, "I wouldn't be the person I am, and you wouldn't respect me for what I am, if I were not to tell you also of the sadness that is in my heart for what happened during the last week. And I am sure that you, too, are sad for the same reasons. What can I do? I belong to a traumatized generation. And to us, as to you, symbols are important." The symbolism of the president's visit to Bitburg was tragically misguided. Wiesel credited Reagan's claim that he hadn't known about the SS graves when he accepted Kohl's invitation to visit the cemetery. "Of course, you didn't know. But now we all are aware. May I, Mr. President, if it's possible at all, implore you to do something else, to find a way, to find another way, another site. That place, Mr. President, is not your place. Your place is with the victims of the SS."

THE WASHINGTON MEDIA corps was willing to blame Don Regan for the public relations disaster the Bitburg affair had become. Pundit after opiner whispered or shouted that Jim Baker would never have allowed such a debacle had he still been chief of staff. Regan resented the charges. "The commitment in question was already on the president's calendar when I arrived at the White House," he recalled. Regan blamed Mike Deaver for not keeping on top of the planning and especially for not checking the roster of the Bitburg dead more carefully. "How the hell did *that* happen?" he demanded of Deaver when the story of the SS graves broke. Washington insiders knew Deaver had a drinking problem, which he admitted after he left the White House and was charged with perjury in an investigation of lobbying activities. Deaver's alcoholism didn't prevent the jury from convicting him (though it might have helped mitigate his sentence), but it lent retrospective credence to the rumors at the time of the Bitburg affair that his resort to the bottle had impaired his performance as deputy chief of staff. Regan reiterated the rumors in pointing the finger at Deaver for the SS oversight. "It was said that he was drinking a quart of Scotch whisky a day and masking his breath with mints while he went about his duties in the White House," Regan wrote. Regan added that he himself hadn't been able to recognize Deaver's impairment because Deaver had disguised it so well. "I never saw the slightest sign in Deaver's behavior that he was drinking to excess; in fact I was then under the impression that he was a teetotaler."

Some in Washington blamed Helmut Kohl for snookering the president. Kohl's constituents included World War II veterans who resented the abasement forced upon Germany by international opinion as a result of the Holocaust. By no means did all of them long for the days of the Third Reich, but more than a few felt that their entire generation was wrongly blamed for the war crimes of the worst among them. A visit by Reagan to a military cemetery, arranged by Kohl, would reassure these voters that the chancellor sympathized with them.

However Bitburg landed on Reagan's schedule, the decision to go ahead with the visit in the face of the public criticism was the president's alone. Reagan characteristically blamed the media for making too much of missteps by his administration. "The press had a field day assailing me because I'd accepted Helmut Kohl's invitation," he wrote in his diary as the controversy was just beginning. "Helmut had in mind observing the end-of-WWII anniversary as the end of hatred and the beginning of friendship and peace that has lasted forty years." The media had inflamed the understandable sensitivities of well-meaning people. "I have repeatedly said we must never forget the Holocaust and remember it so it will never happen again. But some of our Jewish friends are now on the warpath." Yet they wouldn't change his mind. "There is no way I'll back down and run for cover." It would send a very bad signal to the world, besides being unjustified. "Yes, the German soldiers were the enemy and part of the whole Nazi hate era," Reagan wrote. "But we won and we killed those soldiers. What is wrong with saying 'let's never be enemies again'? Would Helmut be wrong if he visited Arlington Cemetery on one of his U.S. visits?"

Reagan's determination didn't prevent him from trying to soften the impact of his cemetery visit. Kohl repeated his invitation to Reagan to visit a concentration camp; Reagan this time accepted. "Helmut may very well have solved our problem," he noted. He sent Deaver to Germany to finalize the plans, with special instructions to make sure no new problems arose.

The furor persisted, however. "The press has the bit in their teeth and are stirring up as much trouble as they can," Reagan wrote. He took pains to publicize that he would visit a concentration camp as well as the military cemetery. "By nightfall the TV press was distorting that statement," he muttered.

Deaver arrived back from Germany and explained that the visit to a camp was firmly on the schedule. But Bergen-Belsen suited Kohl better than Dachau, and he had seen no reason to insist on the latter. Kohl himself called Reagan to confirm the new schedule and to thank the president for his steadfastness. The chancellor was "quite emotional," Don Regan wrote in his notes of the call. Reagan appreciated the message and the emotion. "He told me my remarks about the dead soldiers being the victims of Nazism as the Jews in the Holocaust were had been well received in Germany," Reagan commented to himself. "He was emphatic that to cancel the cemetery now would be a disaster in his country and an insult to the German people. I told him I would not cancel."

Reagan received encouragement from closer to home as well. "I was very *proud* of your stand," George Bush wrote to him. "If I can help absorb some heat, send me into battle. It's not easy, but you are *right*!!"

Reagan valued the support, but the criticism was no less important in making him hold his ground. "The uproar about my trip to Germany and the Bitburg cemetery was cover stuff in *Newsweek* and *Time*," he wrote derisively. "They just won't stop. Well, I'm not going to cancel anything no matter how much the bastards scream." Forty-eight hours later he wrote, "Every day seems to begin with the latest press muckraking over whether I should or shouldn't go to the Bitburg cemetery in Germany. Well, d--n their hides. I think it's morally right and I'm going."

THE PRESIDENT JOINED the other G7 leaders in Bonn in early May. Discussions centered on trade and finance. Japan's Yasuhiro Nakasone proposed a new round of the trade talks that had been going on recurrently since World War II; he sought to head off protectionism, particularly against exports of Japanese automobiles. France's Mitterrand pushed for monetary talks to adjust exchange rates, which had hurt the French economy of late. Britain's Thatcher cemented her mutual admiration pact with the president.

Helmut Kohl spoke with Reagan privately for nearly an hour. Reagan assured him he wasn't upset by the furor in the media. Kohl was pleased. "He said I had won the heart of Germany by standing firm on this," Reagan recorded. The German people confirmed Kohl's assertion. "In all our motoring the streets are lined with people clapping, waving, cheering—all I'm sure to let me know they don't agree with the continuing press sniping about the upcoming visit to Bitburg," Reagan wrote.

On the morning of May 5, Reagan visited the grave site of Konrad Adenauer, the founding father of West Germany, in the hills above the Rhine. Nancy Reagan and Mrs. Kohl laid flowers on the grave. The Reagans and the Kohls then boarded Air Force One for a flight to Hanover. A German helicopter carried them to Bergen-Belsen.

Reagan wasn't used to speaking to hostile audiences. As California governor he had occasionally encountered hecklers, but as president he was insulated from voiced dissent. On this day, however, the dissenters were fully in evidence. They came from Germany, the United States, Britain, France, Israel, and other countries. They were Christians and Jews, civilians and military veterans, the politically active and the heretofore silent. Guards, and reverence for the dead, kept them out of the camp itself, but they shouted in protest from the borders of the memorial. Obviously referring to Bitburg, they chanted, "You don't belong there . . . We don't want you to go in there."

Reagan saw and heard them. He affected unconcern. Asked what he thought of the protests, he shrugged. "It's a free country," he said. But he understood he had one chance to make the situation right, or at least better. A light rain fell from a gray sky as Reagan and Nancy walked beside the mounds of heather that marked the mass graves of those killed at the camp. He stood with bowed head before the obelisk commemorating the victims. He placed a wreath of green ferns at the base of the stone pillar; a ribbon on the wreath read, "The People of the United States of America."

He spoke in a low voice that suited the place and the mood. He talked of the evil that Hitler had wreaked on the world and on the souls buried in this place in particular. "For year after year, until that man and his evil were destroyed, hell yawned forth its awful contents," Reagan said. "People were brought here for no other purpose but to suffer and die—to go unfed when hungry, uncared for when sick, tortured when the whim struck, and left to have misery consume them when all there was around them was misery." Death had ruled at the camp, but death had not ruled forever—which was why he and Chancellor Kohl had come to the camp this day. "We're here because humanity refuses to accept that freedom of the spirit of man can ever be extinguished. We're here to commemorate that life triumphed over the tragedy and the death of the Holocaust— overcame the suffering, the sickness, the testing and, yes, the gassings. We're here today to confirm that the horror cannot outlast hope, and that even from the worst of all things, the best may come forth."

Reagan quoted Anne Frank, who had perished at Bergen-Belsen: "I see the world gradually being turned into a wilderness. I hear the ever approaching thunder which will destroy us too; I can feel the suffering of millions and yet, if I looked up into the heavens I think that it will all come right, that this cruelty too will end and that peace and tranquility will return again." He cited the Talmud: "It was only through suffering that the children of Israel obtained three priceless and coveted gifts: the Torah, the Land of Israel, and the World to Come." In his own voice he added, "Yes, out of this sickness—as crushing and cruel as it was—there was hope for the world as well as for the world to come. Out of the ashes— hope, and from all the pain—promise." The present generation bore witness to the pain as well as to the promise. "We're all witnesses; we share the glistening hope that rests in every human soul. Hope leads us, if we're prepared to trust it, toward what our President Lincoln called the better angels of our nature. And then, rising above all this cruelty, out of this tragic and nightmarish time, beyond the anguish, the pain and the suffering for all time, we can and must pledge: Never again."

No one applauded when Reagan finished. Applause was out of place. But his words took the edge off the protests. Even his critics had to appreciate his seriousness; whatever his other shortcomings, he clearly understood what had happened here and what it meant.

The group proceeded to Bitburg. After all the uproar, Reagan took pains not to draw attention to himself. He neither spoke nor laid a wreath. He deferred to retired American general Matthew Ridgway, who had fought his way into Germany in 1945 with Eisenhower and the U.S. Army. Ridgway shook hands with an equally venerable German officer while a military band played the German equivalent of taps. Michael Deaver made partial amends for his public relations faux pas by narrowly restricting television coverage, ensuring that cameras could not pan from the president to the gravestones showing the SS insignia. Within minutes Reagan and Kohl and their wives had departed.

74

DONALD REGAN THOUGHT the visit had gone as well as it could have, under the circumstances. "Few presidents can have passed through a day of such unrelieved mourning in time of peace," he wrote. "The symbols and memories of untimely death lay all around from morning till night. Reagan went through the ceremonies like a president, shoulders squared, features composed, every gesture correct. It was clear that he felt that he was carrying out a difficult and historic duty." The somberness penetrated Reagan's being. "As we walked to the car after the president's speech at Bergen-Belsen I made small talk about the weather, hoping to divert his thoughts," Regan recalled. "He shuddered. 'It's given me quite a chill,' he said."

Reagan was quietly satisfied with the outcome. "It was the morally right thing to do," he commented that evening. Kohl's reaction confirmed this view. The chancellor and his wife wished Reagan and Nancy goodbye the next day. "They were quite emotional," Reagan observed. "Helmut swore undying friendship."

NANCY REAGAN TOOK a very different view of the Bitburg affair. "I was furious at Helmut Kohl for not getting us out of it," she recalled of the cemetery visit. She had wanted her husband to reconsider. "I urged Ronnie to cancel the visit." She was distressed when he refused, as she was distressed by anything that showed him in an unfavorable light. "And yet I was also proud of Ronnie for following his conscience," she allowed.

She blamed Don Regan for putting her husband in such an embarrassing position, and she mildly blamed her husband for permitting Regan to be where he could do such harm. "If, by some miracle, I could take back one decision in Ronnie's presidency, it would be his agreement in January 1985 that Jim Baker and Donald Regan should swap jobs," she wrote. Speaking for herself, who could have vetoed the swap before Mike Deaver took it to the president, she reflected, "It seemed like a good idea at the time—a little unusual, perhaps, but reasonable." Baker was exhausted as chief of staff, and Regan was eager to step in. "When Baker and Regan suggested the switch, there was no reason to expect that this new arrangement would lead to a political disaster."

Don Regan was experiencing his own doubts about his new position and all it entailed. "I enjoy this job a little more than Treasury because of the excitement and being 'at the point,'" he confided to a friend. "However, it doesn't give me as much time for thinking as Treasury did, and certainly I can't spend nearly the time I want in analyzing as I was able to do at Merrill Lynch." Regan sought to remedy the analytical deficit by devising a second-term strategy for the president. He and his staff produced a document laying out priorities in domestic and foreign policy. These included tax reform and the ongoing budget battle at home, as well as a variety of initiatives abroad: arms-control talks with the Soviets, trade negotiations with America's trading partners, the fight against leftism in Central America and the Caribbean, efforts toward peace in the Middle East.

Regan drew from his experience in the corporate world, where a chief executive's staff would hammer out an action plan and present it to the boss, who would approve some parts of the plan and reject others. Regan deemed the document he handed Reagan a work in progress, with further work to follow the president's reactions. Regan knew Reagan well enough not to expect a line-by-line critique, but he thought the president would take the exercise seriously, read the document carefully, and offer substantive comments. "Instead, Ronald Reagan read the paper while he was at the ranch and handed it back to me on his return without spoken or written comment," Regan recalled.

"What did you think of it?" Regan asked.

"It's good, Don," Reagan said. "It's really good, Don."

Regan expected the president to elaborate. But he didn't. "He had no questions to ask, no objections to raise, no instructions to issue," Regan wrote. "I realized that the policy that would determine the course of the world's most powerful nation for the next two years and deeply influence the fate of the Republican Party in the 1986 midterm elections had been adopted without amendment."

Regan couldn't believe he had anticipated Reagan's desires perfectly. "I was uneasy," he remembered. "Did the president really want us to do all these things with no more discussion than this?" He was tempted to press Reagan to be sure. Did he want his staff to move forward on each of these fronts just as the paper specified? But respect for the president's office bound his tongue. "It is one thing brashly to speak your mind to an ordinary mortal and another to say, 'Wait a minute!' to the president of the United States. The mystery of the office is a potent inhibitor. The president, you feel, has his reasons."

Regan realized that Reagan's leadership style was unique. "Another president would almost certainly have had his own ideas on the mechanics of policy, but Reagan did not trouble himself with such minutiae," Regan wrote. "His preoccupation was with what might be called 'the outer presidency.' He was content to let others cope with the inner details of running the administration." Regan knew that Kennedy had often jumped the chain of command to question mid-level officeholders about details of policy. Nixon immersed himself in the detailed formulation of policy toward China and the Soviet Union. Carter was notorious for micromanagement. "But Reagan chose his aides and then followed their advice almost without question."

The system worked well most of the time, but even when it didn't, Reagan remained unflappable and removed. "Never—absolutely never in my experience—did President Reagan really lose his temper or utter a rude or unkind word," Regan wrote. "Never did he issue a direct order, although I, at least, sometimes devoutly wished that he would. He listened, acquiesced, played his role and waited for the next act to be written." Regan, coming from the private sector, found this behavior baffling. But he couldn't fault the president's results. "Reagan's method had worked well enough to make him president of the United States, and well enough for the nation under his leadership to transform its mood from pessimism to optimism, its economy from stagnation to steady growth and its position in the world from weakness to strength. Common sense suggested that the president knew something that the rest of us did not know. It was my clear duty to do things his way."

75

R EAGAN'S WAY WASN'T always easy to discern. A month after
Bitburg the president confronted a problem he had been preparing for since his campaign against Jimmy Carter. Reagan
had excoriated Carter for failing to secure the release of the fifty-two
American hostages in Iran, and he took pride that their captors had freed
the hostages before having to deal with him as president. The hostage
problem receded from the headlines, but it didn't disappear. Its center of
gravity shifted to Lebanon, where that country's civil war allowed militia
groups to operate with impunity. Hezbollah was the most active; supported by Iran, it waged irregular war against the Israeli occupation of
Lebanon and against countries that supported Israel. The United States
topped the list of Israel's supporters; on this account Americans became
targets of Hezbollah operations, including kidnappings. By the middle of
1985 the group held seven Americans it had seized in Lebanon.

Reagan tried not to publicize the hostages' predicament lest the publicity encourage other kidnappings. He felt deeply for the hostages and their
families, but he discovered what Carter had learned: that the instruments
for freeing the hostages were frustratingly ineffectual or self-defeatingly
expensive. American intelligence agencies couldn't figure out where the
hostages were being held, and their captors seemed to be moving them frequently. Any military rescue operation risked killing the very people it was
supposed to save. "Our options were few, and I spent many, many hours late
at night wondering how we could rescue the hostages, trying to sleep while
images of those lonely Americans rolled past in my mind," Reagan recalled.
"Almost every morning at my national security briefings, I began by asking
the same question: 'Any progress on getting the hostages out of Lebanon?'"

As of the summer of 1985 the answer was no. And that June the hostage problem grew dramatically worse. Two hijackers associated with Hezbollah seized control of TWA flight 847 from Athens bound for Rome. The 153 passengers and crew were mostly Americans. The hijackers forced the plane to reroute to Beirut, where they released some women and children, refueled, and headed for Algiers, where more women and children were released. The hijackers then ordered the plane back to Beirut, where they dumped the body of a U.S. Navy diver, Robert Stethem, whom they had killed, apparently to demonstrate their determination. Several gunmen in sympathy with the hijackers boarded the plane, which returned to Algiers. Some additional passengers were released. The plane flew once more to Beirut.

Reagan had been alerted as soon as American intelligence learned of the hijacking. He followed the crisis as it unfolded. And he learned that the hijackers were demanding that Israel release more than seven hundred Shia prisoners Israel's army had taken in Lebanon, as their condition for freeing the Americans they still held. Israel had indicated confidentially to the American government that it had planned to free the Atlit prisoners, as they were called for their place of detention in Israel, but it was disinclined to do so under duress from the terrorists. Yet it was willing to help the United States if so requested. "The U.S. at the highest level must ask them to do it," Reagan explained in his diary. "This of course means that we, not they, would be violating our policy of not negotiating with terrorists. To do so, of course—negotiate with terrorists—is to encourage more terrorism."

Reagan nonetheless thought there might be a way to shape the discussion in order to satisfy the hijackers and preserve the appearance of refusing to negotiate with terrorists. A Lebanese Shia, Nabih Berri, had emerged as a spokesman for the hijackers; Reagan reasoned that the American government could talk to Berri without breaking its rule against negotiating with terrorists. "I suggested that if Israel said to Berri—we were going to release these detainees anyway, we'll expedite it if you let the Americans go—no one would be giving in to terrorists," Reagan wrote after meeting with his national security team.

George Shultz didn't like the sound of it. Whether through a middleman or not, the United States would be negotiating with terrorists. "You can't square that circle, Mr. President," Shultz said.

In public the president stuck to stated policy. Reporters shouted questions as he stepped off his helicopter returning from a weekend at Camp

David. "Sir, can this be negotiated?" one asked. Another said, "Would you like to see Israel return some of those Shiite prisoners?"

"This is a decision for them to make," Reagan responded. "And the decision isn't so simple as just trading prisoners. The decision is at what point can you pay off the terrorists without endangering people from here on out once they find out that their tactics succeed."

"Are you still opposed, then? Are you still opposed to negotiating with terrorists?"

"This has always been a position of ours, yes," Reagan said.

"So how might this be worked out, then?"

"I can't comment. I think that we're going to continue doing the things that we're doing and just hope that they themselves will see that, for their own safety, they'd better turn these people loose."

In a formal news conference two days later Reagan spoke more vigorously. "America will never make concessions to terrorists," he said. "To do so would only invite more terrorism. Nor will we ask nor pressure any other government to do so. Once we head down that path there would be no end to it, no end to the suffering of innocent people, no end to the bloody ransom all civilized nations must pay."

Yet Israel insisted on blurring the line between negotiating with terrorists and not doing so. "The Israelis are not being helpful," Reagan complained confidentially. "They have gone public with the statement that they would release their prisoners if we asked them to. Well, we can't do that because then we would be rewarding the terrorists and encouraging more terrorism." The next day Reagan grumbled that Yitzhak Rabin, the Israeli defense minister, had "loused things up by establishing a linkage we insist does not exist."

Eventually, the administration and the Israeli government coordinated their stories. The Israelis convinced Reagan that they had indeed intended to release the Shia prisoners and would have done so if the hijacking had not taken place. Reagan took this as sufficient ground for encouraging Hafez al-Assad, the leader of Syria and a new prospective go-between, to pass along a message. "It has been the position of the U.S. throughout this event that the hijacking and hostage-taking is preventing the planned release by Israel of Atlit prisoners," George Shultz cabled the American embassy in Damascus. "Therefore you may inform the Syrians that the President believes that Syria may be confident in expecting the release of the Lebanese prisoners after the freeing of the passengers of TWA 847, without any linkage between the two subjects."

This understanding became the basis for the hostage release. The Americans were taken to Syria, where they boarded a U.S. Air Force plane that flew them to West Germany. The Israelis freed the Shia prisoners over the space of several weeks, saying the decision had nothing to do with the hijacking.

Reagan discreetly celebrated a victory, offset by sorrow at the loss of Robert Stethem. He placed flowers on Stethem's grave at Arlington National Cemetery, then flew to Andrews Air Force Base to greet the hostages and their families. "It was a nice homecoming ceremony and a heartwarming one," he recorded.

But the seven original hostages remained in captivity. And Reagan continued to ask his advisers if there was any progress toward their release.

REAGAN'S FATHER-IN-LAW, Dr. Loyal Davis, had long preached the virtues of regular physical exams. As Reagan aged and then became president, he gave the advice the weight it deserved. A colonoscopy in 1984 resulted in the discovery of a polyp, which was excised and found to be noncancerous. A follow-up exam in March 1985 revealed another polyp, and his doctors scheduled a removal procedure for Friday, July 12, at Bethesda Naval Hospital. The president prepared for the procedure by abstaining from solid food and by drinking GoLytely, a laxative that uncomfortably but thoroughly flushed his digestive system.

Reagan's brush with death in 1981 and the questions that had arisen regarding the chain of command during his surgery sensitized the White House to such matters, and so before being sedated, this time he signed a letter temporarily transferring power, under the Twenty-Fifth Amendment, to Vice President Bush.

The anesthesia took hold, and the surgery went forward. The operating team removed the polyp but in the process discovered another, larger one. Nancy sensed the consequence of the discovery before she heard it. "I sat in the waiting room and talked with Larry Speakes," she remembered of that afternoon. "Ronnie was alert and fine afterwards, and making jokes as usual. But I noticed that the doctors weren't laughing. I also had the feeling they were looking at me funny, especially John Hutton"—Reagan's regular physician—"who seemed to be avoiding my eyes. The doctors suggested that Ronnie lie down, and that I come with them into the other room. Then one of them pulled up a chair and said, 'We have some bad news for you.'"

Since March 1981, Nancy had feared obsessively for her husband's physical well-being. She had gradually managed to fight back the fear, but now it seized her again. "I felt as if I had been hit by a ten-ton truck," she said. She insisted that the doctors tell her all they knew.

They explained that they had discovered a mass the size of a golf ball on the side of the colon. It looked cancerous, though they wouldn't know for sure until the completion of a biopsy. But it had to be removed in any event, lest it turn cancerous. They also had to test Reagan's other organs to see if they showed signs of cancer.

"It was all so sudden I had trouble believing it," she recounted. She listened while Dr. Hutton explained the options. She and Reagan could proceed to Camp David for the weekend, as they had planned, and return Monday to Bethesda for surgery. Or they could wait for ten days, until a scheduled visit by Chinese president Li had been completed. Or they could hold Reagan in the hospital and remove the polyp the next day.

Nancy gave the first two options scarcely a thought. "All I cared about was getting the operation over with as quickly as possible," she said. "Now that we knew about the polyp, I couldn't stand the prospect of letting it stay in Ronnie any longer than we had to."

She took matters into her own hands. "I want to be the one to tell him," she said to the doctors. "And please, when we go in to see him, don't mention cancer. We don't know for sure that it *is* cancer, and there's no point in using that word unless we're positive."

She knew her husband hadn't liked the presurgery preparation, especially the GoLytely flush. And so as she explained the need for a second procedure, she cast her argument in those terms. "As long as we're here, why don't we do it tomorrow and get it over with? Because if we come back next week, you'll have to drink that Go Lightly [*sic*] all over again."

Whether because he hated GoLytely or because he loved his wife, or simply because he wanted to get the operation over with, Reagan assented. The surgery was scheduled for the next morning.

"NANCY REAGAN STAMMERS slightly when she is upset," Don Regan recalled. "And her voice was unsteady when she called me from Bethesda Naval Hospital." Regan remembered the sequence of decisions regarding Reagan's care differently than Nancy did. "In illness of this kind speedy treatment is essential, and so I was concerned—apprehensive would be a better word—when she told me that the operation might be delayed for a day and a half. 'I'm reading something into this,' I said, speaking cautiously because we were on the telephone. 'Am I on firm ground in doing it?'

"'Yes, possibly,' the first lady replied."

Nancy later asserted that her careful language reflected the gravity of her husband's case. "I meant, of course, that Ronnie's condition was probably more serious than I was willing to say over the phone."

Regan thought he heard spousal concern but something else as well in her evasive answer. "I feared two things—first, that President Reagan's condition was more serious than his wife had been able to tell me over the telephone, and second, that the first lady was choosing the date for surgery in consultation with her astrologer. Of the two possibilities the second seemed more likely. Virtually every major move and decision the Reagans made during my time as White House chief of staff was cleared in advance with a woman in San Francisco"—Regan did not then know Joan Quigley's name—"who drew up horoscopes to make certain that the planets were in a favorable alignment for the enterprise." Regan went on: "She had become such a factor in my work, and in the highest affairs of the nation, that at one point I kept a color-coded calendar on my desk (numerals highlighted in green ink for 'good' days, red for 'bad' days, yellow for 'iffy' days) as an aid to remembering when it was propitious to move the president of the United States from one place to another, or schedule him to speak in public, or commence negotiations with a foreign power."

In this case Nancy's astrologer seemed to be influencing the president's medical treatment. "On the telephone from Bethesda, Mrs. Reagan continued to suggest that the removal of the polyp would be delayed. 'Tell Larry'"—Speakes—"'to say that the president will have surgery next week,' she said. It was now Friday afternoon. 'Larry can say the polyp was larger than expected, but he mustn't say a word more than that.'"

Regan sympathized with Nancy but questioned her judgment. "Her tone was insistent and tinged with anxiety. This was not the moment to dispute the wishes of a worried wife. But I did not altogether agree with the advice she was giving me. The risks of withholding the smallest part of this story from the media and thereby creating the suspicion of a cover-up were obvious. So was the danger of making a statement about the timing of the operation that might have to be withdrawn."

Regan called Speakes at the hospital and cautioned him to tell all he knew but nothing more. "No dissimulation. And no alarms."

A short while later he spoke to the senior physician on the case and received his first professional briefing. The polyp had to come out, and the president would be hospitalized for a week to ten days.

By Regan's recollection, it was Reagan who decided on surgery the next day. "Why wait?" the president asked the doctors. "Do the tests and go ahead with the operation. I can function just as well in the hospital as at home."

The surgery was straightforward, and the growth was removed, along with a short section of the president's colon. The more troublesome question was whether the cancer, if any, had spread. A biopsy revealed that the mass was indeed cancerous, but additional tests indicated that the cancer had not spread. Reagan required no chemotherapy or other continuing treatment, although he would need regular tests to see that the cancer had not recurred.

IN HIS DAYS as chief of staff, James Baker had kept in his files a document titled "Rumsfeld's Rules." Donald Rumsfeld had been Gerald Ford's chief of staff, and he shared with Baker what he had learned in the job. Rumsfeld's first rule was "Don't play President." Twelve pages of additional rules followed, culminating in the last: "Don't play President." Baker himself added his own précis of what a chief of staff must never forget: "Nobody elected you."

If Don Regan ever read Rumsfeld's rules or heard Baker's version, he didn't take the lesson. Following Reagan's surgery, the CEO in Regan grew increasingly evident. "President Reagan's chief of staff, Donald T. Regan, is the dominant figure in White House plans for operating the government while Mr. Reagan recovers from abdominal surgery, White House aides said today," the *New York Times* reported on July 15. "The aides said Mr. Regan's role has extended beyond what had already become an increasingly powerful one in running White House operations." The front-page article was accompanied by two photographs, one of Reagan and Nancy in his hospital room, the other of Regan at work.

The former photograph pleased Nancy; the latter did not. Nor did she appreciate the lionization of Regan in the rest of the article. "White House aides said Mr. Regan, who is 66 years old, is emerging as one of the most powerful chiefs of staff in years, and Mr. Reagan's illness has placed the chief of staff squarely in the center of decision-making on domestic and foreign policy." The recent developments consolidated a trend that had been under way since Regan arrived at the White House, the article said. "Even before the illness, Mr. Regan made it plain to the senior White House staff and administration officials that he, and he alone, largely controlled access to Mr. Reagan." With each passing day, Regan's grip on the machinery of the administration grew firmer. "Everyone works for Regan," one unnamed White House aide said.

Nancy resented the general tone of the piece as disrespectful to her husband. But the part that galled her most was a sentence that made it sound as though she herself were subordinate to the chief of staff: "Nancy Reagan, the president's wife, has come to rely increasingly on Mr. Regan, a factor that further solidifies his position."

"For the first few months we got along fine," Nancy wrote of Regan, eliding her anger over the Bitburg affair. "It wasn't until July 1985, when Ronnie had his cancer operation, that Don and I had our first run-in. Within forty-eight hours of the surgery, Don wanted to bring in George Bush and Bud McFarlane to meet with the president. I thought that was much too soon—and so did the doctors. But Don thought it was more important for Ronnie to resume his schedule of appointments. 'Let's wait,' I told Don. 'Remember, he's just had major surgery. I know he's the president, but don't forget that he's also a patient like any other patient. If you push him too hard, he could have a relapse.'"

Nancy took pains to puncture what she saw as Regan's pretensions. "Don came out to Bethesda every day, and he wanted to make the trip by helicopter," she recounted. "That seemed wrong to me. I thought it was inappropriate for anyone other than the president to use the helicopter except in an emergency. The drive to the hospital took about forty-five minutes, and everybody else who came traveled by car. I must have had some inkling, even then, of what increasingly bothered me about Don Regan, which was that he often acted as if *he* were president."

Regan thought Nancy was being overly protective. He perceived the president as far sturdier than the vulnerable invalid of her imagination. Reagan greeted Regan and Fred Fielding, the White House counsel, with a joke when they entered the postoperative recovery room to see if he was ready to reassume the authority he had again surrendered to George Bush during his surgery. "The Russians have dropped the bomb!" Reagan said, referring to the sober expressions on Regan's and Fielding's faces. Regan assured the president that they were simply concerned for his health. Tentatively, Regan handed the president the required letter. "Can you read?" Regan asked.

"Let me see that thing," Reagan said, snatching the letter. He held it at arm's length, as he didn't have his reading glasses handy.

"Do you understand it?" Regan asked.

"Yup," Reagan said. "I'll sign it now." He wrote his name with a flourish.

"Then, in an impressive display of alertness," Regan continued, "he took up where he had left off before he went under the anesthetic." Reagan's last words had been criticism of Bob Dole for not supporting the administration on the budget. "What's the matter with Bob Dole?" Reagan resumed. "He's got to be a leader on this budget." Regan had rarely seen him sharper. "He seemed so strong and clear-minded that I took another minute or two to tell him that all was calm on the international scene. He listened, then thought of something that made his cheerful expression change. 'Any word on the hostages?' he asked."

After some discussion of the hostages, Reagan demanded, "How long do I have to stay here?" Reagan's brother, Neil, coincidentally had recently undergone surgery similar to the president's and been released from the hospital after just a few days. "I want to get out of here soon, Don," Reagan said. "See what you can do."

"Mr. President, forget it," Regan said. "Just follow your doctors' orders."

Though Regan refused to abet Reagan's early release, the president's tone and demeanor made him think he could stand occasional visitors, including Bush and McFarlane. The vice president had been at his summer home in Maine when Reagan's routine procedure turned more serious, and he had flown straight to Washington. He wished to pay his respects to the president, and Regan thought he ought to be allowed to. The visit could take only minutes. McFarlane also wanted a moment of the president's time. The national security adviser said he needed to tell the president something important. Regan put Bush and McFarlane on the president's schedule.

Nancy was outraged when she learned of it. "Why are you doing this?" she demanded of Regan by phone. "It's too much. He needs rest." Regan explained his thinking. She was not persuaded. She took the opportunity to express her displeasure at his plan to use the presidential helicopter for the trip from the White House to Bethesda. Regan replied that the helicopter would conserve valuable time. She brushed his answer away. She said the president's helicopter was for the president.

Regan retreated tentatively. He said he would consult with the president's doctors before allowing the visit by Bush and McFarlane. And he would reconsider the use of Marine One.

He had scarcely put down the phone when he received a call from Edward Hickey, who handled White House transportation and had known the Reagans for years. "I'd cancel the helicopter if I were you, Don," he said. "The first lady's staff are talking about it."

"Why should they talk about it?" Regan responded. "I'm just trying to save time. I've got to go out there seven days a week and it's forty minutes by car each way. That's more than ten hours down the drain in a single week."

"That would be good reason to fly instead of drive under normal circumstances," Hickey said. "But right now circumstances aren't normal. The buzzards are out, Don. Be careful what you're doing."

Regan later recalled being surprised at this comment. He had grown used to gossip around the West Wing, though he didn't like it. But gossip from the East Wing, the realm of the First Lady, was something he hadn't expected. He liked it even less. Yet he sensed that it might be more troublesome than the West Wing whispers.

"Okay," he told Hickey. "Cancel the damn helicopter."

B EFORE HE BECAME president, Reagan derided the potential of
personal diplomacy, especially with leaders of communist countries. The godless commissars were immune to charm, humor,
persuasion, or appeals to a shared humanity; they responded only to force
or its threat.

But as president, Reagan took a different view. He was supremely
confident of his own ability to find common ground with foreign counterparts, even the leaders of the Soviet Union. He wanted to get into a room
with Brezhnev, but the longtime Kremlin boss ignored his invitation to a
summit and then died. Andropov and Chernenko shortly followed him
to the grave.

Then Gorbachev came along, and Reagan thought he would finally
get his wish. Gorbachev responded cautiously at first to Reagan's suggestion of a personal meeting, but as he gained his footing with the Politburo,
he indicated that a summit would indeed make sense. Date and location
would have to be determined, but the principle of a face-to-face meeting
was one he could embrace.

THE POSSIBILITY OF a summit triggered a battle within the American
foreign policy establishment. Henry Kissinger visited the White House
to urge Reagan to move slowly. An opportunity existed, the co-architect
of détente declared, but it must be handled very carefully. "Let it mature,"
Kissinger said. Zbigniew Brzezinski warned against Soviet tricks at a
summit. "They will spring a surprise so as to put the president on the

defensive," Brzezinski told Don Regan. "This is a contest." The president needed to be thoroughly prepared.

The battle raged most heatedly inside the administration. The hard-line anticommunist wing, headquartered in the Defense Department and the CIA, was as opposed to summitry as Reagan once had been. "Caspar Weinberger was utterly convinced that there was no potential benefit in negotiating anything with the Soviet leaders and that most negotiations were dangerous traps," Jack Matlock recalled. Matlock was a Soviet expert from the foreign service who had been pulled from the diplomatic ranks to head the National Security Council's Soviet and European division. He became Reagan's right-hand man in dealing with the Kremlin. He found Weinberger's opposition to summitry irksome but bureaucratically predictable. The business of the Pentagon was weapons development and procurement, not diplomacy and negotiation; the Pentagon's chief could be expected to promote the former and oppose the latter. But Matlock thought Weinberger pushed the opposition too far, for even after Reagan made clear he wanted to meet with Gorbachev, Weinberger resorted to leaks that undermined and implicitly insulted the president. Matlock thought Reagan thought so too, though Reagan rose above the issue. "When leaks that represented his ideas turned up in the press, most often in the *Washington Times* or in comments by columnists and television pundits Rowland Evans and Robert Novak," Matlock said of Weinberger, "Reagan was annoyed, sometimes even infuriated, but he usually tolerated them. He disliked direct confrontation with cabinet members, particularly old friends like Weinberger. He also understood that he would need the acquiescence, if not the active support, of the hardliners in his administration if he was to implement a positive agenda with the Soviet Union."

William Casey lacked Weinberger's long ties to Reagan, but as intelligence director he possessed information and therefore credibility of a sort commanded by no one else in the administration. Casey didn't believe Gorbachev was a sincere reformer in either domestic or foreign policy. "While some Soviet officials have indicated he is sympathetic to the use of pragmatic methods, including tapping private initiative," Casey wrote to Reagan, "his statements and actions underscore his overall commitment to the current economic system and his determination to make it work better." In foreign policy Gorbachev adhered to the traditional Soviet belief in military strength and the ultimate victory of socialism. On this account the United States needed to pursue its own policy of strength, and it needed to convince the Kremlin it would continue to do so. "Achieving this Soviet conviction against the doubts that are accumulating in Moscow will require political victories for your policy agenda in the Congress, the U.S. public, and the Alliance," Casey wrote. "It will require skill and adherence to a durable strategic concept in dealing with all the issues that attach to the U.S.-Soviet superpower struggle." Summitry was distracting at best, pernicious at worst.

George Shultz at State was the strongest voice in favor of a summit. He was also the person with the closest contacts in the Soviet government. He met regularly with Andrei Gromyko, the Soviet foreign minister, who would presumably deliver any message from Gorbachev accepting Reagan's invitation to get together. Shultz tried to crack Gromyko's stolid front. At a diplomatic dinner Gromyko described Gorbachev's campaign against alcoholism; Shultz responded that the Reagan administration was trying to deter drunk driving in America. He repeated a joke then circulating in Russia, according to Shultz's informants. Two men are standing in a long line waiting to buy vodka from the state-run store. The line hardly moves. Finally one says, "I'm fed up. I'm going over to the Kremlin to shoot Gorbachev." He leaves. He comes back a while later. His friend is still in line. "Well, did you shoot him?" the friend asks. "Hell, no," the first man says. "The line there was even longer than this one!" Gromyko didn't crack a smile.

But he eventually raised the issue of a summit. He said Reagan would be welcome in Moscow in November. Shultz rejoined that it was the turn of the Soviet leader to come to the United States. Gromyko said this was out of the question. But Europe was not.

"Are you suggesting Geneva?" Shultz asked.

"If you say Geneva, I'll have to say Helsinki," Gromyko responded.

Shultz took this as progress. He went to Reagan to make sure he was still on board. He detected some doubt, apparently provoked by Weinberger and Casey. Reagan said November might be too soon. Perhaps he should play hard to get.

Shultz pushed back. "Many key people in your administration do not want a summit," he said. "You have to make up your mind. You have to step up to the plate. And when it comes to the divisions in your administration over this issue, you can't split the difference."

A personal meeting had been Reagan's idea in the first place, and he remained convinced that personal diplomacy would afford the best chance for a breakthrough in U.S.-Soviet relations, especially on arms control. In late May the White House hosted a small dinner for Arkady Shevchenko, a Soviet diplomat who had turned double agent before defecting to the West. "Our guest sang for his supper," Reagan wrote afterward. "He confirmed that Soviet leaders do have an inferiority complex about their superpower standing—that they are a superpower only in military power. That will be a factor in arms control talks. He also affirmed that they do nurse a feeling that we may be a threat to them." Reagan knew the United States was not a threat to the Soviet Union, and he judged a face-to-face meeting with Gorbachev the best way to convince him of that fact.

He directed Shultz to set it up. The Kremlin agreed to Geneva, not least because Gorbachev kicked Gromyko upstairs to the ceremonial position of chairman of the presidium of the Supreme Soviet. The foreign ministry went to Eduard Shevardnadze, a Gorbachev man and an individual far less confrontational than Gromyko. In early July the White House and the Kremlin simultaneously announced the November dates they had set for the summit.

THE DECISION ALTERED the dynamics within the administration. As the summit became inevitable, Weinberger shifted from opposition to sabotage. Though the Senate had never ratified the SALT II treaty, the United States—and the Soviet Union—had informally adhered to the limits it imposed on weapons systems. The limits were fairly generous, and during Reagan's first term they didn't inhibit the arms buildup he ordered. But early in his second term a new submarine was commissioned that would push the United States over the SALT II limit on submarine-based missiles unless the president retired an existing submarine. The older vessel was obsolete by the standards of the U.S. Navy, which had no desire to keep it in service. Yet Weinberger and the hawks at the Pentagon, with support from their allies in Congress and elsewhere, argued that it *should* be kept in service. Some contended that it remained essential to American defense; the more candid acknowledged that their goal was to break free from the SALT II limits on this and other systems. Reagan eventually decided to retire the older submarine, in large part to counter Soviet assertions that the American administration was bent on achieving military superiority that could only endanger world peace. But the decision cost him politically with the hawks, who made clear that they would be no pushovers for future arms agreements.

The CIA adopted a different tack. Robert Gates was less hostile to negotiations than Bill Casey, and he was considerably less devious. But he thought the president should be urged to adopt a tough line with Gorbachev. "Bill, I think Gorbachev wants and needs a deal so bad that he can taste it," Gates wrote to Casey. "I've been involved in preparing a number of U.S.-Soviet summits and I have never seen such an open signaling of a desire to do business." This gave the administration an important advantage. "President Reagan goes to Geneva holding better cards than any president meeting his Soviet counterpart since Eisenhower went to Geneva 30 years ago. Our planning should start from that premise and focus on specific, realistic demands we should make of Gorbachev—not to score debating points but to advance U.S. interests in concrete ways—from Nicaragua to Angola to Afghanistan to Kampuchea to Iran-Iraq war to arms control to cultural agreements to human rights." Gates thought the White House fundamentally misunderstood the opportunity. "The meeting is shaping up as a terribly important moment in the Reagan presidency. I fear that the president's staff is approaching the meeting aiming just to survive it and without a clear view of the larger objectives—and opportunities."

Gates recommended that the CIA brief the president on the opportunities he spoke of. Casey agreed. But Robert McFarlane and Jack Matlock got there first. "Even before it was decided when and where Reagan and Gorbachev would meet, Bud McFarlane asked me to think about how we could see that the president had more and better knowledge of the Soviet Union before he faced the Soviet leader," Matlock recalled. "Dealing as he did with Reagan every day, he was struck by the president's spotty command of historical facts. Reagan had had very few contacts with Soviet officials and still tended to base many of his judgments more on generalities, even slogans, than on a nuanced understanding of Soviet reality." Reagan, for his part, recognized his deficiencies and was eager to remedy them with information from experts. "I want the best minds in the country, Republican or Democrat, academics or diplomats, to give me in-depth knowledge," he told McFarlane.

McFarlane and Matlock organized what they called "Soviet Union 101." Matlock oversaw the production of some two dozen papers of a few thousand words each on various aspects of Soviet politics, economics, history, and culture. Fresh papers were delivered to Reagan each Friday. He read them carefully over the weekend. "He would devour them, annotate them," McFarlane recalled. "He would come in Monday like a kid with a new toy. He would quiz his experts, would obsess about getting more information." Matlock remembered that Reagan found some of the papers more compelling than others. "He was interested mainly in the people involved," Matlock said. "His eyes would glaze over when you talked statistics." One crucial question engaged him above all: "What makes this Gorbachev fellow tick?" Both McFarlane and Matlock found Reagan to be an apt pupil. "Very, very quick," McFarlane described him. Matlock, who taught in the Ivy League after leaving government, said, "In many ways he was the best student I ever had."

The CIA got its chance with Reagan a few days before he left for Geneva. Casey suggested an hour's meeting between the president and the agency's top Soviet analysts. Robert Gates led off. "I described for Reagan the severe domestic problems Gorbachev faced and his need for a respite as well as Western economic cooperation and help," Gates remembered. Yet he predicted that Gorbachev would move slowly in dealing with the West, especially the United States. "I said that I thought Gorbachev was not prepared to pay much for some breathing space with the United States—that he likely saw it coming anyway in the defense arena, especially SDI." Gorbachev didn't think Reagan could sustain spending on defense. "I said that the same would be true in the Third World, where support for freedom fighters would decline when Reagan left office. My bottom line: Gorbachev simply intended to outwait Reagan."

Gates didn't think he or his colleagues made much impression on Reagan. "I felt Reagan was alert but not very interested in what I and others had to say," he recounted. There was one conspicuous exception. Kay Oliver described the social stresses on the Soviet system, including alcoholism, crime, corruption, and the revival of religion. Reagan perked up. "He was riveted by Oliver's briefing, I think because she described the Soviet Union in terms of human beings, everyday life, and the conditions under which they lived," Gates wrote. "It was all far more real to the president than the strategic concepts and broad geopolitics the others of us went on about."

Gates recalled another, different reaction from the president. "I was seated closest to him, and about two minutes into my comments I heard a piercing electrical hum. Reagan's eyes got very wide, and he reached up to his ear to adjust his hearing aid. A couple of minutes later, the hum returned and, since I could hear it, I could only guess how loud it must have been in his ear. At that point, in some disgust, he reached up, pulled the hearing aid out of his ear, and pounded it on the palm of his hand a couple of times. As he replaced it in his ear, he looked at me, smiled, and said, 'My KGB handler must be trying to reach me.'"

78

R EAGAN LISTENED TO Gates and Matlock and the others. He
weighed their words against his own experience of human nature
and his discovery that the Soviets were human too. In an action
rare for him, he committed his reflections to a memo, which summarized
the state of his mind just ahead of the biggest meeting of his life. It also
revealed subtleties of thought he declined to share with the public.

"I believe Gorbachev is a highly intelligent leader totally dedicated to
traditional Soviet goals," Reagan wrote. "He will be a formidable negotiator and will try to make Soviet foreign and military policy more effective.
He is (as are all Soviet General Secretaries) dependent on the Soviet-
Communist hierarchy and will be out to prove to them his strength and
dedication to Soviet traditional goals." Gorbachev's pursuit of arms control would be tactical rather than ethical. "If he really seeks an arms control agreement, it will only be because he wants to reduce the burden of
defense spending that is stagnating the Soviet economy."

Reagan believed that the struggling Soviet economy was Gorbachev's
Achilles' heel. It might force him to make concessions on arms he wouldn't
have made otherwise. But Reagan had believed the same thing about
Brezhnev and Andropov and Chernenko, and the Soviet system had outlasted them. It might outlast Reagan himself. He simply couldn't know.
For all he could tell, Gorbachev himself didn't know. Consequently, Reagan wasn't holding his breath awaiting its collapse, and he wouldn't hold
arms control hostage to its collapse. Yet he still thought the vulnerability
of the economy afforded him leverage with Gorbachev, especially on SDI.
"He doesn't want to face the cost of competing with us," Reagan wrote.

He saw Gorbachev as essentially conservative but shrewdly political.

"He doesn't want to undertake any new adventures but will be stubborn and tough about holding what he has." Gorbachev wanted to drive a wedge between the United States and its NATO allies. "That means making us look like the threat to peace while he appears to be a reasonable man of peace." But he also had a domestic constituency, his own hard-liners, to consider. "If he has to make a choice, then he will opt for demonstrating to his own hierarchy that he is a strong leader."

What did this mean for the summit? Reagan conceded that summitry entailed a large dose of public relations, but that didn't make the summitry, or the public relations, any less important. "In the world of P.R. we are faced with two domestic elements. One argues that no agreement with the Soviets is worth the time, trouble or paper it's written on, so we should dig in our heels and say 'nyet' to any concession. On the other side are those so hungry for an agreement of any kind that they would advise major concessions because a successful summit requires that." Reagan granted the sincerity of the two sides but opted for a more basic, pragmatic standard. "My own view is that any agreement must be in the long-term interest of the United States and our allies. We'll sign no other kind." And he judged that success at the summit could come in alternative forms. "In a way, the summit will be viewed generally as a success because we've met, shaken hands and been civil to each other. It can also be a success if we fail to arrive at an arms agreement because I stubbornly held out for what I believe was right for our country."

Reagan imagined himself in the place of Gorbachev and the Kremlin leadership. "What are some of their needs and priorities?" he asked. His study and briefings suggested answers. "I believe they hunger for some trade and technology transfers. There is no question but that we have a tremendous advantage on that front." He intended to exploit that advantage. "Trade is for us a major bargaining chip. We shouldn't give it away."

Human rights would surface at the summit, whether Reagan liked it or not. In fact he did *not* like it, though he would never say so in public. "I'm sorry we are somewhat publicly on record about human rights. Front page stories that we are banging away at them on their human rights abuses will get us some cheers from the bleachers, but it won't help those who are being abused." Reagan approvingly recounted remarks by Richard Nixon, who told of being pressed by Jewish leaders to condition arms agreements upon the Kremlin's letting more Jews emigrate. Nixon refused. He got Brezhnev's signature on the landmark SALT I treaty, and only then, and privately, did he raise the human rights issue. The result was a dramatic increase in Jewish emigration.

Nixon had offered explicit advice to Reagan on dealing with Gorbachev. "He expressed optimism that I might accomplish what he did in 1972, but only if I didn't force Gorbachev to eat crow and embarrass him publicly." Reagan took this to heart. "We must always remember our main goal"—arms reduction—"and his need to show his strength to the Soviet gang back in the Kremlin," he wrote. At the same time, Gorbachev must understand America's strength and this American president's determination. "Another of our goals, probably stated to Gorbachev in private, should be that failure to come to a solid, verifiable arms reduction agreement will leave no alternative except an arms race, and there is no way we will allow them to win such a race."

Reagan didn't expect to solve all America's problems with the Soviets at one outing. But he could make a start. "Let us agree this is the first of meetings to follow. That in itself will give an aura of success. We will have set up a process to avoid war in settling our differences in the future. Maybe we should settle on early 1987 as the next meeting time, and maybe we should discuss offering that it be in Moscow. He can come back here in 1988."

CASPAR WEINBERGER WASN'T invited to Geneva and might not have gone had he been. He still believed the summit was a bad idea, and he distrusted Reagan's ability to stand up to Gorbachev or others pressing for agreements. To forestall such agreements he lectured the president in absentia. The *New York Times* and the *Washington Post* printed a letter, obviously leaked from the defense secretary's office, in which Weinberger warned Reagan against what was awaiting him in Geneva. Weinberger's pretext for writing was an earlier instruction from Reagan to gather information on Soviet violations of existing arms treaties. The violations had been consistent and serious, the secretary reported, and could not be wished away, as advocates of new treaties seemed to desire. "The Soviet violations put us in a particularly vulnerable and dangerous position," he declared. The president must keep this fact firmly in mind as he approached the summit, for the treaty-mongers—in both the Soviet Union and the United States—would conspire to make him forget it. "In Geneva, you will almost certainly come under great pressure to do three things that would limit severely your options for responding to Soviet violations: One is to agree to continue to observe SALT II. The second is to agree formally to limit S.D.I. research, development and testing to only that research allowed under the most restrictive interpretation of the ABM Treaty, even though you have determined that a less restrictive interpretation is justified legally. The Soviets doubtless will seek assurances that you will continue to be bound to such tight limits on S.D.I. development and testing that would discourage the Congress from making any but token appropriations. Third, the Soviets may propose communiqué or other language that obscures their record of arms control violations by referring to the 'importance that both sides attach to compliance.'"

George Shultz read the letter and nearly exploded. Policy differences between Shultz and Weinberger had escalated into a personal dislike that rendered cooperation between the two secretaries nearly impossible. "Shultz detested Weinberger," Robert Gates recalled, adding that Weinberger reciprocated the ill feeling. Shultz suspected the worst of Weinberger, and the leaked letter confirmed his suspicions. "Weinberger's letter must have been written and leaked deliberately to hamstring the president and sabotage the summit," he asserted later. "I was surprised the president tolerated it." Robert McFarlane shared the secretary of state's view. Asked by a reporter whether the Weinberger letter was an attempt to sabotage the summit, McFarlane responded bluntly, "Sure it was." Jack Matlock thought Weinberger's letter represented an attempt to upstage the president. "It was written to be leaked," Matlock recalled. "It was a flagrant attempt to steal the limelight."

The presumed target of the leak kept above the furor. "Reagan himself was pretty calm," Matlock said. The president didn't take this outbreak of bureaucratic politics any more seriously than he took other manifestations of the jockeying endemic to presidential administrations. "Doesn't everyone know what Cap thinks?" he asked his staff dismissively during a meeting.

Many observers judged that Reagan's inability to keep his subordinates in line revealed a failure of leadership. Robert Gates, by contrast, detected a purpose in the president's acceptance of internecine squabbles. "I think Reagan wanted conflict," Gates said. Gates likened Reagan to Franklin Roosevelt, who was famous for pitting members of his administration against one another, in order that the final decision always rest with him. Gates saw Reagan doing the same thing. "It gave him more leverage in the decision process," Gates said. Ken Adelman, Reagan's director of the Arms Control and Disarmament Agency, thought the president's firm sense of priorities allowed him to ignore the infighting. "Reagan was going to do his own stuff," Adelman said.

Whatever the cause, the president initially refused to dignify the Weinberger flap with a statement. But when reporters shouted questions at him on his arrival in Geneva, he exercised his selective hearing to make a point. A reporter inquired if he thought he was being sabotaged by Weinberger. "No," Reagan said.

Was he going to fire Weinberger?

"Do you want a one-word answer or two?" Reagan asked.

Two words, the reporter said.

"Hell no," Reagan said.

L ORD I HOPE I'm ready," Reagan wrote on the eve of his first session with Gorbachev. The president focused on what he would say; his handlers agonized over how he would look. Reagan arrived at the Château Fleur d'Eau ahead of Gorbachev and prepared to greet him at his car. The November morning was windy and cold. The question of the hour was: Should the president wear an overcoat as he stepped outside? His advisers were split. The age issue persisted; Reagan must appear no less vibrant and vigorous than Gorbachev. But it was *cold* outside, and he was, after all, seventy-four. Would Gorbachev be wearing a coat? No one knew. The matter remained unresolved when Gorbachev's limousine suddenly pulled up. Reagan silenced the debate by bounding out coatless. He offered his hand to Gorbachev, who emerged from the car coated, scarved, and hatted. As the cameras of the world's media clicked and whirred, Reagan's team tallied one for their side and prayed against pneumonia.

The summit was scheduled to last two days, with private meetings between the principals alternating with larger sessions including staff. "President Reagan began the conversation by telling the General Secretary that the two of them could really talk now," Reagan's interpreter and note taker at the initial private meeting recorded. "The President indicated that he approached this meeting with a very deep feeling and hoped that both of them could realize its importance and the unique situation that they were in." Reagan said that in the larger sessions they would talk about arms control and other issues of policy. "But he wondered if the primary aim between them should not be to eliminate the suspicions which each side had of the other." To talk about arms without addressing the suspicions would be fruitless. "Countries do not mistrust each other because of arms," he said. "But rather countries build up their arms because of the mistrust between them."

Gorbachev responded that he shared Reagan's desire that the two of them get to know each other. Serious steps were necessary to bridge the differences between the two countries, and these would require "political will at the highest levels." Gorbachev acknowledged the mutual mistrust Reagan spoke of, but he pointed out that cooperation existed at various levels of culture and trade. The general secretary granted that "squalls" in the relationship between the two countries had occasionally been severe. "But he could definitely state that in the USSR there was no enmity toward the United States or its people. The Soviet Union respected the U.S. and its people. The Soviet people and the leadership of the Soviet Union recognized the role of the U.S. in the world and wished it no harm."

Reagan expressed confidence that the American and Soviet peoples would discover more of what they had in common the better they got to know each other. Friendship between them would grow. The role of their governments was to let this happen. "It is not people but governments that create arms." Reagan shared a lesson he had learned in a lifetime of dealing with people. "People do not get into trouble when they talk *to* each other, but rather when they talk *about* each other."

Gorbachev said the overriding issue was the threat of war, specifically nuclear war. "Young people are wondering about whether they will be alive or not, and the older generation, which has suffered so much"—in the war against Germany—"is also thinking about this." If the two sides at Geneva could create an impetus toward eliminating the threat of nuclear war, they would have accomplished a great deal. Failure was unacceptable. "If no such impetus is created, there will be great disappointment, and no statements or press announcements will justify the meeting. People will say that we are irresponsible."

Gorbachev mentioned an issue that was sure to come up in the larger meetings. Bilateral relations were essential, but the Soviet Union and the United States must not forget the interests of other countries. "The Soviet Union has its national interests and the U.S. has them as well. Other countries also have their national interests. In the international context, we cannot speak of advancing some of these interests at the expense of suppressing others." Gorbachev shared a saying he had heard after the announcement of the Geneva summit: "Reagan and Gorbachev should bear in mind that the world does not belong only to the two of them."

Reagan said he had not heard the saying. He agreed that the super-powers should remember the interests of other countries. But he had to point out that the Soviet Union was not always helpful. "One of the things that creates mistrust of the USSR by the U.S. is the realization of the Marxist idea of helping socialist revolutions throughout the world and the belief that the Marxist system should prevail." The United States sup-ported each country's right to self-determination, Reagan said. "But the U.S. feels that the Soviet Union attempts to use force to shape the devel-oping countries to their own pattern, and that such force is often used only by a minority of the people of the country."

Reagan, noting the time, suggested they join the larger group. But Gorbachev wouldn't let the president's assertions go unanswered. "There were some who considered that the American Revolution should have been crushed," he observed. "The same applies to the French Revolu-tion and the Soviet Revolution." People made their own revolutions; these were not imposed from without. "The U.S. should not think that Moscow is omnipotent and that when I wake up every day I think about which country I would now like to arrange a revolution in."

THE TÊTE-À-TÊTE HAD been scheduled for fifteen minutes. "We did an hour, which excited the hell out of the press," Reagan remarked that evening. It also evoked anxiety in Reagan's staff, who wanted to keep the president on schedule. One staffer asked George Shultz if he should break up the meeting. "Are you out of your mind?" Shultz responded. "This is what it's about. The longer they talk, the better it is."

Reagan and Gorbachev gathered their entourages. Gorbachev spoke first before the larger group. He returned to the central issue of war and peace. "If the two of us are unable to tackle this issue," he said, "it is dif-ficult to see how we can deal with others." Gorbachev conceded that the Soviet Union had its own counterpart to the American military-industrial complex. "There are people linked to military affairs in both countries," he said. "There are people who earn their living from these matters." But such people should not be allowed to dictate policy. The overween-ing power of the military hindered economic progress, Gorbachev said. "Soviet and American scholars have shown that one job in the military sector is three times as costly as in the civilian sector. More jobs can be created if the money is channeled into civilian areas."

Gorbachev had been reading Reagan's speeches. He quoted the president as saying that a nuclear war could not be won and therefore must never be fought. Gorbachev said he agreed. Reagan had said the superpowers must treat each other as equals; Gorbachev agreed. Reagan had said cultural exchanges between the two countries conduced to peace; Gorbachev agreed. The general secretary reemphasized the need for cooperation. "We can live in this world only together," he said. "So we both must think how to put relations on a new track."

He hoped the president would not mistake the meaning of his remarks. "If the United States thinks that by saying these things I am showing weakness, that the Soviet Union is more interested than the United States, then this will all come to nothing. The Soviet Union will not permit an unequal approach. But if there is on the U.S. side a positive will, the United States will find the Soviets an active participant in the process."

Reagan reiterated his earlier theme of trust. "If the two sides are to get down to the business of reducing the mountains of weapons, then both must get at the cause of the distrust which led to building these weapons," he said. The United States had shown itself worthy of trust, he asserted. After World War II, when it possessed a nuclear monopoly, it had refrained from employing it. It had reduced its armies from twelve million men to fewer than two million and had cut its navy by half. The Soviet Union, however, had not reciprocated. It had rejected multiple American offers to reduce nuclear arsenals. The Kremlin instead had increased its arsenal even as it promoted world revolution. "The United States watched the Soviet military buildup, including nuclear weapons," Reagan said. "The United States also sees an expansionist Soviet Union. It has a satellite in Cuba just ninety miles off our shores." The expansion continued to the present. "Now we see Afghanistan, Ethiopia, Angola and Yemen—with, for example, 35,000 Cubans in Angola."

Reagan said that Gorbachev overestimated the influence of the military on American policy and spending. "Our budget for humanitarian affairs—for the elderly and handicapped and for other social needs—is greater than our total military budget. Two-thirds of our military spending pays for manpower; only a small percentage is spent on equipment. The total military budget is a very small percentage of our GNP." Yet he agreed that America would be better off economically with an even smaller military. "The United States has no economic interest in continuing a military buildup."

Reagan said that the Soviet buildup provoked fears among Americans—"maybe not fears of war, but that the Soviet Union could acquire such an imbalance of strength that it could deliver an ultimatum." Gorbachev needed to address these fears, as he—Reagan—was willing to address Soviet fears of the United States. "But more than words are needed. We need to get on to deeds."

Reagan was the first to touch on the issue of strategic defense. Gorbachev had said previously that an antimissile shield would be destabilizing and dangerous, for it would give the United States a first-strike capability against the Soviet Union. Reagan denied any offensive intent. He didn't even know whether an antimissile shield would be possible, but he wanted to explore it. "The United States has a research program. The Soviet Union has the same kind of program. The United States has some hope that it might be possible." Reagan suggested that both sides conduct research on an antimissile system. "And if one or both come up with such a system then they should sit down and make it available to everyone so no one would have a fear of a nuclear strike." This would be essential even if the superpowers eliminated their nuclear arsenals. "A mad man might come along with a nuclear weapon. If we could come up with a shield and share it, then nobody would worry about the mad man."

POSSIBLY REAGAN REALIZED this would be the last word before lunch. In Hollywood he had been known for hitting his mark. But whether designed or not, the recess that followed his introduction of the issue of strategic defense served his purpose of framing it as he wished without allowing Gorbachev an immediate rebuttal. Reagan didn't know for certain but could reasonably guess that SDI would be the hardest nut for the two sides to crack, and he wanted an uncontested first blow.

Gorbachev didn't want to give Reagan that advantage. He seemed quite willing to talk through lunch. Yet protocol intruded, and the two sides separated. Reagan relaxed, satisfied he had done well in his first appearance on the summit stage, while Gorbachev simply grew more impatient. So it appeared, at any rate, when the general secretary opened the afternoon session with a blistering rebuttal to Reagan's defense of SDI. "Twenty years ago there was no strategic balance," he said. "The United States had four times as many strategic delivery systems as the USSR, and also forward-based systems. What would the United States have done if the Soviet Union had possessed four times as much? The United States would have had to take steps, just as the Soviet Union did, to establish parity." Gorbachev denied Reagan's assertion that the Soviet

Union had surpassed the United States. "All institutes which study the problem, including the ISS"—Institute for Strategic Studies—"in London, conclude that there is strategic parity. Force structures are different, but they support different strategies."

The Soviet government insisted on maintaining parity, Gorbachev said, but it sought parity at a lower level. "We must meet each other halfway if we are to find a way to reduce strategic weapons. The time has come for us both to muster the political will and realism to make progress and to end efforts to outsmart or overrun the other side. Even now, due to computer technology, one side could get ahead in space. But we can match any challenge, though you might not think so. We know that the United States can meet any challenge from us, and we can meet any challenge from you. But why not make a step which would permit lowering the arms level?"

Gorbachev warned that SDI would trigger an arms race in space. "And not just a defensive arms race but an offensive arms race with space weapons," he said. "Space weapons will be harder to verify and will feed suspicions and mistrust. Scientists say any shield can be pierced, so SDI cannot save us. So why create it? It only makes sense if it is to defend against a retaliatory strike. What would the West think if the Soviet Union was developing these weapons? You would react with horror." Gorbachev cited remarks by Caspar Weinberger that missile defense in Soviet hands would be a threat to the West. "If we go first, you feel it would be bad for the world, feeding mistrust. We cannot accept the rationale which says it is good if you do it and bad if we do it."

Gorbachev said he knew Reagan was very attached to the idea of strategic defense. But he cautioned the president against acting on the idea. "We will have to frustrate this plan, and we will build up in order to smash your shield." Gorbachev took pains to ensure that Reagan understood what he was saying. "If the United States embarks on SDI, the following will happen: first, no reduction in offensive weapons; second, the Soviet Union will respond. This strategy will not be a mirror image of your program but a simpler, more effective system." Gorbachev wanted the president to consider other implications of SDI. Even if the system worked at some level, it would have dangerous consequences. "It will require automation which will place important decisions in the hands of computers," he said. "This could unleash an uncontrollable process. You haven't thought this through. It will be a waste of money and will also cause more distrust and more weapons."

Gorbachev proposed a ban on space weapons as a precursor to reductions in existing offensive systems. "Verification will not be a problem," he added, "if the basic question is solved. We are prepared for full verification of a ban on space weapons. If such a ban is agreed upon, then the two countries can negotiate on their respective proposals for arms reduction." Absent such a ban, arms reduction would be impossible.

Reagan let Gorbachev speak his piece. In this first day's meeting with the general secretary, Reagan came to realize that once Gorbachev developed a head of steam, there was not much chance of stopping him. So he let the steam run out a bit before responding. He began by remarking that the general secretary's presentation corroborated what he had been saying about a lack of trust. He rejected Gorbachev's assertion of present parity, arguing that parity had been posited at the time of SALT I in the early 1970s and that the Soviet Union had outbuilt the United States substantially since then. Turning to the philosophical issues behind the arms race, Reagan said, "Now we are locked in a mutual assured destruction policy. The United States does not have as many ICBMs as the Soviet Union but has enough to retaliate. But there is something uncivilized about this. Laws of war were developed over the centuries to protect civilians, but civilians are the targets of our vast arsenals today."

The president acknowledged that strategic defense was important to him. But he thought it was important to humanity as well. "History teaches that a defense is found for every offensive weapon. We don't know if strategic defensive weapons will be possible, but if they are, they should not be coupled with an offensive force. The latter must be reduced so it will not be a threat. And if strategic defenses prove possible, we would prefer to sit down and get rid of nuclear weapons and with them the threat of war." Reagan reiterated that SDI was defensive. "SDI will never be used by the United States to improve its offensive capability or to launch a first strike," he said. "SDI should not lead to an arms race. We can both decide to reduce and eliminate offensive weapons."

THE TIMING OF the lunch break might or might not have been fortuitous, but the afternoon break was definitely choreographed. The grounds of the mansion where they were meeting included a small house beside Lake Geneva; Reagan had directed that a fire be kept burning in a fireplace there. With the temperature inside the meeting room rising, the president suggested a walk in the fresh air. Gorbachev couldn't refuse without appearing peevish. So off they went. The temperature had scarcely risen from the morning, and within minutes both men felt the chill. Reagan pointed to the house with its inviting fire, and they entered.

Reagan presented a written outline of his thoughts on arms reduction, translated into Russian for Gorbachev to read. The general secretary examined the document carefully. To Reagan's suggestion of reducing strategic arsenals by half, he said he could accept it but only if it was accompanied by a provision to prevent an arms race in space. He observed that the part of Reagan's proposal on limits to intermediate forces in Europe failed to count British and French missiles on the American side of the ledger.

Reagan stuck to his vision of strategic defense but repeated that the United States would share successful technologies with the Soviet Union. Gorbachev asked how the Soviet leadership could rely on such a commitment. Reagan answered that American laboratories would be open to Soviet scientists. Gorbachev judged this insufficient. He again insisted that space weapons be prohibited. Reagan complained that Gorbachev chronically mischaracterized strategic defense, which need not include space-based weapons at all.

They talked for more than an hour but got nowhere. "He's adamant and so am I," Reagan recorded that evening. They returned to the mansion. But before they entered the door there, Reagan invited Gorbachev to visit the United States in 1986. Gorbachev accepted and in turn invited Reagan to the Soviet Union in 1987. Reagan agreed. "I scored one we've worried about—that the meetings should be on an ongoing basis," the president wrote later. "That alone could make the meeting a success."

REAGAN AND GORBACHEV faced off again over dinner and during another series of meetings the following day. Reagan knew that conservatives in the United States—and some liberals too—expected him to speak out on human rights, and so, contradicting his earlier preference, he raised the issue. He said Congress would require satisfaction on human rights before it would approve any arms treaty. Gorbachev reacted with annoyance. He accused Reagan of hiding behind the pressure groups. The president could get what he wanted. Reagan answered that he wished it were so. "You sure are wrong about an American president's power," he said. Reagan repeated his argument that missile defense would not be destabilizing. Gorbachev grew angrier still. "Do you take us for idiots?" he said.

"The stuff really hit the fan," Reagan observed afterward. "He was really belligerent, and d--n it I stood firm." But things calmed down when the formal sessions ended and the staff on both sides set to work crafting a communiqué. "He and I and the interpreters went into a small room and wound up telling stories," Reagan said.

To Reagan this was the most significant part of the summit. "As we flew home I felt good," he recollected. "Gorbachev was tough and convinced communism was superior to capitalism, but after almost five years I'd finally met a Soviet leader I could talk to."

80

GORBACHEV DEPARTED GENEVA less upbeat than Reagan. The Soviet leader later recalled the tension that had character-ized the initial session. "As I reread the minutes, I am amazed at the extremely ideological stands taken by both partners," he wrote. "In retrospect, they read more like the 'No. 1 Communist' and the 'No. 1 Imperialist' trying to out-argue each other, rather than a business-like talk between the leaders of the two superpowers." That first meeting had made him skeptical that anything would come of the weekend. "We had lunch at our residence, and I shared my impressions of my tete-a-tete with Reagan with my colleagues. Reagan appeared to me not sim-ply a conservative, but a political 'dinosaur.'" Gorbachev's impression of his American counterpart didn't improve during the afternoon session. "Ronald Reagan's advocacy of the Strategic Defense Initiative struck me as bizarre. Was it science fiction, a trick to make the Soviet Union more forthcoming, or merely a crude attempt to lull us in order to carry out the mad enterprise—the creation of a shield which would allow a first strike without fear of retaliation?"

The adjournment to the small house with its blazing fire seemed promising at first. "The walk, the change of scene, the crackling of burn-ing wood—all these helped to alleviate the tension," Gorbachev said. But the better mood didn't last. "As soon as we sat down, Reagan rushed back to his old tactics. Seemingly anxious that I might take up SDI again—this time one-on-one—he decided to anticipate my move by taking out a list of arms control proposals and handing them to me. As I understood it, the paper was not intended for discussion but, rather, for acceptance on a 'take it or leave it' basis." Gorbachev naturally resented the pressure.

The only hopeful moment occurred on the walk back to the mansion. "We went outside again and I suddenly felt very cold—maybe in contrast to the warmth by the fire or to our heated discussion. At that point, the president unexpectedly invited me to visit the United States, and I reciprocated by inviting him to Moscow."

Yet that moment was a start. "As it seems to me now," Gorbachev recounted, "something important happened to each of us on that day, in spite of everything. I think there had been two factors at work—responsibility and intuition. I did not have this impression after lunch, and in the evening we were still clinging to our antagonistic positions. But the 'human factor' had quietly come into action. We both sensed that we must maintain contact and try to avoid a break. Somewhere in the back of our minds a glimmer of hope emerged that we could still come to an agreement."

REAGAN HOPED TO build on what he took as the positive spirit of Geneva. He sent Gorbachev a handwritten letter expressing a desire to continue the conversation. "Our people look to us for leadership, and nobody can provide it if we don't," Reagan said.

Gorbachev responded cordially but unforthcomingly. He said that Reagan's attachment to SDI stood in the way of any meaningful agreement between their countries. If the president wasn't willing to reconsider, talk was futile. Yet Gorbachev didn't close the door entirely. "I would like to have you take my letter as another one of our 'fireside talks,'" he said. "I would like to preserve not only the spirit of our Geneva meetings, but also to go further in developing our dialogue."

Reagan and Gorbachev weren't the only ones responding to the spirit of Geneva. Important constituencies in both countries didn't like the spirit at all. Caspar Weinberger rallied opponents of arms cuts to lobby Reagan to break the limits of the unratified SALT II treaty; Weinberger and the others similarly sought an interpretation of the 1972 ABM Treaty that would allow research and development of antimissile systems short of deployment.

Reagan might have resisted the pressure had Gorbachev shown more flexibility on SDI. But when Gorbachev stood fast, Reagan suspected he was being played for a fool. A March 1986 National Security Planning Group meeting heard arguments from George Shultz for continuing to observe the SALT II restraints and from Caspar Weinberger for breaking them. Reagan leaned toward the latter unless the Soviets agreed to a new arms agreement. "We can have a real reduction in weapons or an arms race," he wrote later that day. "But we're not going to sit by and watch them keep on fudging." He heard additional arguments during the following weeks and in May came down on the side of the hawks. He issued a statement that detailed Soviet breaches of the SALT limits and concluded, "Given this situation, I have determined that in the future the United States must base decisions regarding its strategic force structure on the nature and magnitude of the threat posed by Soviet strategic forces and not on standards contained in the SALT structure."

Meanwhile, he rejected calls from Democrats and others to join Gorbachev in a moratorium on nuclear testing. The Soviets had just completed a round of nuclear tests, and so a moratorium would cost them nothing. Weinberger and the hawks convinced Reagan that a moratorium would cost the United States something substantial, namely the reliability of the weapons systems that were due to be tested. Reagan approved the testing.

Yet he winced as he did so. Reagan wasn't used to losing battles of public relations. He had mastered the art of public relations in American politics, but he realized he was losing the global public relations battle to Gorbachev. His refusal to forswear SDI, his decision to break out of the SALT limits, and his order to resume nuclear testing, however justified from the standpoint of American security, made Reagan seem a warmonger when Gorbachev was preaching peace and fewer weapons. In January the Soviet leader had offered proposals that would have resulted in the total elimination of nuclear weapons by the end of the century. Reagan liked the idea and wished he could have proposed it first. "It's a hell of a propaganda move," he wrote. "We'd be hard put to explain how we could turn it down."

But he did turn it down. The hawks in his administration and Congress were pushing him in just the opposite direction—the direction in which he himself had led them until recently. He now wanted to change course, but they didn't. And he wasn't willing to overrule them.

Yet he hoped another summit or two might prepare the way for the kinds of cuts he and Gorbachev both envisioned. Gorbachev seemed willing to meet again. Soviet ambassador Dobrynin came for a visit and relayed Gorbachev's interest in a sequel to Geneva. Reagan reciprocated. "My feeling is the summit will take place, if not in June or July, sometime after the election," he recorded.

COMPLICATIONS AROSE, HOWEVER. In late April a nuclear reactor at Chernobyl in the Soviet Ukraine malfunctioned, leading to an explosion that spewed large amounts of radioactive debris into the atmosphere. The incident was a disaster in human and environmental terms, with dozens of people killed and many thousands exposed to dangerous levels of radiation. It was a debacle, as well, in the way the Soviet government handled it. Gorbachev seems to have wanted to tell the Soviet people as much as the government knew about the accident and its consequences for public health, but the ingrained secrecy of the Soviet bureaucracy prevented even him from finding out what was going on. The residents of the Chernobyl region, consequently, learned more from reports originating outside the Soviet Union, including those put out by the U.S. Environmental Protection Agency, than from their own government.

Reagan offered American assistance and refrained from trying to gain political ground at Gorbachev's expense. But others on the American side made ample use of this opportunity to rail against Moscow for ineptitude and secrecy. Opponents of arms control contended that if the Soviets stonewalled their own people on a matter of such urgency, they would certainly try to frustrate any inspection regime established by an arms-control treaty.

Gorbachev was embarrassed by the cover-up within his bureaucracy and angered by the Western reaction. Seizing on inaccuracies in some of the external reports, he accused the Western media of constructing a "mountain of lies." He blamed the United States for an "unrestrained anti-Soviet campaign." Years later he was still sore. "The tragedy of Chernobyl was exploited as an alleged proof that we had no intention of really 'opening up,' that we remained treacherous and not to be trusted."

Gorbachev took the reaction to Chernobyl, in the context of Reagan's decision on SALT and his continued support of SDI, the MX, and the Pershings, as evidence of American bad faith. "The Americans continued to proclaim in public their readiness for serious arms control negotiations, but in reality they were again undermining the talks and adopting new weapons programs which sent the arms race spiraling upward," he wrote. He was puzzled. "Try as I would, I simply could not understand this behavior." He wondered what had happened to the spirit of Geneva. "Was President Reagan perhaps overruled by the powerful American military-industrial complex?" Did the president fear a political backlash? Whatever the cause, the result was discouraging for future progress. "I finally arrived at the conviction that it was yet another attempt to provoke us and to make us deviate from the new course we had been pursuing since April 1985, returning to a policy of open confrontation. Right-wing circles in the West feared a renewed, dynamic and more democratic Soviet Union, offering peace and cooperation to other nations. Such an outcome did not conform with their strategies of the time."

I N JANUARY 1986, Americans watched as the space shuttle *Challenger* lifted off from the Kennedy Space Center in Florida. Since the dawn of the space age, NASA's launches had drawn large audiences, with tens of thousands watching on the ground and millions on television. The crowds never tired of the spectacle of mighty rockets sending brave men and recently women into orbit, and with each launch American pride received a boost.

On this day the flight proceeded well for the first minute. The launch vehicle rapidly gained speed and altitude; cameras strained to follow it as it rose into the distance. Viewers on the ground regained their hearing from the engines' roar; watchers on television turned to their daily routines. But the attention of all was suddenly wrenched back when the mission experienced a catastrophic malfunction. A critical seal failed, allowing hot gases from one of the rocket engines to escape their normal exhaust route. This triggered a series of events that resulted in the breakup of the vehicle, which disintegrated amid several plumes of smoke and steam. All seven members of the crew were killed.

Reagan had been in the Oval Office preparing to brief the television network news anchors on his State of the Union address, scheduled for delivery that evening. John Poindexter, the recently appointed national security adviser, and George Bush came in and told him what had happened. They went into the study and watched the replay on television. "It was just a very traumatic experience," Reagan said later.

He went ahead and met with the anchors. They talked not about the State of the Union but about the *Challenger* tragedy. "It's a horrible thing,"

Reagan said. "I can't rid myself of the thought of the sacrifice of the families of the people on board. I'm sure all of America is more than saddened."

One of the reporters asked if the president took comfort in knowing that the American space program had suffered fewer deaths than the Soviet program.

"We all have pride in that," he responded. "But it doesn't lessen our grief."

One of the crew was a schoolteacher, Christa McAuliffe, who had been chosen and specially trained for the mission. Her presence had prompted NASA to provide special coverage of the launch to public schools. A reporter asked Reagan what he would say to the children who had been watching.

"Pioneers have always given their lives on the frontier," he reflected. "The problem is that it's more of a shock to all as we see it happening, not just hear about something miles away. But we must make it clear"—to the children—"that life goes on."

Reagan thought of the McAuliffe family. "I can't put out of my mind her husband and children," he said. "The others knew they were in a hazardous occupation." But she was different, and so was her family. "Your heart goes out to them."

HE DECIDED TO postpone the State of the Union address. Instead, he spoke to the American people about the terrible event the nation had witnessed and suffered. "Today is a day for mourning and remembering," he said. "Nancy and I are pained to the core by the tragedy of the shuttle *Challenger*. We know we share this pain with all of the people of our country. This is truly a national loss." The country had lost another astronaut crew nineteen years earlier. "But we've never lost an astronaut in flight; we've never had a tragedy like this."

He read the honor roll of the deceased. He commiserated with their families. "We're thinking about you so very much. Your loved ones were daring and brave, and they had that special grace, that special spirit that says, 'Give me a challenge, and I'll meet it with joy.' They had a hunger to explore the universe and discover its truths. They wished to serve, and they did. They served all of us."

He spoke to the schoolchildren. "I know it is hard to understand, but sometimes painful things like this happen," he said. To the children and their parents and the rest of his audience, he added, "It's all part of the process of exploration and discovery. It's all part of taking a chance and expanding man's horizons. The future doesn't belong to the fainthearted; it belongs to the brave. The *Challenger* crew was pulling us into the future, and we'll continue to follow them."

He almost spoiled the mood with a swipe at the Soviet Union. "We don't hide our space program," he said. "We don't keep secrets and cover things up." America was different. "We do it all up front and in public. That's the way freedom is, and we wouldn't change it for a minute."

His short speech was nearly over. Some in his audience caught the reference to "High Flight," a favorite poem among aviators, but others simply appreciated the lyricism of the closing lines: "The crew of the space shuttle *Challenger* honored us by the manner in which they lived their lives. We will never forget them, nor the last time we saw them, this morning, as they prepared for their journey, and waved goodbye, and 'slipped the surly bonds of earth' to 'touch the face of God.'"

SPEECHWRITER PEGGY NOONAN, the principal drafter of Reagan's speech, watched with proprietary interest. "When the president finished, he looked lost," she recalled. "I knew: He didn't like what he was given."

Reagan thought the speech had been a bust. "I just had this feeling that I'd failed," he told Noonan. But he blamed himself. "I thought that I'd done badly and I hadn't done justice," he said.

Reagan's audience took a different view. Perhaps sorrow and decorum stilled critical voices. But the response was strongly positive, and it grew overwhelmingly so. Before long, Reagan's *Challenger* eulogy was being cited as one of the best speeches he or any other president had ever given.

ONE OF THE secrets of Reagan's success as president was his ability to concentrate on the most important issues, leaving lesser matters for subordinates to handle. By 1986 his agenda in foreign affairs was focused on a single item: arms control with the Soviet Union. He hoped for an agreement on intermediate-range missiles, preferably his zero option, and for at least a start on cuts in long-range missiles and bombers. He continued to insist that any such agreements come without constraining SDI.

Yet he found himself compelled to deal with foreign policy issues having nothing to do with arms control. For more than a decade Washington had eyed Libya's mercurial leader, Muammar Qaddafi, with deepening distrust. A 1974 arms deal with Moscow had marked Libya as a Soviet surrogate in the eyes of those, like Reagan, who were inclined to see Kremlin mischief in the nonaligned world. Qaddafi's rhetorical and apparently logistical support for terrorist activities in the Middle East and elsewhere pushed him further beyond the pale.

Reagan decided, shortly after becoming president, to teach Qaddafi a lesson. Vaguely implicating Qaddafi in a murder in Chicago, he summarily shut the Libyan embassy in Washington, and in response to Qaddafi's assertion of Libyan authority over the Gulf of Sidra, the president ordered the U.S. Sixth Fleet into the gulf. "He's a madman," Reagan wrote to himself. "He has been harassing our planes out over international waters and it's time to show the other nations there—Egypt, Morocco, et al.— that there is a different management here."

Qaddafi challenged the American presence in the Gulf of Sidra, sending fighter planes against the task force. The aircraft carrier *Nimitz* scrambled some of its F-14s to meet the Libyans; when the latter fired on the American jets, they fired back and shot down two of the Libyan planes.

The incident evoked comment in the American media, not least because Reagan's aides didn't inform him immediately of what had happened. The president waved aside the criticism. "There's been a lot of talk and the press has been very concerned because six hours went by before they awoke me at 4:30 in the morning to tell me about it," he said to reporters. "And there's a very good answer to that. Why? If our planes were shot down, yes, they'd wake me right away. If the other fellow's were shot down, why wake me up?"

Qaddafi responded with bluster and what American intelligence considered credible threats to kill Reagan. "It's a strange feeling to find there is a 'contract' out on yourself," Reagan observed. The threats gained additional credibility in October 1981 when Egypt's Anwar Sadat, a bitter opponent of Qaddafi, was assassinated. Reagan privately asserted, working from intelligence reports, that Qaddafi had readied a celebration of Sadat's death ahead of the news. "In other words, he knew it was going to happen."

The threat against Reagan seemed to grow more specific. In November the Secret Service got wind of a possible attack at the National Press Club in Washington, where Reagan was giving a speech. Reagan donned a bulletproof vest and gave the speech, and nothing happened. New reports at Thanksgiving suggested that a band of assassins had crossed into the United States from Canada. The Secret Service was sufficiently alarmed that it vetoed a scheduled appearance by Reagan at Arlington National Cemetery.

The president convened the National Security Council to consider retaliation against Qaddafi. William Casey recommended laying out publicly the evidence of Libya's involvement in terrorist activities, starting with a Qaddafi plot to assassinate the American ambassador to Egypt in 1977.

Reagan was skeptical, saying the American media would never believe the administration, regardless of how much evidence it provided.

Casey pressed the issue, suggesting the release of a map showing terrorist training camps in Libya, with the caption "Terror is Libya's second largest industry" (after oil).

Reagan remained reluctant. Nearly two thousand Americans resided in Libya; most were connected to the oil industry. Reagan was as sensitive as ever to the possible taking of more American hostages, and he feared that any strong action might prompt Qaddafi to seize some of the Americans.

Al Haig, still secretary of state, discounted the likelihood of hostages. "A hostage situation would alarm other Westerners in Libya," Haig said. Libya required those Westerners to keep the oil flowing. Haig suggested economic sanctions. These might include an embargo on oil imports from Libya, a ban on exports to Libya, and seizure of Libyan assets in the United States.

Donald Regan replied that the seizure of Libyan assets could destabilize American relations with other countries of the Middle East. "The Saudis, for example, may get the wrong idea from U.S. sanctions against Libya," he said. Regan added that the big oil companies with operations in Libya wouldn't sit idly while Washington adopted measures that damaged their bottom lines.

Haig answered that the Saudis were among those urging strong action against Qaddafi and that they were prepared to increase their own oil production to offset any losses the United States suffered from a ban on Libyan oil.

Jeane Kirkpatrick reported that international action against Qaddafi, as by the Organization of African Unity, was unlikely. "Qaddafi has intimidated the leaders of black African states," Kirkpatrick said. None dared to oppose him.

Reagan interjected, "The United States dares to oppose him."

But not yet. The meeting ended without a decision. Reagan still worried about the Americans. And he still blamed the media for its distrust of the intelligence the administration shared about Libya. "The press is beginning to charge that we are making up the Qaddafi threat because we won't tell them the sources of our information," he muttered. "I've come to the conclusion that they are totally irresponsible and won't be satisfied (if then) until someone is gunned down by the 'hit men.'"

The Secret Service took the threat seriously, though. When Reagan and Nancy flew to Camp David in early December, the Secret Service rerouted their helicopter. Reports indicated that Libyan sympathizers might have secured heat-seeking missiles that could shoot down the aircraft.

NOTHING CAME OF these reports, either, leaving the president and his aides to wonder whether Qaddafi was simply engaged in disinformation. Yet they continued to monitor Qaddafi's behavior and counter his mischief. When Qaddafi lent support to rebels in Chad and the French government dispatched troops to counter the rebels, Reagan ordered American warplanes and AWACS reconnaissance aircraft to keep an eye on Libyan planes. When Qaddafi was reported to be readying planes to back a coup in Sudan, Reagan sent AWACS to help prepare the Egyptian air force to shoot down the Libyan planes.

Tensions with Libya reached a new height in December 1985 when Palestinian gunmen opened fire at the Rome and Vienna airports. Qaddafi praised the attacks, which killed nineteen and wounded more than a hundred, as vengeance for the massacres of Palestinians at the Lebanese refugee camps three years earlier. American intelligence indicated that Qaddafi's support went beyond cheerleading to funding and perhaps training.

Reagan decided he'd had enough of Qaddafi. After a long meeting with his national security team, he issued an executive order telling the Americans in Libya to leave the country. He froze Libyan assets in the United States. He directed the Sixth Fleet to increase its presence off Libyan shores. Reagan hoped Qaddafi would get the message, but he was ready to do more. "If Mr. Q. decides not to push another terrorist act— O.K., we've been successful with our implied threat," Reagan noted. "If on the other hand he takes this for weakness and does loose another one, we will have targets in mind and instantly respond with a h--l of a punch."

Qaddafi decided to test Reagan's resolve. Libyan batteries fired surface-to-air missiles at American warplanes in the Gulf of Sidra, and Libyan missile-armed patrol boats menacingly approached American ships.

Reagan delivered the promised punch. American planes acting on the president's orders rocketed the missile batteries and sank the boats. "U.S. forces will continue their current exercises," Reagan declared in a letter of notification to the speaker of the House and the president pro tem of the Senate. "We will not be deterred by Libyan attacks or threats from exercising our rights on and over the high seas under international law. If Libyan attacks do not cease, we will continue to take the measures necessary in the exercise of our right of self-defense to protect our forces."

Qaddafi prepared to counter by other means, as the CIA reported to the president. "We learned that in response Qaddafi had directed several of his 'People's Bureaus' in Europe to plan terrorist operations against the United States," Robert Gates recalled. "The Libyans informed a number of ambassadors in Tripoli that a 'state of war' existed with the United States. We quickly began picking up information on Libyan plans to hit us." Qaddafi's agents apparently succeeded in early April, bombing a West Berlin nightclub frequented by American military personnel. One American soldier was killed, along with a Turkish woman. Dozens of Americans were among the hundreds wounded.

Reagan reacted decisively. He ordered air strikes against Qaddafi's headquarters and other assets. Dozens of warplanes from American aircraft carriers and from a base in Britain pounded targets in Tripoli and Benghazi. Shortly after the planes left Libyan airspace, Reagan addressed the American people and the world, explaining the strikes as retaliation for the Berlin bombing and laying out the evidence of Qaddafi's guilt. "On March 25th, more than a week before the attack, orders were sent from Tripoli to the Libyan People's Bureau in East Berlin to conduct a terrorist attack against Americans to cause maximum and indiscriminate casualties," he said. "Libya's agents then planted the bomb. On April 4th the People's Bureau alerted Tripoli that the attack would be carried out the following morning. The next day they reported back to Tripoli on the great success of their mission." The blood of the victims was on Qaddafi's hands. "Our evidence is direct; it is precise; it is irrefutable," Reagan said.

The attack on Libya was part of a larger war against terrorism, he continued. "I warned that there should be no place on Earth where terrorists can rest and train and practice their deadly skills. I meant it. I said that we would act with others, if possible, and alone if necessary to ensure that terrorists have no sanctuary anywhere. Tonight, we have."

The war on terrorism wasn't an evening's outing, Reagan said. "I have no illusion that tonight's action will ring down the curtain on Qaddafi's reign of terror." But he hoped it would give Qaddafi pause about committing new crimes against innocent people. In any event, the attack on Libya wouldn't be America's last strike against terror. "We will persevere."

R EAGAN HAD WON the White House from Jimmy Carter not least by lambasting the Democratic president for abandoning friendly conservative regimes in the face of radical insurgencies. Conservative columnist Charles Krauthammer, noting that Reagan had adopted the contrary position, of supporting conservative insurgencies against radical regimes, in Afghanistan, Nicaragua, Angola, and Cambodia, approvingly conferred the label "Reagan Doctrine" on the policy. Reagan's own take on his strategy lacked Krauthammer's theoretical gloss but was easier to implement: communists and their sympathizers were bad, anticommunists and their supporters were good. Thus his support for the contras in Nicaragua against a leftist government, and for the government of El Salvador against a leftist insurgency.

Thus also his support for the apartheid regime in South Africa. At a time when much of the world sought to isolate South Africa by economic and diplomatic sanctions, Reagan stood by the government of P. W. Botha. Reagan and his administration contended that "constructive engagement" with South Africa would promote democratic reform while preserving the country from the African National Congress, which included elements Reagan deemed alarmingly communist and pro-Soviet. The policy inspired heavy criticism of Reagan; Bishop Desmond Tutu, a black South African cleric who won the Nobel Peace Price for opposing apartheid, denounced Reagan's policy as "immoral, evil and totally un-Christian." Eventually, Congress approved sanctions against South Africa and, when Reagan vetoed the bill, overrode the veto.

REAGAN'S POLICY TOWARD Ferdinand Marcos of the Philippines initially displayed a similar tolerance for right-wing authoritarianism. Reagan had first encountered Marcos in 1969, when he traveled to the Philippines in the service of Richard Nixon. Reagan was impressed by Marcos and enchanted by his wife, the beautiful and flamboyant Imelda. He sympathized when Marcos took stern measures against leftist insurgents during the 1970s, and he brought the Philippine president and Imelda to the White House for a state dinner in 1982. "It's a nostalgic occasion for us," he said in his toast. "Nancy and I often think of our 1969 visit to Manila, when we first experienced that unexcelled Philippine hospitality as the guests of our guests here tonight." Many things had changed in the intervening years, Reagan said. "But one thing remains constant—the basic nature of the Filipino–United States friendship." America and the Philippines had forged ties in defense, economics, and other areas. "I pledge to you, President Marcos, that the United States will do its share to strengthen those ties."

Reagan's support didn't prevent the opposition to Marcos—and to the increasingly egregious Imelda—from growing. A crisis occurred when opposition leader Benigno Aquino was assassinated in 1983. Massive protests followed the murder, giving rise to demands that Marcos step aside. Reagan stood by the president. "I know there are things there in the Philippines that do not look good to us from the standpoint right now of democratic rights," he said in one of his 1984 debates with Walter Mondale. "But what is the alternative? It is a large communist movement to take over the Philippines. They have been our friend since their inception as a nation. And I think that we've had enough of a record of letting— under the guise of revolution—someone that we thought was a little more right than we would be, letting that person go, and then winding up with totalitarianism, pure and simple, as the alternative. And I think that we're better off, for example with the Philippines, trying to retain our friendship and help them right the wrongs we see, rather than throwing them to the wolves and then facing a communist power in the Pacific."

George Shultz cringed at Reagan's conflation of the Philippine opposition with communism. The State Department issued a corrective, explaining that the United States recognized that there were legitimate democratic groups working for change in the Philippines. To Reagan, Shultz argued that unquestioning support for Marcos would discourage the democratic opposition and enhance, rather than diminish, the appeal of the radicals, to the peril of American interests in the Philippines, including rights to bases at Clark Field and Subic Bay. "I went through all of these matters with the president," Shultz recalled. "He agreed with our judgments and our course of action, while hoping, as we all did, that somehow Marcos would shift gears and work with us on reform." Yet the secretary sensed Reagan's reluctance to press Marcos. "I could see that Ronald Reagan wanted to support this man who had been a friend of the United States over many years, a staunch anticommunist, and head of a country that was host to important U.S. military bases."

Reagan listened to Shultz, but he distrusted the State Department as a whole on the Philippines. He thought stories of Marcos's ill health were being exaggerated for political purposes. "I suspect an element of the State Department bureaucracy is anti-Marcos and helps the false reporting along," he wrote in his diary in October 1985. To get to the heart of the matter, he asked Paul Laxalt, the Nevada senator, to travel to the Philippines as his personal investigator. The visit was supposed to be secret, to spare Marcos embarrassment. "This was a complete graveyard trip," Laxalt recalled. But the story leaked. "So, hell, by the time we got there it was public," Laxalt said. "We had this whole crowd of Philippine reporters there. They're a pretty intimidating bunch . . . They obviously didn't like Marcos, and they wondered what the hell I was doing there, an outsider coming in."

Laxalt found Marcos perplexing. "Smart as hell, but he had no idea what was going on," Laxalt said later. "I told him the whole sad story, what our intelligence was revealing." Marcos didn't like what he heard, especially coming from the American president's envoy. "He loved Reagan; it was a long-standing relationship," Laxalt recounted. Yet Marcos seemed healthier to Laxalt than the deathbed stories suggested. Laxalt subsequently related this assessment to Reagan, who was pleased to hear it.

While in Manila, Laxalt suggested a way for Marcos to steal a march on the opposition. Philippine law allowed the president to call a snap election. Marcos had previously considered doing so but put the idea aside. Laxalt raised it anew. "He was telling me how strong he was politically," Laxalt later remembered, "and I suggested to him that maybe he ought to reconsider the snap election. If he's as strong as he told me he was, hell, go through the election. That will solve a lot of your problems in Washington."

Marcos took the advice. In a television interview with American journalist David Brinkley, the Philippine president announced that he would hold a snap election in early 1986, a year ahead of schedule.

Reagan wasn't sure this was a good plan. "It's a touchy mess," he observed privately. But in public he emphasized America's support for the democratic process. "This election is of great importance to the future of democracy in the Philippines, a major friend and ally of the United States in the Pacific," he declared in a written statement. He stressed the importance of elections in neutralizing the communist insurgency. "The Communist Party of the Philippines, through its military arm, the New People's Army, and its front organization, the National Democratic Front, is pursuing a classic military and political strategy intended to lead eventually to a totalitarian takeover of the Philippines," Reagan said. "The Communist strategy can be defeated, but defeating it will require listening to and respecting the sovereign voice of the people." He complemented his words with a promise of new American aid should the election go smoothly and fairly.

REAGAN AWAITED THE elections, hoping for the best. So did the people of the Philippines, many of whom suspected that Marcos would rig the results. Reagan was asked about this possibility. "Mr. President, will the U.S. do anything if Marcos wins through fraud?" a reporter wanted to know.

Reagan refused to engage. "That's up to the Filipino people to determine, whether they think they've had a fair election or not," he said.

Reagan hoped Marcos would win fairly, or at least plausibly, as a credible victory would keep him in power and quiet criticism from the American left. But election day reports indicated widespread corruption of the polling. Members of the media sought Reagan's response. "You called for free and fair elections," a reporter said. "How does the United States respond to these reports of fraud from our observers, and can Marcos ever again make a claim to legitimacy after this?"

Reagan didn't want to be rushed. "Well, I'm going to wait until I have a chance to talk to our observers who are over there," he responded. "I haven't as yet. Whether there is enough evidence that you can really keep on pointing the finger or not, I don't know. I'm sure, you know, even elections in our own country—there are some evidences of fraud in places and areas. And I don't know the extent of this over there—but also do we have any evidence that it's all been one-sided, or has this been sort of the election tactics that have been followed there?"

The next day Reagan met with Senator Richard Lugar and Representative Jack Murtha, who had traveled to the Philippines to observe the election. They said the evidence of fraud was overwhelming. The challenger, Corazon Aquino, the widow of the slain Benigno Aquino, was the apparent victor, though Marcos was claiming otherwise.

Yet the final results had yet to be announced, and Reagan remained publicly neutral. "The determination of the government in the Philippines is going to be the business of the Philippine people, not the United States," he told reporters.

This wasn't quite true. The elections convinced Reagan that Marcos had become more of a liability than an asset. He decided Marcos had to go. But he didn't want to be seen as throwing Marcos overboard. He preferred discretion. When the Philippine National Assembly, against mounting evidence from neutral observers, declared Marcos the victor, the White House protested. "Although our observation delegation has not yet completed its work, it has already become evident, sadly, that the elections were marred by widespread fraud and violence perpetrated largely by the ruling party," a written statement said. "It was so extreme that the election's credibility has been called into question both within the Philippines and in the United States."

Reagan sent Phil Habib, his Middle East fixer, to Manila. Habib soon concluded that Reagan would have to take a higher profile. "The dominant view here is that Marcos is finished," Habib telephoned George Shultz. "But it will have to be the U.S. that gives him the boot." Habib said he had been handed a list of four generally pro-Marcos notables by an aide to the Philippine president. "I went to see them, and all four told me, 'Marcos has got to go, and you Americans have got to get rid of him. You're the Godfather. *You* do it.'" Habib said Cardinal Jaime Sin, the archbishop of Manila, had urged him to persuade Reagan to act. "Tell the president to pick up the phone and tell Marcos to go."

Reagan still hoped not to have to. But the Philippine people forced his hand. Hundreds of thousands poured into Manila's streets to protest the election fraud and demand the inauguration of Cory Aquino.

Marcos had caught Reagan's unspoken drift; amid the protests he wildly blamed the Americans for turning against him. "He called in panic and said that he thought that Weinberger had set the marines loose, and they were coming down the river after him," Paul Laxalt remembered. "I figured, well Jesus, gunboat diplomacy in Manila, for Christ's sake. It was a little weird. So I called Weinberger. Weinberger thinks I'm about half-nuts. 'Hell, no,' he said. So I called Marcos back to reassure him that the marines were not after him."

Marcos demanded to speak to Reagan directly. "The president, of course, couldn't talk to him," Laxalt recalled. Marcos unhappily settled for speaking to Laxalt. He asked for advice. "What would you do, Senator?" he said. Laxalt, on Reagan's authority, told him it was time to give up power and leave the Philippines. "There were long silences," Laxalt recalled. "He was very emotional." Marcos tried to bargain. He spoke of a compromise with Cory Aquino. Laxalt repeated his message, more firmly. "I was very direct," Laxalt said. Marcos didn't know what to say. "There was a long pause," Laxalt recounted. "I thought he'd passed away on me." When Marcos continued to bargain, Laxalt put the matter as succinctly as he could. "Mr. President, cut and cut clean," he said.

Marcos did cut, but he didn't cut cleanly. He fled Manila but tried to stay in the Philippines, forcing Reagan to let him know that this half-measure would not suffice. The United States would offer no protection against the wrath of the Philippine people as long as he remained in the country. Marcos and Imelda then accepted transport by the U.S. Air Force to Hawaii.

Reagan felt badly for the Marcoses. So did Nancy. "I phoned President Marcos and Imelda," he wrote in his diary some weeks later. "Nancy talked to her for an hour. They have not given up on returning to the Philippines and to the office which he claims is still his."

The Marcoses settled for Hawaii. Marcos's health declined, limiting his activities, but Imelda reprised her role as the center of attention, if on a smaller stage. "She's quite something," an employee at an Oahu restaurant she frequented told a reporter. "She'll make reservations for four, then she arrives with an entourage of nine or twelve, and more keep coming all evening to join the group." A clerk at an upscale dress shop remarked, "She always gets very special treatment."

Donald Regan learned a great deal as chief of staff about Reagan that he hadn't guessed as Treasury secretary. He discovered that the president had a passion for order and predictability. "His daily schedule was the centerpiece of his life," Regan wrote. "The scrupulous way in which he observed it, checking off each event with a pencil after it ended and preparing himself for the next, gave his life a regularity and a tangible measure of accomplishment that evidently was deeply pleasing to him. He seemed to feel that his schedule set him free: more than almost any other person in the world, he knew exactly what to expect all day long, every day."

Reagan assumed others valued predictability as much as he did. He interrupted the routine of the White House staff only rarely, and then primarily to deliver a birthday balloon or funny gift. He often didn't know the recipients, but he enjoyed the moments much as he had enjoyed playing the celebrity on his publicity tours as a Hollywood star.

Reagan almost never canceled meetings. He knew that a great deal of effort had gone into the planning and that people might be upset. "He seemed genuinely horrified at the prospect of causing embarrassment or disappointment or inconvenience to another person," Regan said. "If he promised that he would do something, he did it."

Unlike many presidents, Reagan enjoyed cabinet meetings. "He loved the give-and-take of policy discussions at the cabinet councils, when he had a chance to pronounce on the broad general principles that primarily interested him," Regan said. The president especially enjoyed meetings attended by the female members of his cabinet. "The presence of Ambassador Jeane Kirkpatrick or Secretary of Transportation Elizabeth Dole at a cabinet meeting always made for a heightened presidential mood; he was more amusing, more talkative."

Reagan's style of persuasion was gentle, almost passive. With legislators in particular, he appealed to reason. "The president never bullied, never threatened, never cajoled," Regan said. "It was always: Let me explain why I'm for this bill, and I hope that we can count on your vote. He would listen to the reply, making meticulous notes as he went. If the senator or the congressman had some sort of problem with a provision of the bill, Reagan would assure him that he would look into the matter, and he never failed to do so—usually by handing his notes to me and asking for a follow-up." The president didn't win over every waverer, but he got more than his share.

In Regan's experience only Tip O'Neill consistently resisted Reagan's charm. Regan judged this significant, as it belied the popular perception of the president and the speaker. "Although photographs taken after their meetings suggested a sort of underlying Irish camaraderie between the two men, the reality was that they were hammer and anvil," Regan said. "O'Neill seemed determined to dislike Reagan and disagree with him, and sparks flew as a result." Reagan was mystified. "I don't know what the hell's the matter with the man," he told Regan. "I just can't seem to reach him."

Regan recalled an afternoon meeting at the White House, to which Reagan had invited the congressional leaders to discuss the budget. Reagan wasn't a drinker, but on this occasion he slowly sipped an orange blossom cocktail. The guests imbibed more seriously. "It was a relaxed occasion, as it was intended to be, in which to discuss differences in a friendly atmosphere," Regan recalled. Various suggestions were made as to which items could be cut. Eventually, one of the Democrats teasingly suggested, in the casual spirit of the session, that many of the problems could be solved if the president would simply agree to raise taxes. Reagan responded, in similar good humor, "Come on, fellows. You know I'm not going to raise taxes."

O'Neill's reaction shattered the easy mood. "His face flushed," Regan remembered. "With his meaty hand he delivered a karate chop to the table, rattling the glasses. 'All right, goddamnit!' he shouted. 'If that's the way it's going to be, then everything is off the table with me, too!'"

The room fell into a stunned silence. No one had ever expected to see the president of the United States berated in his own house. Reagan himself was taken aback. "Reagan's face flushed—a little pinker than usual because even a small amount of alcohol causes his naturally ruddy color to rise," Regan recounted. "The president's lips pursed, a sure sign of anger. But he held onto his self-control. 'Well, damn it, Tip,' he said, 'I just can't do it.'"

YET THE TWO Irishmen needed each other, not least on the issue that proved to be the centerpiece of Reagan's domestic agenda during the second term. Don Regan had jumped from Treasury to the White House not least to champion tax reform, and at the president's right hand he pressed the issue. He made the case that reducing rates and closing loopholes would be good for the economy, good for the country, and good for the president politically. The economy would benefit from the stimulus of lower marginal rates and the redirection of talent and energy from tax dodges to productive enterprise. The country would benefit from the greater fairness of the principle that equal incomes should pay equal taxes. The president would benefit politically from a big victory on behalf of the American people.

Some of Reagan's advisers were skeptical. Paul Laxalt declared that anything beyond tweaking was a recipe for disaster. "When you open up the whole code, lobbyists from all over the country, and perhaps the world, will be crawling out from under any rock," Laxalt said.

But Reagan went ahead. He addressed the American people to pitch his vision of tax reform, based on the proposal Don Regan's team had crafted. "We have made one great dramatic step together," he said of his first-term tax cuts. "We owe it to ourselves now to take another. For the sake of fairness, simplicity, and growth, we must radically change the structure of a tax system that still treats our earnings as the personal property of the Internal Revenue Service; radically change a system that still treats people's earnings, similar incomes, much differently regarding the tax that they pay; and, yes, radically change a system that still causes some to invest their money, not to make a better mousetrap but simply to avoid a tax trap." The president outlined his plan. The existing system of fourteen tax brackets with rates that ranged from 11 percent to 50 percent would be replaced by a system of three brackets of 15, 25, and 35 percent. Low-income earners would benefit by the expansion of the standard deduction and the personal exemption.

The guiding principle was simplification; the primary value was fairness. Special loopholes, deductions, and exclusions would be dramatically curtailed. The new plan was revolutionary, but it had everything to recommend it. "Comparing the distance between the present system and our proposal is like comparing the distance between a Model T and the space shuttle," Reagan said with a smile. "And I should know—I've seen both." The task would not be easy. The defenders of the status quo would cling to their privileges. But Reagan put his faith in the American people and their insistence that government serve them and not the special interests. "The American dream belongs to you," he said. "It lives in millions of different hearts; it can be fulfilled in millions of different ways. And with you by our side, we're not going to stop moving and shaking this town until that dream is real for every American."

Reagan took his tax reform show on the road. By making his case to the people, he judged, as he had made his case during his first term, he could compel the lobbyists and the interest groups to yield. At Williamsburg, Virginia, he cited the antitax ethos of the American Revolution. "Here the arguments against unjust taxation rang out like a firebell in the night, and the chief arguer, Patrick Henry, gave our movement for independence the one thing it needed to become a revolution—he gave it passion," Reagan said. He quoted a senator who had opposed the Sixteenth Amendment, the one that allowed federal income taxes: "If we pass this amendment, we may very well see the day when the government could think it could take as much as 10 percent of a person's earnings." Reagan's audience groaned for the good old days. The tax code had grown hopelessly byzantine, Reagan said. "It's a system so utterly complex and ultimately inexplicable that half the time the tax professionals themselves aren't sure what the rules are—a system that even Albert Einstein is said to have admitted he couldn't begin to fathom." Reagan grinned as he added, "You know, it's said that his hair didn't look that way until after he experienced his first tax form."

He flew west to Wisconsin. In the blue-collar town of Oshkosh he led a rally for tax reform. "Do the people of Oshkosh want our tax system to be complicated and unfair?" he asked.

"No!" his audience responded.

"Do you want steeply rising tax brackets that punish achievement and hurt the American family?"

"No!"

"Or would you like a dramatic simplification that eliminates loopholes and makes our tax system straightforward, fair for all?"

"Yes!"

"And would you like to see a tax plan that increases personal exemptions, brings tax rates further down, and reduces the tax burden on working Americans and their families?"

"Yes!"

"Well, that's the tax plan that, with your help, we can and will pass this year."

He visited a high school in Atlanta. "Someone might say it's odd to talk about tax policy with young people in their teens," he observed. But he thought otherwise. "I know some of you already have part-time jobs, and I know you keep your eye on the part of the check that shows what Uncle Sam is taking out." Reagan's speechwriters had prepped him on the cultural touchstones of his audience. "The way I see it, if our current tax structure were a TV show, it would either be 'Foul-ups, Bleeps, and Blunders' or 'Gimme a Break,'" he said. "If it were a record album, it would be 'Gimme Shelter.' If it were a movie, it would be 'Revenge of the Nerds' or maybe 'Take the Money and Run.' And if the IRS—the Internal Revenue Service—ever wants a theme song, maybe they'll get Sting to do, 'Every breath you take, every move you make, I'll be watching you.'"

THOUGH REAGAN GOT the popular response he wanted, crafting the new tax law required many months and more than a few strategic compromises. The original plan was dubbed "Treasury I" at the time it was replaced by "Treasury II," a substitute that let some existing loopholes slide while adjusting certain proposed rates. The switch produced tension between Donald Regan, the father of the first version, and James Baker, the sponsor of the second. Baker thought Regan was becoming an impediment to the very cause he supported. "His indecisiveness and lack of political smarts almost killed tax reform," Baker subsequently said of Regan. The friction within the administration encouraged stalling by congressional opponents of reform, including many Republicans. On one test vote in the House, a mere fourteen Republicans sided with the administration, prompting Tip O'Neill to declare that the insurgents had humiliated their own president.

"The president *was* humiliated, and angry," Baker recalled. Yet the revolt focused the administration's attention. Baker urged the president to put his whole weight behind the proposed reforms. "Tax reform is *one of your top two domestic priorities*," Baker wrote to Reagan (the other priority being spending cuts). "It *will likely die if you do not support moving the Ways and Means bill forward* . . . You must keep the process moving forward."

Reagan agreed, and after O'Neill, who supported reform, challenged the president to deliver at least fifty Republican votes, Reagan resorted to retail politicking. He went up to Capitol Hill and met with the House Republicans. "It was a straight talk session with all sides having their say," Reagan recorded afterward. The opponents aired their grievances, which Reagan said he shared in some cases. But he said the bill could be fixed in the Senate. His strategy was subtle. He asked the representatives to vote for a bill he said he would veto if it arrived on his desk in its present form. Yet if they passed it, its flaws could be fixed in the Senate.

The maneuver worked, but barely. A head count revealed that forty-eight Republicans would side with the president. This left him two shy of the demand of O'Neill, who appeared unwilling to relent. Baker summoned reinforcements. "We assembled a team in the office of my old friend, House Minority Leader Bob Michel, and started working the phones," Baker remembered. "It took a lot of calls and a lot of horse-trading. I even agreed to come stump for one representative." But finally they secured the needed votes, and the measure passed the House.

More months were required before the two houses came to agreement, but the result was the most sweeping revision of the tax code since World War II. The top rate on personal income taxes fell to 28 percent, down from 50 percent (and from 70 percent when Reagan entered office). Four-fifths of Americans would fall into the expanded 15 percent bracket. The top corporate rate was slashed from 46 percent to 34 percent. Capital gains would be taxed as ordinary income, eliminating the incentive to shift compensation from the latter category to the former. Many of the most popular tax shelters and deductions were abolished, while the standard deduction was raised and the personal exemption was nearly doubled.

The losers didn't abandon their fight. Representatives of manufacturers forecast that the curtailment of investment tax credits would prevent needed modernization, with baleful consequences for the entire economy. Erstwhile recipients of other tax favors predicted similar ill effects.

Dan Rostenkowski, the Democratic chairman of the House Ways and Means Committee, whose backing for the bill had been vital to its passage, acknowledged the complaints but refused to reopen the issue. "Let the bill take effect and let the American people and businesses make their adjustments," he said. Congressman Richard Gephardt of Missouri, another Democratic supporter of the reform, waved aside the criticism as predictably self-serving. "I think this bill will be blamed for everything, including the common cold," Gephardt said.

Reagan appreciated the unaccustomed Democratic support, and he similarly dismissed the carping. "The journey's been long," he declared at the signing ceremony. "Many said we'd never make it to the end. But as usual the pessimists left one thing out of their calculations: the American people." He called the new tax code pro-business, pro-labor, pro-family, and pro-liberty. He acknowledged the vital contributions of members of both parties in Congress to the success of the tax bill. "I feel like we just played the World Series of tax reform and the American people won," he said, to laughter and applause.

TWO WEEKS LATER the president signed another landmark reform. Immigration had never been a priority issue with Reagan, certainly nothing like taxes. But as California governor he had grown aware of the tension between federal law on immigration and the economic law of supply and demand in unskilled labor. California's southern border, like the borders of Texas, New Mexico, and Arizona, had long been porous, allowing Mexicans eager to work in the United States to slip across without acquiring the documents to make their entry and subsequent residence legal. The system suited employers—agricultural concerns chiefly, but also construction companies and other enterprises—as it provided a pool of low-cost workers who could be counted on not to report mistreatment or unsafe working conditions to authorities. It suited the employers' customers—consumers of farm products, purchasers of new homes—who paid lower prices for goods and services than they would have otherwise. It suited the immigrants themselves, who wouldn't have come to America if it didn't.

But it didn't suit labor unions, which decried the depressing effect the immigrants had on wages. It sometimes didn't suit state and local authorities, who had to provide social services for the immigrants. And it didn't suit the many people in America who thought border laws ought to be enforced or who worried that heavy immigration from Mexico and countries farther south would dilute the traditional character and mores of the American people.

In 1985, Alan Simpson, a Republican senator from Wyoming, sponsored a bill to curtail illegal immigration and bring existing undocu-

mented immigrants in from the cold of illegality. Simpson had tackled
immigration before without success, but this time he got essential help
from Romano Mazzoli, a Democratic congressman from Kentucky. The
Simpson-Mazzoli bill aimed to curtail illegal immigration by imposing
stricter border controls and, crucially, penalties on employers who knowingly hired illegal immigrants. It meanwhile would provide a path to
legal residency for many of the undocumented immigrants already in the
United States.

The bill had to overcome the opposition of employers who liked the
status quo or feared being held liable for honest mistakes in screening job
applicants. Other skeptics fretted that the bill would become the entering wedge for a system of national identity cards—"papers" of the kind
Americans often associated with police states. But Simpson, especially,
and Mazzoli answered the objections, sometimes with logic, sometimes
with amendments to their bill, sometimes with quid pro quos, sometimes
with what Greg Leo of Reagan's Immigration and Naturalization Service
later called Simpson's "velvet-hammered charm."

Reagan let Simpson and Mazzoli do the heavy lifting on immigration reform, but as the bill gained momentum, he assured the sponsors
he was with them. "Al Simpson came by to see if he had my support,"
Reagan recorded in October 1986, shortly after the measure cleared the
House. "They have one or two amendments we could do without but even
if the Senate in conference cannot get them out, I'll sign. It's high time we
regained control of our borders and his bill will do this."

The bill passed the Senate, and Reagan duly signed. "It will remove
the incentive for illegal immigration by eliminating the job opportunities
which draw illegal aliens here," he said in a written statement. The legal
residency route provided by the law was scarcely less important. "The
legalization provisions in this act will go far to improve the lives of a class
of individuals who now must hide in the shadows, without access to many
of the benefits of a free and open society. Very soon many of these men
and women will be able to step into the sunlight and, ultimately, if they
choose, they may become Americans."

The immigration law elicited controversy at once. Some Latino
groups embraced it enthusiastically. Manuel Lopez of the Mexican
American Political Association likened the measure's amnesty provision
to the Emancipation Proclamation. "It enables millions of persons who
came to this country as economic refugees to find a better way of life and
be free," Lopez asserted. Other provisions of the law inspired ambiva-

lence among Latinos, however. Many legal residents hailed the employer sanctions as protection against low-wage illegal immigrants, but others feared that the sanctions would simply discourage employers from hiring Latinos altogether. Employers complained that the burden of protecting the borders was being pushed onto them. "It turns a personnel manager into a special agent of the INS to help stem the tide," a Chicago labor-law specialist declared. Lawyers and officials who dealt with immigrants predicted a boom in forged documents purporting to show the residency required for employment and amnesty. "I think the only people who may ultimately benefit from the legislation will be the people in the business of manufacturing fraudulent documents," Linda Wong, an attorney with the Mexican American Legal Defense and Educational Fund, said. Officials of communities with large Latino populations complained at the prospect of having to raise taxes to pay for services to newly legal residents. "It is another disappointing chapter in Congress's failure to address a major national issue in a meaningful way," the supervisor of Los Angeles County said. Carlos Castaneda of the Carnegie Endowment for International Peace called the new law worse than useless for raising expectations it couldn't fulfill. "The act will undoubtedly exacerbate the racist, xenophobic sentiments that are increasingly common in border areas and other regions with large Mexican communities," Castaneda declared.

N
O MATTER WHAT else he was working on, Reagan never
forgot the American hostages in Lebanon. "He worried about
them personally," John Poindexter recalled. George Shultz put
the matter in stronger terms. "Reagan was agonized over the hostages,"
Shultz said. "It was deep in his gut." The president of the United States
was the most powerful man in the world, yet he was helpless in this crucial matter. "It just drove him crazy," Shultz said. "There were these hostages in Lebanon, Americans being tortured, and he couldn't do anything
about it, and he's their president."

And he constantly searched for ways to secure the hostages' release.
Two weeks after visiting the grave of Robert Stethem and greeting the
survivors of the TWA hijacking, Reagan wrote in his diary, "Some
strange soundings are coming from the Iranians. Bud M. will be here
tomorrow to talk about it. It could be a breakthrough on getting our seven
kidnap victims back. Evidently the Iranian economy is disintegrating fast
under the strain of war."

Bud McFarlane had been pondering Iran for some time. He assumed
that the Ayatollah Khomeini wouldn't live many years longer and that his
successors, presumably more moderate, might seek the protection of the
United States against the Soviet Union, as Khomeini's predecessors had.
McFarlane made contact with certain Israelis, whose government likewise
looked toward moderate elements in Iran for balance against Iraq, Israel's
nearer threat. The Iranians, for their part, engaged in the desperate war
against Iraq, sorely needed parts and replacements for the American-made
military equipment they had acquired under the shah. McFarlane envisioned encouraging the Iranian moderates by supplying them weapons.

The shipments would have to be secret, as any revealed contact with the U.S. government would compromise the Iranians involved. Arms shipments, moreover, would violate America's policy of neutrality between Iran and Iraq, as well as its embargo on weapons to terrorist-sponsoring states, among which the Reagan administration loudly and repeatedly included Iran.

McFarlane tested his idea on top officials of the administration. William Casey liked it, but George Shultz and Caspar Weinberger judged it harebrained and counterproductive. "To reverse our present policy and permit or encourage a flow of Western arms to Iran is contrary to our interests, both in containing Khomeinism and in ending the excesses of his regime," Shultz wrote to McFarlane. "It would seem particularly perverse to alter this aspect of our policy when groups with ties to Iran are holding U.S. hostages in Lebanon." Weinberger denounced the plan with equal vigor. "This is almost too absurd to comment on," he wrote on the note transmitting McFarlane's proposal. "It's like asking Qaddafi to Washington for a cozy chat." In a separate memo Weinberger was equally categorical. "Under no circumstances should we now ease our restrictions on arms sales to Iran," he declared. The proposed reversal of policy would be seen as "inexplicably inconsistent by those nations whom we have urged to refrain from such sales," and it might well simply strengthen the Khomeini regime.

Shultz and Weinberger thought their combined opposition, at a time when they agreed about little else, killed the plan. The president's public statements certainly suggested as much. In a speech to the American Bar Association, Reagan explicitly identified Iran as a sponsor of the intensifying campaign of global terror, which he called "a new, international version of Murder, Incorporated." In a news conference he reiterated his unyielding opposition to any compromise with terrorists. "America will never make concessions to terrorists," he said. "To do so would only invite more terrorism. Nor will we ask nor pressure any other government to do so. Once we head down that path there would be no end to it, no end to the suffering of innocent people, no end to the bloody ransom all civilized nations must pay."

McFarlane persisted, however, cloaking his initiative in deeper secrecy. Secrecy suited McFarlane's personality, Weinberger thought. "McFarlane is a man of evident limitations," Weinberger wrote later. "He could not hide them, but he did attempt to conceal them, by an enigmatic manner, featuring heavily measured, pretentious and usually nearly impenetrable prose, and a great desire to be perceived as 'better than Henry' "—Kissinger, the orchestrator of the opening to China in the early 1970s. "He was very secretive," Weinberger continued. "He seemed to feel that what he did was too important or classified to be discussed with anyone else."

McFarlane took his plan to Reagan, who was then in Bethesda Naval Hospital following his cancer surgery. Records and recollections of the meeting subsequently differed. Don Regan's notes summarized: "Middle East/hostage release/problem." Regan afterward explained, "The hostages were discussed in a general way. The sense of this part of the conversation, as well as I can remember it, was that the Iranians, who had already been helpful in connection with the TWA hijacking, might be disposed to be helpful in other situations if we were more friendly to them." Regan recounted that Reagan had paid close attention to McFarlane's description of the initiative and had asked several questions. The president approved the plan, telling McFarlane, according to Regan, "Yes, go ahead. Open it up."

But Reagan, when asked, said he had no memory of the hospital meeting with McFarlane. His diary nonetheless confirmed and slightly elaborated Regan's recollection. "Bud came by," Reagan wrote on July 18, 1985. "It seems two members of the Iranian government want to establish talks with us," Reagan recorded after the meeting. "I'm sending Bud to meet with them in a neutral country."

McFarlane did not, in fact, meet with the Iranians at this time. He engaged intermediaries instead. One was David Kimche of the Israeli Foreign Ministry, who suggested that Israel would transfer American-made missiles to Iran if the United States would replace them. McFarlane said he would forward the suggestion and return the administration's response.

In early August, McFarlane met with Reagan at the White House. He told of his conversation with Kimche and of the suggestion of the missile transfer from Israel to Iran. As George Shultz, present at the meeting, recalled, McFarlane talked of a strategic opening to Iran but also spoke of the hostages. McFarlane said the Iranians with whom he had been in contact could secure the release of four of the Americans. Shultz argued against the proposal, saying that arms transfers to Iran would be a serious mistake. "I thought that the president agreed, though reluctantly," Shultz wrote.

But Reagan had not agreed, as a diary entry a short while later indicated. "I received a 'secret' phone call from Bud McFarlane," the president, then vacationing at the ranch in California, wrote. "It seems a man high up in the Iranian government believes he can deliver all or part of the seven American kidnap victims in Lebanon sometime in early September. They will be delivered to a point on the beach north of Tripoli and we'll take them off to our Sixth fleet. I had some decisions to make about a few points—but they were easy to make. Now we wait."

Reagan's decisions involved the transfer of TOW antitank missiles from Israel to Iran. McFarlane notified the Israelis, who during the first two weeks of September 1985 delivered some five hundred TOW missiles to Iran. On September 15, one American hostage, the Reverend Benjamin Weir, was released.

Reagan hoped the other hostages would follow. "A call from Bud M. on the secure phone," he wrote in his diary on Sunday, September 15. "Rev. Weir, the Presbyterian minister, has been delivered to our embassy in Beirut and is now aboard the U.S.S. *Nimitz*. We're trying to hold it secret because of the other kidnap victims. An unverified source says they will be delivered in 48 hours. Everything is top secret but suddenly on the TV talk shows they quoted a Reuters story that an anonymous call had reported Weir's rescue. But of course we are stonewalling." Two days later Reagan recorded, "Rev. Weir and his family are at a 'safe house' here in our country. His family was a little hard to handle. They insisted on going to a hotel but we managed to move them when he arrived. So far the secret is holding and they are all together. We've been told by the mystery man in Beirut the others (hostages) will follow."

THE OTHER HOSTAGES did not follow. They remained in captivity when a separate event distracted Reagan while confirming his resolve to bring the hostages home. On October 7 an Italian cruise ship, the *Achille Lauro*, was hijacked off the coast of Egypt by four men affiliated with the Palestine Liberation Front. The hijackers demanded the release of various Palestinians detained by the Israelis. Reagan's diary reveals that he followed every detail of the hijacking with great care, all the more because the hostages included dozens of Americans. He directed the U.S. Navy to ready a rescue team.

The rescue proved unnecessary after the hijackers ordered the ship to Port Said, where they surrendered themselves to Egyptian authorities in exchange for a pledge of safe conduct to a friendly country. Reagan recounted the events in his diary: "Word came that the Italian liner had returned to Port Said—the hijackers were taken by the Egyptians who turned them over to the P.L.O. who took them out of Egypt. They were only four in number but then we learned they had killed an American—a 69-year-old man in a wheel chair. So we never had a chance to launch our rescue attack. The hostages minus one are on their way home."

The murder of the American, Leon Klinghoffer, infuriated Reagan, and he refused to be bound by the Egyptian government's safe-conduct pledge. He ordered the navy into action. "The big news was that our Navy F-14s had intercepted the Egyptian plane carrying the hijackers and forced them down on Sicily—the NATO base in Sigonella," he wrote on October 11. "Americans as well as friends abroad are standing six inches taller. We're flooded with wires and calls." Reagan worked the levers of diplomacy to try to get his hands on the hijackers. "There were other kinds of calls half the night, such as my call to Prime Minister Craxi of Italy asking that we be allowed to fly the four to the U.S. for prosecution here. He explained that he didn't have the authority—Italian magistrates are independent of the government. Well, the upshot is, Italy will prosecute but we are putting in an extradition request just in case."

Reagan was willing to endure criticism from the Arab world for his affront to international law in waylaying the Egyptian plane. "Mubarak is offended and called our act piracy," he wrote. "I think he's playing to his own audience. The Egyptian people are partial to the PLO." If anything, Reagan relished the harsh words. "I called Mrs. Klinghoffer," he wrote two days later. "She and some other passengers had a stop in Rome to identify the hijackers. She told me I'm really hated by them, that every few minutes during the ordeal on ship they were sounding off about me."

THE CONTINUED CAPTIVITY of most of the hostages in Lebanon following the initial delivery of arms to Iran inspired McFarlane and his staff to try again. This time the Iranians wanted HAWK antiaircraft missiles, and McFarlane endorsed the request. He judged that Reagan's previous approval of the TOW missiles would extend to the HAWKs, and he simply informed the president that a shipment from Israel was going forward, rather than asking for fresh authorization.

Reagan didn't object. Following a November 22 meeting of the NSC, he wrote, "Subject was our hostages in Beirut. We have an undercover thing going by way of an Iranian which could get them sprung momentarily." The next day he observed, "We're still sweating out our undercover effort to get hostages out of Beirut."

The second arms delivery was even less successful than the first. This time no hostages came home. McFarlane grew discouraged and told Reagan he wanted to resign. Reagan didn't try to dissuade him. McFarlane's last NSC meeting was on December 5. "Subject was our undercover effort to free our five hostages held by terrorists in Lebanon," Reagan wrote. "It is a complex undertaking with only a few of us in on it. I won't even write in the diary what we're up to."

What the administration was up to was more bartering of arms for hostages. By this time Oliver North, the NSC staffer who was taking the lead on implementing the policy, had reduced the initiative to a formula:

H-hr: 1 707 w/300 TOWs = 1 AMCIT
H+10hrs: 1 707 (same A/C) w/300 TOWs = 1 AMCIT
H+16hrs: 1 747 w/50 HAWKs & 400 TOWs = 2 AMCITs
H+20hrs: 1 707 w/300 TOWs = 1 AMCIT
H+24hrs: 1 747 w/2000 TOWs = French hostage

The 707 and 747 were the transporting planes; the AMCITs were American citizens.

North, unlike McFarlane, refused to be discouraged by the meager results to date. The administration must press forward, he argued, lest the hostages be in greater danger. "We are now so far down the road that stopping what has been started could have even more serious repercussions," he wrote to John Poindexter, currently McFarlane's deputy. "If we do not make at least one more try at this point, we stand a good chance of condemning some or all to death."

Reagan responded to this argument much as he had to previous arguments for sending weapons to Iran. "The president was profoundly concerned for the hostages," McFarlane recalled of a White House meeting at which the new danger to the hostages formed a central part of the discussion. John Poindexter remembered the president weighing the hazards of going ahead but concluding, "I don't think I could forgive myself if we didn't try." Reagan added, "If it becomes public, I think I can defend it, but it will be like answering the question of how many angels can dance on the head of a pin."

The initiative went forward. In January 1986, Reagan described the program in greater detail than he had previously confided to his diary. "This was a day spent on two issues," he wrote on January 7. "One was Qaddafi (Libya), and the other our five hostages in Lebanon." Reagan vented against Qaddafi before continuing: "The other issue is a highly secret convoluted process that sees Israel freeing some 20 Hezbollahs who aren't really guilty of any blood letting. At the same time they sell Iran some 'Tow' anti-tank weapons. We in turn sell Israel replacements and the Hezbollah free our five hostages. Iran also pledges there will be no more kidnappings. We sit quietly by and never reveal how we got them back."

The process turned out to be too convoluted for the Israelis, who recommended streamlining. Prime Minister Shimon Peres feared that Iran was losing its war with Iraq, and he urged the Americans to sell weapons directly to Iran. This appealed to John Poindexter, who had succeeded McFarlane as national security adviser. On January 17, 1986, Poindexter sent Reagan a memo outlining the Israeli plan, along with a draft presidential finding authorizing the direct sales. "Some time ago Attorney General William French Smith determined that under an appropriate finding you could authorize the CIA to sell arms to countries outside the provisions of the laws and reporting requirements for foreign military sales," Poindexter wrote in his memo. "The objectives of the Israeli plan could be met if the CIA, using an authorized agent as necessary, purchased arms from the Defense Department under the Economy Act and then transferred them to Iran directly after receiving appropriate payment from Iran. The Covert Action Finding attached at Tab A provides the latitude for the transactions indicated above to proceed." The finding itself declared, "The USG"—United States government—"will act to facilitate efforts by third parties and third countries to establish contact with moderate elements within and outside the Government of Iran by providing these elements with arms, equipment and related materiel." A previous finding had authorized aid to third countries; this version added the "third parties," understood to be private intermediaries.

Poindexter's memo and the presidential finding nodded to the idea of a strategic opening to Iran, but Reagan read them in terms of the hostages and what it would take to release them. He wrote in his diary that night, "Only thing waiting was NSC wanting decisions on our effort to get our five hostages out of Lebanon. Involves selling TOW anti-tank missiles to Iran. I gave a go ahead."

One thousand TOW missiles were delivered to Iran in February under the terms of the new finding. But no hostages were released. The Iranians instead kept the Americans dangling. "This morning more word about the possibility of getting our hostages out of Lebanon," Reagan wrote in his diary on February 28, a Friday. "This has been a long tragic time for the families. We are supposed to know by next Thursday."

Thursday came and went. March came and went, and April and most of May. "We still don't know whether our hostages will be freed," Reagan wrote on May 27. Robert McFarlane, though no longer national security adviser, continued to pursue the Iran initiative for the president. He had traveled to Tehran in an effort to untangle things and was now reporting in. "Bud's call revealed that two of the Iranians who had involved us were on the phony side," Reagan wrote. "However through them Bud was put in touch with a rep. from the P.M.'s office. Outrageous demands were made by the Hezbollahs such as Israel must leave the Golan Heights and South Lebanon. Kuwait must free the convicted murderers they've tried and imprisoned etc. Bud said no dice so they got back to the original price—sale of some weaponry. Now we'll know possibly in the next 48 hours."

Later that day, Reagan added to his diary entry. "Another call from Bud in Iran," he wrote. "Again they tried to exact some outrageous terms— delivery of the weapons and spare parts before release of the hostages. Bud told them deal was off. They backed down and said we had a deal, but they'd have to get through to the Hezbollah in Beirut. Bud thinks Iran, conscious of the Soviet forces on their border and their own lack of competence, want a long term relationship with us and this could be what's behind their negotiations. Now we wait some more." McFarlane was still thinking strategically, but Reagan remained focused on the hostages and the price of their release. "The deal is the plane carrying the material takes off from Tel Aviv. If at the end of three hours we have not received the hostages, we signal the plane to turn back."

"And that's just what we did," Reagan wrote the next day. "Signal the plane to turn back after over one-half hour. It seems the rug merchants said the Hezbollah would only agree to two hostages. Bud told them to shove it, went to the airport and left for Tel Aviv. This was a heartbreaking disappointment for all of us."

But neither McFarlane nor Reagan could walk away from the bargaining table. The Iranians, perhaps sensing the president's desperation, lowered their offer. In exchange for spare parts for HAWK missiles and additional TOWs, they would arrange the release of one hostage. McFarlane accepted the deal. Reagan was relieved and encouraged. "Saturday good word: one of our hostages—Father Jenco—was released in Lebanon and turned over to the Syrians," he wrote in his diary for July 26. "The release of Jenco is a delayed step in a plan we've been working on for months. It gives us hope the rest of the plan will take place. We'd about given up on this."

Reagan's relief turned to pleasure when he met Jenco and his family. "The high spot of the day: the arrival of Father Martin Jenco, just released by the Hezbollahs in Beirut after being a hostage 19 months," the president wrote on August 1. "His family were all with him and it was an emotional experience."

D URING THE SAME months when he was wrestling with Iran over the hostages, Reagan was battling Congress over the contras. The discovery of the CIA's mining of Nicaraguan harbors had produced another Boland amendment, the most restrictive yet. "No funds available to the Central Intelligence Agency, the Department of Defense, or any other agency or entity of the United States involved in intelligence activities may be obligated or expended for the purpose or which would have the effect of supporting, directly or indirectly, military or paramilitary operations in Nicaragua by any nation, group, organization, movement, or individual," the amendment declared, seemingly categorically.

Yet Reagan refused to be deterred. He judged the Boland restrictions wrongheaded and dangerous to American security, and he mounted a counteroffensive. Regional negotiations begun on Contadora Island in Panama had yielded little so far, but the administration watched them closely. The president's stated desire for peace in Central America required him to express support for the Contadora negotiations, if only to mollify skeptics in Congress. But he and his team had serious reservations as to what the negotiations might produce. The last thing Reagan wanted was a regional agreement that afforded the Sandinistas international legitimacy.

During the spring of 1985, Reagan publicly embraced the Contadora process as part of a strategy to secure new funding for the contras. "In NSC we're putting together an idea for trying to frame our spending request to Congress for the Contras in Nicaragua in connection with peace proposals," Reagan wrote in his diary that April. "I don't believe the Dem. House will vote us the money just on a straight up or down basis."

He expected a struggle. "Tip O'Neill and his cohorts are already bad-mouthing the idea," Reagan continued. "Indeed Tip sounds irrational." He thought the House speaker was waging a personal vendetta against him. "Tip has engineered a partisan campaign to hand me a defeat—never mind if it helps make another Cuba on the American mainland." Reagan chafed at the restrictions the legislature was putting on his ability to conduct diplomacy. He offered another plea for aid to the contras, couching their cause in terms of American obligation. "The United States has a clear, undeniable moral imperative not to abandon those brave men and women in their fight to establish democracy and respect for human rights in Nicaragua," he told the lawmakers. But O'Neill and the Democrats wouldn't budge. "Met with Repub. Leadership—House and Senate," he wrote in May. "I got a little ticked off and told them I was tired of foreign policy by a committee of 535."

Reagan's frustration prompted him to look elsewhere for contra funding. "Over to EOB"—the Executive Office Building—"to address about 150 presidents of major Jewish organizations," he wrote in his diary in March 1986. "Subject Nicaragua. Very well received." A few days later he recounted, "Over to EOB for a pitch on Nicaragua to an overflow crowd of leaders of a number of supporting organizations." At first Reagan asked simply for political help: paid advertisements and other forms of pressure on Congress to reopen the funding pipeline. But when the legislature continued to balk, he requested aid for the contras themselves. "Over to the Mayflower Hotel to the CSIS"—Center for Strategic and International Studies—"conference," he wrote in June. "I made a strong pitch for aid to the Contras and was well received." A week later: "Over to EOB to speak to 200 reps of various groups who are all gung ho for our effort to help the Contras in Nicaragua."

Meanwhile, the president solicited money for the contras from friendly foreign governments. King Fahd of Saudi Arabia visited Washington to discuss the Middle East; Reagan was happy to oblige, but he brought up another subject as well. "We talked of our Mideast peace plan," the president recorded. "He is agreeable to backing King Hussein and I think he sees merit in our proposals. He's also going to increase the funding he is secretly giving the Contras in Nicaragua."

The question of contra funding prompted a special meeting of the National Security Planning Group. Reagan expressed his concern about the Contadora negotiations and made clear he would oppose any settlement that left the Sandinista status quo in place. "We will not agree or settle for any agreement which does not provide for democracy in Nicaragua," the president told the planning group. "The main point of any settlement has to be to go back to the day the revolution against Somoza ended and enable the Nicaraguan people to decide what kind of government they want."

John Poindexter observed that the administration trod a narrow line on the Contadora negotiations. "We have a dilemma," he explained. "For there to be any chance of getting money for the contras, we need a negotiating track. But there is no guarantee we won't get an agreement which we don't want."

Caspar Weinberger preferred to have nothing to do with any Contadora agreement, which would remove what little leverage the administration had with Congress. "We just have to make sure that the negotiations do not get out of our control," Weinberger said. "We need to prevent them"—the Contadora negotiators—"signing an agreement or we will never get anything out of Congress."

George Shultz remarked that the administration wasn't getting anything from Congress as matters stood. The contras were at grave risk. "If we don't get money for the freedom fighters, they will be out of business," Shultz said. Some members of the administration were advocating efforts to persuade the relevant committees in Congress to redirect to the contras funds appropriated for other purposes. Shultz dismissed this idea as inane. "It's breathtaking in improbability," he said. "It would be better to go to other countries."

Weinberger agreed that the administration should solicit funds from other countries, but he wasn't ready to give up on Congress. "Try everything," the defense secretary said. "We should try every country we can find, the committees and the people of the United States. If the contras are out of business in July, we will have to fight there ourselves some day."

Oliver North attended this meeting as an aide to Poindexter and seconded Shultz's suggestion. "The fiscal year 1986 intelligence authorization bill permits the State Department to approach other countries for non-military aid," North said.

"Haven't we approached other countries?" William Casey asked.

"We have, but not with much success," Shultz replied.

"But until now we have not involved the president," Casey answered. "The Saudis, Israelis, South Koreans, Taiwanese all have some interest," he said.

The meeting ended with nothing decided and nothing said about the support the Saudis had already provided to the contras.

Neither did North share that he had devised a separate method for funding the contras. After the February delivery of TOW missiles to Iran, North had taken between $3 million and $4 million from the proceeds and placed it in an account from which the contras could draw. Two months later he sought authorization to continue the diversion. He drafted a memo for Poindexter describing the Iran enterprise and explaining how the profits from the sale of weapons might be disbursed. "$12 million will be used to purchase critically needed supplies for the Nicaraguan Democratic Resistance Forces," North wrote. At the end of the memo North included a recommendation: "That the President approve the structure depicted above."

Poindexter later testified that he couldn't recall receiving this memo. He said he had directed North not to put anything in writing about the diversion of funds to the contras. North denied receiving this direction. Poindexter nonetheless admitted knowing about the scheme, if only in outline. "I had a feeling that something bad was going on, but I didn't investigate it and I didn't do a thing about it," he told Donald Regan after the story broke, according to Regan's recollection. "I really didn't want to know. I was so damned mad at Tip O'Neill for the way he was dragging the contras around I didn't want to know what, if anything, was going on. I should have, but I didn't." Poindexter told Ed Meese much the same thing. "He said that he did know about it," Meese recounted. "Ollie North had given him enough hints that he knew what was going on, but he didn't want to look further into it. But that he in fact did generally know that money had gone to the contras as a result of the Iran shipment."

Still later Poindexter offered a fuller account. He said he had known about North's diversion and approved it in good conscience. "We didn't see anything illegal about it," he said. Indeed, he agreed with North that using the arms proceeds to keep the contras alive was a nice turn of policy. "They were like a gift from Iran, though Iran didn't know that." He said he had made a deliberate decision not to inform Reagan. "I didn't tell the president about it so that he would have plausible deniability." He understood that there was a political risk, but it was a risk worth taking. "It was more important that I take the risk than that the president take the risk," he said.

So the diversion went forward. And Reagan never knew to inquire about it.

PART SIX

THE FROSTY ICELAND AIR

1986–1988

ASIDE EFFECT OF the otherwise successful bombing of Libya was further postponement of action on arms control with the Soviet Union. Gorbachev knew Qaddafi had been a thorn in America's side for years; he asked himself why Reagan had chosen this moment to chastise him. He concluded that Washington was trying to prove a point. "The United States attacked Libya in a show of its might and impunity," he wrote later. Combined with the other provocations after Geneva, especially the breakout from SALT II and the resumption of nuclear testing, the strike on Libya suggested to Gorbachev that the Americans didn't take the Soviet Union seriously. "Did the Americans think we would not notice how they used the fledgling Soviet-American dialogue as a cover for new weapon programs?" He blamed Reagan not for insincerity but for inability to rein in the powerful groups who benefited from an arms race. "Détente or even a simple warming in Soviet-American relations did not conform to the interests of certain people in the West who would use any pretext to undermine the improvement in international relations initiated in Geneva."

Additional complications arose. In August 1986 the FBI sent a request to the White House seeking approval of the arrest of Gennadi Zakharov, a Soviet scientist employed by the United Nations who evidently was doubling as an agent of the KGB. Had Zakharov been a diplomat and enjoyed immunity from arrest and prosecution, he would have been deported. An American diplomat in the Soviet Union might have been deported in a tit for tat, but the issue would have gone no further. Because he lacked immunity, however, he could be arrested and prosecuted.

The FBI was especially eager to make the arrest, as the bureau had been embarrassed by recent revelations of Soviet spying in the United

States. For similar reasons the CIA and the State Department supported the FBI request, and the White House gave its approval. Zakharov was seized in a sting operation.

A week later the Soviets retaliated by arresting Nicholas Daniloff, an American journalist in Moscow, and charging him with espionage. "It is of course a frame up," Reagan told himself. The president wrote to Gorbachev asserting as much. "I can give you my personal assurance that Mr. Daniloff has no connection whatever with the U.S. Government," Reagan declared. The president added, "There are no grounds for Mr. Daniloff's detention, nor for any attempt to link him to any other case. If he is not freed promptly, it can only have the most serious and far-reaching consequences for the relationship between our two countries."

Gorbachev didn't believe Reagan. "Your letter of September 5 prompted me to ask for information regarding the question you raised," Gorbachev replied. "As was reported to me by competent authorities, Daniloff, the Moscow correspondent of the U.S. News and World Report magazine, had for a long time been engaged in impermissible activities damaging to the state interests of the USSR. Now an investigation is being conducted by the results of which we shall be able to make a conclusive judgment about this entire case."

Reagan didn't anger easily, but he grew livid at having his personal word doubted. "Gorbachev response to my letter was arrogant and rejected my statement that Daniloff was no spy," he wrote in his diary. "I'm mad as h--l."

WHAT REAGAN DIDN'T know was that the CIA wasn't telling him the full story. Reagan had asked William Casey if Daniloff was a spy; Casey had assured him Daniloff was not. This was true, but it omitted pertinent information. George Shultz didn't trust Casey or the CIA, and he demanded to learn whatever the agency knew about Daniloff. He was informed that Daniloff had received an envelope from a "Father Potemkin" for transmission to the American embassy. Daniloff delivered the envelope, which contained a message that appeared to be from a source that had previously conveyed valuable information about the Soviet nuclear arsenal. The CIA tried to contact the source through Potemkin, in the process mentioning Daniloff. This likely came to the attention of the KGB, and it might have been what Gorbachev was referring to in his letter to Reagan.

Shultz asked Abraham Sofaer, legal adviser to the State Department, to look into the matter and give his opinion. "The CIA has really reamed Daniloff," Sofaer reported. "Based on my reading of his activities, Daniloff can credibly be prosecuted under Soviet law, and a Soviet journalist who became similarly involved with the KGB in the U.S. could credibly be prosecuted under our law." Sofaer later commented, "The Soviets had done a beautiful job of replicating what we had done to Zakharov."

"This put a whole new light on the case," Shultz recalled. He phoned John Poindexter at the White House and said he had some information to share with the president on the Daniloff case. The national security adviser didn't seem eager to receive the information, for reasons Shultz couldn't fathom, but he couldn't turn away the secretary of state. "I found President Reagan poorly informed about the case," Shultz remembered, "and I felt that Poindexter clearly did not want him well informed."

Shultz had Sofaer tell Reagan what he knew. "I went through the facts," Sofaer said afterward. "I explained the situation." He found Reagan to be an engaged listener. "He kept interrupting me. What about this? What about that?" Yet the president refused to alter his view of the Soviet handling of the affair. "His basic point was, these are the bad guys. They've concocted this record."

Sofaer, a former prosecutor and judge, responded, "You're absolutely right, but it doesn't matter. If it were in a federal court and we concocted the records, and we gave Daniloff the documents, just as we gave them to Zakharov, he would be dead. He'd be prosecuted successfully in your own district courts."

"How can we equate these things?" Reagan protested. He refused to accept Sofaer's explanation. "The president went on and on about that," Sofaer recalled. Sofaer kept at it. "I didn't quit. I just went on. Every time he asked me a question, I told him what I thought. Finally I said, 'Mr. President, you keep talking about the truth. The truth has nothing to do with the judicial system. Sure, you always try to get to the truth, and occasionally you get it, but if you think you always get the truth as a result of a judicial process, you're wrong. That's not what you get. You get a finding. You get a finding of guilt or a conclusion of guilt. You don't get truth. This is not God. This is just people doing our best to make findings. I'm telling you, as a trial judge and a prosecutor, that what you would get out of the system for Daniloff is going to be the same thing you would get out of the system for Zakharov.'"

"That had an impact on him," Sofaer recounted. "I could see that hit him square between the eyes. He's a very practical man. He prides himself, in fact, on being practical. I could see that. But he kept wagging his head the way Reagan always did. 'Well, Abe, it doesn't seem sensible to me to equate a reporter just trying to be a good citizen, with a professional spy.' I said, That's clearly true as a matter of principle, but in this case, with regard to Daniloff, the outcome would be the same."

Reagan remained reluctant, though, and Shultz sensed they had overstayed their welcome. He pulled Sofaer aside, and they turned to leave. "We were heading out the door," Sofaer recalled. "I could see he"—Reagan—"wasn't comfortable with his position. He was anxious about it. He got up and walked us to the door. He didn't want us to leave, almost. He kept asking questions. So I turned around, and I said to him, 'You know, the difference here, the important thing for you to remember, is that Daniloff is an American citizen who didn't do anything wrong. He was brought into this by our own CIA, and he could spend the rest of his life in prison if we fail to understand that a reasonable deal could be made on his behalf.'"

Sofaer remembered Reagan's reaction. "It was like hitting him with a left jab. He's a very emotional man. This man clearly cares about people. He realized that there was a human being involved here. It wasn't just an abstract argument."

But Reagan still rejected any moral equivalence between Zakharov and Daniloff. "Their man is a spy caught red handed and Daniloff is a hostage," he wrote to himself. And he continued to deny, even to himself, that there would be a trade. "Most of the shows dealt with the Daniloff matter," he recorded after watching the Sunday morning news programs. "And a number of the media and press involved launched a campaign that I had blinked and softened—giving in to Soviet demands. That's a lot of crap and they don't know what they are talking about." Three days later he was still complaining about the media. "The press is obsessed with the Daniloff affair and determined to paint all of us as caving in to the Soviets which they of course say is the worst way to deal with them. The simple truth is we've offered no deal and are playing hard ball all the way."

Eduard Shevardnadze was in the country for the autumn session of the UN General Assembly; he dropped down to Washington to discuss the Daniloff case and other matters between the Soviet Union and the United States. Reagan lit into him. "I let the Foreign Minister know I was angry and that I resented their charges that Daniloff was a spy after I had personally given my word that he wasn't. I gave him a little run down on the difference between our two systems and told him they couldn't understand the importance we place on the individual because they don't have such a feeling." Reagan added, "I enjoy being angry."

GORBACHEV ENJOYED BEING angry, too. Or at least he found it politically useful. He had Shevardnadze deliver a letter to Reagan in which he reiterated that the Daniloff case required further investigation. He said he had hoped this could occur in an atmosphere of calm. "However, the US side has unduly dramatized that incident," he continued. "A massive hostile campaign has been launched against our country, which has been taken up at the higher levels of the United States administration and Congress. It is as if a pretext was deliberately sought to aggravate Soviet-American relations and to increase tension."

Gorbachev lamented that things had come to such a pass. The positive spirit of Geneva had been squandered. Yet he wasn't willing to give up on it entirely. "That is why an idea has come to my mind to suggest to you, Mr. President, that, in the very near future and setting aside all other matters, we have a quick one-on-one meeting, let us say in Iceland or in London, maybe just for one day, to engage in a strictly confidential, private and frank discussion (possibly with only our foreign ministers present). The discussion—which would not be a detailed one, for its purpose and significance would be to demonstrate political will—would result in instructions to our respective agencies to draft agreements on two or three very specific questions, which you and I could sign during my visit to the United States." Gorbachev closed, "I look forward to your early reply."

It was an offer Reagan couldn't refuse. Frustrated at the loss of diplomatic momentum after Geneva and eager to bring Daniloff home, the president dropped his insistence on treating Zakharov and Daniloff differently. He let Shultz arrange a deal with Shevardnadze. The American journalist was released without trial from Soviet custody and allowed to leave the country. Zakharov was permitted to plead no contest to the espionage charges and was likewise sent home. Gorbachev gave Reagan political cover by granting Soviet dissident Yuri Orlov and his wife permission to emigrate. And on the day of Zakharov's release the American and Soviet governments announced that Reagan and Gorbachev would meet in Reykjavík, Iceland, the second weekend in October.

A SUMMIT ON LESS than two weeks' notice was unheard of in superpower history. Skeptics of summitry weren't mollified by White House efforts to call the Iceland rendezvous a working meeting—"a pre-summit planning session"—rather than a summit, and anyway the efforts failed. Summits had become media events, at least in the West, and the media refused to forgo the drama and television ratings "summits" provided.

The skeptics lit into Reagan, and for the first time in his career he found himself pilloried from the right. The critics couldn't decide whether the president had let himself be bamboozled by George Shultz and other pro-summit softies in the administration or, more alarmingly, was revealing a heretofore hidden streak of détente-like concessionism. Reagan thought he had inoculated himself against such attacks by swearing full devotion to SDI, with which the conservatives had fallen in love. "Our SDI research is not a bargaining chip," he declared in a national radio address. He said he would talk to Gorbachev about eliminating offensive missiles but not defensive systems. "It's the number of offensive nuclear missiles that need to be reduced, not the effort to find a way to defend mankind against these deadly missiles." Reporters pressed him nonetheless. Would SDI be on the table in negotiations with Gorbachev, perhaps as part of a grand bargain to reduce offensive arsenals? Pouring the concrete around his feet, Reagan replied, "Our response to demands that we cut off or delay research and testing and close shop is: No way. SDI is no bargaining chip. It is the path to a safer and more secure future."

Perhaps the critics weren't listening. Or maybe they wanted to help the concrete harden. In any case, they let Reagan know he would pay dearly if he showed the slightest weakness in Iceland. George Will described an administration "reeling toward a summit" and mocked the logic behind the meeting: "The administration believes the impediment to Soviet reasonableness is Soviet neurosis. A therapeutic U.S. policy can dispel that, especially a policy advocated by a great communicator, especially one who knows communists from the experience of labor-union strife in Hollywood forty years ago." Charles Krauthammer warned that the "snap summit" boded ill for American interests. "All summits are a risk, the Reykjavik summit more than most," Krauthammer wrote. He lashed Reagan for trading Zakharov for Daniloff and feared that a similar lack of principle and courage would be revealed in Iceland. Rowland Evans and Robert Novak blamed Shultz for pushing the president into a "posture of vulnerability" as he approached Reykjavík. "He either gives Gorbachev what he wants or returns empty-handed three weeks before the election," the co-columnists wrote. Republican congressman Jack Kemp agreed that the timing was terrible. "This is the wrong kind of environment going into a critical, high-level meeting next week," Kemp said.

REAGAN'S NATIONAL SECURITY team worked around the clock to prepare the president for whatever Gorbachev might throw at him in Iceland. "We go into Reykjavik next week with very little knowledge of how Gorbachev intends to use the meeting," the NSC staff conceded in a memo to Reagan. "The same was true of Geneva, of course, but the uncertainty is perhaps greater this time around." The NSC group saw no reason to think Gorbachev had altered his long-term goals: "to unravel the Western consensus behind tougher policies toward the Soviet Union, to stabilize US-Soviet relations in a way that gives him greater latitude in his domestic policies, and over time to regain a more favorable position in the global balance of power." Arms control would be a means toward each of these ends. But the NSC authors predicted nothing significant on this front at Reykjavík. The big question was whether Gorbachev would agree to a 1987 summit in Washington, the more likely venue for any major initiative on arms control. The memo posed three possibilities: Gorbachev had already decided to come to Washington, he remained neutrally undecided about further meetings, or he had decided he would come only if he won some significant concessions in Iceland. "It is conceivable that between now and Reykjavik we may see some Soviet probes that begin to tip their hand and to indicate which of these routes Gorbachev will follow," the memo observed. "More likely, however, is that you will have to smoke him out during your discussions."

George Shultz weighed in separately. The secretary of state continued to battle Weinberger for the mind of the president, and he assumed the defense secretary would warn that nothing good could come from Reykjavík. Shultz pushed in the opposite direction. "We should take a positive, self-confident and commanding approach to this meeting," he told Reagan. "The American people are all for it so we should not seem to be playing it down or disparaging its chances for solid progress." Shultz didn't expect breakthrough agreements at Reykjavík; these could await the next full summit, in Washington. Yet he hoped for modest progress, perhaps on human rights but especially on arms control. "Arms control will be key not because that is what the Soviets want, but because we have brought them to the point where they are largely talking from our script. This doesn't mean Gorbachev will be easy to handle in Reykjavik, but it means we are justified in aspiring to accomplish something useful there." A framework for reductions in ballistic missiles was a good possibility; likewise an agreement in principle on intermediate nuclear forces. The president's position, and America's, had never been better. "The policies you set in motion six years ago have put us in the strong position we are in today," Shultz said. "We are now entering the crucial phase in the effort to achieve real reductions in nuclear forces—an historic achievement in itself and a major step toward your vision of a safer world for the future."

GORBACHEV MADE HIS own preparations for Reykjavík. The general secretary judged that the chances for serious movement by Reagan on arms control were slim. "I am convinced," he told the Politburo, "that in the U.S. governing circles they do not want to allow a relaxation of tensions, a slowing down of the arms race. This is most important for them now. Not to allow us to expand our plans. Not to let us increase the dynamism of our system. Not to let us strengthen our democracy." Yet the Soviet Union was winning the battle for the support of the world. "It seems like everybody is turning toward us now, in the U.N. as well as in Stockholm," Gorbachev said. "Truly, there is no way for them to get away from our initiatives." The American ruling circles had noticed the warm reception of the world to Soviet initiatives. "This is what scares the Americans, inspires them to try to undermine our plans, to sow mistrust by the arms race, including among our population, a disillusionment in our policy."

Gorbachev doubted that Reagan could overcome this American resistance, even if he wanted to. "Most likely nothing can really be done with this administration," Gorbachev predicted. He had spoken with various Western leaders, including Pierre Trudeau of Canada. "Trudeau warns us that we will not be able to come to an agreement with Reagan, who is a product of certain forces and who has been appointed and sponsored by them." But Trudeau had urged Gorbachev to look beyond Reagan. "He says you are doing the right thing and have already reached the ears of the Congress."

Gorbachev was not ready to write Reagan off. He realized the president wouldn't be easily persuaded. "In order to move Reagan, we have to give him something," Gorbachev told his associates. "Something with pressure and breakthrough potential has to be done. We have to decide for ourselves what is realistic, in what the USA is bluffing and what we are ready to do, what we can get out of them right now." He said he would lead at Reykjavík with the issue of strategic weapons. "Strategic weapons concern everybody, the most of all other issues. And we must emphasize that we are proposing the liquidation of nuclear weapons, which we already discussed with the President in Geneva. The talks must be devoted precisely to this goal."

Gorbachev guessed that Reagan would insist on pursuing strategic missile defense. The general secretary judged this a winning issue for the Soviet Union even if it blocked a broader treaty. "I will tell Reagan in Reykjavik that our response will be effective. And not from the direction from which you, so to say, expect it. I will look him straight in the eye as I say this: If you do not meet us halfway, well then my conscience will be clean before you and before myself. Now I have to explain to my people and to the whole world why nothing worked out between us." Reagan would bear the blame.

Gorbachev respected Reagan as a negotiator and didn't expect him to give anything away at Reykjavík. "Nothing will come out of it if our proposals lead to a weakening of US security," he said. There had to be something for both sides in any bargain. "Thus the principle is as follows: increased security for all along the way toward equal reduction of armaments levels." Gorbachev was committed to arms control, which he considered essential to the Soviet future. "Our goal is to prevent the next round of arms race. If we do not do this, the threat to us will only grow. And if we do not compromise on some questions, even very important ones, we will lose the main point; we will be pulled into an arms race beyond our power, and we will lose this race, for we are presently at the limit of our capabilities." This conclusion was inescapable, and Gorbachev reiterated it: "If the new round begins, the pressure on our economy will be inconceivable. That is why to avoid the new round of arms race is the task of tasks for us."

Even so, Gorbachev didn't think he would have to accept Reagan's position on strategic defense. "I have read everything available on the SDI," he remarked to his aides. "We should concentrate all our resources on the development of our own anti-SDI." This must be a top priority. "We must not allow the US superiority in this issue. So far, from what I have read up till now, and from what was reported to me, I see that we can reach the result with smaller expenditure. If the Americans do not accept an agreement, then we will tell them that we will be looking for a move which they do not expect."

Gorbachev heard the outcry of American conservatives against the Iceland summit, and he thought it would make Reagan harder to work with. "The rightists are concerned about Reykjavik," he told the Politburo. "They are intimidating Reagan. Once again we hear appeals to expand the borders of freedom, once again they are speaking of a crusade, threatening to send socialism to the scrap heap of history. Reagan is working on placating the right for his agreement to go to Reykjavik. From all this it follows that the meeting will be very difficult. We should not exclude a possibility of failure."

The American president knew he was losing the propaganda battle, Gorbachev said. "Reagan understands—and information from Trudeau confirms this—that the line of action suggested to him by the extremists is not acceptable for the world. He sees a way out for himself in holding a meeting for the sake of a meeting." Yet once in Iceland he would feel pressure to achieve something of substance. "People around the world are inclined to demand a constructive outcome. Reagan needs this as a matter of personal ambition, so as to go down in history as a 'peace president.' The elections are just around the corner."

Yet if Reagan needed a success at Reykjavík, so did the Soviet Union. Gorbachev returned to the necessity of controlling the arms race. "Something needs to be done in this central direction," Gorbachev said. "It needs to be pushed forward. The United States has an interest in keeping the negotiations machine running idle, while the arms race overburdens our economy. That is why we need a breakthrough. We need the process to start moving." Gorbachev sketched the grim alternative. "The most important task is to prevent a new round of arms race. Otherwise, modernization of strategic weapons. Tridents, Minutemen, entering space with weapons. Then a degradation of our ecological, strategic and political security—a loss on all sides, because first and foremost it will lead to a wearing out of our economy. This is impermissible. That is why it is impermissible to cling to particulars, to details, to fail to see the bigger picture behind the details, to confuse one's own head with arguments over details. If they impose a second round of arms race upon us, we will lose!"

ONE PERSON WHO did not prepare for Reykjavík was Nancy Reagan. The First Lady's previous experience of summitry, in Geneva, had been less than satisfactory. "I was nervous about my first meeting with Raisa Gorbachev," she said of the Geneva event. "I didn't know what I would talk about with her." She soon learned that silence was not a problem. "From the moment we met, she talked and talked and *talked*—so much that I could barely get a word in, edgewise or otherwise." The Soviet First Lady seemed to love the sound of her own voice. "My fundamental impression of Raisa Gorbachev was that she never stopped talking. Or lecturing, to be more accurate. Sometimes the subject was the Soviet Union and the glories of the Communist system. Sometimes it was Soviet art. More often than not, it was Marxism and Leninism. Once or twice, she even lectured me on the failings of the American political system. I wasn't prepared for this, and I didn't like it."

For a socialist, Raisa Gorbachev could be quite imperious, Nancy thought. "When she came to tea in Geneva that first day, she struck me as a woman who expected to be deferred to," she said. "When she didn't like the chair she was seated in, she snapped her fingers to summon her KGB guards, who promptly moved her to another chair. After sitting in the new spot for a couple of minutes, she decided she didn't like that one either, so she snapped her fingers and they moved her again. I couldn't believe it. I had met first ladies, princesses, and queens, but I had never seen anybody act this way."

Raisa Gorbachev hosted a tea at the Soviet mission. "The hall was covered with children's paintings, and Raisa insisted that I look at each one while she described the meaning behind it," Nancy recalled. "I felt condescended to, and I wanted to say, 'Enough. You don't have to tell me what a missile is. I get the message!'" Raisa showed her to the room where the tea was served. "Welcome," she said. "I wanted you to see what a typical Russian tea looks like." Nancy took note. "On the table was a lovely antique samovar," she recounted. "And next to it was a mouth-watering array of delicacies: blinis with caviar, cabbage rolls, blueberry pie, cookies, chocolates, honey and jam. I couldn't possibly try everything, and I finally had to give up. It was a beautiful spread, but if that was an ordinary housewife's tea, then I'm Catherine the Great."

Nancy's experience at Geneva inclined her to accede when Jack Matlock of the NSC staff suggested that she stay home from Reykjavík, lest Gorbachev bring Raisa and the business meeting expand to include the social trappings of a regular summit. Reagan never liked being apart from Nancy, but he accepted Matlock's suggestion. The Soviet government was informed that Mrs. Reagan would not be attending. Yet the Gorbachevs either ignored or misinterpreted the hint, for the Kremlin indicated that Mrs. Gorbachev *would* be attending.

"This put me in an awkward position," Nancy remembered. "Should I go simply because she was going?" She weighed the matter carefully. "No, I decided. Raisa's last-minute reversal struck me as a bit of one-upsmanship. I had a full schedule in Washington, as I'm sure she knew, and I didn't want to change it. Besides, I thought it was important, as my son Ron put it, not to be jerked around. I felt that Raisa was testing me, to see if I would cave in and change my mind. But she had to know that schedules are made out long in advance, and I was determined not to give in. This was supposed to be a meeting, not a formal summit, and as far as I was concerned, that's the way it would stay."

DON REGAN JUDGED that Nancy's astrologer had something to do with her decision to stay home from Iceland. By this time Regan realized that not even summitry was beyond the reach of Nancy's faith in the stars. He had felt the pull in the planning for Geneva. "As usual, Mrs. Reagan insisted on being consulted on the timing of every presidential appearance and action so that she could consult her Friend in San Francisco about the astrological factor," Regan wrote. "The large number of details must have placed a heavy burden on the poor woman, who was called upon not only to choose auspicious moments for meetings between the two most powerful men on our planet, but also to draw up horoscopes that presumably provided clues to the character and probably behavior of Gorbachev."

Regan thought all this was ludicrous, but he recognized that it was unavoidable. And he wasn't unhappy when Joan Quigley apparently advised Nancy against making the trip to Iceland. "After extensive consultations with her Friend, Mrs. Reagan decided that she would not accompany her husband to Iceland," Regan wrote. But Quigley influenced the summit nonetheless. "Mrs. Reagan also consulted with her Friend as to the best day for the Presidential departure, and the astrologer informed us that Thursday, October 9, was the most auspicious date. We wrote it into the schedule."

THE ICELAND AUTHORITIES were happy to call the meeting a summit. They and the people of the country were delighted by the attention that surrounded the visit of the American president and the Soviet general secretary. Public opinion appeared to favor Gorbachev. "The Russians are gaining sympathy in Iceland right now because Gorbachev proposed the meeting and because they think he is more sincere in wanting arms control," the marketing director of a Reykjavík hotel told a reporter. Gorbachev also scored points for bringing Raisa. But Reagan benefited from the cachet advantage of American culture in Icelandic life. Two discotheques in Reykjavík were named the Hollywood and the Broadway (a third was called the Kremlin), and the current most popular film was the paean to U.S. Navy aviation *Top Gun*.

The meeting was a boon to the local economy. Hotels got four times the normal rate for rooms; restaurants and taxis enjoyed similar windfalls. The mayor of Reykjavík hoped the superpower summit, as he pointedly labeled the meeting, would lead to a surge in convention business. "If we are good enough for Reagan and Gorbachev, why not for conferences of I.B.M.?" he said. The director of the country's tourism bureau was more cautious, praying for no major problems. "If something bad happens this weekend," he said, "Iceland may as well pack up and go all the way back to the North Pole."

The venue for the sessions between Reagan and Gorbachev was Höfði House, an eighty-year-old mansion that had once housed foreign diplomats and still harbored ghosts, according to local legend. One version described the most active spirit as the shade of a young woman who had worked for a poet who lived in the house, and killed herself, apparently from unrequited love. Another said she was a lost soul whose body had washed ashore on the beach below the house. Still another offered a more manly explanation, claiming that the house was built over an ancient Viking graveyard. Icelandic authorities took no side in the debate. "We do not confirm or deny that the Hofdi has a ghost," a spokesman for the Foreign Ministry explained.

THE TWO LEADERS arrived at Höfði simultaneously at 10:30 on Saturday morning. They shook hands, smiled for the cameras, and proceeded inside, where they repeated the handshake and smiles. With their foreign ministers, George Shultz and Eduard Shevardnadze, they entered the meeting room and set to work.

Gorbachev's proposal to rid the world of nuclear weapons still thrilled the world and continued to put Reagan at a disadvantage in public relations. The general secretary moved at once to press his edge. "I would like to precisely, firmly and clearly announce that we are in favor of such a solution to the problem"—of the arms race—"which would ultimately provide for complete liquidation of nuclear weapons," he said.

This would be a big step, Gorbachev granted, but it was possible. And it could be accomplished only with due consideration for the security interests of both sides. "Any other approach would be unintelligible, unrealistic and inadmissible," he said. He hoped the president felt the same way.

Reagan nodded. "We have exactly the same feelings," he said. Much would depend on the confidence each side could have in treaty enforcement. The president didn't respond at this point to Gorbachev's proposal to abolish nuclear weapons; instead, he employed a one-liner Jack Matlock had helped him with. "There is a Russian proverb," Reagan said: "Doveryai no proveryai"—trust but verify.

Gorbachev smiled and said he knew the proverb. Confidence was crucial, he agreed. He noted that they had come far, literally and figuratively, in getting to Reykjavík. "It is almost exactly midway between Moscow and Washington."

Reagan said he had chosen Reykjavík over London because it was out of the way and consequently more conducive to private conversations. He asked Gorbachev if he had a date in mind for his visit to Washington.

Jack Matlock sat at Reagan's side throughout this session. "Whoops, I thought," he recalled of the president's query about Washington. Matlock judged that Reagan was getting ahead of himself. "Gorbachev was not going to talk dates until he had a clear idea of what sort of agreement would be reached. We had briefed Reagan repeatedly on this point, advising him to play it cool and not appear to want a meeting without results. He would always agree, but at that moment in Reykjavík his eagerness to show Gorbachev the United States got the better of his judgment."

If Gorbachev thought Reagan had tipped his hand, he didn't tip his own by any overt reaction. He said the date of a Washington summit mattered less than the prospects for success there. A major arms-control agreement was important for both sides. "You and I cannot allow the upcoming meeting to fail," he said. "This would be a very serious blow. People would begin to ask what kind of politicians these are who meet with each other, pronounce many words, talk for hours, hold one, two, three meetings and still cannot agree on anything. This would be a scandalous outcome, with consequences which would be difficult to predict. It would evoke disappointment throughout the entire world."

Gorbachev made the first specific proposal of the weekend. As a start toward the elimination of nuclear weapons, he suggested a 50 percent cut in strategic offensive weapons, the ones deliverable by long-range missiles and bombers. He offered the first concession of the weekend when he accepted the American position on intermediate-range missiles in Europe. The Kremlin had consistently rejected Reagan's zero option as giving the Americans something for nothing—as giving up real Soviet missiles for notional American missiles. But the American deployment of Pershings and cruise missiles had begun, and so the calculation was changing. Gorbachev now accepted the zero option. "We are agreeing to a great concession," he said. "I think you understand what a great new step we are taking." He additionally offered a commitment to the ABM Treaty for at least ten years into the future, and he said the Soviets would interpret the treaty to allow testing of SDI technologies, but only in the laboratory.

Reagan hadn't expected so much so soon. But he wanted more. "We are very encouraged by what you have presented," he told Gorbachev. He said he too sought deep cuts in nuclear arsenals. But he had to point out that there remained important differences between the two sides. For instance, Gorbachev had said nothing about intermediate missiles in Asia. Intermediate missiles were mobile, and missiles based in Asia could quickly be moved to Europe.

The larger matter, however, was Gorbachev's insistence that SDI be confined to the laboratory. The American interpretation of the ABM Treaty allowed research and testing, even outside the laboratory, but not deployment of new systems. Reagan asserted that strategic defense was nonnegotiable for the United States. Strategic defense was at the heart of the American position. "The point is that SDI should make the elimination of nuclear weapons possible," he said. He repeated his earlier offer to share SDI technology. "The Soviet Union is also researching defensive weaponry, and both sides would go forward within the limits of the ABM Treaty. If either reached the point that they decided it would be desirable to go beyond the ABM Treaty restrictions, they would conduct testing in the presence of representatives of the other country. For example, if the U.S. were first, Soviet representatives would be invited to witness the testing. Then, if the testing should reveal that a system is practical, we would be obligated to share it." The United States could not abandon SDI, Reagan said. "The reason for this is that we can't guarantee in the future that someone—a madman like Hitler, for example—might not try to build nuclear weapons."

Gorbachev responded that he hoped the president's remarks were simply preliminary. The Soviet side had made major concessions. The president needed to give them due consideration. Regarding the ABM Treaty, he expressed puzzlement. "We are proposing to preserve and strengthen the treaty. You are proposing to renounce it. We want to preserve it; you want to destroy it. We just don't understand this."

Gorbachev said he hoped the United States would not proceed with SDI. But if it did, the Soviet Union was prepared. "We will respond to it, but not in the same way," he said. "If we do so, we will just have the arms race transferred to a new environment. If this is what the U.S. wants, then we can understand why it has made the proposals it has. However, the resulting situation will simply be more dangerous."

Reagan couldn't decide if Gorbachev was being stubborn for effect or willfully perverse. He replied that the general secretary was refusing to consider the essential aspect of strategic defense. "If SDI research is successful, it would make possible the elimination of nuclear weapons," he said. "We are accused of wanting a first-strike capability, but we are proposing a treaty which would require the elimination of nuclear weapons *before* SDI is deployed. Therefore a first strike would be impossible." Strategic defense was a hedge against an uncertain future. "After all, when the use of chemical weapons was prohibited after World War I, we did not reject gas masks. They were the guarantee of our protection against such a weapon in case someone decided to use it."

Gorbachev answered that they had been over this ground in Geneva.

The Soviet side had thought about it thoroughly since then but found no reason to change its views.

Recognizing the impasse, he looked at his watch. It was time for lunch. "We will continue the discussion," he said.

NOT SINCE HIS days with the actors' guild had Reagan gone toe-to-toe in negotiations the way he was going against Gorbachev. And his battles with the bosses of the studios and the other unions, important as they had seemed at the time, were for trivial stakes compared with what he and the Soviet leader were arguing over. He remembered what he liked about bargaining: the give-and-take, the search for language that could bridge gaps, the test of his own mettle against a worthy adversary. The more he talked with Gorbachev, the worthier this adversary seemed. And the more Reagan liked testing himself against him.

By the opening of the afternoon session, both sides understood that SDI was the impediment to the big deal both men wanted. Gorbachev wouldn't let the Americans take SDI out of the laboratory; Reagan wouldn't agree to confine it there.

The question was whether either party would bend. Reagan spoke first. "As I listened to you this morning I had to agree that arms reduction is a matter of the highest priority and that the time for real action has come," Reagan said. An agreement was in reach. Gorbachev merely had to drop his restrictions on SDI. "You are concerned that defense could be used for offense," Reagan said. "I can assure you that this is not the purpose of SDI." The system was purely defensive. Gorbachev had expressed concern that the United States might use SDI to launch a retaliation-proof first strike. "I can say that we do not have the capability for carrying out a first strike, and that this is not our goal."

Reagan said the answer was not less defense but less offense. He made his first novel proposal of the weekend. "The concern you voiced encouraged me to suggest drawing up a treaty eliminating all offensive ballistic missiles," he said. Gorbachev's idea of eliminating nuclear weapons entirely was too much for the present, but ridding the world of ballistic missiles was achievable, Reagan said. And it would resolve the first-strike worries Gorbachev had expressed about SDI. "The question as to the combinations of offensive and defensive systems that would allow one of the sides to make a first strike disappears automatically."

Gorbachev wasn't persuaded. But he shifted the ground, hoping to make a smaller deal. He returned to the subject of intermediate missiles. He reiterated his acceptance of the American zero option in Europe and offered to talk about the intermediate missiles in Asia. "Zero in Europe, and negotiations regarding Asia," he summarized. Would the United States accept that?

George Shultz had been letting Reagan do the talking. But at this point he said, "The problem is that—"

Gorbachev cut him off. "I would like to hear the president's opinion," he said. He repeated: "If a solution is found for Asia, will you agree to the zero option in Europe?"

"Yes," Reagan said.

Gorbachev wanted to nail this down. "Do I understand correctly? If a solution is found regarding Asia, will you agree to the zero option in Europe?"

"Yes," Reagan said again.

Gorbachev nodded, evidently pleased at having secured one solid agreement. "Now, about something else," he continued. "I am referring to the open-ended ABM Treaty." He was back to SDI. "Can we really go and violate it, rather than strengthening it?" he said of the treaty. "If we are really going to have reductions, it is very important for both sides to be certain that no one will create weapons during this time that would undermine stability and parity." He proposed commitments not to violate the ABM Treaty for ten years. This would give both parties confidence while they were reducing their offensive arms. "Otherwise when someone is doing something behind your back during the reductions, a dangerous situation is created." He added, "In the meantime your SDI will be limited to laboratory research."

Reagan shook his head. He defended SDI once more. "I feel certain that this is the best possibility for ensuring peace in our century." He repeated that the United States sought no advantage. "We propose writing it into the treaty that we will share with you the defensive weapons we are able to create."

He grew emotional as he spoke. Some of his feeling might have been feigned, but much was sincere. Reagan had long dreamed of a world without the specter of nuclear war, and finally he was in a position, perhaps, to bring that world into being. "Listen, we are two civilized countries, two civilized peoples," he said. "When I was growing up—that was before your time—countries had rules of warfare directed at protecting the peaceful population. But now that an ABM regime exists, both countries have terrible missiles aimed at each other that can annihilate count-less numbers of people, and primarily noncombatants—women, children. And the sole defense against this possibility is the threat that we are also in a position to carry out such mass extermination. This is an uncivilized situation." Strategic defense promised an escape. "I think the world will become much more civilized if we, the two great powers, demonstrate this example, create defensive systems and eliminate terrible modern armaments. I think that we would then be able to look proudly into the eye of the entire world."

Gorbachev wasn't moved. "I would prefer to reply in a less philosophi-cal spirit, more on a practical plane," he said. The president's insistence on SDI would not rid the world of fear; it would simply push the arms race in a new direction. "Our response will be different, asymmetrical," he said. "We will not deploy SDI. We have another concept." The new race would be expensive, and it would prevent the arms reductions the president said he desired.

Reagan tried again. He reiterated that the two sides could share what they learned from SDI research.

"Excuse me, Mr. President," Gorbachev cut in, clearly annoyed. "I do not take your idea of sharing SDI seriously. You don't want to share even petroleum equipment, automatic machine tools or equipment for dairies. Sharing SDI would be a second American revolution. And revolutions do not occur all that often. Let's be realistic and pragmatic. That's more reliable."

Reagan declared that he was serious. "If I thought SDI could not be shared, I would have rejected it myself," he said.

Gorbachev shrugged and said he didn't think the president knew what SDI entailed.

And on this sour note the Saturday session ended.

Y ET REAGAN WASN'T dismayed. He understood the extraordinary nature of what he was doing. Never in American history had a president negotiated major arms reductions directly with his Soviet counterpart; previous negotiations had always been conducted through intermediaries, with the principals exchanging signatures after the hard work was done. Never in world history had the heads of the two major powers of an era argued matters more portentous for so many people in so many countries across the planet. Almost literally, Reagan and Gorbachev held the fate of humanity in their hands. The power and the responsibility were daunting, even terrifying. An error could have horrendous consequences.

But Reagan wasn't daunted, and he certainly wasn't terrified. At an informal dinner at the American embassy that evening he exuded good cheer. The day's talks hadn't produced an agreement, he observed, but he and Gorbachev had spoken frankly and identified the issues that still separated them. After several months of communicating at cross-purposes, this counted as progress. He went to bed shortly after nine and slept well.

WHAT WAS SUPPOSED to be the last meeting of the weekend, on Sunday morning, commenced with a Gorbachev joke. The Bible said that creation had begun on the first day, proceeded to the second day, and so on. He and President Reagan were now on the second day, and they had a long way to go before they rested on the seventh day. (Gorbachev's note taker discreetly left this comment out of the Soviet transcript of the meeting.)

Gorbachev suggested a review of the progress to this point, and he invited Reagan to go first. The president said that he was disappointed with what had been accomplished. The two leaders had shared their desire to rid the world of nuclear weapons; this was good. Their staffs, working overnight, had mutually accepted a 50 percent reduction in strategic arsenals. This too was good. But vexing details remained to be worked out. On intermediate-range weapons, the two sides had accepted the zero option for Europe but hadn't figured out how Asian missiles affected this result; in other words, they had not reached an agreement they could write into a treaty. The hardest nut was strategic defense. "Here we have differences," Reagan said. "I cannot retreat from the policy I have declared in the field of space and defensive weapons. I simply cannot do it."

Gorbachev shared Reagan's disappointment at the lack of progress. He blamed the president. "We have made major concessions to the United States in the hope that it will be possible to get the arms control talks moving and work seriously on reducing nuclear weapons," he said. "It is my impression that the American side is not taking this position of ours into account." He repeated that the Soviet side had accepted the American zero-option plan for Europe. What had the United States offered of equal substance? Gorbachev questioned whether Reagan really wanted an agreement. "When you listen closely to the American positions you get the impression that the U.S. president and administration are beginning from false premises. You and your people think that we have a greater interest in nuclear disarmament than the United States does, that if you put a little pressure on the Soviet Union it will raise its hands and surrender. This is a dangerous mistake."

Gorbachev stressed that the window of opportunity for meaningful arms reduction wouldn't be open forever. "A year ago it was not the case that the Soviet Union had advanced major compromise proposals, and certainly not two to three years ago. I simply did not have the capability then. I am not certain I will still have it in a year or two to three years. What will happen if we do not make use of this opportunity? Reykjavik will just be mentioned in passing, nothing more. A shame that all that was missed."

Reagan nodded. "I am in the same position," he said. "It is possible that before long I will not have the powers I do now. Why not use the time that we have and make a contribution to the creation of a world free of the nuclear threat?"

Gorbachev threw the question back at Reagan. "When I sit opposite you, opposite the president of the United States, I can look you in the eye with a clear conscience," he said. "We have brought far-reaching proposals. I ask you to appreciate this. One thing is needed to reach agreement: a desire on your side."

The roadblock on strategic reductions was the president's insistence on unlimited testing of SDI, Gorbachev said. He again asked Reagan to reconsider. The Soviet proposal was less limiting than the president appreciated or was willing to admit. "We do not touch the SDI program within the framework of laboratory experiments. I do not think that this point would greatly limit you." He professed knowledge of what the United States had achieved on SDI. "We know that in two or three areas you have had some breakthroughs. We know, and we ourselves are doing a few things. So the laboratory phase should not constrain you."

Reagan said he couldn't give Gorbachev what he asked. He had pledged that he would not bargain away SDI. "I cannot retreat from my position and renounce what I promised our people." He repeated that SDI did not threaten the Soviet Union. The United States was willing to share the technology, which would help both sides protect themselves against third states or nuclear maniacs.

Gorbachev said again that the Soviet side was asking the president not to abandon SDI, simply to reframe it within the context of a strengthened ABM Treaty. "We are giving you this opportunity to show that your idea is alive, that we are not burying it, that the United States can continue laboratory work on SDI, but cannot go beyond the framework of research. As for the nuclear maniac, we can handle this issue somehow within the framework of the ABM Treaty too."

"I'm not sure of that," Reagan rejoined, growing testy. "And anyway, damn it, what kind of agreement are you defending?" The ABM Treaty reinforced the nuclear status quo, which was what he was trying to overturn. "I do not understand the charm of the ABM Treaty, which in fact signifies guaranteed mutual destruction. We are holding talks about elimination of nuclear missiles, about how we should no longer be threatened with the danger that some gloomy day someone will push the button and everything will be destroyed." That's what they should be focusing on, not on freezing the status quo in place. And SDI was part of the solution, especially over the long term. "Even when we destroy these missiles we must have a defense against others. The genie is already out of the bottle.

Offensive weapons can be built again. Therefore I propose creating protection for the world for future generations, when you and I will no longer be here."

Gorbachev thought Reagan accorded the ABM Treaty too little credit. It had been the basis for the nuclear stability of the last decade. Again he asked the president for concessions to match those already made by the Soviet side. "As the American saying goes, 'It takes two to tango.' And it takes two to control arms, to reduce and eliminate nuclear weapons."

Reagan expressed disappointment that Gorbachev seemed to fear that SDI was part of an American effort to gain advantage over the Soviet Union. "It is not true," he said. "We do not have any hostile intentions toward you. We recognize the differences between our systems, but we think that our countries are entirely capable of living in the world as friendly rivals. I understand that you do not trust us, just as we do not trust you. But I am convinced that the historical facts are on our side. Long ago Karl Marx said—"

Gorbachev interrupted: "Earlier you referred to Lenin, and now you've moved on to Marx."

Reagan didn't miss a beat. "Everything that Marx said, Lenin said it too. Marx was the first, and Lenin was his follower." And what they both said was that for socialism to succeed, it had to be triumphant throughout the world. This had been the consistent position of Soviet leaders. "Maybe you have not managed to express your views on this yet, or you do not believe it. But so far you have not said. But all the others said it."

"So you are talking about Marx and Lenin again," Gorbachev said dismissively. "Many people have already tried to bring down the founders of this well-known line of social thought. No one has been able to do this, and I advise you not to waste time on this."

Gorbachev shrugged. "I do not want to argue with you," he said. "I respect your independent nature and your views and ideas. And I am convinced that if you and I have different ideological ideas, that is not a reason for us to shoot at one another. On the contrary, I am convinced that in addition to political relations, purely human relations between us are possible also."

"Unquestionably," Reagan responded. He smiled as he added, "And I would even like to convince you to join the Republican Party."

"An interesting idea," Gorbachev rejoined. He shifted back to SDI, joking that he was doing Reagan a favor. "I think I am even helping the president with SDI. After all, your people say that if Gorbachev attacks

SDI and space weapons so much, it means the idea deserves more respect. They even say that if it were not for me, no one would listen to the idea at all." If these commentators were right, the president should show gratitude. "I am on your side in this matter, but you have not appreciated it."

Reagan didn't consider SDI a joking matter. His smile was gone. "What the hell use will ABMs or anything else be if we eliminate nuclear weapons?" he demanded.

"Mr. President, you just made a historic statement: What the hell use will SDI be if we eliminate nuclear weapons?" Gorbachev responded. "But it is exactly because we are moving toward a reduction and elimination of nuclear weapons that I favor strengthening the ABM Treaty. In these conditions it becomes even more important."

Reagan tried another tack. "I am the oldest man here," he said. "And I understand that after the war the nations decided that they would renounce poison gas. But thank God that the gas mask continued to exist. Something similar can happen with nuclear weapons. And we will have a shield against them in any case."

"I am increasingly convinced of something I knew previously only second-hand," Gorbachev said. "The president of the United States does not like to retreat. I see now that you do not want to meet us halfway on the issue of the ABM Treaty, which is absolutely essential in conditions where we are undertaking large reductions in nuclear arms."

He paused, wearily. "I see that the possibilities of agreement are exhausted," he said. He had gone as far as he could. "I think we can conclude our meeting with this." The two of them had not achieved the results he had hoped for, results the world had hoped for. "But we must take account of the realities. And the reality is that we are unable to work out agreed-upon proposals on these issues. You and I talked about the possibility of major reductions in nuclear weapons, but if the fate of the ABM Treaty is unclear, then the entire conception collapses and we return to the situation that existed before Reykjavik."

He reflected. "Perhaps you will report this to Congress," he said. "We will report to the Politburo and the Supreme Soviet. I do not think the world will stop. Events will unfold, and neither will our relations stop. But we will not succeed in taking advantage of the present opportunity."

Reagan hadn't given in, but he wasn't ready to give up. "Can we go away from here with nothing?" he asked.

"Unfortunately, we can," Gorbachev replied stolidly.

The foreign ministers, Shultz and Shevardnadze, reminded their bosses that they had to issue a communiqué. They exchanged phrases, seeking language that wasn't entirely negative.

Gorbachev grew impatient. "Well, Mr. President," he said, "'X hour' is approaching. What are you going to do?"

Shultz jumped ahead of Reagan. He said he had some phrasing that might suit both sides. He started reading.

Gorbachev cut him off after only a few words. "That is not acceptable to us," he said. But he said he was willing to let Shultz try again, at greater length. "Maybe, if the president does not object, we will declare a break for one or two hours," he said.

Reagan nodded, and the two sides recessed.

91

NOT FOR YEARS had Reagan worked this intensely and long. He was nearly exhausted. He had been counting on being back at the White House for Sunday dinner with Nancy. But he realized he and Gorbachev stood at the brink of one of the great decisions in world history. If they could bridge the gap between them on SDI, they might put the planet on a path to a post-nuclear age. Future generations would thank and revere them. He couldn't leave Iceland without one more try.

The American offer at this point, as sharpened by Shultz with Reagan's approval, was that the two countries would abide for five years by the ABM Treaty's provisions for research, development, and testing. During this time they would reduce their strategic offensive arsenals by 50 percent. During the next five years they would continue to reduce their offensive ballistic arsenals, with the goal of total elimination by the ten-year mark. As long as the reductions proceeded, the two sides would adhere to the ABM Treaty. After the ten years, assuming all offensive ballistic missiles had been eliminated, both sides could deploy strategic defenses if they wished.

Gorbachev opened the afternoon session with his counterproposal. He agreed to the two five-year reductions of offensive ballistic missiles. And he liked the ten-year adherence to the ABM Treaty, although he wanted it embraced at the outset, without the dual five-year formula proposed by the Americans. Yet he continued to insist that research and testing of strategic defense technologies be confined to laboratories. Testing in the field must wait until the end of the ten-year period.

Reagan responded indirectly. "Our position offers a somewhat different formulation," he said. "I hope we can eliminate the difference in the course of our talks." He repeated the proposal Shultz had crafted.

Gorbachev answered that there were definitely differences between the two positions. "Your formula, as I see it, fails to meet our position halfway," he said. "The main aspect of the Soviet Union's approach is that in the period in which the U.S.S.R. and the U.S. are carrying out deep reductions in nuclear weapons, we ought to reinforce instead of impairing or undermining the ABM Treaty." The president's attachment to SDI would have the latter effect. Gorbachev said he was asking no more than was entirely within the spirit of the ABM Treaty. "What we are talking about primarily is the renunciation of testing any space components of ABM defense in space—that is, refraining from any steps which would in effect pave the way to deployment of such systems. I want to emphasize once more that what is prohibited according to our formula does not affect laboratory testing and leaves open the possibility for the American side, like the Soviet side, to conduct any laboratory research relating to space, including SDI research. We are not undermining your idea of SDI; we are permitting that kind of activity, which is already being conducted by the United States and which is impossible to monitor anyway. We are only placing the system in the framework of laboratory research." Gorbachev said he wasn't asking any more than was reasonable. "I think the U.S. could go along with this, especially considering the major steps the Soviet Union has made."

Reagan shook his head. "That doesn't remove the question of what we are to do after ten years if we should want to create a defense against ballistic missiles," he said. He couldn't fathom Gorbachev's stubbornness on strategic defense. "I just don't understand why you object so much to SDI," he said. He added, "As for what the ABM Treaty prohibits and what it permits, the two sides have differences of interpretation here."

Gorbachev was mystified, too, but by Reagan's attachment to SDI. Yet his proposal granted much of what the president sought. "As you see, we are offering a broad formula of what we can do after the ten years," Gorbachev said. "If you should deem it essential to continue SDI, we can discuss that. And so why deal with the question in advance, right now? And why force us to sign SDI? Perhaps we might have other interests."

Reagan stood firm. "We want right now to provide for the possibility of defense in case, ten years from now, when we no longer have missiles, someone should decide to re-create nuclear missiles," he said.

Gorbachev asked Reagan to focus on what the two sides had agreed on and what it would allow them to do. "We will be able to accomplish the historic task of eliminating strategic offensive weapons," he said. He continued, "Why complicate things with other problems which we are uncertain about, the consequences of which are unclear? It would only undermine one side's confidence in whether it was acting correctly by reducing its nuclear forces under conditions where the other side is taking steps which could have aggravating consequences for the entire process." Gorbachev reiterated that SDI was not being eliminated. "The scientific-technical aspect of SDI could still continue, your capability in that sphere. The decision would by no means sound the death knell for your SDI program."

Reagan defended America's pro-SDI interpretation of the ABM Treaty. "We are only proposing such research, development and testing as are permitted by the ABM Treaty," he said. He wondered aloud if there was more to the Soviet resistance than Gorbachev was admitting. "What objection can there be unless something is being hidden?" He repeated yet again his willingness to share SDI technology. "We will make it available to the Soviet side if it wants it." Reagan added that if either side had reason to worry about strategic defense, it was the United States. "If the Soviets feel that strongly about strengthening the ABM Treaty, why don't they get rid of Krasnoyarsk"—where the Soviets had built a radar system the American government deemed in violation of the ABM Treaty—"and the whole defense structure they have built around their capital? They have a big defense structure and we have none. It is a peculiar fact that we do not have a single defense against a nuclear attack."

Gorbachev ignored the allegation. "I still wish you would carefully examine our proposal," he said. "It encompasses elements of both your and our proposals. If it is acceptable I am ready to sign it."

George Shultz intervened. "Would you please give us this formula in printed form in English so that we can examine it carefully?" the secretary of state asked.

Gorbachev nodded. Trying yet again to convince Reagan, he said, "You are proposing SDI. To us, that option is unacceptable. We want to keep the possibility of finding something different. Hence our formula makes it possible to take account of the situation in the future, after the ten years. Summing up our proposal, let me emphasize that the two sides will strictly comply with the ABM Treaty for ten years and will pledge not to exercise the right to withdraw from the treaty. Simultaneously they will continue laboratory research. After the ten-year period, under conditions of the complete elimination of nuclear weapons, the two sides will get together and decide what to do next and come to an agreement." Gorbachev paused. "I don't understand what bothers you about that."

Reagan answered with a query of his own. "If we have eliminated all nuclear weapons, why should you be worried by the desire of one of the sides to make itself safe—just in case—from weapons which neither of us has anymore? Someone else could create missiles, and extra guarantees would be appropriate. Your side and our side are completely eliminating our weapons. I can imagine us both in ten years getting together again in Iceland to destroy the last Soviet and American missiles under triumphant circumstances. By then I'll be so old that you won't even recognize me. And you will ask in surprise, 'Hey Ron, is that really you? What are you doing here?' And we'll have a big celebration over it."

Gorbachev was beyond being amused. "I don't know whether I'll live till that time," he said.

"Well, I'm certain I will," Reagan said.

"Sure you will," Gorbachev said. "You've passed the dangerous age for men, and now you have smooth sailing to be a hundred. But these dangers still lie ahead for me. For a man they come by the age of sixty, and besides, I still have to meet with President Reagan, who I can see really hates to give in. President Reagan wants to be the winner. But in this case, on these matters, there can be no winner—either we both win or we both lose. We're in the same boat."

Reagan's sense of humor was fraying too. "I know I won't live to be a hundred if I have to live in fear of these damned missiles," he said.

"Well, let's reduce and eliminate them," Gorbachev said.

"This is a rather strange situation," Reagan said. "We have both put forth specific demands. You are in favor of a ten-year period. I have said that I will not give up SDI. But both of us, obviously, can say that the most important thing is to eliminate nuclear missiles."

"But you wouldn't have to give up SDI," Gorbachev objected, "because laboratory research and testing would not be prohibited. And so you could continue activities within the framework of the SDI program. Your opponents won't even be able to open their mouths, especially under conditions where we have eliminated nuclear weapons. Anyway, I am categorically against any situation where our meeting results in one winner and one loser. Even if this did happen now, in the next stage, in the process of preparing the text of agreements, it would make itself felt and the loser would act in such a manner that everything would end up destroyed. Therefore equality is essential both at the present stage and in the next. After all, considerable time will pass between the achievement of agreements and the final ratification of the agreements. And only if the document accommodates the interests of the U.S. and the interests of the U.S.S.R. will it merit ratification and support."

Reagan tried a different approach. "Perhaps we can resolve the matter this way," he said. "The question of what research, development and testing are permitted by the ABM Treaty should remain for discussion and negotiation at the meeting in the course of your visit"—to Washington. "We will come to an agreement regarding the ten-year period and breaking it down into two five-year periods, in the course of which nuclear weapons will be eliminated, while everything having to do with testing, laboratory research and the provisions of the ABM Treaty and so on are things we can discuss at the summit meeting."

"But without that there's no package," Gorbachev objected. "All of these issues are interconnected. If we come to an agreement on deep reductions of nuclear weapons, we will have to have assurance, guarantees, that the ABM Treaty will not only be complied with but also strengthened in the course of this crucial period, this historic period when strategic offensive weapons will be eliminated. I repeat, this period is too crucial; it is dangerous to improvise." He added, "I am convinced that preserving the ABM Treaty is also consistent with the interests of the U.S."

Reagan's fatigue and frustration grew more obvious. "It looks like we're not getting anywhere," he said. He reiterated his inability to understand why Gorbachev was so worried about what would happen in ten years, when all strategic missiles would have been eliminated. "Perhaps we ought to take another look at what we disagree about."

George Shultz again intervened. "It seems to me there are two differences between us," he said. "First, what to consider to be permissible research in the course of the ten-year period. Second, it seems to me the Soviet side has in mind an indefinitely long period during which we will not be able to withdraw from the ABM Treaty. We have in mind ten years."

"No," Gorbachev said. "We need absolute clarity here. We believe that in the stage in which we are undertaking actual reductions in nuclear weapons the ABM Treaty needs to be made stronger, not made weaker. Over the period of ten years the two sides will refrain from exercising the right to withdraw from the treaty. After those ten years, we will see. Perhaps we will continue to comply with the treaty. Perhaps some new elements will emerge. But for the period of ten years the treaty must be preserved, in fact made stronger."

"In other words," Shultz said, "for ten years the two sides will not exercise the right to withdraw from the treaty. After the ten years, this aspect will be gone. Then the sides can exercise that right."

Now Eduard Shevardnadze stepped in. "Let me remind you, moreover, that research will not be restricted, but it can only be conducted in the laboratory," he said.

Gorbachev urged Reagan to do what he himself had done in Geneva. "Mr. President," he said, "I remember how things went in Geneva. You and I were sitting in a room drinking coffee, we were in a good mood and we thought we were going to succeed. Secretary of State Shultz came in and told us how things stood. He said that the Soviet delegation would not give its consent to an agreement with respect to certain questions. And then you said to me, 'Pound the table and order your people to come to an agreement!' I went out and in fifteen minutes the agreement had been reached. If we take a break now, and if you achieve agreement in ten minutes, you can consider it another victory for you."

Before Reagan could respond, Shultz asked for additional clarification. At times Gorbachev had spoken of the elimination of ballistic missiles, at times of strategic offensive weapons, at times of nuclear weapons generally. What precisely did the general secretary have in mind?

"The weapons to be eliminated would include all components of the triad," Gorbachev said. "Missiles, including heavy missiles; submarine missiles; and bombers."

Shultz explained that the American proposal dealt with offensive ballistic missiles. "These missiles include not only strategic missiles"—long-range missiles—"but also, for example, intermediate-range missiles and others. What you are talking about are strategic offensive weapons. That is a different category of weapons."

Gorbachev's impatience with details surfaced once more. "I thought that yesterday we had offered, and you had agreed to, an option which calls for a fifty-percent reduction of the entire triad of strategic weapons, including missiles like the SS-18 that you are so worried about," he said. "That option did not come easy to us. But we went along with it in order not to get bogged down in a swamp of levels, sublevels and so on. So let's agree that in this case, again, we're talking not only about missiles but about all strategic offensive weapons."

Everyone was exhausted by now. The clock showed 4:30. Reagan wanted to board his plane and head back toward Washington and Nancy. But he could see that Gorbachev was tired too, and he knew from his union days that fatigue could be the deal maker's friend.

Perhaps Gorbachev was thinking something similar. Surely he could outlast the old man across the table.

They agreed to another recess.

92

THE DISTANCE BETWEEN the two sides was heartbreakingly small. Gorbachev wanted testing on SDI to be confined to the laboratory for ten years; Reagan refused the constraint. What made the heartbreak the more excruciating was that the distance was almost wholly political. No one had shown Reagan evidence that SDI would be ready to emerge from the laboratory before Gorbachev's ten years had expired. He was standing on principle, but the principle had little to do with the technology. He just couldn't be seen as giving ground on SDI.

Reagan again gathered with his team. He made clear he wasn't going to move, but they thought Gorbachev might. Gorbachev, after all, had made big concessions so far. Perhaps he had another in him. Someone suggested giving Gorbachev an additional night to think it over. "Oh, shit!" Reagan burst out. He had no desire to remain in Iceland until Monday. The suggestion was abandoned.

The president summoned the energy for one more try. "We have kept you a long time because it hasn't been easy reaching an agreement between us," he told Gorbachev upon returning to the conference room. "We have sought a formulation which would meet you halfway with respect to your desire regarding the ten-year period. Here is the final option which we can offer." Reagan read essentially the same proposal he had laid out earlier regarding a pledge not to withdraw from the ABM Treaty for ten years and meanwhile to comply strictly with its provisions regarding research, development, and testing. He continued to the question of arms reductions. "In the course of the first five years (until 1991 inclusive), there will be a fifty-percent reduction in the two sides' strategic offensive weapons.

In the course of the following five years of that period, the remaining offensive ballistic missiles of both sides will be reduced. In this way, by the end of 1996 the USSR and the U.S. will have completely eliminated all offensive ballistic missiles. At the end of the ten-year period, each side may deploy defensive systems if they so desire, provided that the two sides do not agree on something else." Reagan put down the paper. "How do you feel about that formula?" he asked Gorbachev.

Gorbachev didn't immediately say no, which Reagan took for a good sign. "I have two questions for you by way of clarifying the American formulation," Gorbachev said. "You speak of research, development and testing permitted by the ABM Treaty. Your formula omits any mention of laboratory testing. Was this done specially?"

Reagan at first dodged the question, saying it had been discussed at the continuing Geneva arms talks.

"What I'm asking is," Gorbachev pressed, "did you omit the mention of laboratories deliberately or not?"

"Yes, it was deliberate," Reagan acknowledged. "What's the matter?"

"I'm simply clarifying," Gorbachev said. "For the time being I'm not commenting. Another question: The first half of the formula talks about the two sides' strategic offensive weapons which will be reduced by fifty percent in the first five years, but in the second part, which talks about the following five years, it mentions offensive ballistic missiles. What is being referred to here? Why this difference in approach?"

Reagan replied that during the break he was told that the Soviet side wanted the special mention of offensive strategic missiles. "That's why we included it in the formula."

"There is some kind of confusion here," Gorbachev said. "When it comes to strategic offensive weapons, we agreed between us long ago that they included all components of the triad—ICBMs, SLBMs and heavy bombers. I don't see what could have changed in this question." Having dismissed details earlier, Gorbachev now stickled. "The wording has to be identical," he said of the two five-year periods.

"I understand, then, that by the end of 1996 all strategic offensive ballistic missiles will be eliminated?" Reagan asked.

"How about airplanes?" Gorbachev insisted. "After all, strategic weapons represent a triad which includes ICBMs, SLBMs and bombers. So it is clear between us what strategic weapons are."

"What I want to know is will all offensive ballistic missiles be eliminated?" Reagan rejoined.

Gorbachev repeated his objection that the first part of the American proposal spoke of strategic offensive weapons, presumably including bombers, while the second part confined itself to missiles.

"Is that the only thing you object to?" Reagan asked. He couldn't tell where Gorbachev was going.

"I'm just trying to clarify the issue," Gorbachev said.

"It will have to be sorted out," Reagan said.

"What we need is for both formulations to be identical," Gorbachev said. "If we talk about all the components in the first case, everything also needs to be clear in the second case."

"Evidently we have simply misunderstood you," Reagan said. "But if that's what you want, all right."

George Shultz spoke up. "We need to be careful here," he said. "When we talk of eliminating all strategic offensive weapons, it does not refer to shorter-range ballistic missiles. I know that the question of them is handled within the framework of a different category, but it is here, it seems to me, that we ought to take decisive measures."

Gorbachev and Shultz tried out wording that might satisfy both sides. After a couple of minutes, Reagan broke back in. "Let me ask this," he said. "Do we have in mind—and I think it would be very good—that by the end of the two five-year periods *all* nuclear explosive devices would be eliminated, including bombs, battlefield systems, cruise missiles, submarine weapons, intermediate-range systems and so on?"

This was more, in fact, than anyone had been talking about. But Gorbachev liked the idea. "We could say that, list all those systems," he said.

Shultz liked it too. "Let's do it," he said.

Reagan was pleased. "If we agree that by the end of the ten-year period all nuclear weapons are to be eliminated, we can turn this agreement over to our delegations in Geneva so that they can prepare a treaty which you can sign during your visit to the U.S."

"Well, all right," Gorbachev declared, sounding suddenly hopeful. "Here we have a chance for an agreement."

Yet there remained the sticking point. "What I am seriously concerned about is another factor," Gorbachev said. "What we are talking about is to comply strictly with the unlimited ABM Treaty for the purpose of pledging not to exercise the right to withdraw from the treaty for ten years. We are doing this under conditions of reducing nuclear weapons. We don't understand, then, why the American side does not agree to having research, development and testing be restricted to the confines of the laboratory." A definite understanding of this matter was essential, lest confusion, ill will, and national insecurity arise. "Hence the ABM Treaty has to be strengthened, which means we cannot remove the mention of laboratories from our text." Gorbachev repeated, "The question of laboratories is of fundamental importance."

Reagan repeated his earlier statement that the American interpretation of the ABM Treaty did not confine research and testing to laboratories. Yet he thought they were splitting hairs unnecessarily. "From the standpoint of the substance of the issue, in my opinion, it is of no importance. Our aim is to safeguard ourselves from a revival of missiles after they have been destroyed, in order to make a kind of gas mask against nuclear missiles." Reagan noticed Gorbachev shaking his head. "I have already spoken of this," he acknowledged. "And I have also spoken of the danger of nuclear maniacs."

"Yes, I've heard all about gas masks and maniacs, probably ten times already," Gorbachev said with a sigh. "It still does not convince me."

"I'm talking about one possibility of what can happen after ten years," Reagan said. "Perhaps there will be nothing of the kind. Perhaps the people who become the leaders at that time will decide that the system is too costly to deploy and will give up the SDI. In any case, the world would welcome it if we could undertake to reduce nuclear weapons and not make this issue a stumbling block. We are asking not to give up SDI, and you are trying to determine now what will happen in ten years."

Gorbachev shook his head. "If we make a stipulation acknowledging the possibility of conducting research work relating to SDI within the confines of the laboratory, that will not mean that the American government will not be able to decide questions relating to the program," he said. "Such a stipulation will not prohibit research, development and testing, including the kind that relates to space weapons. But it would make it possible to guarantee a strict interpretation of the ABM Treaty. It would make it possible to prevent bringing such weapons out of the laboratories, out in the atmosphere and into space. These are completely different things. We are talking about an agreement that is supposed to strengthen peace instead of subjecting it to new dangers."

"I'm not demanding the right to deploy ABMs in space," Reagan said. "I'm only talking about research permitted by the ABM Treaty. By the way, the Soviet Union is not entirely without reproach in this. I'm referring to the Krasnoyarsk radar station. We have differing interpretations of the ABM Treaty—that's a fact."

"What we are talking about is seeing to it that SDI testing takes place only in the laboratory," Gorbachev said. "We cannot go along with allowing it to come out into the atmosphere or into space. That is unacceptable to us. It is a question of principle."

Reagan let his annoyance show. "You're destroying all my bridges to continuation of my SDI program," he said. "I can't go along with the restrictions you demand."

"Is that your final position?" Gorbachev said. "If so, we can end our meeting at this point."

Reagan took a deep breath. He shrugged wearily. "Yes, it is," he said. "The whole thing comes up against the fact that your side and our side differ as to what is permitted by the ABM Treaty and what is not."

Gorbachev made sure he understood what the difference was. "From our discussion I conclude that the U.S. wants to reserve the possibility of conducting tests of the SDI program not only in the laboratory but also outside, in the air and in space. If that's so, there can be no agreement between us."

"But you have to understand that experimentation and research cannot always be kept within the laboratory," Reagan said. "Sometimes it is simply necessary to go outside the laboratory."

Gorbachev tried again. "You must understand me," he said. "To us the laboratory issue is not a matter of stubbornness or hard-headedness. It is not casuistry. It is all too serious. We are agreeing to deep reductions and, ultimately, the destruction of nuclear weapons. And at the same time the American side is pushing us to agree to give them the right to create space weapons. That is unacceptable to us. If you will agree to restricting research work to the laboratory, not letting it out into space, I will be ready in two minutes to sign the appropriate formulation and adopt the document."

"I can't go along with that," Reagan said. For the first time he appealed to Gorbachev as a practical politician. "You and I have different positions, different problems. In your country, nobody can criticize you without winding up in prison. In my country the situation is different. I have a lot of critics who wield great influence. And if I agree to such a formulation, they will launch a campaign against me. They will accuse me of breaking my promise to the people of the United States regarding SDI. So I pledge not to deploy the corresponding systems for ten years, and to restrict ourselves to research permitted by the ABM Treaty. I'm not asking for anything out of the ordinary."

Gorbachev responded in like vein. "If I understand you, Mr. President, you are now addressing me in a trusting manner, as a man who occupies in his country a position equal to yours," he said. "Therefore I say to you frankly and in the same trusting manner: If we sign a package containing major concessions by the Soviet Union regarding fundamental problems, you will become, without exaggeration, a great president. You are now literally two steps from that. If we come to an agreement on strengthening the ABM Treaty and on laboratory research, which will not rule out work within the SDI framework, it will mean our meeting has been a success."

He paused to let Reagan consider how he would look to history. Then he shrugged. "If not, let's part at this point and forget about Reykjavik." He added, "But there won't be another opportunity like this. At any rate, I know I won't have one."

He turned reflective. "I firmly believed that we could come to an agreement," he said. "Otherwise I would not have raised the question of an immediate meeting with you. Otherwise I would not have come here in the name of the Soviet leadership with a solid store of serious, compromising proposals. I hoped that they would meet with understanding and support from your side, that we could resolve all issues. If this does happen, if we manage to achieve deep reductions and the destruction of nuclear weapons, all of your critics will not dare open their mouths. They would then be going against the opinions of the overwhelming majority of people in the world, who would welcome our success. If, on the other hand, we are not able to come to an agreement, it will obviously become the job of another generation of leaders. You and I have no more time."

His voice acquired a bitter tone. "The American side has essentially not made any concessions, not a single major step to meet us halfway," he said. "It's hard to do business on that basis."

Eduard Shevardnadze tried his hand. "Let me speak very emotionally, because I feel that we have come very close to accomplishing this historic task," he said. "And when future generations read the record of our talks, they will not forgive us if we let this opportunity slip by."

Reagan attempted again to reach Gorbachev. "I want to say one thing to you as one political leader to another," he said. "I am being subjected to criticism which began even before I came here. They were saying that

I would make concessions, that I would agree to a lengthy period of time of not withdrawing from the ABM Treaty. And so I ask you as a political leader to take one step which will substantially facilitate our relations and the solution to many questions for both of us. Let me say frankly that if I give you what you ask it will definitely hurt me badly at home."

Gorbachev frowned in resignation. "Let's end it here," he said. "What you propose is something we cannot go along with. I've said all I can."

Reagan appeared equally pained. Even now he wasn't ready to admit failure. He thought if he kept talking, he might squeeze that last concession from Gorbachev. "Are you really going to turn down a historic opportunity for agreement for the sake of one word in the text?" he said.

"You say that it's just a matter of one word," Gorbachev objected. "But it's not a matter of a word. It's a matter of principle." He was angry now. "We cannot agree to a situation in which you are expanding your SDI and going into space with it while reductions of nuclear weapons are going on. If I go back to Moscow and say that despite our agreement on deep reductions of nuclear weapons, despite our agreement on the ten-year period, we have given the United States the right to test SDI in space so that the U.S. is ready to deploy it by the end of that period, they will call me a fool and an irresponsible leader."

He tried once more. "If you agree to restrict research to the laboratory, then there will be a framework. For ten years you will have enough work to do research within the SDI framework and inside the laboratory. And you will be able to say that you are continuing the SDI, that you are not giving it up, if that is so essential to you for the American people."

Now Reagan sighed. "After our meeting in Geneva I was convinced that you and I had established personal contact of the kind the leaders of our two countries never had before," he said. "You and I understood each other very well. But now, when I have asked you a personal favor which would have enormous influence on our future relations, you have refused me."

"There are various kinds of favors," Gorbachev replied. "If you came to me and said you were having trouble with your farmers, they were demanding increased grain purchases by the Soviet Union, that you were asking this as a personal favor, I could understand that. But I can't understand how you can ask the U.S.S.R. to grant the U.S. the right, during the period of deep reductions and elimination of nuclear weapons, to test an ABM system in space, to implement SDI in its entirety, at the same time we were destroying our offensive nuclear potential. If you think about it, that wouldn't even be right for the U.S. It would create nervousness, a lack of trust and is completely unacceptable to us. You don't need that kind of favor either."

"But if you don't have nuclear weapons, you won't have anything to threaten us with," Reagan said yet again. "The defensive system could not be deployed earlier than in ten years' time; we have gone along with that deferment. As for the word 'laboratory,' it has its own particular meaning and subtext. They would simply tell me in that case that I had capitulated, that I had given away what I had promised not to give away. All of the other formulations we have taken from you. We are saying we will comply with the ABM Treaty for ten years. And now I see that nothing is coming of it, and all because of one word which has such specific meaning. I simply don't understand how you can think that I want to gain some special military advantage. After all, it's you, with your actions, who are violating the ABM Treaty. Yet we are not telling you to eliminate what you have. We're not setting that condition and we will not even mention it outside this room."

Reagan sighed once more, wearily. "But now it's a matter of one word," he repeated. "Perhaps you will propose a different formulation? But the text now contains everything you have asked for—not to exercise the right to withdraw from the ABM Treaty for ten years, strict compliance with its provisions and the conduct only of the kind of research, development and testing which are permitted by the treaty. For this reason I want to ask you once more to change your viewpoint, to do it as a favor to me so that we can go to the people as peacemakers."

Gorbachev refused. "We cannot go along with what you propose," he said. "If you will agree to banning tests in space, we will sign the document in two minutes. We cannot go along with something else. We have already agreed to what we could. We are not to blame."

He made ready to leave. "Even though our meeting is ending this way, I have a clear conscience before my people and before you," he said. "I have done everything I could."

Reagan realized the historic opportunity was slipping away. For a rare moment in his life he experienced self-doubt. He scribbled a note and passed it to Shultz. "Am I wrong?" the note asked.

Shultz whispered, "No, you are right."

Reagan then gathered his papers. "It's too bad we have to part this way," he told Gorbachev. "We were so close to an agreement." His voice grew angry and disappointed. "I think you didn't want to achieve an agreement anyway. I'm very sorry."

"I am also very sorry it's happened this way," Gorbachev said. "I wanted an agreement and did everything I could, if not more."

"I don't know when we'll ever have another chance like this and whether we will meet soon," Reagan said.

"I don't either," Gorbachev replied.

93

R EPORTERS HAD BEEN barred from the talks and had received
no word of how the discussions were going. But most assumed,
because Reagan and Gorbachev delayed their departures, that
something was afoot. They crowded the front of Höfði House to assess
the demeanor of the principals as they emerged.

Reagan was their bellwether. He was better known to the media than
Gorbachev, and he was famous for his smile, his wave, and the spring in
his step. The public self-possession acquired in decades before crowds and
cameras sometimes made him a cipher, but it caused reporters to scruti-
nize him all the more closely for hints of how he really felt.

On this day, at this late hour, no scrutiny was required. His face told
everything. He suddenly looked all of his seventy-five years. His features
sagged; his shoulders slumped; his mouth formed a thin, tight line. Larry
Speakes had never seen his boss so. "I was worried about his health,"
Speakes wrote later. Reagan's trademark optimism had vanished. "Reagan was somber," Don Regan recalled, "and for the first time since I had
known him I felt that I was in the presence of a truly disappointed man."

Reporters asked if there would be a joint statement. "There is going to
be *no* statement!" Reagan said curtly.

The president accompanied Gorbachev to the Russian's limousine.
Gorbachev said, "I'm sorry it didn't work out."

"It could have worked out if you had wanted it to," Reagan said, anger
inflecting his disappointment.

"I hope to see you in the United States," Gorbachev said.

"I don't know that there is going to be a meeting in the United States,"
Reagan replied.

Don Regan talked to Reagan in the car on the way to the air field. "Buck up, Mr. President," he said. "I don't know what went on in there, but you're going to have to meet with the staff in a few minutes. It won't look well for you to be seen so grim and angry."

Reagan hardly heard what Regan said. "Don, we came so close," he said. "It's just such a shame." He held his thumb and forefinger half an inch apart. "We were *that* close to an agreement."

"His frustration was palpable," Regan continued. "'Laboratory, laboratory, laboratory,' the president said, repeating the word over and over again. Then he went on: 'It even got to a personal level, Don. I said to Gorbachev: "I think we've developed a good relationship. I'm asking you personally to give me this. You've got your ten years; I understand why you need it. But I promised the American people that I wouldn't trade away their future security, which is SDI." But Gorbachev wouldn't give in even to my personal plea.'"

As he had for many months, Gorbachev bested Reagan in the battle for public opinion. While Reagan drove to the airport for the flight home, lamenting to Don Regan the opportunity lost, Gorbachev held a news conference. A reporter for the *New York Times* found him characteristically impressive. "Mr. Gorbachev, leaning forward in his seat and slashing the air with his right hand at times for emphasis, spoke without notes for an hour before responding to questions," the reporter recounted. "His presentation was polished and at times impassioned."

Gorbachev explained that he had offered far-reaching proposals that would have averted the threat of nuclear war. But President Reagan had rejected them by insisting that he, Gorbachev, agree to an SDI policy "only a madman would accept." In the end the American president had even rejected an agreement on intermediate nuclear forces that he himself had proposed five years earlier. "I said, 'I don't understand how you can abandon your own child,'" Gorbachev recounted.

Yet for all his puzzlement and disappointment, the general secretary professed optimism. "This is not the end of contact with the United States," he said. "It is not the end of international relations." The Soviet Union stood by the offers it had presented. "Let America think. We are waiting. We are not withdrawing our proposals."

THE TROUPER IN Reagan reemerged at the airport. Donald Regan claimed credit. "For much of the way he talked about his disappointment, going over the details of his discussions with Gorbachev," Regan wrote. "His spirits were so low that I finally tried to cheer him up by telling a joke. The only one I could think of was about horses." This finally started to draw Reagan out of his funk, as he couldn't resist horses or horse stories.

Meanwhile, Reagan's speechwriters, in another car, were busy crafting his first public statement after the summit. On reaching the airport, they gathered with the president. "Despite the cheering conversation in the car, Reagan was still subdued and pensive," Regan said. "He shuffled the speech cards, changing the order of his remarks, then shuffled them again; his mind was elsewhere."

But gradually the reality of having to face an audience sank in. "The discipline of a lifetime returned, and he began to study his lines," Regan recalled. He had mere minutes to learn them. He was still studying when the band struck up "Hail to the Chief." Reagan heard the cue. "The president looked around the table at each of us in turn, squared his shoulders and literally marched the twenty steps to the platform that had been set up on the airport tarmac," Regan said. A small crowd of Americans had gathered to see the president; they applauded and waved American flags. Reagan responded as he always did to a friendly crowd. "Color returned to his face," Regan observed. "His smile came back and he read his speech in a strong, confident voice. It was a flawless performance."

"Thank you all," the president said. "It's good to feel so at home. And I want to apologize for being so late. As you know, General Secretary Gorbachev and I were to have concluded our talks at noon, after more than seven and a half hours of meetings over the last two days. But when the hour for departure arrived, we both felt that further discussions would be valuable. So, I called Nancy and told her I wouldn't be home for dinner." The crowd laughed appreciatively. "She said she understood," Reagan continued. "In about six and a half hours, I'll find out." The crowd laughed again.

The president addressed the issue that was on everyone's mind. Reagan's staff and speechwriters had understandably decided to emphasize the positive elements in the meetings with Gorbachev. Reagan responded to their suggestions and carried it off. "The talks we've just concluded were hard and tough, and yet I have to say extremely useful," he said. "Mr. Gorbachev and I were frank about our disagreements. We had to be. In several critical areas, we made more progress than we anticipated when we came to Iceland. We moved toward agreement on drastically reduced numbers of intermediate-range nuclear missiles in both Europe and Asia. We approached agreement on sharply reduced strategic arsenals for both our countries."

Yet they hadn't quite reached the finish line. "There remained, at the end of our talks, one area of disagreement," Reagan said. "While both sides seek reduction in the number of nuclear missiles and warheads threatening the world, the Soviet Union insisted that we sign an agreement that would deny to me and to future presidents for ten years the right to develop, test and deploy a defense against nuclear missiles for the people of the free world. This we could not and will not do."

REAGAN'S EXPLANATION BECAME the administration's line: that the president had pressed for sweeping reductions in nuclear arsenals but had refused to compromise American defense, represented by SDI, to achieve them. The White House interpretation had numerous advantages. It blunted assertions by antinuclear activists that Reagan was an irredeemable warmonger. To be sure, he hadn't achieved the deep cuts he proposed, but in merely putting them on the table, he had gone further than any president before him. It appeased the hawks, who had criticized the quick summit and feared that Reagan would be gulled by the wily Gorbachev. On this point the hawks had to credit Gorbachev as much as Reagan, for by making the laboratory restriction on SDI his price for the cuts, the general secretary had outfoxed himself and inadvertently rescued America. Robert Gates of the CIA was less hawkish than many in America, but he subscribed to this view. "Gorbachev took a very high-stakes, high-risk gamble to set up Ronald Reagan, ambush him, and kill SDI," Gates wrote. But the ambush had failed, and SDI and the American arsenal survived.

The administration's interpretation of what happened at Reykjavík had a final, absolutely critical advantage: it reflected what Reagan actually believed. At every opportunity the president repeated, with perfect sincerity, that SDI was vital to American security, that field-testing was crucial to its development, and that no reductions in offensive weapons warranted giving it up.

Yet not everyone, even in the administration, shared this view. "I felt crushed," Jack Matlock recalled of the moment he learned what had caused Reagan to balk. "Ten years in laboratories would not have killed

SDI; it could have preserved the concept since there was at least that much research needed to determine what technologies were most promising." Matlock declined to blame Reagan, who was no expert on the science and engineering of SDI. Instead, he blamed George Shultz, who did know the state of technology and had been at Reagan's side at the critical moments. "How could Shultz have let this happen?" Matlock asked himself. "Ten years in labs for SDI and elimination of strategic nuclear weapons and ballistic missiles would have been an agreement totally in the U.S. interest. If Shultz had told Reagan that, Reagan might have accepted it. Why had Shultz been so obtuse?"

Matlock wasn't alone in doubting that restricting SDI to labs for ten years would kill the program. "Given the present state of our technology, I think we could abide by these restrictions for ten years," Sidney Drell, a Stanford University physicist and supporter of SDI, said. Norris Smith, speaking for Lawrence Livermore National Laboratory, which was doing SDI research, said that no current projects would be hampered by confining research to the laboratory and that follow-on projects wouldn't be ready for field-testing for two to ten years, depending on the success of the lab tests.

George Shultz thought the critics missed the point of SDI. The secretary of state thought Reagan missed the point of SDI, too, though he was tactful enough not to say so. Reagan denied SDI was a bargaining chip; Shultz thought a bargaining chip was precisely what it was, except that it was a chip that must never be bargained away. Shultz was agnostic on whether SDI would ever work as Reagan hoped it would in shielding America from enemy missiles. But he judged that it had worked brilliantly in bringing Gorbachev to the negotiating table and wringing concessions out of him. "History will show, I believe, that the Reykjavik meetings were a turning point in the modern history of arms control," he told an associate as soon as he got back to the office. And SDI would continue to work only if America held it over the head of Gorbachev and his successors. "Without SDI as an ongoing propellant, these concessions could wither away over the next ten years," Shultz remarked later. As it was, SDI had shown how far Gorbachev was willing to go in arms reductions. "I knew that the genie was out of the bottle: the concessions Gorbachev made at Reykjavik could never, in reality, be taken back. We had seen the Soviets' bottom line."

GORBACHEV CONTENDED THAT it was Reagan who had revealed his bottom line. The general secretary remained upbeat as he reported the outcome of Reykjavík to the Politburo in Moscow. He blamed the failure to reach agreement partly on Reagan. "We had to wage a struggle in Reykjavik not only with the class enemy but also with such a representative of our class enemy, who exhibited extreme primitivism, a caveman outlook and intellectual impotence," Gorbachev said. But the larger cause was a fundamental American misconception of the Soviet system. "It is the belief that the U.S. might exhaust us economically via an arms race, create obstacles for me and for the entire Soviet leadership, undermine its plans for resolving economic and social problems and thereby provoke popular discontent." Reagan had thought this would compel the Soviet side to accept his interpretation of the ABM Treaty; he was shown to be mistaken. In the process, though, he had tipped his hand, revealing how far he was willing to go on arms control.

Public opinion was siding with the Soviet Union after Iceland, Gorbachev said. "The world lays responsibility for the failure to reach agreements at Reykjavik on the United States." Even many Americans thought Reagan was being unreasonable in clinging so tightly to SDI. The situation would only get better. "We did the right thing when we came forth with the initiative of holding this meeting and when we put forth our new proposals," Gorbachev told the Politburo. "Our line fully lived up to expectations. Reagan and his administration found themselves in a quandary. Let them flounder."

94

REAGAN WAS STILL unwinding from Reykjavík when, on November 4, 1986, he received a pair of jolts. The first was the loss of the Senate to the Democrats in the midterm elections. The eight-seat swing wasn't wholly unexpected; presidents' parties typically lose ground at the halfway points of second terms. But the Democratic takeover of the north end of the Capitol meant that the opposition would control both houses of Congress for the rest of Reagan's presidency. He had never been able to charm Tip O'Neill; he wondered if Robert Byrd, the leader of the new Senate majority, would be any easier to deal with.

The second jolt took the president entirely by surprise, although it shouldn't have. American papers picked up a story that had been published in an Arabic-language magazine in Lebanon asserting that the United States had been furnishing military equipment to Iran. Robert McFarlane, the story went on to say, had secretly traveled to Tehran in connection with the arms shipments.

The government of Iran shortly confirmed part of the story. It said McFarlane had been in Tehran. It added that McFarlane and four Americans who accompanied him had been detained before being expelled from the country. Additional news accounts linked the arms deliveries to the recent release of David Jacobsen, an American who had been kidnapped in Lebanon more than a year before.

The White House initially gave the story the back of its hand. "As long as Iran advocates the use of terrorism, the U.S. arms embargo will continue," Larry Speakes told reporters. In response to a direct question as to whether the arms embargo remained in effect, Speakes said, "Yes."

Reagan refused to dignify the story with a public comment of his own. In his diary he blamed the media for more misreporting. "Usual meetings," he wrote. "Discussion of how to handle press who are off on a wild story built on unfounded story originating in Beirut that we've bought hostage Jacobsen's freedom with weapons to Iran." Reagan intended to continue his silence. "Our message will be 'we can't and won't answer any Q's on this subject because to do so will endanger the lives of those we are trying to help.'"

Reagan brought Jacobsen and his family to the White House. The president couldn't resist the opportunity to express his satisfaction at Jacobsen's freedom and his concern for the Americans still in captivity. But the event gave reporters license to question him on his policy toward the hostages and their kidnappers. "Mr. President," one reporter asked, "the Iranians are saying that if you'll release some of those weapons, they'll intercede to free the rest of the hostages. Will you?"

Reagan stuck to his script. "There's no way we can answer questions having anything to do with this without endangering the people we're trying to rescue," he said.

Reporters had uncovered the rift between the State Department and the NSC staff regarding the hostages and relations with Iran. A reporter wanted Reagan to confirm or deny the division: "Could you just tell us whether Secretary of State Shultz agrees with your policy or disagrees and has protested, as has been reported?"

Reagan refused to reveal what advice he had been given. "We have all been working together," he said.

"And Secretary Shultz supports the policy, and so does Cap Weinberger?"

"Yes," Reagan said.

A reporter wanted more detail on how Jacobsen had been freed. "Why not dispel the speculation by telling us exactly what happened, sir?"

"Because it has to happen again and again and again until we have them all back," Reagan said. He returned to the script. "And anything that we tell about all the things that have been going on in trying to effect his rescue endangers the possibility of further rescue."

The reporters continued to push. "Your own party's majority leader"— Robert Dole—"says you're rewarding terrorists," one said.

David Jacobsen stood beside Reagan through all this. His frustration grew with each probing question. Finally he burst out angrily, "In the name of God, would you please just be responsible and back off?"

Reagan nodded agreement with Jacobsen, and the two turned to go inside the Oval Office. A shouted question followed them: "How are we to know what is responsible and what is not?"

Moments later, away from the reporters, Jacobsen said to Reagan, "My God, Mr. President, these people are savages. Don't they realize what they are doing?"

Reagan again nodded, gratified that Jacobsen had said what he himself was thinking. "It was an emotional and heartwarming meeting," he recorded in his diary. He was pleased with his own response to a flap he hoped would blow over. "Now we are off to Camp D," he concluded the day's entry.

DON REGAN DIDN'T think the problem was so easily resolved. He recognized that the arms-to-Iran story hadn't emerged out of thin air, and he guessed that it couldn't be waved away. He urged the president to get ahead of the story by telling everything he knew about it.

The problem was that Regan didn't know how much Reagan knew. He could only guess at the extent of the president's knowledge of the alleged arms-for-hostages deal. As chief of staff, Regan theoretically controlled the flow of information to and from the Oval Office. Theory and practice meshed closely in domestic affairs, but foreign policy often frustrated his efforts to keep on top of things. The national security adviser reported directly to the president; Robert McFarlane and then John Poindexter briefed Regan only intermittently on what they told Reagan and what he told them.

Regan nonetheless believed the president had to face the press. Before Reagan left for Camp David, Regan repeated his advice about telling all.

Reagan again resisted. "Don, you heard what Jacobsen said," he explained. "I *can't* talk."

"Mr. President, I don't care," Regan replied. "We're between the devil and the deep and it's not going to help things to maintain silence. If these hostages don't materialize soon, you're going to have to speak up. You're going to be ripped apart on the weekend talk shows. The Monday morning papers will pick it up. The American people are going to start demanding to know what's going on here."

Reagan still refused. But he said he would reconsider on Monday after he returned from Camp David. He flew to the presidential retreat, where he persisted in blaming the media. "The Saturday night and Sunday morning talk shows continued to hammer on the hostage and Iran arms story giving credence to every rumor and supposed leak," he wrote. "They can do great harm with their irresponsible drum beating."

Don Regan hoped to enlist Nancy Reagan to help in persuading the president to go public. But she declined. "He's not going to talk to the press," she said. She added, according to Regan's recounting, "My Friend says it's, you know, it's just *wrong* for him to talk right now."

Regan had bitten his tongue at the influence of Nancy's astrologer in determining the president's schedule, but this crossed the line into policy. Over the phone he exploded in frustration. "My God, Nancy," he said. "He's going to go down in flames if he doesn't speak up."

On Monday, Reagan met with his national security team. "Subject: the press storm charging that we are negotiating with terrorist kidnappers for the release of hostages using sale of arms as ransom," he recorded. "Also that we are violating our own law about arms sales to Iran. They"— the press—"quoted as gospel every unnamed source plus such authorities as a Danish sailor who claims to have served on a ship carrying arms from Israel to Iran, etc. etc. etc. I ordered a statement to effect we were *not* dealing in ransom, etc., but that we would not respond to charges or Q's that could endanger hostage lives or lives of people we were using to make contact with the terrorists."

Reagan only reluctantly agreed to speak to the leaders of Congress in a private session. He told the lawmakers that the administration had indeed sent arms to Iran but merely in small amounts and not in exchange for hostages. Don Regan watched the visitors as the president spoke. "Some of those men were skeptical," he recalled. "You could see it in their faces. But they had no choice but to accept what the president told them. Ronald Reagan had never lied to them (or in my experience, to anyone). And there is no question in my mind that he thought he was telling the truth."

Reagan sensed the skepticism as well. He wasn't used to having his integrity impugned. He decided that the only way to resolve the matter was to take his case to the American people. "This whole irresponsible press bilge about hostages and Iran has gotten totally out of hand," he wrote to himself. "The media looks like it's trying to create another Watergate. I laid down the law in the morning meetings—I want to go public and tell the people the truth."

TEN DAYS AFTER the story surfaced, the president addressed the American people from the Oval Office. He dispensed with the typical opening joke, though he allowed himself a jab at the media. "I know you've been reading, seeing, and hearing a lot of stories the past several days attributed to Danish sailors, unnamed observers at Italian ports and Spanish harbors, and especially unnamed government officials of my administration. Well, now you're going to hear the facts from a White House source, and you know my name."

His television audience had never seen him more serious. "I wanted this time to talk with you about an extremely sensitive and profoundly important matter of foreign policy," he said. "For eighteen months now we have had underway a secret diplomatic initiative to Iran. That initiative was undertaken for the simplest and best of reasons: to renew a relationship with the nation of Iran, to bring an honorable end to the bloody six-year war between Iran and Iraq, to eliminate state-sponsored terrorism and subversion, and to effect the safe return of all hostages." Iran's cooperation was crucial to achieving these goals.

He went straight to the most damning allegation. "The charge has been made that the United States has shipped weapons to Iran as ransom payment for the release of American hostages in Lebanon, that the United States undercut its allies and secretly violated American policy against trafficking with terrorists." He let the charge hang in the air for a moment, and then, looking straight in the camera, he said, "Those charges are utterly false. The United States has not made concessions to those who hold our people captive in Lebanon. And we will not. The United States has not swapped boatloads or planeloads of American weapons for the return of American hostages. And we will not."

Yet some things needed to be explained. "During the course of our secret discussions, I authorized the transfer of small amounts of defensive weapons and spare parts for defensive systems to Iran," Reagan said. "My purpose was to convince Tehran that our negotiators were acting with my authority, to send a signal that the United States was prepared to replace the animosity between us with a new relationship." But the shipments were no more than a gesture. "These modest deliveries, taken together, could easily fit into a single cargo plane. They could not, taken together, affect the outcome of the six-year war between Iran and Iraq nor could they affect in any way the military balance between the two countries."

As for the hostages: "At the same time we undertook this initiative, we made clear that Iran must oppose all forms of international terrorism as a condition of progress in our relationship. The most significant step which Iran could take, we indicated, would be to use its influence in Lebanon to secure the release of all hostages held there."

The initiative had borne fruit. "Some progress has already been made," Reagan said. "Since U.S. government contact began with Iran, there's been no evidence of Iranian government complicity in acts of terrorism against the United States. Hostages have come home, and we welcome the efforts that the government of Iran has taken in the past and is currently undertaking."

Reagan emphasized Iran's strategic significance. "It lies between the Soviet Union and access to the warm waters of the Indian Ocean," he said. "Iran's geography gives it a critical position from which adversaries could interfere with oil flows from the Arab States that border the Persian Gulf. Apart from geography, Iran's oil deposits are important to the long-term health of the world economy." For these reasons, the United States had to establish a dialogue with Iran. He likened Iran to China in the early 1970s, and his secret policy to that of Richard Nixon. "In 1971 then-President Nixon sent his national security adviser on a secret mission to China. In that case, as today, there was a basic requirement for discretion and for a sensitivity to the situation in the nation we were attempting to engage."

Reagan offered greater detail about his Iranian initiative. "Our discussions continued into the spring of this year," he said. "Based upon the progress we felt we had made, we sought to raise the diplomatic level of contacts. A meeting was arranged in Tehran. I then asked my former national security adviser, Robert McFarlane, to undertake a secret mission and gave him explicit instructions. I asked him to go to Iran to open a dialogue, making stark and clear our basic objectives and disagreements. The four days of talks were conducted in a civil fashion, and American personnel were not mistreated." The dialogue had continued since then, and progress continued to be made. The release of David Jacobsen was the latest sign.

Reagan reiterated that Jacobsen's release had nothing to do with the arms shipments. "We did not—repeat—did not trade weapons or anything else for hostages, nor will we." The Iran initiative did not signal an easing of American policy toward terrorism. "Those who think that we have gone soft on terrorism should take up the question with Colonel Qaddafi. We have not, nor will we, capitulate to terrorists." And the initiative violated no laws. "The actions I authorized were, and continue to be, in full compliance with federal law."

Reagan appealed to Americans' good sense. "As president, I've always operated on the belief that, given the facts, the American people will make the right decision. I believe that to be true now. I cannot guarantee the outcome. But as in the past, I ask for your support because I believe you share the hope for peace in the Middle East, for freedom for all hostages, and for a world free of terrorism."

GEORGE SHULTZ WATCHED Reagan's address with mounting dismay. "The president's speech convinced me that Ronald Reagan still truly did not believe that what had happened had, in fact, happened," Shultz recalled. The secretary of state had gradually realized that his and Caspar Weinberger's strong opposition had not spiked the Iran initiative. John Poindexter had kept the details from him, but Shultz divined enough to conclude that it was a disastrously conceived arms-for-hostages deal.

Yet Poindexter had managed to persuade the president otherwise, Shultz observed. "What had been going on here was a staff con job on the president, playing on his very human desire to get the hostages released. They told the president what they wanted him to know and what they saw he wanted to hear, and they dressed it up in 'geostrategic' costume." The con job worked all too well. "So what Reagan said to the American public was true to him, although it was not the reality."

Shultz was hardly alone in finding Reagan's explanation incredible. A *Los Angeles Times* poll revealed that a scant 14 percent of respondents thought the president was telling the truth about the Iran initiative. By a margin of three to one they rejected his claim that the administration did not negotiate with terrorists. Only one in five respondents believed Reagan's claim that his administration had not violated federal laws in sending weapons to Iran.

Shultz was sorely tempted to resign. By office he was the president's right arm for foreign affairs, but Reagan had rejected his advice in favor of that of Poindexter. He wanted to be a good soldier and support the president's policies, but he was convinced Reagan didn't know what policies Poindexter was making in his name. And Shultz refused to cover for Poindexter.

He agreed to appear on *Face the Nation* but soon wished he hadn't.

Host Lesley Stahl asked an obvious question: "Will there be any more arms shipments to Iran, either directly by our government or through any third parties?"

"It's certainly against our policy," Shultz responded.

"That's not an answer," Stahl observed. "Why don't you answer the question directly? I'll ask it again. Will there be any more arms shipments to Iran, either directly by the United States or through any third parties?"

"Under the circumstances of Iran's war with Iraq, its pursuit of terrorism, its association with those holding our hostages, I would certainly say, as far as I'm concerned, no," Shultz replied.

"Do you have the authority to speak for the entire administration?" Stahl pressed.

"No," Shultz said, reddening with anger and embarrassment.

95

R EAGAN, PRESUMABLY, SPOKE for the administration. The president observed the mounting skepticism and realized he had to answer the questions himself. He called a news conference. "Eighteen months ago, as I said last Thursday, this administration began a secret initiative to the Islamic Republic of Iran," he said in an opening statement. "Our purposes were fourfold: to replace a relationship of total hostility with something better, to bring a negotiated end to the Iran-Iraq war, to bring an end to terrorism and to effect the release of our hostages." Reagan said he had recognized that the initiative entailed great risks for both the American hostages and the administration's Iranian interlocutors. "That's why the information was restricted to appropriate cabinet officers and those officials with an absolute need to know." For the first time the president acknowledged the dissent among his advisers. "This undertaking was a matter of considerable debate within administration circles," he said. "The principal issue in contention was whether we should make isolated and limited exceptions to our arms embargo as a signal of our serious intent." Reagan didn't identify the disputants by name, but all the reporters and many of those watching the news conference on television understood that the prime objector was George Shultz. "Several top advisers opposed the sale of even a modest shipment of defensive weapons and spare parts to Iran. Others felt no progress could be made without this sale. I weighed their views. I considered the risks of failure and the rewards of success, and I decided to proceed. And the responsibility for the decision and the operation is mine and mine alone." Reagan quoted Abraham Lincoln on controversial decisions: "If it turns out right, the criticism will not matter. If it turns out wrong, ten angels swearing I was right will make no difference."

Reagan refused to apologize for the course he had chosen. "I understand this decision is deeply controversial and that some profoundly disagree with what was done. Even some who support our secret initiative believe it was a mistake to send any weapons to Iran. I understand and I respect those views, but I deeply believe in the correctness of my decision. I was convinced then and I am convinced now that while the risks were great, so, too, was the potential reward. Bringing Iran back into the community of responsible nations, ending its participation in political terror, bringing an end to that terrible war, and bringing our hostages home—these are the causes that justify taking risks."

Reagan said he would continue to take risks to enhance American security. But his past policy toward Iran had become counterproductive on account of the heavy and often inaccurate media attention. And so it was being changed. "To eliminate the widespread but mistaken perception that we have been exchanging arms for hostages, I have directed that no further sales of arms of any kind be sent to Iran. I have further directed that all information relating to our initiative be provided to the appropriate members of Congress. There may be some questions which for reasons of national security or to protect the safety of the hostages I will be unable to answer publicly. But again, all information will be provided to the appropriate members of Congress."

He opened the floor to questions. Helen Thomas asked if he thought the credibility of his administration had suffered as a result of the recent revelations, coming soon after the swapping with the Soviets of Zakharov for Daniloff.

Reagan denied, as he had before, that there was any trade of Zakharov for Daniloff. The premise of Thomas's question was simply wrong. As for the Iran enterprise: "There was no deception intended by us. There was the knowledge that we were embarking on something that could be of great risk to the people we were talking to, great risk to our hostages. And therefore we had to have it limited to only the barest number of people that had to know." In language that inadvertently conjured memories of Richard Nixon and Watergate, Reagan continued, "I was not breaking any law in doing that." He explained, "I have the right under the law to defer reporting to Congress, to the proper congressional committees, on an action, and defer it until such time as I believe it can safely be done with no risk to others." He said the relevant congressional committees would receive briefings shortly. He added, as an afterthought to his Nixonesque denial of legal culpability, "We were not negotiating government to government. We were negotiating with certain individuals within that country."

Thomas followed up. "Are you prepared now to disavow the finding which let you make end runs around the Iranian arms embargo?" she asked. "Are you going to tear it up?"

"No, as I say, we are going to observe that embargo," he replied, somewhat confusingly. "And it's part of the same reason that, as I've said, we were doing this in the first place: And that is to see, among the other issues involved, if we can help bring about peace between those two countries, a peace without victory to either one or defeat and that will recognize the territorial integrity of both. And this is something that all of our allies are seeking also. But I think the people understand that sometimes you have to keep a secret in order to save human lives and to succeed in the mission, just as we went into Grenada without prior notice, because then we would have put to risk all of those men who were going to hit the beach."

Another reporter asked about Shultz. Had the president and the secretary of state ever spoken about the latter's resignation?

"There's been no talk of resignation," Reagan said.

Chris Wallace of NBC News wanted Reagan to resolve a seeming contradiction. "Mr. President, you have stated flatly, and you stated flatly again tonight, that you did not trade weapons for hostages. And yet the record shows that every time an American hostage was released—last September, this July, and again just this very month—there had been a major shipment of arms just before that. Are we all to believe that was just a coincidence?"

Reagan sidestepped. "Chris, the only thing I know about major shipments of arms—as I've said, everything that we sold them could be put in one cargo plane, and there would be plenty of room left over. Now, if there were major shipments—and we know this has been going on—there have been other countries that have been dealing in arms with Iran. There have been also private merchants of such things that have been doing the same thing. Now, I've seen the stories about a Danish tramp steamer and Danish sailors' union officials talking about their ships taking various supplies to Iran. I didn't know anything about that until I saw the press on it, because we certainly never had any contact with anything of the kind. And so, it's just that we did something for a particular mission. There was a risk entailed. And Iran held no hostages. Iran did not kidnap anyone, to our knowledge. And the fact that part of the operation was that we knew, however, that the kidnappers of our hostages did have some kind of relationship in which Iran could at times influence them—not always—but could influence them. And so three of our hostages came home."

Wallace wasn't satisfied. "On that first point, your own chief of staff, Mr. Regan, has said that the U.S. condoned Israeli shipments of arms to Iran," he said. "And aren't you, in effect, sending the very message you always said you didn't want to send? Aren't you saying to terrorists, either you or your state sponsor—which in this case was Iran—can gain from the holding of hostages?"

Reagan denied it. "No, because I don't see where the kidnappers or the hostage-holders gained anything," he said. "They didn't get anything. They let the hostages go. Now, whatever is the pressure that brought that about, I'm just grateful to it for the fact that we got them. As a matter of fact, if there had not been so much publicity, we would have had two more that we were expecting."

Sam Donaldson of ABC News was Reagan's least favorite reporter because, to Reagan's thinking, Donaldson was more interested in skewering his subjects than in revealing the truth. Donaldson played to form this evening. "Mr. President, when you had the arms embargo on, you were asking other nations, our allies particularly, to observe it, publicly," he said. "But at the same time, privately, you concede you were authorizing a breaking of that embargo by the United States. How can you justify this duplicity?"

Reagan didn't like being called a liar, even if a synonym was employed. He kept his temper only with difficulty. "I don't think it was duplicity," he replied. "And as I say, the so-called violation did not in any way alter the military balance between the two countries. But what we were aiming for, I think, made it worthwhile. And this was a waiver of our own embargo; the embargo still stays now and for the future. But the causes that I outlined here in my opening statement—first of all, to try and establish a relationship with a country that is of great strategic importance to peace and everything else in the Middle East, at the same time, also, to strike a blow against terrorism and to get our hostages back, as we did."

"Sir, if I may," Donaldson continued, "the polls show that a lot of American people just simply don't believe you. The one thing that you've had going for you, more than anything else in your presidency, your credibility, has been severely damaged. Can you repair it?"

Reagan's anger grew evident. He came close to blaming the media,

Donaldson included, for the whole affair. "Well, I imagine I'm the only one around who wants to repair it," he said. "And I didn't have anything to do with damaging it."

Bill Plante of CBS News spared Reagan more of Donaldson, but the difference hardly mattered. "Mr. President, you say that the equipment which was shipped didn't alter the military balance. Yet several things: We understand that there were 1,000 TOW antitank missiles shipped by the U.S. The U.S. apparently condoned shipments by Israel and other nations of other quantities of arms as an ancillary part of this deal—not directly connected, but had to condone it, or the shipments could not have gone forward, sir. So how can you say that it cannot alter the military balance? And how can you say, sir, that it didn't break the law, when the National Security Act of 1977 plainly talks about timely notification of Congress and also, sir, stipulates that if the national security required secrecy the president is still required to advise the leadership and the chairmen of the intelligence committees?"

Reagan shook his head. "Bill, everything you've said here is based on a supposition that is false," he said. "We did not condone and do not condone the shipment of arms from other countries. And what was the other point that you made here?"

"There were the antitank missiles, sir."

Reagan wasn't used to such sustained skepticism. It seemed to affect him. "Oh no, about the—that it didn't—no, that it didn't violate the—or that did violate the law," he fumbled. "No, as I've said, the president, believe it or not, does have the power if, in his belief, national security can be served, to waive the provisions of that law as well as to defer the notification of the Congress on this."

Plante still wanted to hear about the antitank missiles. "Isn't it possible that the Iraqis, sir, might think that a thousand antitank missiles was enough to alter the balance of that war?" he asked.

"This is a purely defensive weapon," Reagan replied. "It is a shoulder-carried weapon. And we don't think that in this defensive thing—we didn't add to any offensive power on the part of Iran. We know that Iraq has already announced that they would be willing to settle the conflict, as we've said, with no winners or losers. And the other parts happened to be spare parts for an antiaircraft Hawk battery. And, as I say, all of those weapons could be very easily carried in one mission."

Charles Bierbauer of CNN inquired about Israel. "Mr. President, I don't think it's still clear just what Israel's role was in this," he said. "The questions have been asked about a condoned shipment. We do understand that the Israelis sent a shipment in 1985, and there were also reports that it was the Israelis that contacted your administration and suggested that you make contact with Iran. Could you explain what the Israeli role was here?"

"No," Reagan responded, "because we, as I say, have had nothing to do with other countries or their shipment of arms or doing what they're doing. And, no, as a matter of fact, the first ideas about the need to restore relations between Iran and the United States, or the Western world for that matter, actually began before our administration was here. But from the very first, if you look down the road at what could happen and perhaps a change of government there, it was absolutely vital for the Western world and to the hopes for peace in the Middle East and all for us to be trying to establish this relationship. And we worked—oh, it started about eighteen months ago, really, as we began to find out some individuals that it might be possible for us to deal with."

"Can I follow up please, if I may, on that?" Bierbauer said. "The contacts that you're suggesting are with moderates in the Iranian government and in the Iranian system. Barry Goldwater tonight said in his judgment there are no moderates in Iran. I don't mean to suggest that there may not be, but how did you know that you were reaching the moderates? And how do you define a moderate in that kind of a government?"

Reagan dodged once more. "Well, again, you're asking questions that I cannot get into with regard to the answers," he said. "But believe me, we had information that led us to believe that there are factions within Iran, and many of them with an eye toward the fact that they think sooner rather than later there is going to be a change in the government there. And there is great dissatisfaction among the people in Iran."

The next questioner inquired, "Could we turn to U.S.-Soviet relations for a moment, please?"

Reagan seized the chance for a laugh. "I'd be delighted," he said. The room duly chuckled.

The respite lasted only a moment, though, and the grilling resumed. "Mr. President, going back over your answers tonight about the arms shipments and the numbers of them," a reporter asked, "are you telling us tonight that the only shipments with which we were involved were the one or two that followed your January 17th finding and that, whatever your aides have said on background or on the record, there were no other shipments which the U.S. condoned?"

"That's right," Reagan said, then caught himself. "I'm saying nothing," he amended. He nonetheless added, "But the missiles that we sold—and remember, there are too many people that are saying 'gave.' They bought them."

Andrea Mitchell of NBC tried to pin Reagan down. "Mr. President, to follow up on that," she said. "We've been told by the chief of staff, Donald Regan, that we condoned—this government condoned—an Israeli shipment in September of 1985, shortly before the release of hostage Benjamin Weir. That was four months before your intelligence finding on January 17th that you say gave you the legal authority not to notify Congress. Now, can you clear that up—why this government was not in violation of its arms embargo and of the notification to Congress for having condoned American-made weapons shipped to Iran in September of 1985?"

Reagan pleaded ignorance. "Well, no, I've never heard Mr. Regan say that, and I'll ask him about that. Because we believe in the embargo, and as I say, we waived it for a specific purpose, in fact, with four goals in mind. Yes."

Mitchell pushed harder. "Can I just follow up on that for a second, sir, because what is unclear to, I think, many people in the American public is why—if you are saying tonight that there will be no further arms shipments to Iran—why you won't cancel the January 17th intelligence finding so that you can put to rest any suggestion that you might again, without notification and in complete secrecy and perhaps with the objection of some of your cabinet members, continue to ship weapons if you think that it is necessary?"

"No, I have no intention of doing that," Reagan said, leaving his listeners potentially confused as to what he had no intention of doing: canceling the finding or shipping more weapons. "But at the same time, we are hopeful that we're going to be able to continue our meetings with these people, these individuals."

Mitchell sought clarity. "You won't cancel the intelligence finding?" she asked.

Reagan hedged. "I don't know whether it's called for or whether I have to wait until we've reported to Congress and all. I don't know just what the technicality legally is on that."

A reporter brought the American people into the picture. "Do you think—its strategic position notwithstanding—the American people would ever support weapons to the Ayatollah Khomeini?" he asked.

"We weren't giving them to the Ayatollah Khomeini," Reagan said. "It's a strange situation. As I say, we were dealing with individuals, and we believe that those—and some of those individuals are in government, in positions in government. But it was not a meeting officially of the United States head of state and the Iranian head of state. But these people, we believed, and their closeness to the Iran military was such that this was necessary to let them know, number one, that we were serious and sincere in our effort about good relations and also that they were dealing with the head of government over here, that this wasn't something coming out of some agency or bureau, that I was behind it."

"Mr. President," a fresh questioner asked, "you said that you were not swapping, or you did not think you were swapping, arms for hostages. But did it ever occur to you, or did it never occur to you, that certainly the Iranians would see it that way and that they might take it as an inducement to take more hostages, especially in light of the fact that they've released three but taken three more?"

Reagan had been saying for years that Iran was a state sponsor of terrorism. Now the president found himself having to deny that Iran controlled those it sponsored. "No, to the best of our knowledge, Iran does not own or have authority over the Hezbollah. They cannot order them to do something." He decided to qualify this. "It is apparent that they, evidently, have either some persuasion—and they don't always succeed—but they can sometimes persuade or pressure the Hezbollah into doing what they did in this instance. And as I say, the Iranian government had no hostages, and they bought a shipment from us." He repeated that the arms were merely a token of good faith. He said the administration reminded the Iranians of America's antiterrorist policy. "We told them that we did not want to do business with any nation that openly backed terrorism. And they gave us information that they did not. And they said also that they had some evidence that there had been a lessening of this on the part of Khomeini and the government and that they'd made some progress. As a matter of fact, some individuals associated with terrorist acts had been put in prison there. And so that was when we said, 'Well, there's a very easy way for you to verify that if that's the way you feel, and they're being held hostage in Lebanon.'"

"If I can follow up," the reporter said. "If your arms shipments had no effect on the release of the hostages, then how do you explain the release of the hostages at the same time that the shipments were coming in?"

"No, I said that—at the time—I said to them that there was something they could do to show their sincerity," Reagan replied. "And if they really meant it that they were not in favor of backing terrorists, they could begin by releasing our hostages."

Reagan's discomfort had been obvious and growing. He now attempted a counterattack against his questioners. "As a matter of fact, I believe and have reason to believe that we would have had all five of them by this last weekend, had it not been for the attendant confusion that arose here in the reporting room."

"On that point," a reporter rejoined, "you said earlier, and you said just now again, that, but for the publicity, two other hostages would have been returned home by now. As you know, the publicity began in a Syrian-backed, pro-Syrian magazine in Lebanon. My question is, therefore, are you suggesting that someone who was a party to this sabotaged it by deliberately leaking that original report?"

"To our best information," Reagan replied, "the leak came from a person in government in Iran and not one of the people that we were dealing with, someone that would be more hostile to us. And that individual gave the story to the magazine, and the magazine then printed the story there in Beirut."

"Mr. President, there has been an obvious change in policy towards Iran: from refusing to deal with a terrorist state to even sending weapons as a gesture of good will," a reporter said. "Would you consider, in the name of the same geopolitical interest that you invoked with Iran, changing your policy towards Nicaragua?"

"No," Reagan said, more convincingly than on several of his previous answers. But then he wandered back into the weeds. "I believe that I've answered that question, I think, more than once here—that no, we still hold to our position, and Iran officially is still on our list of nations that have been supporting terrorism. But I'm talking about the people that we were doing business with, and they gave us indication and evidence that that policy was changing. And so, as I said, to give them more prestige and muscle there where they were, we made this sale."

A reporter offered Reagan a chance to cut his way out of the thicket. "Mr. President, there is a mood in Washington tonight of a president who is very much beleaguered, very much on the defensive. Why don't you seize the offensive by giving your secretary of state a vote of confidence declaring that all future covert activities will have his support and by shaking up the National Security Council in such a way as to satisfy the concerns in Congress that it has been running a paramilitary operation out of the basement of the White House in defiance of the State Department and the Congress?"

Reagan rambled before finding something to grasp. "The State Department—or the secretary of state—was involved. The director of the CIA was involved, in what we were doing and, as I said before, there are certain laws in which, for certain actions, I would not have been able to keep them a secret as they were. But these people you've mentioned have been involved—do know what was going on. And I don't see that the action that you've suggested has called for it. But what you've disappointed me the most in is suggesting that I sound defensive up here. I've just been trying to answer all your questions as well as I can. And I don't feel that I have anything to defend about at all. With the circumstances the way they were, the decision I made I still believe was the correct decision, and I believe that we achieved some portion of our goals."

"Mr. President, do you believe that any of the additional hostages will be released?" a reporter asked.

"I have to believe that," Reagan said.

"Mr. President, you made an exception for the arms embargo when you thought it was in the U.S. interest to do so. Why shouldn't other nations ship weapons to Iran when they think it's in their interests?"

"Well, I would like to see the indication as to how it could be in their interest," Reagan said. "I know that there are other nations that feel as we do that the Western world should be trying to find an avenue to get Iran back where it once was—and that is in the family of democratic nations and the family of nations that want peace in the Middle East and so forth."

"How, Mr. President—if I may follow up—how does shipping weapons to Iran help bring them back into the community of nations? You've acknowledged that you were dealing with only a small portion of the government."

"I was talking of strengthening a particular group who needed the prestige that that could give them, who needed that, well, that bargaining power, themselves, within their own ranks," Reagan said.

Jeremiah O'Leary of the Republican-friendly *Washington Times* corrected a Reagan misstatement from earlier in the news conference. "Mr. President, I believe you may have been slightly in error in describing a TOW as a shoulder-mounted weapon. It's a ground-to-ground weapon. Redeye is the shoulder weapon, but that's beside the point. TOWs are used to destroy tanks."

"Yes, I know, Jerry," Reagan said. "I know it's a tank weapon."

"I don't think it's fired from your shoulder."

"Well, now, if I have been misinformed, then I will yield on that," Reagan said. "But it was my understanding that that is a man-carried weapon, and we have a number of other shoulder-borne weapons."

"I did have a question, though," O'Leary said. "I just wanted to ask you what would be wrong at this stage of the game, since everything seems to have gone wrong that could possibly go wrong, like the Murphy Law, the Reagan Law, the O'Leary Law, this week—what would be wrong in saying that a mistake was made on a very high-risk gamble so that you can get on with the next two years?"

Reagan stood his ground, eroded though it was. "Because I don't think a mistake was made," he said. "It was a high-risk gamble, and it was a gamble that, as I've said, I believe the circumstances warranted. And I don't see that it has been a fiasco or a great failure of any kind. We still have those contacts. We still have made some ground. We got our hostages back—three of them. And so, I think that what we did was right, and we're going to continue on this path."

96

I T WAS A harrowing experience. Reagan had never spent a more uncomfortable hour in public, on camera. Characteristically, he blamed his interrogators. "They were out for blood," he wrote that night. "Every Q. had a sharp barb." But he thought he had handled himself well. "Our gang seems to feel 'I done good.'"

Reagan remained a sucker for favorable reviews. Optimism had been part of his personality since childhood; whether innate or learned, it helped him survive the uncertainties of life with an alcoholic father. His favorite story, one his inner circle heard so often they couldn't stand it any longer, told of a child who wants a horse for Christmas but wakes to find a pile of manure instead. Undaunted, the child grabs a shovel and starts digging. "There's got to be a horse in here somewhere!" he explains delightedly. Reagan focused on the positive parts of any experience, convinced they held the key to its meaning. This habit constituted one of his great personal strengths, making him almost unsinkable emotionally. It was also central to his political success. Pessimism pervades the thinking of conservatives, who tend to believe the world is going to hell in a handbasket. They might be right, but they aren't fun to be around. Barry Goldwater appealed to people's heads, but he left their hearts cold. Reagan was as conservative philosophically as Goldwater, but his sunny mien made Americans feel good about themselves and their country and made him irresistible at the polls.

Yet Reagan's insistence on seeing the good side sometimes worked against him. His staff buoyed their boss by sharing favorable responses and arranging appearances before friendly crowds. They told him he "done good" even when he hadn't. This kept the spring in his step and the smile on his face, but it also kept him from hearing bad news he needed to hear.

GEORGE SHULTZ WASN'T part of the good-news gang. He deemed Reagan's press conference "disastrous" and shuddered at being associated with the policies that had made it necessary. He groaned to read a devastating review of the administration's actions in the typically supportive *Wall Street Journal.* "If some malicious Merlin were trying to concoct a scheme that, with one stroke of a wizard's wand, would undermine American principles, policies, people, interests and allies," the *Journal's* columnist declared, "it would be hard to conjure up anything more harmful and humiliating than secretly shipping supplies of American weaponry to the world's primary terrorist state in exchange for a handful of hostages." The columnist went on to say, "In the process, Mr. Reagan seems to have cuckolded his own secretaries of state and defense. Secretary of State George Shultz has staked his personal prestige on a global campaign against cooperation with terrorism. Only weeks ago, for example, Mr. Shultz was at the United Nations reassuring Arab ministers that the U.S. was determined to stem the flow of arms to Iran. About the same time Defense Secretary Caspar Weinberger was in Peking urging Chinese leaders to cease shipping arms to Tehran."

Shultz phoned the president after the news conference and told him he had made "a great many factual errors." Shultz asked permission to come to the White House the next day and show Reagan where he had gone wrong. "He was shaken by what I said and agreed to listen to me," Shultz recalled.

The president corrected one of the errors before the secretary arrived. "There may be some misunderstanding of one of my answers tonight," Reagan said in a written statement released less than an hour after the news conference. "There was a third country involved in our secret project with Iran." Reagan didn't name the third country, but after all the publicity, everyone interested understood it to be Israel. The president proceeded, however, to compound a separate error. "Taking this into account, all of the shipments of the token amounts of defensive arms and parts that I have authorized or condoned taken in total could be placed aboard a single cargo aircraft." This was patently untrue, as anyone familiar with the ordnance included in the transfers understood. But Reagan, who was not familiar with the ordnance, as had become clear at his news conference, had been told this by John Poindexter, and he believed it.

Reagan and Shultz met the following afternoon. Don Regan joined them. "The content of our discussion was tough," Shultz wrote later. "I had detailed material on statements the president had made that were wrong. He had accepted as accurate information provided him by the CIA and the NSC staff that was in fact laden with error—all coordinated, insofar as I could see, by Poindexter. For nearly an hour I went at it with the president. We argued back and forth, hot and heavy. I never thought I would talk to a president of the United States in such a direct and challenging way."

Reagan seemed to accept Shultz's good intentions. "But I didn't shake him one bit," Shultz recalled. "To him, the problem was with the press." Shultz mentioned a telephone call from McFarlane a year earlier in which McFarlane described an arms-for-hostages trade. "Oh, I knew about that," Reagan responded. "But that wasn't arms for hostages." Shultz rejoined that no one who saw the evidence would believe him. Reagan held fast. "George, I know what happened, and we were doing the right thing."

Reagan thought Shultz was blowing things out of proportion. "A touchy meeting with George S. and Don R.," he wrote in his diary. "George is very upset about the Iran affair and I fear he may be getting ready to say 'Either someone else is fired or I quit.'" The president remarked to himself, "I don't like ultimatums." Yet he agreed to Shultz's demand for a showdown within the administration. "I've called a Monday afternoon meeting"—Reagan was writing on Thursday—"of him and Don, me and Cap W., Bill Casey, John P. and the V.P. to get everything about the Iran effort out on the table."

Reagan continued to think the problem was primarily a misunderstanding. "We had an NSC briefing," he wrote the next day. "It seems there is a thing having to do with Israel and some Hawk missiles in the Iran mix that has to be straightened out." His confidence remained unshaken. "Ed Meese assured us again that I'm in the clear legally on what we were doing."

REAGAN'S CONFIDENCE WAS tested anew at the start of the following week. "Big thing of the day was two-hour meeting in the Situation Room on the Iran affair," Reagan wrote on Monday night. "George S. is still stubborn that we shouldn't have sold the arms to Iran. I gave him an argument. All in all we got everything out on the table."

Actually, not everything came out at the meeting, as Ed Meese soon revealed. The attorney general had been conducting a quiet investigation, quizzing Poindexter and others. He had more bad news for the president. "After meeting, Ed M. and Don R. told me of a smoking gun," Reagan wrote in his diary. "On one of the arms shipments the Iranians paid Israel a higher purchase price than we were getting. The Israelis put the difference in a secret bank account. Then our Col. North (NSC) gave the money to the 'Contras.'"

Don Regan recalled the moment the president learned of the contra connection. "The president, in person, is a ruddy man, with bright red cheeks," Regan wrote. "He blanched when he heard Meese's words. The color drained from his face, leaving his skin pasty white. The president wore a stern, drawn expression that was new to me—and just as new, I suspect, to Meese, who has known him for more than twenty years." Regan added, "Nobody who saw the president's reaction that afternoon could believe for a moment that he knew about the diversion of funds before Meese told him about it. He was the picture of a man to whom the inconceivable had happened."

"Get to the bottom of this, Ed," Reagan told the attorney general. "We have to go public with what we already know as soon as we can."

Regan suggested that the president appoint a bipartisan commission to investigate. Meese said that an independent counsel might have to get involved.

Reagan asked Meese and Regan what Poindexter had to say for himself. Meese explained that Poindexter admitted to knowing some of what North was doing. But he hadn't wanted to look too closely for fear of what he might find.

"The president looked at Ed Meese in disbelief," Regan recalled. "He shook his head in bewilderment. He was pale and unsmiling." Meese left the room, and the president turned to Regan. "What went on in their minds?" he said. "Do you understand it, Don?"

Regan didn't, but he knew what the consequence had to be. He told the president that Poindexter had to go. Reagan nodded.

Regan relayed the decision to Poindexter, who arrived at the Oval Office the next morning with resignation in hand. "I'm sorry it's come to this, Mr. President," he said.

"So am I, John," Reagan replied.

REAGAN, MEESE, AND Regan agreed that the White House would call another news conference. The president would make a statement before letting Meese field the questions. Reagan told the reporters that he had asked Meese to review the Iran initiative and the allegations surrounding it. The attorney general had delivered his preliminary report. "And this report led me to conclude that I was not fully informed on the nature of one of the activities undertaken in connection with this initiative," Reagan said. "This action raises serious questions of propriety." Without specifying the offending activity, the president said that Poindexter had resigned and Oliver North had been fired from the NSC staff. He said that the Justice Department would continue its investigation and that he would appoint a special review board to conduct its own probe. "I am deeply troubled that the implementation of a policy aimed at resolving a truly tragic situation in the Middle East has resulted in such controversy," Reagan said. "As I've stated previously, I believe our policy goals toward Iran were well founded. However, the information brought to my attention yesterday convinced me that in one aspect implementation of that policy was seriously flawed."

The first question from the first reporter was the obvious one: "What was the flaw?" A second reporter immediately asked, "Do you still maintain you didn't make a mistake?"

"No, and I'm not taking any more questions," Reagan said.

"Why won't you say what the flaw is?" a third reporter demanded.

Reagan quickly exited the room, leaving Meese to clean up. The attorney general delivered his own opening statement. He explained that the president had asked him to examine the allegations surrounding the arms transfers to Iran. He cautioned that his findings were very preliminary. But the president had insisted that he reveal one important aspect of the Iran initiative. "In the course of the arms transfers, which involved the United States providing the arms to Israel, and Israel in turn transferring the arms—in effect selling the arms—to representatives of Iran," Meese said, "certain monies which were received in the transaction between representatives of Israel and representatives of Iran were taken and made available to the forces in Central America which are opposing the Sandinista government there."

The reporters required a moment to absorb what Meese had said. Then they began to shout questions. "How much money, sir, was involved?" one asked.

"We don't know the exact amount yet," Meese replied. "Our estimate is that it is somewhere between ten and thirty million dollars."

"Why wasn't the president told?"

"The president was told as soon as we found out about it. The president knew nothing about it until I reported it to him."

Meese was asked who *did* know about the diversion of funds.

"The only persons in the United States government that knew precisely about this—the only person—was Lieutenant Colonel North. Admiral Poindexter did know that something of this nature was occurring but he did not look into it further."

"What about CIA director Casey?"

"CIA director Casey, Secretary of State Shultz, Secretary of Defense Weinberger, myself, the other members of the NSC—none of us knew."

Some of the reporters were openly skeptical. "What's to prevent an increasingly cynical public from thinking that you went looking for a scapegoat and you came up with this whopper?" one asked.

"The only thing I can say is that we have been very careful to lay out the facts for you and for the American public just as rapidly as we've gotten them," Meese said. "The president felt that in the interests of getting the full story out, that he should make the statement that he did today and that I should appear before you and answer questions. Which I think you will agree is doing everything we can to be sure that there is no hint that anything is trying to be concealed."

The skepticism persisted. "Mr. Meese, how high does this go? In other words, do you believe, and are we being asked to believe, that a lieutenant colonel took this initiative and had these funds transferred and that only Admiral Poindexter knew about it? How high did it go?"

Meese stood by his explanation. "What you have just said is an accurate picture of what we know at this time," he said. "And to the best of our knowledge, and we have checked this rather extensively, it did not go any higher than that."

NANCY REAGAN WAS sometimes candid about her husband's weaknesses. "Ronnie can be too trusting of the people around him," she told Michael Deaver. To a reporter she once said, "I think it's the eternal optimist in him, his attitude that if you let something go, it will eventually work itself out. Well, that isn't always so."

It certainly wasn't so in the autumn of 1986, and as the Iran scandal metastasized to include the contra diversion, Nancy grew increasingly distressed for her husband and angry at his staff. "I'll never forget the expression on Ronnie's face after Ed Meese came to him on the afternoon of November 24 with astonishing and alarming news that although Iran had paid $30 million for American military equipment, less than half of that money had been accounted for," she wrote later. "Oliver North had admitted diverting at least some of the profits to Nicaraguan contras. The news was so shattering that everything just stopped. Ronnie came into our bedroom looking pale and absolutely crushed. 'Honey,' he said, 'I've got some bad news. Ed Meese just came in and told me that money from the sale of arms to Iran went to the contras.' Although I didn't really understand it yet, I could tell from his voice that this was very serious."

Nancy didn't have to understand it completely to know how she felt about it. "If Ronnie was incredulous, I was furious," she wrote. "Later that evening I called Don Regan from my office to let him know how upset I was. I felt very strongly that Ronnie had been badly served, and I wanted Don to know." She also wanted Regan to know that she blamed him. She refused to accept his explanation that he hadn't known what was going on. "He was the chief of staff, and if he didn't know, I thought, he should have. A good chief of staff has sources everywhere. He should practically be able to smell what's going on." She wasn't the first or last to compare Regan's tenure as chief of staff negatively with that of his predecessor. "I can't imagine that this problem would have developed during Ronnie's first term, when the 'troika' of Baker, Meese, and Deaver was in charge. The West Wing was far more open then, and if anything devious had been going on in the White House basement it would have come to light—and certainly to Ronnie's attention. But now all the power of the troika was concentrated in one man."

Nancy's distress deepened during the following weeks. "I must have dropped ten pounds," she said. "I tried to eat, but I couldn't eat much. Every day when we turned on the television, we didn't know what we were going to hear. It was crazy—I was relying on the media for information about what was going on in our own house."

She hated to see her husband in such a fix. "Ronnie was genuinely baffled," she wrote. "He kept expecting that everything would fall into place, that there was a rational explanation for all this. But he couldn't stop it, and he couldn't control it." He couldn't even address it. After appointing the investigative commission he had promised, he imposed silence on himself pending the commission's report. But the silence didn't come easily. "Ronnie was in an impossible bind," Nancy explained. "Holding a press conference would have created the risk of being contradicted by new information, but not holding one created a vacuum and gave some people the impression that Ronnie had something to hide."

The agony wouldn't end. "It was a dark and hurtful time, and it lasted for months," Nancy wrote. "Every time I opened a newspaper or turned on the television, there was the same drumbeat." And it was echoed among the public, where Reagan's credibility and approval remained at record lows. "No matter how often he said that he hadn't known about the diversion of funds, the same message kept coming back: *Oh yes, you did.*"

Nancy did what she could to ensure that Reagan received sound advice, separate from what Don Regan was giving. She contacted Michael Deaver, who brought in William Rogers, secretary of state under Nixon, and Robert Strauss, a Democrat but one of the shrewdest of Washington graybeards. "I didn't normally attend meetings with Ronnie," Nancy observed, "but this was a special situation, and it was held in the residence, and I wanted very much to be there."

Rogers said little beyond predicting that the storm would pass. Nancy found his words unhelpful. Strauss was more to her liking. "Mr. President, let me tell you about the first time I was up here in the residence," Strauss said. "LBJ was in office, and a few of us came to see him about Vietnam. When my turn came to speak, I held back. I didn't tell the president what I really thought. Instead I told him what I thought he wanted to hear. When I went home that night, I felt like a two-dollar whore. And I said to myself: If any president is ever foolish enough to invite me back, I hope I show more character. I came to see Carter on many occasions, and I always told him what I thought."

Strauss paused, then continued. "Now, I have no quarrel with Don Regan. But you've got two serious problems right now, and he's not helping you with either one. First, you've got a political problem on the Hill, and Don Regan has no constituency and no allies there. Second, you've got a serious media problem, and Regan has no friends there, either. It makes no difference how earnest he is, or how much you like him, or how well the two of you get along. He's not the man you need. You're in a hell of a mess, Mr. President, and you need a chief of staff who can help get you out of it."

Nancy Reagan was gratified by Strauss's words. She called him that evening to thank him for being so direct. "Unfortunately, Ronnie wasn't responsive to Bob's message," she recalled.

Nor did he respond to her. "I said to him: I was right about Stockman. I was right about Bill Clark. Why won't you listen about Don Regan?" Reagan loved his wife but on this subject heeded his own instincts. "Until the very end, Ronnie continued to believe that the problems with Don were going to work themselves out," she wrote.

DON REGAN SAW the end coming. Recalling the news conference at which Reagan and Meese revealed the diversion of funds, Regan wrote, "As revelation followed revelation and the reporters, shouting and leaping and gesticulating, began to understand the magnitude of the event, their excitement created an atmosphere that can only be described as primal. Fundamental emotions came into play. The many minds in the briefing room seemed to be thinking a single thought: another presidency was about to destroy itself. The blood was in the water."

The blood wasn't Regan's, but he didn't think the sharks could tell the difference. The media speculated how long he could last, with the balance of opinion predicting days or weeks rather than months. The Democrats predictably demanded his resignation, but so did many Republicans.

Regan thought he could survive the criticism from outside the White

House, but he wasn't sure he could stand the carping from within. He recalled the novel about the Roman emperor Claudius by Robert Graves, in which Claudius asks his grandmother, the scheming Livia, whether she prefers fast poisons or slow ones. She replies that slow poisons are better, as they give the appearance of ordinary disease. "Without stretching things too far," Regan remarked later, "it can be suggested that the most popular poison in twentieth-century Washington is bad publicity. In massive doses it can destroy a reputation outright. When leaked slowly into the veins of the victim it kills his public persona just as certainly, but the symptoms—anger, suspicion, frustration, the loss of friends and influence—are often mistaken for the malady. The victim may realize that he is being poisoned; he may even have a very good idea who the poisoners are. But he cannot talk about his suspicions without adding a persecution complex to the list of his faults that is daily being compiled in the newspapers."

Regan didn't identify his Livia explicitly, but he didn't have to. Everyone in Washington knew that Nancy Reagan distrusted and despised him; most assumed she was trying to have him fired. Regan interpreted a series of leaks damaging to himself as coming from the First Lady and her staff. "Longtime Reagan Advisers Seeking Regan's Ouster," a typical headline asserted in the *Los Angeles Times*. The accompanying story, citing "sources close to the president," explained that Michael Deaver and Stuart Spencer would be meeting with the president. "Deaver and Spencer, supported by First Lady Nancy Reagan, plan to advise Reagan that his presidency will be seriously hampered during his final two years unless he ousts Regan and takes other strong steps to address the Iranian arms-and-hostages scandal, the sources said." The article added helpfully, "Deaver, Spencer and Nancy Reagan have collaborated in the past on crucial personnel problems confronting the president." And it quoted one of the unnamed sources as saying of Regan, "He's got to go because absolutely nobody's for him. Even some of his own staff would like to tell him he has to go, but they don't dare. Everybody's on board on this one except the 'old man'"—Reagan.

The sniping had a temporarily paradoxical effect. Regan had been planning to resign after the midterm elections, but he didn't want to yield to media pressure or give Nancy the satisfaction of driving him from the administration. And he judged that resignation under fire would seem an admission of guilt.

THE PRESIDENT, FOR his part, was equally reluctant to have personnel decisions made for him by others. He continued to blame the media for the scandal—for spoiling a worthy initiative and grossly exaggerating some venial offenses by his staff. "There is a bitter bile in my throat these days," he told *Time* magazine. Switching to the metaphor du jour, he continued, "I've never seen the sharks circling like they now are with blood in the water." Switching again, he added, "What is driving me up the wall is that this wasn't a failure until the press got a tip from that rag in Beirut and began to play it up. I told them that publicity could destroy this, that it could get people killed. They then went right on." Asked whether he felt betrayed by Oliver North, Reagan roundly rejected the idea. "Lt. Col. Oliver North was involved in all our operations," he said. "He has a fine record. He is a national hero. My only criticism is that I wasn't told everything."

Reagan told some visiting Republican lawmakers that he wasn't going to fire people to appease the media or his critics. "So far, only two have been named"—Poindexter and North—"and those two have been let go," he said. "If others are named I'll take action, but I'm not going to change my team." Following the meeting that had been leaked to the *Los Angeles Times*, the president wrote in his diary, "Stu Spencer dropped by with Mike Deaver. They are good friends and honestly want to help me but I can't agree with their recommendation—that the answer to my Iran problem is to fire my people—top staff and even cabinet."

AN UNEXPECTED COMPLICATION distracted the president from questions about his chief of staff. Even as the special commission appointed to investigate the Iran-contra affair commenced its work, the Senate and the House launched their own probes. The Senate committee called William Casey to testify, supposing that if anyone knew about secret activities linked to the contras, it would be the CIA director. But the day before Casey was to appear, he suffered a seizure and had to be hospitalized. Doctors diagnosed and removed a brain tumor, which proved malignant. Casey lost most of his ability to speak. Certainly he could not testify.

Reagan treated the situation matter-of-factly. "Have to begin thinking of a possible Director for CIA," he wrote. "The prognosis on Bill Casey is not too good. Will now have to have radiation in addition to chemotherapy. If we must, our U.N. ambassador Vernon Walters might be a very good choice."

Nancy Reagan wanted her husband to move at once. "With Casey in the hospital, the CIA was left without a director," she said later. "It seemed to me that this especially sensitive position ought to be filled as quickly as possible, especially during a government crisis."

Don Regan pushed back. "It seemed unwise as well as inhumane, I told Mrs. Reagan, for the president to fire a man who was known to be one of his closest friends while the man was lying on what was almost certainly his deathbed," Regan recalled.

"Ronnie and I were not old friends of the Caseys, although it was said in the media that we were," Nancy rejoined afterward. And she continued to press her husband to let Casey go.

Regan found her meddling distasteful and annoying. "Just before Christmas the First Lady rang to ask, for the third or fourth time since Casey's surgery on December 18, what I was doing to get rid of him," Regan recalled.

"Nothing," he responded.

"Why not?" she asked. "He's got to go. He can't do his job. He's an embarrassment to Ronnie. He should be out."

"But, Nancy, the man had brain surgery less than a week ago. He was under fire before he got sick. This is no time to pull the rug out from under him."

Nancy said she had spoken to her stepbrother, a neurosurgeon, who predicted that Casey would never be able to work again.

"That may well be," Regan replied. "But I don't think anyone has told Bill Casey that. Sophie and the family are taking the illness very hard. It's Christmastime. It wouldn't be seemly for Ronald Reagan to fire anybody under these circumstances, much less Bill Casey. We're not going to do it."

Nancy grew angry, by Regan's account. "You're more interested in protecting Bill Casey than in protecting Ronnie!" she said. "He's dragging Ronnie down! Nobody believes what Casey says. His credibility is gone on the Hill."

"All that may be true," Regan granted. "But Bill Casey got your husband elected, and he's done a lot of other things for him, too. He deserves some gratitude and a better break than you're giving him, Nancy. The time will come when he can bow out gracefully. Please be patient."

Regan's refusal to fire Casey confirmed Nancy's judgment that Regan himself had to go. She restated her case to her husband until his patience snapped loudly enough for the media to hear. "An informed source said the Reagans quarreled over Regan earlier in the week, with the First Lady pushing for Regan's dismissal and the president finally saying, 'Get off my goddamn back,'" the *Washington Post* reported. Reagan's spokesman denied both the quotation and the context. Nancy was less categorical. "There was some tension between us over Donald Regan, but Ronnie and I just don't talk to each other that way," she reflected.

98

DON REGAN SURVIVED into the new year. In January the president underwent surgery for an enlarged prostate. The procedure was neither unusual nor particularly stressful, yet it triggered Nancy's anxieties, and she hovered closely about him as he recovered. She tried to persuade him to postpone his State of the Union address, but he said he felt fine and went ahead. His solid performance caused Regan to think he was ready for another news conference, and one was scheduled for the end of February. Nancy exploded at Regan. "I was furious, and on February 8 we had a heated argument about it on the telephone," she wrote afterward. "When it was clear that I wasn't going to change his mind, I said, 'Okay, have your damn press conference!'"

Regan had had enough of Nancy. "You bet I will!" he said. And he hung up.

Nancy was stunned. "It's quite a feeling," she wrote. "You're standing there holding a dead phone in your hand, and there's absolutely nothing you can do. It's infuriating. You want to shake the phone and say, 'Talk to me!'"

She didn't immediately complain to her husband. Once before, following Reagan's cancer surgery, Regan had hung up on her, and she had kept the matter to herself. This time she waited several days. Regan eventually called with a backhanded apology. "My wife said I shouldn't have hung up on you," he said.

"That's right, you shouldn't have," she replied. "Don, don't ever do that to me again." By her subsequent recollection, what she really wanted to say was "Do you need your wife to tell you that you shouldn't hang up on people?" She added, in the later version, "That's when I finally told Ronnie."

The fateful conversation took place at Camp David. "I talked with Ronnie about Don Regan," she wrote in her diary for February 13. "For the first time I think he listened. I told him again how disappointed I was in the whole situation, and how morale had sunk very low in the office."

They spoke more in bed that night and again during the next few days. "I think Ronnie finally understands that he has a real problem, and that something has to be done about it," she wrote on February 16. Another news story prompted her next day's entry: "It broke tonight on the news that Don and I are not speaking because I want him to leave. It's true that we're not speaking, and it's true that I want him to leave. But that's not the reason we're not speaking."

Reagan began to distance himself publicly from his chief of staff. A photo session with visiting Israeli prime minister Yitzhak Shamir led to shouted questions from reporters. "Are you going to fire Regan, or is he talking to Mrs. Reagan, or is she talking to him?" one reporter asked.

"Oh, for heaven's sake!" Reagan responded, laughing deliberately.

"Not true?"

"No, not true, and nobody's getting fired."

After questions on the Middle East, a reporter circled back. "Mr. President, you said nobody is going to get fired. Will Mr. Regan be staying on as your chief of staff?"

"Well, this is up to him," Reagan said. "I have always said that when the people that I've asked to come into government feel that they have to return to private life, that's their business and I will never try to talk them out of it."

"Is that a yes or a no, sir?"

"That's a no-answer. That's not an answer."

YET NANCY THOUGHT it was a message. "That's a pretty broad hint," she wrote in her diary that evening. "But I don't think Don will take it," she added. The report of the special commission, named for its chairman, former senator John Tower, was expected within days. The report's approach gave Nancy further reason to wish Regan gone. "The Tower report comes in on the 26th and Don wants Ronnie to go on television on the 27th to make a speech. Ye gods! You can't prepare a good speech in twenty-four hours. Any fool would know that."

The Tower report proved to be the catalyst for the long-delayed decision. Regan afterward asserted that he and the president had agreed the previous November that he would leave after the report was published. So he was surprised to receive a visit from George Bush three days ahead of the report. "Don, why don't you stick your head into the Oval Office and talk to the president about your situation?" Bush said.

Regan asked Bush why he was offering this suggestion. He supposed the vice president knew about the understanding that he would leave after the report came out.

"Well, the president asked me if I knew what your plans were," Bush said.

Regan went into the Oval Office and sat in his usual chair at the side of the president's desk. He asked Reagan if he wanted to talk about his situation.

"I think it's about time, Don," Reagan said.

Regan later confessed to making no effort to ease the president's task. "All right, Mr. President," he said. "Why don't you tell me? Where's your head on this? What do *you* think I should do?"

"Well, good Lord, Don," he said. "This last weekend the airwaves were filled with all that stuff about Nancy." A ruckus had arisen around a newly appointed White House director of communications, Jack Koehler, who had not told Regan or anyone else that he had been a member of a Nazi youth group during his boyhood in Germany. The newspapers reported that Nancy Reagan had pushed Koehler's appointment and that Regan was saying that it therefore should have been her staff's responsibility to check out his background. The president unsurprisingly took Nancy's side. "She's being blamed for Koehler and she's being seen unfairly," he told Regan. "I was the one who wanted him. She never met him."

Regan didn't respond. The president was clearly uncomfortable. "I think it's time we do that thing that you said when we talked in November," Reagan said.

"I'll stick by that," Regan replied. "I'll go whenever you say."

"Well, since the report is coming out on Thursday, I think it would be appropriate for you to bow out now."

Regan recalled being shocked and answering angrily. "What do you mean *now*?" he said. "This is the Monday before the report. You can't do that to me, Mr. President. If I go before that report is out, you throw me to the wolves. I deserve better treatment than that."

Reagan searched for a way past the tense moment. "Well, what do you think would be right?" he said.

"The first part of next week," Regan responded. "Let the report come out. Let the world see what really happened and where the blame lies. I'm willing to take my chances on that."

Reagan consented, relieved at resolving the issue. But Regan had more to say. He complained about Nancy's meddling in the affairs of the administration. "I thought I was chief of staff to the president," he said. "Not to his wife. I have to tell you, sir, that I'm very bitter about the whole experience. You're allowing the loyal to be punished, and those who have their own agenda to be rewarded."

Regan recalled Reagan's reaction. "The president, who dislikes confrontations more than any man I have ever known, looked at me without anger. 'Well, we'll try to make that up by the way we handle this,' Ronald Reagan said softly. 'We'll make sure that you go out in good fashion.'"

THINGS HAPPENED OTHERWISE. The Tower Commission had done yeoman work; in three months it interviewed more than fifty witnesses, and though it lacked subpoena power and so could not compel testimony, it got all but two of the most important players to talk. Those two, significantly, were John Poindexter and Oliver North.

Reagan was among the willing. He spoke to the commissioners in the Oval Office in late January and again in February. Reagan told them in his first interview that he had approved the initial shipment of TOW missiles from Israel to Iran in August 1985. This contradicted testimony by Don Regan, who said the president had not granted prior approval. As Reagan prepared for his second interview, he met with Regan, George Bush, and White House counsel Peter Wallison to review their records and memories to determine who was right. Regan persuaded Reagan that the president's memory was wrong. The chief of staff said that when he told Reagan about the missile shipments, the president had acted surprised and upset. Wallison pressed Reagan: "Were you surprised?"

"Yes, I guess I was," Reagan said.

"That's what I remember," Regan reiterated. "I remember you being angry and saying something like, 'Well, what's done is done.'"

"You know, I think he's right," Reagan said.

Wallison drafted a memo to Reagan to help organize the president's thoughts for the second interview. "On the issue of the TOW shipment in August," Wallison wrote, "in discussing this matter with me and David Abshire, you said you were surprised to learn that the Israelis had shipped the arms. If that is your recollection, and if the question comes up at the Tower Board meeting, you might want to say that you were surprised."

Reagan was indeed asked about the discrepancy between his testimony and Regan's. He told the commissioners he had changed his mind. He had talked the matter over with Regan and been convinced that Regan was right. He had not authorized the shipment in advance, and he had been surprised when he learned about it. As if to confirm his statement, the president stood up and looked toward Wallison. "Peter, where is that piece of paper you had that you gave me this morning?" Spotting the memo, he grabbed it and read, "If the question comes up at the Tower Board meeting, you might want to say that you were surprised."

"I was horrified, just horrified," Wallison said later. "I didn't expect him to go and get the paper. The purpose of it was just to recall to his mind before he goes into the meeting that on something that he had been all over the lot on for so long, he had seemed to have come to some conclusions." Wallison shook his head. "God, it was just terrible."

The commissioners were astonished and confused. The commission's chief of staff, Rhett Dawson, remembered the reaction of the commissioners—John Tower, former secretary of state Edmund Muskie, and former national security adviser Brent Scowcroft—after the meeting. "Ed and Tower and Brent slumped on the couch or in their chairs just thunderstruck," Dawson said. The commissioners' conclusion that Reagan's memory, or at any rate his testimony, on the subject was worthless received corroboration when the president wrote the board a letter abdicating all reliability. "In trying to recall events that happened eighteen months ago I'm afraid I let myself be influenced by others' recollections, not my own," Reagan said. "I have no personal notes or records to help my recollection on this matter." He declined to mention the diary entries that contained repeated mention of arms and hostages. "The only honest answer is to state that try as I might, I cannot recall anything whatsoever about whether I approved replenishment of Israeli stocks around August of 1985. My answer therefore and the simple truth is, 'I don't remember—period.'"

THE TOWER REPORT, released on Thursday, February 26, confirmed what was by then common knowledge: that the administration had traded arms for hostages and had taken proceeds from the arms sales and sent them to the contras. The report faulted the president himself for not supervising the NSC staff sufficiently. "The president's management style is to put the principal responsibility for policy review and implementation on the shoulders of his advisers," the report stated. "Nevertheless, with such a complex, high-risk operation and so much at stake, the president should have ensured that the NSC system did not fail him. He did not force his policy to undergo the most critical review of which the NSC participants and the process were capable. At no time did he insist upon accountability and performance review."

The report laid most of the operational blame on Robert McFarlane, John Poindexter, and Oliver North, all of whom had left the administration. Donald Regan, the ranking staffer of those who remained in the White House, was treated roughly but briefly. "More than almost any chief of staff of recent memory, he asserted personal control over the White House staff and sought to extend this control to the national security adviser," the report said. "He was personally active in national security affairs and attended almost all of the relevant meetings regarding the Iran initiative. He, as much as anyone, should have insisted that an orderly process be observed. In addition, he especially should have ensured that plans were made for handling any public disclosure of the initiative. He must bear primary responsibility for the chaos that descended upon the White House when such disclosure did occur."

REGAN SOUGHT A period of grace before he resigned, to let the world know that the president disagreed with the report's findings. He didn't expect Reagan to admit that by giving McFarlane and Poindexter a back door to the Oval Office, he had made it impossible for Regan to do his job. Yet neither did he expect the president to toss him overboard bearing all the blame.

But that was exactly what Nancy Reagan wanted her husband to do. And he largely acceded. Reagan began considering successors to Regan; Paul Laxalt suggested Howard Baker, the former Senate majority leader. "It's not a bad idea," Reagan wrote in his diary on the Thursday of the Tower report's release. "I'd probably take some bumps from our right wingers but I can handle that." In this same entry, the president added, "V.P. just came up—another meeting with Don. This time totally different"—different from the angry meeting Bush had reported to Reagan a few days earlier.

"He says he'll hand in his resignation first thing Monday. My prayers have really been answered."

But Nancy didn't want to wait until Monday. The next day, Friday, CNN reported that Howard Baker would succeed Regan as chief of staff. Nancy didn't admit that the leak had come from her staff, but interest and evidence pointed to the East Wing.

Regan decided he'd had enough. He dashed off a one-sentence letter of resignation and sent it to the president. Frank Carlucci, the successor to John Poindexter as national security adviser, urged him to see the president personally. Regan refused. "I'm too mad," he told Carlucci. "There's been a deliberate leak, and it's been done to humiliate me."

Carlucci wouldn't let Regan leave without speaking to the president. So he had Reagan call Regan. Reagan apologized that the Baker appointment had been leaked, but he said he hoped Regan would stay around long enough to help Baker get grounded in the new job.

Regan refused. "I'm sorry, Mr. President, but I won't be in any more. This is my last day. I've been your secretary of the Treasury for four years and your chief of staff for two. You don't trust me enough even to tell me who my successor is and make a smooth transfer. I deserved better treatment than this. I'm through."

Reagan tried to mollify him, but to no avail. "He was understandably angry," the president wrote that night. He signed a gracious letter accepting Regan's resignation. Regan read the letter and tossed it aside. "In my time with President Reagan, I had seen many such letters, and so I knew that someone else had written it for him," he recounted.

Nancy Reagan had her own reaction. "That night, for the first time in weeks, I slept well," she remembered.

99

ON MARCH 4 the president addressed the American people in response to the Tower report. He had never given a more important speech, and he knew it. The final two years of his presidency hinged on whether he could win back the popular confidence that had been essential to everything he had achieved as president. Never had the people been more skeptical of him, nor with better reason. The evidence of his incompetence or culpability continued to mount, making the case for his policy toward Iran and the contras ever harder to defend. Yet he had to say something.

"For the past 3 months, I've been silent on the revelations about Iran," he began. "You must have been thinking: 'Well, why doesn't he tell us what's happening? Why doesn't he just speak to us as he has in the past when we've faced troubles or tragedies?' Others of you, I guess, were thinking: 'What's he doing hiding out in the White House?'" Yet silence had been necessary, he said, because he didn't know all the facts of the matter, and he didn't want to speak until he knew them. "I've paid a price for my silence in terms of your trust and confidence," he acknowledged. "But I've had to wait, as you have, for the complete story." Now that the Tower board had delivered its report, he could break his silence.

"I'm often accused of being an optimist," he continued. "And it's true I had to hunt pretty hard to find any good news in the board's report. As you know, it's well-stocked with criticisms, which I'll discuss in a moment." But there was good news amid the bad. "I was very relieved to read this sentence: 'The board is convinced that the President does indeed want the full story to be told.'" There had been no cover-up. And there would be no cover-up. "That will continue to be my pledge to you as the other investigations go forward."

Regarding the bad news, Reagan didn't blink. "I've studied the board's report," he said. "Its findings are honest, convincing, and highly critical; and I accept them." There would be no buck-passing in this administration. "I take full responsibility for my own actions and for those of my administration. As angry as I may be about activities undertaken without my knowledge, I am still accountable for those activities. As disappointed as I may be in some who served me, I'm still the one who must answer to the American people for this behavior. And as personally distasteful as I find secret bank accounts and diverted funds—well, as the Navy would say, this happened on my watch."

Reagan addressed the issue that had generated the greatest controversy. "A few months ago I told the American people I did not trade arms for hostages. My heart and my best intentions still tell me that's true, but the facts and the evidence tell me it is not. As the Tower board reported, what began as a strategic opening to Iran deteriorated, in its implementation, into trading arms for hostages. This runs counter to my own beliefs, to administration policy, and to the original strategy we had in mind. There are reasons why it happened, but no excuses. It was a mistake. I undertook the original Iran initiative in order to develop relations with those who might assume leadership in a post-Khomeini government. It's clear from the board's report, however, that I let my personal concern for the hostages spill over into the geopolitical strategy of reaching out to Iran. I asked so many questions about the hostages' welfare that I didn't ask enough about the specifics of the total Iran plan."

Reagan remained concerned about the hostages. "Let me say to the hostage families: 'We have not given up. We never will. And I promise you we'll use every legitimate means to free your loved ones from captivity.'" But there would be no more trading arms for hostages. In what amounted to a significant concession of presidential impotence, Reagan said, "Those Americans who freely remain in such dangerous areas must know that they're responsible for their own safety."

The other part of the report involved the money diverted to the contras. "The Tower board wasn't able to find out what happened to this money, so the facts here will be left to the continuing investigations of the court-appointed independent counsel and the two congressional investigating committees. I'm confident the truth will come out about this matter, as well." And he would live with the truth. "As I told the Tower board, I didn't know about any diversion of funds to the contras. But as president, I cannot escape responsibility."

Reagan introduced the new personnel who would forestall future transgressions. "Former senator Howard Baker, my new chief of staff, possesses a breadth of legislative and foreign affairs skills that's impossible to match," he said. "Frank Carlucci, my new national security adviser, is respected for his experience in government and trusted for his judgment and counsel." Reagan's nominee for CIA director, William Webster, awaited confirmation by the Senate. Reagan had previously nominated Robert Gates to replace William Casey, who had at length resigned, still gravely ill. But the nomination ran into trouble when many senators questioned the swap of one CIA insider for another, and Reagan and Gates agreed to withdraw it. Reagan expected no such difficulty with Webster. "Mr. Webster has served as director of the FBI and as a U.S. district court judge. He understands the meaning of 'rule of law,'" he said.

The president said he had ordered a review of covert operations, to ensure that they clearly supported American policy and values. "I expect a covert policy that, if Americans saw it on the front page of their newspaper, they'd say, 'That makes sense.'" He had forbidden the NSC staff to undertake covert operations. "No ifs, ands, or buts," the president said. He had created a new position of NSC legal adviser to ensure compliance with the law. And he pledged to keep Congress informed. "Proper procedures for consultation with the Congress will be followed, not only in letter but in spirit."

Reagan hoped the country could get past the problems that had compelled the Tower report. "What should happen when you make a mistake is this: You take your knocks, you learn your lessons, and then you move on. That's the healthiest way to deal with a problem." He didn't deny the importance of the continuing investigations. "But the business of our country and our people must proceed."

REAGAN'S SPEECH SCARCELY dented the skepticism. A new poll revealed that 85 percent of respondents believed that the White House had engaged in an organized cover-up of the Iran-contra affair, and half said Reagan himself was part of the conspiracy. By one measure the speech did more harm than good. Its focus on foreign affairs, combined with the general distrust surrounding the presidency, drove the approval rating of Reagan's handling of foreign policy to a new low of 33 percent.

Yet Reagan refused to be discouraged, or even to acknowledge the damage he had suffered. His staff continued to cocoon him. "The speech was exceptionally well received, and phone calls (more than any other speech) ran 93 percent favorable," he wrote in his diary. "Even the TV bone pickers who follow the speech with their commentaries said nice things about it."

100

REAGAN'S RESISTANCE TO unpleasant reality took other forms as well. He had known Rock Hudson the way he knew many other Hollywood stars: by reputation chiefly but by occasional encounter as well. And it wasn't unusual that he had acknowledged the actor's passing in October 1985. "Nancy and I are saddened by the news of Rock Hudson's death," Reagan declared in a written statement released by the White House. "He will always be remembered for his dynamic impact on the film industry, and fans all over the world will certainly mourn his loss. He will be remembered for his humanity, his sympathetic spirit and well-deserved reputation for kindness. May God rest his soul."

None denied the graciousness of the president's gesture, but many found the statement late and lacking. Rock Hudson had been visibly wasting for months. "He had been to a White House dinner and had been at my table," Nancy recalled. "I remember sitting across from him and thinking, Gee, he's thin. I asked if he had been dieting, and he said he had been hard at work on a new picture and had lost weight." The tabloid press asserted various causes for his decline. Reagan heard the stories and responded privately. "Called Rock Hudson in a Paris hospital where press said he had inoperable cancer," Reagan wrote in July 1985. "We never knew him too well but did know him and I thought under the circumstances I might be a reassurance. Now I learn from TV there is question as to his illness and rumors he is there for treatment of AIDS."

Hudson confirmed the rumors, revealing that he had been diagnosed with acquired immunodeficiency syndrome a year earlier. The syndrome remained relatively new to doctors and public health officials; not until 1981 had AIDS been clinically described. And because it appeared first in homosexual men, it carried a stigma among those very many Americans who considered homosexuality sinful, perverted, or merely distasteful.

Reagan was more tolerant than many of his generation. His daughter Patti Davis (who dropped her father's last name in favor of her mother's) later said that he had spoken matter-of-factly about Rock Hudson's homosexuality, which had been an open secret in Hollywood for years. And she said that Reagan and Nancy had once left her and Ron in the care of a lesbian couple while they vacationed in Hawaii. As former governor of California in the late 1970s, Reagan visibly opposed a ballot measure that would have barred gay men and women from teaching in California public schools.

Yet Reagan headed a party that included powerful groups appalled by homosexuality. In their view the "gay plague," as they often called it, was the consequence of homosexuals' defiance of nature and God. "They have declared war upon nature, and now nature is exacting an awful retribution," wrote Patrick Buchanan, a conservative pundit (and future Reagan communications director). Televangelist Jerry Falwell declared, "AIDS is God's judgment on a society that does not live by His rules."

Reagan had sometimes catered, if not pandered, to the social conservatives. During the Republican primary season in 1980 journalist Robert Scheer inquired whether Reagan thought gay people had the same civil rights as everyone else.

"I think they do and should," Reagan replied.

Then why, Scheer asked, did some of the candidate's reported comments suggest otherwise?

"My criticism of the gay rights movement is that it isn't asking for civil rights," Reagan responded. "It is asking for a recognition and acceptance of an alternative lifestyle which I do not believe society can condone, nor can I."

"For religious reasons?" Scheer asked.

"Well," Reagan said, "you could find that in the Bible it says that in the eyes of the Lord, this is an abomination."

"But should that bind the rest of the citizens who may not believe in the Bible?" Scheer asked. "Don't we have the right to separation of church and state?"

"Oh, we do, yes we do," Reagan affirmed. But he added, "Look, what other group of people demands the same thing? Let's say here is the total libertarian—or libertine, I should say—who wants the right to just free and open sex."

Scheer expressed puzzlement that self-proclaimed conservatives should want government to intrude in the private lives of consenting adults.

Reagan clearly didn't like the path he was going down. "No one is advocating the invasion of the private life of any individual," he said. "I think Pat Campbell said it best in the trial of Oscar Wilde. She said, 'I have no objection to anyone's sex life so long as they don't practice it in the street and frighten the horses.'"

Reagan spoke little more about gay rights after he secured the nomination and then the election. He quietly allowed money for AIDS research to be included in the federal budget, but he let others in the administration do what little talking executive branch officials did on the subject. He maintained presidential silence on AIDS throughout his first term, even as the death toll mounted into the many thousands.

But eventually reporters flushed him out. "Mr. President," one asked at a news conference in September 1985, "the nation's best-known AIDS scientist says the time has come now to boost existing research into what he called a minor moon shot program to attack this AIDS epidemic that has struck fear into the nation's health workers and even its schoolchildren. Would you support a massive government research program against AIDS like the one that President Nixon launched against cancer?"

"I have been supporting it for more than four years now," Reagan answered. "It's been one of the top priorities with us, and over the last four years, and including what we have in the budget for '86, it will amount to over a half a billion dollars that we have provided for research on AIDS in addition to what I'm sure other medical groups are doing. And we have $100 million in the budget this year; it'll be $126 million next year. So, this is a top priority with us. Yes, there's no question about the seriousness of this and the need to find an answer."

The reporter was skeptical. "The scientist who talked about this, who does work for the government, is in the National Cancer Institute," he said. "He was referring to your program and the increase that you proposed as being not nearly enough at this stage to go forward and really attack the problem."

Reagan defended his policy. "I think with our budgetary constraints and all, it seems to me that $126 million in a single year for research has got to be something of a vital contribution."

Several months later, when Reagan sent his budget to Congress, it included AIDS research as a "high priority" program. On the same day he declared, in remarks to the employees of the Department of Health and Human Services, "One of our highest public health priorities is going to continue to be finding a cure for AIDS. We're going to continue to try to develop and test vaccines, and we're going to focus also on prevention."

In the spring of 1987 Reagan announced the creation of a special commission to study AIDS and seek a cure. "AIDS is clearly one of the most serious health problems facing the world community, and our health care establishment is working overtime to find a cure," he said. "The commission will help us to ensure that we are using every possible public health measure to contain the spread of the virus."

That May he gave his first important address on AIDS. The American Foundation for AIDS Research held a fund-raiser in Washington and invited Reagan to speak. If the audience expected him to be tentative or uncomfortable, they soon discovered their mistake. "Fundraisers always remind me of one of my favorite but most well-worn stories," he began. "I've been telling it for years, so if you've heard it, please indulge me. A man had just been elected chairman of his community's annual charity drive. And he went over all the records, and he noticed something about one individual in town, a very wealthy man. And so, he paid a call on him, introduced himself as to what he was doing, and he said, 'Our records show that you have never contributed anything to our charity.' And the man said, 'Well, do your records show that I also have a brother who, as the result of a disabling accident, is permanently disabled and cannot provide for himself? Do your records show that I have an invalid mother and a widowed sister with several small children and no father to support them?' And the chairman, a little abashed and embarrassed, said, 'Well, no, our records don't show that.' The man said, 'Well, I don't give anything to them. Why should I give something to you?'"

Some in the audience laughed; others thought the parallel between the miserly rich man and Reagan's AIDS policy too close to be funny. Reagan turned serious. "I want to talk tonight about the disease that has brought us all together," he said. "It has been talked about, and I'm going to continue. The poet W. H. Auden said that true men of action in our times are not the politicians and statesmen but the scientists. I believe that's especially true when it comes to the AIDS epidemic. Those of us in government can educate our citizens about the dangers. We can encourage safe behavior. We can test to determine how widespread the virus is. We can do any number of things. But only medical science can ever truly defeat AIDS." Reagan noted the progress that had been made so far. "To think we didn't even know we had a disease until June of 1981, when five cases appeared in California. The AIDS virus itself was discovered in 1984. The blood test became available in 1985. A treatment drug, AZT, has been brought to market in record time, and others are coming. Work on a vaccine is now underway in many laboratories." He explained that the federal government continued to expand its budget for AIDS research. "Spending on AIDS has been one of the fastest growing parts of the budget, and, ladies and gentlemen, it deserves to be." Washington was also removing regulatory barriers to bringing new drugs to market. "I don't blame those who are out marching and protesting to get AIDS drugs released before the t's were crossed and the i's were dotted. I sympathize with them, and we'll supply help and hope as quickly as we can."

A vaccine was the ultimate goal of AIDS research. But because the virus had a lengthy incubation period, developing and testing a vaccine took time. "We will not have a vaccine on the market until the mid- to late 1990s, at best," Reagan said. In the meantime the country had some important questions to answer. "How do we protect the citizens of this nation, and where do we start?" Information was crucial. "I recently announced my intention to create a national commission on AIDS because of the consequences of this disease on our society. We need some comprehensive answers. What can we do to defend Americans not infected with the virus? How can we best care for those who are ill and dying? How do we deal with a disease that may swamp our health care system?" The commission would hear expert testimony and make the appropriate recommendations.

Reagan rejected the notion that AIDS was a gay disease. "I don't want Americans to think AIDS simply affects only certain groups. AIDS affects all of us. What our citizens must know is this: America faces a disease that is fatal and spreading. And this calls for urgency, not panic. It calls for compassion, not blame. And it calls for understanding, not ignorance." He similarly rejected the moralistic finger-pointing that had characterized too much of the discussion of the disease. "Final judgment is up to God; our part is to ease the suffering and to find a cure. This is a battle against disease, not against our fellow Americans. We mustn't allow those with the AIDS virus to suffer discrimination."

Reagan observed that many fears surrounding AIDS were unjustified by the facts. "These fears are based on ignorance. I was told of a newspaper photo of a baby in a hospital crib with a sign that said, 'AIDS—Do Not Touch.' Fortunately, that photo was taken several years ago, and we now know there's no basis for this kind of fear. But similar incidents are still happening elsewhere in this country. I read of one man with AIDS who returned to work to find anonymous notes on his desk with such messages as, 'Don't use our water fountain.' I was told of a situation in Florida where three young brothers—ages ten, nine, and seven—were all hemophiliacs carrying the AIDS virus. The pastor asked the entire family not to come back to their church. Ladies and gentlemen, this is old-fashioned fear, and it has no place in the 'home of the brave.'"

Reagan called for informed tolerance. "The Public Health Service has stated that there's no medical reason for barring a person with the virus from any routine school or work activity. There's no reason for those who carry the AIDS virus to wear a scarlet A. AIDS is not a casually contagious disease. We're still learning about how AIDS is transmitted, but experts tell us you don't get it from telephones or swimming pools or drinking fountains. You don't get it from shaking hands or sitting on a bus or anywhere else, for that matter. And most important, you don't get AIDS by donating blood."

Yet behavior did matter. Reagan might eschew moralism, but he embraced moral values, in particular the value of personal responsibility. In the absence of a vaccine or a cure, the sole way to slow the spread of AIDS was to change the behavior of those infected and those at risk. "As individuals, we have a moral obligation not to endanger others, and that can mean endangering others with a gun, with a car, or with a virus. If a person has reason to believe that he or she may be a carrier, that person has a moral duty to be tested for AIDS; human decency requires it. And the reason is very simple: Innocent people are being infected by this virus, and some of them are going to acquire AIDS and die." Reagan characteristically employed an example to make his point. "A doctor in a rural county in Kentucky treated a woman who caught the AIDS virus from her husband, who was an IV-drug user. They later got divorced, neither knowing that they were infected. They remarried other people, and now one of them has already transmitted the disease to her new husband. Just as most individuals don't know they carry the virus, no one knows to what extent the virus has infected our entire society. AIDS is surreptitiously spreading throughout our population, and yet we have no accurate measure of its scope. It's time we knew exactly what we were facing, and that's why I support some routine testing." Reagan added that he had instructed the Department of Health and Human Services to assess the current incidence of AIDS and project its future. "I've also asked HHS to add the AIDS virus to the list of contagious diseases for which immigrants and aliens seeking permanent residence in the United States can be denied entry."

Some members of the audience didn't like these last comments, about routine testing for the AIDS virus and barring infected immigrants. They booed the president, tentatively at first, then more loudly.

Reagan continued undaunted. He pointed out that potential immigrants were currently denied entry for exhibiting other contagious diseases, many much less deadly than AIDS. "I've asked the Department of Justice to plan for testing all federal prisoners, as looking into ways to protect uninfected inmates and their families. In addition, I've asked for a review of other federal responsibilities, such as veterans hospitals, to see if testing might be appropriate in those areas. This is in addition to the testing already underway in our military and foreign service."

"No! No!" shouted a sizable minority of the audience.

Reagan spoke through the shouts. The states had their own responsibilities, he said. "While recognizing the individual's choice, I encourage states to offer routine testing for those who seek marriage licenses and for those who visit sexually transmitted disease or drug abuse clinics. And I encourage states to require routine testing in state and local prisons. Not only will testing give us more information on which to make decisions, but in the case of marriage licenses, it might prevent at least some babies from being born with AIDS. And anyone who knows how viciously AIDS attacks the body cannot object to this humane consideration. I should think that everyone getting married would want to be tested."

Many in the audience were still upset as Reagan approached the end. "You know, it's been said that when the night is darkest, we see the stars. And there have been some shining moments throughout this horrible AIDS epidemic." He described the dedication of volunteers who cared for AIDS patients, noting especially the work of one San Francisco group that provided over 100,000 hours of support for the city's AIDS sufferers. "That kind of compassion has been duplicated all over the country, and it symbolizes the best tradition of caring. And I encourage Americans to follow that example and volunteer to help their fellow citizens who have AIDS." He quoted a young man in the terminal stages of the disease: "While I do accept death, I think the fight for life is important, and I'm going to fight the disease with every breath I have." Reagan paused, then concluded, "Ladies and gentlemen, so must we."

REACTIONS TO REAGAN'S speech varied dramatically. Activists already condemning the administration for tardy and feeble funding of AIDS research accused him of wanting to add to the victims' burden. "I am outraged and depressed," said Ben Schatz, a lawyer with the National Gay Rights Advocates. Reagan's call for routine testing, while less threatening than the mandatory testing many conservatives were urging, put the country on a dangerous path, Schatz predicted. "All those who test positive are going to get their insurance canceled and go on Medicaid, possibly lose their jobs, their apartments. We've already been through a lot of that in the gay community."

An international AIDS expert who wouldn't let his name be printed pronounced Reagan's speech more of what the country and the world had come to expect of an ignorant and uncaring president. "From the beginning this administration has played with AIDS like a bunch of amateurs," he said. "They haven't listened to the health care experts. There's no national AIDS or education program. They can't even talk about sex." Politics, not public health, motivated the president. "The administration's realization that they have to do something comes when elections are around the corner, not when people are dying."

Conservatives assailed Reagan from the opposite direction. "Routine testing is a cop out," said Republican congressman William Dannemeyer. "It's another illustration of treating the issue as a civil rights issue instead of a public health issue." Reagan had been unspecific about the nature of appropriate public education on AIDS, but Dannemeyer warned him against anything that made homosexuality seem normal. Children and the public should be taught to shun the practices that had brought this plague upon the country in the first place. "We should reaffirm the heterosexual ethic of our society and we should tell them that the homosexual life style is a very unhealthy life style."

The director of continuing education for the California Medical Association thought Reagan had done fairly well. "I would have liked for him to say a great deal more," Mark Madsen remarked. "But I appreciate him coming out and talking about it. Considering this was his first major talk on AIDS, I'd give him a B+ for the effort."

Reagan was an easier grader, as usual, when evaluating himself. "Well received until I mentioned routine testing for AIDS," he wrote in his diary. "A block of the gay community in the tent booed me enthusiastically. All in all, though, I was pleased with the whole affair."

PRESIDENTS COME AND go, but Supreme Court justices abide. John Adams's presidency was forgettable, but the accomplishments of John Marshall, whom Adams appointed chief justice, were indelible. The supporters and enemies of Andrew Jackson watched their hero and bête noire leave the White House in 1837, but they dealt with Roger B. Taney, Jackson's pick to succeed Marshall, until 1864. William O. Douglas was still annoying conservatives thirty years after his sponsor, Franklin Roosevelt, exited office and life.

Reagan had three chances to fill Supreme Court seats. The first two went smoothly, so smoothly that neither Sandra Day O'Connor nor Antonin Scalia suffered a single nay in confirmation votes in the Senate. O'Connor's invulnerability rested on her distinction as the first woman to be nominated to the high court. Reagan realized liberals would be hard-pressed to vote against such a pioneer of women's equality, and none did. Scalia represented a different calculation. Combatively conservative, he was also irrepressibly charming. And he replaced the conservative William Rehnquist, whom Reagan promoted to chief justice upon the retirement of fellow conservative Warren Burger. As a result, Scalia's appointment presaged no swing in the court's philosophical balance. Timing benefited the Scalia appointment as well. In the summer of 1986, Reagan's reelection landslide still daunted the Democrats; few Democratic senators saw advantage in taking on the president over a Supreme Court seat.

Robert Bork's nomination was a different story. The retirement of the moderate Lewis Powell had been expected, and conservatives hoped Reagan would shift the court to the right with Powell's replacement. For decades conservatives had complained about judicial activism, accusing justices of creating law rather than merely interpreting it. Reagan had joined their complaints and now gave the conservatives what they wanted. "Judge Bork, widely regarded as the most prominent and intellectually powerful advocate of judicial restraint, shares my view that judges' personal preferences and values should not be part of their constitutional interpretations," Reagan declared in announcing the nomination on July 1, 1987. "The guiding principle of judicial restraint recognizes that under the Constitution it is the exclusive province of the legislatures to enact laws and the role of the courts to interpret them." Judge Bork would help the high court regain the balance it had lost. "We're fortunate to be able to draw upon such an impressive legal mind, an experienced judge and a man who already has devoted so much of his life to public service. He'll bring credit to the court and his colleagues, as well as to his country and the Constitution."

Bork wasn't obviously more conservative than Scalia, but his nomination came at a moment when the Democrats were more effectively combative than they had been in 1986. They now controlled the Senate and with it the all-important Judiciary Committee, which would conduct hearings on the Bork nomination. Democratic hopefuls for the 1988 presidential race were already jockeying for position, with each tempted to outdo the others in attacking the administration. And because Bork would replace a moderate justice, Democrats realized that his seating could reconfigure the balance of power on the court for decades to come.

They determined to block the nomination. Narrowly partisan calculations entered their thinking: they hoped to embarrass the president and his party ahead of the 1988 elections. Legal philosophy mattered too. Bork's version of judicial restraint had caused him to question federal authority on certain civil rights issues, alarming advocates of equality for minorities and women. His willingness, as acting attorney general in 1973, to fire the Watergate special prosecutor at the order of Richard Nixon, after his two superiors in the Justice Department resigned in protest, caused liberals and not a few moderates to wonder if, notwithstanding his rhetoric of restraint, he was really a pushover for executive power.

The Democratic attacks commenced at once. Senator Edward Kennedy of Massachusetts assailed Bork as hostile to the ordinary people of the country. "Robert Bork's America is a land in which women would be forced into back-alley abortions, blacks would sit at segregated lunch counters, rogue police could break down citizens' doors in midnight raids, schoolchildren could not be taught about evolution, writers and artists could be censored at the whim of the government and the doors of the federal courts would be shut on the fingers of millions of citizens," Kennedy said. Senator Joseph Biden of Delaware, the chairman of the Judiciary Committee, spoke less melodramatically but, for this reason, more persuasively. Biden reflected on Bork's writings and expressed concern that they signaled a mind already closed on critical issues that could come before the court. Biden didn't think he could approve such a nominee. "Unless he can demonstrate that he carries to the court more of an open mind, I would have a tough time," Biden said.

Reagan dismissed the critics as partisan blowhards. "Some talk about Bork and last night's broadcast featuring all the Democratic candidates for president," he wrote in early July. "There was a lot of demagoguery." A few days later he predicted, "We'll get Bork confirmed to Supreme Court but it will be a battle with left-wing ideologues."

Howard Baker was just getting used to Reagan's governing style. "The president had high confidence that he could move anything, whether it was a vote on an issue or a nomination or a treaty," the chief of staff recalled. "He was supremely confident. He took account of the fact that there were big storm warnings about Bork ahead of time but it was very Reagan-like to say, I want to do it anyway, and he did."

Summer delayed the hearings on Bork until mid-September, allowing the opposition to organize. Bork's testimony at the hearings differed in tone and sometimes substance from his published opinions, causing critics to allege a confirmation conversion. Bork explained the discrepancy as contextual. His more provocative pieces had been written when he held academic positions, where provocation was the point, he said. As a judge he had taken, and would continue to take if confirmed, more measured positions. He defended his record on civil rights and women's rights. "Beginning with *Brown v. Board of Education*, I have supported black equality," he told the committee. "I have never said anything or decided anything that should be frightening to women." He denied he was tailoring his testimony to win over wavering senators. "It would really be preposterous for me to sit here and say the things I have and then go on the court and do the opposite," he said. "I would be disgraced in history."

Bork's critics on the committee weren't appeased. "You are not a frightening man, but you are a man with frightening views," Howard Metzenbaum of Ohio declared, referring to a Bork appeals court ruling permitting a chemical company to offer women employees a choice between sterilization and dismissal. After Bork defended his ruling as being neither pro-sterilization nor antiwomen, Metzenbaum continued, "Judge, I must tell you it is such a shocking opinion. I don't understand how you as a jurist could put women to a choice to be fired or sterilized." He added, "I cannot tell you strongly enough that the women of this country are terribly, terribly apprehensive about your appointment." Metzenbaum frowned. "The women's groups are afraid. The fact is, Judge Bork, they do fear you. Blacks as well."

Bork grew testy under the interrogation. "I can't say this enough times," he said. "I supported black equality. I have never said or decided anything that should be frightening to women." On civil rights in particular, he declared, "If I were a black man and knew my record as solicitor general and a judge, I would not be concerned, because my civil rights record is a good one." He again denied he was shaping his remarks to curry senators' favor. "For sixteen years I have been saying one thing about the courts— they have to be guided by the intentions of lawmakers, with some respect for precedent. If I got on the Supreme Court and did anything else, I'd be a fool in history. I suppose that's the best guarantee I can give you."

BY THE END of the hearings the nomination was in peril. Reagan belatedly lit a backfire. He lobbied fence-sitting senators and threatened to leave the ninth seat on the court unfilled if the Senate rejected Bork. He conspicuously denied rumors that he might abandon the nominee. In early October he met with a group of high school principals in the White House Rose Garden. As they walked to the Oval Office, Sam Donaldson shouted a question as to whether Bork's nomination was finished. "Over my dead body," Reagan replied. The president smiled as he related the incident in his diary. "The principals cheered and then moved in on the press gang giving them h--l."

Yet Reagan could count votes, and as the Democrats dug in, he gradually realized the nomination would fail. He didn't abandon Bork, but he nudged the door open for Bork to exit on his own. "Mr. President, fifty-one senators now oppose Judge Bork," a reporter said. "He can't make it. He can't make it, sir. Fifty-one senators have announced their opposition."

Reagan responded to the implied question. "He has a decision to make," the president said. He added, "I have made mine. I will support him all the way."

"Would you accept his decision, whatever it may be?" a reporter pressed.

"Well, obviously I'd have to," Reagan said.

Was the president giving up?

"It would be impossible for me to give up in the face of a lynch mob," Reagan said.

Bork wouldn't give up either. He declined the exit Reagan offered, insisting on a vote of the full Senate. Reagan had no choice but to stand behind him. "Judge Bork and I agree that there are no illusions about the outcome of the vote in the Senate, but we also agree a crucial principle is at stake," the president declared. "That principle is the process that is used to determine the fitness of those men and women selected to serve on our courts. And the ultimate decision will impact on each of us and each of our children if we don't undo what has already been done and see that that kind of performance is never repeated."

Reagan tried to hold the high moral ground, but his exasperation sometimes got the better of him. He met with Republican senators to discuss the Bork nomination. "I assured them I would not soften my requirements for a Supreme Court justice and please the lynch mob," he recounted in his diary. At a Republican fund-raiser a woman shouted, "We want Bork!" Reagan responded, "So do I. What's at issue is that we make sure that the process of appointing and confirming judges never again is turned into a political joke. And if I have to appoint another one, I'll try to find one that they'll object to as much as they did to this one."

In fact he did the opposite. After the Senate handed Reagan the most lopsided defeat of a Supreme Court nomination in history—Bork lost by 58 to 42—the president decided to cut his losses. He quickly nominated Douglas Ginsburg, chosen chiefly for being noncontroversial. Reagan admitted as much in announcing the nomination. "By selecting Judge Ginsburg, I've gone the extra mile to ensure a speedy confirmation," he said. "I've been impressed by the fact that in academia, in government, and on the bench Judge Ginsburg has been enormously popular with colleagues of all persuasions."

But Reagan's haste contributed to a failure of vetting, and within days reporters discovered something the administration had not: that Ginsburg had used marijuana as a young man. Reagan initially dismissed the news as inconsequential. "It was a brief thing back when a lot of people experimented a bit and that's all it amounted to," he wrote in his diary. "I think the fellow who leaked it was a friend at the time who smoked it with him. I don't see any reason why I should withdraw his name."

Another president might have ridden out this new controversy. But Nancy Reagan had made the suppression of illegal drug use her principal public cause, and with Nancy imploring the nation's youth to "just say no," the president could hardly say yes to an admitted user.

Reagan resisted admitting he had erred again. Bill Bennett, the secretary of education and the second most conspicuous foe, after Nancy, of illegal drugs, called Reagan and asked him to pull the Ginsburg nomination. "I told him that was absolutely impossible," Reagan wrote.

But then Ginsburg offered to withdraw, and Reagan went along. "It looks increasingly that he cannot be confirmed and he's taken enough abuse," he wrote.

Reagan finally succeeded on the third try. Anthony Kennedy's past was closely examined for troublesome indiscretions. "FBI check on Judge Kennedy: clean as a whistle," Reagan noted with relief. His personal life appeared a model of decorum. "Lovely wife; beautiful daughter, sophomore at Stanford; son who is a senior at Stanford; and son who is out in business." And he was politically uncontroversial. "So far we've heard encouraging words that he has bipartisan support from Dems and Repubs."

The hearings went smoothly. "They didn't lay a glove on him," Reagan wrote with satisfaction. The holidays pushed back the final decision, but in early 1988 the Senate approved the Kennedy nomination by a vote of 97 to 0.

I N THE SUMMER of 1987, Paul Volcker completed his second term as chairman of the Federal Reserve. Reagan had reappointed him four years earlier because not doing so might have risked another recession ahead of the president's reelection campaign. "The financial market seems set on having him," Reagan wrote in the summer of 1983. "I don't want to shake their confidence in recovery." An additional reason for reappointing Volcker was that he hinted he wouldn't stay for a full four years. "I think we'll reappoint Paul Volcker for about a year and a half," Reagan wrote. "He doesn't want a full term."

Within months of Volcker's reappointment, Reagan was having second thoughts. "Lew Lehrman came by with some disturbing info about Paul Volcker and his strong belief that we should slow our business growth," Reagan wrote in early 1984. Lehrman was an investment banker, conservative activist, and recent Republican nominee for governor of New York. "Paul is obsessed with a fear of returning inflation and according to Lew would seek to use the Fed to slow our recovery." By phone, in person, and through such proxies as Donald Regan, the president pressured Volcker to loosen the reins on the money supply. But Volcker set his own course. "The Fed has pulled the string on the money supply and it's down to one-half the rate of growth in the economy," Reagan grumbled the week before the election. "Don is trying to goose Paul V. into a little action before he brings on more of a lull."

Perhaps Volcker had indeed intended to resign before his second term ended, or perhaps Reagan misinterpreted the signals he sent. Whatever the case, Volcker apparently decided, in the face of the persistent pressure from the White House, that he needed to stick around lest the progress that had been made against inflation be undone. And his stubbornness confirmed Reagan's belief that two terms for Volcker were more than enough. "We're going to see if Alan Greenspan will take the job if Paul will step down gracefully," Reagan wrote in the spring of 1987.

Volcker agreed that the time had come for a change in the leadership of the Fed, and Reagan announced Greenspan's nomination that June. He assured reporters, the markets, and the country at large that the change at the Fed signaled no slackening of the administration's commitment to keep inflation in check. "We've had a miraculous fifty-odd months of bringing inflation down," Reagan declared. "Now there is something of a little surge again, in large part, precipitated by energy prices. But I have perfect confidence in Alan Greenspan and his philosophy and that what he would do would curb that and not let inflation get out of hand again."

Inflation proved to be just one of the challenges Greenspan encountered in his first months on the job. "I felt a real need to hit the ground running because I knew the Fed would soon face big decisions," Greenspan recalled. The economic expansion that had begun after the recession of Reagan's first term was in its fourth year, but signs of instability were growing more evident. The stock market had soared 40 percent since the beginning of the year, with little sign of slowing. "Wall Street was in a speculative froth," Greenspan recounted. The federal budget provided no solace. "Huge government deficits under Reagan had caused the national debt to the public to almost triple, from just over $700 billion at the start of his presidency to more than $2 trillion at the end of fiscal year 1988." Inflation was creeping upward again, from less than 2 percent to nearly twice that. This was still far below the double-digit rises of the 1970s, but it was worrisome all the same. "We were in danger of forfeiting the victory that had been gained at such great misery and cost under Paul Volcker," Greenspan wrote.

To dampen the inflationary pressures, Greenspan persuaded the Fed board to boost interest rates. This was a big step, as the Fed hadn't raised rates in three years. "I couldn't help but remember accounts I'd read of the physicists at Alamogordo the first time they detonated an atom bomb: Would the bomb fizzle? Would it work the way they hoped? Or would the chain reaction somehow go out of control and set the earth's atmosphere on fire?"

The sky didn't catch fire, but the stock market imploded. The Dow Jones average lost 6 percent the first week in October, then 12 percent more the next week. On a single day—Friday, October 16—the Dow plunged 108 points. Greenspan and the rest of the country held their collective breath waiting for the markets to reopen on Monday.

The early news that day was grim. The Dow fell another 200 points in morning trading. Greenspan was scheduled to speak in Dallas, and he boarded a plane to fly west. For three hours he was out of touch. His first question on landing was how things had ended on Wall Street. "Down five-oh-eight," his Dallas host, from the local branch of the Fed, replied.

Greenspan sighed relief, thinking that a loss of 5.08 was far better than he could have expected. But the look on his host's face revealed that the news was not good but very bad: the Dow had fallen 508 points. This was the largest one-day loss in Wall Street's history, bigger than any single day's beating in the crash of 1929. Trillions of dollars had vanished in the blink of an eye.

Greenspan at once appreciated the danger. He had studied the 1929 crash and the ensuing depression, and he knew what the Fed had done wrong. He determined not to repeat the mistakes of his predecessors. "I went straight to the hotel, where I stayed on the phone into the night," he recalled. "The Fed's job during a stock-market panic is to ward off financial paralysis—a chaotic state in which businesses and banks stop making the payments they owe each other and the economy grinds to a halt." The senior people Greenspan spoke with shared his understanding of the crisis and the appropriate remedies. But some of the younger people, shaped more by the inflation of the 1970s than the depression of the 1930s, counseled caution. One suggested that the Fed wait and see what was going to happen.

"Though I was new at this job, I'd been a student of financial history for too long to think that made any sense," Greenspan recounted. "It was the one moment I spoke sharply to anybody that night. 'We don't need to wait to see what happens,' I told him. 'We *know* what's going to happen.' Then I backed up a little and explained. 'You know what people say about getting shot? You feel like you've been punched, but the trauma is such that you don't feel the pain right away? In twenty-four or forty-eight hours, we're going to be feeling a lot of pain.'"

Greenspan flew back to Washington, where Reagan was trying to shrug off the bad news from Wall Street. "Are we headed for another great crash?" a reporter shouted at the president as he crossed the White House lawn. Reagan didn't hear the question. "Are we headed for another great crash?" the reporter repeated. "Stock market," another reporter offered.

"Oh, the stock market," Reagan replied. "Well, I only have one thing to say: I think everyone is a little puzzled, and I don't know what meaning it might have because all the business indices are up. There is nothing wrong with the economy."

So what had caused the collapse? the reporters asked.

"Maybe some people seeing a chance to grab a profit, I don't know," Reagan said. "But I do know this: More people are working than ever before in history. Our productivity is up. So is our manufacturing product up. There is no runaway inflation, as there has been in the past. So, as I say, I don't think anyone should panic, because all the economic indicators are solid."

Greenspan knew the president was trying to be reassuring. And under the circumstances he could hardly speak otherwise. But Reagan's comments reminded him of similar comments by Herbert Hoover amid the crash of 1929. He huddled with James Baker, who had a longer record with the president than he did. The two agreed to approach Reagan together. "We met with Reagan at the White House to suggest he try a different tack," Greenspan recalled. "The most constructive response, Jim Baker and I argued, would be to offer to cooperate with Congress on cutting the deficit, since that was one of the long-term economic risks upsetting Wall Street."

Reagan took the cue. He told reporters he was directing members of the administration to commence discussions with Congress on reducing the deficit. A reporter immediately queried, "Are you willing to compromise on taxes, sir? Are you willing to compromise on taxes?"

Reagan initially hedged. "I presented in my budget a program that provided for $22 billion in additional revenue, which was not necessarily taxes," he said. But, perhaps recalling the worry in the voices of Greenspan and Baker, he added, "I am willing to look at whatever proposal they might have."

Reagan's statement might have reassured the markets. Or it might have been regarded as political fluff. No one ever knew, for his offer wasn't seriously tested. Greenspan and the Fed jawboned banks to keep lending and, most critically, flooded the financial system with new money. The markets stabilized, then began to recover the lost ground. As the memories of Black Monday faded, so did the president's inclination to meet Tip O'Neill halfway on the budget.

I T WAS IN many ways a crisis for the country," Reagan later wrote of the events of that October. "But I confess this was a period of time in which I was more concerned about the possibility of an even greater tragedy in my own life than I was about the stock market." Nancy's routine mammogram had revealed a troubling lump. John Hutton looked after Nancy's health as well as Reagan's; he had accompanied her to Bethesda, and he returned to the Oval Office to break the news to Reagan. It looked malignant, he said, but a biopsy would tell for certain. Reagan was stunned. "Afterward, John told Nancy I reacted to the news with an expression he would never forget," Reagan recalled. "I think the president has always believed that nothing would ever happen to you," Hutton said. Reagan added, "He was right."

The not knowing was the hardest part. "The next ten days may have been the longest ten days of our lives," Reagan wrote. The night before her surgery, Reagan helicoptered with Nancy to Bethesda. He returned to the White House but couldn't sleep. He got up early to fly back to the hospital, but fog grounded his aircraft and he had to take a car. He reached the hospital in time only to kiss Nancy as she went into the operating room.

He and Nancy's brother, Dick, who had driven in from Philadelphia, sat in the waiting room. "Dick and I buried ourselves with newspapers and some sessions with assembled doctors keeping us posted on progress of surgery," Reagan wrote that evening. In due course they learned the results. "The biopsy turned out to be traces of what they called a noninvasive carcinoma—very tiny. Decision was to perform moderate mastectomy." Reagan and Dick were able to see Nancy after lunch. "As can be expected she's feeling bad about losing a breast," Reagan wrote. "We did our best to let her know that was nothing compared to fact the cancer was gone. The doctors are delighted with the operation—it went so well and was so effective. There won't be any chemotherapy or radiation treatment at all."

In his memoir Reagan recounted the incidents of that day more emotionally. "I looked up and saw John Hutton and Dr. Ollie Beahrs of the Mayo Clinic approach us," he wrote. "Their faces telegraphed the news that they were about to give me: Nancy had a malignancy and she and her doctors decided on a mastectomy. I know how desperately Nancy had hoped this would not be the case and I couldn't reply to them. I just dropped my head and cried. After they left, I remained at the table, motionless and unable to speak." He told of visiting Nancy in the recovery room. "She was asleep when Dick and I got there. Suddenly, as we were standing by her bed, there was a little movement of her body. Her eyes didn't open, but I heard a tiny voice say, 'My breast is gone.' Barely conscious because of her anesthesia, Nancy somehow had sensed we were there. She was devastated by the loss of her breast—not because she was worried about herself, but because she was worried about me and how I would feel about her as a woman. 'It doesn't matter,' I said. 'I love *you*.' Then I leaned over and kissed her softly, and repeated that it made no difference to me. But seeing that sadness in her eyes, it was all I could do to avoid breaking up again."

Nancy suffered a second blow ten days later when her mother, Edith Davis, died. The president learned first. "I came home and told her the news," he recounted in his diary. "It was heartbreaking." The next day they flew to Phoenix. "Upon arrival we went direct to the mortuary," Reagan wrote. "We saw Deede looking calm and peaceful in her red robe. This was too much for Nancy who broke down sobbing and telling her how much she loved her. I told her Deede knows that now and that she really wasn't in that room with her body but would be closer to her when we get to her apartment where her long time friends were waiting for us."

The gathering with friends did help. "Nancy was in a better state of mind hearing all of us talk about Deede and our love for her," Reagan wrote that evening. He flew back to Washington but returned to Phoenix for the funeral. Nancy asked him to deliver the eulogy. The service eased her pain a bit more. "Friends from all over the country were on hand," Reagan recounted. "It was most heart warming."

T HE IRAN-CONTRA SCANDAL fairly paralyzed Reagan's poli-
cies toward the Middle East and Central America. The adminis-
tration's violation of its own arms embargo against Iran shattered
America's credibility with much of the world, and its circumvention of
Congress with regard to the contras lost it the support of even many
Republicans on anything touching Nicaragua or its neighbors.

Oddly, though, this was a blessing. By precluding new initiatives
toward other regions, Iran-contra drove Reagan to focus on what he had
always considered the central issue of foreign policy: relations with the
Soviet Union. He had nothing to look forward to in domestic politics;
the Democrats in Congress would simply wait him out. And with foreign
policy narrowed to the Soviet Union, there was no one to dance with but
Gorbachev.

But there were observers watching from the sides of the room. In the
spring of 1987 Reagan traveled to Europe for the annual meeting of the
G7, in Italy. Some of America's allies had been upset by Reykjavík, worried that the president was moving too quickly on arms control. "Margaret Thatcher came down like a ton of bricks," Jack Matlock recalled.
The British prime minister chided Reagan for even thinking of removing the nuclear deterrent that for decades had kept the peace in Europe.
She reminded him that American nuclear weapons had the purpose of
offsetting Soviet advantages in conventional forces. An arms treaty for
Europe that didn't address conventional weapons could leave the Soviets
dangerously dominant. "There was a real point at issue on arms control,
on which I wanted to make my position clear," Thatcher wrote later. "I

was not prepared to see British forces in Germany left without their protection and said so forcefully."

Reagan reassured her that he wouldn't weaken deterrence. He thought she was mollified. "As usual we were on the same wave length," he remarked in his diary.

He traveled from Italy to Berlin. The mayor of West Berlin had asked him to speak on the occasion of the 750th anniversary of the city. Reagan's advisers wanted to hear something ceremonial and innocuous; with Congress still investigating the Iran-contra scandal, they thought the president should maintain a low profile.

Reagan took the opposite view. He insisted on reminding the world of the moral difference between the United States and the Soviet Union. Howard Baker read a draft speech that included a challenge to Gorbachev to tear down the Berlin Wall. Supposing the phrase to be the work of an overzealous speechwriter, Baker sought to strike it out. The State Department seconded his caution. "But Reagan was tough on it," Baker recalled. The language was the president's, he learned. "Those were Reagan's words." And Reagan didn't want them tampered with. "He said leave it in."

The words stayed in. "General Secretary Gorbachev," Reagan declared in front of the Brandenburg Gate, "if you seek peace, if you seek prosperity for the Soviet Union and Eastern Europe, if you seek liberalization, come here to this gate! Mr. Gorbachev, open this gate! Mr. Gorbachev, tear down this wall!"

GORBACHEV GROANED, NOT because he opposed what Reagan was demanding, but because he supported it. Gorbachev had moved cautiously after Reykjavík. His dual reforms, glasnost and perestroika, inspired hope among Russian liberals even as they sowed fear in the old guard. Americans, including Reagan, had often assumed Soviet leaders ruled by diktat, and some, most notably Stalin, did. But Gorbachev lacked the stature of Stalin or even Brezhnev, and he had to feel his way forward. In certain respects he was weaker than Reagan, who at least had the popular mandate conferred by two election victories. Definitely no more than Reagan could he be seen as compromising national security in his relations with the United States.

Reagan and the Americans weren't helping. "In the best tradition of its Wild West, America was again flexing its muscles and accusing the Soviet Union of all sins," Gorbachev wrote in his memoirs. "The Americans (and not only they) employed the mass media to manipulate public opinion, to recapture the initiative in international affairs and to force us to accept their rules. I often discussed the issue with my colleagues. All of us felt that we must not surrender the initiative."

But they did surrender something more valuable than the initiative. Gorbachev decided to unbundle the package deal he had offered at Reykjavík. He announced that the Soviet government was willing to negotiate a treaty on intermediate nuclear forces, or INF, separately from a strategic forces treaty. By delinking INF from what was being hopefully called a Strategic Arms Reduction Treaty, or START, he delinked INF from SDI as well. He had hoped to use Reagan's desire for an INF treaty to persuade him to drop SDI or confine it to the laboratory, but his strategy had fallen short. Moving on, he judged an INF treaty beneficial to the Soviet Union on its own merits. He privately assailed the decision by his predecessors to install the SS-20 missiles that had triggered the whole intermediate forces controversy. "Whatever the arguments advanced at the time to justify the deployment of such missiles, the Soviet leadership failed to take into account the probable reaction of the Western countries," he wrote. "I would even go so far as to characterize it as an unforgivable adventure, embarked on by the previous Soviet leadership under pressure from the military-industrial complex." The SS-20s threatened merely America's allies, but the Pershings the Americans and NATO responded with threatened the Soviet Union itself. In fact they threatened the Soviet Union more gravely than any other American system, as they could reach their targets in as little as five minutes. "Hence I deemed it my duty to avert the deadly danger to our country and to correct the fatal error made by the Soviet leadership in the mid-1970s."

Gorbachev told George Shultz of his decision when the secretary of state visited Moscow. Gorbachev had previously seen Shultz as Reagan's mostly silent partner, but in Moscow he learned to appreciate him as a diplomat of the highest order. "I realized, maybe for the first time, that I was dealing with a serious man of sound political judgment," Gorbachev recalled. They discussed an INF deal and sketched the outlines of an agreement. They shared the hope that a treaty could be signed by year's end.

REAGAN HOPED SO too. But he hoped for more. An INF pact would be very important; it would be more than any president had ever achieved on arms control. But it wasn't enough. Reagan still wanted to lift the nuclear cloud from humanity's future. This had been his goal from the beginning. He had come close at Reykjavík. And with his time in the White House dwindling, he felt a greater need than ever to tackle the big missiles, the ones that threatened Armageddon. "Now we must finish the task," he told the National Security Planning Group. "I don't accept the suggestions of some that it is too late for us to get a START agreement before I leave office." Reagan knew he faced skeptics, even within his administration, and he made clear he wouldn't cut a deal for the sake of a deal. "I want a START agreement," he said, "but *only* if it is a good one, one we can verify and which enhances our security."

Caspar Weinberger remained distrustful of any agreement. He deemed Reykjavík a disaster narrowly averted. He didn't like the idea of an INF accord, though he judged he could no longer oppose it frontally. He definitely didn't want a START deal. He warned Reagan and the planning group against any concessions to the Soviets. Better no START agreement at all than one that required concessions, he said.

George Shultz supported both an INF pact and a START treaty, and he opposed Weinberger. He suspected that Weinberger was opposing START as a way of sabotaging INF. Shultz declared that START was essential to INF. "It is very easy for the Soviets to deploy more missiles, and it is hard for us," he said. An INF treaty would be worthless if not followed by START, he said, for the Soviets could simply deploy new strategic missiles to replace the intermediate missiles eliminated.

Weinberger denied wanting to scuttle either START or INF. "I agree with you on the need for START," he said. "But that is no reason for us to give in to the Soviet demands. We've got a good agreement in INF because we hung tough and we can do the same in START."

Reagan elevated the discussion to the realm of first principles. "You've got to remember that the whole thing was born of the idea that the world needs to get rid of nuclear weapons," he said. "We've got to remember that we can't win a nuclear war and we can't fight one. The Soviets don't want to win by war but by threat of war. They want to issue ultimatums to which we have to give in. If we could just talk about the basic steps we need to break the log jam and avoid the possibility of war—I mean, think about it: Where would the survivors of the war live? Major areas of the world would be uninhabitable. We need to keep it in mind that that's what we're about. We are about bringing together steps to bring us closer to the recognition that we need to do away with nuclear weapons."

Weinberger played to Reagan's desire to eliminate nuclear weapons. "We have to be very careful in this area, Mr. President, because what we want to do is get rid of nuclear weapons, and if we handle this badly, we will not be able to get rid of them," he said. "We can't live with nuclear weapons if they are used. We can't get rid of them because there are no defenses against them. We must do nothing to inhibit our ability to defend against nuclear weapons. We need to defend early; we need to defend our continent, not just a few sites."

Weinberger was among those who had sighed relief that Reagan at Reykjavík had refused to constrain SDI. He worried that Reagan's evident desire for START might cause him to wobble in a future meeting with Gorbachev. He now declared that SDI must not be limited in any way. There could be no restrictions on America's ability to test or deploy.

Frank Carlucci pointed out that at Reykjavík the president and Gorbachev had agreed in principle not to withdraw from the ABM Treaty before 1996.

"Yes, but we're walking back from that, and we're really making progress," Weinberger said.

Reagan interjected, "Why can't we agree now that if we get to a point where we want to deploy we will simply make all the information available about each other's systems so that we can both have defenses? So that if either side is ready to deploy, both agree to make available to the other all the results of their research."

"I don't believe that we could ever do that," Weinberger said. The secretary of defense had never so flatly contradicted this fundamental facet of Reagan's conception of strategic defense. But the president said nothing.

Weinberger's allies joined in. General Robert Herres, the vice-chairman of the Joint Chiefs of Staff, said, "Mr. President, there is great risk in exchanging technical data. Much of our technology is easily convertible into other purposes and into an offensive area."

Ken Adelman took a similar view. "Mr. President, that would be the most massive technical transfer that the western world has ever known," the arms control director said. And it would defeat the purpose of strategic defense. "If they understood our system that well, it would be easy for them to move to countermeasures."

Now Reagan objected. "Once we deploy something, won't they know about the system? So won't they try to counter it anyway? So what difference does it make if they get the information and counter it or if we simply provide it to them?"

Weinberger ignored the president's questions. "The key here is the price that they are asking is too high. We ought to just hold tough."

Technical discussion ensued. The president listened distractedly. Finally he said, "There has to be an answer to all these questions, because some day people are going to ask why we didn't do something now about getting rid of nuclear weapons. You know, I've been reading my Bible and the description of Armageddon talks about destruction, I believe, of many cities, and we absolutely need to avoid that. We have to do something now."

"We certainly need to avoid Armageddon," Carlucci agreed.

"The answer is SDI," Weinberger said.

GORBACHEV WAS PLEASED that George Shultz was the one to greet him when he landed in Washington in early December. America's Geneva negotiators had reached agreement on INF with their Soviet counterparts, producing a signature-ready treaty. Gorbachev belatedly accepted Reagan's Reykjavík invitation for a Washington summit and winged west.

The secretary of state thought the general secretary had never looked better. "He was upbeat, positive, animated and eager," Shultz recalled. "He talked about the changes taking place in his country and his desire to close out the Cold War with the United States." Gorbachev inquired as to American opponents of the INF Treaty. "What about critics in the U.S.?" he asked Shultz.

"The vast majority of Americans support what President Reagan is doing," Shultz answered. There were indeed critics, but the way to deal with them was by making further progress.

"I work very hard," Gorbachev told Shultz. "I drive people and wear them out. I go at it all the way. If I tire, someone else will take over." Shultz didn't expect weariness to be a problem. "He looked as if he would never tire," Shultz wrote.

THE NEXT MORNING Gorbachev and Reagan picked up where they had left off in Reykjavík. "A good rousing meeting" was Reagan's diary description of their opening round. Gorbachev complained about Reagan's Berlin speech. "Mr. President, you are not a prosecutor and I am not on trial," he said. "Like you, I represent a great country and therefore expect our dialogue to be conducted on the basis of reciprocity and equality. Otherwise there will be no dialogue."

Reagan considered Gorbachev's admonishment to be part of the game. "I enjoyed the debate and I think he did, too," the president wrote later. "We agreed to disagree."

They adjourned to the signing ceremony. The East Room of the White House was filled with diplomats, members of Congress and the executive branch, Gorbachev's entourage, and the media. Reagan took the lead. The president was understandably proud. "This ceremony and the treaty we're signing today are both excellent examples of the rewards of patience," he said. "It was over six years ago—November 18, 1981—that I first proposed what would come to be called the zero option. It was a simple proposal—one might say, disarmingly simple." Reagan smiled amid the expected laughter. "Unlike treaties in the past, it didn't simply codify the status quo or a new arms buildup; it didn't simply talk of controlling an arms race. For the first time in history, the language of 'arms control' was replaced by 'arms reduction'—in this case, the complete elimination of an entire class of U.S. and Soviet nuclear missiles." Reagan acknowledged the opposition his proposal had encountered. "Reaction, to say the least, was mixed. To some the zero option was impossibly visionary and unrealistic; to others merely a propaganda ploy. Well, with patience, determination, and commitment, we've made this impossible vision a reality."

Reagan's researchers had scoured Russian literature for an appropriate reference. The president turned to Gorbachev and said, "General Secretary Gorbachev, I'm sure you're familiar with Ivan Krylov's famous tale about the swan, the crawfish, and the pike. It seems that once upon a time these three were trying to move a wagonload together. They hitched and harnessed themselves to the wagon. It wasn't very heavy, but no matter how hard they worked, the wagon just wouldn't move. You see, the swan was flying upward; the crawfish kept crawling backward; the pike kept making for the water. The end result was that they got nowhere, and the wagon is still there to this day." Fortunately, the American and Soviet governments knew better. "Strong and fundamental moral differences continue to exist between our nations," Reagan granted. "But today, on this vital issue, at least, we've seen what can be accomplished when we pull together."

Reagan tallied the accomplishment. All of the Soviet Union's ground-launched intermediate-range missiles would be destroyed, with their more than fifteen hundred warheads. America's entire complement of Pershing IIs and ground-launched cruise missiles, with some four hundred warheads, would be destroyed as well. "But the importance of this treaty transcends numbers," Reagan continued. "We have listened to the wisdom in an old Russian maxim. And I'm sure you're familiar with it, Mr. General Secretary, though my pronunciation may give you difficulty. The maxim is: Doveryai no proveryai—trust, but verify."

Gorbachev smiled for the cameras. "You repeat that at every meeting," he said. The audience of notables laughed.

"I like it," Reagan protested. More laughter. He expressed hope that the INF Treaty would lead to progress on strategic arms but also on conventional weapons, regional conflicts, and human rights. He cited another Russian proverb ("as you can see, I'm becoming quite an expert in Russian proverbs," he said, to further chuckles): "The harvest comes more from sweat than from the dew." He invited Gorbachev to speak.

Gorbachev said he would leave to future generations to pronounce on the importance of this single treaty. But the act of agreeing had a broader significance that was obvious even now. "For everyone, and above all, for our two great powers, the treaty whose text is on this table offers a big chance at last to get onto the road leading away from the threat of catastrophe. It is our duty to take full advantage of that chance and move together toward a nuclear-free world, which holds out for our children and grandchildren and for their children and grandchildren the promise of a fulfilling and happy life without fear and without a senseless waste of resources on weapons of destruction."

He turned to Reagan. "We have covered a seven-year-long road, replete with intense work and debate," he said. "One last step towards this table, and the treaty will be signed." He added, "May December 8, 1987, become a date that will be inscribed in the history books, a date that will mark the watershed separating the era of a mounting risk of nuclear war from the era of a demilitarization of human life."

THE GOOD FEELING of the signing ceremony persisted throughout Gorbachev's visit. But it didn't make additional agreements any easier. Reagan and Gorbachev went straight to the Cabinet Room for a discussion of the next steps. Reagan wanted to talk about strategic arms and press on toward START, but Gorbachev unexpectedly pushed the issue of conventional weapons. He didn't say so, but the principal appeal of a conventional-forces agreement was that it promised greater cost savings.

Reagan answered that he would be willing to talk about conventional arms, though he considered START the priority. Yet in either realm, trust was essential. "It is not armaments that create distrust," he said, "but distrust that creates armaments." He noted that the INF Treaty, historic as it was, still had to be ratified. Anything that caused distrust would jeopardize ratification.

Gorbachev said he had his own ratification problems. The Soviet Union was destroying four times as many missiles as the United States. The Supreme Soviet, which, with two thousand members, was far larger than the American Senate, would ask why he had been so generous to the Americans. Many in his country distrusted the United States and therefore disarmament. "People ask how it is possible to have disarmament when the Soviet Union is ringed with U.S. bases. People ask how Gorbachev can bow down to the U.S." Referring again to Reagan's Berlin speech, Gorbachev said the American government accused the Soviet Union of all sorts of sins, but the Americans themselves had plenty to answer for. "During the forty-five years since the war, so much has piled up that if we just go on with the complaints—on the Soviet side there are all sorts of doctrines to complain about: the Truman Doctrine, the Eisenhower Doctrine, the Carter Doctrine—we will put each other on trial." This was not the constructive approach people wanted. Looking beyond the Reagan years, Gorbachev turned to Vice President Bush. "Unless policy reflects what people want, you can win an election but not succeed in the long term," he said.

The topic of elections prompted Reagan to say that the United States supported Gorbachev's steps toward democracy under glasnost. He said he didn't want to offend the general secretary, but he couldn't resist telling a story he had recently heard from an American academic who visited the Soviet Union. The professor said that as he left his house in his home city, he was taken to the airport by a part-time taxi driver who was about to finish college. He asked the young man what he would do after he got his degree. "He replied that he had not yet decided," Reagan said. In the Soviet Union the professor had ridden in another taxi, similarly driven by a college student. He posed the same question as to what would come next. The driver said he didn't know—"they haven't told me yet."

Gorbachev frowned. He said he knew the president liked anecdotes, and Russia was a land rich with them. But he said he had a request to make of the president: "that you not ask Matlock to collect anecdotes for you."

The meeting ended with nothing accomplished or agreed upon. Yet Gorbachev, referring to the treaty signing, said the day had been a success. "It is a bridge to the future. The Soviet side is ready to build it over. By the time the president comes to Moscow, the two sides of the bridge should be locked together."

"They should meet in the middle," Reagan replied.

Gorbachev said he concurred completely.

TALKS THE NEXT day produced modest progress. Reagan pitched a START package that included 50 percent reductions in strategic weapons and an explicit acknowledgment of the right of both sides to test defensive systems outside the laboratory, including in space. Ignoring the reservations of Weinberger, Reagan proposed that each side commit to share with the other what it learned from the testing.

Gorbachev, as before, rejected the concept of strategic defense. The president's proposal, he said, would simply trigger a new arms race. Gorbachev repeated what he had said at Reykjavík about the Soviet Union's not intending to match the Americans SDI for SDI. "It would develop a response," he said. "But that response would take a different path from SDI." For this reason alone the president's technology-sharing provision was unacceptable.

Gorbachev nonetheless made a crucial concession on SDI. He accepted the principle of 50 percent cuts in strategic arms while saying nothing about confining SDI testing to the laboratory. He insisted only that the United States commit to a period of nonwithdrawal from the ABM Treaty; during that time testing, but not deployment, of SDI could proceed. Gorbachev indicated that the Soviet Union considered SDI a losing proposition, regardless of what the Americans did. "It could wear out the Soviet economy," he said. "It is up to the United States to decide if SDI makes sense for itself in economic terms; the Soviet Union has decided it does not." Should the United States deploy SDI at the end of the nonwithdrawal period, the Soviet Union would respond, but by more cost-effective methods than SDI. "For the Soviet side, it would be less expensive to explore ways other than through SDI-type deployments to ensure its security," Gorbachev said.

Reagan reiterated that SDI was central to his vision of a nuclear-free world. "The secret of nuclear weapons is spreading inexorably," he said. "If the U.S. and the Soviet Union ever reach the point where they have eliminated all their nuclear arms, they will have to face the possibility that a madman in one country or another could develop a nuclear capability for purposes of conquest or blackmail." Reagan knew Gorbachev would cringe, but he trotted out once more the analogy from the period after World War I, when poison gas had been outlawed. "People kept their gas masks," Reagan said. "There will always be a need for defense."

Gorbachev said he needed an American commitment to nonwithdrawal from the ABM regime. "If the U.S. wants the 50 percent reductions, there has to be a commitment of ten years on the ABM Treaty." He observed that nothing would come of SDI before that time anyway.

Reagan refused to limit SDI in any manner. He didn't think he should have to. His voice rising, he said, "I don't want to talk about links to SDI but about 50 percent reductions, about how the hell the two sides are to eliminate half their nuclear weapons. I want to talk about how we can sign an agreement like the one we signed yesterday, an agreement which made everyone in the world so damned happy it could be felt in the room at dinner last night. Let's get started with it!"

"I'm ready," Gorbachev said. But he could not go forward without reaffirmation of the ABM Treaty.

NANCY REAGAN MADE certain to participate fully in this summit. And she found Raisa Gorbachev as insufferable as ever. "Raisa and I hadn't seen each other in two years, but nothing much had changed," Nancy wrote later. While their husbands prepared to sign the INF Treaty, Nancy hosted a reception for Raisa, Barbara Bush, and several other women. "I had a fairly good idea of what to expect, but my guests were taken completely aback when Raisa proceeded to lecture us for the entire hour about the history of Russia, its political system, and how there were no homeless people in the Soviet Union," Nancy recalled. "Later, one of the guests came up to me and said, 'That was the rudest thing I've ever seen.' The others just shook their heads in amazement. I was glad that other people could see what I had been going through." Nancy noted disapprovingly that Raisa didn't ask about her struggle with cancer or offer condolences on the death of her mother. "The Soviets know everything, so I can't believe she didn't know what I had gone through only a few weeks earlier. Maybe I was overly sensitive, but I don't think so."

Nancy grudgingly took Raisa on a tour of the White House. She had extended an invitation three weeks earlier, but Raisa had been slow to respond. "I was offended," Nancy said. "In the circle we moved in, you don't ignore an invitation from the head of state or his wife." Eventually, Raisa said she would come but at a different time than Nancy had mentioned, as her schedule was very demanding. Yet she made time to speak with reporters. One asked her whether she would like living in the White House. She said that it seemed like a museum rather than a regular house. Nancy simmered. "It wasn't a very polite answer," she said, "especially from somebody who hadn't even seen the private living quarters."

Nancy's vexation extended into the state dinner she had arranged for that evening. "The Gorbachevs were understandably tired from their long trip," she recounted. "Because they had specifically requested an early evening, we made several changes in our routine to allow them to leave by ten o'clock, as they had asked." Nancy canceled a private reception she had planned for the Yellow Oval Room. She ordered that coffee be served at the dining tables in the State Dining Room rather than separately in the Blue Room. She told the violinists she had hired for the evening to trim their repertoire. Even Van Cliburn, the musical star of the evening, was urged to keep it short.

"After making all these changes to ensure an early evening, I was slightly annoyed when the Gorbachevs arrived late for dinner," Nancy recalled. Yet that wasn't the worst. "The real holdup came in the receiving line. Maybe it's a cultural difference and she was merely trying to be polite, but Raisa tried to have a real conversation with practically every guest. 'What is your name? How many children do you have?' She seemed very well briefed on who many of our guests were, and she obviously wanted them to know this. But the line was moving like molasses, and I thought I would go crazy."

IF RAISA GORBACHEV registered Nancy's annoyance, she gave no sign. Neither did her husband, who seemed to enjoy himself at the dinner. Nancy seated Richard Perle, the combative assistant secretary of defense, at the same table as Gorbachev, doubtless in part so she, seated at Gorbachev's side, wouldn't have to carry the conversation. Perle, a stout man, had been played by a slim actor in a British television re-creation of the Reykjavík summit. Gorbachev teased him: "When I saw you on television, you were a lot thinner."

Perle responded by asking Gorbachev what percentage of Soviet economic production went to the military.

"That's a secret," Gorbachev replied.

"Are you sure you know?" Perle demanded.

"I know *everything*," Gorbachev said. "I'm head of the defense council, so you're dining with a military man."

"I think you're spending twenty percent, and probably more," Perle said.

Gorbachev turned away, leaving Perle to guess. But he enjoyed the evening. "During those days so full of interesting meetings there were some truly emotional moments," he wrote in his memoir. "One was the dinner at the White House. Van Cliburn gave a recital after dinner. We remembered him as the young pianist who had won the 1958 Tchaikovsky Prize in Moscow for his rendering of the great Russian composer's first piano concerto. After exchanging an affectionate hug with us, Van Cliburn sat down at the grand piano and started softly playing and singing 'Moscow Nights.' This was a genuine gift for the Soviet guests. The song, which had been written by Soloviev-Sedoi for the 1957 Moscow Youth Festival, had become virtually an informal popular anthem. We could not resist the temptation and joined in, Russian and English lyrics blending into one emotion."

Gorbachev's good cheer infused his visit. He worked a Washington street crowd like a seasoned American pol. Ordering his limousine to stop, he leaped out and shook hands. "Hello, I'm glad to be in America," he told the first person he encountered, a woman. "I'm glad to be friends with all of you." To another observer he said, "My people are pushing me very hard to come to a better understanding of the American people." His exuberance took hold. A restaurant owner invited him in for borscht. A group of expense-account lunchers burst into applause when he waved. "Even from the balcony you could sense the charisma of the man," one said. "It was almost like a parade or a celebration. There was a world leader out shaking hands and you kind of felt the world was going to be okay. None of us wanted to let go of the moment. It was such a warm moment, of love. I'm a cynic, but I got chills."

He stirred an audience at a State Department reception hosted by George Shultz. "Today, hundreds of millions of people are gradually realizing that the end of the twentieth century represents a watershed for mankind," Gorbachev said, "a watershed which separates not so much political systems and ideologies but common sense and the will to survive on the one hand, and irresponsibility, national egotism, prejudices—in short, the old thinking—on the other hand. Mankind has come to realize that it has had enough wars and that it is time to put them to an end for good." Peace in the past had been based on a balance of force. This was dangerous. "Peace from a position of force is inherently weak, whatever people say about it. It is in the nature of such peace to be founded on confrontation, hidden or open, and on the permanent danger of flare-ups and the temptation to use force." The world could not afford to continue to indulge this misconception. The INF Treaty represented a first step beyond deterrence toward a new era of security based on trust. "To put it in simple, human language, what we have achieved is—both in Russian and English—the revival of hope."

He gave Reagan a parting gift. For years the president had complained about Soviet shipments of weapons to the Sandinistas in Nicaragua. Gorbachev had countered by criticizing the United States for arming the anti-Soviet mujahedeen in Afghanistan. Gorbachev had already agreed in principle to withdraw Soviet troops from Afghanistan, rendering moot the arms question in that country. Now he told Reagan he would cut off the Sandinistas.

Reagan had hoped for greater progress on START. But he was willing to accept what he got. "I think the whole thing was the best summit we'd ever had with the Soviet Union," he wrote that evening.

107

Reagan usually celebrated St. Patrick's Day. Being Irish was good fun and often good politics. But March 17 wasn't fun in 1988. "First talk was about 23 indictments against Col. North, John Poindexter, General Secord and Hakim," he wrote in his diary, referring to Richard Secord and Albert Hakim, intermediaries in the Iran-contra affair, as well as his former national security adviser, Poindexter, and Poindexter's deputy, North. "Nothing much to say really."

Nor did he say much as the prosecution went forward. When questioned by reporters, he took refuge in the separation of powers: the courts must be allowed to do their duty. Politics constrained him no less than the law, for he couldn't say anything without reminding his constituents of the most egregious blunder of his presidency.

He had more to say on a related but differently embarrassing topic. Don Regan's anger didn't diminish upon leaving the administration; he exacted his revenge in a memoir published in the spring of 1988. He led with the story of Nancy's astrologer, which naturally riveted the attention of the media and the public. Reagan dismissed it, even to himself. "The media are behaving like kids with a new toy," he wrote. "Never mind that there is no truth in it." The next day he recorded, "A short meeting—some talk about this astrology mess Don Regan's book has kicked up. Some gal in L.A. claims she's a visitor to the White House and that she gives us frequent readings. She even claims she advised me on choosing George B. We've never seen her in our lives and don't know her at all."

Reagan was equally categorical in public, at first. During a business awards ceremony honoring ice-cream makers Ben Cohen and Jerry Greenfield, a reporter shouted a question: "Mr. President, will you continue to allow astrology to play a part in the makeup of your daily schedule, sir?"

"I can't," Reagan replied, "because I never did."

White House staffers were more circumspect. They didn't deny the essence of the story, but they said Nancy hadn't consulted her astrologer for months. Joan Quigley thereupon told reporters she had been in contact with Nancy that very week. Marlin Fitzwater, Reagan's new chief spokesman, stood up for the First Lady even while implicitly undercutting the president. "She certainly has every right to consult an astrologer," he said. "There's nothing wrong with it. I object to the implication it is wrong and therefore has to be discontinued."

Nancy declared herself hurt by Don Regan's revelation. "I was taken aback by the vengefulness of the attack," she said in a written statement. "It's come through to me that Don Regan really doesn't like me."

Reagan defended Nancy. To journalists he characterized Regan's account as "a bunch of falsehoods" and said, "I'll be damned if I'll just stand by and let them railroad my wife."

This hardly quelled the chatter. After fresh stories suggested that the signing date of the INF Treaty had been influenced by astrology, Reagan was asked whether this was true. He didn't answer the question, instead asserting that Quigley had nothing to do with his midnight swearing in as California governor in 1967.

The reporter brought him back to the question. "Are you denying that either you or Mrs. Reagan used astrology on any occasion during your time here at the White House to help set the schedule for trips or the signing of the INF treaty?" he asked. "I must say that this goes against what a lot of aides are telling us, sir."

"Well, no, I'm only going to tell you one thing," Reagan said. "And that is that after I'd been shot, which was quite a traumatic experience for my wife—"

"And you?" the reporter interrupted.

"No, I was confident I was going to be all right." Reporters laughed, easing the tension slightly. "But she was getting a great many calls from friends," Reagan continued. "And a friend called and said that—or wished that he'd known what I was going to do that day and so forth because of— he mentioned someone, that all the signs were bad and everything else. And Nancy was—it was a trauma that didn't go away easily. And when suddenly things of the same kind just for a short period there—when I was booked for something of the same kind where the accident occurred, why, she would ask, what does it look like now? And no changes were ever made on the basis of whether I did nor did not conduct this—"

"But why something like the signing of an INF treaty?" the reporter pressed.

"No, it wasn't. Nothing of that kind was going on. This was all, once again, smoke and mirrors, and we made no decisions on it, and we're not binding our lives to this. And I don't mean to offend anyone who does believe in it or who engages in it seriously—"

"Do you believe in it?" a reporter asked.

"I don't guide my life by it, but I won't answer the question the other way because I don't know enough about it to say is there something to it or not."

"Do you think the attempt on your life could have been prevented?"

"No, this friend thought that had I been told that that was supposed to be a horrendous time for me, that I might have done something—well, we didn't."

Reagan and Nancy hoped the to-do would blow itself out. Yet they took little comfort from a prediction by the astrologer herself that it would do the president no lasting harm. Joan Quigley told a reporter that Reagan shared a fundamental strength with Franklin Roosevelt and Abraham Lincoln: "They're all Aquarians. They all have great vision." She added, "Reagan has a lot of Capricorn in his chart, because he's very practical. Also he has three planets in their exaltation, which is a very good quality. It means his life is a very important one."

108

Amid the tizzy, Reagan met with some foreign television correspondents, who found the astrology story bizarrely riveting. "Your former chief of staff has said that astrology played a part in your scheduling, indeed, in summit planning," one of them recounted for viewers in his home country. "How do you think that may change the way Mr. Gorbachev views the president and the administration he's dealing with?"

Reagan wasn't surprised by the question. "I hope Mr. Gorbachev has heard some of the things that I have been saying about those charges," he replied, "because no decision was ever made by me on the basis of astrology."

Gorbachev's reaction mattered to Reagan, because by this time the Soviet leader was one of the few people paying attention to the president. Reagan's power was rapidly dwindling; with the election campaigns to replace him already at full steam, his ability to get even the attention of the American people was diminishing. Domestic initiatives were out of the question; foreign policy was the sole realm in which he still exercised influence.

But his foreign policy goals were shifting. When he entered the White House, his primary objective in foreign policy had been the defeat of communism. The Kremlin had been the enemy, and all efforts were bent toward frustrating its designs. Now the head man in the Kremlin was his partner. Reagan recognized that his goals and Gorbachev's weren't identical, but he had concluded that neither were they antithetical. He had called the Soviet empire evil, but he didn't think of Gorbachev as evil at all. In fact he had come to think of Gorbachev as not very different from himself. He credited Gorbachev with good faith in seeking an end to the arms race and even the nuclear era; he acknowledged that Gorbachev had constituencies that had to be placated, just as he himself did.

Reagan's constituencies were on his mind when he visited Gorbachev in Moscow for their final summit. He understood that a START deal at this late date was unlikely, but he hoped to maintain the momentum he and Gorbachev had built on arms control. He also understood that conservatives in the United States still suspected Gorbachev's motives and that some doubted his own motives or wisdom in getting so close to Gorbachev. Many conservatives seemed to long for the ideological clarity of the days when the American president called the Soviet Union an evil empire.

Not long after the handshake at the start of the Moscow summit, Reagan raised what he called a sensitive topic. It was so sensitive, he said, that if word he had mentioned it leaked to the press, he would deny it. It had to do with religious freedom. Saying he was speaking as a friend, he asked Gorbachev, "What if you ruled that religious freedom was part of the people's rights, that people of any religion—whether Islam with its mosque, the Jewish faith, Protestants or the Ukrainian church—could go to the church of their choice?" Religious freedom, besides being valuable on its merits, would make agreements with the United States much easier. If Gorbachev would guarantee religious tolerance, Reagan said, attitudes in America toward the Soviet Union would change dramatically. "You will be a hero, and much of the feeling against your country will disappear like water in hot sun." Reagan reiterated that he himself would never try to take credit for pushing Gorbachev to make the change. "If anyone in the room would say I had given such advice, I would say that person was lying."

Gorbachev initially waved aside the suggestion. The problem of religion in the Soviet Union was not serious, he said. He himself had been baptized but was not now a believer; this represented an evolution of Soviet society. In the Soviet Union, people were allowed to believe or not, according to their own lights. "This is a person's freedom," he said. The United States was in no position to cast stones, for America was less free than the president suggested. "Why do nonbelievers sometimes feel suppressed?" he asked.

Reagan rejoined that they were not suppressed. He said his own son Ron was an atheist—"though he calls himself an agnostic." He said that in the United States, church and state were so fully separated that prayers could not be said in public schools.

Gorbachev granted that after the Russian Revolution, opposition to religion had gone too far. But those times were long past. "Today the trend is precisely in the direction you mentioned. There have been some conflicts between the authorities and religious activists, but only when they were anti-Soviet. There have been fewer such conflicts recently, and these surely will disappear."

Reagan urged Gorbachev to make that prediction a promise.

Gorbachev again resisted, but less vigorously than before. The conversation ended on a touchingly personal note. Reagan remarked that there was one thing he had always wanted to do for his atheist son. He wanted to serve Ron a gourmet dinner and have him enjoy it. At the dinner's end he would ask Ron if he believed there was a cook. Reagan said he wondered what Ron would answer.

Gorbachev replied that one answer alone was possible: yes.

THEY TALKED ABOUT a START agreement but made little progress. They repeated earlier arguments about SDI but soon realized they weren't getting anywhere. Both realized, though neither said, that Reagan's lame-duck status made it impossible for him to deliver any major agreement on strategic arms, and therefore made it imprudent for Gorbachev to offer any concessions toward such agreement.

The focus of the summit shifted to events outside the formal talks. Reagan spoke with Soviet dissidents, with prominent writers and artists, with Russian Orthodox clerics, and with students and faculty at Moscow State University. His theme was freedom, which he hailed as the key to progress in all realms of human development. "Freedom is the right to question and change the established way of doing things," he declared at Moscow State. "It is the right to put forth an idea, scoffed at by the experts, and watch it catch fire among the people. It is the right to dream—to follow your dream or stick to your conscience, even if you're the only one in a sea of doubters."

Reagan referenced American history in his praise of freedom, but his theme applied as well to perestroika, as his audience understood. They applauded him for siding with Gorbachev and reform. Jack Matlock, by this time ambassador to the Soviet Union, heard the president's speech at Moscow State and marveled at the response. "It was almost electric, the way the speech touched the students there," Matlock said. "He made a tremendous impression that went through the media like lightning." Matlock recalled receiving an ecstatic hug from a Russian intellectual he knew. "This is one of the greatest days in Russian history," the friend said. Matlock gently suggested he might be exaggerating. "No," he replied. "If Reagan thinks we're on the right track, we have a chance."

The crucial moment for Gorbachev came almost casually. "Mr. Reagan and I went on a walk around the Kremlin," Gorbachev recalled. "The American president was greeted by groups of tourists. He answered their greetings good-humoredly, occasionally stopping for a chat." One Muscovite asked the president, "Do you still see the Soviet Union as the evil empire?"

Reagan answered simply: "No."

Gorbachev recalled, "I was standing next to him and thought to myself: 'Right.'"

Gorbachev made sure to describe the exchange and repeat the president's response in a news conference the next day, prompting reporters to ask Reagan what had caused the shift in his views.

Reagan replied, "I think there is quite a difference today in the leadership and in the relationship between our two countries." He added, "I think that a great deal of it is due to the general secretary, who I have found to be different than previous Soviet leaders."

En route home Reagan refined his assessment of the changes taking place in the Soviet Union and the world. "Quite possibly, we're beginning to take down the barriers of the postwar era," he told Margaret Thatcher and an audience of British dignitaries at London's Guildhall. "Quite possibly, we are entering a new era in history, a time of lasting change in the Soviet Union." He couldn't be sure. "We will have to see." But his tone and demeanor indicated he had hopes.

His private response to the summit was equally optimistic and more heartfelt. "What can I say except 'Thank the Lord,'" he wrote in his diary.

109

G EORGE BUSH GREETED Reagan at Andrews Air Force Base. "You made us proud," the vice president declared. "This week an American president strode the hard ground of Red Square and reminded the world through the sureness of his step and the lilt of his words what a bracing thing freedom is—what a moving and bracing thing."

More than good feeling toward the president inspired Bush's words. In a season of Republican primaries that served as a referendum on the Reagan presidency, Bush had garnered sufficient delegates to secure the nomination to succeed the president. Reagan had adopted a public posture of impartiality between Bush and Bob Dole, the vice president's principal challenger, but like everyone else he considered a vote for Bush to be an endorsement of himself. On learning that Bush had won the New Hampshire primary, Reagan noted, "That made my day even if I do have to be neutral publicly."

It wasn't inevitable that the Republican convention would be a celebration of the Reagan years. The shadow of Iran-contra still hung over the president, and the enormous addition to the federal debt during Reagan's tenure continued to give traditional conservatives nightmares. But the organizers of the convention decided the Reagan charisma was good for one more victory, and they placed the president front and center. A series of loyalists paid tribute to his masterful leadership. A documentary recounted his life and touted his accomplishments.

Then Reagan himself spoke. He had never been in finer form. He recounted the dire condition of the country when he had been elected, and he recalled what he and the party had promised to do to remedy things.

"It was our dream that together we could rescue America and make a new beginning, to create anew that shining city on a hill. The dream we shared was to reclaim our government, to transform it from one that was consuming our prosperity into one that would get out of the way of those who created prosperity. It was a dream of again making our nation strong enough to preserve world peace and freedom and to recapture our national destiny." The challenge had been great, but Americans were used to rising to challenges. And so they had risen during the last eight years.

The delegates thrilled to the old Reagan message and incomparable delivery. They wouldn't let him continue. "Reagan! Reagan! Reagan!" they chanted.

He deflected the enthusiasm toward the party's new nominee. "And George was there," he said.

The audience wasn't buying. They wanted their hero. "Four more years! Four more years!" they shouted.

"No, you haven't heard it all yet," he insisted. He described his administration's efforts to reduce red tape, and declared, "George Bush headed up the task force that eliminated those regulations."

From a man who had recently completed his fourth superpower summit, this was almost damning with faint praise. But the delegates eventually took their cue. Some began chanting, "Bush in '88."

Reagan nodded approvingly. Yet he made no more than a passing effort to promote Bush as a leader in his own right. And he undercut even that effort when he told Bush, "Go out there and win one for the Gipper."

He concluded with more of the imagery the Republicans had learned to love. "We lit a prairie fire a few years back. Those flames were fed by passionate ideas and convictions, and we were determined to make them burn all across America." And so they had burned. "But we can never let the fire go out or quit the fight, because the battle is never over. Our freedom must be defended over and over again—and then again."

Reagan said he would be spending more time in California. There was brush to clear on the ranch and fences to mend. "But I want you to know that if the fires ever dim, I'll leave my phone number and address behind just in case you need a foot soldier. Just let me know, and I'll be there, as long as words don't leave me and as long as this sweet country strives to be special during its shining moment on earth."

The delegates were delirious. To a man and woman they applauded and yelled and wouldn't stop. Nearly all wished they could have nominated Reagan again. One delegate waved a sign that read, "Reagan for

King." Phil Gramm, a fellow Texan of Bush's and the designated nominator of the vice president, didn't bother disguising his greater devotion to Reagan. "I've worked with Ronald Reagan for eight years," Gramm said. "I love the president. There won't be another like him for a long time."

REAGAN'S AIDES FREELY acknowledged that his convention appearance was in the genre of political valedictories. None expected any signal accomplishments in the five months left to the president. All realized that his final contribution to the reforms he had set in motion would be the election of his protégé.

Yet some work remained. The political season in America coincided with a renewal of troubles with Iran, triggered, as before, by the bloody stalemate between Iran and Iraq. Reagan's disclaimer in the Iran-contra case that the American weapons shipped to Iran were insufficient to shift the strategic balance between the two Gulf antagonists had been true, if also self-serving. The continued deadlock prompted Tehran to try new tactics. Iranian warships began targeting oil tankers in the Gulf, particularly those loading at Kuwait, which was bankrolling Iraq's war effort. Tehran reasoned that scaring Kuwait's customers would cut the emirate's revenues and curtail its support of Iraq.

Kuwait had no navy to speak of, and so it turned to countries that did possess fleets. The Kuwaitis cannily called on both the United States and the Soviet Union. The Kremlin indicated assent, prompting the Reagan administration to try to preempt the Soviets. "I knew that the Soviet government had already told Kuwait it would help," Caspar Weinberger recalled. "And I was, and still am, convinced that it was not in our interest for Soviet forces to move into an area so vital to us." Neither Weinberger nor anyone else in the administration cared to credit Jimmy Carter by name with the doctrine asserting that Soviet penetration of the Persian Gulf would gravely endanger American security, but they acted on the principle that inspired the Carter Doctrine. "From the outset," Weinberger continued, "I was quite sure that if we did not respond positively to the Kuwaitis, the USSR would quickly fill the vacuum." Weinberger made this case to Reagan, who approved the reflagging of some Kuwaiti ships to American registry, justifying their protection by U.S. Navy vessels.

Administration officials denied that the reflagging suggested any shift in the American policy of neutrality between Iraq and Iran. Kuwait was a neutral, they said, and the United States had long defended neutral shipping rights during wartime. Iran didn't accept the argument, however, and it denounced the reflagging as further evidence of America's malign intent toward the Islamic Republic.

The Iranians weren't the only critics. Democrats on Capitol Hill complained that Reagan was committing America to a conflict that had nothing to do with American security. The war in the Gulf had already swallowed hundreds of thousands of lives, they pointed out, and it might start swallowing Americans if Reagan's new policy was implemented. The warnings gained believability when an Iraqi warplane unexpectedly attacked the USS *Stark*, killing thirty-seven American sailors. Reagan accepted the Iraq government's claim of mistaken identity, not least because no other explanation made sense. But he took precautions that another such accident not occur, ordering American ships to fire on any aircraft that appeared threatening.

The new policy had tragic consequences. The convoy operation inspired the Iranians to send gunboats against American ships. The American vessels responded with force against the gunboats and against Iranian communication facilities on offshore oil platforms. In the summer of 1988 the American guided-missile cruiser *Vincennes* spotted a plane approaching on what seemed a threatening trajectory. The captain ordered the launch of missiles, which destroyed the plane. Only later did the captain and crew discover that they had shot down a civilian Iranian airliner and killed the nearly three hundred passengers and crew. "It's a terrible tragedy," Reagan recorded. He said as much in public, and he ordered an investigation. But he didn't fault the commander of the *Vincennes*. "I don't believe the captain had any other choice but to fire on the plane."

The shoot-down revived memories of the Soviet destruction of the Korean airliner in 1983, though Reagan declined to acknowledge any equivalence. It might have provoked new attacks by the Iranians against American vessels, but after eight years of sanguinary futility the Iranians were ready to quit. So were the Iraqis, and the two belligerents accepted a United Nations–brokered cease-fire.

THE REPUBLICAN REACTION to Reagan's convention speech revealed a serious risk that the president would overshadow the nominee. George Bush, understanding the problem but not knowing how to solve it, vacillated between comments designed to establish his independence of Reagan and remarks that made him sound more Reaganesque than Reagan himself. "I want a kinder, gentler nation," Bush said, suggesting that the program cuts of the Reagan years had gone too far. Yet in the next breath he channeled Reagan the tax cutter, via Clint Eastwood's character Dirty Harry: "Read my lips: No new taxes."

Reagan let Bush find his way. He offered support when the nominee shocked the nation by naming Dan Quayle, a young and undistinguished senator from Indiana, as his number two. "Vice President Bush has made an outstanding selection of Senator Quayle as his running mate," Reagan said, albeit in a written statement released by the White House rather than in person. "I know he will be a great vice president." Reagan made strategic appearances on Bush's behalf, reiterating the accomplishments of his own administration and asserting that only a Bush victory could prevent the Democratic nominee, Michael Dukakis, and the liberals from reversing the good work of the last eight years. He offered Dan Quayle debating tips ahead of the senator's one on one with the Democratic vice presidential candidate, Lloyd Bentsen, and when most observers awarded the victory in the debate to Bentsen, Reagan loyally blamed the media. "Quayle did very well and Bentsen got away with some blatant falsehoods," he wrote.

The Bush team, led by Jim Baker, who had resigned from the Treasury Department to rejoin his old Houston friend, surmounted early questioning of the Quayle nomination to run an aggressive, effective campaign. They portrayed Dukakis as distant and cold, and the Democratic nominee did little to counter the impression. Bush built a lead he carried into the election, which he won handily: 53 percent to 46 percent in the popular count.

Reagan was delighted. "A great evening," he wrote after watching the returns. "About 11 p.m. to bed—happy."

PART SEVEN

A RANCH IN THE SKY

1989–2004

With Bush safely elected, Reagan completed his celebratory final lap. Margaret Thatcher came to Washington to measure the president-elect; she took time to toast her departing comrade-in-arms. "Mr. President, you've been more than a staunch ally and wise counselor," she said. "You've also been a wonderful friend to me and my country." Citing an observation by Winston Churchill that Americans seemed to be the only people who could laugh and fight at the same time, Thatcher added, "Mr. President, you are one of those men—a combination of true valor and gentle good humor."

He visited Simi Valley, California, where on a hilltop not far from his old Malibu ranch he helped break ground for the Ronald Reagan Presidential Library. Charlton Heston led the group in the Pledge of Allegiance, after which Reagan quipped, "Thank you, Chuck. I hope everyone here is suitably honored by your presence. After all, it's not often that you get Moses to lead you in the Pledge." The Southern California crowd chuckled at the reference to Heston's signature part. Reagan rode the laughter with a gibe at his own age: "When I first knew him, he didn't even speak English."

The Senate Republicans threw him a dinner. "What a team we've been, and what a time this has been," Reagan told the diners. "You faced the opposition and fought the tough battles. In fact, when I told Bob Hope I was coming here tonight, he thought I was to do a U.S.O. show." The Democrats had increased their majority in the upper house in the recent elections, disappointing Reagan but allowing him another one-liner this evening. "I think you all know the difference between a Republican Senate and a Democratic Senate," he said. "It's the difference between a super majority and a simple majority." Perhaps the wine had dulled the reflexes, for the laughs were slow. "I'd better just let you think about that one," he said. More laughter, slightly self-conscious.

In early January 1989, Reagan attended a fiftieth-anniversary celebration of the Franklin Roosevelt Presidential Library. More openly than ever, he drew the connection between himself and his political model. "Franklin Roosevelt aroused the interest of young men and women in politics and government and drew them into the national service," Reagan said. "From the brain trusters to the many idealists who staffed the agencies and bureaus of the New Deal, his magic brought thousands to Washington. But I can tell you from personal experience that it didn't stop there. All across the nation, millions of new voters looked at this president who was filled with confidence in the future, faith in the people, and the joy of the democratic rough-and-tumble, and they said to themselves maybe someday they, too, would like to serve the nation in public life. I was one of those millions." Reagan had built a political career bashing what Roosevelt had created, but with his political career ending he acknowledged his debt to FDR. "Franklin Roosevelt was the first president I ever voted for, the first to serve in my lifetime that I regarded as a hero." Reagan told of seeing Roosevelt when the president visited Des Moines in 1936. "What a wave of affection and pride swept through that crowd, as he passed by in an open car—a familiar smile on his lips, jaunty and confident, drawing from us a reservoir of confidence and enthusiasm some of us had forgotten." Reagan recalled his own reaction, and his debt to Roosevelt. "It was that ebullience, that infectious optimism that made one young sportscaster think that maybe he should be more active as a citizen."

In the decades since then, Reagan had reflected on what else he and Roosevelt shared, and he concluded that the most important thing was their faith in the American people. He told of listening to Roosevelt's Fireside Chats in the depths of the Great Depression. "I remember how a light would snap on in the eyes of everyone in the room just hearing him, and how, because of his faith, our faith in our own capacity to overcome any crisis and any challenge was reborn." He said he would like to be remembered similarly. "To my mind, as one who has served in the office FDR once graced so magnificently, no higher tribute can be given a president than that he strengthened our faith in ourselves." Policies went in and out of favor; presidents stepped on the stage and stepped off. But the American people remained. "When the American people are strong and confident, when their leaders hear their voices, America, whatever storms it might be weathering, will make it through. It will survive, and it will prevail."

111

R EAGAN'S DEPARTURE FROM the White House inspired him to seek paying work in the private sector. Fortunately for his bank account, he lacked qualms about capitalizing on his government experience. He and Nancy had scarcely landed in California before the speakers' agency he enlisted began hawking his services on the lecture circuit. His fee was $50,000 per speech, and interest was strong. "You've got to put this into context," a spokesman for the agency explained. "If a business or convention goes out and gets entertainment for a night, they may spend $100,000 to $300,000." At those rates the former president would be a bargain.

Sometimes he received much more. After warming up with events around California, Reagan flew to Japan, where he spoke in favor of Sony's recent acquisition of Columbia Pictures. The deal symbolized the free market in action, and besides, Reagan said, he was "not too proud of Hollywood these days" for producing filthy dreck instead of the good, clean pictures of the golden age. Sony's influence might be healthy. When Reagan's remarks were reported in the United States, he felt obliged to take back what he had said about Hollywood. He told a crowd of industry executives at the Beverly Wilshire that the menu for him that day listed "crow soufflé followed by humble pie." He praised Hollywood's role in broadcasting American values and said, "You are truly great communicators." Yet though he took back his words, he declined to return his speaking fee of $2 million. He defended the payment as justified by what he delivered. He compared it favorably with the $3 million fee an American actor had received for being in a Toyota commercial. Anyway, he needed to regain the ground he had lost while on the government payroll. "I just thought that, for sixteen years, I hadn't made any kind of money," he said.

Another big payday came when he signed a contract with Simon & Schuster to write a memoir. His guarantee against royalties for the memoir and a second, unspecified book was $5 million. The publisher wasn't bothered that Reagan had already written a memoir, published to promote his first campaign for governor. Though the new volume would cover the same ground (sometimes in nearly the same language, as it turned out) for his pre-political years, the publisher guessed that it was his tenure as president of the United States rather than of the Screen Actors Guild that would drive sales. Many conservatives and Republicans would buy the book as a way of voting for their hero one more time; whether they read it was beside the point.

Nancy didn't miss out. The same speakers' bureau that booked Reagan listed her at $30,000 per lecture. And Random House paid her $2 million to get back at Don Regan and her other critics in a memoir of her own.

THE REAGANS' SPEAKING bureau also handled bookings for Oliver North, whose popularity among conservatives rose even while he faced criminal charges of lying to Congress and obstructing justice in the Iran-contra affair. One of Reagan's last chores as president had been to decide whether or not to pardon North. He was tempted, and pressured, to do so. "Rev. Falwell has sent a petition with 2 million signatures demanding a pardon for Ollie," Reagan wrote. George Shultz had far less sympathy for North than Reagan did, but he nonetheless urged the president to pardon North lest a trial reveal secrets of national security. "It was a hell of a presentation and I've ordered that we pursue this further," Reagan recorded.

In the end he decided against a pardon. Elements of the media and the public were still debating Reagan's complicity in the Iran-contra affair; to pardon North preemptively might appear part of a cover-up. Reagan remembered how Gerald Ford's preemptive pardon of Richard Nixon had so weakened Ford as to make him vulnerable to challenge from within his own party, by Reagan himself. Reagan wasn't running for reelection, but he had his reputation to consider. Richard Thornburgh had replaced Ed Meese as attorney general after Meese was splashed with mud in a scandal involving defense contracts. Thornburgh argued that justice should be allowed to run its course in the North case. "I'm afraid he's right," Reagan concluded glumly.

What he didn't realize was how the case was going to follow him. As he packed for California, he was subpoenaed to testify. The subpoena put him in a difficult spot. On one hand, presidents and former presidents, citing executive privilege and the separation of powers, had rarely testified in cases relating to their presidential duties, and Reagan didn't want to establish a precedent that might weaken the office. On the other hand, his refusal to pardon North was premised on the belief that justice must be served, but refusing to testify could hinder the serving. North's defense rested on his assertion that in orchestrating the arms sales to Iran and the diversion of the proceeds to the contras, he had the approval of the president. It was crucial to their case, his lawyers said, to ask Reagan if this was true.

Reagan disagreed. Or at any rate he refused to testify. "I made up my mind I wasn't going," he explained in an interview. "I think it would have set a precedent that a president doesn't have a right to impose on other presidents."

The judge in the case, Gerhard Gesell, chose not to challenge Reagan. "The trial record presently contains no proof that defendant North ever received any authorization from President Reagan to engage in the illegal conduct alleged, either directly or indirectly, orally or in writing," Gesell wrote. This was good enough for him. The former president did not have to take the witness stand.

Reagan nonetheless became a centerpiece of the courtroom arguments. "What's the difference between what Oliver North did and what the president did?" demanded Brendan Sullivan, North's lead counsel. Nothing material, Sullivan said. Yet the legal system was treating the two quite differently. "The president is happily retired in California. Oliver North has spent the last two and a half years in Washington fighting for his reputation." Recalling Reagan's praise of North as a national hero, Sullivan declared, "Oliver North doesn't want to be a hero. He just wants to go home."

The jury wasn't moved. North was convicted of shredding and falsifying documents and of obstructing a congressional investigation. He vowed to appeal and promised, "We will be fully vindicated."

Reagan continued to keep mum. "Because of the likelihood of further legal proceedings, it would not be appropriate for President Reagan to comment," his spokesman told reporters.

THE NORTH CONVICTION, after the judge's ruling that Reagan need not testify, prompted the lawyers for John Poindexter to redouble their efforts to ensure that the former president *did* testify in their client's trial. They battled long and hard and eventually secured a partial victory. The judge in the Poindexter case, Harold Greene, ruled that Reagan did have to testify but could do so in California rather than in Washington, where the trial was being conducted. The testimony would be videotaped and played for the Washington jury.

Judge Greene closed the Los Angeles courtroom to the media but allowed the defense and prosecution to field their full teams. Poindexter sat with his counsel. The CIA and other federal intelligence agencies sent experts to warn the questioners and the president if they were treading on ground that might compromise continuing operations. Reagan received 154 questions from Poindexter's lawyers in advance to prepare for the deposition.

Reagan's testimony did nothing good for Poindexter and nothing good for Reagan's reputation. In eight hours in the witness box over two days, he pleaded ignorance nearly one hundred times, saying he had never known of the events in question or now didn't recall them. He was unable to describe various meetings and conversations in which he had taken part. He could not identify individuals he had worked with, including General John Vessey, his chairman of the Joint Chiefs of Staff for three years. The gist of the Tower Commission report was lost to him.

The defense had hoped to demonstrate that Poindexter's actions had had Reagan's approval, but his foggy testimony failed them, and Poindexter was convicted on multiple counts. (The convictions were later overturned on technical grounds.) Yet Reagan's performance left observers—including the public, after Judge Greene allowed the tapes to be released—wondering about Reagan. Had he been this out of touch while president? Or had he simply aged rapidly in the year since he relinquished the presidency?

On the tapes he looked every one of his seventy-nine years. The old tics were there: the faux-sheepish grin, the duck and nod of the head, the breathy radio voice. But the vibrancy Americans had come to expect of Reagan was missing. His face seemed slack and pasty; his eyes sometimes stared blankly; he tired quickly. He had never been as good in news conferences as in set speeches, or as good as he flattered himself to think he was. Sharp questioning penetrated the thinness of his knowledge base. Yet he had been light on his feet and usually able to dodge the heavy blows. No heavy blows landed this time, but only because his questioners didn't want to make him look any worse than he made himself look. The jury might punish the side that beat up on a confused old man.

The silver lining for Reagan was that his floundering diminished the possibility that he himself might be charged with criminal wrongdoing. Special counsel Lawrence Walsh was moving up the chain of command; after winning indictments against North, Poindexter, and McFarlane, he was said to be investigating Caspar Weinberger and George Shultz. The obvious final target was Reagan. But Reagan's hapless performance in the Poindexter case suggested that any trial of the former president could be a public relations disaster for the entire investigation.

NANCY REAGAN DATED her husband's decline to an incident that occurred just six months after they left the White House. The Reagans were visiting William Wilson and his wife at their ranch in northern Mexico. The two couples were old friends, and Wilson had served as Reagan's ambassador to the Vatican. Reagan loved to ride horseback as much as ever, and he set out with a small party across the rugged terrain of the ranch. He was an able rider, especially on his own horses, but the horse he rode this day turned skittish. It bucked a few times, causing two Secret Service agents to close in and try to calm it. Yet the horse would not be soothed, and it finally pitched Reagan out of the saddle and onto the rocky ground.

He got up and dusted himself off, seeming not much the worse for the tumble. But Nancy insisted that he be flown to a hospital in Tucson for a thorough checkup. Various scans indicated no fractures, and he and Nancy left the hospital to travel to their own ranch, where they celebrated her birthday.

Further tests, however, revealed a blood clot, a subdural hematoma, in Reagan's skull, presumably the result of hitting his head in his fall. Doctors in Los Angeles monitored the condition during the next several weeks and chose not to operate. Reagan appeared to be recovering satisfactorily.

But when he and Nancy traveled to Minnesota in September for their annual physical exams at the Mayo Clinic, his doctors detected a new clot. They recommended surgery, and Reagan consented. The procedure involved drilling a hole in the skull and inserting a tube to drain the gathered fluid. The surgery went smoothly, and Reagan was released from the hospital after several days. His sense of humor survived intact; observing his shaved head, he commented to the attending staff, "I guess my barber can have the week off."

Nancy, as always, took her husband's health problems more seriously than he did. "I was in shock," she recalled of the events surrounding the surgery. "It shows up in the picture that appeared in the press at the time: Ronnie leaving the hospital, taking his hat off to salute the crowd, and me dashing forward trying to cover his partially shaven head with my hand. He didn't care that he had no hair on one side—but I did!"

She went on to say, "I've always had the feeling that the severe blow to his head in 1989 hastened the onset of Ronnie's Alzheimer's. The doctors think so, too."

YET HIS CONDITION often seemed no more than simple aging. Reagan's memoir *An American Life* was published in the autumn of 1990, and he went on the talk shows promoting it. His publicists booked him with interviewers certain to be friendly, and indeed Barbara Walters, Charles Gibson, and William F. Buckley couldn't have been kinder. They pitched him softballs, and when he failed to make contact, they hit the pitches for him. "Mr. Reagan is treated like a well-loved uncle who needs a little help these days in keeping the conversation going," television critic Walter Goodman wrote in the *New York Times*. Reagan looked fit, Goodman said, and his smile still charmed. "Words, however, do not always come easily or always in the right order; when dealing with his time in the White House he often reaches into past scripts for some phrase that has done proven service. The phrases he finds are not always directly on the mark, but no one calls him to task."

The book was a commercial success for Simon & Schuster and a personal triumph for Reagan. It topped best-seller lists and showed how much Reagan's fans still loved their hero. Yet the triumph was bittersweet, in that the interviews revealed that the author was no longer the man his book described.

THE BOOK AUGMENTED Reagan's emerging historical reputation at a moment when the Cold War was coming to an irreversible end. The reform tides Gorbachev had set in motion in the Soviet Union rolled across Eastern Europe in the year after Reagan left office. The Berlin Wall came down metaphorically in November 1989 and concretely in the following months. In the autumn of 1990, just as Reagan's book was hitting the bookstores, West Germany absorbed East Germany into a single federal republic, erasing the border that had long formed the front line of the superpower confrontation. Meanwhile, the communist regimes in the other countries of the Soviet satellite belt crumbled before popular uprisings.

Reagan kept in touch with Gorbachev as the anticommunist revolution unfolded. On a state visit to America in June 1990, Gorbachev invited Reagan to breakfast in San Francisco. Gorbachev liked Reagan better now that they no longer had to spar over strategic defense; he also understood that the former president had continuing pull in American politics and might be helpful to Gorbachev's agenda. The San Francisco meeting went well, and Gorbachev invited Reagan and Nancy to visit Russia in the autumn.

Reagan emerged from the California meeting more taken by Gorbachev than ever. He shortly published an opinion piece in the *New York Times* under the headline "I'm Convinced That Gorbachev Wants a Free-Market Democracy." Reagan recounted his own role in the changes that were taking place in Eastern Europe. "Three years ago today I stood in front of the Berlin Wall and urged Mikhail Gorbachev to tear it down," he wrote. "This was not a spur-of-the-moment idea. Rather, it reflected my belief that both my relationship with Mr. Gorbachev and the effects of his policy of glasnost at home had reached a point where I could publicly call for this act of East-West reconciliation." Reagan noted that Gorbachev had not responded positively at once, but he gave the Soviet leader credit for making the ultimate outcome possible. "Glasnost had let the free speech genie out of the bottle in the Soviet Union; Mr. Gorbachev's call for perestroika, or reform, held the promise of better times for his citizens." Reagan told of his recent meeting with Gorbachev. "He was every bit as warm, earnest and optimistic about his country's future potential as I remembered him from our previous meetings." Yet he faced daunting challenges: rampant nationalism in the Soviet republics, consumer complaints over lack of goods in the stores, political opposition led by Russian leader Boris Yeltsin. Reagan thought Gorbachev deserved America's support. Glasnost and perestroika had started Russia on the right path, but greater change was coming, and it behooved the United States to support

Gorbachev during the transition. There was no limit to what the positive results might be, in Russia and elsewhere. "Like the chips of the Berlin Wall that are being sold everywhere these days, democracy seems to be sweeping the world."

REAGAN AND NANCY accepted Gorbachev's invitation to Russia, and they expanded the trip into an eleven-day tour of Europe. They touched down in Germany, where Reagan was invited to have a whack at the Berlin Wall. "Darned hard," he remarked after several unproductive blows with hammer and chisel. A German onlooker responded, "German quality work." They entered East Berlin through the Brandenburg Gate and were greeted by the president of the East German parliament, who said, "Mr. President, we have much to thank you for." Reagan replied, "Berlin is going to be Berlin once again."

From Germany they traveled to Poland, where the Polish government newspaper hailed Reagan as the "real father of perestroika" and dubbed his European tour the "symbolic harvest" of his support of freedom as president. Reagan met Lech Wałesa, still the leader of the now-divided Solidarity movement. Reagan urged the opposing factions to keep their differences within bounds. "To protect the liberty you have won, you will need a full measure of the tolerance and openness that are Poland's tradition," he said.

The good feelings followed them to Moscow, where Gorbachev embraced his erstwhile partner in diplomacy and praised him as a statesman of true vision. "I'm sure you must have sensed by now during your stay here in this country that we, and people in Soviet society, hold you in tremendous respect and esteem," Gorbachev said.

Reagan returned the compliment by praising Gorbachev to the Supreme Soviet. As in Poland he cautioned against demands of too much too soon. "These are yeasty times, times of ferment," he said. "Freedom can bring out passions between groups of people that may boil over. When they do, cool and calm decisions are called for by leaders, so as to lower temperatures all around." Reagan cited the anguish of America's Civil War and said he hoped the Soviet peoples would spare themselves anything similar. "Reason must prevail over passion if there is to be a climate conducive to the settlement of disagreements." He observed that the United States and the Soviet Union had long eyed each other with distrust, but things had changed between them. Cooperation was evident in joint efforts to settle a crisis in the Persian Gulf, where Iraq had recently invaded and occupied Kuwait. Reagan was pleased that the superpowers were on the same side of this issue, and he hoped their cooperation could be a model for responses to other crises. "Together, our great size can be used in the service of all humankind to persuade those whose passions have reached the danger point to cool down again."

REAGAN TURNED EIGHTY in February 1991. Merv Griffin hosted a black-tie dinner party at the Beverly Hilton that doubled as a fund-raiser for the Reagan Library foundation. Nearly a thousand guests drawn from Reagan's two worlds, Hollywood and Washington, paid as much as $2,500 apiece to honor the former president. Charlton Heston, Elizabeth Taylor, and Jimmy Stewart mingled with George Shultz, Caspar Weinberger, and Paul Laxalt. Margaret Thatcher traveled from London, where she had resigned as prime minister the previous November following a revolt within her Conservative Party. She offered a toast: "Twenty-five years ago, in a famous speech, you quoted President Franklin Roosevelt, who said we all have a rendezvous with destiny. Certainly you had such a rendezvous. Thank God you were on time." Dan Quayle represented George Bush, who was busy directing a war in the Persian Gulf, where the crisis had not been resolved peacefully. Bush nonetheless sent videotaped congratulations. "They'll get you on Mt. Rushmore yet," he predicted. Lech Wałesa, similarly speaking via video, expressed gratitude for what Reagan had done for Poland. The San Diego Marine Corps Band supplied music.

Reagan thanked the guests for coming. He blew out the eight candles on his four-decker cake and accidentally smeared frosting on his tuxedo. He shared his birthday wish with the group: "That God will watch over each and every one of our men and women who are bravely serving in the Persian Gulf, and their families, wherever they may be. And may they know that we as a nation stand firmly behind them." He closed the evening by holding hands with Nancy and leading the group in singing "God Bless America."

THE DINNER RAISED $2 million for the Reagan Library, which opened to the public six months later. Many of the same group reconvened at Simi Valley for the dedication. They were joined by an additional two thousand people, mostly Republicans, and several hundred members of the media. All of America's living presidents were there: Nixon, Ford, Carter, and Bush, along with Reagan. The Republican presidents praised Reagan unstintingly. "He believed that America was on the right side of history, standing with the forces of good against the forces of evil in the world," Nixon observed. "And some have dismissed him, therefore, as an ideologue. But Ronald Reagan has been justified by what has happened." Ford lauded Reagan as "a national leader who was able to articulate the highest hopes and deepest beliefs of the American people." Bush called him "a political prophet leading the tide toward conservatism." Carter, the outlying Democrat, couldn't resist noting that poverty and unequal opportunity survived the Reagan years, but then he too joined the celebration, praising his successor as one under whom "our nation stood strong and resolute and made possible the beginning of the end of the Cold War."

Reagan accepted the plaudits and added his own. "Within the course of only a few short years I have seen the world turned upside down and conventional wisdom utterly disproved," he said. "Visitors to this mountaintop will see a great jagged chunk of the Berlin Wall, hated symbol of, yes, an evil empire, that spied on and lied to its citizens, denying them their freedom, their bread, even their faith. Well, today that wall exists only in museums, souvenir collections and the memories of a people no longer oppressed. It is also a reminder that a strong America is always desirable—and necessary in our world."

NOT THREE YEARS out of office, Reagan had ascended to the realm of Republican legend. The party faithful loved him for the policies he had pursued in office, but they loved him even more for the vision he had conveyed of America's inherent greatness. He made Americans feel good about themselves, and Republicans feel best of all.

Yet a few issues raised doubts, even among conservatives. On the tenth anniversary of his shooting, Reagan endorsed a handgun regulation bill named for James Brady, who had never recovered from the brain damage he incurred that day. The Brady bill would require a seven-day waiting period for the purchase of handguns, during which time state and local authorities could check the criminal and mental backgrounds of prospective purchasers. Reagan had previously supported waiting periods but only in the context of state laws. His support for the federal bill marked a significant concession to the big government he had long decried.

He explained his change of heart in an opinion piece in the *New York Times*. He recounted his own near brush with death at John Hinckley's hand, and he described the permanent injury to Brady, as well as the wounds to police officer Thomas Delahanty and Secret Service agent Tim McCarthy. "Four lives were changed forever, and all by a Saturday-night special—a cheaply made .22 caliber pistol—purchased in a Dallas pawnshop by a young man with a history of mental disturbance," Reagan wrote. "This nightmare might never have happened if legislation that is before Congress now—the Brady bill—had been law back in 1981." He acknowledged the argument for leaving gun control to the states as one he had often made himself. But the state-by-state approach wasn't working. "Criminals just go to nearby states that lack such laws to buy their weapons." The current system had to change. "Every year, an average of 9,200 are murdered by handguns," he wrote. "This level of violence must be stopped." He recognized that no law could prevent all mayhem, but the country had to start somewhere. "If the passage of the Brady bill were to result in a reduction of only 10 or 15 percent of those numbers (and it could be a good deal greater), it would be well worth making it the law of the land. And there would be a lot fewer families facing anniversaries such as the Bradys, Delahantys, McCarthys and Reagans face every March 30."

Opponents of gun control reacted sharply. "I felt somebody had stabbed me in the back," the former head of Sportsmen for Reagan, a campaign group from 1980 and 1984, said. The director of the Citizens Committee for the Right to Keep and Bear Arms shook his head and declared, "This action on his part leads one to the conclusion that, well, he's just another politician, after all." The director added, hopefully and in topic-appropriate terms, "He's no longer a kinetic force in American politics." A spokesman for the Oregon State Shooting Association announced that Reagan's turnabout made him suspect the former president's entire party. "Every time I look at a Republican," he said, "I'm going to wonder if he is telling me what he believes, or is he telling me what I want to hear to get my vote."

THE BRADY BILL passed, but not for another two years, suggesting that Reagan, indeed, was not the kinetic force he had been. On other issues, too, his influence waned. Though George Bush had campaigned as a Reagan conservative, he governed as a throwback to the era when Republicans took balanced budgets seriously. Not long after Reagan left office, the heady economic growth of his final six years slowed and then reversed, carrying the country into recession. As recessions do, this one cut into government revenues, causing the sobering deficits of the Reagan years to become alarming. Investors feared for the economy's future and their own. And the Gramm-Rudman-Hollings Act, passed during Reagan's tenure, mandated automatic and painful spending cuts if Congress and the president didn't come to terms.

Bush preferred spending cuts to tax increases, but the easy trimming had been accomplished in the Reagan years, and the Democrats, who still controlled both houses of Congress, insisted on tax increases to accompany any spending cuts. After much anguish and doubtless unspoken laments that he had permitted himself his Dirty Harry moment, Bush agreed to a deal with the Democrats that combined spending cuts with tax increases.

It was a bold decision. It enraged the Republican right. "Read My Lips: I Lied," screamed the *New York Post*. The libertarian Cato Institute called Bush's reversal the "Crime of the Century." But the bargain bore fruit when its terms took hold, shrinking the deficit and helping fuel the rapid economic growth of the 1990s, which, together with additional tax increases under Bill Clinton, diminished the deficit further. By the end of the decade, the federal budget showed a surplus for the first time since the 1960s.

Yet Bush's retreat on taxes confirmed the belief of Reagan conservatives that he had never been one of them. The Reaganites remembered Bush's branding of Reagan's policies as "voodoo economics," and the conservatives who didn't abandon Bush at once made clear that they might do so any day.

Amid the complaining at Bush's apostasy, few conservatives noticed that his compromise on the budget followed the practice, if not the rhetoric, of his predecessor. Reagan had consistently advocated lower taxes, and in the aggregate he had achieved lower taxes. But he had tolerated modest increases in taxes when they were necessary to secure the best available bargain with Congress. Reagan was a conservative, but he was also a pragmatist. He took what he could get, never holding practical results hostage to ideological purity. James Baker heard Reagan say as much many times. "If Reagan told me once, he told me fifteen thousand times," Baker recalled: "'I'd rather get 80 percent of what I want than go over the cliff with my flags flying.'"

ON ANOTHER SUBJECT as well, Bush followed Reagan's example. In July 1991, Bush and Gorbachev signed the Strategic Arms Reduction Treaty. The START pact mandated deep cuts in strategic forces like those Reagan and Gorbachev had begun discussing in Geneva and nearly agreed to in Reykjavík. Gorbachev dropped the last of his insistence on linking START to restrictions on SDI, which had progressed more slowly than Reagan and its enthusiasts had hoped. The START process did not eliminate nuclear weapons, as Reagan had dreamed, but it marked a major step toward dispelling the nuclear specter that had haunted the world for much of his lifetime.

AFTER BUSH WON renomination in 1992, despite the complaints of conservatives, Reagan was happy to address the Republican convention on his successor's behalf. He looked remarkably hale for a man of eighty-one, and if his movements and gestures lacked some of the sureness and vigor of earlier times, his delivery was still polished and his voice strong. His speech, like so many of his speeches over the years, was a paean to American exceptionalism. He had never had better occasion to trumpet America's virtues. The last stage in the unraveling of the Soviet empire was the disintegration of the Soviet Union itself; at the end of 1991 the Soviet government voted itself out of business and ceded power to the republics that had formed the union. America's Cold War foe of nearly half a century was no more. And the communist ideology that had tested democratic capitalism had finally and conclusively failed its own test.

Reagan didn't gloat. But he took pride in his country and what it had achieved. America, he said, was the world's moral compass, the guardian of freedom, the beacon of opportunity. And after all America had accomplished, its best days were ahead. "The changes of the 1990s will leave America more dynamic and less in danger than at any time in my life," he predicted. Humanity expected more of America than ever. "We remain the one nation the rest of the world looks to for leadership." He urged the party and the country to remain true to America's roots. "May all of you as Americans never forget your heroic origins, never fail to seek divine guidance and never lose your natural, God-given optimism."

The delegates were transported by the sight and words of their hero. They interrupted him again and again, shouting, "Reagan! Reagan!" and "Thank you, Ron!" They waved printed banners emblazoned "Reagan Country" and hand-lettered signs reading, "We Love You, Ron."

Not all Americans loved Reagan as much as the Republicans did, but even many Democrats confessed to a modest liking. He was, after all, a likable fellow. Yet his legacy as president evoked a decided ambivalence. A poll conducted at the time of the Republican convention revealed that only 43 percent of respondents approved of the job Reagan had done in office, while 50 percent disapproved. Another poll had respondents rate Reagan's presidency; 33 percent declared it below average, 39 percent called it average, and 28 percent said it was above average.

Some of the unhappiness reflected the recent recession. Economists debated whether the downturn had its roots in the deficits of the Reagan years, but stalled growth and rising unemployment typically sour voters on the president's party, and Reagan's reputation took a hit along with Bush's.

Reagan's legacy suffered also from the continuing investigation into the Iran-contra scandal. The indefatigable Lawrence Walsh had reached the cabinet level in his probe of the Reagan administration; in June 1992 he persuaded a grand jury to indict Caspar Weinberger for perjury and related felonies. Although the chances of an indictment against Reagan himself seemed slim, the continuing attention to the great blunder of his administration cast a shadow over his time in office.

Reagan tried to ignore the investigation. He carried on the routine he had established since leaving Washington. He and Nancy split time between the ranch and a home in Bel Air. He kept an office in Century City and spent his normal working hours, ten to three, there. "This is not retirement," his spokeswoman said. She added, inadvertently contributing to her boss's reputation for not overtaxing himself, "This is as bad as the White House—worse." Traveling dignitaries—Lech Wałesa, Václav Havel of Czechoslovakia, among others—dropped by to share news of the world and enjoy the Pacific view from Reagan's thirty-fourth-floor suite.

Reagan and Nancy remained physically active. They went rafting in Wyoming and yachting among the islands of southeastern Alaska. Reagan lifted weights in a home gym, played golf with friends, and rode horse-back and cut brush at the ranch. He and Nancy kept tabs on their health with regular checkups at the Mayo Clinic. His office in August 1992 declined to release details of their latest exams, beyond saying, "Their physicians found them both to be in excellent health."

113

For Reagan, this wasn't true. A month earlier he had testified before the Walsh commission, and from the start of the questioning it was painfully obvious that his memory was disappearing. He couldn't remember some of the most basic information about who had worked for him and what they did. "You were reelected in 1984 and began your second term in January of 1985," Walsh said by way of introductory refreshment. "At that time the State Department was headed by Secretary Shultz, George Shultz. Would that be correct, sir?"

"I think so but I can't swear anymore," Reagan said. "I know there were changes that came along and so forth in there but I think that you're right."

"And Edwin Meese started as counselor to the president during your first term of office and then became attorney general during your second term of office," Walsh said. "Would that be approximately correct?"

"I take your word for it here," Reagan replied. "I don't remember the times in which those changes and things were made but that is true of Ed."

"During your second term was Bud McFarlane the national security adviser?"

"I can't tell you or remember when Bud left that job."

"Would it have been approximately December 5th, 1985?"

"I can't remember. I just know that I had him in that position for a while and I know that he did rather well."

"Could you tell us a little bit about how the work was divided between Don Regan and Bud McFarlane?"

"No I can't. I just have to tell you that all of this and every day—the whole history of this took place after we were—I was out of the governor's office and Nancy and I started talking on how little we could remember about what took place because there was always—you were in motion always and that was what led to—in the president's job, that's what led to the diaries was because we remembered that we just couldn't pin down the happenings in those eight years when I was the governor."

Walsh inquired about other staffers and their backgrounds with the former president. "Mr. Deaver—was he in the California administration with you?"

"I'm going to have to think."

"Well, don't—"

"I honestly can't swear to that. I'd hate to have him hear me say that."

"Judge Clark had been in your administration?"

"Yes."

"And then he subsequently became secretary of Interior?"

"I think that Deaver was in both areas but I can't be sure."

The Walsh investigators had subpoenaed and won access to Reagan's diaries. Walsh showed the former president transcripts of various entries to jog his memory. He asked Reagan to read one from February 26, 1985.

"NSC briefing report," Reagan read. "Assad seems to be making an effort to get four kidnap victims back from Hezbollah." Reagan seemed unfamiliar with the reference.

"You don't happen to remember this particular incident and what President Assad was trying to do? Does that come back?"

"No. And you know something, I'm trying to remember now who was Assad."

Walsh read another entry himself. "Heartbreaking photos of kidnap victims," he quoted Reagan.

"I don't recall that at all," Reagan said.

"Would you remember in June of 1985, June 14th, that there was a hijacking of a TWA flight and the whole flight was captured?"

"I don't have a memory of that."

"It may prove to have some importance to you because there was the thought that Iran had been instrumental in getting the hostages—in getting the flight released."

"I would have to be reminded of that. I'm quite sure it happened but I don't have any memory of it."

And so it went, agonizingly. Again and again Walsh tried to trigger Reagan's memories; again and again the memories wouldn't come. Walsh asked if Reagan remembered that Vice President Bush had headed a counterterrorism task force. "I had forgotten about that," Reagan replied. Walsh read from Reagan's diary about his meeting with McFarlane after his surgery in July 1985. "I have no memory of that either," Reagan said.

The interchange grew more excruciating. Walsh asked Reagan more questions he couldn't answer; Reagan shook his head in frustration. "I'm very embarrassed," he said. "I'm sorry."

Walsh tried to reassure him. "This was a long time ago," he said, though it had been only several years.

"It's like I wasn't president at all," Reagan said.

REAGAN'S DEPOSITION WASN'T released until years later, and so the public had no inkling of the extent of his mental deterioration. He continued to appear in public and to deliver prepared speeches, which he could read almost as well as ever. He commented occasionally on matters of public policy. After Bill Clinton defeated George Bush in the 1992 election, aided by the wild-card and sometimes wild-eyed candidacy of Texas billionaire Ross Perot, the Democrats moved to undo an aspect of the Reagan legacy that had long irked them. Clinton's secretary of defense, Les Aspin, announced in May 1993 the termination of the Strategic Defense Initiative. Critics of SDI pointed out that a decade after Reagan initiated the program, it had produced little of substance to show for the $30 billion it had consumed. The exotic technologies SDI proponents had promised never panned out, and the Democrats thought they never would. Surveying the changes in world politics in recent years, Aspin told a Pentagon news conference, "Today we are here to observe another point of passage, which is the end of the Star Wars era. The fate of Star Wars was sealed by the collapse of the Soviet Union." Missile defense wasn't being abandoned, Aspin said, but it was being reconceptualized. The kind of threat the Reagan program had been intended to deal with, a mass attack from the Soviet Union, had "receded to the vanishing point." The threat now was from single missiles from potential rogue states. Consequently, missile defense would be ground based, rather than space based, and would focus on intercepting single missiles rather than waves of missiles.

Reagan decried the decision. "I may not be a Rhodes Scholar, but I know this," he told graduates at the Citadel in South Carolina: "If we can protect America with a defense shield from incoming missile attacks, we should by all means do so." Reagan credited SDI with helping to win the Cold War, and he thought it had a continuing mission. "If the new administration in Washington thinks we are no longer at risk, they need to open their eyes and take a long, hard look at the world."

AT TIMES IT seemed that Lawrence Walsh's pursuit of the Iran-contra story would never end. Begun in 1987, the Walsh expedition outlasted Reagan's presidency, then George Bush's. It suffered a setback when Bush, before leaving the White House, pardoned Caspar Weinberger, who was about to come to trial, and Robert McFarlane, who had pleaded guilty to a misdemeanor charge of withholding information from Congress. Walsh had hoped the Weinberger trial would bring new evidence to light; instead, he found himself struggling to keep a decreasingly popular investigation afloat. It lasted another year, but in early 1994 Walsh published his final report on the Iran-contra affair.

The report exonerated Reagan of criminal wrongdoing but blamed him for allowing the misconduct of others. "It was concluded that President Reagan's conduct fell well short of criminality which could be successfully prosecuted," the Walsh report declared. "Fundamentally, it could not be proved beyond a reasonable doubt that President Reagan knew of the underlying facts of Iran/contra that were criminal or that he made criminal misrepresentations regarding them." Yet he had much to answer for, the report said. "President Reagan created the conditions which made possible the crimes committed by others by his secret deviations from announced national policy as to Iran and hostages and by his open determination to keep the contras together 'body and soul' despite a statutory ban on contra aid. In the Iran initiative, President Reagan chose to proceed in the utmost secrecy, disregarding the Administration's public policy prohibiting arms sales to nations supporting terrorism. He also chose to forgo congressional notification under the National Security Act and the Arms Export Control Act. Having bypassed accountability to Congress, the President failed either to establish an effective system of accountability within the Administration or to monitor the series of activities he authorized."

On the diversion of funds from Iran to the contras, the report said, "No direct evidence was developed that the President authorized or was informed of the profiteering on the Iran arms sales or of the diversion of proceeds to aid the contras. Yet it was doubtful that President Reagan would tolerate the successive Iranian affronts during 1986"—the reneging on agreements to release hostages—"unless he knew that the arms sales continued to supply funds to the contras to bridge the gap before the anticipated congressional appropriations became effective."

Reagan and his supporters pronounced the Walsh verdict the worst form of prosecutorial misrepresentation. In a written statement Reagan characterized the report as an "encyclopedia of old information, unwarranted conclusions and irresponsible speculation." Reagan's statement went on to say that Walsh's report was a "self-administered pat on the back and a vehicle for baseless allegations that he could never have proven in court." Reagan's lawyer, Theodore Olson, branded the Walsh report a "fantasy" and a "purely speculative theory based upon misinterpretations of several key facts." Walsh's allegations about President Reagan were, Olson said, "refuted by overwhelming evidence."

FOR REAGAN, THIS might have been the last of the long, regrettable story if Oliver North hadn't chosen to run for the Senate. North's conviction had been overturned on appeal when the appellate court determined that evidence in his trial might have been tainted by his testimony to Congress, for which he had been granted immunity. North took the appeals court judgment as exoneration and launched a political career based in part on Reagan's characterization of him as a national hero. But he drew Reagan's ire when he began portraying himself as the Iran-contra scapegoat and asserted that Reagan had ordered him to lie to Congress about the contra diversion.

Reagan initially refused to respond. He had no wish to give the Iran-contra story further legs. Moreover, he reasoned that criticizing North might be interpreted as intervening on behalf of North's Republican opponent in the Senate primary in Virginia. But Paul Laxalt told Reagan he owed it to the country and to himself to set the record straight. Reagan agreed and gave Laxalt a letter intended for publication. The former president reiterated that he didn't like stepping between Republican candidates. "But I do have to admit that I am getting pretty steamed about the statements coming from Oliver North," he wrote. "I never instructed him or anyone in my administration to mislead Congress on Iran-contra matters or anything else. And I certainly didn't know anything about the Iran-contra diversion. In fact, as you know, the minute we found out about it, we told the American people about it and called for investigations. And the private meetings he said he had with me just didn't happen."

THE FIRMNESS OF Reagan's tone impressed many readers and caused North to claim he hadn't said or meant what had been reported. What neither North—who won the Republican nomination but lost in the general election after Nancy Reagan declared, "He lied to my husband, and he lied about my husband"—nor the great majority of Americans knew was that Reagan's statement was unsupported by anything he himself could still recall. His memory of the events he spoke so confidently about in his letter to Laxalt was gone.

Americans learned soon enough. Nancy had noticed continuing changes in her husband's mental abilities but had hesitated to speak to anyone about them. "One small leak to the press, and the media would begin homing in on the ex-president, testing him at every turn," Michael Deaver said, characterizing her feelings and his own. Yet she couldn't shield him forever. Others began to notice. Phil Gramm later recalled approaching the former president at a public event. Reagan looked at him with a slightly puzzled expression. "I don't remember your name," he said. "But I remember what you did." Gramm assured him that was plenty. At his eighty-third birthday party in February 1994, Reagan stumbled badly over his lines in front of a large and friendly Washington crowd. They tried to ignore the slips and explain them away, but obviously something was wrong.

Even so, Nancy waited until their regular checkups in August to investigate thoroughly. John Hutton, still Reagan's primary physician, notified the Mayo doctors of his memory lapses, and they added several neurological assays to the standard protocol. Their conclusion was that Reagan was in the early stage of Alzheimer's disease.

The diagnosis was a shock, though not a great surprise. Deciding how to deal with it, personally and publicly, required some time. Reagan chose to inform the American people himself. "My Fellow Americans," he wrote in a letter released on November 5. "I have recently been told that I am one of the millions of Americans who will be afflicted with Alzheimer's Disease." He explained that he and Nancy had decided to share this diagnosis with the public so that others might benefit through greater awareness of the disease and deeper understanding of what it entailed. "At the moment I feel just fine," he continued. "I intend to live the remainder of the years God gives me on this earth doing the things I have always done. I will continue to share life's journey with my beloved Nancy and my family. I plan to enjoy the great outdoors and stay in touch with my friends and supporters." He recognized that the burden of Alzheimer's often weighed heavily on the families of patients. "I only wish there was some way I could spare Nancy from this painful experience. When the time comes I am confident that with your help she will face it with faith and courage."

Reagan had delivered several valedictories by now. But this one carried a moving definitiveness. "In closing let me thank you, the American people, for giving me the great honor of allowing me to serve as your President. When the Lord calls me home, whenever that may be, I will leave with the greatest love for this country of ours and eternal optimism for its future."

Readers of this letter, many with tears in their eyes, could imagine Reagan's characteristic grin and sideways duck of the head as he bade them farewell: "I now begin the journey that will lead me into the sunset of my life."

O N THAT DAY Reagan passed from politics into history. His
public appearances became fewer and more fleeting, as Nancy
understandably sought to protect him from embarrassment and
discomfort. He visited the Reagan Library to see the Christmas exhibit.
He rang in the new year with old friends at Walter Annenberg's estate in
Rancho Mirage. At his office in Century City he occasionally posed for
photographs with newlyweds or visiting schoolchildren.

But as the last of his memory faded, his world grew ever smaller.
Travel outside California ceased. Trips to the ranch, long his source of
greatest joy, now caused him distress. He didn't know why he was taken
there or what he was supposed to do. Nancy put an end to them and in
1996 listed the ranch for sale.

He ceased to recognize even his oldest friends. Mike Deaver recalled
his last visit to Reagan, in 1997. "He looked great when I opened the
door and stepped in—a blue suit, flawless French cuffs, just the right tie,"
Deaver wrote. "But it didn't take long to realize that Ronald Reagan had
no idea who I was or any interest in why I had walked into his office. A
book was in his hands; his attention to it was total. Finally, I slipped over
to his side to see what it was. He was reading a picture book about Traveler, Robert E. Lee's famous horse. I was heartbroken."

Though Reagan forgot the world, the world didn't forget him. The
1996 Republican national convention nominated Bob Dole to oppose Bill
Clinton, but the delegates found greatest joy in feting Ronald Reagan.
A special video, featuring testimonials by Henry Kissinger, Billy Gra-
ham, auto industry executive Lee Iacocca, and others, paid tribute to Reagan's life and accomplishments. The beaming images of Reagan in his

prime, combined with the knowledge of his current affliction, left the delegates in tears. The lights went up after the video to reveal Nancy standing before the convention; her appearance elicited further tears and additional applause. She spoke briefly, thanking them for their support for her husband and herself in their difficult time. She quoted his remarks to the previous convention, when he had told the delegates never to lose America's natural optimism. And she closed, "Ronnie's optimism, like America's, still shines very brightly. May God bless him, and from both of us: God bless America." The delegates melted once more.

The country as a whole honored him. Congress voted unanimously to name a large new federal office building on Pennsylvania Avenue for the former president, prompting some to wonder whether Reagan, the avowed foe of government growth, would have approved. His name was prefixed to Washington's National Airport, again raising eyebrows, this time especially among the air controllers he had fired. More obviously fitting was the christening of a new aircraft carrier, the symbol of American military power, as the USS *Ronald Reagan*.

The nation learned in early 2001 that he had fallen at home and broken his hip. Many familiar with the complications that often follow such falls expected to read his obituary shortly. But he was discharged from the hospital in time to celebrate his ninetieth birthday in February. Later that year he passed John Adams to become the longest-lived president in American history.

He held on for three more years. He died on June 5, 2004, at the Bel Air house, at the age of ninety-three.

In DEATH HE retraced his journey from California to Washington and back. First services were held at the Reagan Library in Simi Valley. Nancy was joined by Michael Reagan, Ron Reagan, and Patti Davis. Maureen Reagan had died of cancer three years earlier. The retired pastor of the Reagans' church, Bel Air Presbyterian, gave the eulogy.

Reagan's casket lay in the library for that afternoon and the next day as thousands of visitors—many famous, most not—paid their respects. The casket was flown to Washington, where the ritual was repeated in the Capitol Rotunda.

The public funeral service took place in the National Cathedral. Four thousand mourners filled the pews; millions watched the live coverage on television. Former presidents Ford, Carter, Bush, and Clinton attended.

Margaret Thatcher, Mikhail Gorbachev, and Lech Wałesa arrived from abroad. Tony Blair, Thatcher's successor, represented the British government. Secretary-General Kofi Annan brought condolences from the United Nations.

President George W. Bush delivered the principal eulogy. "Ronald Reagan believed in the power of truth in the conduct of world affairs," Bush said. "When he saw evil camped across the horizon, he called that evil by its name. There were no doubters in the prisons and gulags where dissidents spread the news, tapping to each other what the American president had dared to say. There were no doubters in the shipyards and churches and secret labor meetings where brave men and women began to hear the creaking and rumbling of a collapsing empire. And there were no doubters among those who swung hammers at the hated wall that the first and hardest blow had been struck by President Ronald Reagan."

At the end of the service Nancy and the children accompanied the casket to Andrews Air Force Base for the return west. Back in California they laid her husband and their father to rest on the hilltop beside his library. "He is home now; he is free," Ron Reagan said. Patti Davis spoke of her father's final affirmation of love for her mother. "When he opened his eyes, eyes that had not opened for many, many days, and looked at my mother," she said, "he showed us that neither disease nor death can conquer love."

"IN HIS LAST years he saw through a glass darkly; now he sees his savior face to face," George Bush had said at the Washington service. "And we look for that fine day when we will see him again, all weariness gone, clear of mind, strong and sure and smiling again, and the sorrow of this parting gone forever."

Bush was speaking of the hereafter, but an approximation arrived in 2011, on what would have been Reagan's hundredth birthday—or, by the reckoning he liked to employ, the sixty-first anniversary of his thirty-ninth birthday. The tears had dried; the darkness of his last decade had lifted; the time that had passed since his departure from office allowed a clearer view of what his life and his presidency meant.

The celebrations were less restrained than at the moment of his passing. Reagan had become sufficiently iconic that civic and corporate groups could safely attach themselves to his memory without fear of alienating clients or customers. The Tournament of Roses included a Reaganthemed float in its annual parade in Pasadena. The National Football League hailed the Gipper in a video aired just before kickoff at the Super Bowl. A similar tribute played before the Daytona 500 car race. The Professional Golfers' Association tipped its cap to Reagan. The U.S. Postal Service issued a Reagan stamp. A measure was introduced in Congress to put Reagan's image on the $50 bill. Initiatives were launched to name something for Reagan in every county in the country.

In a more analytical vein were the symposia and conferences that weighed his achievements and measured his contribution to the landmark events of his time. None of the participants could deny that America and the world had changed dramatically during the Reagan era. The nation's politics took a sharp turn to the right; after a half century of liberalism, Americans rediscovered the virtues of conservatism. The international order was transformed by the collapse of Soviet communism; the end of the Cold War completed what American presidents had been attempting since 1945.

From the vantage of the Reagan centennial, with the twentieth century receding into the past, it wasn't unreasonable to measure Reagan against his political hero, Franklin Roosevelt. And by that measure, he fared quite well. What Roosevelt had been to the first half of the twentieth century, Reagan was to the second half. Roosevelt entered office amid a crisis of the private sector, when the conservative status quo had lost legitimacy. Roosevelt tipped the balance to the left, launching the age of liberalism in American politics. In foreign affairs he asserted America's world leadership and defeated the first of the century's two modes of totalitarianism, fascism. Reagan entered office amid a crisis of the public sector, when the liberal status quo was floundering. Reagan tipped the balance back to the right, reviving conservatism as the more credible force in American politics. In foreign affairs he confirmed America's world leadership and set the century's second form of totalitarianism, communism, on the path to extinction.

An additional parallel appeared in the fact that while the magnitude of the accomplishments of the two presidents was impossible to deny, the meaning of those accomplishments continued to provoke vigorous debate. The New Deal was the salvation of democracy, in the minds of Roosevelt's liberal supporters, and the onset of socialism, to his conservative critics. The Reagan revolution was the restoration of freedom, in the view of Reagan's conservative admirers, and the abandonment of the weak and vulnerable, to his liberal opponents.

In certain respects, Reagan's accomplishment was greater than Roosevelt's. During the formative stages of the New Deal, Roosevelt enjoyed rubber-stamp majorities in Congress. After Pearl Harbor, Roosevelt as commander in chief met almost no resistance as he redesigned American foreign policy. Reagan, by contrast, had to struggle with a Democratic House during his entire presidency and with a Democratic Senate during his last two years. Nothing in international affairs gave him anything like the carte blanche in foreign policy enjoyed by Roosevelt.

The key to Reagan's success, like that to Roosevelt's, was his ability to restore Americans' faith in their country. Reagan was called the "great communicator" with reason. He was the most persuasive political speaker since Roosevelt, combining conviction, focus, and humor in a manner none of his contemporaries could approach. Reagan's critics often dismissed the role of conviction in his persuasiveness; they attributed his speaking skill to his training as an actor. But this was exactly wrong. Reagan wasn't acting when he spoke; his rhetorical power rested on his wholehearted belief in all the wonderful things he said about the United States and the American people, about their brave past and their brilliant future. He believed what Americans have always wanted to believe about their country, and he made them believe it too.

It helped that his beliefs relentlessly flattered the American people. Reagan blamed the country's problems not on the people but on their government, as though the government—in a democracy, of all systems— existed apart from the people. His message was an easy sell. He asked next to nothing of the people, neither the soaring sacrifice of John Kennedy's inaugural nor the quotidian adjustments sought by Carter. He promised Americans the gift of tax cuts, which he delivered without insisting on conservatism's traditional precondition, spending cuts.

Reagan's focus was no less important than his conviction. Focus is often the inverse of expertise, and Reagan understood that at the highest levels focus is far more important. He refused to clutter his mind with details that might distract from his major goals. From the start of his political career to the finish, his major goals were always the same: to shrink government at home and defeat communism abroad. Everything else was secondary. Reagan communicated effectively not least because he gave essentially the same speech again and again. The particulars and the anecdotes varied, but the message never did.

Yet the anecdotes were crucial. Reagan told stories and jokes better than any president since Lincoln. He understood the disarming power of humor: that getting an audience to laugh with you is halfway to getting them to agree with you. He was not a warm person, but he seemed to be, which in politics is more important. Many people loathed his policies, but almost no one disliked *him*. Democratic elections are, at their most basic level, popularity contests, and Reagan knew how to be popular.

Also vital to Reagan's success was his ability to get other people to do his dirty work for him. He was accounted a terrible manager, unwilling to fire people, unable to keep track of what was being done in his name. If he had been the chief executive of a large corporation, these would have been damning failures. But in a president they can be essential to success. Whatever William Casey was up to in the months before the 1980 election, none of it touched Reagan. Reagan likely gave Casey no encouragement to stall the hostages' release. But he didn't have to. He knew what kind of person Casey was and what Casey was capable of doing.

In the matter of Iran-contra, Reagan understood full well the connection between the arms deliveries and the release of the hostages. His diary makes this quite clear. But he distanced himself from the details, leaving them to John Poindexter and Oliver North. Poindexter didn't inform Reagan what North was doing, because every signal he got from Reagan told him the president didn't want to know. By remaining in the dark, Reagan eventually managed to convince himself that the dealings were something other than arms for hostages. His outrage at the accusations of bargaining with terrorists was emotionally sincere, if logically incredible. As for the contra connection, Reagan didn't know about the diversion of funds, again because he didn't want to know. He set the moral tone of the administration, which placed the survival of the contras above nearly everything else, including the repeatedly legislated will of Congress. He left it to his subordinates to figure out how to keep the contras alive. He let Poindexter and North work out the details, and he let them take the fall when the scandal broke. Even if his memory hadn't failed by the time the Walsh investigation got to him, there was little chance of his being prosecuted. There were no fingerprints and no smoking gun.

A related talent was Reagan's ability to say one thing and do something else. In an individual this is hypocrisy; in a president it is realism. Reagan's political philosophy was adamant conservatism. He valued freedom over equality, the individual over the group, the private sector over the public sphere. In every speech he gave, he preached the conservative gospel. But Reagan's political practice was flexible pragmatism. He opposed abortion, but as California governor he relaxed the state's abortion laws. He favored lower taxes, but he accepted tax increases when necessary to achieve the best bargain with Congress. He believed communism to be evil, but he forged an alliance with the leader of the most powerful communist country in the world.

Reagan's pragmatism was a reflection of his ambition. Throughout his life and career he had constantly sought larger stages; when he reached the largest stage in American politics, the presidency, he sought the still larger stage of history. He wanted to make a mark, not merely to make a statement. He understood that the purpose of politics is to govern, not to preserve ideological purity. He pursued the ends of Barry Goldwater by the means of Franklin Roosevelt. Like Roosevelt and other successful presidents, he realized that progress comes in pieces. If he got four-fifths of his ask in a negotiation, he took it and ran. He knew he could return for the rest.

Reagan's timing—some called it his luck—was no less essential to his success than his ability. In historical terms, his life and career couldn't have been timed more effectively. The century after Reagan's birth was an American era in world affairs. The United States came of age as Reagan came of age. He lived through World War I, with its false step toward American global leadership; he survived the Great Depression and experienced the annealing it afforded the American character. He went to Hollywood's version of war as the United States went to war against Japan and Germany. He became aware of the communist threat in the film industry as America discovered the communist threat in the world at large. His political career blossomed as the struggle against communism matured, and his career culminated as the Cold War reached its climax.

Timing in human affairs is often a matter of coincidence, the overlapping of lives and moments. Reagan's moment in power overlapped with the moments of two men who were crucial to his success. Paul Volcker was Jimmy Carter's gift to Reagan; it was Volcker who squeezed the inflationary expectations out of the economy and put it on the path to solid growth. And he did so at just the right time for Reagan. If Volcker had taken charge of the Fed two years earlier, the economy might have improved sufficiently that Carter and not Reagan would have been elected in 1980. If Volcker had arrived two years later, the recession that routed the Republicans in the 1982 elections could have swept Reagan from office in 1984.

In a similar way, Mikhail Gorbachev was Moscow's gift to Reagan. Reagan had tried without success to engage Brezhnev, Andropov, and

Chernenko in arms talks; only the emergence of Gorbachev provided him with a counterpart willing and able to negotiate seriously. Perhaps the demise of the Soviet Union was predestined; the system there had been broken for years. Yet the timing of the demise depended on someone willing to acknowledge the undeniable. Had Brezhnev, Andropov, and Chernenko collectively lived but a few years longer, Reagan would never have found his partner. To one of his successors would have gone the distinction of pushing the Soviet Union to the edge.

Presidential reputations, however, reflect what did happen, not what might have happened. Herbert Hoover might have been a great president if not for that nasty depression. In Reagan's case, of the two goals he set for himself—shrinking government and defeating communism—he accomplished half of the first and all of the second. He cut taxes and regulations but failed to cut spending; the result was the economic recovery but also the doubling of the federal debt. He defeated communism definitively, with the help of Gorbachev and George Bush. By the early 1990s communism was a dead letter in world affairs. The Communist Party still ran China, but it was communist in name only. Residual communist regimes in Cuba, Vietnam, and North Korea didn't matter to anyone except their own suffering people.

"I KNOW IN my heart that man is good," Reagan had said at the dedication of his library. "That what is right will always eventually triumph." These lines of the Reagan creed were etched over his grave at the Reagan Library.

But the closing words of his poignant farewell to the American people were the ones that were better remembered, that captured the belief that made him irresistible to so many. The shadow of forgetfulness was growing long across his path, yet his optimism and faith in his country remained undiminished as he wrote, "I know that for America there will always be a bright dawn ahead."

ACKNOWLEDGMENTS

The author would like to thank the many people without whom this book would not have been possible. Duke Blackwood, Mike Duggan, Jennifer Mandel, and Ray Wilson made research at the Reagan Library a pleasure. The archivists and librarians at the Library of Congress, the Seeley Mudd Library at Princeton University, the Hoover Institution at Stanford University, and the University of Texas at Austin were thorough professionals. My colleagues and students at the University of Texas at Austin have allowed me to test ideas on them, as have audiences who have heard me speak about Ronald Reagan these last several years. Jonathan Hunt took time from his own research to track down some elusive sources.

Kris Puopolo at Doubleday has been a model editor, prodding and applauding at just the right moments. Dan Meyer made the production process as smooth as it could be. Bill Thomas has supported my work for years, and continues to do so.

Special thanks to those individuals who personally conveyed to me their experiences and knowledge of Reagan and his presidency. These include Ron Reagan, George H. W. Bush, George Shultz, James Baker, Edwin Meese, Robert McFarlane, John Poindexter, Robert Gates, Jack Matlock, Ken Adelman, Bobby Ray Inman, Phil Gramm, Henry Nau, Gilbert Robinson, Harrison Schmitt, Hans Mark, Ben Barnes, Greg Leo, Lawrence Freedman, Gary Sick, Douglas Brinkley, and Larry Temple.

SOURCES

The most important source of information on Ronald Reagan is Reagan himself: his speeches, diaries, letters, and memoirs. Reagan spoke a great deal in his lifetime, and he wrote much more of what he said than is commonly appreciated. He started speaking while an actor in Hollywood in the 1930s and 1940s; he kept speaking as spokesman for General Electric in the 1950s and 1960s; he spoke as governor of California in the 1960s and 1970s; he spoke as a candidate for president in the late 1970s and then as president in the 1980s. At first he wrote his speeches unaided, but even after he acquired assistants, he put his pencil to every draft, making sure that what came out of his mouth was what was in his head and heart. The unfriendly critique of Reagan is that he was merely an actor, mouthing lines written by others. The truth is more nearly the opposite: few presidents paid closer personal attention to what went into their speeches than Reagan. And the speeches of few presidents shed more light on the presidential mind than Reagan's. Reagan's speeches—delivered in person, over radio, and on television—are an important source for the present book. Portions or all of some early speeches were printed in contemporary newspapers; after he became a national figure in the 1960s, an increasing number aired on radio or television. Few of his radio speeches survive in audio form, but hundreds of radio scripts from the 1970s, most in his own handwriting, are preserved at the Reagan Library. A great many have been published in *Reagan, in His Own Hand*, edited by Kiron K. Skinner, Annelise Anderson, and Martin Anderson. After Reagan entered the White House, essentially every word he spoke publicly was recorded and transcribed; these are most readily available through the Public Papers of the Presidents, a part of the digital American Presidency Project.

Reagan kept a diary while president. The purpose was to facilitate the writing of his presidential memoir, and in fact selections from the diary were published in that memoir. Yet as often occurs with diaries, the entries took on a life of their own. Reagan often forgot the audience over his shoulder and revealed himself in ways he wouldn't have to the public. The diaries have been preserved at the Reagan Library; they have been published almost in their entirety as *The Reagan Diaries*, edited by Douglas Brinkley.

Reagan was a letter writer of the old school. Even as governor and president, he eschewed dictation when feasible, preferring pen and paper. He wrote to friends and acquaintances but also to people he didn't know who had written to him regarding some aspect of public policy. These letters are the personal counterpart to his public speeches; occasionally, he said more in letters than he felt he could say in public, but as a rule they demonstrate the remarkable consistency between the public Reagan and the private man. An illuminating selection of the letters is *Reagan: A Life in Letters*, edited by Kiron K. Skinner, Annelise Anderson, and Martin Anderson.

Reagan wrote two memoirs. The first, *Where's the Rest of Me?*, was a campaign biography published during his run for governor in 1965. Written for a California audience during the liberal 1960s, it deals, sometimes cheekily, with his childhood and youth and especially his years in Hollywood. His second memoir, *An American Life*, published in the more conservative 1990s, falls sedately into the genre of presidential memoirs. Both books are reasonably accurate regarding the events they portray, but they are more valuable as reflections of how those events appeared to Reagan.

Reagan's presidency produced scores of millions of pages of memos, papers, meeting notes, proposals, reports, agendas, itineraries, and the like. The principal repository for these is the Reagan Library, where a substantial portion of the whole has been processed and declassified but much remains under seal of one sort or another. Yet the available and steadily growing documentation allows an ever fuller, if still interim, assessment of Reagan's presidency.

In the digital age, virtual archives are an essential tool for any historian or biographer. The American Presidency Project, mentioned above, is one such archive. Others of note for foreign policy are the National Security Archive and the Cold War International History Project. Both employ researchers who painstakingly pry open refractory archives, using the

Freedom of Information Act and similar instruments, and they make the results of their labors available to other researchers. More focused is the Reagan Files, created and curated by Jason Saltoun-Ebin, which provides a window on recent declassification of national security documents from the Reagan years. The Gorbachev Foundation Archive affords access to records relating to Reagan's adversary and eventual partner in superpower diplomacy. The digital archive of the Margaret Thatcher Foundation does the same for Reagan's favorite prime minister.

As governor and as president, Reagan attracted many talented, strong-minded men and women to his administrations. They didn't always agree, and after they left office, several tried to settle old scores in print. The result is an embarrassment of memoir riches—embarrassing in extent to the historian and biographer, embarrassing at times personally to the various authors. Most of Reagan's senior cabinet secretaries and White House staff told their stories: Alexander Haig, George Shultz, Caspar Weinberger, Donald Regan, James Baker, Edwin Meese, Michael Deaver, Robert McFarlane. Several others with less central roles in the Reagan administration, including Martin Anderson, Robert Gates, Peggy Noonan, and Larry Speakes, have also recounted their experiences. Precisely because these individuals often disagreed strongly, their dueling perspectives highlight the contours of the Reagan presidency in a way the memoirs of a more congenial group might not have.

Of particular note is the memoir of Nancy Reagan, who exerted a powerful influence on her husband yet one that has often been misunderstood. Nancy Reagan cared little for politics per se; her interest lay almost completely in the fact that the love of her life was the most powerful politician in America. She had no policy agenda as such, aside from her war on drugs; her sole interest was in protecting and promoting her husband. She pursued this interest fiercely and, for the most part, effectively. And afterward she wrote one of the most candid and at times self-critical memoirs in recent American political history. Biographers of her husband are deeply in her debt.

Reagan's children wrote memoirs too. Those by Michael Reagan, Maureen Reagan, and Ron Reagan are the most revealing of family dynamics in the Reagan household. Patti Davis has written with sensitivity about her father's struggle with Alzheimer's disease during his final decade.

The memoirs of some of Reagan's foreign counterparts illuminate the effect the American president had on world affairs. The most important of these are by Margaret Thatcher and Mikhail Gorbachev.

Reagan's associates left collections of papers at the Reagan Library and elsewhere. The persons closest to Reagan and whose papers were available at the time of the research for this book include James Baker, with papers at the Reagan Library and Princeton University; William Casey, at the Hoover Institution at Stanford University; Michael Deaver, at the Reagan Library; Edwin Meese, at the Reagan Library and the Hoover Institution; Donald Regan, at the Reagan Library and the Library of Congress; George Shultz, at the Reagan Library; and Caspar Weinberger, at the Library of Congress.

Reagan's associates and contemporaries have in many cases conveyed their impressions of Reagan and his actions in interviews. The Bancroft Library at the University of California at Berkeley has recorded and transcribed many such interviews. The Miller Center at the University of Virginia has compiled a separate collection of interviews. Deborah Hart Strober and Gerald S. Strober have gathered and edited scores of interviews to produce *Reagan: The Man and His Presidency* (1998). The present author has made use of all three collections and has conducted numerous interviews of his own.

The secondary literature on Reagan and the Reagan years is large and growing fast. Nearly every author writing on American public life in the last third of the twentieth century deals with Reagan, as do many authors discussing the major events of international relations during this period. Of works dealing with Reagan specifically, several merit particular mention. Lou Cannon covered Reagan as a reporter from the beginning of Reagan's political career to its close; his *Governor Reagan* and *President Reagan* remain the starting point for any understanding of Reagan's role in public life. Steven F. Hayward has written at comparable length on Reagan, with a broader focus. Hayward's two-volume *The Age of Reagan* is as fully history as biography; the first volume, which covers the years 1964 to 1980, sets the stage for the Reagan presidency, the subject of the second volume. Richard Reeves recounts the White House years with a journalist's eye for detail in *President Reagan*; the book is especially good on the interplay of personalities in the administration. Edmund Morris enjoyed unprecedented access to Reagan as president, attending meetings in the White House and conducting lengthy interviews with the president and his associates. Morris's *Dutch* disappointed and at times infuriated readers who expected a standard presidential biography rather than the impressionistic rendering Morris provided. Yet readers willing to invest the energy to sift the fact from the fiction can find illuminating material here. Sean Wilentz places Reagan at the center of *The Age of Reagan*, which assesses the conservative turn in American politics embodied and energized by the fortieth president.

NOTES

PROLOGUE

1   "TONIGHT": *New York Times*, Oct. 27, 1964. Similar ads in *Los Angeles Times* and other papers.

3   "Anytime you and I question": Reagan campaign speech, Oct. 27, 1964, Reagan Library.

6   "I have never aspired": *Washington Post*, Nov. 26, 1964; *Los Angeles Times*, Nov. 29, 1964.

CHAPTER 1

9   "When I was eleven": Reagan, *An American Life* (1990), 33.

10 "The parades, the torches": Reagan, *Where's the Rest of Me?* (1965), 13.

10 "Nelle tried so hard": *American Life*, 34–35.

11 "While my father was a cynic": Ibid., 22–23, 30.

11 "The Klan's the Klan": Anne Edwards, *Early Reagan* (1987), 53.

11 "You'll like it here": *American Life*, 30.

11 "I was forever the new kid": Ibid., 23, 34.

12 "Summoning my courage": Ibid., 35.

12 "He had a wry, mordant humor": *Rest of Me*, 9.

13 "That prodded me": *American Life*, 41.

13 "'Twas the night": "Hallowe'en," Nov. 6, 1925, in *Reagan, in His Own Hand*, edited by Kiron F. Skinner, Annelise Anderson, and Martin Anderson (2001), 423–24.

13 "Mark had": "Yale Comes Through," Nov. 17, 1927, in *Reagan, in His Own Hand*, 424–26.

14 "For a teenager": *American Life*, 41.

14 "There's something": Ibid., 42–43.

16 "I think the realization": Ibid., 26.

16 "The chief business of America": David Greenberg, *Calvin Coolidge* (2006), 4.

17 "'I would have been fine'": *Rest of Me*, 21-22.

18 "I had never seen Eureka College": Ibid., 23.

18 "Dutch?": Edwards, *Early Reagan*, 87–88.

18 "The head of Northwestern's Drama Department": *Rest of Me*, 44.

18 "War-weary, young": Ibid., 29.

19 "I'd been told": Ibid., 28–29.

20   "I became the younger brother": Neil Reagan interview, Bancroft Library.
20   "Anytime I heard": Edwards, *Early Reagan*, 101.
20   "My principal academic ambition": *American Life*, 53.
20   "the A.E.F. suicide club": "Killed in Action," May 7, 1931, in *Reagan, in His Own Hand*, 430–32.

CHAPTER 2
22   "After we moved to Dixon": *American Life*, 58–59.
24   "Well, it's a hell": *Rest of Me*, 41.
24   "By my senior year": *American Life*, 59.
25   "This is the big time": *Rest of Me*, 46.
25   "How the hell": *American Life*, 64–66.
27   "Well, Felix": H. W. Brands, *Traitor to His Class: The Privileged Life and Radical Presidency of Franklin Delano Roosevelt* (2008), 259.
27   "His strong, gentle, confident voice": *American Life*, 66.
28   "I soon idolized FDR": Ibid.
28   "I was shocked": Ibid., 68.
30   "One summer's day": Ibid., 72–73.

CHAPTER 3
36   "Max": *American Life*, 79–81; Reagan to Ron Cochran, May 12, 1980, in *Reagan: A Life in Letters*, edited by Kiron K. Skinner, Annelise Anderson, and Martin Anderson (2003), 29–31.
37   "mortgage lifter": Cass Warner Sperling and Cork Milner, *Hollywood Be Thy Name: The Warner Brothers Story*, with Jack Warner Jr. (1998), 81.
38   "Who the hell": Scott Eyman, *The Speed of Sound: Hollywood and the Talkie Revolution, 1926–1930* (1997), 70.
38   "The making of any animal pictures": Susan Orlean, *Rin Tin Tin: The Life and the Legend* (2011), 83.
39   "The motion picture presents": Harry Warner quoted in Neal Gabler, *An Empire of Their Own: How the Jews Invented Hollywood* (1988), 196.
39   "Where in hell": Reagan, "The Making of a Movie Star," *Des Moines Register*, June 13, 1937, in *Reagan, in His Own Hand*, 435–36.
40   "Kid, don't worry": *American Life*, 86.
41   "Some day when the team's up against it": Reagan as George Gipp in *Knute Rockne: All American* (1940).
41   "Look": *American Life*, 93–94.
44   "He was such a sunny person": Edmund Morris, *Dutch: A Memoir of Ronald Reagan* (1999), 153–54.
44   "When Clark Gable": Ibid., 154.
44   Hollywood gossip and bits of circumstantial evidence: Ibid., 162–63.

CHAPTER 4
47   "When do I fight?": Stephen Vaughn, *Ronald Reagan in Hollywood: Movies and Politics* (1994), 71–72.
47   "There was Harry Warner": Ibid., 62.
48   "If any more stuff": Ibid., 43.
50   accepted Hitler's assurances: Gabler, *Empire of Their Own*, 338.
50   "A lot of Jews": Ibid.

50 "Are we making it": Ibid., 340, 343.
51 "I started preparing": *American Life*, 95–96.

CHAPTER 5
53 "live in infamy": Roosevelt address to Congress, Dec. 8, 1941. Unless otherwise noted, public statements by presidents are taken from the Public Papers of the Presidents, hosted by the American Presidency Project, www.presidency.ucsb.edu.
54 "I didn't have a burning desire": *American Life*, 75.
54 "any time after that date": Vaughn, *Ronald Reagan in Hollywood*, 107.
56 "Jack, we've got enough pilots": Jack L. Warner, *My First Hundred Years in Hollywood*, with Dean Jennings (1964), 281–82.
56 "If we sent you overseas": Vaughn, *Ronald Reagan in Hollywood*, 107.

CHAPTER 6
60 "At the end of World War II": *American Life*, 105.
61 "I was well fixed": *Rest of Me*, 139–41.
61 "Set Your Clock at U-235": Vaughn, *Ronald Reagan in Hollywood*, 122; Paul Lettow, *Ronald Reagan and His Quest to Abolish Nuclear Weapons* (2005), 5.
62 "I expected great things": *Rest of Me*, 165.
62 "I think your speech": *American Life*, 106–7.
63 "It sounded good to me": *Rest of Me*, 166–68.

CHAPTER 7
68 "I couldn't do that": Vaughn, *Ronald Reagan in Hollywood*, 140.
68 "The CSU strike was a phony": *American Life*, 108.
68 "Now!": *Rest of Me*, 171–74.
69 "We wangled a meeting": Ibid., 148–52.

CHAPTER 8
76 "shocking piece of legislation": Truman radio address, June 20, 1947.
76 "We went into that meeting": House of Representatives, 80th Cong., 1st sess., *Hearings Before a Special Subcommittee of the Committee on Education and Labor: Jurisdictional Disputes in the Motion-Picture Industry* (1948), 349.
77 "I am no longer neutral": Vaughn, *Ronald Reagan in Hollywood*, 142.
77 "We were scared to death": *Rest of Me*, 173.
77 "Reagan spoke very fast": Reynold Humphries, *Hollywood Blacklists* (2008), 70.
77 "Ronnie Reagan has turned out": Marc Eliot, *Reagan: The Hollywood Years* (2008), 192.
78 "Eddie Arnold and I": *Rest of Me*, 175.

CHAPTER 9
81 "It is estimated": *Washington Post*, Oct. 19, 1947.
81 "Some of the most flagrant": *Los Angeles Times*, Oct. 19, 1947.
82 "Our committee's job": *New York Times*, Nov. 8, 1947.
82 "The committee is well aware": House of Representatives, 80th Cong., 1st sess., *Hearings Before the Committee on Un-American Activities* (1947), 1.
83 "Ideological termites": Ibid., 10–16.
83 "I think you should tell": Ibid., 55, 60, 66.
84 "Communism is so completely opposed": Ibid., 70–72.

85   "You really lay it on the line": Ibid., 68.
85   "At meetings": Ibid., 165, 168, 170.
85   "They are well organized": Ibid., 205.
85   "I think there is communism": Ibid., 211–12.
86   "with a brief interlude": Ibid., 213–18.

CHAPTER 10
90   "I don't care to read": *Hearings Before the Committee on Un-American Activities*, 290–95.
94   "With no vested right": *New York Times*, Oct. 26, 1947.
95   "Members of the Association": Larry Ceplair and Steven Englund, *The Inquisition in Hollywood: Politics in the Film Community, 1930–1960* (1983 ed.), 455.

CHAPTER 11
96   "to protect the industry": Vaughn, *Ronald Reagan in Hollywood*, 153–54.
97   He reported having encountered: *San Jose Mercury News*, Aug. 25, 1986. The basis of the *Mercury News* article was a newly released FBI file on Reagan.
97   "I don't go in for red-baiting": *Rest of Me*, 170–71.
97   "follow the Communist Party line": *San Jose Mercury News*, Aug. 25, 1985. The names of the actors Reagan identified were redacted when the FBI file was released, but Seth Rosenfeld successfully appealed the redaction. Seth Rosenfeld, *Subversives* (2012), 127–28, 559. Rosenfeld's book provides the fullest account of Reagan's relationship with the FBI.
98   "In all the battles": *Rest of Me*, 158.
98   "I think we both measured": Maureen Reagan, *First Father, First Daughter* (1989), 55.
99   Years later Reagan was asked: Morris, *Dutch*, 267.

CHAPTER 12
102   "At the present moment": Truman address to Congress, March 12, 1947.

CHAPTER 13
105   "His wife, Jane Wyman": Edwards, *Early Reagan*, 356.
105   "Reagan was a lonely guy": Ibid., 357.
106   "We got along well": Stephen Michael Shearer, *Patricia Neal: An Unquiet Life* (2006), 78.
106   "To the finder": Reagan to Jack Warner, Dec. 1948 (no day given), in *Life in Letters*, 136–37.
107   "The president of the United States": Shearer, *Patricia Neal*, 78.
108   "Spence was the most charming": Nancy Reagan, *My Turn* (1989), 79.
109   By at least one account: Edwards, *Early Reagan*, 394.
109   "There was a lot of political talk": Ibid.
109   "I can't do that": Nancy Reagan, *My Turn*, 95–96.
110   "I wish I could report": Ibid., 97, 106.
110   "The truth is": *Rest of Me*, 236.
110   "That hurt": Nancy Reagan, *My Turn*, 97–99.
111   "Gradually I came out": *Rest of Me*, 237.
111   "I began to believe": Nancy Reagan, *My Turn*, 99–100.
111   "Your letter led me to believe": Reagan to Florence Yerly, Dec. 17, 1951, in *Life in Letters*, 139–40.

113 "Go ahead and count": Nancy Reagan, *My Turn*, 103.
113 "I spent the entire day": Ibid., 101.

CHAPTER 14

114 "I don't feel that strangers": Reagan to Jack Warner, May 3, 1950, in *Life in Letters*, 137–38.
116 "Let me make one thing plain": *Rest of Me*, 223.
117 "conspiracy so immense": David M. Oshinsky, *A Conspiracy So Immense: The World of Joe McCarthy* (2005 ed.), 197.
118 twenty million viewers: *Encyclopedia of Television*, edited by Horace Newcomb (2004 ed.), 1:136.
118 "Have you no sense of decency": Oshinsky, *Conspiracy So Immense*, 463.

CHAPTER 15

119 "A star doesn't slip": *Los Angeles Times*, Aug. 27, 1950.
120 "I sat down": *Rest of Me*, 245.
121 "the fattest TV deal": *Los Angeles Times*, April 27, 1954.
121 "In the old days": *Washington Post* and *Times Herald*, April 3, 1955.
122 "We have Fred Astaire": *Los Angeles Times*, Oct. 27, 1957.
124 "never suggested": *Rest of Me*, 263, 266.
125 "Suddenly, realization dawned": Ibid., 269–70.
125 "Looking back now": *American Life*, 128–29.
126 "The men would all stand": Earl Dunckel interview, Bancroft Library.
126 "I still can't think": *American Life*, 128.
126 "He was interested": Thomas W. Evans, *The Education of Ronald Reagan: The General Electric Years and the Untold Story of His Conversion to Conservatism* (2006), 53, 75.
127 "Ron had the dope": Edwards, *Early Reagan*, 171.
127 "One day I came home": *American Life*, 132.
128 "Well, no, I haven't": Ibid., 136.

CHAPTER 16

135 "dime store New Deal": Goldwater obituary, *Washington Post*, May 30, 1998.
135 "Sometimes I think this country": Ibid.
135 "you have too often": Ibid.
136 "I needn't remind you": Goldwater acceptance speech, July 16, 1964, American Presidency Project.
136 "The stakes are too high": Gary Donaldson, *Liberalism's Last Hurrah: The Presidential Campaign of 1964* (2003), 247.

CHAPTER 17

138 "I've never had a mail reaction": *Los Angeles Times*, Nov. 29, 1964.
138 "It's 14 months away": Ibid.
139 "The conservative philosophy": *Los Angeles Times*, Nov. 11, 1964.
139 "I hope I could turn it down": *Los Angeles Times*, Nov. 15, 1964.
140 "I have some other thoughts": *Washington Post*, Nov. 26, 1964.
141 "I have a dream": Martin Luther King Jr., "I Have a Dream," Aug. 28, 1963, americanrhetoric.com.
142 "Because, Bill": Randall B. Woods, *LBJ: Architect of American Ambition* (2006), 480.
142 "I, too, learned to shout": *Los Angeles Times*, Aug. 14 and 15, 1965.

CHAPTER 18

145   "Each individual": *Los Angeles Times*, Jan. 13, 1965.
145   "I don't believe": *Los Angeles Times*, April 24, 1965.
146   "I'm all for it": *Los Angeles Times*, April 8, 1965.
146   "socialized medicine": *Los Angeles Times*, April 23, 1965.
146   "The most startling fact": *Washington Post*, June 17, 1965.
147   "He is developing": Buckley syndicated column in *Los Angeles Times*, Dec. 17, 1965.
148   "citizen politician": *Los Angeles Times* and *New York Times*, Jan. 5, 1966.
149   "Of course, the chairman": Lyn Nofziger interview, Miller Center.
149   "I will have no word of criticism": *Los Angeles Times*, Jan. 5, 1966.
149   "blanket indictments": *Los Angeles Times*, April 8 and Sept. 24, 1965.
149   "I resent": *Los Angeles Times*, March 7, 1966.
150   "I believe": *Los Angeles Times*, March 12 and June 2, 1966.
150   "I was not a big fan": Michael Deaver interview, Miller Center.
151   "The California primary results": *Los Angeles Times*, June 14, 1966.
152   "Pat is a nice man": Lyn Nofziger interview, Bancroft Library.
152   "Boy, I dream": *Los Angeles Times*, July 3 and Sept. 24, 1966.

CHAPTER 19

154   Warren Weaver Jr.: *New York Times*, Nov. 10, 1966.
154   "I am honored and flattered": *Washington Post*, Nov. 21, 1966.
155   "This is the document": *New York Times*, Dec. 29, 1966.
155   "Government is the people's business": Reagan inaugural address as governor, Jan.
      5, 1967, Reagan Library.
157   "He had the underlying philosophy": William Clark interview, Miller Center.
158   "My father was a very private person": Ron Reagan interview with author.
158   "All of those guys": Deaver interview.
159   "RECORD TAX HIKE": *Los Angeles Times*, March 9, 1967.
159   "I'm willing to take": Lou Cannon, *Governor Reagan* (2003), 200.
160   "It is a very profound": *Los Angeles Times*, May 10, 1967.
161   "I am satisfied": *Los Angeles Times*, May 24, 1967.
162   "I am confident": *Los Angeles Times*, June 14, 1967.

CHAPTER 20

165   "noncandidate": *New York Times*, April 3, 1968.
165   "Naturally I was interested": *Los Angeles Times*, April 17, 1968.
165   "I'll wait till such a thing happens": Reagan press conference notes, March 5, 1968,
      Reagan Library.
166   "At close range": *New York Times*, April 28, 1968.
166   "The nation is totally out of control": *Los Angeles Times*, May 19, 1968.
167   "I do not believe": *Washington Post*, July 6, 1968.
167   "I have not solicited": *Los Angeles Times*, July 25, 1968.
168   "I won't be a reluctant candidate": Cannon, *Governor Reagan*, 266.
168   "Young man": Nofziger interview, Miller Center.
168   "At that point": *New York Times*, July 28, 1968.
168   "This nation cannot survive": *New York Times*, Aug. 8, 1968.

CHAPTER 21

169   "The overwhelming majority": *Los Angeles Times*, June 17, 1966.

170   "Don't Loot the Colleges": *Los Angeles Times*, Feb. 12, 1967.

170   "I wouldn't miss this": Clark interview, Miller Center.

170   "A funny thing happened": *Los Angeles Times*, Feb. 12, 1967.

171   "You are a hero to some": Cannon, *Governor Reagan*, 290.

171   "extreme emergency": *Los Angeles Times*, Feb. 6, 1969.

173   "After the property was cleared": *Los Angeles Times*, May 21, 1969.

173   "In the past eleven months": *Los Angeles Times*, June 14, 1969.

174   "I remember one": *Los Angeles Times*, June 25, 1969.

CHAPTER 22

175   "cowardly little bums": *Los Angeles Times*, Feb. 27, 1970.

175   "Appeasement is not the answer": *Los Angeles Times*, April 8, 1970.

175   "There comes a time": Ibid.

176   "It isn't very important": *Los Angeles Times*, April 22, 1970.

177   "That sound you hear": *Los Angeles Times*, Feb. 8, 1970.

CHAPTER 23

179   "Mandated by statute": Reagan's second inaugural address, Jan. 4, 1971, governors
      .library.ca.gov.

180   "I believe that the government": Cannon, *Governor Reagan*, 352–53.

180   "Nixon sent several people": Deaver interview.

180   "I remember": Cannon, *Governor Reagan*, 356.

182   "the most significant foreign policy achievement": Robert Dallek, *Nixon and Kiss-
      inger: Partners in Power* (2007), 293.

183   "Seize the day": Nixon toast, Feb. 21, 1972.

183   "sovereignty, equality, non-interference": Raymond L. Garthoff, *Détente and Con-
      frontation: American-Soviet Relations from Nixon to Reagan* (1994 ed.), 327.

CHAPTER 24

186   "Walter Cronkite": Deaver interview.

187   "Finally, one day": Ibid.

188   "When we withdrew": Reagan radio commentary, April 1975 (no day given), in
      Reagan, in His Own Hand, 48–49.

189   "The Russians want": Reagan radio commentary, Oct. 1975, in *Reagan, in His
      Own Hand*, 26–31.

191   "some activities": *Report to the President by the Commission on CIA Activities Within
      the United States*, June 1975, 10.

191   "In any bureaucracy": *Washington Post*, June 3, 1975.

CHAPTER 25

193   "We were on a plane": Deaver interview.

194   "Our nation's capital": *New York Times*, Nov. 21, 1975.

195   "I was trembling": Nancy Reagan, *My Turn*, 183.

CHAPTER 26
196 "For thirty-five years": Michael Reagan, *On the Outside Looking In* (1988), 30, 33, 96, 122–24.
199 "He looked at me quizzically": Ibid., 142–43.
199 "The consultants were very nervous": Maureen Reagan, *First Father, First Daughter*, 146–47.
199 "They felt we made Dad": Michael Reagan, *On the Outside*, 142–43, 147.

CHAPTER 27
201 A Gallup survey: *New York Times*, Dec. 12, 1975.
201 "We've got to go out there": Nofziger interview, Miller Center.
201 "The press could see it": Deaver interview.
202 "That was the start": Nofziger interview, Miller Center.
202 "Nancy was most unhappy": Ibid.
204 "What Sears thought": Ibid.
204 "The Southern Reagan thing": Deaver interview.
205 "The Republican party needs to lose": *Washington Post*, Aug. 19, 1976.
205 "You know, Mr. President": James A. Baker III, *"Work Hard, Study . . . and Keep Out of Politics!": Adventures and Lessons from an Unexpected Public Life* (2006), 2–3.
206 "Sure, there's disappointment": *New York Times*, Aug. 20, 1976.
206 "He damn near took us down": James Baker interview with author.

CHAPTER 28
208 "We might never have lost to Carter": Baker interview with author.
208 "Once upon a time": Radio script, Nov. 16, 1976, in *Reagan, in His Own Hand*, 262–63.
210 "The campaign goes on": Radio script, July 6, 1977, in *Reagan, in His Own Hand*, 366–67.
210 "They interviewed a product": Radio script, Nov. 16, 1976, in *Reagan, in His Own Hand*, 342–43.
210 "How much do you miss dinosaurs?": Radio script, July 6, 1977, in *Reagan, in His Own Hand*, 329.
211 "The EPA back in 1972": Radio script, May 15, 1978, in *Reagan, in His Own Hand*, 333–34.
211 "The harp seal": Ibid., 335.
211 "That cost figure": Radio script, Dec. 22, 1976, in *Reagan, in His Own Hand*, 307–8.

CHAPTER 29
213 "For too many years": Carter address, May 22, 1977.
215 "Although there is no instance": Jeane Kirkpatrick, "Dictatorships and Double Standards," *Commentary*, Nov. 1979.
217 "The tear gas had created": Carter, *Keeping Faith* (1982), 434.

CHAPTER 30
218 "A troubled and afflicted mankind": *New York Times*, Nov. 14, 1979.
219 "Giscard d'Estaing": Cannon, *Governor Reagan*, 453.
220 "My opinion of the Russians": H. W. Brands, *The Devil We Knew: Americans and the Cold War* (1993), 160.
220 "the most serious threat": Carter State of the Union address, Jan. 23, 1980.

222 "It was a big surprise": Baker interview with author.

223 "I'm paying": *Washington Post*, Feb. 24, 1980.

223 "The bad news": Baker, *Work Hard*, 91.

CHAPTER 31

224 "Bush is very competitive": Baker interview with author.

224 "Every time I weighed my options": George Bush interview with author.

225 "All the old Ford guys": Baker interview with author.

225 "figurehead": Cannon, *Governor Reagan*, 475.

225 "As I had done so many times": Michael Deaver, *Behind the Scenes* (1987), 96.

225 "Can you support my policy positions?": Baker interview with author.

226 "He and I have come": *New York Times*, July 17, 1980.

226 "The major issue": Reagan acceptance address, July 17, 1980, American Presidency Project.

228 "noble cause": *New York Times*, Aug. 19, 1980.

228 "The only good news": Cannon, *Governor Reagan*, 481.

229 "I was the only Republican": Baker interview with author.

229 "All you have to do": Nofziger interview, Miller Center.

229 "There you go again": Reagan-Carter debate, Oct. 28, 1980, American Presidency Project.

CHAPTER 32

231 "October surprise watch" and "Our business": Senate Foreign Relations Committee, *The "October Surprise" Allegations and the Circumstances Surrounding the Release of the American Hostages Held in Iran* (1992), 33, 35.

231 "The Iranians know": Stef Halper to Ed Meese, Oct. 19, 1980, in *"October Surprise" Allegations*, 239–44.

232 "I believe": Casey to Reagan and Meese, Nov. 2, 1980, in *"October Surprise" Allegations*, 234.

232 "Precautions must be taken": Casey memo, Oct. 27, 1980, Reagan Library.

232 In a 1991 book: Gary Sick, *October Surprise: America's Hostages in Iran and the Election of Ronald Reagan* (1991).

233 others that appeared to be critical: *"October Surprise" Allegations*, 13–15.

233 "The great weight": Ibid., 114–17.

234 "If true": Lee F. Hamilton, "Case Closed," *New York Times*, Jan. 24, 1993.

234 "Mr. President": Douglas Brinkley, "The Rising Stock of Jimmy Carter: The 'Hands On' Legacy of Our Thirty-Ninth President," Bernath Memorial Lecture to the Society for Historians of American Foreign Relations, March 30, 1996, published in *Diplomatic History* (Fall 1996).

234 Brinkley said Carter: Douglas Brinkley interview with author. Kai Bird, in *The Good Spy: The Life and Death of Robert Ames* (2014), 242–47, provided evidence of a Casey effort to influence Arafat, though Bird noted that the alleged agent in the effort, Jack Shaw, denied anything untoward.

235 "I can categorically assure you": Bush to Moorhead Kennedy, May 9, 1991, George Bush Library, College Station, Tex. Kevin Phillips, declining to take Bush at his word, in *American Dynasty* (2004) laid out the case for a Bush connection to efforts to prevent the preelection release of the hostages. Characterizing the available testimony and documents as "fascinating in evidentiary potential yet appalling in implication," Phillips nonetheless drew no firm conclusion (290).

235   "In this regard": Memorandum for the record by Paul Beach, Nov. 4, 1991, Bush Library.

235   "If the White House knew": Robert Parry, "Second Thoughts on October Surprise," June 8, 2013, Consortiumnews.com.

235   In 2013, Ben Barnes: Ben Barnes interview with author.

236   "personal business for private interests": Undated memo, Connally Papers, Lyndon Baines Johnson Library, Austin, Tex.

236   "I am sure that you will find": Nixon to Paul-Louis Weiller, June 30, 1980, Connally Papers.

236   "Governor Reagan": Memo, July 21, 1980, Connally Papers.

236   "not be helpful": Barnes interview.

237   "absolute fiction": Sick, *October Surprise*, 225.

237   "You know . . . Abe Lincoln": Reagan victory speech, Nov. 4, 1980, American Presidency Project.

CHAPTER 33

241   "He's got a briefcase": Nofziger interview, Miller Center.

241   "There was absolutely nothing wrong": Stuart Spencer interview, Miller Center.

242   "If you were sitting": Ibid.

242   "I've always assumed Ed Meese": Deaver, *Behind the Scenes*, 124.

242   "Everyone assumed": Spencer interview.

242   "She was the reason": Baker interview with author.

243   "The President is elected": Nofziger interview.

243   "President Reagan understood": Baker, *Work Hard*, 125.

243   "Of all the advisers": Nancy Reagan, *My Turn*, 238.

244   "At times, Ronald Reagan": Deaver, *Behind the Scenes*, 39–40.

245   "Ed reacted": Spencer interview.

245   "I want you to make it right": Baker interview with author.

245   "Counselor to the President for Policy": Memo by Baker, initialed by Meese, Nov. 13, 1980, James A. Baker Papers, Mudd Library, Princeton University.

245   "You've got the policy": Baker interview with author.

246   "It was a good, lawyerly way": Baker, *Work Hard*, 128.

246   "Who's boss?": Interview excerpt in Richard Darman memo, Jan. 10, 1981 [misdated as 1980], Reagan Library.

246   "The president liked the issues": Edwin Meese interview with author.

246   "At the outset": Edwin Meese III, *With Reagan* (1992), 80.

246   "It was primarily": Nofziger interview.

246   "It really worked well": Baker interview with author.

247   "He was one of the smartest people": Phil Gramm interview with author.

247   "He was extraordinarily talented": Baker interview with author.

CHAPTER 34

250   "It would cap off": Martin Anderson, *Revolution* (1988), 331–32.

250   "He was tall": Robert M. Gates, *From the Shadows* (1996), 215.

250   "You know, I've never been able": Baker interview with author.

251   "God, he must have been bitter": Anderson, *Revolution*, 332.

251   "Bill Casey came to CIA": Gates, *From the Shadows*, 199, 201; Robert Gates interview with author.

251   "The DCI": Memorandum for the record, Nov. 14, 1980, CIA Historical Collec-

tion on Ronald Reagan, Intelligence, and the End of the Cold War, accessed Sept. 8, 2012, www.foia.cia.gov/Reagan.asp.

252 "The briefings in general": Memorandum for the record, Nov. 21, 1980, CIA Historical Collection on Ronald Reagan.

253 "Economic prospects": "USSR: Economic Issues Facing the Leadership," Jan. 1981, CIA Historical Collection on Ronald Reagan.

254 "My theory of the Cold War": Richard Allen interview, Miller Center.

CHAPTER 35

255 "We sat": Nancy Reagan, *My Turn*, 231.

255 "The atmosphere in the limousine": *American Life*, 225–26.

256 passengers reported a shaking: *Washington Post*, Jan. 21, 1981.

257 "It distorts": Reagan inaugural address, Jan. 20, 1981.

CHAPTER 36

259 "Ronald Reagan?!": David A. Stockman, *The Triumph of Politics: The Inside Story of the Reagan Revolution* (1987), 53–55.

261 "I'd worked out": Ibid., 80.

261 "It's Raygan": Donald T. Regan, *For the Record: From Wall Street to Washington* (1988), 154–57.

262 "To this day": Regan memo, March 11, 1981, in ibid., 159.

263 "a report on the state": Reagan address, Feb. 5, 1981.

CHAPTER 37

265 "about the size": Stockman, *Triumph of Politics*, 110, 112–13.

266 "Stockman was possessed": Regan, *For the Record*, 172–73.

266 "By now it was clear": Stockman, *Triumph of Politics*, 119.

267 "I would not forget": Caspar Weinberger, *Fighting for Peace* (1990), 20–21.

267 "I had become": Stockman, *Triumph of Politics*, 117–18.

268 "I became a little troubled": Weinberger, *Fighting for Peace*, 49.

CHAPTER 38

270 "I'm bringing home more dollars": Reagan address, Feb. 18, 1981.

CHAPTER 39

274 "I had met Governor Reagan": Margaret Thatcher, *The Path to Power* (1995), 372.

275 "Mrs. T told me": Nicholas Henderson, *Mandarin* (1994), 384–90.

CHAPTER 40

278 "I'm certainly not thinking": Reagan news conference, Jan. 29, 1981.

279 "Your hard line": Reagan interview with Cronkite, March 3, 1981.

CHAPTER 41

282 "People often ask me": Nancy Reagan, *My Turn*, 244.

283 "Everybody who served us": Ibid., 245.

283 "Thank God for Camp David!": Ibid., 253, 259.

284 "Doing for people": Reagan address to Building and Construction Trades Department, AFL-CIO, March 30, 1981.

285 "There's been a shooting": Nancy Reagan, *My Turn*, 3–4.

286   "Rawhide is okay": Transcript of Secret Service radio traffic, March 30, 1981, United States Secret Service press release, March 11, 2011, secretservice.gov.

286   "I felt a blow": Diary entry for March 30, 1981, in *The Reagan Diaries*, edited by Douglas Brinkley (2009). Diary entries below are taken from this collection and are identified by date alone. Some of Reagan's abbreviations have been spelled out to aid in the reading. The most important exceptions are "d—m!" and "h—l!" The spirit of Nelle Reagan apparently hovered over the president as he wrote his diary entries, and her spirit is honored here.

287   "I'm having a hard time breathing": Del Quentin Wilber, *Rawhide Down: The Near Assassination of Ronald Reagan* (2011), 109–10.

287   "I hope they are all Republicans": Ibid., 120.

288   "I walked in": Nancy Reagan, *My Turn*, 6.

288   "Who's minding the store?": Baker, *Work Hard*, 144.

288   "I love you": Wilber, *Rawhide Down*, 144–47.

CHAPTER 42

290   "They might view the transfer": Baker, *Work Hard*, 146.

290   "This is very bad": Alexander M. Haig Jr., *Caveat* (1984), 159.

290   "Constitutionally, gentlemen": Ibid., 160.

291   "Perhaps the camera": Ibid., 163–64.

292   "I can't breathe": Nancy Reagan, *My Turn*, 9.

292   "It's okay, Dad": Ron Reagan, *My Father at 100* (2011), 202.

292   "Get Well Soon": Nancy Reagan, *My Turn*, 10–11.

293   "God bless you, Mr. President": Chris Matthews, *Tip and the Gipper* (2013), 73.

293   "It heightened his sense of mission": Ron Reagan interview.

293   "Whatever happens now": Diary entry for March 30, 1981 (written April 11).

293   "I don't know what you're worried about": Nancy Reagan, *My Turn*, 20–21.

293   "Everyone said it was just a coincidence": Ibid., 44–48.

CHAPTER 43

296   "You wouldn't want to talk me": Reagan address to Congress, April 28, 1981.

298   "Stockman and I wrote the Reagan budget": Gramm interview.

298   "We embrace": Reagan address to Congress, April 28, 1981.

CHAPTER 44

300   "Am I lobbying people?": *New York Times*, May 5, 1981.

300   "We never anticipated": Diary entry for May 7, 1981.

301   "Then we shot ourselves": Baker, *Work Hard*, 179.

301   "Schweiker and I": Stockman, *Triumph of Politics*, 200–201.

301   "They gave us": Ibid., 204.

302   "I was apoplectic": Baker interview with author.

302   "Our success": Baker, *Work Hard*, 180.

302   "Look": Stockman, *Triumph of Politics*, 205–7.

303   "And that was that": Baker, *Work Hard*, 181.

CHAPTER 45

304   "A university like this": Reagan commencement address at Notre Dame, May 17, 1981.

305   "Tip O'Neill is getting rough": Diary entry for June 23, 1981.

305   "Tip was bluster": Diary entry for June 18, 1981.

305 "I'll reluctantly give in": Diary entry for May 28, 1981.
305 "Jim Wright is playing games": Diary entry for July 18, 1981.
306 "I'd intended to make": Reagan address to the nation, July 27, 1981.
307 "All of them told": Diary entry for July 28, 1981.
307 "The bill is done" and "the most sweeping": *New York Times*, July 29, 1981.
308 "I cannot imagine anything": Weinberger to Regan, July 30, 1981, Caspar Weinberger Papers, Library of Congress.
308 "the greatest political win": Diary entry for July 29, 1981.
308 "They represent a turnaround": Reagan remarks and news conference, Aug. 13, 1981.

CHAPTER 46
309 "Mr. President": Question-and-answer session with reporters, Aug. 13, 1981.
309 "We're still miles apart": *New York Times*, Aug. 3, 1981.
310 "Negotiations are still going on": Diary entry for June 21, 1981.
310 "This morning at 7 a.m.": Reagan remarks to reporters, Aug. 3, 1981.
312 "I don't care": *New York Times*, Aug. 4, 1981.
312 "I'm sorry": *Washington Post*, Aug. 6, 1981.
312 "United Airlines is still flying": *Washington Post*, Aug. 8, 1981.
312 "crisis made in heaven": *Washington Post*, Aug. 7, 1981.
312 "I can understand": Reagan to Mrs. Browning, ca. Sept. 1981, in *Life in Letters*, 328.
313 "I am more grateful": Reagan to Jerry McMillan, Sept. 29, 1981, in *Life in Letters*, 329.

CHAPTER 47
314 "The scent of victory": Stockman, *Triumph of Politics*, 291–97.
316 "My job was to establish": Regan, *For the Record*, 180–81.
317 "I was wondering": Anderson, *Revolution*, 250–51.
318 "He knew what he knew": Gramm interview.
318 "I was sitting": Anderson, *Revolution*, 250–51.
318 "Volcker, possessed": Regan, *For the Record*, 191–93.

CHAPTER 48
320 "Another bomb": Diary entry for Oct. 16, 1981.
320 "A very dark picture": Diary entry for Nov. 2, 1981.
320 "Kemp-Roth was always a Trojan horse": *Atlantic Monthly*, Dec. 1981.
321 "We even autographed": Baker, *Work Hard*, 166.
321 "one of the most cynical pieces": Associated Press, Nov. 11, 1981.
321 "The networks hammered us": Baker, *Work Hard*, 168.
321 "I don't know who the hell else": Baker interview with author.
321 "Today was different": Stockman, *Triumph of Politics*, 4–5.
322 "He was disloyal": Baker interview with author.
322 "I'm reading an article": Diary entry for Nov. 11, 1981.
322 "I had lunch": Diary entry for Nov. 12, 1981.
322 "The president's eyes were moist": Stockman, *Triumph of Politics*, 1–4.

CHAPTER 49
324 "He was frustrated": Gates, *From the Shadows*, 209; Gates interview.
324 "I would like to tell you": Casey to Reagan, May 6, 1981, CIA Historical Collection on Ronald Reagan.
325 "It was the appointment from hell": Gates, *From the Shadows*, 211.

326   "He customarily lied": Bobby Ray Inman interview with author.
326   "We believe that Soviet military leaders": "Soviet Goals and Expectations in the Global Power Arena," NIE 11-4-78, July 7, 1981, Reagan Library.

CHAPTER 50
328   Bobby Ray Inman recalled: Inman interview.
329   "There are 33 states": Minutes of NSC meeting, Feb. 6, 1981, Reagan Library.
330   "They are not men of great stature": Minutes of NSC meeting, Feb. 11, 1981, Reagan Library.

CHAPTER 51
333   "antisocialist elements": *Pravda*, Sept. 1, 1980.
333   "The United States is watching": Carter statement, Dec. 3, 1980.
333   "The Polish people must be allowed": Reagan remarks at welcoming ceremony for Margaret Thatcher, Feb. 26, 1981.
333   "We waited eagerly": Gates, *From the Shadows*, 227–28.
334   "Polish Patriots Day": Ibid., 231.
334   "desperate dilemma": Ibid., 232.
334   "Now we must take on": Diary entry for July 14, 1981.
335   "Your Holiness": Excerpt of telephone conversation transcript, Dec. 14, 1981.
335   "Lunched with Cardinal Casaroli": Diary entry for Dec. 15, 1981.
335   "All the information": Reagan news conference, Dec. 17, 1981.
336   "There is widespread resentment": Minutes of NSC meeting, Dec. 21, 1981, Reagan Library. Remarks at this meeting and many others are quoted in Martin Anderson and Annelise Anderson, *Reagan's Secret War* (2009).
341   "Mr. President . . . would you light": Deaver, *Behind the Scenes*, 142–43.
341   "As I speak to you tonight": Reagan address, Dec. 23, 1981.

CHAPTER 52
344   "We who were going to balance": Diary entry for Dec. 8, 1981.
344   "While one or two": Diary entry for Dec. 10, 1981.
344   "I'm not sure he sees": Diary entry for Dec. 14, 1981.
344   "Met with Senate leaders": Diary entry for Dec. 18, 1981.
345   "They're so used to spending": Diary entry for Dec. 22, 1981.
345   "Except for Jack Kemp": Diary entry for Jan. 11, 1981.
345   "In other words": Regan, *For the Record*, 193–95.
346   "Downplay deficits": Undated memo, Baker Papers, Princeton.
346   "Both parties in Congress": Baker, *Work Hard*, 187.
347   "I told our guys": Diary entry for Jan. 22, 1982.
347   "The press has done a job": Diary entry for Feb. 22, 1982.
347   Gallup showed: ropercenter.uconn.edu.
347   "It reflects the constant media": Diary entry for April 2, 1982.
347   "We met at Blair House": Regan, *For the Record*, 202–3.
348   "There will be blood": Diary entry for April 23, 1982.
348   "The D's are playing games": Diary entry for April 26, 1982.
348   He made a last offer: Diary entry for April 28, 1982.
348   "The philosophical difference": Reagan address, April 29, 1982.
349   "People are confused": Diary entry for May 4, 1982.
349   "The president listened": Baker, *Work Hard*, 187.

349   "I thought they were going to break": Baker interview with author.
349   "A compromise is never": Diary entry for May 20, 1982.
349   "The tax increase": Diary entry for Aug. 4, 1982.

CHAPTER 53
350   "I suspect bureaucratic sabotage": Diary entry for Nov. 16, 1981.
350   "The press is not going to let up": Diary entry for Jan. 4, 1982.
351   "We are now at a watershed": Minutes of NSC meeting, Feb. 10, 1982, Reagan Library.

CHAPTER 54
356   "Central America is really": Diary entry for Oct. 16, 1981.
356   "There is no question": Diary entry for Nov. 16, 1981.
356   "We have decided": Ibid.
356   "We have problems": Diary entry for Feb. 3, 1982.
356   "The guerrillas have a really": Diary entry for Feb. 15, 1982.
357   Walters had orders: Haig, *Caveat*, 136.
357   "Maybe we'll be sending": Diary entry for March 9, 1982.
357   "They are uptight": Diary entry for March 11, 1982.
357   "In the commitment to freedom": Reagan address, Feb. 24, 1982.
359   "If he had just given": *Washington Post*, Feb. 25, 1982.
360   "As in Vietnam": *New York Times*, Feb. 25, 1982.
360   "It was extremely well received": Diary entry for Feb. 24, 1982.
360   "Met with National Security Council Planning Group": Diary entry for April 5, 1982.
360   "Within a relatively short period": Minutes of NSC meeting, Nov. 3, 1982, Reagan Library.

CHAPTER 55
363   "I'm disturbed by the reaction": Diary entry for April 23, 1981.
363   "I am convinced": Reagan letter to congressional leaders, Aug. 5, 1981.
363   "I have proposed this sale": Reagan news conference, Oct. 1, 1981.
364   "We did some getting acquainted": Diary entry for Sept. 9, 1981.
364   "He told me he wouldn't": Diary entry for Sept. 15, 1981.
364   "Frankly, I'm gratified": Reagan exchange with reporters, Oct. 15, 1981.
365   "The president was our chief negotiator": Reagan-Baker exchange with reporters, Oct. 28, 1981.
365   "Are we a vassal state": *New York Times*, Dec. 21, 1981.
366   "No, it's just friends": Reagan interview, Dec. 23, 1981.
366   "Sharon is a brawny man": Haig, *Caveat*, 329.
366   "He fears they may": Diary entry for Jan. 30, 1982.
366   "We are trying to persuade": Diary entry for Feb. 6, 1982.
367   "Many of his people resisted": Diary entry for April 25, 1982.
367   "I'm afraid we are faced": Diary entry for June 2–11, 1982.

CHAPTER 56
369   the Argentine regime was funding: Inman interview.
369   "Our only hope": Margaret Thatcher, *The Downing Street Years* (1993), 179.
369   "Talked for forty minutes": Diary entry for April 5, 1982.
370   "There could be no question": Thatcher, *Downing Street Years*, 181.

370 "The United States Secretary of State": Minutes of cabinet subcommittee meeting, April 7, 1982, Cabinet Files, British National Archives, nationalarchives.gov.uk.

370 "She rapped sharply": Haig, *Caveat*, 272.

370 "We cannot sacrifice our honor": Ibid., 277–78.

371 "Both sides want our help": Diary entry for April 6, 1982.

371 "We're friends with both": Question-and-answer session with reporters, April 5, 1982.

371 "senior administration officials": *Washington Post*, April 14, 1982.

371 "a most irresponsible act": Diary entry for April 14, 1982.

371 "The safest thing": Question-and-answer session with reporters, April 14, 1982.

371 "That would only be in keeping": Reagan remarks and question-and-answer session, April 30, 1982.

372 "Spent half an hour": Diary entry for April 15, 1982.

372 "It was not Britain": Thatcher, *Downing Street Years*, 202.

372 "As of noon": Diary entry for April 17, 1982.

372 "The shooting could start": Diary entry for April 23, 1982.

372 "Mr. President, was the British attack": Exchange with reporters in Washington, May 1, 1982.

373 "It was the only time": Inman interview.

373 "Mr. President, how could you": Exchange with reporters in Knoxville, May 1, 1982.

374 "Our intelligence community confirmed": *American Life*, 359.

374 "Whether or not such attacks": Thatcher, *Downing Street Years*, 221.

374 "I talked to Margaret": Diary entry for May 13, 1982.

374 "Hundreds have been killed": Haig, *Caveat*, 294.

374 "The prime minister is adamant": Diary entry for May 31, 1982.

374 "The Prime Minister said": Memo of conversation, June 4, 1982, Prime Minister's Files, British National Archives, nationalarchives.gov.uk.

375 "On distant islands": Address to Parliament, June 8, 1982.

375 "The speed with which the end": Thatcher, *Downing Street Years*, 235.

CHAPTER 57

376 "She believed absolutely": *American Life*, 360.

376 on the hook for the two thousand contras: Inman interview.

376 "He had grandiose ideas": Baker interview with author.

376 "He was a swashbuckler": Inman interview.

376 "He was somewhat contemptuous": Anderson, *Revolution*, 307.

377 "To me, the White House": Haig, *Caveat*, 85–94.

378 "Sit down and work it out": Baker interview with author.

378 "Al thinks his turf": Diary entry for March 24, 1981.

378 "Of course he wouldn't reveal": Diary entry for Nov. 1, 1981.

379 "I think we can get a lid": Diary entry for May 31, 1982.

379 "I was startled to hear reports": Haig, *Caveat*, 299–301.

379 "You can say Haig needs a win": *New York Times*, April 15, 1982.

379 "Shortly after my return": Haig, *Caveat*, 302.

379 "He was suspicious of everybody": Baker interview with author.

380 "Mr. President": Haig, *Caveat*, 312.

380 "The Al H. situation": Diary entry for June 14, 1982.

380 "Dear Al": Haig, *Caveat*, 314.

380 "He gave me the most intense grilling": George Shultz interview with author.

381 "Al Haig has resigned": George P. Shultz, *Turmoil and Triumph* (1993), 3–4.

381 "The only disagreement": Diary entry for June 25, 1982.

CHAPTER 58

382 "President Reagan and I": Shultz, *Turmoil and Triumph*, 9.

383 "We're walking on a tightrope": Diary entry for June 16, 1982.

383 "I was pretty blunt": Diary entry for June 21, 1982.

384 "Habib never ceased": Shultz, *Turmoil and Triumph*, 45.

384 "Let me say I'll be firm": Reagan exchange with reporters, Aug. 1, 1982.

384 "all out assault": Minutes of NSC meeting, Aug. 4, 1982, Reagan Library.

386 "Menachem, this is a holocaust": Geoffrey Kemp interview in Deborah Hart Strober and Gerald S. Strober, eds., *Reagan: The Man and His Presidency* (1998), 207.

386 "Our purpose will be to assist": Remarks to reporters, Aug. 20, 1982.

387 "Today has been a day": Reagan address, Sept. 1, 1982.

388 "What some call the West Bank": *American Life*, 433–34.

388 "I was horrified": Reagan statement, Sept. 18, 1982.

389 "I finally told our group": Diary entry for Sept. 19, 1982.

CHAPTER 59

390 "The big day!": Diary entry for Oct. 22, 1982.

391 "I really like him": Diary entry for Dec. 21, 1982.

391 "We had good meetings": Diary entry for Jan. 27, 1983.

391 "Still Israel dragging their feet": Diary entry for March 18, 1983.

391 "D--n them": Diary entry for April 18, 1983.

391 "Lord forgive me": Diary entry for April 19, 1983.

392 "There can be no sadder duty": Reagan remarks, April 23, 1983.

392 "Mr. President": Reagan news conference, Sept. 28, 1982.

393 "Israel is pursuing": Brezhnev to Reagan, June 9, 1982, Reagan Library.

394 "Your expressions of concern": Reagan to Brezhnev, July 1, 1982, Reagan Library.

394 "Armageddon in the prophecies": Diary entry for May 4, 1983.

395 "The world must have been simpler": Diary entry for Aug. 10, 1983.

395 "This could be seen": Diary entry for Sept. 11, 1983.

395 "The president's face turned ashen": Robert C. McFarlane, *Special Trust* (1994), 263.

395 "There are no words": Reagan remarks to reporters, Oct. 23, 1983.

CHAPTER 60

396 "This must not be allowed": Diary entry for Jan. 4, 1983.

397 "Based on the President's directives": Sapia-Bosch and North to William Clark, April 5, 1983, Reagan Library.

397 "The CIA sent briefers": Shultz, *Turmoil and Triumph*, 296–97.

397 "Our message": Clark interview, Miller Center.

398 "Venezuela couldn't go along": Diary entry for April 11, 1983.

398 "On the small island of Grenada": Reagan address, March 23, 1983.

399 "I had never really gotten along": Nancy Reagan, *My Turn*, 242–43.

399 "We both had the searing memory": Shultz, *Turmoil and Triumph*, 328.

400 "I asked McFarlane": *American Life*, 450–51.

401   "I believe Maggie Thatcher": Howard Baker interview, Miller Center.

401   "Early this morning": Reagan remarks, with Eugenia Charles, Oct. 25, 1983.

402   "I can't say enough": Reagan address, Oct. 27, 1983.

403   "It didn't upset my breakfast": Reagan comments, Nov. 3, 1983.

CHAPTER 61

404   "Nancy is very depressed": Diary entry for May 19, 1982.

404   "He got a lot of sustenance": Meese interview.

404   "I can't help feeling": Ron Reagan, *My Father at 100*, 86, 104.

405   "He was not a real Bible thumper": Ron Reagan interview.

405   "It bothers me": Diary entry for Oct. 4, 1981.

405   "Thank you for your prayers": Reagan address, March 8, 1983.

CHAPTER 62

412   "Back to Washington": Diary entry for Sept. 28, 1981.

412   "It is absolutely essential": National Security Decision Directive 35, May 17, 1982, Reagan Library.

412   "We're going to have trouble": Diary entry for Nov. 15, 1982.

413   "The United States wants deep cuts": Reagan address, Nov. 22, 1982.

413   "Tip O'Neill has mounted": Diary entry for May 15, 1984.

CHAPTER 63

414   "The United States does not start fights": Reagan address, March 23, 1983.

415   "When he was governor": Weinberger, *Fighting for Peace*, 296.

417   "Several years earlier": Ron Reagan, *My Father at 100*, 207.

417   "To those who traipse": Weinberger, *Fighting for Peace*, 291.

417   "R&D on Ballistic Missile Defense": National Security Decision Directive 35.

418   "Would it not be better": Weinberger, *Fighting for Peace*, 304.

418   "Much of it": Diary entry for March 22, 1983.

418   "I guess it was O.K.": Diary entry for March 23, 1983.

418   "Ron, it will make you look": Robert McFarlane interview with author.

418   "The reports are in": *American Life*, 572.

CHAPTER 64

419   "He looked more like a cadaver": Shultz, *Turmoil and Triumph*, 126.

420   "No bureaucracy involved": Diary entry for Feb. 15, 1983.

420   "We both share": *American Life*, 576.

420   "I have considered its contents": Ibid., 576–78.

420   "Their only function": Ibid., 580–81.

421   "I speak for all Americans": Reagan statement, Sept. 1, 1983.

421   "Our first emotions": Reagan remarks, Sept. 2, 1983.

421   The CIA and military intelligence: David E. Hoffman, *The Dead Hand: The Untold Story of the Cold War Arms Race and Its Dangerous Legacy* (2009), 82; Robert Gates, *From the Shadows*, 267.

421   "This Soviet attack": National Security Decision Directive 102, Sept. 5, 1983, Reagan Library.

422   "Despite the savagery": Reagan address, Sept. 5, 1983.

CHAPTER 65

426 "Each of us recognizes": Reagan statement, Jan. 15, 1983.
426 "The National Commission considered": Report of the National Commission on Social Security Reform, Jan. 1983.
426 "After months of debate": Reagan State of the Union address, Jan. 25, 1983.
427 "Today we reaffirm": Reagan remarks, April 20, 1983.

CHAPTER 66

431 "There is renewed energy": Reagan State of the Union address, Jan. 25, 1984.
432 "From my seat": Regan, *For the Record*, 225–26.
433 "I want to speak": Reagan State of the Union address, Jan. 25, 1984.
433 "Three years had taught me": *American Life*, 588–89.
434 "I'd like to talk to him": Diary entry for Feb. 22, 1984.
435 "They are utterly stonewalling us": Diary entry for May 11, 1984.
435 "What would I think": *American Life*, 601–2.

CHAPTER 67

436 "In the last fifteen years": Reagan address, May 9, 1984.
437 "Dear Bill": *New York Times*, April 11, 1984. The *Times* bowdlerized "pissed" for publication.
438 "Says he was never briefed": Diary entry for April 10, 1984.
438 "Central America is a region": Reagan address, May 9, 1984.
439 "We've got to find a way": McFarlane, *Special Trust*, 68.
439 "The purpose of this meeting": Minutes of National Security Planning Group meeting, June 25, 1984, National Security Archive.

CHAPTER 68

444 "Barry is upset": Diary entry for April 24, 1984.
445 "Our first go": Diary entry for April 26, 1984.
445 "We get along very well": Diary entry for April 27, 1984.
445 "This was Big Casino day": Diary entry for April 28, 1984.
446 "We believe in the dignity": Reagan remarks at Fudan University, April 30, 1984.
446 "It was a darn good speech": Diary entry for April 30, 1984.
446 "I think they have": Reagan question-and-answer session with reporters, May 1, 1984.
447 "We stand on a lonely, windswept point": Reagan remarks at Pointe du Hoc, June 6, 1984.
449 "Every man who set foot": Reagan remarks at Omaha Beach, June 6, 1984.
450 "Believe me": Reagan message to officers and men of USS *Eisenhower*, June 6, 1984.

CHAPTER 69

451 "I do not know": *New York Times*, Aug. 22, 1981.
451 "I never use the words": *New York Times*, Oct. 10, 1983.
452 "environmental extremism": Reagan interview, Jan. 20, 1982.
452 "He's the best thing": *New York Times*, Oct. 10, 1983.
452 "I think that's a decision": Reagan interview, Sept. 26, 1983.
452 "Here is the truth": Mondale acceptance speech, July 19, 1984, American Presidency Project.
453 "One of the key tests": Reagan-Mondale debate, Oct. 7, 1984, American Presidency Project.

454   "I have to say": Diary entry for Oct. 6–7, 1984.
454   "We left Louisville": Diary entry for Oct. 8, 1984.
454   "It was the worst night": Nancy Reagan, *My Turn*, 266.
455   "I never had one difference": Baker interview with author.
455   "Jesus, Nancy Reagan": Paul Laxalt interview, Miller Center.
455   "Fitness Issue": *Wall Street Journal*, Oct. 9, 1984.
455   "The president's advisers": *Washington Post*, Oct. 12, 1984.
455   "Age may have been a factor": *New York Times*, Oct. 10, 1984.
456   "Mr. Reagan is a mentally alert": *New York Times*, Oct. 11, 1984.
456   "It was the same old stuff": Baker interview with author.
456   "Let Ronnie be Ronnie": Nancy Reagan, *My Turn*, 267.
456   "Mr. President, I want to raise": Reagan-Mondale debate, Oct. 21, 1984, American Presidency Project.
457   "It's morning again in America": Reagan campaign commercial, youtube.com.

CHAPTER 70
459   "The press is now trying": Diary entry for Nov. 7, 1984.
459   "Tip O'Neill told me": Diary entry for Jan. 21, 1985.
459   "The Soviets are afraid": Minutes of National Security Planning Group meeting, Nov. 30, 1984, Reagan Library.
461   "We and the Soviet Union": Minutes of National Security Planning Group meeting, Dec. 5, 1984, Reagan Library.
462   "He could well be": Diary entry for Dec. 12, 1984.
462   "I hope we're making them realize": Diary entry for Jan. 30, 1985.
462   "I believe we'll have": Diary entry for March 4, 1985.
462   "Tip surprised me": Diary entry for March 7, 1985.

CHAPTER 71
463   "Awakened at 4 A.M.": Diary entry for March 11, 1985.
463   "We knew a lot about him": Gates, *Out of the Shadows*, 327–28.
464   "If Gorbachev is chosen": Ibid., 329.
464   "I think it was Jim Baker": George Bush and Brent Scowcroft, *A World Transformed* (1998), 4.
464   "Gorbachev started": Shultz, *Turmoil and Triumph*, 529.
466   "As you assume your new responsibilities": Reagan to Gorbachev, March 11, 1985, Reagan Library.
466   "President Reagan told me": Shultz, *Turmoil and Triumph*, 531–32.
467   "Gorbachev will package": Bush and Scowcroft, *World Transformed*, 4.

CHAPTER 72
469   "I reflected": Regan, *For the Record*, 236–45. Also Baker, *Work Hard*, 209–10.
472   "Possible Secretary of State": Undated notes, Baker Papers, Princeton.
473   "How would we approach": Regan, *For the Record*, 249; Baker, *Work Hard*, 211.
473   "It's time for a change": Baker, *Work Hard*, 211.
473   "In my innocence": Regan, *For the Record*, 251.
474   "Mr. President, I've brought you": Ibid., 249–56; Baker, *Work Hard*, 211–12.

CHAPTER 73

477 "I feel very strongly": Reagan news conference, March 21, 1985.

477 "President Reagan apparently believes": *New York Times*, March 30, 1985.

478 "in a spirit of reconciliation": *New York Times*, April 12, 1985.

478 "All it would do": Reagan remarks to editors and broadcasters, April 18, 1985.

479 "To equate the fate": *New York Times*, April 19, 1985.

479 "But, Mr. President": Wiesel remarks at White House ceremony, April 19, 1985.

480 "The commitment in question": Regan, *For the Record*, 287–91.

480 "The press had a field day": Diary entry for April 5–14, 1985.

481 "Helmut may very well": Diary entry for April 15, 1985.

481 "The press has the bit": Diary entry for April 16, 1985.

481 "quite emotional": Regan notes, April 19, 1985, Donald Regan Papers, Library of Congress.

481 "He told me my remarks": Diary entry for April 19, 1985.

481 "I was very *proud*": Bush to Reagan, undated, included in Reagan diary entry for April 19, 1985.

481 "The uproar about my trip": Diary entry for April 22, 1985.

482 "Every day seems to begin": Diary entry for April 24, 1985.

482 "He said I had won the heart": Diary entry for May 2, 1985.

482 "In all our motoring": Diary entry for May 3, 1985.

482 "You don't belong there": *New York Times*, May 6, 1985.

483 "For year after year": Reagan remarks at Bergen-Belsen, May 5, 1985.

CHAPTER 74

485 "Few presidents": Regan, *For the Record*, 295.

485 "It was the morally right thing": Diary entry for May 5, 1985.

485 "They were quite emotional": Diary entry for May 6, 1985.

485 "I was furious": Nancy Reagan, *My Turn*, 63.

486 "If, by some miracle": Ibid., 312.

486 "I enjoy this job": Regan to Michael McCarthy, Nov. 4, 1986, Regan Papers, Library of Congress.

486 "Instead, Ronald Reagan": Regan, *For the Record*, 298–300.

CHAPTER 75

488 "Our options were few": *American Life*, 492.

489 "The U.S. at the highest level": Diary entry for June 17, 1985.

489 "You can't square that circle": Shultz, *Turmoil and Triumph*, 656.

490 "Sir, can this be negotiated?": Reagan exchange with reporters, June 16, 1985.

490 "America will never make concessions": Reagan news conference, June 18, 1985.

490 "The Israelis are not": Diary entry for June 20, 1985.

490 "loused things up": Diary entry for June 21, 1985.

490 "It has been the position": Shultz, *Turmoil and Triumph*, 664.

491 "It was a nice homecoming": Diary entry for July 2, 1985.

CHAPTER 76

492 "I sat in the waiting room": Nancy Reagan, *My Turn*, 271–73.

493 "Nancy Reagan stammers": Regan, *For the Record*, 3.

494 "I meant, of course": Nancy Reagan, *My Turn*, 275.

494 "I feared two things": Regan, *For the Record*, 3–5.

495   "Rumsfeld's Rules": Undated memo [late 1980], Baker Papers, Princeton.

495   "Nobody elected you": Baker interview with author.

495   "President Reagan's chief of staff": *New York Times*, July 15, 1985.

496   "For the first few months": Nancy Reagan, *My Turn*, 312–13.

496   "The Russians have dropped": Regan, *For the Record*, 10–15.

CHAPTER 77

499   "Let it mature": Regan notes of meeting with Kissinger, March 13, 1985, Regan Papers, Library of Congress.

499   "They will spring a surprise": Regan notes of meeting with Brzezinski, July 23, 1985, Regan Papers, Library of Congress.

500   "Caspar Weinberger was utterly convinced": Jack F. Matlock Jr., *Reagan and Gorbachev* (2004), 114–15.

500   "While some Soviet officials": Gates, *From the Shadows*, 331–32.

501   "I'm fed up": Shultz, *Turmoil and Triumph*, 564–66.

502   "Our guest sang": Diary entry for May 26, 1985.

503   "Bill, I think Gorbachev": Gates to Casey, Sept. 3, 1985, in Gates, *From the Shadows*, 342.

503   "Even before it was decided": Matlock, *Reagan and Gorbachev*, 132–33.

503   "I want the best minds": McFarlane interview.

503   "He would devour them": Ibid.

504   "He was interested mainly": Jack Matlock interview with author.

504   "Very, very quick": McFarlane interview.

504   "In many ways": Matlock interview.

504   "I described for Reagan": Gates, *From the Shadows*, 343–44.

CHAPTER 78

505   "I believe Gorbachev": Reagan memo, undated [Nov. 1985], in Anderson and Anderson, *Reagan's Secret War*, 223–27.

507   "The Soviet violations": Weinberger to Reagan, Nov. 13, 1985, in *New York Times*, Nov. 16, 1985.

508   "Shultz detested Weinberger": Gates interview.

508   "Weinberger's letter": Shultz, *Turmoil and Triumph*, 598.

508   "I was surprised": Shultz interview with author.

508   "Sure it was": *Washington Post*, Nov. 17, 1985; Shultz, *Turmoil and Triumph*, 598; McFarlane interview.

508   "It was written to be leaked": Matlock interview; Matlock, *Reagan and Gorbachev*, 150.

508   "Reagan himself was pretty calm": Matlock interview.

508   "I think Reagan wanted conflict": Gates interview.

509   "Reagan was going to do": Ken Adelman interview with author.

509   "No": *New York Times*, Nov. 18, 1985.

CHAPTER 79

510   "Lord I hope I'm ready": Diary entry for Nov. 18, 1985.

510   "President Reagan began": Memo of conversation of first private meeting at Geneva, Nov. 19, 1985, Reagan Library.

512   "We did an hour": Diary entry for Nov. 19, 1985.

512   "Are you out of your mind?": Shultz interview, Miller Center.

512 "If the two of us": Memo of conversation of first plenary meeting at Geneva, Nov. 19, 1985, Reagan Library.

514 "Twenty years ago": Memo of conversation of second plenary meeting, Nov. 19, 1985, Reagan Library.

517 Reagan presented a written outline: Matlock, *Reagan and Gorbachev*, 158–59.

517 "He's adamant": Diary entry for Nov. 19, 1985.

517 "You sure are wrong": Matlock, *Reagan and Gorbachev*, 161–62.

518 "The stuff really hit the fan": Diary entry for Nov. 20, 1985.

518 "As we flew home": *American Life*, 640–41.

CHAPTER 80

519 "As I reread the minutes": Mikhail Gorbachev, *Memoirs* (1996), 405–9.

520 "Our people": Reagan to Gorbachev, Nov. 28, 1985, Reagan Library.

520 "I would like": Gorbachev to Reagan, Dec. 24, 1985 (translation by State Department), Reagan Library.

521 "We can have a real reduction": Diary entry for March 24, 1986.

521 "Given this situation": Reagan statement, May 27, 1986.

521 "It's a hell of a propaganda move": Diary entry for Jan. 15, 1986.

521 "My feeling is": Diary entry for April 8, 1986.

522 "mountain of lies": Matlock, *Reagan and Gorbachev*, 189.

522 "The tragedy of Chernobyl": Gorbachev, *Memoirs*, 412.

522 "The Americans continued": Ibid., 412–13.

CHAPTER 81

524 "It was just a very traumatic experience": Peggy Noonan, *What I Saw at the Revolution* (1990), 254–55.

525 "Today is a day": Reagan remarks, Jan. 28, 1986.

526 "When the president finished": Noonan, *What I Saw*, 257–58.

CHAPTER 82

527 "He's a madman": Diary entry for June 1, 1981.

528 "There's been a lot of talk": Reagan remarks and question-and-answer session, Aug. 20, 1981.

528 "It's a strange feeling": Diary entry for Aug. 6–Sept. 3, 1981.

528 "In other words": Diary entry for Oct. 6, 1981.

528 "Terror is Libya's second largest industry": Minutes of NSC meeting, Dec. 8, 1981, Reagan Library.

529 "The press is beginning to charge": Diary entry for Dec. 8, 1981.

530 "If Mr. Q. decides": Diary entry for Jan. 7, 1986.

530 "U.S. forces will continue": Reagan to speaker of the House and president pro tem of the Senate, March 26, 1986.

530 "We learned that in response": Gates, *From the Shadows*, 353.

531 "On March 25th": Reagan address, April 14, 1986.

CHAPTER 83

532 "immoral, evil and totally un-Christian": *New York Times*, Dec. 5, 1984.

533 "It's a nostalgic occasion": Reagan toast, Sept. 16, 1982.

533 "I know there are things": Reagan-Mondale debate, Oct. 21, 1984.

534 "I went through all of these matters": Shultz, *Turmoil and Triumph*, 613.

534 "I suspect an element": Diary entry for Oct. 22, 1985.
534 "This was a complete graveyard trip": Laxalt interview.
534 "He was telling me": Ibid.
535 "It's a touchy mess": Diary entry for Nov. 14, 1985.
535 "This election": Reagan statement, Jan. 30, 1986.
535 "Mr. President, will the U.S.": Reagan exchange with reporters, Feb. 7, 1986.
535 "You called for": Reagan interview, Feb. 10, 1986.
536 "The determination of the government": Reagan news conference, Feb. 11, 1986.
536 "Although our observation delegation": Reagan statement, Feb. 15, 1986.
536 "The dominant view": Shultz, *Turmoil and Triumph*, 630–31.
536 "He called in panic": Laxalt interview.
537 "There were long silences": Shultz, *Turmoil and Triumph*, 637; Laxalt interview.
537 "I phoned President Marcos": Diary entry for April 26, 1986.
537 "She's quite something": *New York Times*, Nov. 16, 1988.

CHAPTER 84
538 "His daily schedule": Regan, *For the Record*, 303–5, 309–12.
540 "When you open up the whole code": Ibid., 14.
540 "We have made one great dramatic step": Reagan address, May 28, 1985.
541 "Here the arguments": Reagan remarks in Williamsburg, May 30, 1985.
541 "Do the people of Oshkosh": Reagan remarks, May 30, 1985.
542 "Someone might say": Reagan remarks at Northside High School, Atlanta, June 6, 1985.
542 "His indecisiveness": Baker interview with author.
542 "The president *was* humiliated": Baker, *Work Hard*, 229.
542 "Tax reform": Baker to Reagan, Dec. 2, 1985, Baker Papers, Princeton.
543 "It was a straight talk session": Diary entry for Dec. 16, 1985.
543 "We assembled a team": Baker, *Work Hard*, 230.
543 "Let the bill take effect": *New York Times*, Oct. 23, 1986.
544 "I think this bill": *Washington Post*, Oct. 23, 1986.
544 "The journey's been long": Reagan remarks, Oct. 22, 1986.
545 "velvet-hammered charm": Greg Leo interview with author.
545 "Al Simpson came by": Diary entry for Oct. 16, 1986.
545 "It will remove": Reagan signing statement, Nov. 6, 1986.
545 "It enables millions": United Press International, Nov. 7, 1986.
546 "It turns a personnel manager": *Crain's Chicago Business*, Oct. 27, 1986.
546 "I think the only people": Associated Press, Oct. 30, 1986.
546 "It is another disappointing chapter": United Press International, Oct. 17, 1986.
546 "The act will undoubtedly exacerbate": *New York Times*, Nov. 13, 1986.

CHAPTER 85
547 "He worried about them personally": John Poindexter interview with author.
547 "Reagan was agonized": Shultz interview with author.
547 "It just drove him crazy": Shultz interview, Miller Center.
547 "Some strange soundings": Diary entry for July 17, 1985.
548 "To reverse our present policy": Shultz, *Turmoil and Triumph*, 793–94.
548 "This is almost too absurd": *Report of the Congressional Committees Investigating the Iran-Contra Affair* (1988), 148.
548 "Under no circumstances": Weinberger, *Fighting for Peace*, 363–64.

548   "a new, international version": Reagan remarks, July 8, 1985.
548   "America will never make concessions": Reagan news conference, June 18, 1985.
548   "McFarlane is a man": Weinberger, *Fighting for Peace*, 360, 364.
549   "Middle East/hostage release/problem": Regan, *For the Record*, 22–23.
549   "Yes, go ahead": *Tower Commission Report* (New York Times ed., 1987), 26.
549   "Bud came by": Diary entry for July 18, 1985.
549   "I thought that the president agreed": Shultz, *Turmoil and Triumph*, 796.
549   "I received a 'secret' phone call": Diary entry for Aug. 11–Sept. 1, 1985.
550   delivered some five hundred TOW missiles: Ibid.
550   "A call from Bud M.": Diary entry for Sept. 15, 1985.
550   "Rev. Weir and his family": Diary entry for Sept. 17, 1985.
551   "Word came": Diary entry for Oct. 9, 1985.
551   "The big news": Diary entry for Oct. 11, 1985.
551   "I called Mrs. Klinghoffer": Diary entry for Oct. 12–14, 1985.
551   He judged: *Tower Commission Report*, 158.
551   "Subject was our hostages": Diary entry for Nov. 22, 1985.
552   "We're still sweating": Diary entry for Nov. 23, 1985.
552   "Subject was our undercover effort": Diary entry for Dec. 5, 1985.
552   "H-hr: 1 707": *Report of the Congressional Committees Investigating the Iran-Contra Affair*, 171.
552   "We are now so far": Ibid.
552   "The president was profoundly concerned": Ibid.
552   "I don't think I could forgive myself": Poindexter interview.
553   "This was a day": Diary entry for Jan. 7, 1986.
553   "Some time ago": Poindexter to Reagan, Jan. 17, 1986, National Security Archive.
553   "The USG": "Finding Pursuant to Section 662 of the Foreign Assistance Act of 1961," Jan. 17, 1986, National Security Archive.
553   "Only thing waiting": Diary entry for Jan. 17, 1986.
553   One thousand TOW missiles were delivered: *Report of the Congressional Committees Investigating the Iran-Contra Affair*, 185.
554   "This morning more word": Diary entry for Feb. 28, 1986.
554   "We still don't know": Diary entry for May 27, 1986.
554   "And that's just what we did": Diary entry for May 28, 1986.
555   "Saturday good word": Diary entry for July 26–27, 1986.
555   "The high spot of the day": Diary entry for Aug. 1, 1986.

CHAPTER 86
556   "No funds available": Boland Amendment, Oct. 12, 1984, *Report of the Congressional Committees Investigating the Iran-Contra Affair*, 51.
556   "In NSC we're putting": Diary entry for April 3, 1985.
557   "Tip O'Neill and his cohorts": Diary entry for April 4, 1985.
557   "Tip has engineered": Diary entry for April 24, 1985.
557   "The United States has a clear": Reagan report to Congress, April 10, 1985, Reagan Library.
557   "Met with Repub. Leadership": Diary entry for May 21, 1985.
557   "Over to EOB . . . to address": Diary entry for March 5, 1986.
557   "Over to EOB for a pitch": Diary entry for March 10, 1986.
557   "Over to the Mayflower Hotel": Diary entry for June 9, 1986.
557   "Over to EOB to speak": Diary entry for June 16, 1986.

557 "We talked of our Mideast peace plan": Diary entry for Feb. 2, 1985.

557 "We will not agree": Minutes of National Security Planning Group meeting, May 16, 1986, Reagan Library.

559 North had taken between $3 million and $4 million: *Tower Commission Report*, 53–54.

559 "$12 million will be used": *Report of the Congressional Committees Investigating the Iran-Contra Affair*, 199.

559 "I had a feeling": *Tower Commission Report*, 54–55.

559 "We didn't see anything illegal": Poindexter interview.

CHAPTER 87

563 "The United States attacked Libya": Gorbachev, *Memoirs*, 413–14.

564 "It is of course a frame up": Diary entry for Sept. 3, 1986.

564 "I can give you my personal assurance": Reagan to Gorbachev, Sept. 4, 1986 (dated Sept. 5 by time of delivery), Reagan Library.

564 "Your letter of September 5": Gorbachev to Reagan, Sept. 6, 1986, Reagan Library.

564 "Father Potemkin": Shultz, *Turmoil and Triumph*, 733; Gates, *From the Shadows*, 366–67.

565 "The CIA has really reamed Daniloff": Shultz, *Turmoil and Triumph*, 733–34.

565 "The Soviets had done": Abraham Sofaer interview, Miller Center.

565 "This put a whole new light": Shultz, *Turmoil and Triumph*, 734.

565 "I went through the facts": Sofaer interview.

566 "Their man is a spy": Diary entry for Sept. 12, 1986.

566 "Most of the shows": Diary entry for Sept. 14, 1986.

566 "The press is obsessed": Diary entry for Sept. 17, 1986.

566 "I let the Foreign Minister know": Diary entry for Sept. 19, 1986.

567 "However, the US side": Gorbachev to Reagan, Sept. 15, 1986, Reagan Library.

CHAPTER 88

568 "a pre-summit planning session": Briefing book, undated, Reagan Library.

568 "Our SDI research": Reagan radio address, July 12, 1986.

568 "Our response to demands": Reagan remarks at White House briefing, Aug. 6, 1986.

569 "reeling toward a summit" et seq.: *Washington Post*, Oct. 3, 1986.

569 "We go into Reykjavik": "Gorbachev's Goals and Tactics at Reykjavik," undated [Oct. 4, 1986], Reagan Library.

570 "We should take": Shultz memo to Reagan, Oct. 2, 1986, Reagan Library.

570 "I am convinced": Anatoly Chernyaev, notes from Politburo session, Sept. 22, 1986, and notes of Gorbachev conversation with assistants, Sept. 29, 1986, Gorbachev Foundation Archive via National Security Archive.

571 "Most likely nothing": Chernyaev notes on Gorbachev's instructions to the Reykjavik Preparation Group, Oct. 4, 1986, Gorbachev Foundation Archive via National Security Archive.

572 "The rightists are concerned": Chernyaev notes from Politburo session, Oct. 8, 1986, Gorbachev Foundation Archive via National Security Archive.

573 "I was nervous": Nancy Reagan, *My Turn*, 338–40, 344.

574 "As usual, Mrs. Reagan": Regan, *For the Record*, 335.

575 "After extensive consultations": Ibid., 383–84.

CHAPTER 89

576 "The Russians are gaining sympathy": *New York Times*, Oct. 10, 1986.

577 "We do not confirm or deny": *Washington Post*, Oct. 5, 1986.

577 "I would like": Memorandum of conversation at first Reagan-Gorbachev meeting, Oct. 11, 1986, Reagan Library; transcript of Reagan-Gorbachev summit in Reykjavík, morning of Oct. 11, 1986, Gorbachev Foundation Archive via Foreign Broadcast Information Service FBIS-USR-93-061, May 17, 1993, 1–5.

577 "Whoops, I thought": Matlock, *Reagan and Gorbachev*, 220.

578 "You and I cannot allow": Memorandum of conversation at first Reagan-Gorbachev meeting, Oct. 11, 1986; transcript of Reagan-Gorbachev summit in Reykjavík, morning of Oct. 11, 1986, 1–5.

578 "We are agreeing to a great concession": Memorandum of conversation at first Reagan-Gorbachev meeting, Oct. 11, 1986; transcript of Reagan-Gorbachev summit in Reykjavík, morning of Oct. 11, 1986, 1–5.

580 "As I listened to you this morning": Memo of conversation of Reagan-Gorbachev meeting, 3:30–5:40 p.m., Oct. 11, 1986, Reagan Library; transcript of Gorbachev-Reagan talks, afternoon of Oct. 11, 1986, Gorbachev Foundation Archive via Foreign Broadcast Information Service FBIS-USR-93-087, July 12, 1993, 1–6.

CHAPTER 90

584 "Here we have differences": Memo of conversation, Oct. 12, 1986, 10:00 a.m.–1:35 p.m., Reagan Library; transcript of Reagan-Gorbachev talks, part 3, morning of Oct. 12, 1986, Gorbachev Foundation Archive via Foreign Broadcast Information Service FBIS-USR-93-113, Aug. 30, 1993, 1–11.

CHAPTER 91

589 "Our position offers": Memo of conversation, Oct. 12, 1986, 3:25–4:30 and 5:30–6:50 p.m. (memo dated Oct. 16, 1986), Reagan Library; transcript of Gorbachev-Reagan talks, part 4, Oct. 12, 1986, Gorbachev Foundation Archive via Foreign Broadcast Information Service FBIS-USR-93-121, Sept. 20, 1993, 2–8.

CHAPTER 92

596 "Oh, shit!": Matlock, *Reagan and Gorbachev*, 233.

596 "We have kept you a long time": Memo of conversation, Oct. 12, 1986, 3:25–4:30 and 5:30–6:50 p.m.; transcript of Gorbachev-Reagan talks, part 4, Oct. 12, 1986, 2–8.

603 "Am I wrong?": Shultz, *Turmoil and Triumph*, 773.

CHAPTER 93

605 "I was worried about his health": Larry Speakes, *Speaking Out* (1988), 142.

605 "Reagan was somber": Regan, *For the Record*, 392.6

605 "There is going to be *no* statement!": Speakes, *Speaking Out*, 142–43.

606 "Buck up, Mr. President": Regan, *For the Record*, 392–94.

606 "Mr. Gorbachev, leaning forward": *New York Times*, Oct. 13, 1986.

606 "only a madman": Ibid.

607 "For much of the way": Regan, *For the Record*, 392–94.

607 "Thank you all": Reagan remarks at Keflavík, Oct. 12, 1986.

608 "Gorbachev took a very high-stakes": Gates, *From the Shadows*, 407.

608 "I felt crushed": Matlock, *Reagan and Gorbachev*, 237–38.

609 "Given the present state": *Washington Post*, Oct. 14, 1986.

609 "History will show": Shultz to Jacalyn Stein, Oct. 13, 1986, George Shultz Papers, Reagan Library.

609 "Without SDI": Shultz, *Turmoil and Triumph*, 775.

610 "We had to wage a struggle": Working notes of session of the Politburo of the Central Committee of the Communist Party of the Soviet Union, Oct. 14, 1986, Volkogonov Collection via National Security Archive, Library of Congress.

CHAPTER 94

611 "As long as Iran": *New York Times*, Nov. 5, 1986.

612 "Usual meetings": Diary entry for Nov. 7, 1986.

612 "Mr. President": Reagan remarks and informal exchange with reporters, Nov. 7, 1986.

613 "My God, Mr. President": Regan, *For the Record*, 29.

613 "It was an emotional": Diary entry for Nov. 7, 1986.

613 "Don, you heard": Regan, *For the Record*, 30.

613 "The Saturday night": Diary entry for Nov. 8–9, 1986.

614 "He's not going to talk": Regan, *For the Record*, 30.

614 "Subject: the press storm": Diary entry for Nov. 10, 1986.

614 "Some of those men": Regan, *For the Record*, 34.

614 "This whole irresponsible press bilge": Diary entry for Nov. 12, 1986.

615 "I know you've been reading": Reagan address, Nov. 13, 1986.

617 "The president's speech": Shultz, *Turmoil and Triumph*, 816, 819.

617 *Los Angeles Times* poll: *Los Angeles Times*, Nov. 18, 1986.

618 "Will there be any more": Shultz, *Turmoil and Triumph*, 822–23.

CHAPTER 95

619 "Eighteen months ago": Reagan news conference, Nov. 19, 1986.

CHAPTER 96

630 "They were out for blood": Diary entry for Nov. 19, 1986.

631 "disastrous": Shultz, *Turmoil and Triumph*, 827.

631 "If some malicious Merlin": *Wall Street Journal*, Nov. 13, 1986.

631 "a great many factual errors": Shultz, *Turmoil and Triumph*, 831.

631 "There may be some misunderstanding": Reagan statement, Nov. 19, 1986.

632 had been told this by John Poindexter: Regan, *For the Record*, 36.

632 "The content of our discussion": Shultz, *Turmoil and Triumph*, 832.

632 "A touchy meeting": Diary entry for Nov. 20, 1986.

632 "We had an NSC briefing": Diary entry for Nov. 21, 1986.

632 "Big thing of the day": Diary entry for Nov. 24, 1986.

633 "The president, in person": Regan, *For the Record*, 42–43.

633 "I'm sorry it's come to this": Ibid., 45–47.

634 "And this report led me": Reagan remarks, Nov. 25, 1986.

634 "In the course": *New York Times*, Nov. 26, 1986.

CHAPTER 97

636 "Ronnie can be too trusting": Michael K. Deaver, *Nancy: A Portrait of My Years with Nancy Reagan* (2004), 99.

636 "I think it's the eternal optimist": Ibid.

636   "I'll never forget": Nancy Reagan, *My Turn*, 317–22.

638   "As revelation followed revelation": Regan, *For the Record*, 47–48.

639   "Without stretching things": Ibid., 61.

639   "Longtime Reagan Advisers": *Los Angeles Times*, Dec. 13, 1986.

640   "There is a bitter bile": *Time*, Dec. 8, 1986.

640   "So far, only two": Regan, *For the Record*, 59.

640   "Stu Spencer dropped by": Diary entry for Dec. 17, 1986.

640   "Have to begin thinking": Diary entry for Dec. 22, 1986.

641   "With Casey in the hospital": Nancy Reagan, *My Turn*, 323.

641   "It seemed unwise": Regan, *For the Record*, 73–74.

641   "Ronnie and I": Nancy Reagan, *My Turn*, 323.

641   "Just before Christmas": Regan, *For the Record*, 74.

641   "An informed source": *Washington Post*, Dec. 6, 1986.

642   "There was some tension": Nancy Reagan, *My Turn*, 324.

CHAPTER 98

643   "I was furious": Nancy Reagan, *My Turn*, 326.

644   "I talked with Ronnie": Ibid., 327.

644   "Are you going to fire Regan": Reagan exchange with reporters, Feb. 18, 1987.

644   "That's a pretty broad hint": Nancy Reagan, *My Turn*, 328.

645   "Don, why don't you": Regan, *For the Record*, 107.

646   "Were you surprised?": Lou Cannon, *President Reagan* (1991), 709–10.

647   "In trying to recall": *Tower Commission Report*, 29.

648   "The president's management style": Ibid., 79.

648   "More than almost any": Ibid., 81.

648   "It's not a bad idea": Diary entry for Feb. 26, 1987.

649   "I'm too mad": Regan, *For the Record*, 416.

649   "He was understandably angry": Diary entry for Feb. 27, 1987.

649   "In my time": Regan, *For the Record*, 417.

649   "That night": Nancy Reagan, *My Turn*, 333.

CHAPTER 99

650   "For the past 3 months": Reagan address, March 4, 1987.

652   85 percent: *Washington Post*, March 11, 1987.

653   "The speech was exceptionally": Diary entry for March 4, 1987.

CHAPTER 100

654   "Nancy and I are saddened": Reagan statement, Oct. 2, 1985.

654   "He had been to a White House dinner": Nancy Reagan, *My Turn*, 281.

654   "Called Rock Hudson": Diary entry for July 24, 1985.

655   Patti Davis . . . later said: *New York Times*, April 3, 2013.

655   "They have declared war": Randy Shilts, *And the Band Played On: Politics, People, and the AIDS Epidemic* (2007 ed.), 311.

655   "AIDS is God's judgment": John C. Purdy, *God with a Human Face* (1993), 38.

655   "I think they do": *Los Angeles Times*, March 6, 1980.

656   "Mr. President": Reagan news conference, Sept. 17, 1985.

656   "high priority": Reagan message transmitting fiscal year 1987 budget, Feb. 5, 1986.

657   "One of our highest public health priorities": Reagan remarks, Feb. 5, 1986.

657   "AIDS is clearly": Reagan statement, May 4, 1987.

657   "Fundraisers always remind me": Reagan remarks, May 31, 1987.
661   "I am outraged and depressed": *Los Angeles Times*, June 3, 1987.
661   "Well received": Diary entry for May 31, 1987.

CHAPTER 101
663   "Judge Bork, widely regarded": Reagan remarks, July 1, 1987.
663   "Robert Bork's America": *New York Times*, July 5, 1987.
664   "Unless he can demonstrate": *New York Times*, July 2, 1987.
664   "Some talk about Bork": Diary entry for July 2, 1987.
664   "We'll get Bork confirmed": Diary entry for July 6, 1987.
664   "The president had high confidence": Baker interview, Miller Center.
664   "Beginning with *Brown v. Board*": *Washington Post*, Sept. 20, 1987.
664   "It would really be preposterous": *Washington Post*, Sept. 17 and 19, 1987.
665   "Over my dead body": Diary entry for Oct. 5, 1987.
665   "Mr. President, fifty-one senators": Reagan exchange with reporters, Oct. 8, 1987.
666   "Judge Bork and I agree": *Washington Post*, Oct. 14, 1987.
666   "I assured them": Diary entry for Oct. 15, 1987.
666   "We want Bork!": *Washington Post*, Oct. 14, 1987.
666   "By selecting Judge Ginsburg": Reagan remarks, Oct. 29, 1987.
666   "It was a brief thing": Diary entry for Nov. 5, 1987.
667   "I told him": Diary entry for Nov. 7, 1987.
667   "FBI check on Judge Kennedy": Diary entry for Nov. 11, 1987.
667   "They didn't lay a glove": Diary entry for Dec. 16, 1987.

CHAPTER 102
668   "The financial market": Diary entry for June 6, 1983.
668   "I think we'll reappoint": Diary entry for June 7, 1983.
668   "Lew Lehrman came by": Diary entry for Feb. 23, 1984.
668   "The Fed has pulled the string": Diary entry for Oct. 31, 1984.
669   "We're going to see": Diary entry for March 16, 1987.
669   "We've had a miraculous": Reagan news conference, June 11, 1987.
669   "I couldn't help": Alan Greenspan, *The Age of Turbulence* (2007), 102–6.
670   "Are we headed": Reagan exchange with reporters, Oct. 19, 1987.
671   "We met with Reagan": Greenspan, *Age of Turbulence*, 109.
671   "Are you willing": Reagan remarks and question-and-answer session, Oct. 20, 1987.

CHAPTER 103
672   "It was in many ways": *American Life*, 693–94.
672   "Dick and I buried ourselves": Diary entry for Oct. 17, 1987.
673   "I looked up": *American Life*, 694–95.
673   "I came home": Diary entry for Oct. 26, 1987.
673   "Upon arrival": Diary entry for Oct. 27, 1987.
673   "Friends from all over the country": Diary entry for Oct. 31, 1987.

CHAPTER 104
674   "Margaret Thatcher came down": Matlock interview.
674   "There was a real point": Thatcher, *Downing Street Years*, 586–87.
675   "As usual": Diary entry for June 9, 1987.

675   "But Reagan was tough": Baker interview, Miller Center.

675   "General Secretary Gorbachev": Reagan address in Berlin, June 12, 1987.

675   "In the best tradition": Gorbachev, *Memoirs*, 439.

676   "Whatever the arguments": Ibid., 443–44.

676   "I realized": Ibid., 440.

677   "Now we must finish": Minutes of National Security Planning Group meeting, Sept. 8, 1987, Reagan Library.

CHAPTER 105

680   "He was upbeat": Shultz, *Turmoil and Triumph*, 1008–9.

680   "A good rousing meeting": Diary entry for Dec. 8, 1987.

680   "Mr. President, you are not a prosecutor": Gorbachev, *Memoirs*, 447.

681   "I enjoyed the debate": *American Life*, 698.

681   "This ceremony": Reagan remarks at INF Treaty signing, Dec. 8, 1987.

683   "It is not armaments": Memorandum of conversation, president's meeting with Gorbachev, 2:30–3:15 p.m., Dec. 8, 1987, Reagan Library.

684   "It would develop a response": Memorandum of conversation, 10:55 a.m.–12:35 p.m., Dec. 9, 1987, Reagan Library.

CHAPTER 106

686   "Raisa and I": Nancy Reagan, *My Turn*, 346–48.

687   "When I saw you on television": Ibid., 350.

687   "During those days": Gorbachev, *Memoirs*, 448–49.

688   "Hello, I'm glad": *Washington Post*, Dec. 11, 1987.

688   "Today, hundreds of millions": Gorbachev, *Memoirs*, 449.

689   "I think the whole thing": Diary entry for Dec. 10, 1987.

CHAPTER 107

690   "First talk was about": Diary entry for March 17, 1988.

690   "The media are behaving": Diary entry for May 3, 1988.

690   "A short meeting": Diary entry for May 4, 1988.

691   "Mr. President, will you continue": Reagan remarks, May 9, 1988.

691   Joan Quigley: *Los Angeles Times*, May 11, 1988.

691   "She certainly has": *Los Angeles Times*, May 10, 1988.

691   "Are you denying": Reagan remarks and question-and-answer session, May 17, 1988.

692   "They're all Aquarians": *Los Angeles Times*, May 10, 1988.

CHAPTER 108

693   "Your former chief of staff": Reagan interview, May 19, 1988.

694   "What if you ruled": Memorandum of conversation, May 29, 1988, Reagan Library.

695   "Freedom is the right": Reagan remarks, May 31, 1988.

696   "It was almost electric": Matlock interview.

696   "Mr. Reagan and I": Gorbachev, *Memoirs*, 457.

696   "I think there is quite a difference": *New York Times*, June 2, 1988.

696   "Quite possibly, we're beginning": Reagan remarks, June 3, 1988.

696   "What can I say": Diary entry for June 1, 1988.

CHAPTER 109

697 "You made us proud": Bush remarks greeting Reagan, June 3, 1988, American Presidency Project.

697 "That made my day": Diary entry for Feb. 16, 1988.

698 "It was our dream": Reagan convention speech, Aug. 15, 1988.

698 "Reagan for King": *Los Angeles Times*, Aug. 16, 1988.

699 "I knew that the Soviet government": Weinberger, *Fighting for Peace*, 389–90.

700 "It's a terrible tragedy": Diary entry for July 2, 1988.

701 "I want a kinder, gentler nation": Bush acceptance speech, Aug. 18, 1988, American Presidency Project.

701 "Vice President Bush has made": Reagan statement, Aug. 16, 1988.

701 "Quayle did very well": Diary entry for Oct. 5, 1988.

701 "A great evening": Diary entry for Nov. 8, 1988.

CHAPTER 110

705 "Mr. President, you've been more": Thatcher toast at state dinner, Nov. 16, 1988.

705 "Thank you, Chuck": Reagan remarks at groundbreaking of Reagan Library, Nov. 21, 1988.

705 "What a team": Reagan remarks at dinner hosted by Senate Republicans, Nov. 29, 1988.

706 "Franklin Roosevelt": Reagan remarks at Franklin D. Roosevelt Library, Jan. 10, 1989.

CHAPTER 111

707 "You've got to put this": *Los Angeles Times*, Jan. 28, 1989.

707 "not too proud of Hollywood": *Los Angeles Times*, Nov. 8, 1989.

708 $5 million . . . $30,000 . . . $2 million: *Los Angeles Times*, Jan. 28, 1989.

708 "Rev. Falwell has sent": Diary entry for Nov. 29, 1988.

708 "It was a hell of a presentation": Diary entry for Dec. 21, 1988.

709 "I'm afraid he's right": Diary entry for Jan. 19, 1989.

709 "I made up my mind": *Los Angeles Times*, April 1, 1989.

709 "What's the difference": *Los Angeles Times*, April 20, 1989.

709 "We will be fully vindicated": *New York Times*, May 5, 1989.

710 he pleaded ignorance: *Chicago Tribune* and *New York Times*, Feb. 23, 1990; video of deposition, C-SPAN video library.

712 "I guess my barber": *New York Times*, Sept. 10, 1989.

712 "I was in shock": Nancy Reagan, *I Love You, Ronnie* (2000), 180.

712 "Mr. Reagan is treated": *New York Times*, Nov. 7, 1990.

713 "I'm Convinced That Gorbachev": *New York Times*, June 12, 1990.

714 "Darned hard": *New York Times*, Sept. 13, 1990.

714 "real father of perestroika": *New York Times*, Sept. 16, 1990.

714 "I'm sure you must have sensed": *New York Times*, Sept. 18, 1990.

CHAPTER 112

716 "Twenty-five years ago": *Washington Post* and *Los Angeles Times*, Feb. 7, 1991.

717 "He believed that America": *New York Times* and *Los Angeles Times*, Nov. 5, 1991.

718 "Four lives were changed": *New York Times*, March 29, 1991.

718 "I felt somebody had stabbed me": *New York Times*, March 30, 1991.

719 "Read My Lips: I Lied": Mark J. Rozell, *The Press and the Bush Presidency* (1996), 73.

719 "Crime of the Century": Cato Institute Policy Analysis No. 182, Oct. 12, 1992.

720 "If Reagan told me once": Baker interview with author.

720 The START pact mandated: Hoffman, *Dead Hand*, 367–68. Hoffman's book is the best account of the struggle to restrain the arms race during the years of Reagan, Gorbachev, and Bush.

720 "The changes of the 1990s": Reagan address at the 1992 Republican National Convention, youtube.com; *New York Times*, Aug. 18, 1992.

721 43 percent: *New York Times*/CBS News poll, *New York Times*, Aug. 16, 1992.

721 33 percent: *Los Angeles Times* poll, *Los Angeles Times*, Nov. 4, 1991.

721 "This is not retirement": *New York Times*, Aug. 17, 1992.

CHAPTER 113

723 "You were reelected in 1984": Reagan deposition, July 24, 1992, *Washington Post*, June 20, 1999.

725 "Today we are here": *New York Times* and *Washington Post*, May 14, 1993.

725 "I may not be a Rhodes Scholar": *New York Times*, May 16, 1993.

726 "It was concluded": *Final Report of the Independent Counsel for Iran/Contra Matters*, Aug. 4, 1993, published Jan. 18, 1994.

727 "encyclopedia of old information": *New York Times*, Jan. 19, 1994.

727 "But I do have to admit": *Washington Post* and *New York Times*, March 18, 1994.

728 "He lied to my husband": *Washington Post*, Oct. 29, 1994.

728 "One small leak": Deaver, *Nancy*, 181.

728 "I don't remember your name": Gramm interview.

728 "My Fellow Americans": Reagan letter, Nov. 5, 1994, Reagan Library.

CHAPTER 114

730 "He looked great": Deaver, *Nancy*, 174.

731 "Ronnie's optimism": Nancy Reagan remarks to Republican national convention, Aug. 12, 1996, reaganfoundation.org.

732 "Ronald Reagan believed": CNN.com, June 11, 2004.

732 "He is home now": MSNBC.com, June 12, 2004.

732 "In his last years": CNN.com, June 11, 2004.

737 "I know that for America": Reagan letter, Nov. 5, 1994.

INDEX

ALSO BY

H. W. BRANDS

THE MAN WHO SAVED THE UNION
Ulysses Grant in War and Peace

Ulysses Grant emerges in this masterful biography as a genius in battle and a driven president to a divided country, who remained fearlessly on the side of right. He was a beloved commander in the field who made the sacrifices necessary to win the war, even in the face of criticism. He worked valiantly to protect the rights of freed men in the South. He allowed the American Indians to shape their own fate even as the realities of Manifest Destiny meant the end of their way of life. In this sweeping and majestic narrative, bestselling author H. W. Brands now reconsiders Grant's legacy and provides an intimate portrait of a heroic man who saved the Union on the battlefield and consolidated that victory as a resolute and principled political leader.
Biography

TRAITOR TO HIS CLASS
The Privileged Life and Radical Presidency of Franklin Delano Roosevelt

A brilliant evocation of the qualities that made FDR one of the most beloved and greatest of American presidents. Drawing on archival material, public speeches, correspondence, and accounts by those closest to Roosevelt early in his career and during his presidency, H. W. Brands shows how Roosevelt transformed American government during the Depression with his New Deal legislation, and carefully managed the country's prelude to war. Brands shows how Roosevelt's friendship and regard for Winston Churchill helped to forge one of the greatest alliances in history, as Roosevelt, Churchill, and Stalin maneuvered to defeat Germany and prepare for post-war Europe.
Biography

ALSO AVAILABLE

The Age of Gold
American Colossus
Andrew Jackson
The First American
The Heartbreak of Aaron Burr
Lone Star Nation
The Murder of Jim Fisk for the Love of Josie Mansfield

ANCHOR BOOKS
Available wherever books are sold.
www.anchorbooks.com